THE STORY OF
THE STUDENT CHRISTIAN MOVEMENT
OF GREAT BRITAIN AND IRELAND

TISSINGTON TATLOW, 1933.

by Alice M. Burton, R.B.A.

THE STORY OF
THE STUDENT CHRISTIAN MOVEMENT
OF GREAT BRITAIN AND IRELAND

by

TISSINGTON TATLOW
M.A. Trin. Coll. Dub., D.D. (Hon.) Edin.

STUDENT CHRISTIAN MOVEMENT PRESS
58 BLOOMSBURY STREET, LONDON, W.C.1

First Published October 1933

Printed in Great Britain

CONTENTS

LIST OF ILLUSTRATIONS

Note.—The photographs of people, with few exceptions, were taken
when they were in the service of the Movement.

PROLOGUE

THIS story of the rise and development of the
Student Christian Movement has seemed worth
telling and I believe the present is the appropriate
time to tell it.

It is a story of the thought and activity of students
to whom God was a great reality and who were inspired
by the vision of a world made new in Christ. It has
been told in a colloquial style as being in keeping with
the free and easy ways of students, and this explains
the element of informality which runs through the
book.

I have written the story with more than one group
in mind. Many in the churches who have had occasional contacts with the life of the Movement through
attendance at one of its conferences, the reading of a
newspaper article or the perusal of one of its books
will, I believe, be interested in a coherent account of
it. No attempt has been made to record all its doings,
but rather to pick out what has been significant in its
life and to indicate why its influence in relation to
foreign missions, the growth of the spirit of unity and
the development of international co-operation among
Christians, has been so considerable.

The life of the Christian Church, both at home and
abroad, has been deeply influenced by the Movement,
for it is after student days that the fruit is garnered
from the seed sown in university and college. Thousands of men and women engaged in responsible work
all over the world owe much of their inspiration and
their training in active Christian service to participation
in the Student Christian Movement while at college.
The story should be of even deeper interest to those

who shared in the life and leadership of the Movement in bygone years.

It is also intended for leaders in the Student Movement of this and succeeding generations. I have had in mind in writing the fact that it is the story of how the Movement has won a base in the universities and colleges of this country, a base which ought to be used to win far greater Christian triumphs in the future than in the past. This explains why there is so much detail about matters of organization in the book. They have been included in the hope that they will be useful to the ever-changing leaders of the Movement. Continuity is one of the Movement's great problems. A student generation is of only three years' duration. Much is inevitably lost in the process of handing on the work of the Movement, and this is the justification for having gone more into detail in some matters than would have seemed necessary were student life more continuous.

I hope many students will read the book even though they may not be called to leadership in the national Movement. There is much in it for those who have little interest in organization but who love the coming of Christ's Kingdom.

Now that the story of the Movement is written down one sees more clearly than ever what a terrible disaster the World War has been. In the middle of the War Dr Barnes, who was then Master of the Temple, wrote a paper on *The Student Christian Movement and the Future of the Nation*, in which he warned us that it had taken the United States half a century to recover from the effects of the Civil War and that the results of the World War would be no less great. " We look to the future ; and even the most optimistic must needs be appalled. The country will stagger under the burden of at least some four thousand millions of debt. The State will be in desperate need of men of ability and enthusiasm to rebuild our civilization, and the natural leaders of the next generation will have been blotted out. . . . When the war ends there will be before us half a century of slow and painful reconstruction. For years prejudice, ignorance, violence and apathy will be far more formidable foes than in the recent past. Both in public and private life second-rate men will inevitably be in positions of which they are unworthy."

Much of the early promise of the Movement has been unfulfilled because of the War, and very many men who showed in its service great promise of future leadership in the cause of Christ have not lived to help now when they are sorely needed.

The Movement arose in a day of opportunity, it was the response of students to needs both in the universities and in the world. Its rise coincided with great developments in the educational life of the nation. The fact that eight new universities and half a hundred colleges of all kinds have been created since the Movement began bears witness to the extent of this development. The influence of the Student Movement in the whole process has been considerable, whether we look at the institutions themselves or at the lives of the men and women whom they have trained. " The Student Christian Movement," writes Sir Michael Sadler, " has been one of the chief influences which have fostered ideals of corporate obligation in the modern universities. It has been indispensable during a critical period of development and growth in our university life."

The expansion of the student world is not a phenomenon confined to our own country. This book deals only with the Student Movement in Great Britain and Ireland, but occasional references in it to the World's Student Christian Federation will bring the reminder that universities and institutions of higher learning have been multiplying rapidly in almost every land.

While the Movement began in a day of opportunity in the universities, it was a day of still greater opportunity outside them at home and abroad. It was towards Asia and Africa that the Movement at first directed its attention, and its influence has been felt in the length and breadth of these continents as thousands of university men and women poured into them from Europe and America, carrying with them all that Western thought and science had to offer, and introducing with the Christian gospel all those ideals of human worth and possibilities which are the fine flower of the Christian view of the world. The exploration of Africa was drawing to completion. National consciousness was beginning to stir in India, and the ancient civilization of China, secure against change as it seemed, was soon to be in the throes of the greatest revolution in history. The world stage was set for vast changes.

At home the Movement set itself to prepare men and women to tackle the great problems of the day. It shared in the growth of social consciousness and sought to inspire in its members the hope of the redemption of society. It felt keenly the schism in the body of Christ and made experiments in Christian co-operation which have done much to promote the desire for Church unity. It fostered the love of truth and engaged the minds of its members on the adjustment of growing knowledge to the permanent elements in the Christian gospel. Since the World War it has conserved all these interests, recreated its work—which had almost been wiped out in the men's colleges by the War—and reconstructed and rejuvenated its central administration and leadership. It is ready for advance.

It is again a day of opportunity. The abiding fact is not the World War and its aftermath. Science has given to mankind the promise of material wealth undreamed of fifty years ago, and men are beginning to think of human life in terms of leisure, rather than of toil. Yet civilization is straitened because it cannot use its treasures. We are beginning to see that only those can inherit the earth who seek first the Kingdom of God. There never was greater need or greater opportunity for a spiritual movement among students than at the present time. The object of this book is not to embalm the history of the past, but to use it to inspire oncoming youth to greater achievements in the future.

The Student Christian Movement has difficulties with which it must cope, but difficulties have never daunted young men and women, and our difficulties in the British Isles are far less serious than those of Student Movements in many other countries.

The time is ripe for advance ; for one student who was concerned about the meaning of life and ready to listen to a prophetic voice, when I joined the Movement nearly forty years ago, there are a dozen to-day. Recent contact with the leaders of the Movement in our own and many other lands leads me to the belief that the great days of the Student Christian Movement lie ahead. Faith in God and belief in the spiritual potentialities of man, courage to attempt great things, together with consecration and prayer as their realization is sought, will bring its reward in the future as in the past.

THE STORY OF THE
STUDENT CHRISTIAN MOVEMENT
OF GREAT BRITAIN AND IRELAND

CHAPTER I

THE ORIGINS OF THE MOVEMENT

"HOW did the Movement begin?" is a question often asked of those who lead it. It is not easy to answer, for the roots lie deep; religious movements among students have been much interrelated and they are as old as the universities.

A student movement was started in 1528 when Peter Faber, Ignatius Loyola and Francis Xavier shared a room at the College of St Barbe in Paris—a movement which made Xavier a missionary and Loyola the founder of the Society of Jesus. In North America there are records of religious societies in the colleges from 1706 onwards, and some of these became linked, in time, with similar societies in Great Britain. The formation at Oxford of the Holy Club, as fellow-undergraduates derisively called it, by John and Charles Wesley, George White-field, James Hervey and a few of their friends set spiritual forces in motion which became a power in the New as well as in the Old World. These are among the influences which ultimately produced among their fruits the Student Christian Movement of Great Britain and Ireland. It is not to be traced to a single source; many streams of religious and missionary fervour combined to give it being. These developed on both sides of the Atlantic and mingled in the latter part of the nineteenth century.

The first interest of the Movement was foreign missionary work, and the earliest record of students organizing themselves in relation to the modern missionary enterprise comes from America. A group of Williams College students, in August 1806, caught in a thunderstorm, took shelter under a haystack and began a discussion, as students will. Their talk was about how they might undertake " the evangelization of the heathen " ; from talk they turned to prayer, after which they joined hands, saying together, " We can do it if we will."

Samuel J. Mills, James Richards, Francis L. Robins, Harvey Lommis and Bryon Green, who composed the group, while still students formed " The Brethren Society," having as object " to effect in the person of its members a mission or missions to the heathen." This was not the first missionary society, but it was the first student missionary organization, and it was marked by the personal note which is characteristic of all student religious organizations ; the members did not combine to move other people but to further their own action— " to effect in the person of its members a mission or missions to the heathen."

Near Williams College to-day, there stands a monument to the memory of this student prayer-meeting and what came of it—a pedestal supporting a globe, with the names beneath of the five students. It is the only monument in the world to the memory of a prayer-meeting.

While there were several missionary societies in the Old World, there were none in the New, and when the first members of " The Brethren Society " were ready for service they corresponded with the London Missionary Society. Samuel Mills, however, was convinced that they should be sent as missionaries by American Christians, and the students petitioned the Joint Association of the Congregational Churches of Massachusetts, in 1810, with the result that the " Board of Commissioners for Foreign Missions "—the first missionary society in America—was founded.

During the next forty years student societies in America were remarkable for their missionary character.

" The Brethren Society " was carried by members of the original group to Andover Seminary, where it existed from 1810 to 1863, and from 1870 to 1872. This society had three hundred and seventy-two members, of whom two hundred and seventeen became missionaries. In the early forties it was joined by Mr Wilder, the father of Robert P. Wilder the founder of the Student Volunteer Movement for Foreign Missions of the United States and Canada, the link between the haystack prayer-meeting of 1806 and the present-day missionary movement among students being thus preserved.

An observance inherited from these early days of the Student Movement in America is the Universal Day of Prayer for Students. Its forerunner was " the Concert of Prayer for Colleges," which was started as the result of a letter written on June 17th 1815 by a committee of the " Church of Christ in Yale College," to the " Praying Society of Brown College," saying : " We are happy to inform you that a Concert of Prayer for a revival of religion in all the colleges in the U.States is established in this and some other seminaries commencing at 9 o'clock Lord's Day morning. We hope it may meet your approbation to join with us at this time for the same glorious cause." Students in Yale, Harvard, Dartmouth, Williams, Brown and Middlebury were joining in this concert before the end of 1815.[1]

In Great Britain the evangelical movement, in the latter part of the eighteenth and of the nineteenth centuries, gave rise to the major portion of the modern missionary enterprise, resulted in the formation of a large number of religious organizations outside the ecclesiastical life of the period, and burst forth in more than one religious revival, the most important of which affected in turn large sections of the population of England, Ireland, Scotland and Wales between the years 1856 and 1862. The evangelical movement affected the life of the

[1] I am indebted to Dr Clarence Shedd of Yale University for this and other information about early student religious societies in U.S.A.

universities and led to the formation of a number of student societies, as well as of a considerable number of religious organizations of all kinds, some of which were in contact with student life.   One such was the Children's Special Service Mission, with its services for boys and girls holiday-making at the seaside.   These services influenced boys who went later to the universities and returned as undergraduate helpers.   They were a training-ground for the leaders of student religious societies for at least fifty years ; many of the early leaders of the Student Christian Movement took part in them.

It should be remembered, when thinking of happenings round about 1860, that the modern universities, university, technical and most of the teachers' training and theological colleges had not yet come into existence. In England, there were Oxford and Cambridge, dating back to the twelfth century, and the recently founded universities of London and Durham, and Owens College, Manchester, which began to give university instruction in 1850.   Scotland possessed four universities, St Andrews, Aberdeen, Glasgow and Edinburgh, which were each from three to four hundred and fifty years old. Ireland had Trinity College, Dublin, dating from the time of Queen Elizabeth.   In Wales there was the small university of Lampeter.   Aberystwyth, the first of the modern university colleges in Wales, was not created until 1872.   The student field was, therefore, a small one compared with that of to-day.

There are a few student societies which have an unbroken record of work up to the present.   The Cambridge University Church Missionary Union was founded in 1858, and on November 24th, 1862, the Daily Prayer Meeting was commenced, conducted by undergraduates, who met to pray " for the outpouring of God's Holy Spirit on the university," a prayer-meeting conducted daily ever since, during term.

The Edinburgh University Medical Students' Christian Association was founded in 1865.   The earliest minute-book available is dated 1874, when the Association had thirty-eight members. Its first page seems strangely modern in recording that " it was resolved that the secretaries should make another attempt at obtaining a list of good lodgings for the benefit of strangers and others," and that at the Annual Meeting of the Association, Professor Crum Brown " adverted to the tendency there is in many to make the teaching of science appear as antagonistic to that of religion, and showed how unfair and unwise it is to pass final judgment on scientific questions regarding which our knowledge is as yet so imperfect."

The same year the Senatus granted the Association permission to hold weekly meetings " within the walls of the university." These meetings were " for the study of the Bible with prayer and praise." Two meetings were also held during the session, when addresses—one on " Revivals " and the other on " Prayer—its Sphere "— were followed by discussion. Three medical professors, Dr Grainger Stewart, Dr Moir and Professor A. R. Simpson, had occasional social meetings at their houses, where the members got to know one another. The Association commenced the holding of services on Sundays in the wards of the Royal Infirmary in 1875, an activity referred to in the minute-book with constant enthusiasm for a number of years.

The Glasgow University Students' Christian Association was founded about the same time as the Edinburgh Association. A secretary is said to have taken its minute-book to New Zealand in 1869, at any rate no early records are available. In 1874 the Medical Prayer Union was started in London with a senior section for qualified men and a junior section which united Christian Associations in the medical schools of London; it was in the succession of work started in 1849.

Mr D. L. Moody, already famous as an evangelist in America, came to England and conducted his first mission, at York, in 1873. It began with an attendance of eight persons, but later in the same year he was at the Barclay Church, Edinburgh, making a deep impression on that city and attracting the ablest students to his meetings. The following year Moody was in London addressing 14,000 people nightly in the Agricultural Hall at Islington, having secured the interest of prominent members of both the Church of England and the Free Churches, as well as of all sections of London society. He left behind him permanent results in the changed lives of thousands of men and women.

A few days before Moody commenced his Edinburgh campaign a New College student, popular but not hitherto regarded as outstanding, read a paper to the Theological Society of his college on " Spiritual Diagnosis," in which he maintained that preaching was not the most important work of the ministry, but that personal dealing with those in spiritual anxiety would yield better results, that practical religion should be treated as an exact science. The paper made a deep impression, it was also a turning-point in the life of the writer, Henry Drummond. Immediately afterwards he came into contact with Moody, and found abundant opportunity for practice in personal dealing.

More student religious societies were formed. A conference between Christian groups in Oxford and Cambridge was held in 1877, and as a result the Cambridge Inter-Collegiate Christian Union was founded in 1878, and the Oxford Inter-Collegiate Christian Union in 1879. The Oxford and Cambridge Conference was an annual event for many years, and men from Edinburgh, Glasgow, Durham, and Dublin came to it. An immense impetus was given to the work of the Cambridge Inter-Collegiate Christian Union when Mr Moody visited Cambridge in November 1882 and conducted a series of meetings. There was a good deal of opposition from undergraduates in the initial stages, and his first meeting was broken up, but Moody persevered and a profound spiritual impression was made on the University. One outcome of this movement was the decision of two of the best-known figures in the University to go to China as missionaries.

It does not require much imagination to realize the extraordinary interest that was aroused, at a time when very few missionaries were being provided by the universities, by an announcement that the Captain of the Cricket XI and the Stroke of the Cambridge Boat were both going out as missionaries. These two men were C. T. Studd and Stanley P. Smith. Studd was one of the leading cricketers of the day ; and no undergraduate was ignorant of the part the Studd family had played in a famous cricket match the previous summer, when Cambridge University beat Australia by six wickets. The three Studd brothers made 295 runs between them; C. T. Studd made 118 runs in the first innings, 15 not out in the second, and took eight wickets. Studd and Smith were soon joined by five other men—W. W. Cassels,[1] Curate of All Saints', Lambeth; Montagu Beauchamp,[2] a well-known rowing man; D. E. Hoste,[3] an officer in the Royal Artillery ; A. T. Polhill-Turner, a theological student at Ridley Hall, Cambridge, and C. H. Polhill-Turner, an officer in the 6th Dragoon Guards. Both the Polhill-Turners, like C. T. Studd, were Etonians, and were well known as cricketers. The group became famous as " the Cambridge Seven." They offered their services as a group to and were accepted by Dr Hudson Taylor, the leader of the China Inland Mission.

Studd, Smith and others arranged missionary meetings at Cambridge; one of these was a notable gathering on December 2nd, 1884, when the Rev. F. E. Wigram, honorary secretary of the Church Missionary Society, met a number of graduates and undergraduates at the invitation of the Cambridge University Church Missionary Union, who desired to offer for missionary work. Mr Stock wrote that " that meeting marked the commencement of a movement which has given the society

[1] Subsequently first Bishop in Western China ; died 1925.
[2] Afterwards the Rev. Sir Montagu Beauchamp, Bart.
[3] Afterwards Director of the China Inland Mission.

a large number of its best missionaries in all parts of the world." [1]

The spiritual movement in Cambridge, of which the most spectacular result was the departure for China of " the Cambridge Seven," firmly established organized Christian activity among undergraduates in the University, and provided one of the two chief bases of the Student Christian Movement. The other base was to be in Edinburgh University.

In 1884 Edinburgh University celebrated its tercentenary. The share of the students in this event was a meeting planned by the Students' Representative Council. This meeting prepared the ground in the University in a wonderful way for the spiritual movement which was to find remarkable expression before the year ended.

The meeting was held in the Synod Hall of the United Presbyterian Church, and was presided over by the Rector of the University, Sir Stafford Northcote, the obvious Chairman, as in the Scottish universities the Rector is the choice of the student body and not of the Senatus. The students invited to address them, from among the University's guests, the following : James Russell Lowell, Professor Beets, Count de Lesseps, Professor Pasteur, Professor Virchow, Professor von Helmsholtz, Professor de Laveleye, and Count Saffi. Two thousand students, nearly the whole University, were present. They came early and enlivened the time of waiting by singing and making a good deal of noise. On the platform were some of the most eminent men of the day, including Robert Browning. The meeting took a wholly unexpected turn in that several of the speeches were of a definitely religious character. Count Saffi, the distinguished Italian scientist and statesman, said :

> I have come to England to see your great things. I have seen your buildings and sights in London ; there is nothing which we have not in my country. But a friend

[1] *The History of the Church Missionary Society*, by Eugene Stock, vol. iii. p. 350.

took me to the City of London and I saw the crowded busy streets. He took me again on the Sunday, and we found the streets deserted, and then I was informed that no business was done in the City of London on Sunday. That is the greatest thing I have seen in England.

He finished an eloquent speech with the words : " Oh, my Italy ! would that thou hadst a Faith like that."

Professor de Laveleye of Belgium gave clearest expression to the call to the acknowledgment of God which sounded throughout the addresses, when he closed the last of the speeches with the words :

> Remember the wonderful and profound word of Jesus, which would put an end to all our troubles and our discords, if it were but listened to : " Seek first the Kingdom of God and His righteousness, and all other things will be added unto you."

The meeting made a profound impression upon the University. A few months later the Principal, Sir Alexander Grant, in his inaugural address at the opening of a new session, called upon the students to recognize and sustain the distinctively Christian character of the University, and his sudden death shortly afterwards deepened the impression his words made upon the student body.[1]

The Edinburgh University Medical Students' Christian Association had an unusually successful session that winter, as did also a similar organization among the Arts students. Some of the student members of these organizations took part in evangelistic meetings on Sunday evenings in the town, conducted by an Edinburgh graduate, Dr Moxey, which strengthened their spiritual life and deepened in them the desire to win their fellow-students for Christ. It was to one of these men, G. Purves Smith, a medical student, that Professor A. R. Simpson communicated the contents of a letter he had received from Mr J. E. Mathieson of Mildmay, London, saying that he was coming to

[1] See for an account of this period *The Year of Grace*, 1884, *in the University of Edinburgh*, by Professor A. R. Simpson.

Scotland hoping to address the students about foreign missions, and was bringing with him C. T. Studd and Stanley P. Smith. Purves Smith and a few of his fellow-students determined that the meeting should be " a thorough students' affair," and they insisted that prominence should be given to Studd and Smith in the meetings and not to the senior members of the party. The Medical Students' Christian Association appointed a sub-committee of six medical students—Terry, Moss, Bailey, Orr, Masterman and Purves Smith—to arrange the meeting, and it is interesting that all these men except one became medical missionaries. They made their plans well, advertised the meeting widely in the University, and were full of expectation.

We had committed ourselves to great things, we had done all in our power to make it a success, and then on the morning before the meeting we prayed that God's Holy Spirit would put it into the minds of the students to come. Our prayers were answered far above our asking. For twenty minutes before the appointed hour men were rushing up the steps of the Assembly Hall asking if there was room. . . . As soon as Studd and Stanley Smith entered the hall they were loudly cheered. We had made it plain on our notices, that they were going to China as missionaries, and our men had come to hear what Studd, who had made the biggest score in cricket at Cambridge, had to say about religion. They admired their consecration. Again and again through their addresses they were cheered. Stanley Smith was eloquent but Studd couldn't speak a bit—it was the fact of his devotion to Christ which told, and he, if anything, made the greatest impression.[1]

Professor Charteris, who was in the chair, announced that if any would like to shake hands with Studd and Smith and wish them Godspeed, they could come forward as soon as the Benediction had been pronounced.

All the men were students and we wondered who would have the courage to do so, but no sooner had the Benediction been pronounced, than there was a stampede for the platform. A great impression had been made and men

[1] Memorandum by Dr G. Purves Smith.

C. T. STUDD AND STANLEY P. SMITH

were crowding round Studd and Smith to hear more
about Christ. Deep earnestness was written on the faces
of many. A great religious movement had had its birth
and it was all so evidently the work of the Spirit of God.
Many of these students were our best men.[1]

Professor Greenfield, one of the medical professors,
urged the students to secure Studd and Smith for a
further visit; this was arranged for the following term,
and a committee of students was appointed to make
arrangements, representing the Medical, Arts, Law, and
Theological faculties in the University, and in addition,
all the other colleges in the City of Edinburgh.

While the student leaders were considering not only
arrangements for Studd and Smith's mission, but how
it could be followed up, Professor Henry Drummond
delivered to the Medical Students' Christian Association an address on " The Contribution of Science to
Christianity," and after the lecture Professor Simpson
asked Purves Smith, " Why do you not get him to
continue the student meetings for you ? " Professor
A. R. Simpson knew, as the students did not, of Henry
Drummond's evangelistic work twelve years before,
while he was himself a student. Mrs Simpson invited
the student leaders and Drummond to meet at dinner
and talk the matter over, when it was arranged that
after a mission to be conducted on January 18th,
19th and 20th, 1885, by Studd and Smith, Drummond
should commence a series of meetings for students.

The mission was attended by large numbers of
students. On at least one occasion there were 1700
men present. Large numbers, including many of the
leading students in the University, decided to follow
Christ. A week later, on Sunday, January 25th, to an
audience of a thousand students, in the Oddfellows'
Hall, Edinburgh, with Professor Greenfield in the
chair, Drummond began a series of addresses, prolonged through ten years, which is the most famous
series of a religious character which has ever been

[1] *Ibid.*

delivered anywhere to university men. Drummond captivated his audience from the first, taking as his opening subject, "Seek ye first the Kingdom of God and His righteousness; and all these things shall be added unto you."

Henry Drummond entered the University of Edinburgh as a lad of fifteen in 1866. His undergraduate course was without special distinction. He cared little for classics or philosophy, but was interested in geology, gaining the class medal. He was a *persona grata* in the social life of his fellow-students. He also read general literature more widely than most of them. He became a theological student at New College, Edinburgh, in 1870, spent a semester three years later at the University of Tübingen, and on returning the same winter to Scotland, came under the spiritual influence of Mr Moody, and took part as a speaker in evangelistic meetings. His power as a speaker and his gift of reaching individuals attracted Moody's notice, with the result that under pressure from Moody, which Drummond for a time resisted, he spent the next two years in evangelistic work, chiefly among young men in Scotland, England, and Ireland. He was then twenty-three years old.

In 1876 Drummond returned to New College and completed his theological course, and the following year he began work as a lecturer on Natural Science in the Free Church Theological College, Glasgow. Six years later he published *Natural Law in the Spiritual World*, and shortly after seeing the book through the Press, started on an exploring expedition into tropical Africa. When he returned to Scotland it was to find himself famous. Dr William Robertson Nicol wrote at the time of his death : "It may be doubted whether any living novelist has had so many readers, and perhaps no living writer has been so eagerly followed and so keenly discussed on the Continent and in America." [1]

[1] *The Contemporary Review*, April, 1897; art.: "Henry Drummond."

Of Drummond's writings and his life this is not the place to speak, but it is surely appropriate to attempt to set down the sources of Drummond's influence with students and the secret of his power. His style of evangelistic address was unique. "It had no theological pre-suppositions, and was designed to affect not creed but life. He made his appeal to the heroic side of a young man's character. He never spoke of the guilt of sin in a man's conscience, but often of the power of sin in a man's life. He did not warn his hearers against the danger of losing their soul, but with terrific intensity he warned them against the danger of losing their life." [1]

Dr Moxey wrote of him shortly after his famous Edinburgh Student meetings had begun : " In Professor Drummond we seem to have found, or rather God sent us, the very man most likely to draw the students to a meeting, and to preach the Gospel to them once they were there. His present scientific popularity made them curious to hear him ; his youthful face and unconventional, almost boyish manner, won their goodwill, and inclined them to hear him ; and his simple and striking way of lifting up Christ, apart from any thought-distracting considerations *about* Him, such as the naming of repentance, faith, etc., concentrated their attention on the Son of God ; and as they saw His love and their own ingratitude side by side, hearts were broken and wills surrendered." [2]

Professor D. S. Cairns remembers Drummond as :

A slenderly built, tall, graceful man, who walked with a curious springy step, and who was always faultlessly dressed. It is hopeless to describe any human face in words, and I shall not try to describe Drummond's. A friend once told me that he was dining in a London club with Drummond and Richard Holt Hutton, the well-known editor of *The*

[1] *The Woman at Home,* June, 1897; art.: Professor Henry Drummond.

[2] *The Christian,* Feb. 19th, 1885; art.: " Students' Meetings in Edinburgh," by Dr D. A. Moxey.

Spectator. Drummond had to go early and when he left Hutton said : " That is the most beautiful face I have ever seen." Certainly I have seen few faces that were so expressive and alive, sympathy, vitality, tenacity, refinement and a certain distinction are the characteristics remembered best. . . . A sense of humour lies near the great virtues . . . and this Drummond had in abounding measure. . . . He certainly had the student's faith in the place of the pure " lark " in the perfect life.[1]

Professor Cairns thinks that his main service was that he translated the Gospel to many :

To many it had become a thing concerned mainly with future salvation, or something bound up with the traditional doctrine, the foundations of which they felt were being shaken by the advance of science and progress of criticism, and Drummond showed them that it was first of all a thing of present life and experience as real as science, an actual present possession in the light of which all other forms of life were mean and vulgar and unworthy of a man. . . . The central emphasis was laid on the living Christ as the one way to truth and life.   This was the real centre of Drummond's Gospel and of his own life. . . . Drummond was a man raised up by God, and trained by His Providence to preach the everlasting Gospel to students in an age of transition. And his power came to him through his implicit trust in that Providence of the Father, his devotion to Christ the Son and his confident faith in the leading of the Holy Spirit.[1]

Professor Cairns believes that :

It was one of the largest secrets of his power over us all that he interpreted and mediated the soul of the older evangelism to men who were willing and eager enough to recognize the truth that was in it, if they could hear it freed from elements that did not commend themselves to their best standards of life and thought. . . . His ideal and spirit are working on throughout the country in the Student Christian Movement.   This has been reinforced by other streams, but the Movement, as a whole, is exactly the kind

[1] *The North American Student*, November, 1913 ; art. : " Recollections of Henry Drummond," by Professor David S. Cairns.

of thing that he would have delighted in and rejoiced to serve.[1]

Drummond's interest was not in students only. Often he would slink away on a Saturday afternoon to some football field in the East End of Glasgow where, as he said, he was " the only man with a collar in the whole crowd." He was sought after for West End drawing-rooms in London, where he would sometimes preach the gospel to society, but he preferred Pleasant Sunday Afternoons for canal boatmen, or evangelistic meetings for thieves and ex-convicts. He was concerned with the social obligations of Christianity and was one of the earliest promoters of the university settlement movement.

It was Drummond who first gave British under-graduates an interest in student campaigns, both inside and outside the universities. Under his leadership and that of other professors interested by him, deputations of students visited different universities. The first three deputations went to Aberdeen, St Andrews and Glasgow. Later deputations visited London and Oxford. A visit of a remarkable character was paid to Aberystwyth, which changed the tone of the whole college; another result was the founding of the Christian Union there.

Drummond also founded and guided the Students' Holiday Mission, which was a student organization for the purpose of carrying on evangelistic work in connec-tion with the Churches.

The Churches took great interest in the students' missions, and the Church of Scotland and the Free Church Assemblies each received a deputation of students. That to the Church of Scotland was intro-duced by Professor Charteris and welcomed by the Moderator, the Lord High Commissioner with his suite

[1] *The North American Student*, November, 1913; art.: " Recollec-tions of Henry Drummond," by Professor David S. Cairns. Extracts have been drawn from less accessible sources, since the most important source is readily available—*The Life of Henry Drummond*, by George Adam Smith.

being present. That to the Free Church was introduced by Professor Greenfield and received by the Moderator, Principal Rainy. Ministers from various parts of Scotland testified to the Assemblies of the good work that had been done in their churches by the students.

In the summers of 1889 and 1890 there were gatherings of students from both England and Scotland in his home at the invitation of Mr R. W. Barbour, of Bonskeid, Pitlochry, a devoted friend of Professor Drummond. These gatherings, though small, were representative and paved the way for the larger conferences which came later.

While foundations for the Movement were thus being laid in Great Britain, student activity had proceeded apace in the United States of America. A student had gone from Columbia University to study at Edinburgh in 1849-50; he wrote home describing the work of the recently founded Y.M.C.A., and as a result the first Y.M.C.A. in America was founded at Boston on December 22nd, 1851. It was not until 1858, however, that a Student Y.M.C.A. was organized : it was at the University of Virginia. This Y.M.C.A. was one in name, aim and methods with the city organization, but the official Y.M.C.A. was not at first willing to admit college branches. In 1870, however, the tide turned, and at the Indianapolis Convention of the Y.M.C.A. a resolution was adopted, stating " that this convention hails with joy the organization in some of our academies and colleges of Young Men's Christian Associations."

Curiously enough, the Y.M.C.A. branches then, and for some years, included a considerable number of women,[1] who do not seem to have desired a more comprehensive title for the Association !

At first college branches joined the ordinary Y.M.C.A.,

[1] From 1872 onwards many Student Young Women's Christian Associations were formed in U.S.A., but the National Y.W.C.A. was not created until 1880.

but at its Louisville Convention, June 1877, the Inter-Collegiate Y.M.C.A. was formed. It is of interest to recall that among the student delegates from twenty-one college Y.M.C.A.'s were included some from three Negro colleges, Fisk, Howard and Walden.

The work of Moody first brought British and American students in touch. J. E. K. Studd,[1] Captain of the Cambridge University Cricket XI in 1884 and a brother of C. T. Studd, went to America in the autumn of 1885 and told throughout the American colleges the story of " the Cambridge Seven," conducted many evangelistic meetings, and was instrumental in the conversion of John R. Mott, who as a student at Cornell University went to hear him speak.

In 1887 Henry Drummond visited America—it was a second visit, the first in 1879 being on geological work —and went to nearly two score of universities, Professor A. R. Simpson, Professor Greenfield, G. Purves Smith and J. C. Webster, both students, being with him and sharing in addressing student audiences. The speakers almost invariably told the story of spiritual revival in Edinburgh University and then proceeded to preach the Gospel to their audience.

Between the visits of J. E. K. Studd in 1885 and Henry Drummond and his companions in 1887, an event of great importance had taken place. D. L. Wishard, the college secretary of the Y.M.C.A., and C. K. Ober, the general secretary, conveyed to the colleges in touch with the Association in North America an invitation from Mr Moody to a Student Summer School during July at Northfield. The object of the school was " the study of the Bible and such methods of Christian work as are adapted to college life." The meetings were " not to exceed two hours a day, the balance of time being devoted to just such recreation as students need after the work of the college year." The cost was to be £1 a week. Two hundred and fifty

[1] Now Sir Kynaston Studd, Bart., Lord Mayor of London, 1928-29.

C

students from ninety colleges and twenty-six States came and remained for twenty-six days.

One student had come to this Northfield gathering after special preparation and with a definite aim in view. Robert P. Wilder had been one of three delegates from the Philadelphian Society of Princeton College three years before at a small conference of theological students held at Hartford, Connecticut. On their return to Princeton they, with two other students, met and drafted the Constitution of " The Princeton Foreign Missionary Society." Membership was open to any student subscribing to the covenant : " We, the undersigned, declare ourselves willing and desirous, God permitting, to go to the unevangelized portions of the world." In this Wilder was leader.

Robert P. Wilder and his sister, Grace Wilder, had been fired with missionary zeal by their father, who had retired to live at Princeton after thirty years' missionary service in India. In the autumn of 1885 and the spring of 1886 Robert and his sister met night after night to pray for a widespread missionary movement in the colleges and universities of America. The volunteer band grew in Princeton, but was limited to that college; when, however, Moody issued his invitation to Northfield the Wilders saw the opportunity and Robert went there, leaving Grace to pray, after agreeing with her that their prayer should be that the band of twenty-three student volunteers might grow to one hundred before the Northfield Student Conference closed.

Half July passed and there was no mention at Northfield of foreign missions, then Moody arranged a meeting addressed by ten students ; three Americans, sons of missionaries, and the others, an Armenian, a Norwegian, a Dane, a German, an American Indian, a Siamese and a Japanese. This meeting was the spiritual high-water mark of the gathering. Men went from the meeting alone, or in little groups, on to the hillside above the river. As a result Wilder's volunteer band grew, until ninety-nine students had signed the declaration. The members met the last night to plan for the future, and as they were praying for guidance the hundredth man came into the room and knelt among them, signing the declaration before the meeting broke up.

Next autumn Robert P. Wilder and John N. Forman, one of the first to become a volunteer, spent a year touring the American and Canadian universities and colleges. They visited one hundred and sixty-two colleges, meeting a warm response everywhere, and enrolled 2106 volunteers, of whom 500 were women. The following year a summer conference was held at Northfield of the " Student Volunteers for Foreign Missions." During a year when no special speaker visited the colleges 600 students joined as a result of the personal work of the volunteers.

In 1888-89 Wilder again visited the colleges to conserve, as well as extend, the Movement. Volunteer bands were linked up with the college Y.M.C.A. and Y.W.C.A. and became their missionary departments, and the Movement was definitely organized with an Executive Committee of three—John R. Mott of the Y.M.C.A., Miss Nettie Dunn of the Y.W.C.A. and Robert P. Wilder, representing both the Inter-Seminary Missionary Alliance and the Canadian Inter-Collegiate Missionary Alliance. This Executive began its work in January 1889, with Robert E. Speer, W. H. Hannum and R. S. Miller as secretaries.

The Volunteer Movement held its first convention [1] in Cleveland, Ohio, 1891, assembling five hundred and eighty-one students from one hundred and fifty-one colleges. The following year it changed its membership declaration to read : " It is my purpose, God permitting, to become a foreign missionary."

The news of this Movement and its careful organization by the American students, as well as information about the Student Department of the Y.M.C.A., was brought to Great Britain by Drummond, Studd and

[1] This was the first of the gatherings in U.S.A. which are the parallel of those known in the S.C.M. as " quadrennials."

others, and later by undergraduates from Oxford, Edinburgh, Aberdeen, Glasgow and Dublin universities, who had accepted invitations to attend the Northfield Summer Conference of the American Student Y.M.C.A.

The British students were impressed by the skill with which the Americans were organizing, and were anxious to secure a visit from Wilder to help them to organize a movement in Great Britain. He was invited first in 1887, but was unable to accept the invitation. Mr J. N. Forman, however, visited a number of British colleges at the expense of American students that year. Two years later a group of medical students, led by O. O. Williams, an Aberystwyth College man who had come to study medicine at the London Hospital, decided to hesitate no longer but to start a missionary movement in Great Britain similar to that in America. The plans for a Students' Foreign Missionary Union were drafted by a group which included O. O. Williams and Dr Howard Taylor, and they made plans to initiate the Union at a Missionary Convention for Young Men which took place at the Metropolitan Tabernacle, London, on Tuesday, October 15th, 1889, the Rev. C. H. Spurgeon being one of the speakers. One thousand five hundred students attended, and Dr Howard Taylor, who had just qualified at London Hospital, introduced the proposal to form the Students' Foreign Missionary Union. In a paper which was distributed among the students its objects were given as follows :

1. To band together students who feel called to foreign missionary work ;
2. To urge the claims of the heathen upon Christian students everywhere, and to advocate the formation of Missionary Associations in connection with the various universities and colleges where they do not already exist.

Dr Taylor, who was on the eve of sailing for China, spent a few weeks before departure in visiting a number of universities on behalf of this Union. Several branches were formed, and at the end of six months one hundred and forty-two men had signed the declaration which formed the basis of membership : " It is my earnest hope, if God permit, to engage in foreign missionary work." The claim has been made for each of several men that he was the first student volunteer in the British Isles. The entry in the first roll of those who signed this declaration is this : " No. 1. Taylor, F. Howard, M.D. Lond. ; M.R.C.P., Lond. ; B.S. Lond. ; F.R.C.S. Eng., London Hospital." This organization had no one who could travel for it, and soon began to decline as its members left college, but the seed of the Student Volunteer Movement was planted in Great Britain and it was not to perish.

CHAPTER II

THE STUDENT VOLUNTEER MISSIONARY UNION

THE Student Volunteer Movement grew rapidly in the United States and Canada, and seven thousand students had joined by 1891. The British students who had been guests at the Northfield Student Conferences were deeply impressed by the organization of the Movement in America and determined to have the help of the man to whom it owed more than any other. They invited Robert Wilder several times to visit Great Britain, and at last, his course completed and his appointment as a missionary to India made, he promised to come.

Robert Wilder arrived in London in July 1891, after the university term had ended, and made his way to the Church Missionary Society to visit Mr Eugene Stock. Wilder's father was founder and editor of *The Missionary Review of the World*, a monthly periodical which essayed to survey the foreign missionary work of all the Churches. He had corresponded for some years with Mr Eugene Stock, the editorial secretary of the Church Missionary Society, and it was natural that one of his son's first acts should be to call on Mr Eugene Stock at Salisbury Square.

Wilder had in his possession letters of introduction to Prebendary Webb Peploe, Rev. F. B. Meyer and others, and one of his first questions to Mr Eugene Stock was how to get into touch with these men. The reply was : "They are just now assembling at Keswick for the Convention and you had better go there." This Convention [1] was a great gathering of some three thousand

---

[1] The Keswick Convention is still held, though less representative in character than at this period.

people, which met in the Lake district for a week to hear Bible readings and addresses on the devotional and spiritual life by men drawn from the Evangelical party of the Church of England and from like-minded groups in the Free Churches in England and Scotland, and whose chief message was the need for holiness of life and the possibility of such through a complete surrender of heart and life to God, with the resultant gift of the Holy Spirit.

Mr Stock introduced Robert Wilder to Mr Miles MacInnes, of Rickerby, Carlisle, a director of the London and North Western Railway Company and a well-known figure in religious circles. Mrs MacInnes was a grand-daughter of the first Sir Fowell Buxton, one of the leaders of the successful anti-slavery movement of the last century. They received Wilder in their house at Keswick and there began a life-long friendship. Their son Rennie,[1] an undergraduate at Cambridge and already a leader in the Cambridge Inter-Collegiate Christian Union, took a leading part in the subsequent founding of the Student Volunteer Missionary Union.

It was the custom to close the Convention week by a missionary meeting on the Saturday morning. Wilder was invited to speak and gave, Mr Eugene Stock wrote afterwards, " a brief but thrilling account of the Student Volunteer Movement in America."

This address reached many students, some were in camp at Keswick under the leadership of Professor Laidlaw of Edinburgh University, while many Oxford and Cambridge men were present with their families or in house parties, attending the Convention. Among the Scottish students was Donald Fraser,[2] who early in the Convention had passed through a deep spiritual experience. He came to the Saturday missionary meet-ing but the tent was full and, unable to find a seat, he crept inside the tent behind the platform and leaned

[1] Later the Right Rev. R. MacInnes, Bishop in Jerusalem, died 1931.
[2] Later the Very Rev. Donald Fraser, D.D.

against the wooden supports. Wilder's address moved him deeply and then and there he dedicated himself to the mission field.

Fraser himself wrote, years afterwards, to Wilder of his experience :

> I and several others had gone up with a very indefinite faith, and God had met with us and we had come into the wonder of forgiveness. On the Saturday you spoke to this prepared atmosphere, and there was an immediate response. What struck us most was the opportunity of influencing our fellow-students during our college course, and doubling our own lives should we be allowed to lead one other into the foreign field. I do not know how the Cambridge men were caught, or what they did, but I remember waiting behind with others to ask you to come to Glasgow.[1]

At the close of this meeting the President of the Cambridge Inter-Collegiate Christian Union, C. T. Horan,[2] and Rennie MacInnes, invited Wilder to visit Cambridge University, while Lord Kinnaird[3] and Mr R. A. Hill, who was secretary to Professor Henry Drummond, invited him to visit Edinburgh.

Illness prevented Wilder from working until after Christmas, but in January 1892 he began a tour which proved to be memorable. The first place he visited was Edinburgh, where his most important meeting was one held in the Oddfellows' Hall, with Professor Henry Drummond in the chair and five hundred students present. He went on to Glasgow, where, as a result of his work, about twenty students sent their names to the Free Church of Scotland Foreign Missions Committee as willing to undertake missionary work. Aberdeen was also visited and twelve Student Volunteers secured. Then he turned south, going first of all to Cambridge, where, on 6th February 1892, he gave a Bible reading in an undergraduate's rooms in Corpus Christi College

[1] *The Student Movement*, vol. xv. p. 150.
[2] Later the Rev. Canon Horan.
[3] Arthur, 11th Baron Kinnaird.

on " The State of the Heathen." The meeting was described by one present as " a tremendous success." The following evening, Sunday, he spoke at a meeting of the Cambridge Inter-Collegiate Christian Union to two hundred and twenty undergraduates, giving an account of the Student Volunteer Movement in America. The next night Wilder described, as its founder, the Student Volunteer Movement in America to the Cambridge University Church Missionary Union in the Henry Martyn Hall, with the Rev. H. C. G. Moule [1] in the chair. Louis Byrde [2] described this as " a most wonderful address, which created such an impression that a number of men immediately came forward and decided to be foreign missionaries."

These meetings were supplemented by numerous talks in men's rooms, where the main subject of discussion was the foundation of a Student Volunteer Missionary Union, first of all for Cambridge, and then for the British Isles ; for both Wilder and the Cambridge men had the idea of a national movement in mind. They do not seem to have been aware at this stage that the Students' Foreign Missionary Union had this object in view.

Wilder wrote that " probably the most important meeting held at Cambridge was the one we had at Corpus Christi College in the rooms of Louis Byrde, where six of us, C. T. Horan, President of the Cambridge Inter-Collegiate Christian Union, and Rennie MacInnes, its treasurer, Ernest Millar, H. A. Kingdon, Byrde and I discussed the advisability of starting a Student Volunteer Missionary Union in Great Britain. They were unanimously in favour of forming a definite organization." They formed the Cambridge Student Volunteer Missionary Union, but it was decided not to draw up a Constitution immediately, but to delay a little until the leaders of groups in Edinburgh and London could be consulted.

[1] Later Bishop of Durham.
[2] Later the Rev. Louis Byrde, C.M.S., China.

One fruit of Wilder's visit to Cambridge was a letter to the C.M.S. signed by fifty-four undergraduates, who asked to be kept in touch with the Society and informed of openings abroad. Sixteen of these were ultimately sent out as missionaries.[1]

Wilder next visited Oxford, where he addressed several meetings under the auspices of the Oxford Missionary Union, at the most important of which the Rev. F. J. Chavasse[2] took the chair. He then fulfilled engagements in London and made inquiries as to the condition of the Students' Foreign Missionary Union. O. O. Williams wrote : " he was asked by the Cambridge men to look us up, find out who we were, what we were like and what we *were doing*, which by that time was very little." Indeed, Wilder subsequently reported the Students' Foreign Missionary Union " to be in a very dying state."

The Students' Foreign Missionary Union was certainly doing very little and the reasons are not far to seek. The men who had started it and given it its early impetus were most of them medical students who, by this time, were either qualified or too busy with their final year of study to do much work. In addition, as has since been demonstrated again and again in London, it is impossible for students to find the time to organize corporate activities in so large and scattered a student field, much less promote a national movement. The leaders of the Union tried to solve their problems by spending much time in the framing of constitutions, but that did not touch the real needs of the situation.

Robert Wilder met twenty-one students on March 11th at 48, Highbury Park, the house of Dr James Maxwell, head of the London Medical Missionary Association, an organization for the training of missionaries. Those present asked for the recognition of the Students' Foreign Missionary Union as the parent society, which

---

[1] *History of the Church Missionary Society*, by Eugene Stock, vol. iii. p. 373.
[2] Later Bishop of Liverpool.

they desired Oxford, Cambridge and Edinburgh to join. O. O. Williams, however, knowing that the London students had tried for two years to establish a general Union but had failed, and doubting their capacity to take the lead at this juncture, pointed out the danger of their standing in the way of establishing a general Union and carried the meeting with him. A report of it was embodied in the following letter by W. Blair Neatby to H. G. Warren of Corpus Christi College, Cambridge, one of the officers of the Cambridge group :

March 15th, 1892.

My Dear Sir,

At a general and special meeting of the members of the S.F.M.U. in and around London on March 11th, the following resolutions were passed unanimously :

1. That this meeting, representing the London members of the Students' Foreign Missionary Union, agrees to enter into negotiations with the various branches of the Union in England, Scotland and Ireland, with a view to reorganizing on the lines suggested by Mr R. P. Wilder, viz. :

(1) An executive of four, representing England, Scotland, Ireland and London, to be appointed annually by the members, the executive to have full power.

(2) The executive to appoint an organizing secretary annually.

(3) An advisory committee of five.

(4) Alteration of the wording of the pledge " I am willing and desirous," instead of " It is my earnest hope."

2. That this meeting appoints Mr Parrott, Mr Neatby and Mr D. W. Roberts to carry out these negotiations so as to secure all completed by the end of the month.

Although the Union has made steady progress during the last two years, our membership now being 218, it has been long and generally felt that we ought to be able to do more to stir up missionary zeal among our fellow-students ; and a few of us were glad a few days ago to have the benefit of Mr R. P. Wilder's experience of the work in America. He told us at our own request that many in Cambridge, Glasgow and Edinburgh thought our organization too elaborate ever to work quite satisfactorily, and thought that it was indispensable that we should have an organizing secretary, whose duty it should be to go from University to University, and from College to College, laying before students everywhere the claims of the foreign field. The lack of such a secretary we have long felt in London. We were given to understand that if the Union would consent to some such simple organization as that suggested by Mr R. P. Wilder, 60 men in Cambridge and others in Scotland were ready to cast in their lot with us, and so make a united stand in the three kingdoms. A special meeting of the 75 London members was according called, and the above resolution passed *nem. con.*

We were requested to put the matter before you, and learn your own views on the subject. If the various bodies of members at the different centres are of one mind with us we may hope to set a larger movement on foot after the summer.

It was the feeling of all that no alteration should be made in our name, or in Rule 7 (as to voting powers) ; but that there should be no constitution and no subscription. £50 have already been promised by one gentleman towards the expenses of an organizing or travelling secretary, and with an advisory committee of representative and well-known Christian men, we ought to have no difficulty in raising £200 or £300 a year to defray all expenses.

.   .   .   .

We are sure you will feel with us the need for earnest prayer that the blessing of our God and Father may rest abundantly on this effort for the spread of the Gospel of our Lord Jesus Christ, and that He will guide us all into the knowledge of His will.

Faithfully yours,
W. Blair Neatby.

When the contents of this letter had been communicated to Wilder he went at once to Edinburgh to make preparations for a conference. On March 23rd he wrote to Louis Byrde of Corpus Christi College, Cambridge, already virtually the General Secretary of the incipient movement :

Met Edinburgh men yesterday, they will issue invitations at once to you, Glasgow, London, Aberdeen, Wales and Ireland. As a result of my five meetings January 26-29, I hope Oxford will be represented. A Glasgow deputation has secured two Volunteers at St Andrews, we hope

ROBERT P. WILDER

that one of them will be present at Edinburgh, April 2nd
and 3rd. Are there not Volunteers at Durham? I had
a good time with the Glasgow men last night, they will
send 3 or 4 to Edinburgh.

God blessed the Copenhagen[1] meetings wonderfully, it is
a long story and I am worn out so I shall tell you about
them when we meet.

To-day one hundred pounds were promised towards the
expenses of a field secretary, if we have one; this added to
the London £50 gives us a good start. I went for this
money with much fear. I told the man of the proposed
conference, etc., and asked for £100; he promised it.
Praise God! You are right. Do nothing to antagonise
the London men. They have been most magnanimous,
they have sent letters to Glasgow and Edinburgh giving
my suggestions plus a few of their own.

The invitation to the places Wilder mentions to a
conference in Edinburgh on April 2nd and 3rd, 1892,
was issued from the United Presbyterian College,
Edinburgh, by J. M. Grieve on behalf of the Edinburgh
Students' Foreign Missionary Union. The Students'
Foreign Missionary Union in London was represented
by O. O. Williams, London Hospital; Cambridge by
Louis Byrde, Ernest Millar and C. T. Horan; Oxford,
Edinburgh, Glasgow, Aberdeen, St Andrews and
Belfast were also represented. Professor Drummond,
who was to have been in the chair, was absent
through illness, and Wilder was elected chairman in
his place.

After prolonged discussion and prayer, the Student
Volunteer Missionary Union of Great Britain and Ireland was inaugurated. The London delegate of the
Students' Foreign Missionary Union quickly gave way on
the question of name, as it was clear to all that the word
" Volunteer " was playing a considerable part in the
movement and should be included in the title of the
organization.

The official record of the conference in the minute-

---

[1] Wilder had been taking a series of meetings in Scandinavia
just before his tour in Great Britain.

book of the Student Volunteer Missionary Union reads as follows :

> After prayer had been offered, various plans, etc., were fully discussed, the result being The Students' Foreign Missionary Union became merged into the new body which was then formed and called the Student Volunteer Missionary Union, the Declaration of which was " I am willing and desirous, God permitting, to become a foreign missionary."
>
> It was agreed
> (1) The Association shall be called the Student Volunteer Missionary Union.
> (2) The membership shall consist of all students who shall sign the following Declaration " I am willing and desirous God permitting to become a foreign missionary."
> (3) The officers of the Union shall consist of an Executive Committee, Advisory Committee, Travelling Secretary, General Secretary (when necessary) and local and corresponding secretaries.
> (4) The Executive Committee shall consist of four members, one for England and Wales, one for Scotland, one for Ireland, and one for London ; each of these constituencies shall elect its own representative, the votes being given by each centre in the proportion of one vote for every ten members or fraction of ten members ; three members of the Executive shall form a quorum.
> (5) The work of the Executive shall be as follows : (1) It shall elect a Travelling Secretary, an Advisory Committee of five gentlemen and a General Secretary (if necessary). (2) Its members shall each superintend their respective constituencies, and arrange the tour of the Travelling Secretary.
> (6) Officers shall hold their posts for one year, but each officer shall be eligible for re-election.
>
> F. V. Thomas and R. M. Robertson were appointed to act as an Executive Committee *pro tem.* and to receive nominations and votes from each centre for their representative on the International Executive Committee.

Plans were already on foot to revive the London Union, which now became the London branch of the S.V.M.U., and a meeting was held in Morley Hall, situated in Regent Street opposite the Polytechnic, on

Friday, April 8th, " to consider the claims of the heathen on students." The chair was taken by Lord Kinnaird and addresses were given by the Rev. R. Wardlaw Thompson, secretary of the London Missionary Society, Ernest Millar, Louis Byrde, Stanley Hersee, all of Cambridge, and Robert Wilder. What the exact membership at this date was is not clear, but it is known that the membership of the Students' Foreign Missionary Union immediately before the Edinburgh Conference was 223, while sixty-eight Volunteers' names were enrolled with Louis Byrde at Cambridge.

The Executive Committee of the new Union was constituted on May 24th, 1892, as follows : Scotland : J. H. Maclean, Glasgow University ; London : O. O. Williams, B.Sc., Aberystwyth College and London Hospital ; England and Wales : Louis Byrde, Corpus Christi, Cambridge. Ireland did not elect a representative. Two days later Wilder addressed the General Assembly of the Free Church of Scotland in Edinburgh on the subject of the Student Volunteer Movement.

One of the first acts of the newly formed Executive was to decide that women students should be admitted to the S.V.M.U. Women had not been enrolled in the Students' Foreign Missionary Union. It also issued a form to each Student Volunteer asking for the following particulars : " Name, college, home address, age, date of entering the Union, university, denomination, missionary society preferred, mission field preferred, when do you hope to go, in what capacity do you hope to go—i.e. lay, ordained, medical, etc.— have you been in communication with the secretary of the missionary society mentioned above ? " Student Volunteers will notice that this form has undergone very little alteration in the intervening years.

The leaders and members of the Union proceeded to take all the opportunities that came to them of addressing meetings on foreign missions, whether of students or the general public. They conceived their task to be to move students to offer in large numbers for missionary service, and to arouse the Christian public to the duty of furnishing the missionary societies with sufficient funds to send them out, and to the privilege of following the Volunteers with their interest and prayers on the mission field. We read of meetings being held for the public in Derby, Carlisle, Penrith, Buxton and in a number of places in Scotland and Wales. Several students who took a prominent part in these meetings became in later life well-known leaders, as, for example, Dr S. Lavington Hart, an outstanding missionary of the London Missionary Society, and Harrington C. Lees, who became Archbishop of Melbourne.

From the first the object of the Union was to secure candidates for the missionary societies. It has sometimes been asked whether the S.V.M.U. ever thought of sending out missionaries itself; apparently this was once discussed by the Executive, but the objections were so obvious that the idea was quickly set aside.

The choice of Maclean, Byrde and Williams as an Executive proved a happy one. Dr Williams, writing years afterwards, says : " We united Church and Chapel, we united the new and old universities, we united England, Scotland and Wales, we based ourselves on unity and refused to quarrel with the orthodox or the unorthodox. We respected all views and only asked the missionary students to unite, and we only ran the missionary idea and the pledge to take up mission work. We had, therefore, nothing to discuss except the missionary idea." [1]

O. O. Williams brought to the group knowledge of successful student work in Aberystwyth (having taken his B.Sc. there before he entered the London Hospital), experience of the difficulties of London, and he also represented to a considerable extent a training and outlook not far removed from that of a large number of the students yet to be reached in the student centres outside Oxford and Cambridge.

J. H. Maclean had a first-class mind, was a fully

[1] Memorandum, 1913.

equipped Scottish Presbyterian theological student, ready to work extremely hard for the cause and quite unready to be rushed into ill-considered action.

Louis Byrde, the leader of the trio, was essentially a man of action. He was educated at Bedford Grammar School and had been an enthusiast for missions while at school, where he had started the Bedford Schoolboys' Missionary Union, stirring up its members to make articles for the annual C.M.S. sale, where they had their own stall. L. B. Butcher says that almost his first introduction to him was when he went to Bedford as a schoolboy " and was met by the request to make a fretwork bracket for the sale, and he would take no denial ! "

Byrde was a member of the Church of England; his own religious experience was simple, direct and vivid. To win men to a personal faith in Jesus Christ as Saviour and Lord, to lead them to dedicate their lives to His service and to consider in a special manner the claims of the foreign mission field, was the main thing for which he lived during his Cambridge days. He was neither a thinker nor to any extent a reader ; he was, however, a painstaking and regular Bible student, a man of prayer and a man of action.

Like all the Cambridge men who were prominent in Christian work among their fellow-students at this time Byrde laid great stress upon unflinching witness at all times to the power of Christ and upon keeping an adequate time every day—with most of these men it was at least an hour each morning—for Bible study, private prayer and communion with God.

His activity was amazing, as two thousand letters (which have come into the hands of the writer), addressed to him at this period by students all over the world, testify. His room at Cambridge was the office of the Student Volunteer Missionary Union for a year; he looked after the finances of the Union, acted as secretary to the Executive, planned visits by students all over the United Kingdom, and carried out several tours of visitation himself. He refused to see difficulties, and

D

he refused to see them because of his profound conviction that in seeking to enrol men to spread the knowledge of Jesus Christ in the non-Christian world, he and his colleagues were doing what God had called them to do and that, therefore, they could count upon the gift of the Holy Spirit. And no one who reads the record of those days can doubt but that God was indeed with them.

The leaders determined to keep their contact with the Volunteer Movement in America, and the summer the S.V.M.U. was founded O. O. Williams, Louis Byrde and F. V. Thomas went to the Northfield Student Conference to study at first hand the work in the United States. This conference, Byrde writes, "was a wonderful inspiration and means of opening the eyes of the delegates to the possibilities of organized Christian work in the colleges."

The American and British leaders decided at this Northfield Conference to alter the S.V.M.U. declaration. Hitherto it had been, " I am willing and desirous, God permitting, to become a foreign missionary." It was decided that henceforth the declaration used on both sides of the Atlantic should be : " It is my purpose, if God permit, to become a foreign missionary." The object of the change was to strengthen the declaration. Henceforth much emphasis was laid, in Great Britain at any rate, upon the word " purpose." Students who had difficulties in the way of leaving home, or who were not sure whether they had really decided to become missionaries or not, often sought advice from travelling secretaries as to whether they should join the S.V.M.U. Such students were invariably faced with the question : " Is it your *purpose* to become a foreign missionary ? " They were told that obstacles might be removed, however great, but that nothing would really set them on the road towards the mission field unless it was their purpose to go there, and that until they had such a purpose they should not join.

The American and British leaders took the occasion

of their meeting in 1892 to discuss the extension of the Movement outside the English-speaking countries. It was D. L. Wishard who first pictured clearly the idea of a world-wide Student Christian Movement. In a pamphlet he published in 1884 he wrote, the Movement " will continue to spread until the students in the old universities of Great Britain and Europe and the students in the missionary colleges in the Orient and the Dark Continent are united with the students of America in one world-wide Movement of Christ for the students of the world and the students of the world for Christ." This idea of extension, which was to produce the World's Student Christian Federation three years later, was in the thought and talk of both American and British leaders at this time.

CHAPTER III

THE S.V.M.U. BEGINS ITS WORK

THE leadership in starting the S.V.M.U. had been in the hands of the Cambridge men and there it was to remain for a little longer, for it was the Executive of the Cambridge S.V.M.U. that decided a travelling secretary should be secured and that delegates should be sent to the conference at Northfield.

A minute-book records meetings of the Cambridge branch between February 7th and December 7th, 1892, then follows a number of blank pages, on which probably Byrde had intended to write the minutes of the national committee, for it did meet, but no entries were ever made. The first minutes of the national organization that are preserved are in this book, but are dated September 20th, 1894; thus the book became Minutebook No. 1 of the S.V.M.U., and was used as such until it was filled and No. 2 commenced.

It has, however, been possible to study the history of the Union from May, 1892, not only in the reports and pamphlets issued by the Union, but in correspondence addressed by the members of the Executive and the travelling secretary to Louis Byrde. This correspondence is complete, as apparently Byrde never destroyed a letter; he kept all, important and unimportant alike, in the envelopes in which they reached him, with the name of the writer and often a note of the contents written across the corner of the envelope.

In August, 1892, the Rev. A. T. Polhill-Turner,[1] one of the Cambridge Seven, who had been at work for seven years in China under the China Inland Mission,

[1] Now the Rev. A. T. Polhill (name changed), Vicar of Furneaux Pelham, Buntingford, after forty years' service in China.

was appointed travelling secretary, although there was some hesitation about choosing a man no longer a student. There was a long correspondence between the members of the committee as to Polhill-Turner's salary and expenses. His remuneration was fixed at £3 per week with travelling expenses. The Scottish representative thought the salary rather high, although it would seem to have been a modest stipend for a married man !

The Executive decided that its first activity should be a campaign in Wales ; among those who took part were Polhill-Turner, Norman Bennett, Louis Byrde and E. H. Elwin [1] of Oxford. They began with the theological students, as entry to these colleges proved easiest. Byrde says of his first visit : " Two of us went to Bala College (Calvinistic Methodist Theological College), where we had several meetings. After the first one, in which we could not find our depth at all, we decided to give a Bible Reading, and the subject chosen was ' Assurance of Salvation.' This produced a great stir among the men, and they set to work to search their Bibles ; some of them saying that they had been studying commentaries and all that sort of thing, and omitting the text of the Bible. Subsequent meetings began a real missionary revival." [2]

Other meetings of this campaign were held in Trefecca and Aberystwyth. Polhill-Turner was left to follow it up, and visited Bala, Aberystwyth, Bangor, Carnarvon, Brecon, Cardiff, Carmarthen, Lampeter, Trefecca and Pontypool. Altogether fourteen colleges and preparatory theological schools were visited in Wales. Polhill-Turner records that he received a great deal of kindness and hospitality from principals and professors, but many of the students viewed the new Movement with distrust. Aberystwyth and Cardiff proved most encouraging ; at the latter place seven students joined the S.V.M.U., including three women, " the first ladies on our roll." The result of the

[1] Later Bishop of Sierra Leone.   [2] Memorandum by L. Byrde.

campaign in Wales was the registration of thirty Student Volunteers.

Polhill-Turner spent November and December in London, and visited University College, Pastors', Richmond, New, Hackney, Cheshunt and Regent's Park Colleges, also Harley House. He went to five hospital medical schools—Guy's, St Thomas's, Middlesex, London and St Mary's—the average attendance at these hospital meetings being twenty men. The London School of Medicine for Women was also visited and seventy students attended the meeting. A short visit to Oxford completed the term's work.

What was the purpose of the S.V.M.U., the call of which Polhill-Turner carried to the colleges? Let the answer be in his own words :

> As a Missionary Union . . . it aims at banding together all students whose hearts are stirred up by the Holy Spirit to obey our Master's parting command to take the Gospel to every creature. Its aims are higher and grander than those of any past movement, and under God's blessing it promises remarkable success. Feeling the pulse of Christian students where I have visited, I have found that they seem just ripe for such a movement, welding into one Union our university, college and hospital students—Episcopalian, Presbyterian, Wesleyan, Baptist and Methodist alike—united into a brotherhood hitherto thought impossible, *all one in Christ Jesus.*
>
> Our work is as *student to student*—a call coming from one of themselves—so to speak—a call to full personal consecration of all our talents to our Master and His blessed service. Bring a man to that point of full consecration; let him be filled with the Holy Ghost and on fire to save souls ; then the missionary question will be solved. If our hearts are melted with Divine Love and respond to that heart of Love which is going out over all heathen lands, it will not take much urging to send us abroad to Christ's " other sheep." [1]

It was characteristic of the spirit of the Movement that the first article published in *The Student Volunteer*—a

[1] *The Student Volunteer*, January 1893 ; art. : " The Opening Campaign."

quarterly magazine edited by J. H. Maclean, the forerunner of *The Student Movement*—which first appeared
in January 1893, was on the subject of " Prayer and
Foreign Missions." In this article Louis Byrde traced
in the Gospels and Acts of the Apostles, the history of
the early Church as " the story of missionary enterprise,
with every footstep marked with an act of prayer." As
the early disciples " laid firm hold on their omnipotent
Leader, Who had promised His abiding presence till
the work was done," so the writer urged the Student
Volunteers to recognize that the same great truth was
valid for them. He pointed out how the missionary
revival of modern times began in prayer, and then
addressed the members of the Union :

> Brother Volunteers, the evangelization of the world is
> possible in this generation. Are we then pleading daily
> with God to thrust forth His labourers into the fields white
> long ago to the harvest ? Why should not the world hear
> the good tidings of salvation within the next few years ?
> Why not ? I ask.

He passes on to an appeal to Student Volunteers " to
keep the Morning Watch, or some definite fixed time
for communion with God," and who of us who knew the
man can doubt but that he was writing out of the heart
of his own experience when, in speaking of " the hour
before we meet with men," he declared " we can plead
in secret with the Lord of the Harvest—for the world,
that His Gospel may be preached far and wide ;—for the
Church, that the Holy Spirit may stir up many to consecrate their all to Him ;—for ourselves, that we may
be daily filled with His Spirit, and so be always equipped
for His service." The practice of the early leaders of
keeping a prolonged period at the beginning of each
day for prayer and Bible study was a great source of
spiritual strength to the young Movement.

The challenge which the Movement presented to
students was embodied in the Declaration : " It is my
purpose, if God permit, to become a foreign missionary."

In this Declaration lies the whole secret of our Union. Every great and enduring Movement has its great underlying principles ; many sections of the Christian Church have formulated their " Confessions of Faith " ; many organizations have their list of objects, or " programmes " ; and it is surely a right thing for us to band ourselves together for a common purpose and to express that purpose in so concise a creed. . . . Some like to call our form a " covenant." . . . Others prefer to think of it as a " pledge," but we are content to call it a " declaration." Having made our purpose sure in the sight of God and of our own conscience we manifest it to others. We throw ourselves at once into our life work, and determine to influence others to the same decision. United, then, in this great purpose, constrained by the Love of Christ, and depending on the power of the Holy Spirit, we make it our endeavour to fulfil the purpose and Will of God.[1]

It is round this declaration that the S.V.M.U. has built up its work. The Watchword " The Evangelization of the World in this Generation," which was adopted later, played its part for some years, as we shall show, in strengthening the work of the Union, but its real strength lay from the first in the Declaration and the use that was made of it.

Another element of strength which early manifested itself was the determination of the leaders to educate students in facts regarding the non-Christian world. They themselves displayed remarkable knowledge of missionary history and literature. This was specially marked in the case of the Oxford and Cambridge men, and was largely the result of the numerous missionary study bands which had been carried on in these two universities during the years that intervened between the departure for China of the Cambridge Seven and the foundation of the S.V.M.U. The first number of *The Student Volunteer* contained notes on missionary books; these notes were continued in subsequent numbers and were then followed up by articles on the non-Christian religions, written by such competent authorities as

[1] *The Student Volunteer*, March 1893 ; art. : " Our Declaration."

Dr A. Murray Mitchell, Professor T. M. Lindsay, Principal T. Witton Davies and Professor Legge.

In the second term of the Union's first year, namely January to Easter 1893, Polhill-Turner, after speaking at Eton on the invitation of Dr Warre—Polhill-Turner being himself an old Etonian—went to Scotland and held his first meeting in New College, Edinburgh. " It was a meeting for Volunteers ; over forty were present and all very hearty." A number of other meetings were held in Edinburgh, and Professor Henry Drummond, Dr Hugh Barbour and Professor Grainger Stewart took part as speakers as well as Polhill-Turner. Among other meetings was a special one for Irish Divinity students studying in Edinburgh, presided over by J. S. Stevenson.[1] The meeting " was certainly characterized by genuine Irish enthusiasm ; and they proposed writing to their friends in the various Irish colleges to prepare for my visit to Ireland."

Visits to St Andrews, Aberdeen and Glasgow followed, and traces were found everywhere " of the most wonderful changes brought about eight years ago from Messrs Studd and Stanley Smith's visit before leaving for China." The number of meetings held in each place was considerable ; for example, a programme of eighteen meetings was carried through in Glasgow in ten days, apparently in very bad weather : " My ten days at Glasgow reminded me of the reply of the Greenock waiter who, when asked, ' Does it always rain here ? ' replied, ' No, Sir; sometimes it snows.' " There were seventeen student volunteers at this date in Glasgow.

The Union took stock of its numerical strength on May 1st 1893 and recorded its membership as four hundred and ninety-one. Of these twenty-five had sailed, thirteen were accepted for the mission field, fifty had left college, forty-six belonged to missionary institutions, while three hundred and seventeen men and women were present students in the universities, theological colleges and medical schools. It is interesting

[1] Later the Rev. J. Sinclair Stevenson, B.D., of Gujarat.

to note that the faculty most largely represented in the
Union was medicine.   One hundred and thirty-three of
its members were medicals, one hundred and twenty
theological and ninety-seven arts.

From Scotland, Polhill-Turner travelled to Ireland,
visiting Belfast, Londonderry, Dublin, Cork and Galway.
During this term he spoke at eighty meetings.   The
Irish meetings were all smaller than those in Scotland :
most of them were attended by from twenty to twenty-
five students.

While the travelling secretary was engaged in visitation, Byrde, Maclean and Williams were in correspondence on the subject of a conference.   Influenced to some
extent by the success attending the presence of groups
of students at the Keswick Convention, and still more
by their knowledge of the influence of summer conferences on the growth of the Movement in America, they
decided to hold a summer conference.   As many students
were already accustomed to go to Keswick, it was chosen
as place, and the date, July 19th to 24th, 1893, the week
before the Keswick Convention.   Tents were ordered
from Messrs Langdon of Liverpool, who to this day
supply annually the tents used at Swanwick.   They
were pitched in a small paddock—now built over—at
the end of one of the streets in Keswick, within a few
minutes' walk of the Convention tent and the Drill Hall.
The latter held about five hundred people and was hired
for the meetings of the Conference.

A visitor to that Drill Hall during the students' conference would have found it a stuffy and ill-ventilated
building, and if coming in unawares, might not at first
sight have recognized the conference as one of students,
for visitors to the Keswick Convention were not excluded, and one's first impression was of a large number of old ladies in bonnets !   A glance at the platform,
however, reassured one.   The chairman and speakers
were most of them obviously undergraduates.

No one knows exactly how many students attended
this conference; the number of men in camp was ninety.

England sent forty-two, Scotland forty-one, Wales four, and Ireland three. About forty per cent. were members of the Church of England, thirty per cent. Presbyterian and thirty per cent. Free Church, and whenever the denominational statistics of a summer conference have been taken any year since, the proportions have been almost exactly the same. In addition to the students in camp there were a number of students living in the town of Keswick, who attended the meetings, but of these no record was taken.

The day's programme opened at 7.15 a.m. with a prayer-meeting with a short address. From 9 to 10 a.m. various aspects of the work of the S.V.M.U. were dealt with. 11.30 to 1 p.m. was devoted to the discussion of Christian Union work, which was arranged not by the S.V.M.U. but by members of a number of College Christian Unions or Associations which were already in existence, though they had not yet been federated to make a movement. The afternoon was kept free for recreation. There was a Bible Reading at 6 o'clock and a general meeting at 7 p.m.

The evening meetings were missionary in character and were addressed by missionaries and missionary secretaries, with the exception of one evening when the speaker was Mrs Isabella Bird Bishop, F.R.G.S., one of the most famous women travellers and writers of her day. Her address, which dealt with what she had seen of the need for and the value of missionary work on her travels, was a remarkably interesting one. Mrs Bishop was deeply interested in the Conference, as a letter she wrote after its close to Louis Byrde makes clear.

The leaders had been happy in their choice of speakers, the Rev. R. W. Stewart of China, who was killed in the Boxer Rising in China, and Bishop Hill of West Africa both made a profound spiritual impression on the students. An immense amount of valuable advice was given to Student Volunteers by Mr Eugene Stock, Dr Hudson Taylor and others.

Dr Hugh Barbour, an early member of the Edinburgh

Medical Students' Christian Association and a friend of Henry Drummond, opened a discussion on " How to get alongside a university man," and what he said might well be reproduced for the benefit of students to-day. He urged that those who hoped to win university men for Christ must be good students, must throw themselves into the athletic and social life of the university and must not neglect the freshmen. He stressed the value to the freshman of a hearty welcome. " A Cambridge man said that ' the first thing that interested me was, when a man told me where I could get the best biscuits,' and that was the beginning of a friendship that went deeper." The speaker passed to the value of sympathy and perseverance :

> Most of us know some fellow in our year who is going off the rails, and we are perhaps the only person who can keep him straight. We are to be the influence through which God is to work, so that that man may be won for Christ. And we must make up our minds for a great deal of time, work and patience ; and, above all, a great deal of going out of ourselves in order that, as far as we can, we may lay our life alongside of the man we wish to win.

He spoke of all a student might do for the man he wished to win :

> Someone says that may mean great trouble on my part. But when we remember the great trouble our Friend has taken with us during all the years of our life, it will seem a very small thing to us. Another man will say, it may make a great demand on my time. But if we look back on the years of our life and see how much time our Friend has given to us, in order that we might be led to consecrate our lives to Him ; how many years He has been following us ; all the providences He has laid round about our life ; then the amount of time another man demands from us will seem a very small sacrifice.

But if missionaries and professors contributed much to the conference, the leaders of the Movement contributed no less. " The working up of a S.V.M.U. branch in college," " Bible training for personal work,"

" Missionary literature," " The Bible and Foreign Missions," " The evangelization of the world in this generation," were topics introduced with ability by the student leaders themselves. J. H. Maclean also con-contributed one of the Bible Readings.

What was the theological position represented by the speakers at the conference ? Theologically the platform was a broader one than that of the Keswick Convention. The majority of the speakers were evangelical, in the sense that there was no High Churchman or strong Institutionalist included among the speakers. They invariably approached their subject from the point of view of experimental religion, or as some of them would have said, from the point of view of Bible Christianity.

As to the Bible, although probably the majority would have declared for verbal inspiration, this theory was not part of the platform of the conference, nor was it the position of J. H. Maclean, who counselled students to avail themselves of the work of Biblical scholars and reminded them that " we must not take all parts of Revelation as of equal authority." He concluded his address by urging that none should " be afraid of what is called the intellectual study of the Bible. We are to love God with our *mind* as well as with our heart and soul." Another of the Bible Readings was given by Mr J. Vernon Bartlet.[1]

It has sometimes been assumed that the Student Movement started exclusively in a single school of thought. That, however, was not so, for although the majority of its early members had probably thought very little about theology and their strength lay in a vivid spiritual experience, initiated in most cases by a definite conversion, there was also a group of speakers and students who held what were at that time regarded as advanced views in relation to Biblical scholarship.

The Executive gave an account of its year's work to

[1] Later Professor J. Vernon Bartlet, D.D., of Mansfield College, Oxford.

the conference, and reported having held five committee meetings—at Cambridge, London (twice), Glasgow and Chester. It had published five missionary pamphlets, including a prayer cycle, and three numbers of *The Student Volunteer*. Byrde had acted as General Secretary and done a vast amount of work. The membership of the Union was over five hundred. The groups of Volunteers in each college met regularly for prayer and the study of the mission field, including non-Christian religions, held missionary meetings for all students who would attend, kept in touch with other Christian societies in colleges where these existed, sought to enrol new Student Volunteers and in many places sent a deputation of Volunteers " to plead the missionary cause in churches, Sunday schools, etc., or at public meetings."

The report also made reference to " the general influence on the Church which the Union is exerting. Testimonies are not wanting of the interest with which the Movement is regarded by the Churches, especially by some denominations, and the stimulus which they have felt from hearing about a Movement so hopeful."

The Union, however, had to face a certain amount of suspicion both from inside and outside the colleges. In Oxford the Union was very closely related to the Oxford Inter-Collegiate Christian Union, and the secretary wrote in this connection :

> I am truly sorry at our lethargy, but you must remember we are an independent lot as you are (at Cambridge), and are guided by the counsels of older men who look at the S.V.M.U. with suspicion and have said so. . . . We proposed having the S.V.M.U. on our O.I.C.C.U. card and but three of us spoke for it; all the rest against. . . . I only tell you this in confidence to show you the Movement, if it is to grow, must come from the men themselves, and God being with us, I trust we shall be able to do so. . . . Do you Cambridge brothers remember us in prayer. Our Missionary Union is growing, we had Wigram last night and about 60 to meet him. The dear man evidently does not wholly approve of the S.V.M.U. I know not how your men look at it, but I do wish men would decide the

matter for themselves and then throw their whole heart into this side.

Mr Wigram, the honorary secretary of the C.M.S., was probably more sympathetic than the Oxford undergraduates realized, but the leaders were so impetuous and so eager to thrust everyone out to the mission field that a missionary secretary might well be forgiven a little caution. The Union was received with great cordiality by most of the secretaries of the Missionary Societies, and among early friends were Dr George Smith, C.I.E., Mr Eugene Stock, the Rev. R. Wardlaw Thompson, Miss G. A. Gollock and Dr Hudson Taylor.

CHAPTER IV

THE INTER-UNIVERSITY CHRISTIAN UNION IS STARTED

WHEN the earlier of the modern student religious societies were founded, just before and after 1860, the universities, as already indicated, were few in number, but by the last decade of the century there had been an immense increase in the number of educational institutions of higher learning. The men from the ancient universities of England and Scotland leading the S.V.M.U., on investigating the English college field in 1893, found university colleges in Leeds (Yorkshire College), Sheffield (Firth College), Birmingham (Mason College), Liverpool, Bristol, Nottingham and Reading, and a College of Science in Newcastle. In London, in addition to University and King's Colleges and the medical schools attached to the hospitals, there were two engineering colleges and three music colleges—the Royal College of Music, Royal Academy of Music and Trinity College of Music. There were the military colleges of Woolwich and Sandhurst, and also a naval college. Several agricultural and veterinary colleges and half a dozen technical colleges had been founded, while there had been a considerable increase in the number of colleges for training teachers, some twenty-five being then at work.

In Scotland a university college at Dundee, a couple of technical colleges and some additional teachers' training colleges had started.

Wales had founded university colleges at Aberystwyth, Bangor and Cardiff, with some training colleges.

In Ireland there were university colleges at Belfast, Londonderry, Galway and Cork, with two new colleges in Dublin—the Royal College of Science and the Royal College of Surgeons.

This field was to gain further in size and importance within a few years as one university college after another received its charter and became a university, while still more technical, training and fine art colleges sprang into existence. This new field was unknown to the men from the older universities but they were determined to enter it.

The proposal to start an inter-collegiate Christian organization with the object of deepening the spiritual life of students who were already Christians and of winning others for Christ was discussed at an inter-university conference held in Glasgow in January 1893, at the annual Oxford and Cambridge conference later in the year,[1] and was decided upon at the summer conference at Keswick, 1893. The summer conference devoted the larger portion of three mornings to the subject, and agreed to found " The Inter-University Christian Union." The following constitution was drawn up :

1. The Union shall be called the Inter-University Christian Union.

2. The object of the Union shall be to unite in work and interest the various Universities, Colleges, Medical Schools, etc., of the United Kingdom, by means of conferences, deputations, correspondence, and such other means as may be thought effective.

3. The management of the Union shall be entrusted to an Executive Committee of three, who shall appoint a General Secretary.

4. The Secretaries of the Associations affiliated to the Union shall form a General Council : and they or their Delegates shall meet at an annual Conference to elect the Executive Committee.

5. Applications for affiliation to the Union shall be submitted to the Executive, by whom the application shall be decided.

[1] The O.I.C.C.U. and C.I.C.C.U. had held a joint conference annually for many years.

E

In addition to this constitution, the following suggestions for its working were agreed:

1. That Christian Associations should report to the Union the name and address of secretary for C.U. for the year.
2. Deputations shall be sent to start Christian Unions and to stimulate the existing ones by personal testimony and practical discussions.
3. Funds to be obtained, but at first at any rate expenses of delegates to be borne locally.
4. Students should be interested in the Annual Conference and encouraged to attend.
5. That we have the same General Secretary as the Student Volunteer Missionary Union.
6. Transference of Christians by introduction.

The men who chose the title for the new union all came from the ancient universities, and it did not apparently occur to any one that it was unsuitable, although the leaders already had in their mind, as letters of the period show, the desirability of founding Christian unions in colleges which were not of university standing, training colleges being especially mentioned as important. The following year the name was changed to the British College Christian Union and the initials B.C.C.U. soon became familiar in student circles.

The first Executive of the Inter-University Christian Union consisted of one arts student and two medicals : Frank Anderson, Exeter College, Oxford ; O. O. Williams, London Hospital and B. L. Livingstone-Learmonth, Edinburgh University. No officers, however, were appointed, though the committee met and discussed policy. This rather tame start was due to the fact that although there were some who saw the value of a union as a means of bringing existing religious societies together, few realized that the main thing to be done was to start Christian Unions where none existed. An early document tells us that the Inter-University Christian Union was started "amid much diffidence and indecision."

The appointment of Donald Fraser of Glasgow University as travelling secretary of the S.V.M.U. in succession to Polhill-Turner proved to be of great importance to the Inter-varsity Christian Union. Fraser soon saw the importance of the new union. Its committee consisted of a trio who knew practically nothing about the English student field as a whole, but he was moving about that field in the interests of the S.V.M.U. and found that he was constantly working at a serious disadvantage through lack of preparation in the colleges for his missionary work. Unlike Oxford, Cambridge and the Scottish universities, the more recently founded English colleges had no Christian societies organized among their students. Christian men among them had no opportunity of meeting to help one another in the Christian life, no organization to provide a base from which they could try to win their fellow-students for Christ or interest them in missionary work abroad.

Fraser did his own work as S.V.M.U. travelling secretary, and also a great deal of pioneering work which resulted in the founding of a number of Christian Unions. He became convinced as the year 1893-94 wore on that the new Inter-University Christian Union must have a travelling secretary of its own. He became that secretary a year later.

To hark back a little ; it was in May 1893 that Maclean wrote to Byrde suggesting Fraser as a suitable man to appoint as travelling secretary of the S.V.M.U. Byrde replied that Fraser might be the man that they wanted, but he would like to write to him about his spiritual qualifications for the work. This drew from Maclean the response :

As to Fraser, you may write him if you please, but I don't know that you will get very much satisfaction. Some of the most spiritual men are, from humility and other causes, the least able to give clear answers when catechized about their spiritual state. On this please yourself. Let me just assure you again that he is a man of great zeal and real spiritual power; he will do all his work in simple dependence upon the Holy Spirit.

As to his English you need have no fear.

I trust we shall be guided by God in this matter. But while praying to Him we must use common sense in looking about; so far as I can see the leadings are in the direction of Fraser.

The reference to Fraser's English is amusing, he spoke with a distinct Scottish accent but was always an accomplished speaker and one of the few born orators the Student Movement has had on its staff. Byrde was satisfied, and less than a fortnight later Maclean wrote, "Fraser has accepted the post of travelling secretary." They had chosen a man of vision, power and great gifts of leadership.

Fraser's letters indicate some of the difficulties of this pioneering. From Bristol he wrote: "I have tried to get an entrance into the Arts faculty at the University College but so far have been unable. I asked several men if they knew a Christian man in college to whom I could go. They answered they did not think there was one."

Fraser did not lack courage, for he pursued these inquiries by standing in the corridor of the college and stopping men as they passed and asking whether any of them knew of a Christian man.

From Nottingham he wrote that he could not get into the University College but had met Professor Grainger; "he is intent on starting Sunday services for the students—but on the very broadest lines. I encouraged him, because if we get these professors enthusiastic we shall get the council moved to sanction religion."

In the meantime there had been correspondence between Byrde and a student at Owens College, Manchester, who after inquiries wrote:

I am sorry to tell you that the Principal says it is against the rules of the college and he does not like to grant permission [to hold a religious meeting], although he says he

has the greatest sympathy with the object and with anything which will tend to raise the moral tone of the college,
because of the number of applications of the like nature
which he would receive.

The same Principal was approached by another
Student Movement man, T. E. Alvarez of Oxford, a
fortnight later, and he likewise wrote to Byrde saying
that the Principal said : " He could not see his way to
establish such a precedent " as to permit a meeting.
Subsequently a meeting was held outside the college,
with the result that Fraser writes :

> My meeting with Owens proved rather a failure.   Only
> two men turned up. . . . However, these places are not
> finished.   I must get an entrance.

Passing to Leeds he wrote of the University College
there :

> I saw the Principal of Yorkshire College in his den, he
> was very polite, but said they had already considered the
> question of religious meetings, and owing to the strictly
> undenominational character of the college could not allow
> a room for one.   He could not give any advice officially,
> not even as to what student I could go to, to arrange a
> private meeting in their rooms, but he advised me to see
> Dr Simon at Bradford College,[1] as some of his students
> attended the Yorkshire College, but he would be very glad
> to hear of my success, etc., etc.   If I can I shall see what
> can be done to-morrow.

Similar quotations could be added from letters and
reports of other secretaries during succeeding years.
It took about five or six years to secure a footing for
Christian Unions among the students of most of the
university colleges which were the forerunners of the
great modern universities.   The task of the travelling
secretary was made very difficult through refusal of
permission to put up notices in colleges or hold a meeting within college walls.

When travelling secretaries did get into the colleges

[1] A Congregational theological college.

the first experience was usually great apathy and a very small meeting. A common experience in a university college which numbered several hundred students was to get an attendance of from six to a dozen students after really hard work. There was little opposition. The only meeting in England that was deliberately broken up by sustained noise was one for students at Owens College, Manchester. This was when another attempt was made after Fraser's first abortive effort.

Fraser had a lively time during his first meeting at Aberdeen University. He arrived there during the Rectorial election and met the first and second year medical students after a lecture :

> The men were in great spirits in the fever heat of the Rectorial election and ready for any fun. So when I appeared alone on the platform I was greeted with volleys of jokes, whistling, etc. For a quarter of an hour or more I spoke, sometimes having almost to shout to be heard. I was very uncomfortable. However, when I began to dwell upon the necessity of knowing Christ before being a foreign missionary, etc., the rowdy men began to clear out and at the end I had five minutes of solemn talk.

This visit was not in vain for eleven meetings were held, two daily prayer-meetings started, one for the medical and the other for the arts students, and the Christian Association considerably strengthened.

Fraser's next letter is from Dublin, three weeks later, and he writes that in the intervening three weeks he had addressed forty-four meetings and had travelled about 700 miles. He asked for prayer, saying : " I have a very heavy week before me—and am already feeling rather worn." Travelling secretaries do often feel worn, it is a very exacting life. The travelling secretary is almost invariably a man or a woman who has started work immediately on graduation. He is plunged into a continual stream of engagements : addresses, committee meetings, talks with individuals ; always trying to lift a situation on to a higher plane ; expected by every new college to be fresh and concerned alone with its problems ; hampered all the time by correspondence ; constantly packing and unpacking his luggage and making journeys ; always meeting new people. There are probably few people in the Student Movement who are more lonely at times than travelling secretaries, but all over the world now are thousands of men and women who owe an incalculable debt to the band of men and women who, each for one, two or three years, have given their time and strength to the Student Movement as a travelling secretary before they entered upon their life work.

In the beginning of 1894 Fraser spent three or four weeks in London and also paid a visit to Cambridge. Here, according to a letter to Byrde from W. Holdgate, one of the Cambridge leaders, Fraser had his heart's desire, which was to be " progged " ! Oxford and Cambridge both possess that interesting institution a proctor, a member of the staff of the University whose duty it is to wander about the town at night with two assistants known as " bull-dogs," to see that members of the University are not out without their caps and gowns, or smoking with their caps and gowns on, or visiting forbidden places of entertainment, staying out too late or committing similar crimes. When an undergraduate is detected departing from the paths of virtue the proctor's bull-dogs give chase, followed by the proctor. When the sinner is caught, his name and college are taken, he appears before the proctor next day and is suitably dealt with—in most cases he is fined. This institution, peculiar to Oxford and Cambridge, is a source of amused interest to most other university men. Holdgate wrote, " Donald Fraser, coming from the meeting with me on Sunday, earnestly desired to see a ' proggins.' Within five minutes of that time he was progged by Jackson of Jesus, in this street "— Malcolm Street, Cambridge.

It was in this academic year, 1893-94, that the Movement acquired its first office. Byrde applied to the secretary of the Y.M.C.A., 186 Aldersgate Street,

London, to know whether they had a room they could
lend as an office. The Y.M.C.A. had little space to
spare, but eventually a partition was erected in one of
its rooms and a tiny office, which Byrde describes as " a
little wooden box only just big enough to hold a desk
and two chairs," became the nominal headquarters of
the Student Movement. The real headquarters remained
as before—Byrde's rooms. At first these were at
Cambridge, but by this time he had been ordained and
was curate at St Peter's, Islington, accordingly he conducted most of the work of the Movement from his
lodgings at 49 Duncan Terrace, Islington. The
occupant of the Aldersgate Street office was Mr V. G.
Levett, a young clerk on the Stock Exchange, who gave
an hour every evening to routine correspondence, the
sending out of magazines, literature, etc.

In the New Year (1894) Miss Hodges became travelling secretary for the women's colleges. She was not
a college woman, none being available. She was introduced to the Movement by Miss G. A. Gollock, a
member of the staff of the Church Missionary Society.
It was largely due to Miss Gollock that a woman was
appointed. Some months before she had written to
Mr Byrde, saying : " There is a remarkable movement
on foot just now among the women students of the
various colleges—it is small as yet but of vital importance. They wish, at a large meeting shortly to be held,
to develop the S.V.M.U." The letter asks for an
appointment in order that she may be brought up to
date as to the latest facts about the S.V.M.U. This
meeting was held later at Westfield College, and among
those who had a share in arranging it were Agnes de
Sélincourt and Ruth Rouse, who later came to play a
large part in the work of the Student Movement all
over the world.

Miss Gollock was visiting as C.M.S. secretary a
number of women's colleges at this period and her help
and advice proved very valuable. Indeed, so many
demands were made upon her that we find Byrde

apologizing for their number, to which Miss Gollock replied : " Yes, I am busy, but this work is very near my heart and as long as you need such help as I can give, please claim it freely." It is thirty-nine years since Miss Gollock wrote that sentence. In the intervening years her help has been sought again and again and her help has never failed.

This spring a joint letter was issued to theological students by the S.V.M.U. and Inter-University Christian Union proposing a " Theological College Missionary Alliance," its object being " to unite the theological colleges of Great Britain and Ireland for (1) the promotion of the spirit of Christian living ; (2) the increase of spiritual life ; (3) the development of Christian effort at home and abroad." The scheme suggested National Councils for Northern England, Southern England, Wales, Scotland and Ireland, with an Executive consisting of a delegate appointed by each National Council. The methods of work proposed were conferences, " seasons of united prayer and the use of other means for the increase of spiritual life," inter-college visitation, the organization of missionary societies in colleges having none, and "co-operation of the Alliance with the S.V.M.U. and the Inter-University Christian Union in holding an international college conference."

Colleges were asked to write their opinion and to send a delegate to the summer conference at Keswick. Subsequently the matter was discussed and decision deferred for a year to give the colleges time to consider the proposal.

About this time Agnes de Sélincourt wrote to Louis Byrde of a plan conceived by a group of Cambridge women to found " a missionary settlement in which women from our universities could live together and unite in educational, medical and evangelistic work," and asked his approval for the insertion in *The Student Volunteer* of a letter setting forth their plan. The letter duly appeared,[1] sketching the plan for a settlement in

[1] *The Student Volunteer*, November 1894, p. 161.

Bombay to carry on work among Parsees. It was signed by L. M. Cooke and E. M. Yeo of Newnham College and C. A. J. Skeel, C. Ruth Rouse, A. J. Hillyard and Agnes de Sélincourt of Girton College. The plan found support and the Missionary Settlement for University Women, Bombay, was founded. It had its own committee that was in close liaison with the Student Movement, and when Ruth Rouse was appointed a secretary in the summer of 1896 it was as travelling secretary for the S.V.M.U., the B.C.C.U. and the Missionary Settlement for University Women.

The Second Summer Conference was held at Keswick from July 30th to August 3rd 1894, under the joint auspices of the Inter-University Christian Union and the Student Volunteer Missionary Union. One hundred and forty-three men and thirty-nine women were present, representing twenty-nine colleges and fourteen Christian Unions. This is smaller than the number of students attending the Convention at Keswick the previous week, one hundred and ninety-two men and forty-one women having been present.

There were delegates at the Student Conference from France, Germany, Holland, the United States of America and South Africa. The two delegates from America were John R. Mott and Robert E. Speer, whose addresses made a deep impression. The programme differed considerably from the more general doctrinal and spiritual programme of later years. More than half of the time of the conference was devoted to the nature of the work and problems of a Christian Union, and of the S.V.M.U. in college. The only speakers other than Student Movement leaders were the Rev. G. H. C. Macgregor, Canon Taylor Smith,[1] Professor Lloyd Snape and the Rev. Alexander Connell. Robert Speer gave Bible Readings which were the basis of his subsequent book, *The Man Christ Jesus*.

A report of this gathering was published, prefaced

[1] Later Bishop of Sierra Leone and subsequently Chaplain-General of the Forces.

by an interesting impression of the conference which, it declares, was remarkable for its spirit of unanimity, " a deep and all-pervading prayerfulness which seemed to prevail " and " a great feeling of expectation . . . were it only to stand by and see God working." " Again, something which gave a wonderful impetus to the conference was the presence of our French, German and American brothers." A warm tribute is paid to Mr Mott.

The idea of the Federation was still in the minds of the leaders. After commenting on the value of the contribution from the visitors from other lands, several of whom addressed the conference, the report says, " It is plain that very soon some sort of international Christian Union for mutual support and help will have to be considered," while *The Student Volunteer* the following term remarked, "the presence of foreign delegates was of great significance—too great to be yet estimated rightly. Ours is a Movement in which the students of the world can join hands and help one another."

The conference was important from the woman's point of view; only six women had been present in 1893, but this year two houses and some rooms were taken and over fifty women students were present. They represented universities and colleges in Glasgow, Edinburgh, London, Oxford, Cambridge, Dublin and Belfast. Forty of them were Student Volunteers and the majority were medical students, the largest delegation coming from the London School of Medicine for Women. The question of founding a separate intercollegiate union for women was discussed. It was decided, however, that women's unions should be affiliated to the same organization as the men's and this was done, but no woman was appointed as yet, either to the Committee of the Union or as an officer.

The S.V.M.U. travelling secretary was able to tell the conference that :

This foreign mission Movement has spread into 60 colleges, and has enrolled in its ranks over 700 students, and we are in the midst of the largest, most influential, and most permanent missionary revival that Great Britain has ever seen. There has been no noise about it; many people do not know of its existence. Yet, without sound, the full spring-tide of missions seems to be rising, touching and reaching places which hitherto have been standing high and dry beyond the reach of previous movements. From the first there has been little criticism of the Union; the Church of Christ has accepted it as the work of God. We are not aware of a single missionary Board which has stood aloof, sceptical and refusing to believe in us. Now they are even becoming enthusiastic about us. We have the approval of the heathen too; in their darkness and help-lessness they are glad to see us waking up to help. We have the approval of Christ Himself, for we believe this Movement has been begun and continued by Him.[1]

This gathering was representative of the different schools of thought in the Presbyterian and Free Churches and of the Evangelical school of thought in the Church of England. Most of the speaking was of a distinctly Evangelical character, but there was also a frank recogni-tion of the value of modern Biblical scholarship. Pro-fessor Lloyd Snape of Aberystwyth, one of the speakers, said to the conference: " We have had occasion to thank God for the Higher Criticism and will have again. The essential truths of Christianity can never contradict those got by Science. God has ever new truth to reveal to man." [2] The school of thought which was unrepre-sented was the High Church party in the Church of England.

On the last day of the conference a general council of representatives of the Christian Unions affiliated to the Inter-University Christian Union was held and a committee for the ensuing year was elected. B. L. Livingstone-Learmonth, Edinburgh University and J. R. Gillespie, Queen's College, Belfast, were elected, while for the third place R. F. Drury, Wadham College, Oxford, and Douglas M. Thornton, Trinity College,

---

[1] *Report of the Second Students' Conference*, 1894, p. 37.
[2] *Ibid.*, p. 55.

Cambridge, were proposed. It was decided to leave to the retiring committee and the two men elected the task of choosing between Drury and Thornton. The minute-book of the Union records for the guidance of those who had to decide " that Mr Drury was gifted with literary talent which might be useful in getting out literature on college Christian work. Re Mr Thornton, he took up a Fallen Women's Home finding it £80 in debt, and has cleared the debt and now has a balance in hand—bespeaks business capacity." Mr Drury[1] was chosen.

At this meeting, among the decisions reached was one " that more rigid discipline should exist through the camp at night in regard to singing, etc." How many a committee since that date has passed a similar minute but without influencing to any great extent the joyous souls who at the midnight hour, and later still, burst forth into song !

The question of continuing to hold the summer conference at Keswick was discussed. The expense of lodgings due to the Convention and its visitors and, still more, the feeling among some of the theological students that it was undesirable to associate the Movement too closely with one particular school of thought, were given as reasons for leaving Keswick. Others felt that if the conference was held elsewhere speakers would be more difficult to secure and that there would be a loss of valuable spiritual influence. Further, as a number of students attended the Convention, to leave might mean loss of touch with many students. It was decided to remain at Keswick.

The Student Movement owes a great deal to the Keswick Convention and its supporters. Not only did its early leaders derive from the Convention itself much spiritual help, but it owed a great deal to the sympathy, encouragement, money and prayers of many Christian men and women attending the Convention who recognized the importance and possibilities of a

[1] Now Vicar of Darlington.

Christian movement among students. Friends of the Movement invited students to join their house parties at Keswick, thus making it easy for them to come. This year (1894) the students needed financial help and members of the Convention came forward with it, providing £300, to which the students added £200. It was this money which enabled the Inter-University Christian Union to appoint Donald Fraser as their travelling secretary, taking him over from the S.V.M.U.; the latter Union appointed Frank Anderson, Exeter College, Oxford, travelling secretary in his place. The two Unions jointly appointed Crayden Edmunds, St John's College, Cambridge, as general secretary, and at the same time enlarged *The Student Volunteer*, increased its price to 2d. a copy, and published five issues in the year, which now attained a circulation of 1600 copies.

The same autumn the Unions left the office in the Y.M.C.A., 186 Aldersgate Street, and took a room at the top of a new building at 93 Aldersgate Street, E.C., at a rent of £25 a year. The office was a small room with windows down one side. It was fitted with a roll-top desk, a couple of tables, a tumble-down cupboard and a set of pigeon-holes; a number of open, wooden packing-cases, all in a rather untidy state, used to keep pamphlets and correspondence in, took up most of the floor space. Fortunately the committee was a small one and there were no clerks to be accommodated. As a matter of fact, the first year the Movement was at 93 Aldersgate Street the committee meetings were not held in London, but in Glasgow in October and in Edinburgh in December. The first meeting at Aldersgate Street was on March 18th 1895. The first general secretary answered letters, kept accounts, packed up parcels of literature and acted as messenger and post boy.

The minutes of the executive meetings in 1894-95 do not contain much of interest. Questions as to the nature of the student field, lists of universities and colleges to be entered, the number of students in them, the existence or not of Christian Unions, the nature of the work to be done, finance and summer conference plans, occupied the attention of the committee.

In the colleges Frank Anderson for the S.V.M.U. and Donald Fraser for the Inter-University Christian Union (which we now know as the S.C.M.) were engaged in securing Student Volunteers, promoting Bible study, doing evangelistic work and starting new Christian Unions.

Donald Fraser did two things for the Movement. He intensified the appeal for volunteers to give their lives to meet the need of the world for Christ, and he demonstrated the need for Christian Unions and the possibility of establishing them amid the new and little organized student life of the English university colleges. He had zeal, courage and vision combined with all the persuasiveness and charm of the Highlander and left his mark permanently on the Movement.

Serious attempts were made at this period to widen the range of speakers at summer conferences. Amongst those invited to that of 1895 were Archdeacon F. W. Farrar, Dr George Adam Smith, the Rev. C. Sylvester Horne, Dr John Watson (Ian Maclaren), Dr Berry of Wolverhampton and the Bishop of Ripon (Dr Boyd Carpenter). The only one of these who accepted was Dr George Adam Smith, but he was prevented from fulfilling the engagement. The failure to secure any of these speakers was largely due to the fact that those asked were all busy men who did not realize the significance of the Movement. None of them, except Dr George Adam Smith, had links with the leaders. It was many years before the Movement could get its invitations accepted by any except those who knew it through contact with it at Keswick, or with the Oxford and Cambridge Inter-Collegiate Christian Unions. The continual stream of polite refusals used to be very disheartening at times.

The field which the Union set out to cultivate according

to a pamphlet issued at the time, consisted of thirty universities and university colleges, eighteen medical schools, forty-four training colleges and thirty technical colleges, military schools, agricultural colleges, etc.— altogether at the lowest estimate one hundred and twenty-two colleges, exclusive of theological colleges, " in these there must be a student population of at least forty thousand,[1] banded together by kindred sympathy, kindred temptations and a kindred occupation. They are the flower of Britain's sons. They are to be our lawyers, our physicians, our scientists, our members of Parliament, and the future leaders of our nation's social and religious life. They will be our representatives on sea and land, our ambassadors to foreign Courts and the rulers of our Colonies and Indian Empire."

The S.V.M.U. developed its work from a general missionary appeal for service to a consistent plan to promote missionary interest through missionary reading, missionary study and the enrolment of Volunteers. The committee decided to appoint an Advisory Council and secured as members the Rev. Professor T. M. Lindsay, Dr James L. Maxwell, the Rev. R. Wardlaw Thompson, General Hutchinson, C.B., C.S.I., Mrs Bannister, Mrs Hatt Noble and Miss Blane.

The S.V.M.U. Executive the same year decided to hold its first great missionary conference. The minute on the subject does not say much : " Resolved that an international conference be held in January 1896 at Liverpool, and that Messrs Fraser and Anderson be requested to undertake the arrangements jointly." The conference proved to be a notable event to which we shall return later. This summer (1895) the Union sent Richard Burgess and J. Rutter Williamson as its delegates to the Northfield conference in the United States.

A word as to the relation of the S.V.M.U. and the Inter-University Christian Union. The reader may be somewhat confused by the way this record seems to pass

---

[1] This estimate puts the number at that time much too high; thirty thousand would be nearer the correct number.

from one Union to the other, and at times seems to be concerned with the doings of both Unions jointly. This is true to the facts. While the two Unions were organized separately, each with its own constitution and its own travelling secretary or secretaries and its own branches in the colleges, yet they worked in the same field, appealed to the same students and, by agreement, shared an office, general secretary and summer conference. This arrangement was maintained for five years, when reorganization took place.

The Inter-University Christian Union made some important changes at the summer conference at Keswick, 1895; it changed its name to the British College Christian Union; it decided to give a woman a place for the first time on its executive committee. The committee was not enlarged, the three members elected being R. F. Drury, Durham University, W. E. S. Holland, Magdalen College, Oxford, and Emmeline Stuart, Queen Margaret College, Glasgow. The S.V.M.U. at the same time elected Agnes de Sélincourt as a member of committee, and Ruth Rouse became editor of *The Student Volunteer*, attending both the S.V.M.U. and B.C.C.U. Committees.

Among the matters discussed at Keswick was the basis of the Union. There was some difference of opinion, but ultimately the following resolution was passed :

That all Associations henceforth to be affiliated, such as shall be formed by the British College Christian Union, shall have the doctrinal position in clause 2 of the B.C.C.U. constitution included in their constitutions, but those which have been already constituted shall add merely an assent to it in the minutes together with a notice of their affiliation.

The " Clause 2 " referred to in this resolution was itself amended at the conference to read as follows :

The object of the Union shall be to unite in work and interest, by means of conferences, deputations, correspondence, and such other means as may be thought effective, the various universities, colleges, and medical schools,

F

etc., of the United Kingdom, the aims and work of which are in full harmony with a belief in Jesus Christ as God the Son and only Saviour of the world.

The amendment consisted of the addition of the last two lines, and thus gave the Movement its first doctrinal basis.

The executive committee gave some consideration the following year to the question of the basis, some fearing that there was inadequate security for the Union being conducted permanently on " evangelical lines." In order to safeguard this the committee resolved to advise the next summer conference to appoint an advisory council of senior people similar to that which had been appointed by the S.V.M.U., and they also advised that new members of executive should be nominated by the retiring executive and appointed by the annual conference. The former of these suggestions was not adopted, the latter was acted upon until 1929, though long before this the right to nominate had also been extended to college Unions and Student Volunteers.

The sense in which the word " evangelical " was used above is important, its meaning being non-Unitarian. This was not the usual sense in which the word was used. The reason for this unusual and un-English use of the word may be traced to American influence. It is quite clear that its use here is not intended to describe the Low Church party in the Church of England and that there was no prejudice against High Churchmen. Indeed, at the same committee meeting instructions were given to the travelling secretary to cultivate any of the High Church theological colleges that were open to him. Further, referring later to the support the Union received from the Archbishop of Canterbury (Dr Benson), it was pointed out that he would not have given such support " unless he had distinctly understood that it stood on an evangelical basis."

There was much talk at the summer conference about

the coming Liverpool conference, and the students promised their hearty support. It was decided to invite the theological colleges, of which there had been much visitation by travelling secretaries, to throw themselves into the work of the Movement. The scheme for a Theological Colleges Missionary Alliance, discussed and deferred at the 1894 summer conference for further discussion, was given up and the following resolution passed : " That the theological colleges shall be embraced in the British College Christian Union ; that they shall be affiliated through their missionary or similar societies ; that a committee of four shall be appointed to look after their interests, one of these to act as general secretary of the Theological College section and advisory secretary to the Executive Committee of the Union." Douglas M. Thornton was appointed. The first step towards bringing theological colleges into the movement was thus taken.

Representatives of six nations discussed at Keswick the possibility of bringing into closer union the Movements which they represented : " it was not till some of the same delegates, and others, met in Sweden a fortnight later, that the World's Student Christian Federation was actually formed, but the main lines of its plans were sketched out at Keswick."[1]

This is not the place to tell the story of the founding of the Federation, but let it be here recorded that on 17th August 1895, accredited representatives of the Student Movements of the United States of America and Canada, Great Britain, Germany, Scandinavia and " a Union of Christian Associations in mission lands " met in council at the Castle of Wadstena in Sweden and agreed that the organizations which they represented should henceforth be united in a single Federation, each national organization to preserve its own liberty and suit its operations to the needs of its own field, each at the same time to unite with others for mutual help and to join with them in carrying the

[1] *The Student Volunteer*, Nov. 1895, p. 80.

Movement into lands which it had not yet reached. A committee of eight members—J. Rutter Williamson and Frank Anderson being the British representatives —was appointed, with Dr Karl Fries of Sweden as chairman and Mr John R. Mott of the United States of America as general secretary.

The Federation was founded as a federation of men's Movements, but the British Movement immediately took this question up through its representative, J. Rutter Williamson, and asked for recognition of the inclusion of women students. The secretary of the Federation replied that " so far its policy had been to confine itself to men's colleges, this being distinctly understood in America." The British Movement, however, pointed out that at the time at which it was affiliated to the Federation, women's Christian Unions in British colleges were an integral part of it, hence women could not be excluded from the Federation, and when a year later they sent two representatives to the Federation committee at Northfield, 1896, the only recorded instruction given these delegates was to support strongly the recognition of women students in the constitution of the Federation.

It must not be supposed, however, that the men leaders in Great Britain were advanced feminists. Both the men and women were feeling their way very slowly and cautiously in the matter of joint work at this time, and among other questions the advisability of holding mixed summer conferences was discussed. The decision reached was " that the practice of holding mixed conferences of men and women students be continued with caution."

CHAPTER V

THE LIVERPOOL CONFERENCE

THE first public event in the life of the Movement was an "International Students' Missionary Conference," which the S.V.M.U. held in Liverpool from January 1st to 5th 1896. For over two years the leaders of the Movement had been distressed to find that the Churches were not responding to the growing interest in the colleges, and that the work was being seriously handicapped by the rejection of Volunteers by some of the missionary societies through lack of funds. The Churches needed to be roused to appreciate the strength of the Movement and to make some corresponding sacrifice in order to send those who were ready to go. The idea grew in the minds of the leaders that they must make a demonstration of the strength of the Movement as a challenge to the Church.

Another reason for holding a conference was the evidence they had of movements among students in the colleges of Scandinavia, Germany, France and Switzerland which seemed to point to the possibility of a missionary awakening in these countries. Student Christian Movements had been started in their universities and close friendly relations had been established with them by means of visitation and correspondence, and an opportunity of helping to extend the missionary movement seemed to be offered to the British leaders.

With these two aims specially in view, and the conviction that such a gathering would strengthen the missionary purpose and enthusiasm of the Volunteers in our own colleges, the need of holding a great international students' conference grew upon us. When it was originally proposed in Executive, the members were at first afraid that the scheme was too big to realize and were not inclined to support it. Then we spent some time in prayer and when we rose from our knees everyone was heartily in favour of it.[1]

The Student Volunteer Movement in America had already held two missionary conferences, at the last of which, Detroit, 1894, Donald Fraser has been a delegate. He had seen the labour involved in gathering, housing and holding a conference for thirteen hundred delegates, yet if one was to be held for the British Isles it must be on somewhat the same scale.

The S.V.M.U. Committee and staff was very small. The Committee consisted of four men and one woman —it was the first year a woman had served. These were A. K. Boyland, Trinity College, Dublin, Donald Fraser, Glasgow University, R. Burgess, Trevecca College, Wales, Agnes de Sélincourt, Girton College, Cambridge. There were two travelling secretaries, J. Rutter Williamson, M.B., Edinburgh University, and Emmeline Stuart, M.B., Queen Margaret College, Glasgow. *The Student Volunteer* was edited by Ruth Rouse of Girton College, Cambridge. A general secretary, L. B. Butcher, Sidney Sussex College, Cambridge, was shared with the British College Christian Union. No wonder this small group shrank from the responsibility of planning a big conference. The day of conferences had not yet dawned in Great Britain and no organization, student or senior, had hitherto attempted to secure free hospitality for a conference in a city. The decision once reached, however, preparations for the conference were pushed forward with both rapidity and skill.

Liverpool was chosen because of its central position, and the Christmas vacation because it was a time when all colleges in Great Britain and on the Continent were on holiday at the same date, which did not immediately precede or follow an examination period, and which

[1] *Make Jesus King*, Report of Liverpool Conference, p. 2.

would allow students to return straight to college and help others to feel the thrill and share the inspiration they had received. The churches of Liverpool were sympathetic and arrangements were made for a conference on a big scale; the leaders aimed at securing the attendance of a thousand students. No part of the preparation was carried out with greater thoroughness than the preparation by prayer. That there should be widespread prayer for the conference was, in the view of the leaders, " the only hope we have for ultimate and far-reaching success." They said that the Movement had been " forced into this great attempt by the Holy Spirit," that the idea of the conference was born of God and that to God they must turn for guidance and help in carrying through what was a great undertaking.

J. H. Maclean, who was sailing for India in the autumn, left England in time to visit Leiden, Amsterdam, Utrecht and Kampen in Holland on his journey, and wrote that he thought a dozen students might go to the Liverpool Conference ; in Germany he spoke to students at Bonn, Heidelberg, Halle, Göttingen, Erlangen and Tübingen ; and paid brief visits to the universities at Zürich and Basel. He found in Holland, Germany and Switzerland that university students did not think of becoming missionaries—the societies securing their candidates from less educated circles than those of university students, and training them at missionary institutions—but that there were signs of dawning missionary interest among a few of them.

Correspondence about delegations took place with the Continental students who had been at the summer conferences of the three previous years, with good results.

Throughout the British Isles both the travelling secretaries of the S.V.M.U. and Frank Anderson, the travelling secretary of the British College Christian Union, worked up delegations wherever they went, literature and *The Student Volunteer* were used to the same end.

When the conference assembled in the Philharmonic Hall, Liverpool, at 7 p.m. on New Year's Day, 1896, to receive the greetings of the Bishop of Liverpool (Dr Ryle) on behalf of the Church of England, the Rev. Charles Garrett, on behalf of the Free Churches and Principal Rendall, on behalf of the University College, there were nine hundred and twenty-seven persons present, seven hundred and fifteen of whom were students, and Donald Fraser, who responded on behalf of the students, was justified in saying, "I am not sure that Europe has ever seen a more representative gathering of students or that the world has seen a more international one than that before us." Seventy-four universities and colleges in Great Britain and Ireland were represented by five hundred and eight men and one hundred and thirty women ; there were in addition twenty members of staff, while twenty nationalities— African, American (U.S.A.), American (South), Canadian, Chinese, Corsican, Danish, Dutch, French, German, Hungarian, Jamaican, Japanese, Jewish, Moravian, Norwegian, Spanish, Swedish, Swiss and Syrian—were represented by seventy-six men and one woman, fifty-seven of whom had travelled to England to attend the conference. Forty-four missionary societies were represented by one hundred and eighty persons. All the important societies were included except the Society for the Propagation of the Gospel and the Universities Mission to Central Africa. The Movement had as yet only touched part of the Church of England.

There was a strong desire that the conference might have the practical result of bringing into touch missionaries and officials desiring recruits for particular fields and students likely to fill these posts. To further this, missionaries were provided with pink badges to serve as introductions, and an introducing committee worked hard. White badges were worn by officers of the conference, red by foreign delegates, and blue by stewards.

The conference was a great spiritual occasion. Not

only did it make a profound impression upon those present—seniors and students alike—but its influence extended far and wide, both in the colleges and outside them, through those who were present. It was widely reported in the Press, and the report, *Make Jesus King*, a well printed and handsomely bound volume, had a large circulation, in two editions. It was out of print inside a year and copies exchanged hands at five times the amount of the published price. The Report derived its title from the words of a cable sent in 1889 by five hundred Japanese students gathered at a conference for the development of the Christian life, to a student conference at Northfield, America. The further transmission of this cable to Sweden led to the holding of the first Scandinavian Student Conference in 1890.

Devotional meetings, with an address and prayer, began the day; the second period the first two mornings at the conference was devoted to sectional meetings, with four to six speakers each, when the needs of different countries and much information about mission work in them were presented. Africa, India, China, South America and the Jews were so treated in a series of meetings on the first morning, while evangelistic, educational, medical missions and the Missionary Settlement for University Women were dealt with on the second morning. This laid a foundation of information and appeal. At the evening meetings there were addresses dealing with the spiritual life, with the claims of Christ and the need of the world. A writer in *The Student Volunteer*[1] records this impression:

> There remain in our memory pictures of heathen darkness and cruelty, heathen enlightenment and conversion, stamped on our hearts in a way new to us; partly due, no doubt, to the unique character of the audience and surroundings; more, we trust, to the working of the Holy Spirit, convincing Christian hearts of the awful need of the non-Christian world.

[1] *The Student Volunteer*, January 1896, p. 5.

The Rev. Egerton Young told us his strange and wonderful story of work for God among the Red men ; of long snow journeys, cold, exposure, and isolation—hardships gladly endured for Christ's sake, and more than repaid by the joy of carrying the Gospel to these vanishing races of North-West America ; of the necessity of simplicity, and the difficulties of speaking by interpreter (" interrupter ") ; of the horrible degradation and sufferings of the women under brutal husbands and sons, changed afterwards beyond recognition by the power of the Gospel.

Mr C. T. Studd pleaded for China's millions. In Great Britain, with one-tenth of the population, we have 30,000 ordained clergy in the Church of England alone, while China has only 2000 workers of all kinds, men and women. He cited terrible instances of the cruelty and utter lack of love in the Chinese heart ; more terrible still the utter lack of hope, written so plainly on their faces, that the face of a Mohammedan Chinaman is bright and hopeful compared with others.

We heard of work among the Mohammedans, from the bigoted East on the one hand to West Africa on the other, where many of the followers of Mohammed are quite ready to listen to the Gospel. Mr G. L. Pilkington pointed out the possibilities of working from Uganda into the great Soudan with its unevangelized millions. The Rev. H. Carless and Dr George Smith reminded us of our special duty to preach Christ to the Mohammedan world, for it was the deadness of Christ's Church that gave Islam its first opening. Miss Gollock, from her winter's visit to India, told the same heart-breaking story of open doors and none to enter in, of missionaries compelled to come home, broken down in health, because brothers and sisters in Christ would not come out to help.

And yet from all parts of the world came the same news, that the Gospel of Christ is ever powerful to raise men and women from the grossest darkness, ignorance, and sin, to lives of consistency and devotion to their Lord that put us Christian students utterly to shame.

Towards the close of the conference a Report was presented by the Executive of the Student Volunteer Missionary Union showing that 1038 students (832 men and 206 women) had joined the Union; 286 of these were medical students; 212 members had already become missionaries, sailing under 42 societies to 27 countries. Stress was laid in the Report on the growth of " deeper intelligence on missionary questions," and on what the Union had done to " weld together men of various denominations, creeds and types of thought," as " limitations are fast disappearing." " The intercollegiate bond has become international : correspondence, visitation and a common purpose have united us in a world-wide student movement."

The Report dealt with the problems of the Union and put first the serious crippling in sight if Christian people did not respond by greater liberality. The Report called Volunteers to " aggressive campaigns " in the Churches to secure their support as missionaries. The danger of premature decisions to sign the Declaration were mentioned, but " from the beginning of the Movement in this country the signing of the Declaration has been carefully safeguarded. Hasty decisions are discouraged ; students are urged not to sign until after prayerful deliberation." The two hundred and eighty-six medical volunteers were declared to be " an insignificant number in face of the wide usefulness of the medical missionary " ; while the fact that there were only eleven volunteers out of the 4100 training college students in Britain was a problem to be faced.

The Report announced the decision to adopt the Watchword which for three years " had been the inspiration of the American Movement," " The Evangelization of the world in this generation."

This they (the Executive) have done because they believe that He who said " Preach the Gospel to every creature " wished His followers in every age to do it. By evangelization we do not mean conversion, nor do we mean to disparage, but to emphasize the value of educational missions. What is meant is simply this : " The presenting of the Gospel in such a manner to every soul in this world that the responsibility for what is done with it shall no longer rest upon the Christian Church, or on any individual Christian, but shall rest on each man's head for himself." We believe that such a Watchword presented to ourselves and the Church at this crisis will do much to waken the Church to the possibility and urgency of immediate and thorough evangelization.

The decision to adopt the Watchword had been reached in the small hours of the morning in the Mitre Hotel, Liverpool, as the Executive discussed and prayed over the matter at a meeting convened the previous night—one of many similar meetings—when the project was discussed. The entry in the minute-book simply records that discussion and prayer was long and then—" finally it was decided in humble dependence on God's power to adopt it."

The Report presented to the conference, Rutter Williamson told of the World's Student Christian Federation formed the previous August, following which Donald Fraser spoke words of welcome to the foreign delegates. " The outburst of enthusiasm when he stopped speaking was ample corroboration of his words." Speeches followed by delegates from Germany, Norway, Holland and France.

There were separate meetings for ministers, business men and professors and tutors. At the latter " about twenty representatives from all the leading universities were present " and discussed " how best may the spiritual life and work of the students be promoted without that interference which might defeat its own object ? " Professor A. R. Simpson [1] of Edinburgh was in the chair. This was an enthusiastic meeting and long exceeded the time allotted to it.

The conference closed with a consecration meeting. There were several speeches—deeply moving speeches, but " earnest prayer had gone up that there might be no excitement that night, no emotion, no burst of feeling ; only a quiet waiting upon God. And those prayers were answered, for the wonderful stillness of that great gathering was truly a stillness in the knowledge of the presence of God."

---

[1] Afterwards Sir Alexander Simpson.

TISSINGTON TATLOW	W. H. T. GAIRDNER	AGNES DE SÉLINCOURT
HENRY DRUMMOND	JOHN R. MOTT	FRANK LENWOOD
DONALD FRASER	DOUGLAS M. THORNTON	C. RUTH ROUSE

The service closed with a period of prayer, during which this pledge of consecration was used :

I take
God the Father to be my God,
Jesus Christ to be my Saviour,
The Holy Ghost to be my Comforter,
The Word of God to be my rule,
The people of God to be my people,
I give myself to Thee, body, soul and spirit, all I am, and all I hope for.
I do this deliberately, sincerely, freely and for ever.

The Rev. W. E. Burroughs, B.D., Central Secretary of the Church Missionary Society, an experienced and sympathetic observer, writing an impression after the conference, expressed himself surprised at the extent of the Movement and, like many others, said the sight of the audience was one " to thrill, to impress, to solemnize." The unity and love, joy and peace of the gathering were marked.

The stand taken was upon the Master's divine imperative order, to view the Church of Christ as existing for the evangelization of the world, to press upon every saved soul, on every consecrated life, his or her individual responsibility in this matter, a responsibility only to be met by personal service abroad if the God of Providence and of Grace opened the way, and, failing that, by personal service in this cause at home, no less needful, though too often forgotten. And this note struck at our first meeting, vibrated right on to the end, only with a crescendo of gathering depth and fulness, until we reached that wonderful consecration meeting on Sunday night, when impressions were made, and steps taken, and resolutions recorded whose final issues and results only heaven and eternity will disclose ! [1]

Members of the public had been allowed to attend the conference, and on the closing night the crowds waiting for admittance were so large that an overflow meeting was held in the Gordon Hall.

[1] *Make Jesus King*, " After the Conference," the Rev. W. E. Burroughs, p. 194.

On one day during the conference Sir George Williams, the founder of the Y.M.C.A. and a devoted friend of the Student Movement, gave a luncheon in St George's Hall, when the entire conference sat down together, some Liverpool friends who had been invited by Sir George making the total party one thousand persons.

Careful attention was given to the literature exhibit, which was housed in the supper room of the Philharmonic Hall. Model missionary libraries, varying in price from £1 to £20, were there for inspection; there was an exhibit of charts and diagrams setting forth the various aspects of the need of the world; specimen copies of almost every missionary leaflet, booklet or magazine in print in Great Britain were gathered on pyramidal stalls all down the room. There was also a bookstall where literature could be purchased. It was claimed for the exhibit that " it was the most complete set of missionary literature ever brought together in any country." The hymns sung were chosen by a Cambridge undergraduate, F. Theodore Woods,[1] Trinity College, Cambridge, who acted as organist of the gathering. The chairman was Donald Fraser, and by the common consent of all the manner in which he chaired the conference added very greatly to its spiritual effectiveness. It was a time when chairmen were always senior men, and the sight of a youthful chairman was a great novelty. His chairing was a great triumph for Fraser in the eyes of the missionary leaders present.

The financial session of the conference was a remarkable occasion. When the conference was planned the Executive estimated that it would cost £400. The actual cost was £862. Of this amount £600 was provided by students and senior friends before it opened, but the leaders needed, in addition to its cost, £700 for the year's work of the Union, so they asked the conference to contribute £900. A financial statement was

[1] Later, in succession, Bishop of Peterborough and of Winchester.

made by the General Secretary, L. B. Butcher. This was followed by speeches from Mr Eugene Stock and Dr George Smith, who commended the work of the S.V.M.U. to the support of the Church, and Mr Sherwood Eddy then spoke of the spiritual significance of giving. Slips of paper were handed round and the company was led in prayer that all might be definitely shown how much they should give, whether it was to be much or little, or even nothing. As the slips were collected they were brought to the chairman, who began reading out the amounts (without names). He ceased after a little, but it was evident a large sum had been given. Dr A. T. Pierson was then called upon to give an address but he said further speaking would be out of place " after God has drawn so close in this solemn hour of self-denying consecration," and he closed the meeting with prayer and the blessing. Next morning the leaders announced that £1641 had been promised and that they had decided to devote a portion of the money towards the extension of the Student Volunteer Movement on the Continent and in Australia.

Mr Mott was at that time in India, having started on his first world tour for the World's Student Christian Federation. He has often described how puzzled he was at receiving £200 by cable with a request to visit Australia. But the explanation soon came, and Mott re-arranged his plans and spent the money as desired in visiting the Australian and New Zealand universities, where there were notable results, followed by the founding of the Australasian Student Christian Movement.

No account of the conference would be complete without a reference to the kindness of the Liverpool Y.M.C.A., which lent its buildings for the purposes of an office and the services of its secretary, the late Mr T. Jameson, as local Conference secretary. The student leaders of that period were never tired of talking of the kindness of Mr Jameson, and I recall that twelve years later, when another conference brought us into contact again with Mr Jameson, he was never tired of extolling the ability, economy and devotion with which a very small group of men and women organized and carried through the conference. " They gave us all a lesson in skilful organization and in the economical spending of money " was his comment.

The contribution made by Dr A. T. Pierson, Mr G. Sherwood Eddy, Mr Harlan P. Beach and the Rev. Egerton Young, all of whom had come from North America to speak at the conference, was a valuable one. Dr George Smith, C.I.E., LL.D. wrote :

> The organization of the conference was perfect, the practical management of the great meetings was wise and efficient, the humility and self-consecration of the Executive were evident fruits of the Spirit of God, and the impulse given, alike to the students and the crowds of Christian people, was remarkable.[1]

The memory of the conference and the prayer, thought and trouble given to its preparation were to inspire the Movement's leaders for years to come in organizing similar gatherings for each generation of students.

The conference received much attention from the Press, and most of the religious and missionary weeklies and monthlies had a full report and a leading article on it.   The S.V.M.U. had secured publicity for itself and its cause through its first " Quadrennial."

In the universities and colleges the conference gave a great stimulus to both the work of the S.V.M.U. and the British College Christian Union.

The influence on the Continent was considerable; during the conference a Volunteer Movement was formed by the Norwegian students, plans laid to bind French and Swiss students in a missionary union, a German Student Volunteer declaration was drawn up, and the foundations of the Dutch Student Christian Movement laid.   Soon after the conference Donald Fraser visited Paris, Montaubon, Neuchâtel, Geneva,

[1] *Make Jesus King*, p. 195.

Lausanne and Basle, and helped to organize a Franco-Swiss Student Volunteer Movement at a conference of forty volunteers at Geneva, when an Executive of four was elected and M. Daniel Couve of France was appointed as travelling secretary.

Fraser then went to Holland, where he found that the eleven Dutch students who had been at Liverpool had held a conference at Delft and founded the Dutch Student Christian Movement. Scandinavia came next, where Fraser visited Copenhagen, Lund, Stockholm, Uppsala and Christiania, speaking to students on the Christian life and missionary service. Towards the end of the visit a conference was held at Copenhagen at which an S.V.M.U. for Scandinavia was organized.

Fraser found Germany " specially difficult because of the deadness and worldliness of student life." A conference of students from six universities gathered at Halle to meet him, and " two days were spent in organizing a missionary union for Germany."

Is it surprising that to this day the Liverpool Conference is referred to as an historic event in Continental religious life?

G

CHAPTER VI

DOUGLAS THORNTON AND THE PROMOTION OF MISSIONARY STUDY

THERE were missionary bands in Cambridge before the formation of the S.V.M.U. These seem to have been an outcome of the missionary interest stirred by " the Cambridge Seven." At these, members read to one another papers on various missionary topics, but there was no attempt at detailed and scientific study of any mission field or non-Christian religion. The importance of a knowledge of missions was recognized by the promoters of the S.V.M.U., and one of the American delegates to the Liverpool Conference, Mr Harlan P. Beach, received special attention from them. He was a man who, after considerable experience as a missionary in China, had become educational secretary of the Student Volunteer Movement in the United States. Speaking at the conference of their experience in America, he said :

> We found that a large number of our volunteers were renouncing their purpose, and a careful inquiry was made into the causes for this. It was found that in the majority of cases men and women had moved from their purpose through the lack of missionary information. They had at first been swept into the movement by a wave of enthusiasm ; and it was decided that, in order to retain them, we must educate them to get them on a stable basis.

After various experiments the Americans were issuing specially prepared text-books and suggestions to leaders of study bands. Beach reported on the whole experiment as satisfactory and advised Great Britain to follow their example. The study work had educated a large body of students in knowledge of some parts of the mission field, it had steadied and confirmed their interest, it was proving a valuable preparation for those going abroad and it was creating supporters for the missionary enterprise from among those remaining at home.

Beach commended his cause as educational secretary by the competence of his own work—he was afterwards appointed the first Professor of Missions at Yale University—his own books and missionary atlas were at one time widely used, and he was what the Americans themselves described as " a great human." We all liked him.

When the Liverpool Conference was over, Beach went to stay with Professor A. R. Simpson in Edinburgh, and some years after, in America, I heard him give an amusing account of one episode during this visit. He had never before been a guest in a private house in Great Britain and was, as he himself confessed, extremely anxious to do the right thing. The evening he arrived in Edinburgh it was snowing and very cold. Professor Simpson kept him up very late talking, and he went to his bedroom feeling, as Americans with their steam-heated houses always do, that British private houses were extremely chilly. In his bedroom he found a hip bath with some cold water in it, which, of course, had been put ready for the morning, as was the custom in many houses at that time ; bath-rooms with hot and cold water laid on were a later luxury. Beach had heard of the British love of cold baths and, being anxious, as he said, to do the right thing, took the bath —cold as it was—although it went much against the grain.

Next morning, when the manservant called him, Beach was already awake and observed the look of surprise on the valet's face when he noticed that the bath had been used. The valet called in another man and between them they carried the bath away, emptied it, brought it back, putting in a little more cold water and leaving a large can of boiling water beside it.

Beach's comment was : " I guess I realized then that I had done the wrong thing, but I was not going to give myself away, and if it was not a British custom to take a cold bath before going to bed, I decided to make it an American custom, for the time being, carried into Great Britain. I took that cold bath every night I stayed with Professor Simpson." Beach had a delightful sense of humour and roared with delight as he told me the story against himself, five years later, sitting in the dusk one night when the day's work was over, at the Northfield Student Summer Conference.

Harlan Beach could tell a story very effectively in a meeting. Addressing a large audience of students at Northfield and speaking to them of the danger of thinking one had achieved anything of value in the realm of character just because one's feelings were stirred, I heard him say, " Why, I remember a friend of mine, a very worldly man, who took a tour in Europe, saying to me ' You know, Beach, when I visited some of those old churches in Italy, with their age and silence and solemnity, I felt that good that I believe if I had died then I should have gone straight up to heaven.' " Beach paused a moment, and then rapped out to his audience : " ' Gentlemen, you scratch the back of a pig and he feels fine ; that ain't religion.' "

If Beach pressed the value of systematic missionary study there was a man ready with hearing ears. Douglas Thornton was already a force in the Movement. He was serving on the committee as advisory secretary in relation to theological colleges and had been one of the literature secretaries responsible for the splendid exhibit of books at the Liverpool conference. The Executive decided to increase the amount of missionary study and to improve its quality, resolving on February 25th 1896 :

> That there be initiated an aggressive educational policy and that it be cautiously introduced into the colleges.
> That this policy be directed from the office by a system of frequent correspondence and occasional visits.

That a common text-book with possibly an alternative be employed.

That Mr D. M. Thornton be asked to undertake the duties of Educational Secretary for the ensuing year.

Thornton set to work at once after his appointment as educational secretary on a missionary study text-book, and his volume *Africa Waiting* was the first of a long series of study text-books published first of all by the Student Movement, and later by a body arising out of the Student Movement,[1] for the use of study circles throughout the British Isles.

Thornton did not wait until his text-book was ready to set students to work. He imported crates full of *The Cross in the Land of the Trident*, a study book on India by Harlan P. Beach, provided model libraries and " suggestions for leaders," with the result that 500 students engaged in its study. The aim of " the educational policy," as it was called, was thus set forth :

1. To promote in the individual student or volunteer that knowledge of missionary principles and facts which is the basis of all permanent interest and intelligent prayer.

2. To ensure that Christian students, upon whom, as upon all Christians, the evangelization of the world rests, shall be acquainted no less familiarly with this missionary knowledge than with any other necessary branch of learning.

3. To meet the growing interest in missionary work, by preparing students to speak effectively on missions in personal conversation and in public addresses.

4. To equip future missionaries by making them familiar with the religious, moral, political and social condition of different nations, the missionary results of the past and the methods of the present.

A flood of speeches, articles and a few pamphlets, all by Thornton, quickly made the missionary study work of the S.V.M.U. its most important activity.

No record of the origin of systematic missionary study, or indeed of the Student Movement as a whole, would be complete without some account of Douglas Thornton. His was the most creative mind that has ever yet been

[1] The United Council for Missionary Education.

brought to bear upon its work. While he set a standard in missionary study, which not only influenced the Student Movement but all the churches throughout the British Isles, his mind also ranged over all the questions with which the Student Movement was concerned. It still seems almost incredible that he was an officer of the Movement for only two years, with a preliminary year on the Executive. Before giving an account of the Movement's activities at this period, which will contain many references to him, let me attempt a brief sketch of the man himself.

Thornton was a great Churchman. He was born into a family in the Evangelical tradition of the Church of England. He was in no sense, however, a party man. While an enthusiastic exponent of the Evangelical tradition he did much to create the comprehensive character of the Student Movement, and no man did more to prepare the way in it for the advent of the High Churchman.

His great passion was foreign missions. He thought the calling of a missionary the greatest that could come to any man. All his Cambridge days he was preparing for the time when he would join the ranks of the missionaries of Christ's Church. He knew an amazing amount about religious conditions all over the world; but it was the task of winning the Mohammedan world that fascinated him. A Pan-Islamic movement was steadily uniting Islam, and was making great progress in Africa; this religion was the most defiant of Christianity in the world. While still an undergraduate Douglas studied Islam, in Africa, India, China and Turkey, and decided that Cairo was the best centre in the world from which to attack the task of winning the Mohammedan world for Christ. He was not content to study alone, his interest was infectious, and scores of men at Cambridge were drawn by his enthusiasm to similar study. Instant in season and out of season, he used the vacation to help at seaside services for children, and his sand maps and missionary talks were famous.

I first saw Douglas at a student summer conference. He was a commanding figure, standing well over six feet, broad shouldered and erect ; a handsome man with impressive manners and a rather grand air. I never saw him shy or disconcerted, he was equal to any occasion. Here is an example of his assurance. We were in bed in the camp leaders' tent before the Summer Conference began at Curbar, having come up early to make final preparations ; in the early morning the first arrivals awakened us. " It's the Irish delegation, they were coming early this morning," said Douglas, and then, after a moment or two, " I say, you fellows, we must welcome these men to camp." He got up and went out. A minute later I stuck my head out of the tent. There was Douglas, a gigantic figure in a long white cotton nightshirt which reached to his toes— pyjamas were a later fashion—shaking hands without a trace of self-consciousness and welcoming with friendly words the astonished students, who were strangers to Thornton and had no idea who he was. His aplomb was so perfect that the Irishmen did not even have the courage to smile !

It is recorded of Douglas that as a boy at Marlborough he lived as a consistent Christian, but it was not until the end of his first year at Trinity College, Cambridge, that he had a spiritual experience at the Convention at Keswick which gave him his power ; what befell must be told in his own words, for he retained to the end of his life the sense of spiritual power which came to him there.

It was crowded and stifling. The meeting began. H. B. Macartney rose up full of the Holy Ghost. He electrified everyone in a word, so it seemed to me. This is something of what he said : " Now it seems to me what all we people want to-night is to get into the presence of God at once. If we wish to speak about God the Holy Ghost, let us believe in Him and receive Him. Shall we all say, ' I believe in the Holy Ghost ' ? " We all did. . . . I confessed my faith in Him, and He came in all His fulness into my soul. Immediately I seemed to see Jesus . . . the truth seemed so easy now. " We live in Christ and Christ in us." No sooner had he finished than I felt impelled to testify, so out I went, and as the door in the side was locked, I jumped out of the top of the window into the market-place. (There was an open-air meeting going on at the time.) " Let me speak to-night," I said, and I did.

The experience thus described remained with him until he died at Cairo on September 8th 1907, still a young man—he was thirty-four years old.

Douglas was a great talker. His almost constant theme was religion. I have heard him discuss all kinds of theological, ecclesiastical and missionary questions, but in all the talk, I never heard him raise any question as to the reality and power of the living Christ. To him Christ was a present leader, who revealed His will through the study of the Bible and through prayer : one Who was made known through the Holy Spirit to a man's spirit, bringing power to work and witness for Him to the world.

Thornton believed in the duty and privilege of constantly bearing witness to Jesus Christ as the Saviour of men. He spoke to his college friends about Christ with the result that many owed their conversion to him. There are numerous stories about his work in the open air. Once in Cambridge the attention of a large crowd in the open air was riveted by his suddenly seizing a child of a year old out of its mother's arms and holding it shoulder high, exclaiming "Except ye be converted and become as little children, ye shall in no wise enter the Kingdom of Heaven."

On another occasion, a Queens' man was known to be speaking in the open air. Some agnostic undergraduates passed a note round at dinner to collect objectors. The result was a goodly attendance of scoffers, who interrupted the speaker with uncomplimentary remarks. Thornton to the rescue ! Up he marched to the interrupters. " Look here ! if you fellows have no care for your own souls, might you not have some for the souls of these people ? They are anxious to have their souls saved ; is it gentlemanly on your part to prevent them having the opportunity ? " This un- expected line of attack carried the undergraduates with him, they were silent through the service and asked him to their rooms to open out to him their doubts and difficulties. His downright earnestness and unconven- tionality carried the day.

It was always so with him. A few years later, when he was a missionary in Cairo, we find Gairdner half laughing at him and half worshipping because, descend- ing the Great Pyramid one day, he was overheard preach- ing Christ to his dragoman. On another occasion, when a friend saw him off by train from Cairo to Upper Egypt and found for him an empty carriage, Thorn- ton came up, looked in and exclaimed : " An empty carriage ! Why, man, I want to fish ! " and before the train had started the friend on the platform found him- self ignored by Thornton, who was hard at work in a carriage full of Egyptian officers and Effendis. And men were not put off, they wanted this man, a whirl- wind of conviction, to talk to them about his Lord whom he served with such passionate devotion.

The Student Christian Movement owes an immeasur- able debt to Douglas Thornton for the vision he brought to it of what it might become. He had prophetic insight. In the days of small things he saw great things. The question of the right basis for the Movement engaged his attention, both when he was in it and after he had gone to Cairo, because he saw that what was to become a many-sided body must be adequately based. He gave much thought to winning the co-operation in the Movement of all parties in the Church of England, at one end of the scale tackling the problem of the best means of establishing the Movement in the theological colleges, and at the other, visiting the Bishop of London to secure his interest in the Movement. Although he knew his term of office in it would be brief, he threw himself with immense energy into the task of establish- ing its missionary work on a basis of sound knowledge,

and " the educational policy " he laid down became the
basis of all the missionary study in the Movement, and
later of the missionary study in the Churches throughout
the British Isles.   Is it any wonder that a senior man
referred to him as " the young man who deals in worlds
and archbishops ? "

There was nothing hectic about Douglas Thornton
for all his schemes.   He was orderly in his habits of
thought, as he was in dealing with correspondence or
in preparing memoranda, as he loved to do.   Poise,
purpose and unceasing industry were what struck one
about him.   He was excellent company, he loved music
and played the piano and sang—he had a well-trained
tenor voice—and he loved talk.   Temple Gairdner
speaks of his " gorgeous laugh and his love of fun."

Thornton was an able man, but he was not primarily
a scholar : " the point," says Gairdner, " at which
ability in him flamed forth into genius was not an
intellectual but a moral and spiritual one, his genius for
consecration to the Kingdom of God."   The Watchword
of the S.V.M.U. made a great appeal to him.   He made
it the Watchword of his life—" this glorious watchword
which has become our own, and now dominates our
lives."   His zeal for the Watchword broadened his outlook until it embraced the whole world, and even after
he was absorbed in the exacting task of learning Arabic
and carrying on the work of a missionary he filled long
letters with surveys of need in all parts of the world.

Douglas was a splendid friend and believed that he
that hath friends must show himself friendly.   Always
a prolific letter writer, he poured himself out on paper
to friends in all parts of the world.   He was a man with
a great heart, and love was to him the greatest thing in
the world—God's love and that same love shed abroad
in the heart of man.   He was one of those selected to
give parting messages at the Liverpool Conference :
" I have for you," he said, " a message from these
gatherings which is an eternal fact, a glorious call, and
a blessed experience.   We have heard the fact, ' God

is love'; the call comes to each, 'Beloved, let us love one another; for love is of God.' God grant that the experience may be ours to-day and for ever—the love of God shed abroad in our hearts."

And as he loved men, so he prayed for them. "I do not forget to pray for you" was an assurance in many of his letters. "I know of nothing that bridges distance," he said, speaking to a company of students, "that makes the farthest corner of the world seem near, that shows us more and more of the love of God and the extent of God's blessing so much as this marvellous prayer life." When he died in 1907 I wrote in *The Student Movement*, "He was the greatest prophet the Student Movement has ever had." Now, twenty-six years later, I believe that judgment still to be true.[1]

[1] See *The Student Movement*, art.: "Douglas Montagu Thornton," by T. Tatlow, vol. x. p. 27, and *D. M. Thornton*, by W. H. T. Gairdner.

CHAPTER VII

THE APPROACH TO THE CHURCHES WITH THE WATCHWORD

THE Watchword which had been adopted during the Liverpool Conference was constantly in the minds of the leaders of the S.V.M.U. They saw that unless a great change took place in the attitude of the Churches to foreign missions the Watchword could not be accomplished. They were a small and inexperienced group and the task in view was a great one —the moving of the Christian Church in Great Britain and Ireland to new endeavours. They allowed the Liverpool Conference and its report *Make Jesus King*, which had a considerable circulation, to make an impact upon the Churches and missionary societies for nearly a year. Then at Christmas 1896 the Executive reconsidered how it could best press the policy of trying to intensify the missionary ardour of the Church. Douglas Thornton urged that " the time was now ripe "—a phrase constantly used by him—for making a special approach to the Churches, particularly in view of the approaching Lambeth Conference of the Bishops of the Anglican communion planned for the following summer.

What the Executive desired was that the Watchword should be adopted by the Churches as their missionary policy. They considered whether it was within the province of the S.V.M.U. to approach the Churches and whether it would meet with the approval of the general body of Volunteers and of the Advisory Council. " It was felt that in all forward Movements the executive committee had to be in advance of the main body of Volunteers ; and that further, it was probable that the

92

majority of the members of the Union would sympathize with such an advance, considering it a natural outcome of the adoption of the Watchword at the Liverpool Conference." [1] Subsequently the committee passed three resolutions :

> Resolved that believing the evangelization of the world in this generation to be the duty of the whole Church of Christ, we should rejoice to see each body of Christians severally adopting the Watchword of our Union as their policy.
>
> Resolved that God has placed us in a unique position and we see no likelihood of any other society arising within this generation better able to present our Watchword to the Christian Church in this country.

Before passing their third resolution they considered whether there were likely to be any bad results arising out of taking such a step as suggested. "Two were suggested : (1) that the action might appear to be presumptuous ; and (2) that it would involve an amount of work which could not be undertaken without detriment to the work already being carried on in the colleges." With regard to the first of these objections, it was decided that the proposed action would not be presumptuous provided it was undertaken in a proper way. "With regard to the second, it was pointed out that a forward movement in the Churches would react favourably on the colleges, and the following resolution was passed : "Resolved that we regard such presentation by us to be a duty for consideration among others."

The committee recorded the following reasons for this resolution :

1. The need for the practical accomplishment of the Watchword to be undertaken without delay.
2. Our unique position as a Union.
3. The eventful nature of this decade.
4. The completion of our expressed purpose.
5. The consequent reaction in an increase of Volunteers.
6. The present widespread interest in the Watchword.

[1] S.V.M.U. Minutes, December 1896.

The committee, having decided that a decision to go
forward would necessitate a large number of private
interviews, adjourned their meeting to the following
day. On resuming the meeting, J. Rutter Williamson,
the chairman, said that he had in the interval consulted
the Rev. R. Wardlaw Thompson, secretary of the
London Missionary Society, and Dr James Maxwell,
both of whom thought that the step would certainly
arouse opposition as " the churches strongly objected
to any organized effort to wake them up, and the step
might arouse prejudice against the S.V.M.U." Both
counselled the leaders to seek advice as to the best
method of approach to each Church. The third resolution was then agreed upon :

> Resolved—that provided suitable and sufficient assist-
> ance can be secured for the working out of the details, an
> approach be made to the Christian Churches of this country
> with a view to their adoption of our Watchword as their
> policy.

R. F. Drury, G. T. Manley and F. W. S. O'Neill
agreed to give time to the work, and it was decided to
seek the co-operation of the officials of the missionary
societies and the editors of missionary magazines. The
question of the relation of the general body of Student
Volunteers to this decision was discussed, and while it
was decided not to take any immediate steps to enlist
students in the work of presentation, it was agreed to
approve the action of a group of Irish Presbyterian
Volunteers who, having been refused for lack of funds
by the Irish Presbyterian Church, had gone to particular
congregations to plead for extra funds to enable the
Church to send them out.

The leaders began at once to interview senior friends
in all the Churches and a good deal of useful advice was
given to them. One of their best friends was the Rev.
George Robson, D.D., of the United Presbyterian
Church, and afterwards editor of *The Record of the
United Free Church of Scotland*, one of the most competent

missionary authorities of the day. He was cordially in favour of approaching the Churches, and thought that the best method of approach would be to draw up and present a memorial. He suggested that it should contain a short history of the Movement, the reasons for the adoption of the Watchword, the results of its adoption and the justification for the Watchword. He advised that the Memorial be submitted to leaders in the different Churches for their approval.

Professor Charteris of the Church of Scotland, Professor T. M. Lindsay of the Free Church of Scotland, and Dr Berry of Wolverhampton, agreed with Dr Robson that a memorial would be the best method of procedure. F. W. S. O'Neill, who brought this advice to the Executive, also brought in his pocket a draft of a proposed Memorial. Both the idea and the outline were approved in general, and Rutter Williamson and G. T. Manley were associated with O'Neill as a subcommittee to draft the Memorial for final approval by the Executive.

The Memorial was written in Manley's rooms at Christ's College, Cambridge, Douglas Thornton being called in to help the sub-committee. It was decided to seek the advice of a number of senior friends, and among those who saw an early draft of the Memorial and helped the committee with advice were : the Rev. H. C. G. Moule, Mr Eugene Stock, Miss Gollock, Professor Ellis Edwards, the Rev. W. T. A. Barber, Mr Duncan Maclaren and the Scottish professors already referred to. The most interesting, as well as the most influential, friend at this period was Dr Temple, the Archbishop of Canterbury. The Lambeth Conference provided an immediate objective, and Thornton and Manley were delegated to see the Archbishop. After their interview Manley wrote :

> We took the draft of the Memorial, and he read it through until he came to a paragraph which stated that the first missionary of the Church of England after the Reformation was in the nineteenth century. " That's not true," was

his characteristic remark. He promised kindly to take the matter up, saying, " I only hope you'll get the Bishops to take it up. I've been trying to move them for the past ten years, but they are hard to move." [1]

Thornton's own observation on this interview with Dr Temple is as follows :

Temple accepts our watchword as an aim to put before the Church, and a possibility. He will bring our appeal before the Assembly at Lambeth, and let the Bishops hear it anyhow. He thinks they will be too old to adopt it as policy, as most of them are over fifty and have not a generation to live. He intimated to us that we had a call to draw together Christian forces. And added, " You may be able to rouse the Church, but . . . I can't." What a confession ! and what an inspiration ! And now to prayer.

This was the Memorial as finally drafted and issued.

MEMORIAL

OF THE

STUDENT VOLUNTEER MISSIONARY UNION

TO THE

CHURCH OF CHRIST IN BRITAIN

INTRODUCTION

BEFORE Christ left the earth, He commanded His followers to preach the Gospel to every creature. The early Church, inspired by the hope of the appearing of her Ascended Lord, carried the message far and wide throughout the then known world. Now, on the threshold of the twentieth century, a new horizon stretches out before us. For the first time in history God has made known to us His earth in every part. One by one, He has unbarred the gates of almost all the nations, that His Word might have free course. To-day Providence and Revelation combine to call the Church afresh to go in and take possession of the world for Christ.

[1] *D. M. Thornton*, by W. H. T. Gairdner, p. 39.

MISSIONARY AWAKENING

The last hundred years have witnessed a remarkable revival of the missionary spirit in the Church, and now a little army of 11,000 soldiers valiantly faces, in a thin and scattered line, the hosts of heathendom. Our Lord, Who said, "All power is given unto Me in heaven and in earth," is in these latter days raising up a new force, to fill the broken ranks and join in the Great Crusade for the evangelization of the world. The Universities and Colleges, which are the training-ground of the leaders of thought and action, have recently become centres of an awakening zeal for the cause of Christ. In Britain and America students are dedicating their lives as never before to the work of Foreign Missions.

STUDENT VOLUNTEER MISSIONARY UNION

The Student Volunteer Missionary Union of Great Britain has, since 1892, banded together 1300 men and women under the Declaration: "It is my purpose, if God permit, to become a Foreign Missionary"; and, already, 300 of these are serving their Commander in the forefront of the fight. This Union is not a society for sending out missionaries, but acts as a handmaid to the Church by influencing students to devote themselves to the service of Christ in heathen and Mohammedan lands. Besides having this direct object, the Union presses upon all Christian students the duty of supporting the work abroad by real sacrifice, systematic missionary study, and definite prevailing prayer.

ADOPTION OF THE WATCHWORD

An International Conference, held at Liverpool at the beginning of 1896, was attended by 715 students from twenty-three different nations, and was marked by the presence and the power of God. Here, after careful thought and earnest prayer, the British Volunteers fell into line with their American brothers by adopting as their watchword,

"THE EVANGELIZATION OF THE WORLD IN THIS GENERATION."

Now, as Volunteers waiting to be sent, we bring this watchword of the Student Missionary Movement on both

H

sides of the Atlantic before the Church of Christ, praying that God may guide His people to carry it into practical effect.

EXPLANATION OF THE WATCHWORD

But it will be asked, What does the watchword mean? Simply that the good news of salvation was intended by God to be made known to the 1500 millions of His present human family, and that the responsibility for this gigantic undertaking lies on all who have been redeemed by His Son. God has "committed unto us the word of reconciliation," and from whose lips shall the heathen now living ever hear that word, if the Christians of the present day fail to discharge the debt? Surely He who said that " repentance and remission of sins should be preached in His name unto all nations," wished His followers in every age to carry the message of His love to the whole fallen race.

We do not understand evangelization to mean, on the one hand, conversion, which is the work of the Holy Spirit, or, on the other hand, a mere hurried proclamation of the truth of Christ. We understand it to mean that the Gospel should be preached intelligibly and intelligently to every soul in such a manner that the responsibility for its acceptance shall no longer rest upon the Christian Church, but upon each man for himself. Hence the watchword is perfectly in harmony with the leavening influences, educational, medical and pastoral, now in operation in the mission-field.

ACCOMPLISHMENT OF THE WATCHWORD

As regards the probability of its achievement within the duration of an average life we hazard no prophecy. Our marching orders require instant obedience, without reference to the time that may be occupied. But there is abundant evidence that the Church has the men and the money that are needed. If the missionary enterprise of Reformed Christendom were carried out on the scale of the Moravian Church, we should have a force of 500,000 heralds of the Cross, who could be maintained at a cost of one-half the annual savings of Great Britain alone. This vast number is far in advance of what is required on the highest estimate of the need, especially as the heathen are more and more responding to the voice of Christ and going forth themselves to tell their countrymen of Him.

The Present Opportunity

When we look at the condition of the world around, there are many indications that the hand of God is visibly preparing the way for the coming of His Kingdom, and that the time is ripe for an advance of our Captain's armies all along the line. The awakening which has been taking place in many of the Universities and Colleges of the Home lands is spreading to those of Australia, Africa and Asia. Students of the West are telling the story of the love of Jesus to their brothers of the East, and these in turn are becoming lights in the dense surrounding night. We are realizing our common brotherhood and clasping hands across the seas to " Make Jesus King." The Bible is now in the languages of nine-tenths of the human race. The blight of Turkish rule is a solemn challenge to the Church to win back for God's Kingdom lands of Bible scenes. The leaves of the Tree of Life are beginning to heal Africa's open sore. China's conservatism is already becoming the sure anchorage of the truth of Christ. The troubled cry of India rings loudest at this juncture in our ears. By entrusting to our rule that mighty Empire, God has placed us in a position of unique privilege and dread responsibility. This trust, if we abuse it, may be taken from us, and we may for ever lose the honour of leading the way in the path of obedience to the will of our Risen Lord.

Need of Spiritual quickening in the Church

Let us, however, frankly own that with heathenism so vast and so strongly entrenched, the evangelization of the world in this generation is an impossibility, unless the Church ceases to be so engrossed with things of time. But if, as we believe, it is God's purpose for the Church, what need we more ? Dare we lower our expectations, seeing they are from Him ? It is true that for its accomplishment a great upheaval of Christendom must take place. There must be a return to Our Lord's conditions of discipleship, forsaking all and losing life itself. Even now we see a widespread search for deeper consecration and for a clearer discernment of the mind of Christ. But before the testimony of the Cross can be everywhere accompanied with the Holy Spirit's power, God must be given complete sovereignty over the lives of His children, that so the promise may be fulfilled : " The nations shall know that

I am the Lord, saith the Lord God, when I shall be sanctified in you before their eyes."

APPEAL TO LEADERS OF THE CHURCH

We venture to ask you, who are called to the holy office of guiding the counsels and action of the Church, to recognize our watchword as expressive of the present duty of the Church, and to ACCEPT IT AS YOUR MISSIONARY POLICY. We beseech you to enlarge your borders, and to direct your plans with a view to carrying the Gospel to all men speedily. In the name of a thousand Volunteers, we entreat you to use your influence, by voice and pen, to rouse the Church to a realization of the present crisis, to claim her sons and daughters, and her wealth to send them forth, and thus redeem the shame of centuries.

APPEAL TO MEMBERS OF THE CHURCH

Fellow-Christians, we ask you to take the part God allots you in the evangelization of the world in this generation, for the work cannot be done unless each fills his place in the universal plan. We beseech you to yield yourselves, your children and your substance, to Him who bought you with His precious blood, and then to go forth or stay as His Spirit may direct. We entreat you to give yourselves continually to prayer that the Lord of the harvest may thrust forth a multitude of labourers into His harvest-field.

CONCLUSION

This our appeal we lay before you, respectfully and hopefully, under the solemn constraint of a deep conviction of the present duty of the Church to accomplish the Great Commission of her Lord.

God grant that the whole Church may hear the voice of Him who has waited all these years for the preaching of His Gospel to a lost world, and yield complete and glad obedience ere this generation shall have passed away.

Signed, on behalf of the Student Volunteer Missionary Union,

Executive—

HOWARD HENRY, *Trinity College, Dublin.*
G. T. MANLEY, *Christ's College, Cambridge.*
A. T. ROBERTS, *Bala College, Wales.*
AGNES ROBSON, *Queen Margaret College, Glasgow.*
J. RUTTER WILLIAMSON, *Edinburgh University.*

Secretaries—

W. R. MILLER, *St Bartholomew's Hospital, London.*
J. H. OLDHAM, *Trinity College, Oxford.*
F. W. S. O'NEILL, *Presbyterian College, Belfast.*
RUTH ROUSE, *Girton College, Cambridge.*
D. M. THORNTON, *Trinity College, Cambridge.*

The Memorial was presented in person by leaders of the Union to several of the missionary societies, whose committees received them and heard them speak. In almost every case a resolution was passed. The Church Missionary Society resolved :

That this Committee, rejoicing in the Divine blessing vouchsafed to the S.V.M.U. in its efforts to influence the students of both sexes in Universities and Colleges all round the world, and thanking its leaders warmly for the Memorial now presented, desire to express their hearty concurrence with the Union in setting before themselves and the whole Christian Church the great aim embodied in the Watchword of the Union, " The evangelization of the world in this generation." [1]

The Standing Committee of the Society for the Propagation of the Gospel received Douglas Thornton and W. R. Miller, gave them ten minutes each to speak and questioned them for forty-five minutes, after which it passed this resolution :

Agreed that the Standing Committee, having heard the statement from the deputation of the S.V.M.U., desires to express its gratitude to Almighty God for the noble effort which is being made to promote the missionary spirit in universities and colleges, especially in leading young men and women to give their lives definitely to the work of the foreign mission field. The Standing Committee earnestly commends the subject to the consideration of the Bishops assembled at the Lambeth Conference. [2]

Rutter Williamson saw the Bishop of Newcastle (Dr Jacob), who was a warm advocate of missions, and

[1] Extract from the proceedings of C.M.S. Committee, April 13th, 1897.
[2] Extract from the proceedings of S.P.G. Committee, June 17th, 1897.

secured his promise to mention the Watchword at the Lambeth Conference. Copies of the Memorial were then posted with a covering letter to every bishop attending at Lambeth. Foreign missions were assigned a more prominent place than at any previous Lambeth Conference, and the report of the committee on foreign missions of the Conference contained these words :

> Your Committee observe with gratitude to God that a very large number of students in Universities and Colleges throughout the world have realized so keenly the call to missionary work that they have enrolled themselves in a Student Volunteer Missionary Union, and have taken as their watchword " The Evangelization of the world in this Generation." A large number of these students are members of the Anglican Communion, and it seems the plain duty of that Communion to provide channels through which such newly-awakened zeal may find outlets in earnest, sound, wise work.

The Free Churches were also sympathetic. The Wesleyan Methodist Missionary Society received Thornton and Miller on April 28th, and the Rev. Marshall Hartley wrote afterwards to the S.V.M.U. :

> I have great pleasure in informing you of the satisfaction with which the committee of our missionary society this morning received a deputation of your Union and heard the statements made in your behalf. I believe everyone present was moved to sympathy with you in your object, and to gratitude to God for the movement which your Union represents. The following resolution was unanimously and heartily adopted :
>
> " The Committee has heard with great sympathy and rejoicing the appeal of the Student Volunteer Missionary Union to the Churches. It desires to express its heartfelt gratitude to God for the signs of a great and growing enthusiasm for foreign missions among the cultured youth of Great Britain and declares its determination to do its utmost to impress the people of the Wesleyan Methodist Church with this burning message of duty and privilege."

The Congregational Union, Baptist Missionary Society, London Missionary Society, Friends' Foreign

Mission Association, Presbyterian Church of England, South American Missionary Society and British and Foreign Bible Society all passed sympathetic resolutions and issued the Memorial to their supporters. Many of the societies printed it in their magazines and wrote articles on it.

In Scotland the Church of Scotland Foreign Mission Committee passed a sympathetic resolution and Rutter Williamson made a brief speech to the General Assembly of the Church on May 27th, copies of the Memorial having been sent to its members. In the Free Church of Scotland and the United Presbyterian Church of Scotland the same course was followed, Frank Anderson speaking in each General Assembly and Miss Rouse at the Women's Missionary Meeting.

In Wales the Memorial was printed in both Welsh and English and circulated by the Calvinistic Methodist Church.

The following year the leaders continued their approach to the Churches and the spring meeting of the Federation of Evangelical Free Churches received a deputation, as did the Baptist Union in the autumn, while the Archdeacon of Glendalough (Dr Galbraith), a loved leader in the Church of Ireland, moved and carried a sympathetic resolution at the General Synod of that Church.

The results of " the Approach to the Churches " disappointed the leaders of the S.V.M.U., they wished the Churches to adopt the Watchword, and consequent upon its adoption to enter upon a phase of missionary activity which would transcend anything of the kind hitherto known in Christendom. What had happened was that the Churches had pushed forward their missionary leaders and missionary societies to receive the Memorial and to reply to the students on their behalf, with the result that in the judgment of F. W. S. O'Neill, a judgment approved by the committee, the missionary leaders said in effect: " This is what we have all along been working for, what more can we do ? "

Rutter Williamson expressed the mind of the Executive when he pointed out to his fellow-members " our appeal was not to missionary leaders but to the whole Church, and while it was not our place to suggest methods we could point out that for the accomplishment of the Watchword there was needed not an increase of missionary interest and giving, but a complete change of attitude towards the question." That was what the leaders wanted, and the sympathy and encouragement they received did not blind them to the fact that they had not achieved what they sought, namely, " a complete change of attitude towards the question."

The resolution of the Church Missionary Society was the one which caused most distress to the committee, because the Church Missionary Society referred to the evangelization of the world in this generation as being " the aim " of the Church. What was necessary in the students' judgment was to bring home to people's consciences that it was " a duty."

If it was the doubt whether all suitable Student Volunteers would be sent abroad by the societies which led to the Approach to the Churches being made, it was the adoption of the Watchword which became the spearhead of the Approach and gave it urgency, and we must look more closely at the Watchword. It was not a sudden impulse induced by the Liverpool Conference that led to its adoption. It had been before the leaders of the S.V.M.U. for three years, and Robert Wilder, John Mott and Robert Speer, who had influenced them and helped them in no small degree, were convinced that it had given inspiration and edge to the Volunteer Movement in the United States.

There have been differing estimates of the real value of the Watchword to the Movement, some thought that it added little to the missionary driving force of the Movement, which was considerable ; while there were others who were convinced that for at least two student generations it added greatly to the force of the S.V.M.U. in Great Britain. I believe those who think it was of great value are right.   It was a time when mottoes were popular, and almost every member of the Movement was in the habit of displaying upon his walls and keeping in his Bible, motto texts and cards.   Men lived for the fulfilment of this Watchword.

The Watchword was expounded by the Union's leaders with remarkable consistency in *The Student Volunteer*, missionary magazines, at college and at public meetings. The point was made again and again that evangelization does not mean Christianization ; " The aim is to bring Christ within the reach of every individual that He may have an opportunity of intelligently accepting Him as a personal Saviour."

" The Evangelization of the world in this generation " was pressed as a *duty*. " This is the only generation which is given us to evangelize, and Christians of to-day are the only ones to whom the heathen of this generation can look for the Gospel.   Christ's command for us applies to this, the one generation in all eternity, for which we are responsible."

While the leaders of the S.V.M.U. declared that they did not intend to raise the question of the probability of its accomplishment, they did deal with the question of its possibility, and it was this question that interested a good many missionaries and missionary society secretaries, and gave rise to a good deal of speculation and calculation as to the number of missionaries that would be required to preach the Gospel effectively to all the world.

The fullest exposition of the Watchword from the British point of view was contributed in a series of four articles by G. T. Manley, a member of the Executive and Fellow of Christ's College, Cambridge, to *The Student Volunteer* during 1897.   The first article expounded the thesis that disciples who really loved their Master must seek to obey His command to carry the Gospel into the whole world.   In the second article Manley sketched briefly the history of evangelization from Pentecost to the present day, and in the third commenced by quoting the words, " All authority hath been given unto Me in heaven and on earth.   Go ye *therefore* and make disciples of all nations."

The covenant of power, he wrote, is so linked with the God-given Watchword of the Church, as to prove beyond all doubt its possibility, and, to make it doubly sure, each several account gives some new promise for our need. Are we afraid our feeble faith may fail ?   Lo, He is with us alway.   Are wonders needed ?   Signs shall follow them that believe.   Are the nations held fast in the bondage of sin ?   To us is entrusted the Gospel of its remission.   Are we unworthy to be ambassadors of God ?   The Holy Ghost shall come with power, and we shall be Christ's witnesses unto the uttermost ends of the earth.   Thus do all the forces of heaven wait on the evangelization of the world.

He then proceeded: " Is it possible in this generation ? Most distinctly we answer, Yes."   Recalling what had been achieved in Uganda he concluded that 6000 missionaries would be required to reach " the two hundred millions " of people in Africa.

The other eight hundred millions of the heathen world are bound by ancient and established, but false religions, and amongst them greater density of population, greater intelligence, and greater ease in travelling, bring more men within the influence of one worker ; but the tyranny of caste and the prevalence of scepticism make fewer accept the Gospel.   And yet in India 179,207 boys attend Protestant mission schools superintended by 75 Europeans (and Americans), thus in each master's lifetime 10,000 boys will come under his influence, learn the primary truths of Christianity, and have every chance of further instruction. Again, the five great universities, and the numerous colleges, which annually pour out thousands of students, will, in the future, be a mighty force.   It has been estimated by a recent writer that, were sufficient Volunteers forthcoming from their ranks 9000 Europeans would be required to lead them in order to evangelize their country in this generation.   It will also be remembered that during Mr Mott's tour in India over one hundred of them had thus offered themselves and formed a first beginning of the S.V.M.U. in India.   But besides native help, no less than

twenty-seven thousand Europeans would be required for
the evangelization of the civilized races.

Manley thought that " thirty-three thousand Western
Christians, if volunteering within the next five years,
would be a minimum sufficient to lead the forces of the
Native Churches in a great Movement for the Evangelization of the World in this generation." He said, however, that these figures were only an indication, and
declared that " taking an outside limit, few would doubt
that one hundred thousand men could cope with the
material difficulties of the task, and for the rest, God's
help would be vouchsafed, as in the past, in answer to
our prayers. Britain's share would be thirty-three
thousand men, or one in every three hundred Protestant
Church members, or one in a hundred of every regular
Communicant." The cost he estimated at ten millions
per annum, which could be provided if all communicants contributed twopence per day each. The amount
would be " one-sixth of what Christian England spends
on war, one-fourteenth of what she pays for alcohol."

In a final article Manley dealt with the objections,
that the Watchword is presumptuous, implies hasty and
imperfect evangelization, and is impracticable. He
urged that the early disciples went to the uttermost
parts of the known world, that the difficulties lay in
man's slowness of heart and indifference, but that
" once the Church is awakened, the power material and
spiritual are ready to her hand."

A message addressed to members of the Union,
written by Rutter Williamson,[1] is in even more urgent
terms.

Fellow-Volunteers, this (Memorial) has been issued in
your name. Will you make it your own? Will you
become distributing centres of the message contained in
the Watchword? Will you let it be your life inspiration?
Will you stand within the field of its spiritual force? Will
you let the Holy Ghost press its claim upon your spirit

[1] *The Student Volunteer*, Summer number, 1897, p. 80.

till you have been impregnated with its spiritual magnetism? It has spoken already to many as a strong cry for deeper consecration. We have unitedly asked the Church of Christ to send us forth without delay. Is our life ringing out an appeal many times louder than even our words?

He then writes words characteristic of the whole spirit in which these men and women presented the Watchword.

As a Union we believe that the Watchword expresses, not merely an ideal, but states a present duty of the Church, which, if realized as such, is easily possible of accomplishment . . . it is not a mere quickening of interest in missions we seek. It is a definite, sustained and comprehensive appropriation of the opportunities presented before us to-day for evangelizing the whole world *in this our generation.*

These were not mere words. The men who adopted the Watchword and expounded it to the Colleges and the Church, subordinated all other interests to their supreme interest—the evangelization of the world. Several of them were intimate personal friends of mine, with whom I spent long hours at a time at work and play. Their references to the Watchword were so constant as to leave no doubt as to the hold it had upon them. The two I knew best were Douglas Thornton and Temple Gairdner; their biographies are available, and bear witness to the passion of their devotion. The men, as I knew them, were exactly like the men portrayed. I find no exaggeration in what is written of them.

Of the ten men and women who signed the Memorial to the Churches as leaders of the S.V.M.U., nine became missionaries, and two of them are still at work on the mission field, Dr W. R. Miller in Africa and the Rev. F. W. S. O'Neill in China.

From " Liverpool 1896 " for a decade the leadership in calling the Christian Church in the British Isles to greater devotion to missionary work was in the hands of the Student Movement. During this period it arrested the attention of the Churches, planted in them the missionary study movement and raised the intellectual standard the societies required of those appointed missionaries. The Watchword was in the forefront of all that the student leaders wrote and said during this period.

Critics of the Watchword soon appeared, not among undergraduates but among senior men. The first considered criticism of it came from Professor Warneck of Halle, editor of the *Allgemeine Missions Zeitschrift*, who was accepted as the greatest authority of the day on modern missions. Dr Warneck was concerned lest the missionary enterprise should come to be dominated by a type of leader who believed in the preaching of the Gospel as a witness more than in thorough work which would lead to the building up of the Christian Church in all parts of the world. He doubted the wisdom of sending out great numbers of missionaries, and criticized Dr Hudson Taylor's demand for 1000 more missionaries for China, with a view to enabling every family to hear the Gospel in three years. Dr A. T. Pierson, a popular American advocate of missions, whose books had a wide circulation, was associated in his mind with this desire for hasty proclamation, and Dr Pierson used the idea of hastening the Second Advent as an argument for world-wide evangelization. While Dr Warneck was reflecting on this subject the S.V.M.U. and its Watchword came to his attention, and, connecting the two, he came to the conclusion that there was a danger that the S.V.M.U. might bring about a change of missionary policy with the result that missionary societies would make the proclamation of the Gospel their end rather than the conversion of men and women to God, and the building up of the Christian Church. Dr Warneck dismissed the explanation of the Watchword given in the Memorial which disclaims the idea of " a mere hurried proclamation of the truth," on the ground that the explanation demanded a work impossible " in this generation."

This attack by Dr Warneck greatly concerned the leaders of the Union, but they took no public notice of it. A spirited defence of the Union and its Watchword, however, was written by Dr Robson and printed in *The Missionary Record* of the United Presbyterian Church.[1]

He declared that Dr Warneck had misread the Watchword, and said:

> From our own knowledge, indeed, we feel warranted in saying that many of those who have taken a prominent part in the Union in this country, and are now in the mission field, as well as those who are now leading in the Movement and will soon go out, would unite with Dr Warneck in disowning that particular theory of the missionary enterprise to which his criticism is directed.

Dr Robson concluded his article by saying that in his judgment Dr Warneck had failed to appreciate adequately the significance and promise of the Movement among the students.

> In its origin, in its manner of growth, in its claim on the best intellects with the fullest culture for missionary service, in its ever increasing appreciation of the task of missions and loyalty to Church lines of action, and in the broadening out of its work among students of all nations, as well as in its actual contribution to the ranks of service, it has proved itself a deep and true movement of the Spirit of God. We are not aware of any friend of missions who has carefully followed the steps of the movement, and has been in personal touch with it, who has not been led with a grateful heart to that conclusion. And we do not think that the Union is misinterpreting the will of Christ or the signs of the times in proclaiming it to be the duty of the Church to seek the evangelization of the world in this generation.

This defence by Dr Robson and his confidence in them greatly helped and comforted the student leaders. When men grow older they tend to care less and less

[1] See *The Missionary Record*, October, 1897.

about what is said regarding them and their work;
this is not so with younger people who are winning
their experience and feeling their way. The seeming
confidence and bumptiousness of youth frequently
covers a quaking heart and very few young people are
insensitive to criticism from whatever quarter it comes,
and usually pay far more attention to it than most of
their elders seem to realize. As one looks back now
one recalls how pathetically grateful the students were
for the support of men like Archbishop Benson, Bishop
Jacob,[1] Dr Robson, Mr Eugene Stock, and many
others. Some of these did little more than make a
friendly reference to the Movement in a sermon, but
others gave constant and considered advice.

In 1899 Mr Mott published, through the S.V.M.U.,
his book *The Evangelization of the World in This Generation.*
It ran through several editions, and at the suggestion
of Henry T. Hodgkin, then Chairman of the S.V.M.U.,
a paper-covered edition, attractively printed on good
paper, was produced by the Union and sold for six-
pence on railway station bookstalls throughout England.

Mott was aware of the criticisms of the Watchword
which had arisen and dealt with them in his book. He
began with definition, and Mr Eugene Stock, the
foremost student of missions in England, approved
what he wrote. Reviewing the book in *The Student
Movement,*[2] he said: "the expression 'in this generation'
is admirably explained, in words which every student
volunteer should copy into his notebook for ready use."

The evangelization of the world in this generation means
the preaching of the Gospel to those who are now living.
To us who are responsible for the preaching, it means *in
our life time*: to those to whom it is to be preached, it
means *in their life time*. The unevangelized for whom we
as Christians are responsible live in this generation; and
the Christians whose duty it is to present Christ to them
live in this generation. The phrase "in this generation,"

[1] The Bishop of Newcastle.
[2] *The Student Movement*, vol. iii. p. 11.

therefore, strictly speaking, has a different meaning for each person.

Mr Mott's power in piling up an appeal comes out in the second chapter of his book where he deals with the obligation to evangelize the world. He concludes the chapter with this summary :

> Because of the infinite need of men without Christ ; because of the possibilities of men of every race and condition who take Christ as the Lord of their lives ; because of the command of our Lord which has acquired added force as a result of nineteen centuries of discovery, of opening of doors, of experience of the Christian Church ; because of the shameful neglect of the past ; because of the impending crisis and the urgency of the situation in all parts of the non-Christian world ; because of the opportunity for a greatly accelerated movement in the present ; because of the danger of neglecting to enter upon a great onward movement ; because of the constraining memories of the Cross of Christ and the love wherewith He loved us—it is the solemn duty of the Christians of this generation to do their utmost to evangelize the world.

Mr Mott then proceeds to deal with difficulties which, he says, are of three kinds, namely, difficulties external to the Church on the mission-field, within the Church on the mission-field and within the Church in Christian lands. In the two chapters which follow he gives historical illustrations of the triumph over difficulties. A striking chapter follows on " Facilities and Resources." " Why," he asks, " has God provided us with such wonderful agencies ? "

> Not that the forces of evil might utilize them. Not for the purpose of promoting strife and avarice. Not for us to waste or leave unused. . . . The hand of God, in opening door after door among the nations of mankind, in unlocking the secrets of nature and in bringing to light invention after invention is beckoning the Church of our day to larger achievements. If the Church, instead of theorizing and speculating, will improve her opportunities, resources and facilities, it seems entirely possible to fill the

earth with the knowledge of Christ before the present
generation passes away.

The two concluding chapters bring together opinions
from missionaries and other experts and urge that more
highly qualified missionaries, more zeal and knowledge,
and self-denial in the Church at home, and above all,
more prayer, are essential factors in carrying out the
evangelization of the world in this generation. The
book was written with immense passion and conviction
and contains a great deal of historical fact as well as
appeal. It is well worth reading at the present day.

CHAPTER VIII

THE BIRMINGHAM CONFERENCE AND THE FORMATION OF THE THEOLOGICAL COLLEGE DEPARTMENT

THE Student Movement owes more to the leadership of theological students than to the students of any other faculty, yet there has been no type of college with which the Movement has found it more difficult to establish the right relationship than the theological college. There is nothing surprising in this, since theological students during their training are apt to be sensitive about anything that seems to imply criticism, and a religious Movement which sets out not only to relate theological students to itself for the purpose of keeping them in touch with what other students are thinking and doing about Christianity, but which also has suggestions to offer to theological students which it believes to be for their benefit, could not escape the odious charge of " trying to do theologicals good ! "

When the Student Movement turned its attention to the theological colleges it found that there were twenty-two Church of England theological colleges and five university divinity faculties on a Church of England foundation, thirteen Presbyterian, twelve Congregational, nine Baptist and eight Methodist theological colleges, with a total of about three thousand students in them. The travelling secretaries always sought opportunities to speak in theological colleges from the foundation of the S.V.M.U. In 1894 the Movement began to turn its attention to theological colleges, as such. The proposal to create a Theological Colleges Missionary Alliance that year and its abandonment the following summer has

already been recorded.[1]   During the year the Alliance
was under discussion in the theological colleges, Frank
Anderson, the British College Christian Union travelling secretary, visited a number of them, chiefly Presbyterian and Nonconformist colleges.   An extract from
his private report explains why the Church of England
colleges were not also entered.

> I walked out about six miles to Cuddesdon Church of
> England college, I saw the Principal but could get no
> promise of an opportunity of addressing the students. . . .
> I visited a Church of England Missionary Training College
> at Dorchester about nine miles from Oxford.   I saw both
> the Principal and the senior student but could get no
> promise of a future meeting. . . . Next, Salisbury . . . I
> could not enter the theological college. . . . My next point
> was Lichfield, on the evening of my arrival I saw two of the
> students who I think would have arranged a meeting for
> me in the theological college but the Principal withheld his
> consent.   The case at Lincoln, which I visited the following
> day, was very similar and no opening offered. . . . At
> Leeds I was unable to get an opening in the Clergy School
> though I had an interview with the Principal on the subject.

The idea of sharing in a Movement which welcomed
Nonconformists and Presbyterians was novel to most
members of the Church of England and deeply repugnant
to some, and it took time to convince the Church of
England theological Principals that their colleges should
have a place in the Movement.   The failure to secure
an entry to these colleges was a great disappointment to
the early leaders, the majority of whom—as was Frank
Anderson—were members of the Church of England.
The reason the Movement was not admitted was partly,
as I have said, the novelty of the idea of an interdenominational body, partly the fear of compromising
principles held with deep conviction, and partly because
the Churchmen who had thrown in their lot with the
Movement were almost to a man products of the
Evangelical party.   It was not until later that the High

[1] See pp. 57, 67.

Churchman and the non-party Anglican came into the Movement.

The Committee blundered when, on abandoning the Alliance, it decided that missionary societies in theological colleges should be affiliated to the B.C.C.U., for this meant that the same circulars and literature which were issued to Christian Unions were issued to theological colleges, and as the leaders of the Union were undoubtedly critical of theological students as a class, it tended to enhance the impression that the Movement thought the theological colleges unspiritual places to which it had a special mission. There was a good deal of truth in this from whatever angle we look at it. The leaders did think that the spiritual life of many theological students needed deepening and, being very uncompromising men, did not hesitate to say so. We find, for example, the following suggestions for work in theological colleges : [1]

1. That every theological college ought to have from two to five days of meetings some time in term each year for deepening of spiritual life.

2. That influences should be brought to bear on the faculties as to the need of more emphasis on the spiritual life of the students.

3. Every theological college should be engaged in town mission work.

4. Every theological college ought to be engaged in some foreign missionary work :

(a) There should be a weekly prayer-meeting for foreign missions with occasional addresses from missionaries.

(b) Professors must be made to cease to take for granted that all men are going to the home field.

(c) Funds should be raised by students preaching to support a missionary or mission work.

(d) The missionary society should seek to develop a missionary spirit in the students.

The question will be asked how far the Student Movement leaders were right. It is a difficult question

[1] Minute Book, January 1896.

to answer. A year later, as a S.V.M.U. travelling secretary who had just completed three years in an engineering school and whose only knowledge of theology was such as had been acquired through making theological reading somewhat of a hobby, I was sent to visit a considerable number of theological colleges. Most of these were Presbyterian and Nonconformist colleges, and I was keenly interested in what was to me a novel type of institution, but was somewhat taken aback by the amount of professionalism and lack of vital spiritual interest met with in some of these colleges. There were theological colleges in which there was no attempt to secure corporate worship, and many were the midnight talks with men who were seeking spiritual help to assist them during the difficult process of adjusting their pre-college spiritual experience to the intellectual studies in which they were engaged. One's own experience of a theological course, three years later, and further knowledge of the difficulties of the theological student, have modified certain of the opinions formed ; but there was need of change, and the Student Movement has produced considerable changes in many of the theological colleges, although some of the changes are not consciously associated with it in the minds of the theological students of the present generation. In many of the Presbyterian and Nonconformist colleges, services and devotional meetings which have become part of college life derive their origin from the Student Movement.

Douglas Thornton had been appointed in 1895 as one of a committee of four to advise the British College Christian Union Executive as regards their activities in theological colleges. On his advice a Call to a Week of Prayer for theological colleges in the Lent term 1896 was issued. This Call described the missionary movement among students, gave some information about theological colleges, laid stress on the importance of the work to which the men in them were called, and suggested as subjects for intercession : 1. A great deepening of personal religion among theological

students.   2. The promotion of the spirit of true unity.
3. The evangelization of the world.   This Call was
signed by the committee and endorsed by the Bishop of
London (Dr Temple), Professor Marcus Dods, Principal
A. M. Fairbairn, Professor R. Flint and others.

Twelve theological colleges were brought into direct
contact with the Movement this winter, but the committee was not satisfied with this progress and decided
the following year to appoint a special travelling
secretary for theological colleges, choosing for this office
F. W. S. O'Neill, Assembly's College, Belfast. O'Neill
visited fifty-three colleges and the number of affiliated
societies rose to twenty-eight.

Fred O'Neill's diary is an interesting document for
several reasons.   It shows how little the problems of
theological students change from generation to generation ; it throws light on the activities of the Movement
in theological colleges thirty-two years ago ; and there
are references to a number of men who later became
well known.   He tells of a Bible study circle started
at Bala Bangor College which Miall Edwards [1] agreed
to lead, how kindly he was received at Ridley Hall by
Theodore Woods,[2] records an interesting conversation
with Dr R. F. Horton, who urged that the one way to
create a missionary pastorate was to create first of all
really good missionary literature, and he has a good
deal to say about W. Nelson Bitton,[3] the student
president of Hackney College, " a fine fellow."   He
was taken by Frank Lenwood, a student at Mansfield
College, to see Principal Fairbairn, whom he found
" greatly interested in the B.C.C.U. and the World's
Student Christian Federation but thought there ought
to be much more union between colleges, especially
between colleges in the same place, as, for instance,

[1] Afterwards the Rev. Professor D. Miall Edwards, D.D.
[2] Afterwards Bishop of Peterborough and Winchester in succession.
[3] Afterwards the Rev. W. Nelson Bitton, Secretary of the
London Missionary Society.

Wycliffe Hall and Mansfield College. He would much like to see missionary study started in Mansfield College." O'Neill wrote appreciatively of the friendliness and good tone of the Methodist Colleges, especially Handsworth. Following in his footsteps a year later, I learned to look forward to visits to the Methodist Colleges for the same reason.

O'Neill as theological travelling secretary for a year had no successor for some years, as it was decided that so many of the theological colleges had been brought into touch with the Movement that it would be unnecessary to appoint a special secretary, and it was arranged that I should visit as many as possible as S.V.M.U. travelling secretary.

A visit by a S.V.M.U. travelling secretary did not seem to meet the need, and accordingly I wrote a report urging that a conference for theological students should be arranged, when questions of interest to them might be considered and when consideration could be given to their relationship to the Student Movement. This suggestion was taken up by Douglas Thornton with enthusiasm and was backed by Temple Gairdner, the travelling secretary of the B.C.C.U. The Theological committee that advised the Executive of the B.C.C.U. and that Executive itself approved the proposal and the Conference was handed over to a committee to carry through consisting of Douglas Thornton, W. H. T. Gairdner and myself. We liked the coincidence that we were all three Trinity men—Trinity, Cambridge, Trinity, Oxford, and Trinity, Dublin. It was symbolic. No trio could have been more different in qualities or more united in spirit. The working up of delegations and making arrangements for hospitality and halls fell to my share, Thornton and Gairdner shaped the programme and policy of the conference. They set out to gain the support and co-operation of a body of theological students in creating a demand from within the theological colleges for a place in the Student Movement.

It was decided to hold the conference from April
12th to 16th 1898, in Birmingham. The difficulties
encountered were considerable; there was no money
and the expenses were bound to be heavy, the whole
of the first list of speakers failed, and as the conference
had to be arranged within four months it seemed as if
it would be impossible in so short a time to find suitable speakers who would be disengaged in Easter Week.
Again, how could we find speakers who were well
known to theological students and at the same time
acquainted with the aims and purpose of the Student
Movement, and always the anxious question remained—
whether the banquet being prepared, the guests would
come ? Would theological students find time and
money to come in sufficient numbers for the conference
to fulfil its purpose ? As Gairdner truly says in the
preface to the Report of the conference : " These
anxieties sufficed to cast the promoters of the enterprise
upon God."

It was a wonderful little fellowship, that trio, how
many consultations and prayer-meetings we had together
in a dingy hotel in Birmingham or in a room in the
Y.M.C.A. !

We went to Malvern for the Easter week-end immediately before the conference, and there Gairdner wrote
a report for presentation to the conference, a report on
which much depended, for it was an attempt to make
an *apologia* for the presence of the Student Movement
in theological colleges. It was the big gun we were
going to fire at the conference. Gairdner would write
a few paragraphs and present them to Thornton. Now
Thornton was a man who loved a blue pencil, and I
can see him sitting very erect with Gairdner's manuscript before him, wielding his blue pencil with Gairdner
looking over his shoulder, murmuring in accents of
increasing anxiety, " Oh, Douglas, oh, Douglas," as
Thornton slashed away at his manuscript with that blue
pencil, usually using it to score out a paragraph and
put against it the word, " Re-write." And then the

wonderful Easter Communion in the magnificent old Priory, when we knelt together, having agreed to commit in a special way at that hour our enterprise to God !

Financial difficulties were met by the generosity of Lord Overtoun. Gairdner being a Glasgow man, it was decided he should go and ask Lord Overtoun for £100. When he returned we asked him what had happened. Here was his account, " I went in to see the old man and told him about the conference, and I just had it on the very tip of my tongue to ask him for £100, when he interrupted me by saying, ' I'll be very glad to give you £200, Mr Gairdner.' "

As to speakers, in spite of the failure of our first list, the conference was strong in speaking, and the Report reads extremely well. The first morning the subject was " The Call to the Ministry." This was treated in two sections. The topic " Its prophetic office " was dealt with by a young Scotsman none of us had ever heard of before, who gave a magnificent address which many of the students declared was alone worth coming to Birmingham to hear. The young minister was the Rev. John Kelman. Among the other speakers were Dr Fairbairn, Rev. J. H. Jowett, Rev. W. T. A. Barber, Rev. F. B. Meyer, the Rev. W. E. Burroughs and Mr Eugene Stock,.

On the fourth day of the conference the Report was presented. It surveyed the theological field of the country, spoke of the origin and results of the S.V.M.U. and of the B.C.C.U., reviewed the connection of the S.V.M.U. with theological colleges, pointed out that of the two hundred and eight-seven students who signed the Declaration in 1892, one hundred and fifteen were theological students, and that of the one thousand five hundred and one students who had joined up to the present, six hundred and twenty-six were theological students. The Report then told the story of the connection of the B.C.C.U. with theological colleges and stated quite frankly that its purpose was to deepen and strengthen the connection between the Student Movement and the theological colleges of the country.

This conference, then, the first of its kind in this country, has been convened in the earnest hope that here theological students will recognize fully the great possibilities that now lie before this Movement; will thus voice the demand for their share in it; and that they will aid their committee in suggesting methods whereby they may become living members, vitally concerned in, and essentially contributing to its success.

The value of the Movement was declared to be the intercourse it created with other colleges.

It will repay us to dwell further on this point. The life of a theological college is often one of extraordinary isolation, no bond or union has hitherto existed between these colleges, which even in the same denomination are often ignorant of each other's doings.

The World's Student Christian Federation was explained, and how inclusion in the Movement

gives the theological colleges a direct lot and portion in the Student Christian Movement which has now spread throughout the world. Such an inclusion must be an inspiration to the theological student who will feel that he has in this a new proof of the advance of the Kingdom of Christ—that he belongs to a faith, which, so far from falling back, is claiming the intellect and power of many countries.

The final section dealt with the future; the most effective link between each college in the Movement was discussed and the creation of a homogeneous society in each college, as far as possible co-extensive with the college, was suggested. The function suggested for it was the organization of devotional Bible study.

During years when of necessity we pass through so much critical and intellectual study of the Bible, there seems to be room for some systematic attempt to help one another to study the living Word of God devotionally and with a view to personal spiritual growth—the way in which we shall one day assuredly have to minister it to the souls of men, during years when the most devoted men have felt how easily the intellectual study of theology can chill the warm, spontaneous spirituality with which they entered college. Is there not a call for the adoption of every possible counter-acting force ?

The Watchword of the S.V.M.U. was put forward and the conference asked to consider :

(a) How may this ideal be accepted by the future ministers and clergy of our country ?
(b) What steps can they take in the work of gaining its acceptance by the whole Church of Christ ?

and a plea was made for " an organized and systematic attempt to acquire a deep and sympathetic knowledge of Foreign Missions ; as those who study some great campaign grasp the positions of the opposing armies, and watch the ordered advance which is slowly driving the enemy off the field."

It was suggested that chairs of foreign missions might be founded in theological colleges, also that foreign missions might be made a subject at the examination of candidates for ordination. The Report ended with an appeal for men for the mission field.

The afternoon of the day the Report was presented the gathering was divided into four sectional conferences, to consider it : these were followed by a general meeting of delegates. Theological students are very much more sophisticated as regards all kinds of religious effort than other students, so that the Report was of vital importance ; if it did not meet with approval the conference might fail. The sectional conferences happily all decided to recommend the adoption of the Report, at the same time using the occasion to air their views about the Student Movement and its proper relation to the theological colleges. The result was that the leaders of the Movement acquired a mass of first-hand information as to the thought of theological students about the Movement and about the different topics presented in the Report.

One incident occurred which very nearly wrecked the conference. A friend of Douglas Thornton's had pressed very earnestly that the Nicene Creed should be recited by the whole conference as a demonstration of their fundamental unity in the Faith. This suggestion was put to the members of the Theological Committee at the conference by Thornton ; there was reluctance by the Nonconformist members, but Thornton had great weight and he was insistent, and they agreed, so the Nicene Creed was printed on cards ready for distribution. It was decided, however, to refer the final decision whether or not it should be used to the sectional conferences, and while the Anglican, Presbyterian and Methodist members were in favour of its recitation, the proposal met with disfavour from a number of the Baptist and Congregationalist students, who felt that they were being rushed into an action which was not in harmony with their traditions. A few protested with a good deal of violence and were only pacified by the withdrawal of the proposal, the Executive having decided that unless the conference was practically unanimous, the Creed should not be used.

As far as establishing the Movement in theological colleges was concerned the Report and debate on it was vital, hence the space given to it. As for the general line of the addresses, a summary in Douglas Thornton's closing speech, as chairman of the conference, will suffice :

> We believe that God's Holy Spirit has guided us to a definite course and plan throughout the conference. The first day was spent in considering the questions that concern the theological student in regard to his call when he becomes a minister . . . then we were led to a wider outlook and were shown what we may attain to by God's grace as soul winners for Christ. . . . We were led further to see that the ministry of soul winning is by no means confined to this country but that there is a greater need than ever in non-Christian lands for ministers of the Gospel.

The second day was devoted to the consideration of what should be our equipment for this service; we were brought face to face with the Holy Spirit of God, and shown how necessary is His fulness for our own life, character and work. The profound depths of prayer life and study of the Word next opened out before us. . . . We were privileged on the evening of that day to have the duty of the Church of Christ brought before us as we saw the scope of the Kingdom of God, there was an opportunity for looking upon the fields white to harvest. . . . It has been some encouragement to us to hear how the Spirit of God is stirring not only the men of our own universities and colleges, but theological students throughout the world. . . . Our last day, from the beginning to the end, been has given to the consideration of the Watchword of the S.V.M.U.

The conference was attended by one hundred and sixty-nine students and twenty-four professors, lecturers and speakers ; forty-one theological colleges (in which are included six university divinity faculties) were represented. Most of the Nonconformist and Presbyterian colleges of the country were represented, the absentees were representatives of the Church of England colleges. Of twenty-three Church of England colleges only Ridley Hall, Lichfield, St John's Hall, Highbury, Wycliff Hall, the C.M.S. College, Islington and St Boniface College, Warminster were represented, and not all the students from these were delegates of their college.

The Movement, however, had more friends in Anglican colleges than this attendance suggests. The Rev. H. F. Stewart, Vice-principal of Salisbury Theological College, wrote saying that "any movement which has for its object the spread of the Kingdom has my warm sympathy and earnest prayers." Dr Bernard[1] wrote from the Divinity School of Trinity College, Dublin : " The meeting I feel sure will be a very important one : and I trust that it may be productive of permanent results and the quickening of missionary zeal and the organization of missionary enterprise both abroad and

[1] Afterwards Archbishop of Dublin.

at home." And we were greatly cheered by a very sympathetic letter from Dr Wilkinson, the saintly Bishop of St Andrews.

On the other hand, some of the Church of England Principals disapproved of their students joining the conference. " I am afraid," wrote the Rev. Winfrid O Burrows,[1] of the Clergy School, Leeds, in a letter typical of several, " I cannot see my way to joining in a conference about the deepening of the spiritual life in our theological colleges with people who do not accept the Church Catechism and its teaching about the entrance into that spiritual life. We differ in first principles, *a fortiori*, I cannot suggest to one of the students to go."

Other Principals wrote at length explaining their difficulties and hesitations about an organization not exclusively Church of England. This was a help as it gave insight into the mind of a group of men in the Church of which the leaders of the Movement knew little : the letters were eagerly read and discussed.

The conference immensely heartened Thornton and Gairdner, not only because the experience convinced them that the theological colleges would come into the Movement and pull their weight in it, but because it brought younger men, and especially Frank Lenwood, to the fore as leaders, a vital matter as the two former were on the point of departure for the mission field.

Lenwood became chairman of the Theological Committee, and very characteristic were the letters to him of the two men who were leaving the Movement. Gairdner wrote :

I thank God that I retire from this work, and especially from the theological work, with a heart at rest. Time was, prior to Birmingham, when I thought Thornton and myself were almost the only ones who had it at heart enough to lead it (don't imagine that I was under any delusion as to the poorness of that leadership as far as I was concerned). And our chief prayer before Birmingham was for leaders. Now I recognize, and recognize with unmixed joy, that I

[1] Afterwards Bishop of Chichester.

can go leaving behind me leaders not only more capable but who have the cause far more at heart than ever I had. I can't tell you how grateful I am for this, or how I admire the goodness and love of God in this matter.

Thornton's mind worked on the incident of the Nicene Creed and the unwillingness of some to join in its recitation, and he wrote a very characteristic letter.

CROYDON,
August 23rd 1898.

MY DEAR LENWOOD,

. . . In my former letter on the relation of our theological colleges to the Student Christian Movement [1] in Britain, I pointed out that all affiliated Unions of the B.C.C.U. are committed upon affiliation to accept as a *minimum* the basis of "a belief in Jesus Christ as God the Son and only Saviour of the World." I suggested, however, that for theological students this basis did not express the extent of their common belief, and should not, therefore, necessarily be the only basis for them in years to come.

I pointed out what I felt to be the lesson of our apparent failure to obtain absolute unanimity on a fuller form of confession of faith on the last day of the conference : that it did not necessarily show that the Nicene Creed was not undoubtedly the heritage of all Christian theological students, but only that at the present some students were not convinced of all the truth that it embodies in the form of words ; [2] in fact, that it betrayed a weakness, which had best be remedied by careful education showing that every member of the Christian Church can claim those formulated words as their Christian heritage.

At the same time I pointed out that the Theological section of the B.C.C.U. had for three years been committed to " the development of the spirit of true unity " as one of the three phases of its work ; that the week of prayer had led on to the desire for conference, and conference to a further desire for federation and co-operation ; so that its

[1] Observe that although " British College Christian Union " was the title of the movement, the name it was to be given later is used by Thornton.

[2] I would add : " and still more of the advisability of accepting it as a profession of faith."—D.M.T.

next work lay along the lines of defining the extent to which that federation and co-operation should go.

That which had been the first desire of my heart—namely, the unifying of the name of the branch associations wherever advisable and possible,—is on its way to fulfilment, with all the attendant advantages that it will bring. That which had been the second,—namely, the promotion of local (shall I say preparatory?) conferences—is laid down as part of the future policy of the Committee. And now a third suggestion, which has in it the nature of a grounded conviction, is put before you as I leave the work—viz., the determination and discernment of the extent of the common faith that God has given us all in Jesus Christ.

It will not be the work of a day or a year, I know, to break down barriers of self-isolation and let the flow of many pent-up revelations be known to brother men. Free, mutual understanding on all points of difference, accompanied by genuine sifting of traditional beliefs within the crucible of an open mind may not be welcome everywhere. But it must come in this enquiring age. And no one who has let the spirit of the Watchword dominate his thought and life can fail to see whereto this movement tends. God will not let a band of men and women have a great ideal without accompanying it in every case with nearer visions of the truth in Christ. We cannot go and teach to men the opposites of thought. We must approximate together in the message that we give.

Now looking at the Student Movement broadly, and considering each national movement in particular, there is little doubt that Britain has a larger point of contact and influence with the world than any other nation. And so we are bound to lead in matters of this sort. However difficult the task of federation here it must be done. And we must be devising means by which the antitypes of men may meet. The recent conference has led the way. To my mind it has clearly shown the growing need for formulating unity. Meanwhile let us continue to promote a common fellowship, and thus remove the obstacles to mutual sympathy and understanding in the Lord.

And just as circumstances led us tremblingly to adopt the present basis of our Union, let us not be fearful if we find it necessary among theological students to go further. Hitherto they have not collectively contributed anything to the message of the movement. But now the time has come. In future they will be represented far more fully on the councils of the Union. It is theirs to lead the way as preacher-prophets to the rest.

I. I propose therefore that someone, who is capable of doing so, shall during the coming year make a point of *conferring with Principals* of the leading theological colleges of each leading denomination. That the situation be placed before them by him carefully ; with a view to ascertaining :

(*a*) their attitude towards Creeds [1] as the heritage of the Church ;

(*b*) their opinion as to whether a fuller Creed would be a greater rallying ground and strength to the Theological section of the B.C.C.U. ;

(*c*) if so, what Creed would be the best to take as the common expression of our faith (whether new or old).

I imagine, however, that all would gravitate towards a form, if any, which is historical, and of universal acceptance. It would be time enough to devise means, whereby to put this question before theological students generally, after our hands were strengthened by knowing the minds of our leaders on this point.

II. With a view to definiteness, I submit that sooner or later *a statement be drawn up by the Theological Committee*, something in the form of the S.V.M.U. memorial ; that the form it should take be guided largely by the advice of Principals and other candid friends to whom it is submitted ; that its contents contain what is felt to be the *message of theological students to the Church of Christ in Britain* ; that its object be to demonstrate the need for federation among Christian bodies as illustrated by the case of theological colleges.

Yours very sincerely,

D. M. THORNTON.

It was decided that the constitutional question which had been in mind for some time must be taken in hand. The theological colleges were affiliated to a body whose concern was to establish Christian Unions in the universities and colleges and the theological committee was

[1] Creed is used here in its broadest sense.—D.M.T.

K

a sub-committee of its Executive. The S.V.M.U. was a separate organization working in the same field as the B.C.C.U. and sharing the same office and general secretary but had no constitutional link with it. Such link seemed desirable, and the Theological Colleges must be offered a place of their own in the Movement.

The ball was started by a memorandum in which I stated the case for a single movement with departments. This was revised by Gairdner, who made no substantial alterations, and then by Thornton, who made some suggestions for elaborating the suggested Constitution I had appended to my document. The only change of interest to a later generation is that all through the document, where I had written " women students " he erased " women " and substituted " lady " !

The proposal to bring the S.V.M.U. into organic relations with the B.C.C.U. had from the first brought G. T. Manley into the field. He thought it would hamper the effectiveness of the S.V.M.U. and wanted it to remain an entirely separate organization. It was a mighty battle between Manley and Thornton, both men immensely tenacious of their point of view ! While the question was under discussion Gairdner, who was travelling for the B.C.C.U., wrote to me as travelling for the S.V.M.U. about some college visitation, warning me that I should have to do work for both organizations, and remembering how Manley wanted to keep separate work interrelated at every point, he burst out on the topic. The letter is typical of Gairdner's style :

> 93, Aldersgate Street,
> London, E.C.,
> *Nov.* 1897.

Dear Old Chap,
There is loads for you to do in London so gird up your loins.

I hope to have entrance into two important training colleges, perhaps more. You may have to do in some B.C.C.U. work, in some S.V.M.U. (Oh, Manley, learned above men [1] and acquainted with the realms of pure mathematics, don't you know that according to Aristotle πολιτική *must* be less αὐριβής than μαθηματική ?   Look then at the practical working of these two Unions and allow that they must work together, that they are working together and that they must also establish a formal co-operation.   Facts are stronger than fictions as well as stranger ; and " fictions " I pronounce thy theories with regard to the independence of the S.V. and B.C.C.U. to be.   Wherefore be good at the December Executive, when this matter must be brought up.)

To return : [here followed suggestion about certain colleges to be visited] I am simply teeming with ideas for the better organization of certain departments of our work. I am quite sure the time for this has arrived.

Yours affectionately,

W. H. T. G.

Manley had the courage of his convictions and resigned when the two committees decided to make a united movement.   The Constitution I had drafted was adopted without substantial change, and with some subsequent modifications remains the Constitution of the Movement to this day.

Three departments were created—the Theological College Department, the S.V.M.U., and the General College Department, each having its own executive committee, each having certain rights guarded for it by the Constitution, each having its own budget and each appointing members to a General Committee to which was entrusted the co-ordination of the work of the departments, the organization of summer conferences, the administration of the office, and the oversight of the whole movement—the whole organization to work under the title British College Christian Union.   In some ways it was a clumsy arrangement, especially as regards finance, but a great advance upon the previous position.   Subsequent changes have improved the Constitution and made it more efficient for its purpose.

---

[1] He had been Senior Wrangler at Cambridge.

The scope of the magazine, under the guidance of Miss Lilian Stevenson who was Editor from 1896-1900, was widened to include the work of the whole Movement in its scope, it was enlarged and its title changed to *The Student Movement*.   The new Constitution was adopted at the business meeting of both unions at the Summer Conference, 1898.

CHAPTER IX

THE APPROACH TO THE CHURCH OF ENGLAND

THE failure of the Movement to interest the Church of England theological colleges in the Birmingham Conference greatly stirred Douglas Thornton. His deep love for both the Church and the Movement drove him to action, and he was ably seconded by Gairdner. It is true that some of the leaders of the Church of England and also its chief missionary societies had shown much sympathy with the Movement. Thornton had spoken with success upon it to the Church Congress at Shrewsbury in 1896, his address, said Mr Eugene Stock, "moved all hearts." The Archbishop of Canterbury (Dr Benson) had referred to the S.V.M.U. in his last sermon, which he preached in Armagh Cathedral on 27th September 1896, saying :

> As I watch with anxiety what I can take in of the field, I cannot but think that the cold shade of recent negative years is passing away from over many minds. It cannot be for nothing that some 2000 men, who in very many seats of education claim the name of students, have bound themselves together to recognize, and, as God shall give openings, to act on a fact that they find impossible for themselves to ignore, the fact that each of them has, at least, some duty, whatever it may be, on the side of Christianization of God's earth. . . .

The Lambeth Conference had made a friendly reference to the Movement and the new Archbishop of Canterbury (Dr Temple) was a warm friend, but this was only a beginning. The Church knew little of the Movement, and the most important group to reach, the theological colleges—staff and students—were in the main ignorant of the Movement and distrustful and aloof.

On the other hand, the leaders of the Movement had always had a kind of instinct for inclusiveness. The world mission of Christianity was a vast task. It needed the united effort of all who named the name of Christ as Saviour and Lord. And as they saw that important bodies were standing aloof and considered how to win them, they were forced to reflect seriously on the whole question of the relationship of the Christian bodies to one another. The Church of England was seriously divided ; even the two great missionary societies were not in full sympathy with one another ; and neither Church party—Evangelicals nor High Churchmen—had any dealings with the Nonconformist Churches as such. Those Evangelicals who were in close touch with Non-conformists had very little feeling for the Church of England, with some rather rare exceptions.

What was the small and uninfluential Student Movement to do in the face of this situation ? Thornton, Gairdner, S. F. Hawkes and I spent much time in talking over the situation, and Hawkes who was still at Oxford, stressed the fact that many men who expected to take Holy Orders hesitated to join the Movement lest it be regarded as disloyal to the Church for them to do so.

We decided that we must put the whole position to some Churchman of weight and ask him if we could hope to win all parties in the Church of England. Dr Creighton, the Bishop of London, was selected as one of the outstanding personalities in the Church and he was asked if he would see Gairdner and Thornton. He heard them fully and sympathetically and as a result of the interview the following letters, intended for such use as the Movement wished to make of them, were exchanged :

93, Aldersgate Street,
London, E.C.
November 30th, 1898.

My Lord Bishop,

In view of the importance of the work in which the Student Christian Movement is engaged and more particularly that branch of it which affects Theological Colleges, it would be a source of strength to us to know that we have Your Lordship's sympathy and approval of the principles upon which the Student Movement in this and other lands undoubtedly rests. The Basis on which we affiliate any College Christian Association (in the case of a Theological College, an association that is co-extensive with the college) is as follows : " A Belief in Jesus Christ as God the Son and only Saviour of the world." And the main specific objects for which we thus unite men in different Theological Colleges are :

1. Intercession for each other and students in all lands.
2. The study of missions while at college, with a view to the adoption of the Watchword, " The Evangelization of the world in this generation," as an ideal and an aim.
3. The promotion of the spirit of true unity by the deepening of the spiritual life.

Such is our Basis and such our objects. In Your Lordship's opinion, does this Basis constitute a definite enough bond between those associations which come together for the above specific objects ?

Do you think it embodies the central ideas of Christianity adequately enough for us conscientiously to ask those to federate upon it whom we know to hold much fuller conceptions of what should be accepted as Catholic faith and practice ?

Do you feel that such could conscientiously associate themselves with colleges of any denomination without compromising the highest views of Churchmanship ?

The desire of this world-wide Movement is to create among Christian students of all shades of thought (subject to assent to the Basis) an atmosphere of mutual knowledge and one where the influence of nationality upon Christian ideals can be widely studied. May we venture to ask you to express your opinion as to whether our work makes for consolidation rather than disintegration ; and whether we seem to be promoting an expression of existing unity in the Church of Christ which when realized must promote that unity of the Church whatever it be that exists in the mind and will of God ?

I am,

Your Lordship's obedient servant,

W. H. T. GAIRDNER.

To the RIGHT HON. AND RIGHT REV.
THE BISHOP OF LONDON.

Fulham Palace, S.W.
December 2, 1898.

My dear Mr Gairdner,

The practical point on which you ask my opinion is this : Do I think that members of Theological Colleges in connexion with the Church of England would in any way compromise their position as thorough and loyal members of that Communion by joining the British College Christian Union, which aims at uniting students of all denominations for the purpose of promoting missionary zeal ? I do not think so. I regard the basis of a " belief in Jesus Christ as God the Son and only Saviour of the world " as one which is independent of the question of ecclesiastical organization. When practical work is to be done we must recognize that it must be done by each of us according to the principles of the ecclesiastical organization to which we belong. But the object of your Union is to prepare the way for practical work, by prayer, by study, by spiritual endeavour. These are objects and methods which are common to all Christians. They can be pursued in different ways. But all may unite in resolving to pursue them. Such union for the general purpose of promoting missionary work does not involve any surrender of individual convictions about the best form in which the Christian Truth can be expressed. It is in the Mission field especially that forms of organization are subjected to the most searching test. No one religious body can undertake all the work that is to be done. Combination among students might help to remove misunderstandings, which are too often engendered by the ignorance which comes from exclusiveness.

Your endeavour has my warm sympathy.

I am,

Yours truly,

M. LONDON :

Bishop Creighton in the interview had urged that the Student Movement should keep clear of any matter which was a subject of ecclesiastical controversy. This led to an examination of policy and to the conclusion that there was only one action of the Movement which was likely to cause difficulties in the future, and that was the Communion Service which had been held in an Anglican Church at each summer conference, and was attended by almost all the students present.

While the summer conference was at Keswick the student leaders never thought about this question. They followed the example of the Keswick Convention, where members of all denominations were in the habit of attending the Communion Services at St John's Parish Church. When the conference moved to Curbar in 1897 the Vicar, who was a Low Churchman, invited all the students on Sunday to Holy Communion in his Church, and most members of the conference communicated. The following year the conference moved to Ripon and the Bishop of Ripon, on his own initiative, invited the conference to the Cathedral, saying that he would like to preach to it, and preach he did. Dr Boyd Carpenter was an eloquent preacher and few who heard it, I imagine, will ever forget his wonderful sermon from the text, " He that followeth Me shall not walk in darkness but shall have the light of life." The sermon was followed by a Celebration of Holy Communion to which the whole conference was invited to remain.

The majority of members of the Committee were very reluctant to give up these united Communion Services, but it was nevertheless decided unanimously at Christmas 1898 that we must do so if we were not to risk being plunged into ecclesiastical controversy, as we sought to draw in the different elements in the Church of England.

The following summer we decided to go to Aberystwyth for our summer conference, and a request came from the students there that as the conference was moving to a centre where the largest body of Christians was the Calvinistic Methodists, a united Communion service for the whole conference should be held in the chief Calvinistic Methodist Church in the town. All realized that to do this would have caused far greater difficulties with Anglican theological students than did the acceptance of the Bishop of Ripon's invitation the previous year, and we were thankful that we had determined our policy before the invitation came.

The discussion of these matters caused the Movement to think out its position. It had begun in close contact with the Keswick Convention : that convention was on an undenominational basis, that is to say, it did not recognize or provide for denominational loyalties, on the contrary, it instructed speakers from its platform to deal only with topics on which they knew there was agreement between them and the other speakers. The more this method of co-operation was discussed the clearer the student leaders became that it could not be their basis of co-operation : men ought not to be asked to suppress their convictions simply because others disagreed with them. We could not be undenominational ; we must be inter-denominational. We were united by tremendous verities. We acknowledged the same Lord and Master, we had an immense amount in common ; if there were differences amongst us on important matters we must respect one another's convictions, we must try to understand one another and learn from one another. Thus a new basis for co-operation not hitherto tried had been devised which was to have far-reaching results for the Christian Church at home and abroad.

For some time Thornton had had his eye upon the Junior Clergy Missionary Association of the S.P.G. He had been impressed with the keenness and ability of a group of sixty clergy he had addressed just before Christmas 1897. And early in the New Year he arranged with their president, the Rev. M. R. Neligan, to meet a few of their leaders at luncheon at St Stephen's Vicarage, Paddington, to talk over the work of the

Student Movement with them. Finding that the luncheon could not be arranged before he left for America to attend the Cleveland Conference of the Student Volunteer Movement, he left me to attend it as the representative of the Student Movement. I went in fear and trembling; my theological course was still ahead of me and I knew very little of ecclesiastical matters. I had only just passed my twenty-second birthday and remember feeling very young and inexperienced.

The men whom I met were all a good deal older than I was, but they were very friendly and we had in common our interest in foreign missions. My instructions were to try and get the Junior Clergy Missionary Association to introduce the Movement to the theological colleges, but these men felt that before they could do anything they must know more about the Movement. The result of our luncheon party was a suggestion we agreed to put to our respective organizations—that we should each appoint seven representatives to a round-table conference to discuss the Movement, its basis, objects and methods of work.

The men chosen by the Junior Clergy Missionary Association were: the Rev. M. R. Neligan, Vicar of St Stephen's, Paddington, the Rev. J. O. F. Murray, Dean of Emmanuel College, Cambridge, the Rev. C. F. Andrews, Fellow of Pembroke College, Cambridge, the Rev. St Clair Donaldson, head of the Eton Mission, Hackney Wick, the Rev. E. J. Palmer, Fellow and Chaplain of Balliol College, Oxford, the Rev. A. B. Mynors, Rector of Langley-Burrell, and the Rev. L. B. Radford, Rector of Forncett-St Peter.

The Student Movement representatives were: Frank Lenwood, Corpus Christi and Mansfield Colleges, Oxford, Henry T. Hodgkin, King's College, Cambridge and St Thomas's Hospital, London, S. F. Hawkes, Wadham College, Oxford, H. C. Duncan, Edinburgh University, C. A. Werner, King's College, Cambridge, G. H. Moule, Clare College, Cambridge and Tissington Tatlow, Trinity College, Dublin. Three were members of committee and four secretaries; four were Anglicans with one Congregationalist, one Presbyterian and one member of the Society of Friends.

It was suggested that we should ask the Bishop of Stepney (Dr Winnington Ingram) to act as our chairman. This he consented to do and the earlier meetings were held in his house at Amen Court, E.C., and later, when he became Bishop of London, the meetings were held at Fulham Palace. He was a delightful friendly chairman and made us all feel at home.

We were immensely cheered to find that the Junior Clergy Missionary Association had taken us seriously and appointed a first-class group to meet us. To realize how first class the group was it is only necessary to recall the positions they subsequently occupied. Mr Neligan became Bishop of Auckland, New Zealand, Mr Donaldson became Archbishop of Brisbane and is now Bishop of Salisbury, Mr Palmer became Bishop of Bombay and is now assistant Bishop in the Gloucester Diocese, Mr Radford is Bishop of Goulburn, New South Wales, Mr Murray was afterwards Master of Selwyn College, Cambridge, Mr Mynors became known to the whole Church as the organizer of the Pan-Anglican Congress, 1908, and Mr C. F. Andrews is known all over the world as the Englishman who is more trusted than any other by the people of India.

The first round-table conference, in the autumn of 1899, was of a very friendly character and devoted chiefly to getting to know one another. We described the Movement, its ideals and what it wanted to achieve in relation to theological colleges, but chiefly we learned to understand one another and the differences in point of view represented in the conference. Mr Neligan, reporting to a conference of delegates of the Junior Clergy Missionary Association, said :

> None of us will ever forget that conference. . . . Nothing but good can come of such gatherings. We get to see each other's point of view, to understand them, to appreciate them, to feel a warmth of love for men differing from us on

many points, and in consequence to grow tolerant, to get a practical basis for our prayers for unity, and to know for a fact that the love of God is broader than the measure of man's mind. . . . Of the good feeling shown at our meeting, it would be impossible to speak too fully. I do think we tried, and were enabled by the Blessed Spirit, to keep the Apostle's injunction, " Let not every man look on his own, but on the things of another."

As a Student Movement group we were so accustomed to meet men of different denominations that we did not realize at first how novel the experience was for several of the men we were meeting, but this dawned upon us as we heard them questioning Lenwood and Hodgkin. The immediate result of the conference was to secure a representative of it to the International Student Missionary Conference, London, January 1900.

A second conference was held in April 1900 when we pressed for help in introducing missionary study into Church of England theological colleges, but nothing practical came of the conference from our point of view.

We met again in September, and as G. H. Moule had sailed as a C.M.S. missionary to Japan, Tom Jays, St Thomas's Hospital, took his place. Otherwise there was no change in the composition of the conference. On this occasion the question of Baptism was discussed, our friends asking why the S.M.V.U. did not make Baptism the basis of membership for the S.V.M.U. Mr Palmer's summary of the Student Movement reply is as follows :

1. Because through lack of teaching on Baptism, many of their members would be unable to regard the appropriation of the benefits of that sacrament as a natural way of expressing their sense of union with Christ.

2. Because the Basis was, unhappily, but necessarily, a safeguard ; and the fact of Baptism would not be the kind of safeguard which they required.

3. Not a point of their Basis. Because, some of the men who had done most for the Union could not accept a Basis of which Baptism was an essential part ; in fact, they could not so frame their Basis as to exclude members of the Society of Friends.

This is a specimen of the kind of subject which was discussed. Later we discussed the Watchword of the S.V.M.U. and the Church and the interdenominational position. The result of these conferences was that the Student Movement and the J.C.M.A. interchanged delegates at their conferences for two or three years and friendship was established with a group of men, a number of whom rendered great service to the Student Movement in after years. It became clear, however, that the group was not one which could do very much about getting access to theological colleges, which was what we were keen about, so the conferences came to an end.

This history of the Movement is only an outline and cannot hope to tell of all the service which has been rendered to it by men who are named and many more who are unnamed in these pages, but Mr Neligan, Mr Donaldson and Mr Radford helped the Student Christian Movement in New Zealand and Australia, Mr Palmer and Mr Andrews in England and India, and Mr Murray in Cambridge, at summer conferences and in other ways. They are men to whom the Student Movement owes a debt of gratitude.

These conferences proved of great value as they forced the leaders of the Student Movement still further along the line of thinking out its interdenominational position ; they also gave it a number of valuable and understanding friends. It is curious to reflect that the man who had most difficulties about sharing in an interdenominational body should have been Mr C. F. Andrews. He said at the last conference that he was sure the Movement was most devoted in its work, but that his principles as a Churchman prevented his sharing in it. It was after service in India that he widened his point of view and became a warm friend.

Although there were sections of the Church of England which had hesitations about the Student Movement, representative men in the Church were always ready to listen and to devote time and trouble to understanding the Movement.   If they took time to consider their position, and also to confer with one another behind the scenes, when they gave their support it was given with understanding and conviction, which meant that it was support worth having.

It is necessary to an understanding of the discussions centring round the interdenominational position of the Student Movement to recall something of the setting in which the Movement had to do its work.   While the relationships of the Nonconformist Churches in England to one another were close and friendly, there was almost no contact between the Church of England and the Free Churches.   The Free Church Council was the body in the public eye as representing the Free Churches. The average Church of England member knew extremely little about the Free Churches except the doings of the Free Church Council, which was a highly political body.   There was bitter controversy between the Church and Nonconformity on the subject of religious education in the elementary schools of the country.   The Education Bill of 1902 is famous for the storm of religious controversy it raised.   The average clergyman was prone to think that the Nonconformist Churches were largely Unitarian, but he had, as a rule, little or no first-hand knowledge of them.   The Nonconformist regarded the Church of England as dry and formal, using written prayers from a love of formalism and, perhaps, from a lack of true spirituality. The leaders did not know one another.   I remember the Archbishop of Canterbury asking me whether I had ever met the Rev. John Clifford, D.D., one of the leading Free Churchmen of the day, and one who crossed swords with Churchmen in *The Times* on the subject of religious education in the schools.   Learning I knew him, the Archbishop was anxious to know what sort of man he was.   He had read his letters in *The Times* but had never met or even seen him.   This sort of thing became incredible in later years, and the same Archbishop, before he died, knew personally and even intimately many of the leading men in the Free Churches.

There was no practical move towards corporate unity at the beginning of the century, and a zealous Church of England clergyman would feel he ought to take any opportunity he could find of bringing Nonconformists to Confirmation, while on the other hand it would not occur to him to do anything to promote conference between Churchmen and Nonconformists with a view to corporate bodies discussing with one another their mutual relationship to the question of reunion. The result of this was that it came as a later idea to the average Student Movement member that reunion would come not by a stream of proselytes trickling from one religious body into another, but by the denominations discussing with one another the problem of reunion and how to achieve it. Young Churchmen and Nonconformists never met one another at this time apart from the Student Movement. They knew nothing of each other's traditions, and the more theologically-minded among them started almost any discussion on religious questions with the assumption that the more they talked, the deeper would their differences be found to be. The reverse was in fact our experience in relation to the majority of the questions discussed, and gradually men came to realize how deep were their agreements in relation to the great Christian doctrines, the Bible and even the Church, although here there were important differences in relation to the nature of the Church, its ministry and sacraments.

When it became clear that our conferences with the Junior Clergy Missionary Association were not helping us in bringing the Church of England theological colleges into the Movement, we debated the matter in September 1902 and " Mr Tatlow said he had come to the conclusion that the only way we could reach the Church of England colleges was through the Principals, and that without them it would be impossible to get any of these colleges to affiliate." [1] This would seem to those who know these colleges, an obvious conclusion, but the Executive did not know these colleges and experience in the Nonconformist colleges led away from such a conclusion as in their case the students were all-important and to win them in any college was to secure it for the Movement.

As to the Church of England colleges we now knew where we stood. The difficulty of winning the theologicals was twofold : the men who were in charge of the majority of these colleges represented an element in the Church which the Student Movement had hardly touched, and Church of England theological students did not want to meet Nonconformist theological students. In December 1902 we find the Theological Committee discussing vigorously what should be the basis of appeal to Church of England theological students to come into the Movement. Frank Lenwood thought that the Theological College Department " must cling to the idea even if it offended some that the Department was a federation of theological colleges," while E. J. Cox of St Aidan's College thought this a bad line of approach to Church of England theological students ; the Department should be given up and a standing committee of the General College Department for dealing with theological colleges substituted. He urged that what made the difficulty was that theological students " conceived our aim to be to bring theological students in touch with other theological students." They did not wish to meet Nonconformist theological students, and if this thing which they did not like was got out of the way, they would be ready to come in touch with the Movement as a whole. The one hope was to interest them in the Movement and keep it dark that they were going to meet theological students of other denominations. Cox carried his point at the time, and the Committee decided " to cease in any way to press a union of theological colleges as theological colleges."

[1] Theological College Department Minutes, September 1902.

L

The next year the question of the Anglican colleges continued to receive attention. E. J. Cox had given place to E. S. Woods [1] of Ridley Hall on the committee, and he, W. F. Lofthouse [2] and J. H. Oldham took the lead in re-discussing the question whether the aim of the committee was to form a union of theological colleges or a union of theological students. This led on to a restatement of the aims of the Theological College Department as follows :

(1) In view of the greatness and urgency of the demands made upon the Church by the problem of world evangelization and by the necessity of dealing with social problems at home, to unite theological students of Great Britain and Ireland in a common devotion to these tasks.

(2) To keep these claims before them by promoting missionary and social study, and by other means.

(3) To enable theological colleges to take their share in the world-wide Student Movement, receiving its inspiration and making their own special contribution to it.

(4) To help and further through interchange of experience all practical Christian activities carried on by the students of such colleges.

(5) To associate itself with the general policy of the Student Movement, in emphasizing the supreme importance of Bible Study as the foundation of all social and missionary endeavour.[3]

While this study of the Church of England colleges was proceeding, the Department had been active in other directions. The Department had no travelling secretary, but after the Birmingham Conference depended upon a gathering each Easter composed of two men from every affiliated college for the promotion of its policy. This gathering was continued until 1903, in which year delegates from twenty-eight colleges in England and Wales met at Handsworth College. It was the last of this annual series of Theological Student Conferences.

[1] Afterwards Bishop of Croydon.
[2] Afterwards the Rev. Principal Lofthouse, D.D.
[3] Theological College Department Minutes, September 1904.

In the case of the affiliated colleges the Movement had made its influence felt by developing systematic missionary study, student missionary campaigns and corporate devotional activities. It had been helped in visitation by Executive members, the travelling secretaries of the S.V.M.U. and occasionally by those of the B.C.C.U.

In Scotland the situation differed from that in England. The Movement found the Scottish theologicals a hard nut to crack. Theological students, even of the same Church, had little contact with one another and there were historic reasons, as there were in England, although of a different kind, why colleges of different denominations did not look with wholly friendly eyes upon one another.

Then the men who had been strong supporters of the Christian Unions at the universities were not afterwards to be found in the theological colleges, the reason being that as a rule men taking a university degree in preparation for theology were related closely to Church life before they went to the university and while there devoted all their spare energies to it. It was in Scotland that the Movement found most acute the difficulty of persuading Christian men whose influence was sorely needed in the university to disentangle themselves sufficiently from Church work to find time to share in what the Christian Union was trying to do for the spiritual life of their fellow-students.

It is easy to see, therefore, that when a travelling secretary visited the Presbyterian theological colleges in Scotland he did not find a very sympathetic attitude towards the Movement since his audience consisted of graduates most of whom had not felt moved while at the university to join the non-theological section of the Movement—the Christian Union—in the theological part of which they were now asked to show an interest. The tide only began to turn when an increasing number of prospective theological students were brought into the Christian Unions at the universities.

The first Scottish committee in connection with

theological students was formed as a result of a conference held in Edinburgh in 1902, when representatives from most of the Scottish theological halls and from three Irish colleges were present. The object of the committee was to bring the theological halls into closer contact with one another and with the Student Movement and to be the medium for interchange of experience in home mission work and in pleading for foreign missions. This committee did not exert much influence for the next three years. It existed.

The Theological College Department Executive, still studying its problem, began to be uneasy about its Easter Conference for theological students. Scotland did not support it ; Church of England theological students from three or four Evangelical colleges only attended, though many more came to the summer conference, and some of the leaders of the Movement said that "the whole Theological College Department was really a withdrawal from the heart of the Student Movement " and that this was accentuated by not bringing theological students other than those studying theology in the universities to the summer conference. The result of discussion was that the theologicals returned to the summer conference at Matlock 1904, and have shared in the summer conferences ever since. Sectional meetings for theological students became a permanent feature at these conferences.

This return to the summer conference at once led to a fuller sharing by the department in the life of the whole Movement. The first thing the Executive did that autumn was to ask the General Committee that the name " British College Christian Union " be abandoned, and that the organization be renamed " The Student Christian Movement." The General Committee refused to change the name. This was, I think, largely for practical reasons. It was easy for the theologicals to press the change ; they did not have to face practical questions ; but the General Committee had a good deal of literature, stationery and the like printed

with the name " British College Christian Union."
The theologicals, however, unanimously moved again
at their meeting in December 1904, that they were of
opinion that the name of the Union should be changed
to " The Student Christian Movement of Great Britain
and Ireland." They came back to the discussion of the
name in April 1905, urging that the chief reasons in
favour of a change were : that the name B.C.C.U. was a
hindrance in the work of the Theological College
Department, it was inadequate to suggest either the
significance of the Movement or the range of its activities, and it " had failed to take hold of the public."
They decided again to press the change upon the General
Committee which at last moved, and by a majority of
90 per cent. the change in name was made at the business
meeting at the summer conference.

In the autumn the Department acquired a travelling
secretary, Malcolm Spencer, Corpus Christi and Mansfield Colleges, Oxford, being appointed in September
1905, no one having occupied this position since
F. W. S. O'Neill's year of office in 1896-97. Mr Spencer
combined the work with the charge of a congregation
at Darwen, the Committee doubting whether there
would be sufficient work to demand Mr Spencer's
whole time !

The instructions which were given to Malcolm
Spencer, as Travelling Secretary, were very carefully
thought out by the Committee, the following being a
summary.

1. To obtain as full reports as possible about the Theological colleges.
2. To take as a large part of his message the ideas embodied in the book *Preparation for the Christian Ministry.*
3. To make a careful investigation of missionary study,
whether there is a demand for fresh Study Outlines, and
along what lines study should be developed.
4. To report on Bible Study in the colleges.
5. To investigate the possibility of utilizing the preaching
undertaken by theological students along Student Missionary Campaign lines.

6. To investigate the extent to which social work is being done by theological students.

7. To consider the question as to how the Student Missionary Campaign could be put on a permanent basis.

8. To keep the question of students joining the S.V.M.U. to the front.

9. To make known the literature of the Movement, especially *The Student Movement*.

10. To note the openings in the colleges for further visitation.

It seems enough for one man, without the care of a congregation, and it was.

Malcolm Spencer's appointment was a successful one. He was patient, persistent, conciliatory and full of ideas : he neglected no item in the programme outlined for him.   As regards his programme, it should be noted that the book referred to, *Preparation for the Christian Ministry in View of Present-day Conditions*, was a publication of the Movement, consisting of a series of essays, dealing with subjects the Executive thought of importance to theological students, by men in whom they had confidence.   Much care was given to the planning of the book ; various aspects of the spiritual and intellectual training of the minister and his work at home and abroad were dealt with by the Very Rev. J. H. Bernard and the Revs. D. S. Cairns, H. Gresford Jones, Robert E. Speer, A. E. Garvie, W. P. Paterson, H. S. Woollcombe, W. H. Findlay, W. D. Mackenzie and J. H. Oldham. The book was well received by the religious Press, and Dr Robertson Nicol, in a front-page article in the *British Weekly*, said that it had changed his whole impression of the Movement and shown him its importance.   This was, perhaps, the most important public notice that the Theological Department had hitherto received and it pleased the Executive and proved a help to its work.

Malcolm Spencer visited forty theological colleges in his first year, and the steady advance of the work of the Department under his care renewed the determination of the Executive to advance the relations of the Movement and the Church of England. The General and Theological Committees of the Movement, acting jointly, appointed an Anglican sub-committee to this end and we met on June 5th, 1906, when there were present: S. F. Hawkes (in the chair), and the Revs. J. Battersby Harford, T. Woods, E. S. Woods,[1] W. G. Hardie,[2] J. Russell Darbyshire,[3] C. F. G. Masterman,[4] F. A. Evelyn, A. W. Davies and T. Tatlow.

The committee was unanimous in thinking that not enough had been done in the past to make members of the Church of England at home at the summer conferences. It suggested that liturgical prayer should find some place on the programme; that a daily celebration at 7.45 a.m. should be arranged; and that evensong should be said daily in the meeting tent at 3.30 p.m. The Committee also arranged an afternoon meeting, asking one of their number, Canon Masterman, to give an address on " What can an English Churchman do to help the Student Christian Movement? "—with a discussion to follow.

An immediate outcome of this meeting was a movement, emanating from Oxford, which resulted in the following letter being addressed to the General Secretary. It was printed and circulated widely with the summer conference literature :

To the GENERAL SECRETARY,
*Student Christian Movement of
Great Britain and Ireland.*

July 1906.

Dear Mr Tatlow,
We think that members of the Church of England ought to give careful consideration to the work of the Student Christian Movement, and the World's Student Christian Federation, to which it is affiliated. We hear that you propose to make special arrangements at the Summer Conference this year for Church of England Students, and we

[1] Afterwards Bishop of Croydon.
[2] Afterwards Bishop of Jamaica.
[3] Afterwards Bishop of Glasgow.
[4] Afterwards Bishop of Plymouth.

think that there could be no better way in which such students could make themselves acquainted with what the Movement is doing than by coming to the Conference. This would not commit them in any way till they have had an opportunity of judging whether it is a Movement with which they ought to identify themselves. We are glad to know that you would welcome and provide for men of strong Church convictions, and would give them the fullest opportunity of talking over any difficulties that they may feel with regard to the aims and methods of the Movement.

Yours faithfully,

CHARLES BIGG,
Canon of Christ Church, Oxford.

H. MONTAGU BUTLER,
Master of Trinity College, Cambridge.

STUART A. DONALDSON,
Master of Magdalene College, Cambridge.

J. O. F. MURRAY,
Warden of S. Augustine's College, Canterbury.

W. SANDAY,
Lady Margaret Professor of Divinity, Oxford.

H. S. WOOLLCOMBE,
Head of the Oxford House.

Appended to the letter was a notice of the arrangements as suggested above for Anglicans.

When the summer conference assembled there was a more representative Anglican group than ever before and the meeting for Anglicans was a decided success. Canon Masterman spoke as " a strong Churchman— that is, a Churchman who is definitely and strongly convinced that the sacramental system of our Church provides the best framework for the protection and development of Christian character, and who is convinced that this is so because it is the divinely appointed system." He asked whether such could throw themselves whole-heartedly into the Movement, and answered yes, we all have the same aim, " the development in ourselves and the extension throughout the world of the highest type of Christian character." The difference between us is one of method.

We must respect one another's methods of worship

and ways of drawing near to Christ and encourage one another in loyalty to our own communion. " We cannot organize reunion on a basis of disloyalty."

Canon Masterman thought that strong Churchmen could help to maintain the interdenominational character of the Movement because, " from our very nature, we constitute a particularly indigestible element in any undenominational organization." He asked for a cordial and encouraging welcome. " It is our duty to respond with an equally cordial and ungrudging enthusiasm." He thought Bible circles could surely be joined, that with other Christians Churchmen might seek " the guidance of the Spirit in the reading of the Bible without any surrender of our convictions."

The World's Student Christian Federation was a great union of Christian students outside which Churchmen could not stand without injury to themselves. The Movement could do much for them in giving a wider outlook and in teaching them " in the intercourse of camp life that loyalty to our Lord Jesus Christ and the communion of the Holy Spirit are manifestly present in the lives of men, with whom, as English Churchmen, we do not agree on important questions." [1] The conference had been a challenge to a new enthusiasm to live for the extension of Christ's Kingdom.

Canon Masterman's address made an excellent impression. There was much informal talk between Churchmen of all schools at the conference and a consensus of opinion that we must continue to work for the inclusion of the theological colleges, and the conviction that they would come in as the members of staff came to understand the Movement. Apart from the theologicals, the Dean of Westminster (Dr Armitage Robinson) had taken the conference by storm with an address on the maintenance of the spiritual life which was long quoted as one of the finest delivered at a student conference, and Canon Kempthorne had given a series of Bible readings. A

[1] Canon Masterman's address is given in *The Student Movement*, vol. ix., pp. 44-45.

new chapter had been opened in the relationship between the Movement and the Church of England.

At the new year I was invited to attend the Annual Conference of Schoolmasters and Lecturers and Tutors in Oxford and Cambridge—the gathering known as "Dons and Beaks." Here I spoke about the Student Movement and made friends with William Temple,[1] whom I met for the first time. My report to the Student Movement Committee says :

> After lunch I was introduced to Mr Temple of Balliol, son of the late Archbishop of Canterbury. We went for a long walk which occupied most of the afternoon, and discussed the Student Movement and a great many other topics. He is a man who, when he is entirely won for the Student Movement, will I think be of great service to us. A speech he made in the morning was listened to with marked attention, and was referred to many times by other speakers. I judge that he is regarded as a man of considerable influence. I found him very friendly and, judging by his point of view on the many topics we discussed, I believe he will feel thoroughly at home in our Movement. I have secured from him a promise to be present at Conishead next summer.

The prophecy proved correct. Dr Temple has always felt and still feels thoroughly at home in the Student Movement.

While the Anglicans were paying attention to the relationship of the Church of England students to the Movement, Free Churchmen on the same committee were dealing with Nonconformist students. A letter over the signatures of Theodore H. Robinson,[2] Regent's Park College, and S. Spicer Harman, Lancashire College, was circulated, giving some account of the spirit of the summer conference and speaking of the activities of the Movement which would be suitable in Free Church colleges. What they thought on the denominational

---

[1] Afterwards Archbishop of York.

[2] Afterwards Professor T. H. Robinson, University College Cardiff.

question may be gleaned from a paragraph which deals with this ; contact meant that

> The horizon was greatly enlarged, and that in not one direction but in many when delegates met as members of different denominations. This point needs a strong emphasis. The hobgoblin of sectarianism has been effectively laid in the Student Movement, not because Anglicans and Free Churchmen met on a common basis and agreed to be silent on controversial points, but because they met as Anglicans and Free Churchmen of intensely strong convictions, agreeing sympathetically to recognize their divergencies, not to conceal them. It was there shown that unity is possible without uniformity, and is, perhaps, the truer for its absence.

While we were sometimes acting separately as Anglicans and Free Churchmen at this period, each group knew fully what the other group was doing and there was on the Committee constant backing of one another by conference, prayer and mutual advice. It was an element of great strength in the situation that the Committee during this whole period was united as to its policy.

The Scottish Theological Council had maintained its existence for some years and Spencer wrote of it : " In 1905 we met with grave doubts as to whether it was worth while. In 1906, after considerable discussion, we confirmed the worth-whileness of the Council, but no one dared prophesy in advance that the decision would be favourable."

In 1907 the Council took on a new lease of life. The hard work a number of men had put into it in previous years bore fruit and the Council discussed not itself but the work of the college societies (most of them missionary societies) that were represented, and the influence of the Movement began to grow among Scottish theological students.

The High Church element, absent on the Executive of the Theological College Department for so long, was supplied at last and Neville Talbot was elected a member at the business meeting of the Department, July 1907. The same autumn the Principal of Ridley Hall, the Rev. A. J. Tait, wrote to say that the conference of principals of Church of England theological colleges at their next meeting intended to discuss the relation of theological colleges to the Student Movement. As a friend of the Movement he asked for advice, and here is the reply sent him :

> 93, Chancery Lane, W.C.,
> *October 21st,* 1907.

My dear Tait,

I wish we had been given a little more time to go on making friends with individual members of the staff of theological colleges, but as the matter is going to be raised, all I would do is to urge upon you not to press them too much. I hope that nothing more will be done than simply to hear a statement from you and perhaps one or two of the others who have been to our conferences, and that no attempt will be made to pass resolutions. I feel that we have everything to gain and nothing to lose by acting slowly. I believe intensely in the blessing this Movement may be and will be to our Church, but I am rather afraid of a set-back if we try to hasten too much. The progress made in view of the history of relationships with non-Anglican bodies has been extraordinary and all our best Anglican friends caution us to move slowly. The real danger we have to face is that men should become prejudiced against the Movement without understanding it. There are doubtless reasons for such prejudice, yet we are really in a very comfortable position—we want to be thoroughly understood. We want that men should know everything about us before they come to decisions. We are free of the difficulties of some people in that there are certain things they want to hide. We want to hide nothing. Our only fear is that men may make up their minds about us before they know enough.

> Yours very sincerely,
>
> TISSINGTON TATLOW.

We received no communication from the Principals' Conference, but at the Quadrennial Missionary Conference at Christmas the Church of England theological colleges were well represented.

The following year we felt that a further step might be taken, and towards the end of the Baslow Conference, July, 1908, decided at a meeting of members of Church of England theological colleges that a letter should be sent to the principals of all Anglican theological colleges. It was pointed out therein that while " the main opportunity of experiencing the enthusiasm of the Movement is offered by the annual summer conference, the intervals between the conferences afford to colleges and individuals other opportunities of being drawn into the current and of sharing the help that is already brought to many."

The letter offered a visit by a travelling secretary who could tell something of the Movement at home and abroad, and went on to speak about the formation of missionary and social study circles, giving information about appropriate literature and concluding with the hope that " the students of the Church of England would take their proper place in the World's Student Christian Federation." The letter was signed on behalf of the meeting by G. E. Aickin, Chaplain of St Aidan's College; N. S. Talbot, Balliol and Cuddesdon Colleges; E. S. Woods, late Vice-Principal of Ridley Hall, who were members of the Executive Committee of the Theological College Department, and also by W. H. Frere,[1] Warden of the College of the Resurrection, Mirfield, and by three students, W. W. Hambidge, House of the Sacred Mission, Kelham; C. S. James, Wells Theological College; and F. J. King, St Augustine's College, Canterbury.

The next eighteen months saw the affiliation of the House of the Sacred Mission, Kelham, and the creating of further friendships. At last the final stage was reached when at the invitation of Canon J. O. Johnston of Cuddesdon, President of the Conference of Principals of Church of England Theological Colleges, I joined their conference, on January 11th and 12th, 1910, as a visitor. An evening session was devoted to the Student Movement. I spoke describing it, explaining what it

[1] Afterwards Bishop of Truro.

meant by interdenominationalism, the nature of its Basis and the summer conferences. I was followed by Canon B. K. Cunningham of Farnham, who spoke of what he had known of the Movement and its value as providing a meeting-place for theological men, where prejudice might be removed and where they might get to know one another before entering their life work as either clergy of the Church of England or Free Church ministers.

Fourteen colleges were represented, and after the speeches a friendly round-table conference took place when many questions about the Movement were asked. Canon Johnston of Cuddesdon, Mr H. L. Goudge of Wells and Mr Abbott of Salisbury expressed themselves as being in favour of the Movement. Father Kelly of Kelham was a great help and most amusing. He took up a superior attitude on being appealed to once or twice, taking care to explain to the principals that he was not in the same box as most of them since he and his college were part of the Movement. He was not a man in doubt!

Two practical questions emerged. One was whether the Student Movement was right in using the word "affiliation" to describe the relationship of a theological college to the Movement. It was clearly not a well-chosen word, and the word "association," which was suggested by the meeting, was later adopted by the Movement and incorporated in its Constitution as describing the link between a theological college and the Theological College Department of the Movement. The other matter debated was of a good deal more importance—what the Movement could do for a one-year graduate college. Several colleges had hesitated about joining the Movement because they were colleges with a one-year course, which meant a very fully organized life for their students. The Movement was perfectly satisfied to have students from these colleges attend the summer conference, observe the Day of Prayer for Students, and only take up any particular Student Movement activity if it seemed to fit the life of the college. As a matter of fact, the representatives of both Wells and Farnham said that they had had mission study circles on Student Movement lines for some time.

After the Theological College Department had had time to receive a report of this conference I wrote the following letter to Canon Johnston at Cuddesdon :

93, Chancery Lane, W.C.,
June 3rd, 1910.

My dear Canon Johnston,

At the Conference of Principals of Church of England Theological Colleges, held at Lincoln last January, I was asked to refer one or two questions arising out of the discussion held there on the subject of the Student Movement to the Executive of our Theological College Department, and ultimately to communicate their replies to you in order that you might forward them to the Heads of Theological Colleges.

You will remember that the discussion centred round one or two points :

1. Our use of the word " affiliation."

2. The relationship of the Movement to a one-year graduate college.

3. What the Student Movement expected of a college on affiliation.

To take up these points in order :

1. We readily agree that " affiliation " is an unfortunate word to have used to describe the relationship which theological colleges bear to one another when associated for the purpose of forming the Theological College Department of this Movement, and we equally readily agree that the word " association " is the proper word. It is a slow business altering our Constitution, but as soon as possible the word will be altered. In the meantime, as you and I have already agreed, we propose putting a footnote to the list of Theological Colleges composing this Movement, which is circulated in our " Brief Statement," to the following effect :

In view of the fact that the word " affiliated " has a technical meaning which makes its use in the case of theological colleges unsuitable, the Executive proposes on an early occasion to move an amendment to the Constitution whereby the term " associated colleges " should be substituted for " affiliated colleges."

2. With reference to one-year graduate colleges, we are quite prepared to affiliate or associate these colleges on the

understanding that activities of the Student Movement which are organized in other colleges having a longer course cannot be organized in these. We are content that in the case of these colleges someone should be appointed to act as Student Christian Movement representative, so that we may have a duly qualified person to communicate with, and that the college undertakes to do its best to send some of its members to one of the Summer Conferences of the Movement, always provided that it has not got a term of its own running during the dates of the Conference.

3. I have really covered my third point under the second heading. Perhaps I may amplify it to this extent by saying that the Executive feel that if a college is represented at the Summer Conference, they are prepared to leave it an open question whether any of the activities, such as mission study, or the study of social problems, which have been promoted by the Movement, be taken up in the college. This is a question for the college and not for the Movement. Also we would hope that the requests for intercession, issued by the Student Movement, would be especially remembered in theological colleges. In the case of both Mirfield and Kelham (these colleges are already affiliated) regular provision is made for bringing requests for prayer on behalf of students before members of the college.

With reference to the appointment of the Student Christian Movement representative in a college, who is appointed and how he is appointed is left entirely to the college to decide. We understand that in the case of graduate colleges the person who would decide this would be the Principal.

We hope that, seeing that the only points raised as possible difficulties by members of the Conference at Lincoln have been fully met, the way is now clear for theological colleges of the Church of England to associate themselves with the Movement, and we venture to hope that the majority of them will do so.

> Believe me,
>
> Yours very sincerely,
>
> TISSINGTON TATLOW.

Canon Johnston circulated this letter to the principals of the theological colleges of the Church of England with a covering letter, saying that he hoped that the letter "removes the chief difficulties which were felt about our relation to the Movement. For my part, I certainly think it does, and I venture to suggest that, if you still hesitate to connect yourself with it, a visit to one of the summer conferences at Baslow will very probably remove that hesitation. It was only by such a visit that I myself came to understand the strength and importance of this Movement."

It was not long after this that all the colleges represented at the principals' conference "associated" themselves with the Movement.

The Student Movement has cause to be grateful to a number of men in this connection, but two men will always be remembered with special gratitude—Father Kelly and Canon Johnston. They attended right through a number of Student Movement conferences, thrashed out with the utmost candour and friendliness all points which they thought were of importance in relation to both the work and policy of the Movement and its bearing upon the desire to associate Church of England theological colleges, and they established themselves in the affections of all those who were brought into close contact with them. An important epoch had closed in the life of the Movement. The approach to the Church of England began in 1898, and after twelve years' steady work the Movement was successful in winning the support of all its most important theological colleges, and the enrichment of its life which came in both making the effort and achieving the result was well worth the time and energy involved.

Far-reaching influences were set to work when the Movement began to bring representative Christian men of all denominations together. The growth of understanding, mutual appreciation and fellowship has wrought great changes in religious life in England and opened many doors hitherto shut, and that this is so is due in no small degree to the contacts and co-operation resulting from the activities of the Student Christian Movement.

M

CHAPTER X

THE WORK OF THE MOVEMENT DEEPENS AND EXPANDS

WE must now turn back and look at some of the general features of the life of the Movement, while the men who led it were following up the Liverpool Conference in the colleges and among the churches, reorganizing the whole, adding a new department—the Theological College Department—and giving it its basis.

The conference method was first developed by the Student Movement, which was the first religious organization in the world to use it as one of its chief activities. The Churches followed the Movement, not the Movement the Churches, in this matter.

The first Irish Student Movement conference was held in Dublin in February 1895 ; Welsh students organized the first held in their country at Aberystwyth, September 28th to 30th, the following year; while Scotland, where there had been student gatherings at Bonskeid and elsewhere in pre-Student Movement days, held its first S.C.M. conference in Edinburgh from January 7th to 9th, 1898. The existence of some Christian Unions in Scotland, Ireland and Wales before the formation of the Student Movement and their inclusion in it as foundation members meant that these countries were more prepared than England, outside the two older universities, to develop corporate activities, as they had men accustomed to the leadership of Christian Unions who were ready to do the necessary work.

These conferences all adhered closely to the interests of the Movement, especially in relation to missionary work and the cultivation of the spiritual life of students, with the exception of Wales, where there was an element in the conference provided by the Welsh students themselves that was interested in the relation of Christianity to social problems.   There were addresses on university settlements, temperance work and " on the special needs of Wales," as well as the topics which were at this time usual in Student Movement conferences.   Mr Richard Roberts [1] spoke on the origin and history of the Student Movement.   The gathering was a small one, only thirty students coming from outside Aberystwyth.

The Irish students held their second conference a month or two later, in Belfast, when there were two hundred students present from four of the five student centres in Ireland—Dublin, Belfast, Londonderry and Galway.

There were a few united activities among London students at this period.   A meeting for women students was held every autumn, when new students from all the colleges were invited; eighty attended in 1896.   This meeting has been one of the most continuous of all London activities.   The S.V.M.U. had a London Committee from the first and organized joint meetings for Student Volunteers, while the Medical Prayer Union, of which more will be said later, held an annual missionary breakfast in May and an annual meeting to which it sought to bring as many London medical students as possible.

When the Liverpool Conference, 1896, was over Miss Rouse, who gave up the post of editor of *The Student Volunteer* a few months later in order to become a travelling secretary, and W. E. S. Holland, each toured throughout the British Isles and devoted much time to the formation of Christian Unions in England. Holland visited the medical schools at Guy's, St Bartholomew's, St Mary's and St Thomas's Hospitals, where there were already branches of the Medical Prayer Union, and sought openings in Middlesex and University

[1] Afterwards the Rev. Richard Roberts, D.D., of Montreal.

College Hospitals. He addressed " the second meeting of the newly formed King's College Christian Union and met the committee of the new Union at the Central Technical College." Writing in *The Student Volunteer* he asked prayer :

> That God will minister an entrance into the many un-opened colleges of London, especially the medical schools at St George's and Charing Cross Hospitals ; and the Art, Veterinary and Technical Colleges. It is difficult to see how, in a vast centre like London, colleges on a non-religious basis can be opened up except by the direct inter-position of God, in bringing across one's path, often in the most unexpected and apparently casual way, the names of Christian students at one or other of these places. Three of the Christian Unions—those at St Thomas', Middlesex and Westminster Medical Schools—struggling for a difficult existence, call for our earnest intercession.

Holland reported about the same time that after many unsuccessful attempts a Christian Union had been started among the men at University College, Nottingham, and that this meant that the only one of the six great Midland and Northern provincial colleges without a Union was Firth College, Sheffield. When he began his work a few months earlier, the only one in existence was the Christian Union at University College, Liverpool. He had been successful in the formation of Unions at Mason College, Birmingham; Owens College, Manchester; Yorkshire College, Leeds; and University College, Nottingham.

Miss Rouse was equally active among women students, but it must be remembered that she was also concerned with promoting the work of the S.V.M.U., while Holland had a fellow traveller in the men's colleges, who specialized on foreign missions, Walter R. Miller, who had just qualified as a doctor at St Bartholomew's Hospital.

The travelling secretaries at this time each visited between sixty and seventy colleges in the course of their year's work. Rutter Williamson, who was a very methodical man, left on record the fact that from

October to April he had visited sixty-eight colleges, addressed eighty-four meetings with audiences totalling 5197 persons, and had travelled 6732 miles.

There are features of the work of the Movement which have persisted since then. Glasgow University Christian Union, for example, was the first Union to secure Christian Union rooms, which it did in a house in Bank Street in 1895. " Vacant posts " was printed from time to time in the pages of *The Student Volunteer*, giving the openings overseas for men and women under the missionary societies, while Edinburgh University had a whole-time secretary, Harold Nuttall.

In 1897 the Movement decided to leave Keswick and to hold its summer conference at Curbar in Derbyshire. This step was taken partly because Keswick had become increasingly expensive, partly because there was no suitable building to hold the women students who had increased in number, and partly because some of the leaders were anxious to avoid associating the Movement permanently with a particular school of thought.

While I had attended two of the Keswick Conferences of the Movement as an undergraduate, I came to Curbar as an incoming secretary. At Easter 1897, I was invited, through Howard Henry, the representative of Ireland, on behalf of the Executive, to become travelling secretary of the S.V.M.U., having signed the declaration after the previous summer conference in August 1896. I had taken my degree in Arts and was finishing a three years' course in the Engineering School at Trinity College, Dublin. I accepted and went to the summer conference at Curbar as travelling secretary.

What a shrimp I felt in a tent that contained Douglas Thornton, Temple Gairdner, W. E. S. Holland and Rutter Williamson. They all seemed so competent and all-knowing ! My first gleam of hope came when Williamson, coming into the tent after a meeting at which I had made a brief speech on missionary reading, and not knowing I was in a corner, said, " I say, you fellows, I think that chap Tatlow will do ; he can speak."

But the man to whom I shall always be most grateful is John Mott. He came to Curbar direct from India and was worn out. Williamson looked after him and he did not appear for some days, then Williamson called me and said, " Mott is going to have a talk with you about your work." He took me upstairs at Cliff College, where the women students and some speakers were lodged, opened a door, said, " Here's Tatlow," and left me with a grim-looking individual with one of the worst black eyes I've ever seen ! Mott had had a fainting fit and fallen against a wash-stand. I don't remember a word of what Mott said except his parting remark, " Well, good-bye, Mr Tatlow. I'm very glad to have met you, and I feel sure you'll make a great success of your work as a travelling secretary." I was comforted, perhaps I shouldn't make a hopeless mess of it after all. I learnt a lesson too. Mott has always got the best out of men by his optimism and confidence in them. I have never forgotten this.

The Curbar Conference was good, but not eventful. The things I remember are Harry Waller,[1] a Cambridge rowing " blue," being very jolly and efficient as camp manager, and his assistant, William Bracecamp, being hospitable with a large teapot ; the fearsome cold of the river when some of us took a plunge at 6 a.m. daily ; and the segregation of the men from the women. I was accustomed to the easy relations of men and women in Ireland and felt rather baffled by finding that it wasn't done to chat to women one knew in a friendly way. I remember to this day the consternation I caused, all unwittingly, by going to Cliff College after supper to find someone's luggage, and remaining for half an hour sitting on a table talking to my country-women, Miss Stevenson and her sister. Times, happily, have changed !

The women students on the committee very seldom spoke unless they were specially appealed to for their opinion by the men. Questions about the women's

---

[1] Afterwards Bishop of Madras.

colleges were invariably referred to the women members to discuss among themselves, and when a proposal had to be made to the committee one of the women generally acted as spokesman for the rest. On the other hand, every detail of the men's work used to be discussed fully, the women being expected to listen patiently even though time might be taken up with matters of detail, which ought really to have been given to some much bigger questions relating to women's colleges instead of these being relegated to informal discussions among the women, usually during lunch or tea.

The men and women on committee did not mix very much with one another and at meal times the two sexes generally separated. They were also rigidly separated at summer conferences, men not being allowed for years to go near where the women were living, and it not being considered desirable for men and women to have anything to do with one another socially during the days of the conference.

The programme of the Curbar Conference provided addresses on the Christian Life, Bible readings and a number of addresses on methods of Christian Union work, the Morning Watch, the use of time, personal work, systematic giving, the choice of a life-work, work among schoolboys, and the memorial of the S.V.M.U. to the Churches. These topics were all dealt with by Student Movement leaders. There were special meetings for presidents and secretaries of Christian unions and of missionary bands, and a training class for leaders of Bible circles. Dr Handley Moule, the Rev. Charles Inwood, the Rev. H. E. Fox, the Rev. R. Wright Hay, Mr John R. Mott and Miss G. A. Gollock were the chief speakers among the visitors, but the Movement itself had a fine body of speakers in its leaders, and the addresses which made most impression on the conference were Rutter Williamson's (the Chairman) on " Reality," Temple Gairdner on " Giving " and " The Use of Time," W. E. S. Holland on " Personal Soul Winning," and Miss Rouse and Fred O'Neill on " The

Watchword." J. H. Oldham spoke on prayer and Douglas Thornton introduced his new missionary study text-book, *Africa waiting*. At no time has the Student Movement produced a finer group of speakers from its committee and secretariat.

Gairdner was the most striking of the speakers. Dealing with the time question, his address was first and foremost a plea for first-class work in college. Perhaps he felt that the enthusiasm of the Movement was such that it might unduly deflect men's energies from study. " Have you not noticed," said Gairdner, " sad cases, when the bright Christian face has gradually lost its light, and dulness entered into the alert, keen, spiritual life ? Enquire and you will very likely find that slackness crept into that man's studies. I have known such cases, and sad it has been. The sluggard intellectually is almost bound to become the sluggard spiritually." He set a very high standard for Christian work in college and then declared that the men who did their college work well and Christian work well were not so much giants as " men who have learned the secret of the economy of time." Concerning this point, he said, " I speak as one who is set to catch a thief because he is personally acquainted with the profession. With sympathy I speak, and with shame. Come, then, and before God look into this matter." As he expounded the ways in which students waste time he revealed in a very human way his knowledge of men. Equally striking was his address on " Giving." Both of these were quoted for years afterwards and had a deep influence on the Movement at this time.

There were three hundred and thirty-three students at the Curbar Conference. They represented seventy-three colleges and constituted the largest summer conference the Movement had held. The international element, which is never lacking in Student Movement conferences, was represented by Australian, German, Finnish, Bulgarian, Dutch and Danish students. The women were accommodated in Cliff College and in rooms in the surrounding villages. The men camped on the banks of the Derwent. The meetings were held in a tent pitched on the asphalt tennis courts of the college.

Leaving Keswick had greatly increased the financial anxiety of the leaders, especially as the expenditure of the Movement was rising rapidly. The budget at this time for the joint work of the S.V.M.U. and B.C.C.U. was about £1200. The reason Gairdner was chosen to deal with the subject of giving was that the leaders felt that they must train the colleges in giving so that they would support the Movement while at college and would also help to provide additional funds for the missionary societies. The Financial Session at the Curbar Conference produced nearly £600, practically all of this amount being promised by students.

The best insight that can be given into the kind of advice to the leaders of Christian Unions at this stage will be to reproduce the " gleanings from the Presidential Conferences," which were held each afternoon, these gleanings being printed in *The Student Volunteer* for October 1897 :

Work among New Students. Every fresher should have an opportunity presented to him of deciding for Christ. This should be the work of the whole C.U., not of a few members only. Get to know the freshers as friends, showing them true kindness for its own sake, in the spirit of Christ, not as a bait. Win them to and for Christ, not to swell the numbers of the C.U. Don't let the work drop after the first fortnight, leaving them stranded high and dry as " all right " ; get them to begin definite work.

Intercollegiate Relations. Pray for other colleges, learn as much about their needs and circumstances as possible. Take in *The Student Volunteer*. Keep in touch with the office, answering all communications promptly and accurately.

General Meetings. Let each meeting have a definite purpose. It is better to have no meeting at all than one which aims at nothing in particular. The way to get men to attend a meeting is to give them a meeting worth coming to. Determine outside speakers by the subjects you want, not *vice versa*. Have no applause or votes of thanks, but be sure to thank the speaker privately and let him know of any cheering results. Among the general meetings there should always be an evangelistic, a missionary, and a devotional meeting.

The College Daily Prayer Meeting is universally allowed to be the most spiritually helpful of all. It draws men together, breaks down reserve, and has an effect on all the other meetings of the C.U. Let the members realize the privilege of taking part ; keep the prayers short. One-sentence prayers are often helpful.

The Travelling Secretary's Visit should be prepared for by much prayer. Post the Travelling Secretary up beforehand about the Christian work in the college and its weak points. Try to get on with your college work beforehand, so that it will not suffer because of his visit. The whole work is God's work. The Travelling Secretary does not come to do, but to reap and to begin. Follow up the work.

Work among Schoolgirls and Schoolboys. Students have an immense influence with these, which should be used for Jesus Christ. A few hints : Love them, respect them, be real and natural with them ; above all, keep in constant communion with God when with them. Remember that there is such a thing as " spiritual heredity."

After the Curbar Conference I proceeded to visit the universities and colleges in the interests of the S.V.M.U. while Gairdner started work as B.C.C.U. travelling secretary. With the coming of Gairdner, B.C.C.U. problems were tackled with a new seriousness. Douglas Thornton was giving his mind to missionary study as the best means of making the colleges missionary and also devoting much thought to some of the wider problems of the Movement, while the man who first brought a highly trained and reflective intelligence to bear upon the work of the Christian Unions was Temple Gairdner. Those who had gone before him as travelling secretaries, Donald Fraser, Frank Anderson, W. E. S. Holland, had largely been occupied in breaking new ground and starting the Christian Unions. This was difficult and exacting work, as has already been indicated, for the reason set down in one of my own reports as a travelling secretary : " One is met with the same difficulty in all the Midland and University Colleges in England, namely, they are non-residential, and in consequence there is practically no social life."

The man who every two or three days was passing on to a new centre, either to found a new Union or to keep a recently started one in existence, and at the same time was carrying on a correspondence with student leaders all over the British Isles, had his hands full. When Gairdner became travelling secretary he took his full share in pioneering work but he also began at once to tackle some of the problems of the Christian Unions. For example, the men who joined the Unions at Oxford and Cambridge found in them a very strong religious tradition, the fruits of the Evangelical Movement, and if they did not already know clearly what the object of a Christian Union was, they soon discovered. Not so the men in the new non-residential colleges in England. While a few here and there came from homes where they had had some religious training, the majority of students had had none. Further, in the case of the men asked to lead these new Unions, they had had no experience of organizing Christian work and were very much at sea as to the object of a Christian Union. After some months on tour and thinking out the problems of these men, Gairdner wrote a pamphlet " The Goal of a College Christian Union," which had a wide circulation and a deep influence upon both the men's and women's Christian Unions. Because of its influence and of the conviction of the Committee that Gairdner had written what was wanted, it is worth quoting from this document.

Troubled by the fact that so many Unions seemed to aim at " simple existence," Gairdner began by saying :

> The important thing is to have a worthy ideal : then, and not till then, is the gradual realization of it, even though slow and apparently insignificant, fully sanctified.

> " Not failure but low aim is crime."

The Divine and therefore Perfect End.

First, let us observe that the idea underlying the whole world-wide student movement is the idea which should underlie each College Christian Union. For, since we are members of one body, that which applies to the whole applies to every part. And it is a solemn thought that by this law the fulfilment of the end of the world-wide movement depends directly upon whether this or that little College Christian Union fulfils *its* part in the attainment of that end. Now the idea that underlies the world-wide movement is nothing less than to " *make the Colleges strongholds and distributing centres of Christianity.*"

If we isolate a generation of College students we see that a College may be viewed as a vast storehouse of potential energy. Here for a few years is energy accumulating in one place which is soon to be distributed into every corner of the earth. A few years hence it would be a hopeless task to attempt to influence as a body the ministers, doctors, lawyers, business men, officers, artists, and teachers who will then be scattered throughout the country exerting that quality of influence with which they have left College. Yet God has given us the opportunity of actually influencing these very persons in the most direct way while they are all gathered together at one time and into one place! They are here members of a corporate body, and are thus capable of receiving any impressions, good or bad, that are brought to bear upon them.

As disciples of the Lord Jesus Christ we desire that these students shall be influenced and won for Him, and for His cause. We desire that these great forces, when released, shall work for, and not against, the Kingdom of Heaven. How many solutions to our greatest national and international problems should we see if the world of college students were confessedly and unreservedly on the side of Jesus Christ! Nothing, then, that comes short of *this* is or can be the aim of our national movement or of any single branch of it. "THE COLLEGES FOR CHRIST—EACH OF ALL AND ALL OF EACH," this is the goal of our prayer and effort: and while the National Movement as a whole is responsible for the " each of all," " *all of each* " is the goal of the College Christian Unions.

In explaining this he adapted some words from Mr Gladstone's farewell to the University of Oxford,

and said that while this ideal did not mean the making
of every student a decided Christian, conversion being
beyond man's province, it did mean adopting as a duty
and an aim " a college, God-fearing and God-sustaining."

Gairdner was the first man who conceived the idea of
a Christian Union influencing an entire college. At this
time the Christian Unions were most of them tiny little
groups of people who felt that they were banded to
help one another in the Christian life and draw in a
few each year from among the freshmen. They had
no hope of influencing the college as a whole. This
wider hope Gairdner did not see realized in his time
in the Movement. It was some years before Christian Unions expected not only to win men to Christ
and build them up in Him, but also expected to influence
the life of the university or college as a whole.

In his pamphlet Gairdner asked the question, " How
can a college be thus reached as a whole and won ? "
He answered that the Movement rightly dealt with the
organization of work for new students, special missions,
committees and different departments of work, but that
methods would not win a college.

> There is something that must be in and around and
> underneath all these things ; something apart from which
> they are nothing. A Union must be possessed by the Holy
> Ghost. Watch a Union during one of the days of the Holy
> Ghost. Members seem to be feeling after deeper life and
> almost daily there are instances of one or another finding it.
> What is the cause of this strange movement ? Track the
> causes back and you will invariably find that one or two
> members, perhaps just one, have laid hold on a fuller life in
> God ; have begun and are continuing to draw upon the
> mysterious resources of lonely prayer, strenuously, per-
> sistently ; are making fresh discoveries in the infinite
> domain of the Word of God. It is not, as a rule, that the
> Spirit falls upon a whole Union at one time and in one
> place, still less upon a whole College—although these
> things have been in the past, and may again be granted to
> our more persistent prayer ;—but His fire is wont to spread
> " from centre to circumference," from the one to the many.
> Now every several member is a centre ; every member may

be the spring of influence which shall go far beyond himself; to every member by himself are put these three questions :

" Is it the will of God that there should be an awakening in my College ? "

" If so, with whom shall it begin ? "

" And when ? "

Then will follow the patient work done by such students. Kindled themselves, they communicate the flame to a member here, another there. One by one the other members of the Union feel the presence of a new spirit, and yield to its influence. They in turn work outwards ; and thus from the centre to the circumference the fire spreads.

With a Union so possessed, is it possible but that the whole College shall be influenced ?

Gairdner thought that the increased spirituality would be manifested first in prayer and secondly in work for the souls of men. He was troubled that as the new Christian Unions sprung up in the colleges they were so separate from the life about them, and he wrote :

Here is the argument for Christian students taking part in the social life of the College—not for the sake of courting popularity, but for the sake of greater human contact and enlarged sympathy. How can athletic students be won if Christian students avoid games ? . . . Many Colleges have little enough social life. Should not members bring Christian influence to bear upon what there is ? . . . If we fear that thus the religion of the Cross will become popular or lose its power, we may remember that the bearing of the Cross is really heavier for a Christian student in such sets as these than when he is sheltered within the circle of his own Christian friends ; and that even if a College were so won as to become almost entirely Christian, the bearing of the Cross would still be possible, and indeed inevitable, in the daily self-humiliation of the Christian life.

Gairdner also gave his mind to the nature of the Bible study circles which were the most general activity of the Christian Unions. The methods had been learned from America and the first Bible study text-books were imported from the American Student Movement. He realized that the Movement must have its own text-books if they were to be suited to the needs of British

students.   He wrote the first series of studies published
by the Student Movement in England for circles, a
pamphlet entitled *Studies in Prayer*.   This being successful, he was asked by the committee to write the first of
the Movement's Bible study text-books.   It was upon
the *Gospel of St John*.   From that time the Movement has
prepared its own study text-books for use in Bible circles.

Gairdner was specially interested in the Fine Art and
Music Colleges.   An artist himself—he was heart and
soul a musician—he was anxious to win the students
in the Fine Art and Music Colleges, and when a group
of women students led by Miss Lilian Stevenson of the
Slade School of Art began to consider how best to
pioneer the Movement in these colleges, the one man
who understood what was at issue was Gairdner and
he took a prominent part in the founding of the Art
Students' Christian Union.

Like Thornton, Gairdner had interests in the Movement outside his own department, and as recorded
elsewhere took a prominent part in the founding of the
Theological Department and assisting with the first
steps in bringing the Church of England theological
colleges into the Movement.

The life of Gairdner has been so well told in a
biography [1] by Miss Padwick that readers may be
referred to it for a study of him, but reference must be
made here to the deep impression left by his spiritual
leadership on the corporate life of Student Movement
committees.   During the year he was a secretary and
the following year, when he was on the committee as a
member, he led quiet half-days at almost all the meetings
the committee held.   His gift for this kind of service
was so obvious that no one thought of another leader
as long as he was available.   His poise and sanity, his
scholarship, his deep sense of the presence of God with
those gathered together in Christ's name, his passionate
earnestness and complete lack of self-consciousness made
him a wonderful leader.

[1] *Temple Gairdner of Cairo*, by Constance E. Padwick.

He had a failing which I think endeared him to us although it undoubtedly distressed him, and that was his extraordinary forgetfulness. I remember that Harry Duncan, the general secretary, had a new pair of brown shoes that he was very proud of yet a little anxious about, lest they were over-worldly for a Christian man. It was a time when we thought of such things! At the Ripon Conference in 1898 Gairdner's shoes being soaked, he borrowed this precious possession of Duncan's, who, knowing him to be very forgetful, said to him, "Now, Gairdie, promise that you won't forget to give me these shoes before you leave the conference." Gairdner went off a day early. Duncan's shoes could not be found, but next morning there came a postcard, still preserved, with these words on the back :

> Dear Harricus,
> I simply had to go off in your shoes. Forgive. I'll send them to the office at once. One has need of faith just now.   W. H. T. G.

The last sentence referred, of course, to the conference that had just closed, but there were not wanting those to point out to Harry Duncan that it was an appropriate reference to him and his shoes, still in Gairdner's possession !

While he was a travelling secretary, all his possessions came back one after another to the office : shoes, Bible, sponge, tooth-brush, waistcoat, trousers. This was a great delight to a newly appointed office boy, who used to feel each parcel carefully, saying, for example, " I think it is Mr Gairdner's sponge this morning, sir."

Walking down New Street, Birmingham, one day with Willie Holland, carrying a heavy bag, Holland, who was curate at the Parish Church, asked him to preach and fixed a date with him. Knowing Gairdner's forgetfulness, he said, " Put it in your diary at once." Gairdner put his bag down on the pavement, pulled out his diary, made the entry and then walked on, forgetting that he had left his bag on the pavement. This forgetfulness

FOUNDERS OF THE WORLD'S STUDENT CHRISTIAN FEDERATION
STANDING BEFORE THE DOOR OF WADSTENA CASTLE, AUGUST 12, 1895
Left to right—J. RUTTER WILLIAMSON, JOHANNES SIEMSEN, JOHN R. MOTT
K. M. ECKHOFF, KARL FRIES, L. D. WISHARD

tried him greatly but, as I say, it was a human weakness that endeared him to us all.

The Movement was widening its interests all this time. It followed the growth of the World's Student Christian Federation with great interest. When the Federation was founded at the Castle of Wadstena, Sweden, in August 1895, John Mott started at once on his first world tour in the interest of student work and sent back reports, which were reproduced in the magazine. Donald Fraser was keeping the Movement informed about student work in South Africa. Ruth Rouse visited all the Scandinavian countries, including Finland, in March and April, 1897, and started the Movement among women students in them. Delegates continued to go to the Quadrennial Conferences of the Student Volunteer Movement in the United States, Douglas Thornton was the delegate to Cleveland in 1898; and Miss L. M. Cooke visited South Africa, doing work among women and girls parallel to that which Donald Fraser had done among the men two years earlier. Rutter Williamson visited the United States, 1898-99, to act as a travelling secretary, and Miss Rouse visited America at the same time. One result of all this was that the magazine contained as much information about the Federation at that period as it has ever contained.

The Movement was also learning about the field in which it worked. A series of articles was begun in October 1898 which continued for several years and described universities both in the British Isles and on the Continent. The first of this series was an article on Cambridge University contributed by Tom Inskip.[1] *The Student Movement* took the place of *The Student Volunteer* as a magazine, and its issues were increased from seven to nine per annum, the price being raised from 1s. to 1s. 6d.

At the end of my year as S.V.M.U. travelling secretary I was offered the travelling secretaryship of the General

[1] Afterwards the Rt. Hon. Sir T. W. H. Inskip.

College Department in succession to Gairdner, and at the same time the General Committee offered me the general secretaryship. This office had been held in succession by Crayden Edmunds, L. B. Butcher, J. H. Oldham and H. C. Duncan, who each served for one year. I had realized during my year of office as travelling secretary that it was an impossible arrangement having a new general secretary every year, and that if there was ever to be an orderly office, appointments for a longer period would have to be made. It was impossible for a man to learn in a week or two how to administer an office, organize conferences, arrange visits of secretaries, undertake publishing and oversee the account-keeping of the Movement and then pass his knowledge on at the end of twelve months to another man, with a view to the same thing being repeated over again.

It was suggested to me that if I became general secretary I should agree to hold office for at least two years and organize the second quadrennial conference. I accepted the general secretaryship and began my work on August 1st 1898, having by that time a good knowledge of the colleges of the British Isles and having learned a tremendous amount, especially from Thornton and Gairdner. I set to work with Mr Walter Saunders, C.A., who had been auditor of the Movement's books for a couple of years, to try and provide a more accurate and satisfactory method of book-keeping, began the filing of the Movement's letters for the first time, bought a little furniture to take the place of a couple of Tate's empty sugar boxes in which literature and letters used to be kept, and engaged the first typist to become a regular member of the staff. The total staff in the office then consisted of a book-keeping clerk, office boy and typist.

As the office at 93 Aldersgate Street had obviously grown too small, I found new offices at 22 Warwick Lane and very nearly produced strained relationships, on grounds of extravagance, between myself and the committee, by renting two floors. It was apparent, however, to everyone when the work for the quadrennial conference of 1900 began that we could not possibly have organized the conference in a smaller space. As a matter of fact we outgrew Warwick Lane very quickly, two floors and all!

About this time I made my first direct contact with the Federation, officially representing the S.V.M.U. at the conference of the Federation, which was held at Eisenach, Germany, from July 13th to 17th, 1898.

As I began my work as general secretary the first London secretary, H. W. Oldham, who had been a student at the Central Technical College in London, began work.

On February 13th 1898 the first Universal Day of Prayer for Students was observed by the ten national Student Movements affiliated to the Federation.

The summer conference of 1898 was held at Ripon, where we met in the Grammar School, one hundred and eighty-five women occupying the house and one hundred and eighty men camping near at hand. It was during this conference that a committee was appointed of women from Newnham, Somerville, Froebel, Bedford and Durham University with a view to the ultimate formation of an organization among schoolgirls which should have an evangelistic and missionary aim and "probably be known as the Junior Students' Christian Union." It was out of this beginning that the Federation of University Women's "Camps" for School-girls ultimately grew.

The one notable event in the following winter was a mission in Edinburgh University, from February 8th to 13th, 1899, conducted by John Mott. The M'Ewan Hall, which had recently been presented to the University, was engaged for a religious meeting for the first time, and the mission which had begun in the Oddfellows' Hall was closed by a meeting in it, when 1800 students were present. A deep impression was made upon the whole University, and as it was the most notable evangelistic meeting within the memory of the leaders of the Student Movement at that time, it raised their expectations as to what could be done among students.

John Mott was at this time preparing for his first visit to the Russian universities and asked me to discover who could best help him to understand the Holy Orthodox Church of Russia. I took him to see Bishop Creighton, who not only understood the Orthodox Church, but had been present at the Coronation of the Czar.

We went to London House, St James's Square, on Ash Wednesday 1899, and the Bishop gave Mott some valuable advice, a personal introduction to the Procurator of the Holy Synod, and lent him some volumes about Russia which had been given him by the Czarina. They were books specially prepared for her and printed privately at the time of her marriage, describing Russia and various aspects of Russian life. As these books were in English, their loan was of great service. They were beautifully printed and bound in dark crimson leather.

The death of Bishop Creighton was a great loss to the Movement. Thornton, Gairdner and I had each met and talked with him about the Movement and he was beginning to know it and be interested in it. We felt his death keenly for we knew he was a wise man and had hoped he would have been a regular helper and adviser. His last service to the Movement was to welcome the S.V.M.U. Conference in January 1900 to London. The advertisement of his name as a speaker brought me a vigorous letter of protest from Lord Kinnaird, a lifelong and generous friend of the Movement, who deplored our asking " a ritualist like the Bishop of London " to speak for the Movement. The Bishop's presence was warmly welcomed by the students and he made an excellent speech, with cordial references to the Movement, which delighted us all.

The summer conference in 1899 moved to Aberystwyth; the women were in the recently built Alexandra Hall, the men in a camp at the back of the town, and the meetings were held in the University College. The outstanding feature of the programme was the speaking of the Rev. G. A. Johnston Ross, then minister of Westbourne Grove Presbyterian Church, London. He was unknown outside his own Church, and I alone had heard him speak, but I knew he would bring in an element of intellectual vigour which the programme of the summer conferences lacked. He was an immense success and the result of his contribution was to give the leaders an appetite for a keen intellectual element in the speaking which would relate it to the best thought of the day.

The Aberystwyth Conference marked a new stage in the development of the summer conference, and in their report a year later the Committee of the Movement said truly "the Aberystwyth Conference gave a fuller place to thought in the Christian life." Mr Johnston Ross's success with students led to his being called later to St Columba's, Cambridge, where he exerted considerable influence, and also did valuable work for the Movement. America then called him and he became a "star" preacher in the American universities, as well as a professor at Union Theological Seminary, New York.

One visitor at the Aberystwyth Conference who was immensely popular was Count Moltke of Sweden. He was a valued senior friend of the Swedish Student Movement. Soon after he arrived I went to look for him in camp, very anxious that some special attention should be paid him. He was Controller of the King of Sweden's household and one of the outstanding personalities of his own country. I was rather taken aback to find a group of students rolling him down a hill near the camp, wrapped in a blanket. He seemed to enjoy the fun, however, and I suppose it was a novelty for a man accustomed to be treated with great respect. He was a fine gentleman and an outspoken Christian.

The S.V.M.U. announced its decision in March 1899 to hold a second missionary conference.

> The purpose of the conference is to bring together carefully selected delegations from the collegiate centres of Great Britain and Ireland, and the Continent of Europe, and leaders of the missionary enterprise at home and abroad, to consider, in the face of the needs of the world, the relation of Christian students to the great problem of its evangelization, and unitedly to undertake, in His strength, greater things for the extension of the Kingdom of Jesus Christ.[1]

One reason for this decision was " that the Liverpool Conference by its far-reaching results demonstrated the permanent value of such gatherings," and another was the slackening of volunteering. The Liverpool Conference had been held because students were volunteering in such numbers that it seemed as if they could not hope to be sent abroad unless the Churches did far more for foreign missions. The London Conference was held because the number of students joining the S.V.M.U. each year was decreasing instead of increasing.

The leaders regarded prayer as the chief means of preparation for the conference. Sunday, November 19th 1899, was appointed as a day of prayer for it, to be observed by all the members of the Movement. Prayer calls were distributed to people all over the world who it was believed would use them, and the preparatory literature and articles in the magazine laid great stress on the importance of prayer, as was the case in the preparation for the Liverpool Conference.

The organization of the gathering was the work of a handful of people. There was a Conference Executive consisting of H. C. Duncan, Edinburgh University, the chairman of the conference, Garden Blaikie, a theological student at Cambridge and A. G. Fraser, who was travelling secretary, with myself and Loftus Wigram, a Cambridge man appointed as an assistant secretary for three months to help me with the conference work.

[1] *The Student Movement*, vol. i. p. 131.

The Committee of the S.V.M.U. planned the programme. The Conference Executive seldom met as it was difficult to get together. Wigram and I were left to secure hospitality and finance the conference on our own lines.

There was so much difficulty about securing speakers that in the autumn before the conference, W. E. S. Holland suggested to the Committee that I should be given a free hand to invite anyone I thought was suitable. No one would guess from a study of the report of the conference that this had ever happened in relation to the speakers, for in spite of the fact that at one time we were almost in despair owing to the number of refusals, there were over fifty speakers at the conference, and a study of the list shows that a large number of the outstanding men in touch with the missionary enterprise were speaking at it. The list included among others : the Archbishop of Canterbury (Dr Temple), the Bishop of London (Dr Creighton), the Bishop of Newcastle (Dr Jacob), the Revs. R. J. Campbell, Alexander Connell, Robert Bruce, T. W. Drury, Prof. Alexander Martin, Prof. A. R. S. Kennedy, Richard Glover, J. H. Bernard, George Robson, W. T. A. Barber, Robert F. Horton, J. H. Ellison, J. O. F. Murray, H. E. Fox, Robert Laws, C. E. Wilson, F. L. Denman, John Sharp, E. P. Rice, Thomas Barclay, Robert E. Speer, R. Wardlaw Thompson, Principal H. R. Reichel, Dr Duncan Main, Dr George Smith, Dr Grattan Guinness and Mr W. Barbrook Grubb.

Invitations were sent to the Student Movements in the United States and Canada as well as to the Continental countries. Descriptive leaflets were printed and circulated in French, Norwegian and Swedish. The result was that 131 men and 20 women, representing 25 countries outside the British Isles, attended the conference, of which number 95 men and 14 women came to England specially for it.

We met from January 2nd to 6th, 1900, in Exeter Hall, London. The conference was more than double the size of the Liverpool Conference, the total attendance being 1619 persons, of whom 1311 were students (879 men and 432 women). The missionary societies were all represented with the exception of the S.P.G., our widening links with the Church of England being typified by the presence of official delegates from the Universities' Mission to Central Africa.

It will interest a later generation to notice the small number of men and women who came from the university colleges, which were the forerunners of the modern universities in England. A total of 114 men and women came from Newcastle, Sheffield, Leeds, Liverpool, Manchester, Birmingham and Bristol. The largest delegation came from Edinburgh, which sent 201 students, Cambridge being next with 158 men and women. As far as faculties were concerned, the Arts 402, Theologicals 320, Medicals 301, were the largest groups. Only 79 were training-college students and 61 science students.

Being given so much freedom of action, I decided to make a special effort to get members of the teaching staffs to the conference, and invited a number with some of the speakers to stay as our guests at the Hotel Victoria, Northumberland Avenue. The Student Movement leaders responsible for running the conference joined this party. Arrangements were made at the hotel for a special dining-room to be placed at the disposal of our guests. We had about fifty members of staff with us; the whole thing was a great success. With the exception of Edinburgh University, where there were close connections between members of staff and the Christian Union, very little had been done elsewhere to cultivate these, and a new day dawned at the London Conference in the relation of the Movement to the teaching staff of our universities and colleges. From then onwards the Movement has always given a good deal of attention to the cultivation of members of staff, realizing that it is of the utmost importance that they should understand not only the Christian Union which they saw in their own college, which might at times possibly be a poor affair, but also the genius of the Movement as a whole. We began definitely and consciously at the London Conference to make efforts to secure the help and advice of principals, professors and lecturers all over the college field.

There was a splendid exhibition in the Examination Hall on the Victoria Embankment, which was described as " a remarkably complete collection of accurate missionary literature, maps and diagrams." Mrs C. A. Flint helped with the loan of large numbers of books she had collected in connection with her circulating library for the C.M.S. Libraries were shown from the value of £5 up to £63. This department was organized under the guidance of G. H. Moule, the educational secretary, Lilian Stevenson, the editorial secretary, and Jessie Mothersole.

Anyone who has organized a conference of 1600 persons in London and undertaken to provide all those who were not Londoners with beds will realize what an undertaking this was. It was not possible to make an impression on London and ask through the Press for help in securing beds as it had been possible in Liverpool, and at one time it looked as if there would be a bad breakdown in the matter of hospitality, but we worked hard and prayed hard in the office, and there was a bed for everybody on the opening night of the conference. The work being done by a very few people we had to keep at it night after night until the early hours of the morning, and several of us became well known customers at the Press Restaurant in Fleet Street between 1 and 2 a.m., where we used to go to get a meal. On at least one occasion I did not vacate the office for thirty-six hours on end. The pace was too hot for one or two and they had to be sent home in cabs ! I remember being grateful for the toughness of A. G. Fraser, who never turned a hair, no matter how long he was expected to work.

On the opening night of the conference it was possible to announce that a sufficient sum of money had been raised to pay all expenses and that gifts made at the conference would be used towards extending the work of the Movement.   The conference raised about £900 at its financial session.   It was announced that the first £150 would be sent to the South African Movement.   The reason this Movement was selected for help was that we were in the midst of the Boer War.   The South African Movement was composed of both Boers and English.   It needed help and the committee was anxious to express its sympathy with it in some tangible form.

The war affected our relations with the Dutch Movement.   This Movement, which had grown out of the previous conference held in Liverpool, felt deeply in the debt of our Movement in Great Britain, which it regarded as its mother-movement, but the sympathies of the Dutch being with the Boers it was acutely distressed by the war, and felt it right to refuse to send delegates unless our Movement denounced the war publicly.   Most of us had never thought about the question of war at all and were inclined to be rather shocked by the small group of people in England who were opposed to it and who were known as " pro-Boers."   The invitation to the Dutch to "London, 1900," had been given without it occurring to anybody that it might not be acceptable and the attitude of the Dutch came as a surprise to us all.

There were prolonged discussions as to what reply we should make, and in the end our two Federation representatives, Frank Lenwood and G. H. Moule, were deputed to reply.   It is not possible to give the Dutch letter, which does not seem to have been preserved. My recollection is that it was a brief letter simply saying that as long as England was doing such a wrong thing as attacking a small nation like the Boers, they did not feel they could send any delegation to England unless we were willing to dissociate ourselves as a Movement from the action of our Government.   As this was the first experience our Movement had of dealing with a public issue of this kind, it will be of interest to give the actual text of the letter sent to the committee of the Student Movement in Holland :

22, Warwick Lane,
London, E.C.,
December 1899.

Dear Brothers in Christ,

We are exceedingly grieved to hear that you have decided that you cannot come to the London Conference. We fully realize the naturalness and nobility of the feeling that has prompted this decision. In a similar case it is not unlikely that we might have been inclined to act just in the same way.

But there are two ways of looking at this matter. The first is practical. Is your attitude the wisest for the future ? We see, of course, that if there is strong feeling in all your local Unions, that of itself might possibly be sufficient reason for declining to come. And we should not wish to ask you to re-open the question, if to do so would be to endanger your own Union. But may we point out that your action greatly endangers the future of the S. African Movement. It will be difficult for it to recover from this awful blow in any case. Will it not be much harder, if far away from the scene of strife, Dutchmen and Englishmen have found it impossible to meet ? Our countries are hostile ; we as Christians are not hostile ; shall we not try and be one of the links that is not broken even by national hostility?

But let us turn to the theoretical side. There are certain things that we must say—without any thought as to whether they will alter your action.

1. Your letter requires us, if we are to welcome you, to make a pronouncement publicly against England. Because you do not expect us to do this (which you consider would be meeting you half-way) you feel that you cannot come.

It is quite true that we can make no such pronouncement. Many of our own members consider the war horrible, but necessary. This may be incredible to you, but you will understand it better if you realize that the impression current in England about the Boers is much the same as that current in Holland about England. You think we are oppressing the Boers. Serious men—many of them Christian men—in England firmly believe (whether right or wrong) that the Transvaal Government is corrupt and that its treatment of Uitlanders is a menace to Cape Colony.

You think we are quite wrong, and it is only natural that you should think so.   But are you sure the Boers had no faults at all ?   At any rate you will understand that we cannot, in our present state of knowledge, declare our country entirely in the wrong.

Could you not suspend judgment ?   Is there *no* possibility that England had some justification for her action ? It would be an act of the greatest heroism, of the truest Christianity, for you to suspend judgment.   Is it too late ? You are not showing your feeling against England alone, but against a small band of men in England who are trying to spread Christ's principles of peace.   It is perhaps the one place where at the present moment England and Holland might join.   Can you not help us, and help the whole of the World's Federation, by an act of Christian self-sacrifice ?

2. It is possible that the feelings of *some* of our countrymen in going into this war have been unworthy.   It is to us a very great grief that this is so.   We desire to replace these spirits of evil by the Spirit of Christ.   Are you not withholding your presence from a body of men, who, whatever some of them think of the present war, hate as much as you could hate the greed of men, and the desire for territory ?   It would make it much easier for us to show this, if you could come, not giving up any of your principles, but consenting for the time being to admit that the men with whom you joined were not actuated by low and cruel impulses.   If you refuse, your mere absence will mean the loss of opportunities of mutual knowledge and understanding.

We fully recognize the greatness of the sacrifice you as friends of the *smaller* country engaged would be making, and that it is much harder for you than it would be for us. Is it too hard ?

But if you feel in the presence of Christ that you cannot come, that you are bound to make your protest, that you cannot suspend judgment, may we ask you *for the future*, as our brothers in Christ, not to visit upon *us* as Christians what you regard as our national crime (and we as our national misfortune).

The future peace between our countries depends upon the mutual knowledge and love of our best men, and therefore upon Movements like this more than upon anything else.   May we beg that at the earliest moment possible you will put aside your natural anger against England sufficiently to resume the old relationship with us ? We write all this for the sake of you and of ourselves, and for the sake of the South African Movement. Only in all things may Christ be glorified.

Your brothers in Christ,

F. Lenwood.
G. H. Moule.

There were two Dutch students present at the conference, but they were not an official delegation from Holland. The South African Student Movement was represented at the conference by a Boer. Later, when we healed our breach with the Dutch Movement at the Versailles conference of the Federation in the middle of 1900, the healing was partly due to the fact that a Boer representative of the African Student Movement had come to England on his way to Versailles and was on terms of close friendship with the British delegates.

The programme arranged for the London Conference expounded the fundamental reasons for missionary work. The first of three outstanding speeches on this topic was the Archbishop's on " Evangelization the Primary Duty of the Church." Dr Temple had no notes. He walked to the front of the platform, leant heavily on his stick, and dealt with the missionary duty of every Christian in pungent terms which none could mistake. Alexander Connell, a delightful Highlander, who was one of the leading ministers in the English Presbyterian Church, dealt with the same subject from a different angle, while the Bishop of Newcastle (Dr Jacob) expounded with sympathy the Watchword of the S.V.M.U.

There was provision in a series of sectional meetings for a comprehensive survey of the actual social conditions in all the non-Christian lands and of the variety of methods being employed in their evangelization. The programme had also much to say about the kind of men and women needed as missionaries and their preparation. The whole programme was a broad and balanced presentation of the missionary enterprise.

The committee was so impressed by the high level of the addresses that it decided to publish a report giving them in full. *Students and the Missionary Problem*, a handsome volume of nearly 600 pages, edited by Lilian Stevenson, ultimately appeared. It was bound in red and known in the Movement for many years afterwards as " the red elephant."

There was more variety in the choice of speakers, and a greater breadth of outlook than ever before at a student conference.

> Speakers of quite opposite ecclesiastical types were at one in declaring that the missionary enterprise is the same for all the Churches, and that in it we must learn from and aid one another. The views presented of heathen life and religion were marked, without exception, by intellectual breadth. It was recognized that, in spite of all the wickedness and darkness of the world, there may be found in all the creatures of God's image some mark of their origin, some spark of goodness, some glimmering of the light of truth. Full justice was done to the value of the great ethnic religions, while it was plainly admitted that they have no sufficient revelation of God, and above all no true message of salvation. A fine sympathy was shown with the converts from heathenism, for whom in many lands the confession of Christ involves the loss of nearly all that men hold dear. It was conceded that we should not be too ready to demand heroism from others, but should rather rejoice that there are over the world many Christians who have not yet openly confessed their faith, but whom Christ will own as His disciples. It was to many a new and welcome thought that the statistical returns of Missions give a very inadequate impression of the immense extent to which the religion of Jesus Christ has influenced the world. The interpretation of the term " evangelization " accepted by the Conference was eminently sound : " Evangelization is the offer to sinful men of Jesus Christ the Saviour King through the lips and lives of redeemed men and women." It was agreed that the Gospel must be seen and felt as well as heard, and that the task of the evangelist, both at home and abroad, is to make Christ a living Reality to the people. [1]

[1] *The Student Movement* ; art. : " Impressions of the London Conference," vol. ii. pp. 112 and 113.

London is not a good centre for a conference. It was agreed afterwards that there were too many distractions, and while the attendance at the meetings was good, a certain number of the delegates tried to crowd a great deal of sight-seeing as well as the conference into their short time in London. The foreign delegates were entertained to luncheon each day of the conference in Exeter Hall, a few of the British delegates being invited to meet them, but most of the members of the conference saw little of one another. The gathering was, however, regarded as a definite success, both by the leaders of the Movement and of the Missionary societies.

CHAPTER XI

THE MOVEMENT DISCUSSES AND ALTERS ITS BASIS

THE story of how the Student Movement came to adopt, amplify and revise its basis is both interesting and instructive, for the basis has been the focusing point of much thought and discussion which has enriched the life of the Student Movement, kept it abreast of the needs of students, and helped to train a considerable number of men and women in the fuller understanding of the fundamentals of the Christian faith, and how to relate them to the thought of the day.

For the first three years of the Movement's life no one took any interest in its basis, chiefly because all were engaged in establishing its position among Christians and not in any serious attempt to win the hostile, indifferent or even doubting, to the Christian faith. But in 1895, when the Movement was pushing on into the university colleges which were the forerunners of the modern universities, the leaders came sharply up against the problem of the considerable number of students whose position was compounded of doubt about and hostility to Christianity, and a basis which should make clear the Movement's religious position became important.

It also became important for specifically doctrinal reasons, as in the same year the travelling secretary, Frank Anderson, reported that in some of these colleges he had been asked whether the Union would admit Unitarians as members.

The basis adopted at the summer conference of 1895 was " A belief in Jesus Christ as God the Son and only Saviour of the world." The basis was chosen to make clear the Movement's belief in " the Incarnation and Atonement of Jesus Christ." The words " God the Son " were deliberately chosen instead of " Son of God."

Unions already in affiliation were not required to adopt the new basis, but were advised to do so. New Unions were required " to print it in their rules." This decision having been reached in 1895, the basis came in for practically no consideration for nearly three years.

The Student Movement had as yet no proper constitution; the leaders had drawn up " objects " (see p. 49). These had been agreed to at the summer conference by the representatives of the Unions present, and the committees elected at the summer conferences administered the Movement as they thought best with due regard to these objects. It was not laid down what use should be made of the basis ; consequently most Unions simply incorporated it in the Constitution of the Christian Union without any indication as to how it was to be used. A few Unions used it as a test of membership. Some of the original Christian Unions did not adopt it at all.

Up to 1898 there was practically no reference on the General Committee to the subject of the basis, but in that year three causes contributed to bring it into the forefront of the General Committee's attention. The first of these was the interest of the theological colleges in the subject, especially the Church of England colleges, and their request as they were asked to join the Union, to know what its basis was and what use was made of it. Second, the fact that it was challenged as a satisfactory basis by several Christian Unions, notably those at Nottingham, Cardiff and the Royal Academy of Art, London. Third, the decision of the S.V.M.U. and B.C.C.U. to reorganize and enter into constitutional relationships.

The Nottingham Christian Union, learning all this, asked what the Union meant by the basis and how far the General Committee expected it to be used as a membership test. The General Committee decided that

o

the Nottingham Christian Union "must assent to the basis of the B.C.C.U., but it need not require each member to hold it as his own position." This was minuted as being "the reaffirmation of the previous decision."

At Easter the following year there was a meeting of the members of the committees of the S.V.M.U., the General College Department and the Theological College Department to "discuss the basis of union of the Movement, and its use in local Christian Unions." Temple Gairdner was in the chair and an outline of his introduction of the subject will show the way in which these basis discussions were tackled from the first.

(I) *History*. What gave rise to the sense of need of a basis in F. Anderson's year of office? The discussion at Keswick, 1895. Sketch of history since 1895. The B.C.C.U. compared with kindred organizations in this matter.

(II) *Scriptural*. The basis of the Early Church as studied in St John's Gospel—St Paul's writings—St John's Epistles —contrast between Old and New Testaments.

(III) *Intention of the Basis*. Primarily inclusive or primarily exclusive?—it may, indeed must, be both ; but one may predominate—which? Query (1) which seemed uppermost in the minds of original promoters—(2) for which has it been most useful?

(IV) *Application of the Basis*. Primarily individual or primarily collective ?—a test or a goal ? This is the point of practical importance—can only be solved by mastering II—analogy of Christ's method with men and that of the Christian Church.

(V) *Possible Solutions*. What is chiefly necessary for us to do in this matter at this time?

We need not follow Gairdner through his long elaboration of this syllabus, but there are points which are still of interest. In reply to the question whether in the minds of the original promoters the basis was intended to be inclusive or exclusive, he said that there was no doubt they adopted it with a view to the exclusion of error, but added that since that time the basis had been looked upon as a bond of union and that this should be its chief use. Individual Christian Unions were affiliated if their constitution included the basis of the Movement.

"What does this really mean for the Union affiliating?" he asked. "It may mean one of three things. Either that all do agree, that all must agree, or that the majority hold it and that it was awkward for a man to become a leader if he did not hold to the basis." He then went on to indicate what in his view were the alternatives:

> Either we regard the work of the Union as being the work of the earthly Christ, viz., taking up and encouraging any who may have any leaning whatsoever towards Him, or the Union may take the attitude of most Churches, who only admit into full membership on a declaration of some definite belief or beliefs. Or again, either we must treat a student who wishes to join as a child is treated to-day in the Christian Church, or treat them as grown men in the mission field, where they are not admitted until they have reached a certain stage of faith. Or yet again, either we emphasize the value of turning to Christ as a Person, or we emphasize the mystery as a starting-point of the new life. In the latter case we do not necessarily pronounce about the salvation of those who have not got to this position.

Gairdner summed up his argument by saying that there seemed to be two possible lines of action:

> To admit Unions to membership of the B.C.C.U. who allow students who cannot accept the basis to join, but whose leaders hold to the basis; or to admit to membership only those Unions which require all their members to give their full assent to the basis.

He thought that both lines of action had their dangers. "The first tended to feebleness and the second tended to harshness and exclusiveness."

The record of the debate shows that the leaders in the discussion were Frank Lenwood, A. G. Fraser, W. E. S. Holland, T. Tatlow and Beatrice Glass.

Some of those taking part were emphatic that the basis had not originally been intended as an individual test, pointing out that Donald Fraser, who had taken a very prominent part in the discussion when the basis was chosen, "had objected very strongly to individual tests." After a long discussion the minutes continue :

Mr Tatlow thought that the points at issue were being mixed. He asked the Executive to hear him while he stated the way in which he considered the basis should be used. He thought that on a student wishing to become a member of a local Union the secretary should hand him a copy of the constitution in which the basis was distinctly set forth, and that the said secretary should ask him if he gave such assent to these rules as to feel that he could join a Union whose rules and basis were such as he saw set out on the aforesaid card. Mr Tatlow pointed out that the student would by joining demonstrate that he did not consider the basis wholly unsatisfactory while, at the same time, he was free to retain his own private interpretation of such a basis. The Executive expressed their approval of this method of applying the basis.

The point of view set forth was prophetic, for the use of the basis then indicated as desirable was virtually that which after many experiments the Movement came to adopt, but this was not to happen for many years. The committee on this occasion passed the two following resolutions :

Resolved : I. That the act of joining a college Christian Union be taken as expressing assent to the basis of the B.C.C.U. II. That the interpretation of the basis be left to the judgment and conscience of the individual.

The departure from the policy at first suggested was in the use of the word " assent," in the first of these resolutions. The word was ambiguous and ultimately came to be used as a synonym for " belief." There were members of the committee who foresaw that this might happen and that the basis would then be used as a test of individual membership. They tried to modify the test by moving that the word " general " be inserted before " assent " ; the amendment was, however, lost.

This meeting, which contained conservative and progressive elements, as has always been the case when the basis has been discussed, was one of great interest ; however keen the discussion became there was never any trace of irritation or ill-feeling, or anything to break the unity of the Spirit. That there had been some nervousness beforehand is indicated by the closing words of the minutes of the meeting, which read :

> The meeting was closed with thankfulness to God for the spirit of unity that had prevailed and the grace that had enabled the different members of Executive to see each other's position.

This is perhaps the best place to record the fact that although there have been many basis discussions during the thirty-four years that have intervened since this minute was written and the present, there has never at any time been any breach in the spiritual unity of the Movement's leadership. Differences of opinion have sometimes been very strong, indeed so much so that it has been necessary to adjourn committees without any decision being taken in order that some reconciliation might be found between the different points of view prevailing. Sometimes this periodic discussion and adjournment has continued for several years, the leaders all sharing the conviction that the Spirit of God would lead them to the truth, and that they must continue to take time for further thought and prayer to fit themselves for the reception of that truth. All recognized that the limitation was not in God but in us, and that if we faithfully persevered in seeking the mind of the Spirit, we should learn what road to take, and should find that the diversity of points of view would lead in the end to something richer than would be the case if the views of one group triumphed over those of another.

Again and again a decision could have been reached if a vote had been taken, sometimes the minority has been numerically a very small one, but that is not the way things have been done amongst us. Minorities have always known that they need not be nervous or irritable because they would not be silenced by being out-voted. We have been a body of men and women aware of our limitations, deeply anxious to do the right thing, believing in one another and trusting one another's good faith, and above all believing that God was with the Movement. The only possible course, therefore, has seemed to be to take time to thrash out such big questions as that of the basis until we were united as regards the course we should take.

The result of this has been an absence of anything like contending parties on the General Committee of the Movement : and as a method it has produced such a spirit of fellowship and goodwill that it has unquestionably brought out the best in men. In such an atmosphere men and women could not be merely argumentative; each one in his own heart has had to ask himself again and again whether the position for which he stood was being held to because he believed it was true, or for some other less worthy motive.

Let it not be thought that people's attitude was one of indifference to truth ; on the contrary opinions were expressed with directness and pungency, and it often took a long time to find our way to a decision. Again and again we found that the decision made was one which neither group had foreseen in advance, but which was arrived at by all parties contributing in such a way that a new and unexpected position was reached which was a higher synthesis of all the elements of truth held by the various groups in the meeting. Again and again these discussions drove the committee to corporate prayer, and often it was after a period of silence and prayer that the proposal which was to unite us was made.

I have chosen to say this here, although this method has not been applied only to basis discussions. In all the years I have been in the Movement I have never known a vote taken if anyone thought the matter being

dealt with too important to decide by vote. If everyone thinks a decision on the topic before us should be
reached and they are ready to let the majority decide,
we vote. On matters of formal business we vote.
But if there is any group, however small, or even one
man or woman, who thinks the subject under discussion
too important to be dealt with by a vote, no vote is
taken. I have never known anyone silenced against
their conviction by a vote on the controlling committees of the Movement.

In May 1899 Mr Mott came to England, and hearing
of the discussion about the basis expressed a wish to
meet the committee to discuss with the members their
policy, in view of its bearing upon the Federation.
The minute which deals with the interview describes
Mr Mott's address prior to the discussion. It begins
very characteristically.

> Mr Mott said that the world had now grown very small,
> and that more and more it was observed that what was
> done in one part of the world affected another part more
> than had ever been the case before in the world's history.

Mr Mott has an unrivalled gift of making the obvious
sound really impressive. I do not say this cynically, it
is a really valuable gift. He was strongly in favour of
a personal basis. He said that when the Federation
was founded at Wadstena this was in the minds of the
founders of the Movement, although it was not made
explicit at the time. As secretary of the Federation,
with this understanding, he had pressed for a personal
basis in the six countries the Movements in which he
had had a share in founding. He explained that by a
personal basis was meant that control or voting power
in the Christian Unions should be in the hands of
students who themselves accept Jesus Christ as their
personal Saviour and Lord, that is to say, " Those
who themselves believe in the deity of Christ and have
acted upon that belief in accepting Christ as Saviour
and Lord." He developed with great clearness and

forcefulness his reasons for thinking a personal basis desirable, and stressed what he regarded as the special responsibility of the British and American Student Movement, concluding : " We have providentially been given organizing ability, a vision of the possibilities of the world-wide Movement, courage, aggressiveness and spiritual resources, in a greater degree than most other races."

The result of Mr Mott's speech was that the Committee passed two resolutions modifying those previously accepted.   They are as follows :

Resolved that in the opinion of this meeting the affiliation of a College Christian Union to the B.C.C.U. should be taken as indicating on the part of each of the members of that Union, a belief in Jesus Christ as God the Son and as his only Saviour.

Resolved that in the opinion of this meeting College Christian Unions not now affiliated to the B.C.C.U. should be required to adopt the following membership article, or its equivalent, in order to become affiliated : " members of the Christian Union of . . . College, are those who by joining the Union acknowledge their belief in Jesus Christ as God the Son and their only Saviour, and express their desire to promote the objects of the Union."

The meeting at which these resolutions were accepted, not being a regular meeting of the Executive, the matter came up again for discussion the following September, when the members of the committees of all the departments were summoned to meet at Farnley House, Eton Avenue, Hampstead, the home of Mrs Armitage, a very good friend of the Movement.   At this meeting there was more discussion of the real difficulties than at the meeting with Mr Mott.

The position was this ; the Movement had been founded by men who believed whole-heartedly in the doctrine of the Incarnation as held by the Church Catholic.   All were convinced that this was the rock upon which the Student Movement was founded, and no one desired to substitute another foundation.   The difficulty with which the leaders were faced lay in the fact that there were a number of students in every college who had only begun to think during college days about this and other Christian doctrines. Most of those who came into the Christian Unions had had a genuine spiritual experience, but had had little opportunity of thinking out its intellectual implications. Some, as a result of their temperament, had no difficulty in accepting on authority the orthodox theology. But others, and many of them the finer and richer personalities, were feeling their way and seeking to make their own the theology presented to them ; such found great difficulty in accepting a personal basis so early in their experience. It was not that they disbelieved, but that they were not yet ready to make the tremendous positive statement demanded by the basis.

What was to be done with these students ? One proposal was that they should be invited to become associate members, but although this was discussed at the time and more than once in later years, the students always came to the same decision : " We do not want to seem to divide people, all of whom want to follow Christ, into sheep and goats ; besides, if we did, many people who would have to join the goats would be among the best people in College." If these people, some of whom were the most active Christians in College, were debarred from being members because their intellectual position had not been thought out by them, some fine characters, without the help of whom the Christian Union would not be able to do as much in College as it otherwise could, would be lost to it; while others whose spiritual experience, though genuine, tended to be eclipsed by their difficulties, would feel rebuffed, and would turn away from the help the Movement might bring them.

All these things received consideration in the discussion, but the tendencies of the period and of the school of thought in which most of the leaders had been brought up, reinforced by the impression made

by Mr Mott, led them to be more concerned with safeguards than with the needs of a large class of students.
Frank Lenwood was the chief advocate of the need of
making allowance " for men who might be feeling
after a full belief in Christ." But having voiced the
need of a class of students which was to become more
insistent as the years passed, he turned to a criticism of
the actual words of the basis proposed by the resolution, and the discussion took on a new phase. That
phase was really an attempt at compromise. The
nature of the compromise was to make subscription to
the basis a matter of personal religion rather than
theological subscription. The meeting ultimately passed
a resolution that the basis should be in the following
words : " That the B.C.C.U. affiliates those Christian
Unions in British Universities and Colleges whose
members, by the act of joining, declare their belief in
Jesus Christ as personal Saviour and God." The
travelling secretaries were instructed to bring this
basis to the attention of the Christian Unions, with a
view to interesting them in it, having it discussed and
securing their approval of it.

Some members of the committee, however, on
further reflection became dissatisfied with the proposed
basis, and the matter was re-discussed by a small committee which had been engaged in drafting the Movement's Constitution. As a result this sub-committee
inserted in their suggested Constitution a Basis clause
as follows :—

> The basis of the Union shall be—" a belief in Jesus Christ
> as God the Son and personal Saviour." Those joining
> any affiliated Christian Union, or signing the S.V.M.U.
> declaration shall be understood in so doing to accept this
> basis.

The Committee were not able to meet again until
the opening of the summer conference at Matlock in
July 1900. Here once more they re-discussed the
question as to whether the Union should insist on a

personal application of the basis or not, and decided that it should. Once again the wording of the basis was reconsidered, but was not altered. This tendency to reopen the whole question after definite decisions, caused the committee to recognize that they had probably not yet found the best line of policy, and that in any case if the basis had caused them so much thought and discussion the colleges would not be likely to want to reach a decision without adequate time for reflection and discussion. They, therefore, decided to ask the Business Meeting to pass the Constitution with the exception of the clause containing the basis. They were asked to discuss this clause, but to agree not to vote upon it for a year.

Frank Lenwood, as chairman of the Business Meeting, presented the question of the basis to the Conference.

> " Some," he said, " were at first inclined to maintain that the ideal form of Christian Union was one where, although the prevailing tone was one of unmistakable confession of Jesus Christ, there might yet be room for what I may call a ' nursery ' for those who had not come so far as that. But as we thought it over and discussed it with prayer, even those who had held this position became convinced that all the voting members of a Christian Union should be confessing Christians, and that the basis, if real, must mean not a mere vote of a majority of the whole Union, but the actual personal confession of every one of the members."

He then explained that they felt that the first basis had been unnecessarily theological, and that they proposed as being less so the words, " a belief in Jesus Christ as personal Saviour and God." The Committee thought that by these words they would avoid " the appearance of a full theological statement." He invited the meeting to discuss separately the two points : (1) the personal application of the basis, and (2) the wording of the basis.

I quote further from his speech because he was not speaking for himself but presenting, and doing it very well, the position of the General Committee for which he was the spokesman.

We frankly admit the argument that in some cases personal application of the basis may occasion hardship, since there are men who know Jesus Christ and yet find confession a peculiarly difficult thing. But we believe that such hardships, even where they are genuine, are outweighed by the great advantage of a personal basis. For (a) *the basis means nothing unless it is personal*. If the basis be a thing accepted by a mere vote of the general Union, what majority will satisfy our requirements? Will it be a two-thirds majority or a bare majority, or any proportion, which will secure that the Union maintains its purpose? There can be no half-way house between acceptance of this basis on the part of every member and no basis at all. What can be the meaning of a basis accepted for the Union if each of the members will not accept it for himself? (b) *The practical value of the basis to a Christian Union* is very great. Everyone admits that there must be some provision calculated to keep the Union from drifting away from its original purpose, the service of Jesus Christ, and everyone will agree that it would be an unfortunate thing if the majority of members were to be those unwilling to accept the basis for themselves. But we would go on to point out that a minority, or a single man, if a good worker and an energetic thinker, may exercise an influence which would wreck the working of the whole Christian Union, and might seriously affect the movement in Great Britain.

Have we moreover recognized sufficiently the influence of uncertainty on the main points of our faith in checking the whole work of a Union? On the central Executive we differ on many points, but we all unite in one thing, and upon that unity we can always reckon. If a single man of that body of 15 or 16 were out of sympathy with this one aim, he would reduce the spiritual force of our Executive by something, if fractions may express it, nearer to two-thirds than one-fifteenth, and if we are to go forward for the objects of this Union we must have the members of the Union united on this point.

People say, "Oh, but the Union is not a Church," without seeing that they give us one of our strongest arguments. The difference which concerns us at present between a Union and a Church lies in the fact that the student body is constantly changing. The way in which student organizations alter from generation to generation is notorious ; and if a Church needs a certain definite standard of membership, as most Churches have felt they do, surely a union of men here to-day and gone to-morrow needs it far more !

And (c) I should like to insist on the *danger of too hasty admission to the man who is admitted*. While it is possible that you may cause hardship to a man by requiring a basis, quite as often you may do considerable harm to him by admitting him without any such profession. For you may give him the impression that there is nothing more in the way of knowledge of Jesus Christ to which he need attain, and you deprive him of just that stimulus to honest enquiry which the basis supplies.[1]

The form of basis proposed Lenwood sought to expound as not being theological, at any rate not too theological. It was a clever but not very convincing explanation, but that was not his fault.

There were three points of view expressed in the discussion which followed, that of those who objected to any personal declaration of faith as a test of membership ; those who thought that the wording of the basis clause as proposed by the committee was not satisfactory but who were in favour of such a clause involving a test ; and those who were satisfied with the clause presented by the executive. While there were differences of opinion the meeting was of a harmonious character and did not justify the fear of one member of committee that if the basis was discussed, " the scenes of the Council of Nicea would be repeated."

This meeting accepted the new Constitution apart from the basis clause, with the exception of an article making secretaries of the Movement full voting members of the committee. This was referred back for reconsideration by the Executive, which declared later its opinion that this clause should stand, and subsequent history has surely borne out the wisdom of this decision. There has never been any cleavage between student

[1] *The Basis of Membership of the British College Christian Union*, pp. 5-7.

committee members and secretaries, and a visitor to any meeting of the committee would find it difficult to detect who were secretaries and who were not. The only limitation that has ever been put upon secretaries was one imposed some years later by a Standing Order, which debars secretaries from voting on any question relating to the status or payment of a secretary.

During the winter there was a certain amount of discussion in the Christian Unions on the subject of the basis, the General Committee also continued its discussion, which revealed some uneasiness as to whether the best words had been chosen, and whether or not the basis should be used as a test of membership. Those uneasy on this point were quieted by the promise that Christian Unions already in the Movement would not be forced to adopt a personal basis unless they wished to do so. It was intimated that more than one Scottish Christian Union would probably not adopt a personal basis if one was decided upon by the Movement.

The adjourned discussion was resumed next year at the business meeting on July 26th, 1901, at Matlock. Henry Hodgkin submitted the basis as proposed the previous year on behalf of the Executive, namely : " The basis of the Union shall be a belief in Jesus Christ as personal Saviour and God. Those joining any affiliated Union or signing the Declaration of the Student Volunteer Missionary Union declare in so doing their personal acceptance of this basis."

Hodgkin took much the same line as Lenwood the previous year in introducing the basis, and commended the wording as, inclusive and brief, simple and untheological, expressive of what the relation between a soul and Jesus Christ should be.

It was decided to take first the question whether the Union should have a personal basis or not, and the discussion showed that the students were far more interested in this point than in the wording of the basis. It was again urged against a personal basis :

(1) That students seeking for truth would be repelled if asked to accept a personal basis, nor would they care to keep in touch with the Union unless they could become full members ; (2) that many students come up to college as Christians, but know little of the intellectual side of Christianity, and would probably hesitate to accept the basis. (3) That it is a definition of Christianity, and that the Union should not attempt such a definition.[1]

All the objections to a personal basis were variations of the main objection that " a personal basis will exclude from membership students who were just the very persons the Union wishes to help." In favour of the personal basis it was contended that a basis means nothing unless it is accepted by each voting member ; that without a basis there would be no guarantee that the Union would remain true to what all regarded as central ; that those who join the Union should be brought face to face at once with its central conviction. Four colleges stated that they had already adopted a personal basis and found it a help, these were Yorkshire College, Leeds (men), University College, Liverpool (women), Somerville College, Oxford, and St Thomas's Hospital, London.

The conference, before taking a vote on whether there should be a personal basis, turned to discuss the wording of the basis. The student members hitherto vocal took very little part, but several senior friends were eager to speak and were allowed to do so. There was considerable criticism of the wording proposed, " a belief in Jesus Christ as personal Saviour and God." The word " personal " was distasteful to a number who thought that it had become rather a shibboleth in some quarters, others thought the wording " crude and man made." The Rev. J. O. F. Murray, Dean of Emmanuel College, Cambridge, who was present as a representative of the Federation of the Junior Clergy Missionary Association of the S.P.G., made a deep impression by his suggestion that a " happier form of words would

[1] *The Student Movement*, vol. iv. p. 6.

be ' I desire in joining this Christian Union to express my faith in Jesus Christ as my Saviour, my Lord, and my God, and my determination, by the grace of God, to make His Will in all things the law of my life.' " It was decided to adjourn the meeting for three days and then have a final discussion and take a vote. During the interval the General Committee held several meetings at which the question of the wording was reconsidered. It was evident both in camp and among the women students that Mr Murray's suggestion had made a favourable impression.

On July 29th the conference re-assembled in business session and I was put forward as the spokesman of the General Committee to move, with the permission of the conference, an amendment to its original proposal. The amendment was a modification of Mr Murray's proposal and read as follows :

> *Basis of Membership.* I desire in joining this Union to declare my faith in Jesus Christ as my Saviour, my Lord, and my God. Any student in becoming a voting member of an affiliated Union, or signing the declaration of the Student Volunteer Missionary Union shall be understood thereby to express his acceptance of the above.

It was pointed out that the belief of the committee that the wording previously proposed was the best was shaken because :

> (1) While none of the students now in college spoke either for or against the actual wording of the basis, the older and more experienced persons present were opposed to it ;
> (2) several had expressed the opinion that the word " personal," as used in this connection, had become associated with a particular school of thought ;
> (3) the Executive felt the full force of the criticism that the wording they had proposed was crude.

Further discussion showed that the new wording was much more popular with the conference than the original proposal.

Before the final vote was taken, by the desire of the Executive, I moved a preliminary resolution :

That this conference considered it desirable that the B.C.C.U. shall have a personal basis.

The vote was taken by ballot, the result being as follows :

In favour of a personal basis 226 ; against 14 ; neutral 2. The amendment was then put to the meeting and accepted by a show of hands, and a final vote was taken as to whether the article of membership as amended should be included in the constitution of the Union. The vote was taken by ballot, the result being as follows : In favour 225 ; against 6 ; neutral 8.

The whole discussion was on a high level. There are many who think that the Student Movement is always seen at its best when discussing a big question like its basis. I fully endorse this opinion, which holds good both as regards meetings of the General Committee and of the Movement in its business meetings. The majority of the Christian Unions throughout the country adopted the new basis at once.

The General Committee took occasion to propose the addition to the Constitution of a clause defining the object of the Union in the following words :

(2) *Object.* The object of the Union shall be to lead the students of British universities and colleges to become disciples of Jesus Christ ; to unite them in seeking a fuller spiritual life ; and to enlist them in the work of extending Christ's Kingdom throughout the whole world.

It also proposed that the clause in the Constitution which stated that the Union should have three departments should be amplified by defining the objects of each of these departments. Accordingly for the existing clause, simply naming the departments, the following was substituted :

IV. *Departments.* The Union shall have the following departments :

1. The Student Volunteer Missionary Union, the object of which shall be to unite those students whose purpose it

P

is, if God permit, to become foreign missionaries ; to bring before all students the claims of the foreign mission field as a life work ; and to emphasize the responsibility of the whole Church of Christ with regard to the Watchword, " The Evangelization of the world in this generation."

2. The General College Department, the object of which shall be to organize affiliated Christian Unions in universities and colleges (other than Theological Colleges), and to aid such Unions in the promotion of Christian life and effort among students.

3. The Theological College Department, the object of which shall be the same as those of the two previous departments in so far as they are applicable to theological colleges.

This Constitution worked very well. There was nothing controversial about it except the basis and its personal application, and here no immediate problem arose, since Christian Unions which liked the change, and they were the majority, adopted the new basis, while those which did not availed themselves of their right not to make the change. The Union settled down to what proved to be twelve years' work under the Constitution it had adopted.

CHAPTER XII

FOUR YEARS OF CONSOLIDATION, 1900-1904

THE excitement of founding, and to some extent establishing the Student Christian Movement was over. A summer conference was no longer a novelty, and even a big Student Volunteer Missionary Union conference was no new thing, two having now been held, and as a result the Movement, and very specially the committee, settled down to the task of consolidating the organization as a united Movement and to the business of extending its operations throughout the entire student field.

The effect of entering upon a quiet period, which seems to have been inevitable as one looks back, was very marked upon the leaders, and their Reports presented at the summer conferences tended to be in a minor key. They spoke of " a distinct want of *esprit de corps* " in the Christian Unions and also about " general apathy." It is doubtful, however, whether they were right in their diagnosis. Each year a new committee came into office with new secretaries, and had little means of comparing its position and work with that of its predecessors. The new leaders found a certain number of Christian Unions at work but had no knowledge of their past history, and if they were not effective it was not surprising that they should say so in their Report, and often imply, as student committees invariably do, that there was a Golden Age behind them which they no longer enjoyed. To the historian it is clear that the Movement was beginning to enter upon its real work, the task of establishing itself in all the universities and colleges of the country, especially in the university colleges which were the forerunners of the modern universities, and also of creating a spirit which should be its own.   A word should be said about each of these things.

In the year 1900 the Movement was controlled by four committees inter-related by Constitution, and it had a staff of six secretaries. Among all the members of these there was not one who had been educated at a modern university or university college. All the members of committee and secretaries came from Oxford, Cambridge, one of the Scottish or Irish universities, or from a London Hospital. The Movement, however, had 97 affiliated Christian Unions, which means that the majority of Christian Unions were in colleges unrepresented on the committees. They were all newly formed and much more difficult to make effective than Unions in the older universities. It was not surprising that the committee members and secretaries kept their attention upon them rather than upon the Unions from which they themselves came. Most of these Unions had been recently founded, they were beginning their work, and the man from the residential college was learning for the first time what is now so well understood in Student Movement circles, namely, the real difficulty of carrying on a Christian Union in a non-residential college.

The committee members knew practically nothing about life in non-residential colleges, and hearing reports from travelling secretaries, they not unnaturally compared what they heard with what they knew of the Christian Union each in his own university, and in consequence were very downhearted about the smallness and the weakness of the majority of Christian Unions in the Movement. They would have probably been no less conscious of the difficulties but been a good deal less depressed if they had known more about modern university college life and had been aware that many of the difficulties and failures were not peculiar to the Christian Union, but were shared by all college societies. In many places, even though the Christian

Union might appear to the visitor a somewhat small and struggling organization, yet it was often much stronger and more effective than the Debating Society or some of the other student organizations. The Movement was really setting itself to one of its great tasks, that of building effective Christian Unions in non-residential universities and colleges founded on a secular basis.

Further, the Movement was also facing the task of generating an atmosphere and an outlook of its own. The Christian Unions which sprang up in places like Cambridge and Edinburgh prior to the organization of the Movement, were the outcome of the Evangelical Revival of the eighteenth and nineteenth centuries ; and while they manifested new features, and were in a very real sense part of a new movement, yet the theology on which they lived was the theology of a day which had passed. The Student Movement had to shake itself free of the theory of the verbal inspiration of the Bible and of somewhat distinctive eschatological views, and to acquire an open-minded love for truth and an absence of fearfulness, if it was to be ready to meet the questionings of the modern mind and to offer something more than spiritual devoutness to the student body. The majority of students were exposed to every kind of influence running counter to the Christian faith, while only a small proportion of them had been brought up in a definitely Christian atmosphere. It is easy in looking back to recognize in what was happening the providential overruling of God.

The real difficulty that faced the Executive, although it was slow to realize it, lay in the fact that the background of the major portion of its constituency was different from its own. The majority of students, at any rate of those who came under the influence of the Movement in the older universities, were untouched by intellectual difficulties. Most of them had received a Christian training and the difficulties they had to face were spiritual and moral rather than intellectual.[1]   In the new universities and university colleges intellectual difficulties bulked large.   A letter appeared in the pages of *The Student Movement* of February 1901, from the pen of Stephen Band of Liverpool University College, in which he put his finger upon the weak spot in the life of the Movement.   He called attention to the fact that while it frequently deplored prayerlessness, neglect of Bible Study, and an imperfect sense of responsibility for the spiritual welfare of fellow-students, it was not concerned about things that profoundly affected the outsider, and lacked sympathy with the intellectual difficulties of students.   He spoke of it as an anomaly that men of undoubted sincerity who were materialistic in their outlook, should pass through a university possessing a " strong Christian Union " and yet not find a single Christian Union member with sufficient sympathy or knowledge to appreciate their difficulties, and to put the Christian position to them from an intellectual standpoint.   " It is of little use to hurl texts at the heads of such men, or to ask them where they will go to should they die within the next few hours.   Cannot such men be met on their own ground and shown the inadequacy of their theory of the universe in a sympathetic and competent manner ? "

Band went on to speak of common methods of personal work and asked for zeal mixed with discretion, declaring " we are exhorted to hold forth the lamp of truth, not to push it rudely into everyone's face."

This letter drew a response from other students, and a demand for the help of those " who could combine keen evangelical fervour with intellectual depth, and who would be able and willing to state the Christian position from an intellectual standpoint."   It took some time for the leaders of the Movement to adjust themselves to these demands and to find senior men who

[1] This statement applies to the men only, intellectual questioning about Christianity was rife among women students at the Oxford and Cambridge Colleges.

were able to help at conferences and in general meetings. I tried to get Apologetics given a place at the summer conference but the General Committee was not ready to take this step. The objection of the Committee was not that they did not approve of an intellectual pre- sentation of Christianity; many of them were able men who had no reason to be ashamed of their scholar- ship; but they were trained in a different school of thought, valued the spiritual intensity of the summer conferences very highly, and were afraid that this might be lost if a distinctively intellectual element were introduced.

All this kind of thing had to be learnt by the leaders, and worked into the life of the Movement before marked advance could be achieved in that major portion of the field where this kind of work, owing to the circum- stances, was of vital necessity. But the leaders were ready to learn and to act. They nominated Stephen Band of University College, Liverpool, a member of the committee, and he was the first student from a non-residential English University college elected to it. Later he became a travelling secretary.

Though somewhat depressed, the leaders settled down with great faith, courage, and perseverance to their task. As the committee said in its *Annual Report*, 1899-1900: "The Aberystwyth Conference gave a fuller place to thought in the Christian life, and the London Conference did the same for foreign work." Both these conferences lengthened the ropes and the Committee was busy pretty well all the time strengthen- ing the stakes. They pegged away at improving the Bible Study work of the Movement, and issued a number of excellent text-books written by Student Movement secretaries. Some of these are still a model for the text-books of to-day. They sought to improve the general meetings in the Christian Unions, and were insistent upon the importance of personal religion, and in this connection declared that "the daily prayer- meeting is the touch-stone of the life of a Christian

Union." They were hampered by financial difficulties through all these difficult years, and there are constant references to the anxiety caused by their straitened resources.

In 1901 the discussion at the summer conference at Matlock, during three sessions, of the basis of membership, a topic already dealt with, proved a real help in that it was the first time men and women from the new university colleges had been given an opportunity of discussing a big subject, which they knew to be a thoroughly live one in the colleges from which they came. The discussions were on a high spiritual level and the general result was to draw people together, to teach them to express themselves and make them feel that they were part of a living Movement. By 1903 signs of faithful work since the Aberystwyth Conference of 1899 were showing results. A considerable number of non-members had begun to attend the Bible circles, and as a result these had in some places become a means of leading students into the Christian life. The attendance at summer conferences was increasing and so was the total membership of the Movement.

Another factor which brought encouragement to the Movement was the improved position of the Student Volunteer Missionary Union. The Union had passed through very difficult years from about 1897, owing to a steady decrease in the number of students joining it. This decrease lasted for several years. We find the Executive reporting to its constituency, July 1900, that " the primary work of the Union seems to be almost at a standstill, for the Union exists to lead students to give their lives to the work of Christ abroad, and the number of those signing the declaration has been steadily decreasing, as has been pointed out in previous reports."

The following year they reported, "Whatever the cause may be, the fact remains that we have again to report a further falling off in the number of those joining the Union"; while the travelling secretary,

Tom Jays, wrote that " in the majority of colleges there is a decided lack of definiteness among those considering the claims of the foreign field."

No doubt the main cause of the decrease was the decline of the evangelical movement, which had probably reached the highest point of its last phase with the work of Mr D. L. Moody in London and Cambridge, and the steady growth of that intellectual questioning which was to become widespread in later years.

Early in 1902 the committee decided to send a letter to all Student Volunteers still at home, "laying upon them the need of a deeper consecration of life to their great missionary purpose, especially with a view to their helping while still at home to lay upon their fellow-students the supreme claims of the mission field upon their life and service." This letter, together with the prayer and faith which was behind it, produced some effect in the colleges.

Another helpful factor was the resolute tackling of missionary study work in the Christian Unions. The missionary study movement, initiated by Douglas Thornton, was beginning to wane, partly because it was not being pushed with anything like his vigour, and partly because the novelty was beginning to wear off. The Executive were depressed about it, and I well remember one meeting when it was almost decided to give up this method of work. Much of the morning had been spent discussing the situation regarding missionary study. Some were doubtful if it could be established in the new colleges, and I had been advocating the importance of trying hard to make a success of it.

The discussion was adjourned for luncheon, and I went upstairs to the general office in Warwick Lane to transact some piece of business in connection with my work as general secretary, which post I was about to relinquish to enable me to return to Dublin University for a post-graduate course in theology. Hugh Weir followed me upstairs and said, " If you don't rescue the educational scheme [1] by taking it on yourself it will die." It had not occurred to me that I might find time to do any work for the Movement while studying theology, but I told Weir that I would do anything I could to save missionary study. After lunch he proposed that I should be Educational Secretary—that was the title then given to the missionary study officer of the Movement—and I subsequently agreed to take charge of this department, which I did for two years while I was a graduate student of divinity at Trinity College, Dublin, for a third year while in a curacy in West London, and for a few years after I had returned to the general secretaryship.

It seemed clear that a new method must be introduced ; students had drifted into a slipshod use of the study text-book and simply reproduced its chapters at the meetings. I produced *Outline Studies*, showing how to use both the text-book and a selection of additional books to prepare three or four brief papers for a meeting. I also interviewed the full delegation from each Christian Union at the following summer conference about missionary study, interesting them in the subject chosen— it was Japan the first year—discussing how to recruit a band, conduct it and secure the use of books for reference. Stress was laid on extra reading and the importance of real study. This interviewing proved a big job, but one or two willing helpers were found, a special tent provided, and every afternoon a succession of interviews, each of half an hour's duration, were arranged with all the colleges. The result was that twenty-eight colleges started missionary study bands for the first time the following winter. Missionary study was not only saved but rapid progress was made, the number of students in study circles being doubled in about a year, and, most important of all, missionary study again made popular. The committee's Annual Report at the end of the year said, " Missionary study work has been taken up by a

[1] Missionary study was referred to for years as " the educational scheme."

larger number of colleges than in any previous year, and has been almost everywhere satisfactory."

This considerable expansion in missionary study was without doubt one of the causes which led to a definite increase in the number of Student Volunteers. Another factor was the careful attention given to the presentation of missionary interests at the summer conferences, with the result that the Matlock Conference of 1902 was more missionary than those of the previous three years. A year later the S.V.M.U. Committee was able to say, " 181 students have joined the Union during the year, which is a larger number than for some years past." The previous year the number had been 130, while a year before the number joining had only been 92 students.

In the spring of 1901 Miss Cable, a Student Volunteer who had been appointed to missionary service in China, but was delayed from sailing by war, asked that nurses should be admitted to the S.V.M.U. After some months' consideration, it was decided that nurses were not properly within the sphere of a student organization, but that the proposal to form some kind of missionary organization amongst them was one that should be encouraged. Edith Overton was appointed as representative of the S.V.M.U. on a small committee led by Miss Fairfield which was formed to create the Nurses' Missionary League. Later the link of representation was severed to economize the time of S.V.M.U. secretaries who were appointed whenever representatives were wanted, students being too busy to attend committee meetings. Those who founded the League and took the lead in establishing it were all members of the Movement —prominent among these being Miss Jean Macfee, who was an art student at Bedford College, London. The Nurses' Missionary League has gone steadily forward from the day of its foundation, and is now a valuable auxiliary to the medical work of the missionary societies.

During this period immense emphasis was laid on the importance of Bible study, and a very large proportion of the time of the Committee of the General

College Department was devoted to surveying the Bible study work in the colleges, considering how it could be improved, discussing methods of Bible study, different types of text-books and possible authors. Indeed, it was during this period that the foundations of the Bible study department were laid, and there has not been any very marked departure either from the type of Bible study text-book that was then produced or from the methods that were then worked out. Bible schools and the systematic training of leaders in Bible circles came later. There is hardly any other aspect of Bible study work which did not originate during this period.

It was at this time that the Movement gave consideration to the relation of the Bible and its authority to modern Biblical scholarship. For a number of years the views of those who had been trained in the verbal inspiration school of thought, and in the school of thought which is the outcome of modern Biblical scholarship, existed side by side. Then the modern view gained ground, and the day rapidly approached when the Movement would take its stand definitely and clearly for the modern view of the Bible. The Movement at this time was being criticized vigorously in some quarters for its sympathy with the progressive point of view. *Studies in Isaiah*, by Frank Lenwood, published by it, was reviewed in a hostile spirit in one of the missionary magazines by a senior friend who had been an early friend of the Student Volunteer Missionary Union and a member of the Senior Advisory Committee. He expressed deep regret that the Union should publish " this sort of book." The book was a devotional study of the first Isaiah with hardly any critical references in it. It was the recognition of two writers in the Book of Isaiah which aroused his deep disapproval.

In June 1901 I visited the United States of America at the invitation of Mr Mott, in order to represent the Movement at the Jubilee of the Y.M.C.A. in North America, and to speak at the Lake Geneva (Wisconsin) and Northfield (Mass.) Student conferences. I returned to find that there was a special sub-committee sitting on policy, and the minutes of that summer record, " that they had met after Mr Tatlow returned from America and that he had brought home a number of new and valuable ideas."

I was much impressed by a Leaders' Training Conference which I attended in the United States and felt sure that we ought to give more help to Christian Union officers, and I urged the starting of an Officers' Conference. But although the committee was convinced that this was one of " the new and valuable ideas " I had brought home, they could not be persuaded to start the Officers' Conference in 1902. The Minute-book shows that I continued to press vigorously the desirability of following the American example, and in 1903 the Officers' Conference was first held, under the title "Presidents' and Secretaries' Conference," only these officers being at first admitted to it.

Another outcome of this visit to America was the more vigorous promotion of evangelistic work. The American colleges were active in this direction, but while the leaders in Great Britain gave much time to discussion and prayer about a spiritual awakening in our own student field, they were not doing much to prepare for it. Most of the Christian Unions were pitifully small; they consisted for the most part of men who came from Christian homes who did not expect to influence their college. The prevailing attitude regarded college as a spiritual wilderness and the Christian Unions as spiritual oases existing for the benefit of convinced Christians.

The students in the English university colleges regarded them for the most part as institutions which delivered lectures with a view to their students securing degrees. The majority of the students never thought of corporate activities, either religious, social or athletic, as a vital part of student life. They had to attend lectures and as soon as lectures were over they went home.

Probably most of the students thirty years ago travelled only a short distance to college and did actually
live at home. Year by year, however, these colleges
attracted more and more students, and attracted them
from farther afield. One result of this has been to
create a large body of students who live in lodgings.
These students, being separated from the interests of
home life, were one factor in creating a corporate spirit
by forming societies and clubs of one sort or another.
They were joined by the more enterprising spirits
among those living at home, and were helped by
members of staff who had been educated at either
Oxford or Cambridge, and who knew how rich and
varied the corporate life of a university could be.
Members of staff, however, have not done all they
could for the modern universities on their social side ;
while individuals have helped greatly, on the whole
there has been too little attempt on the part of the
average member of staff in the modern university to
mix with and get to know the students.

Another factor which has helped to promote corporate life has been the Student Christian Movement.
Thirty years ago the leaders of the Student Movement
might have drawn a good deal more comfort than they
did from the fact that if the Christian Union did not
flourish, neither did any other society, and indeed in
more institutions than one the first student society to
be firmly established and to show an interest in the life
of the university or college as such was the Christian
Union. It took some years to do this, but it was done.

The Student Movement did it in two ways ; first of
all through the work of its travelling secretaries, men
and women who in an unending succession have given
one or two years each after leaving the university and
before entering upon their life work, to travel for the
Student Movement. They almost all came from Oxford,
Cambridge, or one of the Scottish universities, and one
and all worked with a capacity, industry and faithfulness which, as one looks back over the succession, is

past all telling. Most of these men and women had
themselves lived an easy college life, were accustomed
to a great deal of social activity, an unlimited amount
of athletic opportunity, and a considerable degree of
comfort. When they became travelling secretaries they
were often appalled at first by the difficulty of the work
they had undertaken, but one and all they never failed
to buckle to with a will, and morning, afternoon and
evening, week after week, month after month, during
their term of office, they moved from place to place
addressing the Unions, advising committees, helping
individuals, ceaseless in their thought and prayer for
those they had been chosen by fellow-students to try
and help. And they have their reward, for not only
did they in time establish the Christian Unions and
through them do much for the corporate life of the
university, but they also have caused the title of travelling
secretary of the Student Christian Movement to be held
in honour throughout the universities and colleges of
the British Isles.

The second factor which the Student Movement
brought to bear upon the situation was through its
summer conferences. At first these were attended only
by the students from the older universities and colleges
of the United Kingdom. But very soon men and
women began to appear from the new university colleges
—Yorkshire College, Leeds, Mason College, Birmingham, University College, Liverpool, University College,
Nottingham, and University College, Bristol. None
of these students had ever been at a conference before.
It was hard to persuade them not to bring their Sunday
clothes to camp; many were the men who turned up in
black coats and bowler hats. They looked with surprise at the undergraduates from the older universities,
with their shorts and blazers, but they themselves turned
up in shorts next year; blazers came later, for this was
a time when most of the modern universities were not
in being, and when the university colleges had no
blazers. But none need laugh at the modern university

men; a Scottish travelling secretary donned a frock-coat and tall hat for his first visit to Oxford !

The man from the new university college learnt a great deal from the man from the ancient university, while the man from the ancient university was also a learner, for the man from the new university taught him a great deal about life, and the mixing was certainly for everybody's good all round.

The committee became deeply concerned at this time about the question of spiritual awakening. How was this to be achieved in such a way that far more students might be reached ?

The situation in the older universities was different. In these there were memories of important spiritual awakenings in the past and in most of them a continuous attempt to win men for Christ. The Movement was led by men from these universities, but their chief pre-occupation was with the Movement, not in their own universities but in the new university colleges.

Prayer and discussion regarding " a spiritual awakening "—that is the phrase used again and again in the minute-books—took place at every meeting of the Executive of the General College Department for the years 1901, 1902 and 1903, but for the most part the expectant committee found disappointment. In October 1901 the minutes contain a long discussion about the great lack of spiritual life in the Unions. In April 1902 the travelling secretary reported that " there seems no prospect of a spiritual awakening in the colleges." But by the end of this year a demand had begun to arise for help from the Executive in arranging evangelistic work, while the following year the reference to college missions increased, although there continued to be very doleful references to the unsatisfactory prayer-meetings.

Too often there is barely a quorum of two or three at the meetings. . . . What is chiefly needed is a deeper sense of the need for and the value of prayer, and especially of intercessory prayer ; the spirit that will impel students to meet together, and that will prevent such meetings from

becoming barren and formal. We all wish that the excellent custom of having special weekly prayer-meetings
for members of committee were universally adopted.
When such are held they are found to be peculiarly helpful.[1]

The following year, 1904, there were signs of a
desire for spiritual awakening, and the thought was
very much in the minds of the leaders of the Movement
throughout the year. But we had not discovered how
to give a lead and precipitate the desire for spiritual
awakening into action by means of witness-bearing and
prayer towards bringing it about. This was the position when we assembled at Conishead Priory for the
summer conference.

The day a summer conference begins those responsible for its planning are always much concerned about
its spiritual outcome. One morning at the beginning
of the conference at Conishead, being at leisure shortly
before lunch, I went into a tiny bedroom I was occupying to pray for the conference, making intercession
specially that the desire for a spiritual awakening should
grip those present. I felt pressed in spirit to secure
the prayers of others, and there and then decided that
I would pray daily for a spiritual awakening, and if I
found anyone who seemed to share my concern I would
invite him to join me.

I went downstairs and ran into Henry Hodgkin in
the hall. He was chairman of the conference, and I
knew that here was someone who would share my
concern, so I told him what had happened. He told
me he had had an identical experience and had made
the same resolve. "This is of God," said Tommy
Hodgkin; "we are not the only people to whom He
is speaking. We shall find many who will want to
pray with us." Within twenty-four hours there was
a large group praying together. We met daily under
a big tree in the grounds, and I have seldom been in a
praying group which had more conviction that God
was about to speak in no uncertain manner.

[1] Minutes of General College Department Committee, July 1903.

Q

After about five days the committee responsible for the conference, without any lead from either Hodgkin or myself, met and decided to add a second address at the evening meeting because they were not sure that the chosen speaker would prove effective with all the different types at the conference and that one of us in the Movement should speak. They were not thinking of the question of spiritual awakening in making this decision. I don't think most of the committee knew of the prayer-meeting. They decided, however, that I should speak at the evening meeting. It came as a call from God to try and share with the conference the longing for the awakening for which our group was praying.

The subject chosen was, " Are we true to the ideal which we set before ourselves as a Union when we adopted the basis ? " I was ill and felt unfit to speak when the evening came. I turned to Hodgkin and Winifred Sedgwick to support me. I can recall to this hour the feeling of weakness and incapacity to grip an audience with which I began the address. But the thing was of God and the audience was moved more deeply than I have ever seen a student conference moved before or since.

The address began by pointing out that when adopting the basis, " I desire in joining this Union to declare my faith in Jesus Christ as my Saviour, my Lord and my God," great emphasis was laid on the fact that it would be a valuable ground of appeal—an appeal to men to accept Jesus Christ as Saviour and Lord, and yet there had been no appreciable increase in the membership of the Movement for about four years, that it was drawing into its ranks only those already Christians.

> These are not the fruits of our warfare for Christ ; they are the results of the work of the Churches or the product of Christian homes. We can take no credit for nine-tenths of the entire membership of our Unions. We gather in only those who can be won without serious effort. We

are failing to do what we proposed doing and what we believe we ought to do.

Tribute was paid to the improvement in Bible and Missionary study and to the better organization of the Unions, but the address pressed the point that men and women were not being won in any appreciable numbers.

While we hesitate, men and women are passing away from college unreached, and as time goes on they are becoming harder to win. Others who may touch their lives later on will not find them as easy to speak to of Christ as we would have found them. Neither will others find it as easy to get into close touch with them as we did. We touch men while in college in a way in which we shall never touch them afterwards.

Then came from one's heart and experience the question whether it is vital for men definitely to take Christ as their Saviour.

We are not likely to take very serious action unless we are convinced that this matter is vital. Is it vital? We speculate a good deal on this point. We wonder if men who have failed in righteousness in this life have a chance after death. We rest a great deal on the good nature of God apart from moral considerations. We good-naturedly hope for the best for men. But none of these considerations are likely to lead us to engage in the work of winning men to Christ.

It was suggested that there is only one true way to put the question, " Is it vital to be in Christ ? "

Is it vital to me to be in Christ? . . . If there are any here to-night who come to the conclusion that it is not vital for them to be in Christ, I have nothing more to say to them on this matter ; but to those who answer that it is vital, I have this to say : if it is vital for you to be in Christ, dare you conclude that it is not vital for any man or woman in your college ?

The view of Jesus as to whether He regarded men's attitude towards Himself as vital or not was then examined, and the address closed with an appeal to hear " the call to win men for the Kingdom which echoes through every page of the New Testament, and that the call is revealing not merely a duty, but a privilege and a joy."

It is a privilege to be allowed to share with God the work of saving men. It is a joy to see men saved. Well might Dr Stalker write that " the humblest Christian worker who is really pained with the sin of men and rejoices in their salvation, is feeling, in his degree, the very passion which bore the Saviour of the world through His sufferings, and which has throbbed from eternity in the heart of God." . . . Let us consecrate ourselves afresh to-day to this service for the sake of the men and women in our colleges. God is with us. He means us to go forward in the name of His Son and win men. I plead with you to lay aside, here and now, all worldly standards of probability, and to refuse the dull estimates of worldly common-sense and joyfully to expect in the future what is not suggested by the experience of the past.

The ground was prepared and prayer answered. When the address ended the whole conference spontaneously knelt in prayer and remained in prayer for a long period, indeed the meeting was never closed; after a time the chairman quietly slipped from the chair and it was over an hour before that silent prayer-meeting had completely broken up.

In the autumn the address was printed and circulated with a letter from the members of the General Committee to the Unions, saying that, " at the Conishead Conference we were led, under what was manifestly Divine guidance, to consider how far we had been true to the ideals contained in our basis, namely, that of winning students to Christ, and we were convicted as a Union of grievous failure up till now."

The letter went on to say that the leaders were encouraged by the way they felt God had dealt with them at the conference, that the Movement had been brought to a crisis because they now realized vividly that they were called to advance in this new direction. They called the Union to prepare by meditation, study and prayer for this work, and declared that God would guide all in their respective colleges as to which of the varying means they should use for the accomplishment of the ideal of winning men.

Missions, evangelistic meetings, singly and in series, literature, and other means will in time be used, but we feel sure we are right when we express the conviction that the chief means used must be the personal work done by individual members among their college friends and acquaintances. Did not Christ teach that His Kingdom would spread and His salvation find men as a result of the personal witness-bearing of His followers ? [1]

The effect of this spiritual movement was felt throughout the year, and the following summer when reporting the committee wrote :

It cannot be regarded as mere coincidence by those who believe in an almighty God that the call to evangelize should have been sounded among the Christian students of Great Britain just a few months before the outburst of revival in Wales. That revival, coming at the end of a period of dulness, discouragement and spiritual death, produced in Christian hearts through all the world a new hope and expectant activity, and though the influence in its Welsh form did not spread out of Welsh circles, men and Churches on every hand have received the vision of a new power in Christianity to conquer men and purify the world of its sin. When this new breath of God began to blow, it found many of our C.U.'s with sail set, and anxious to use its power to the full. . . . Not a few colleges record special efforts to bring before their fellow-students the reality of the truths of the Gospel, while many could tell of results of personal dealing with individuals which defy statistics.

During the year missions were conducted by John Mott at both Oxford and Cambridge. Dr Kelman and the Rev. J. Harry Miller at Edinburgh, Dr James Denney at Queen Margaret College, Glasgow, and Lenwood at Manchester conducted evangelistic meetings, while week-end conferences with an evangelistic aim were held at Aberystwyth, Alexandra and Trinity Colleges,

[1] *Letter and Address to Members of the B.C.C.U.*, September 1904.

Dublin, and Armstrong College, Newcastle. Results differed; in some places they were very striking, as in Mott's mission at Oxford, in others they were less spectacular, but everywhere men and women were led into the Christian life.

The real significance of this episode of the prayer-meeting under the tree at Conishead was that it was the genesis of college missions and "religion and life" weeks, which have been a regular part of the life of the Movement ever since.

In the meantime the S.V.M.U. had been tackling its problems very soberly. The years prior to the S.V.M.U. Conference, London, 1900, had been years of great disappointment to the leaders of the Union owing to a decrease each year in the number of Student Volunteers, and this when a large increase was looked for. The tide turned in 1901 and

> there can be no doubt that the revival of volunteering, which began in 1901, and which has grown ever since, began in prayer. The Executive in that year were granted anew the spirit of prayer; and in two letters to volunteers in college, and to all members of the Union, they call for more earnest and believing prayer, and the result was a movement onward and upward.[1]

Henry T. Hodgkin became chairman of the S.V.M.U. in 1901 and his influence was a potent factor in causing a deepening of the corporate prayer life of the S.V.M.U. committee. Not only was there prayer, but there was a revival of missionary study, and by the time of the Edinburgh Conference, 1904, fully one-third of the membership of the entire Movement was in missionary study circles.

As the time for another quadrennial conference drew on there was much questioning as to whether another should be held. The committee agreed that " it would be a grave step to deprive a student generation of the

[1] Report of the S.V.M.U. Executive to the Edinburgh Conference, 1904.

inspiration and stimulus of such conferences as those held at Liverpool and London," but it shrank from the publicity of another great conference, when the Union would probably have its praises sung in the religious press while the failure to win Student Volunteers in large numbers was a call to humiliation. The discussions of the committee resulted in the decision to hold a conference in Edinburgh from January 2nd to 6th 1904, and to lay emphasis at this conference on humiliation rather than achievement, and to avoid a great demonstration by selecting delegations which should be representative rather than large. Again the influence of Hodgkin in relation to this decision was considerable. One big change was that the missionary societies and the large body of guests usually at quadrennial conferences were not invited. The conference, although it was reported in the press, was thought of as a private meeting of the S.V.M.U. and its adherents meeting quietly together in the presence of God to pray, not in a spirit of discouragement but of humiliation and hope, that the Union might rise to the call of the Watchword and yet arouse the colleges to an adequate enthusiasm and dedication to missionary service to achieve it.

The conference met in the Assembly Hall of the United Free Church of Scotland, with the use of the buildings of New College. It had most of the features of previous conferences. There was a literature exhibit and bookstall in the New College common-room with a very complete set of model libraries. Foreign delegates were entertained to lunch and tea daily in the Rainy Hall, with some British students to meet them. There were 709 British students and 98 foreign students, a total of 807, at the conference. The three largest groups of students were Arts 243, Theology 165, and Medicine 138; twenty-four foreign countries were represented. Many of the foreign delegates were invited to speak, and there was much encouragement because the representatives of Holland, France, Switzerland, Finland, Australasia and South Africa were able to report that well-established Student Christian Movements had grown up in their countries since the Liverpool Conference. In addition to these there were representatives present from Austria, Hungary, Italy, Belgium, the Levant, West Africa and Russia. In each of these lands there was the germ of a Student Movement nonexistent eight years before.

There was a financial session devoted to extending the work of the whole Student Movement, the conference being already paid for. This produced promises of £880, with payment to be spread over four years.

J. H. Maclean, who sailed in 1895, before the Liverpool Conference, and accordingly had never been at a quadrennial gathering, wrote an interesting impression of the conference, summing up its most notable elements as being " humility, consecrated ambition, sanity, and prayerfulness." He noted that the spirit of humility and confession which " found definite expression more particularly at the meeting for humiliation and prayer on Sunday afternoon . . . involved no lowering of the standard. Leaders showed that they were only disappointed and humbled, not discouraged. Once more they came forward with their Watchword and appealed for such lives as would make its realization possible."

The chairman of the conference was Henry T. Hodgkin of King's College, Cambridge, and St Thomas's Hospital, London. His leadership of this conference was the crowning act of nearly five years' leadership in the Movement. He was the most effective man amongst us for several years. Principal Rainy was the most notable figure among the Edinburgh public men who welcomed the conference, and Mr John Mott was the outstanding figure among the speakers. The Rev. G. A. Johnston Ross, the Very Rev. George Robson, the Rev. Professor W. P. Paterson were the best known of the small group of speakers called upon to address the conference. Not very much was said about the need of the world, that was assumed. The speakers dealt with such topics as the need for a larger missionary programme in the colleges, every Christian man a missionary, the missionary possibilities of the students of the world, the Holy Spirit, God's ways of guiding men, the consecration of personality, the Watchword, and the need of prayer in our work. The address which was perhaps the most direct and searching was John Mott's on " The Watchword as a spiritual force."

The number of students who had signed the Volunteer declaration since its commencement was, at the opening of the conference, 2185, of whom 920 had become missionaries. It was calculated that of those who could have sailed 62 per cent. had reached the mission field. Another 10 per cent. had offered to the missionary societies and had been rejected on various grounds, usually health.

The S.V.M.U. Executive prepared an official interpretation of the meaning of the Student Volunteer declaration, and used it for the first time at the Edinburgh Conference.

This Declaration is not to be interpreted as a " pledge," for in no sense does it imply that he who signs it is withdrawn from the subsequent guidance of the Holy Spirit. But it is more than a mere expression of willingness or desire to become a Foreign Missionary. It is the statement of a definite life purpose formed under the direction of God. The student who signs this Declaration fully purposes to spend his life as a Foreign Missionary. Towards this end he will shape his plans ; he will steadily set himself to prepare for this great work ; he will do all in his power to remove obstacles which may stand in the way of his going ; and in due time he will apply to a Missionary Society to be sent out. Only the clear leading of God will prevent his going to the foreign field. It is the duty of every Christian to face this question, but let no one decide it without careful thought and earnest prayer. And having faced the question, let him think to a conclusion, " Understanding what the will of the Lord is."

The Edinburgh Conference was organized by W. P. W. Williams, who was general secretary from 1902-1903 and who remained to complete the arrangements for the conference, but I had returned to the general secretaryship three months before, after an interval of three years. The first two of these years I had spent at Trinity College, Dublin, taking its Divinity Testimonium. While doing this I prepared several courses of missionary study for the use of students and also edited *The Student Movement*. The third year was spent in London as curate of St Barnabas, Kensington. On ordination I retired from the editorship, but remained in charge of the missionary study work of the Movement. An invitation due to the initiative of Henry Hodgkin to return to the general secretaryship for five years came from the General Committee about six months after I had gone to St Barnabas', and with the Bishop of London's consent I accepted it and returned to the office on September 1903. The following January I resumed the editorship of *The Student Movement*. The S.V.M.U. insisted that I should retain the office of missionary study secretary. I was not idle !

The Movement's staff at headquarters at this date consisted of a general secretary, accountant, junior clerk, typist and office boy, and in the field a travelling secretary for men's colleges for general work, a travelling secretary for men's colleges appointed by the S.V.M.U., a London secretary for men's colleges, and two travelling secretaries for women's colleges who shared the work, both general and S.V.M.U. A total of six secretaries with an office staff of four people.

The Movement's finances were a struggle to raise; the total amount required when I returned as general secretary was £1260 a year. We arranged at this time the first meetings to gain the support of senior friends; these were held at Oxford, Cambridge, Hampstead, Manchester, Birkenhead and Glasgow.

There was a great deal of discussion about whether the summer conferences were sufficiently spiritual in tone; a number of Cambridge men who had been at Keswick and come on to Matlock, where our conferences were held from 1900-1903, criticized them unfavourably. Others, however, pointed out that there were thousands of experienced Christians at Keswick, which created a remarkable atmosphere, and that people who came to the student conferences should not expect to find them identical with Keswick. Three of the Cambridge men were invited to a meeting of the General Committee to state their views. It came out clearly in the discussion that spiritual results to be traced to the summer conferences were apparent all over the college field. The significance of this point was pressed vigorously by the women members of the committee, none of whom agreed with the opinion of the Cambridge visitors.

The vigorous disagreement of the women helped to make them vocal. The custom of letting the men do all the talking and of asking one woman to speak for the rest, after a meal or some other interval when they got together and discussed their views, had led to a sub-committee of the women becoming the recognized way, not only of dealing with questions relating to the women's colleges, but of making the women's contribution to the work of the committee. The chairwoman of the sub-committee usually spoke for the women. At this time, however, Evelyn Lea Wilson [1] " reported that the ladies suggested that the women's sub-committee should be abolished." [2] This provoked the question from the men : with whom shall the chairmen of the different departments correspond when making up the agenda for committee meetings ? " It was finally decided that no one person should be spokesman for the ladies."

The women were very forbearing, then and later, for the men would discuss their colleges and problems at great length and be obviously impatient when a woman's question emerged. It was some years before the women established their right to speak as freely as the

[1] Afterwards Mrs G. F. Saywell.
[2] B.C.C.U. Minutes, March 1904.

men. Lilian Stevenson, Adelaide Wynne Wilson, Evelyn
Lea Wilson, Nancy Borrow were always listened to
with interest by the men, but it was not until Zoe
Fairfield joined the staff of the Movement four years
later that the emancipation of the women was complete. Zoe Fairfield fought no battle, but simply took
her place in the councils of the Movement with complete ease, and the women followed her example.

The women led in creating a technique for the
summer conference. They suggested that the students
should be divided into companies with an officer in
charge and should wear labels bearing their name and
college. The men consented to companies and labels
for the women, but said the men would dislike both.
Companies and labels were so obviously successful that
H. C. Duncan and I tried to get the committee to
extend them to the men. We were defeated at first,
but within a year or two the men were in companies
and wearing labels, and companies and labels prevail to
this day !

CHAPTER XIII

THE STUDENT MISSIONARY CAMPAIGN

WHEN student hearts and minds are stirred on any great issue they always go campaigning in relation to it outside as well as in the colleges. Long before the Movement was organized Professor Henry Drummond used to guide students doing evangelistic work. When the S.V.M.U. began, students carried its ideals at once to young people's societies in the Churches. The Liverpool Conference gave a considerable impetus to this kind of work as it provided a clear objective—the accomplishment of the Watchword. Edinburgh students gave a fresh lead, hiring a removal van and carrying out a missionary caravan tour. Next year, finding the furniture removal van unwieldy, they had a caravan of their own built at a cost of £38, "including a tent and utensils." Relays of students manned the caravan during the whole of September 1897, visiting eighteen villages and holding forty-seven meetings in churches and public halls. Lantern lectures on mission fields were delivered on week nights, and addresses on the Volunteer Movement and the Watchword at Sunday services. Three years later they reported that they had approached one hundred ministers, of whom ninety-seven had welcomed their help in their congregations. Edinburgh students used their caravan for many years.

Another active body of students was the Irish Presbyterian Volunteers, working from Belfast.

In Wales Bala College students gave a lead in campaigning, and a year or two later the Welsh Calvinistic Methodist Volunteers memorialized their Church Assembly as a result of the London S.V.M.U.

Conference, asking that a student volunteer be appointed to work up missionary interest in the churches and offering to provide half his salary for at least two years. The memorial was signed by 235 Welsh students and endorsed by Principal T. C. Edwards of Bala and Dr Owen Prys.

Under the title, " The Field Campaign," work among young people's societies in the Churches in England, especially in Christian Endeavour Societies and Wesley Guilds, was initiated by students, and London Non-conformist theologicals were specially active.

After the London S.V.M.U. Conference—the second quadrennial—the Union announced that it had decided " to adopt the Field Campaign as part of its policy, doing its best to secure the perpetuation of Student Volunteer influence and principles in campaigns already started by Student Volunteers, and to initiate new campaigns where desirable." It was due to American influence that this decision was taken. Mr Earl Taylor had spoken at the London Conference with enthusiasm of the work being carried on by the American Student Volunteer Movement among the young people's societies in the Churches. Malcolm Spencer wrote in *The Student Movement* [1] of the wonderful proportions which this American Field Campaign had assumed and advocated its adoption by Great Britain, told of the beginnings of campaigning by students in Leicestershire and Liverpool among Christian Endeavour Societies and among Wesley Guilds. He asked those ready to help to send him their names. This was the commencement of work which was to result in a few years in establishing missionary study in the Churches. The decision of the S.V.M.U. to make the promotion of missionary campaigns part of its work meant that it began to study how to prepare students for taking part in campaigns and how to organize the campaigns with both thoroughness and expedition. The Executive of the S.V.M.U. put on sale a library of sixteen books, issued by different

[1] *The Student Movement*, vol. ii. p. 136.

publishers with whom they made terms, at a price considerably less than the published value of the books. This was sold by campaigners to the young people's societies visited which, as a rule, had no missionary libraries.

The Theological College Department began to take an interest in campaigns, its committee recognizing that it would give it a *raison d'être* which theological colleges would understand. It soon found campaign work, with its accompaniment of college missionary study circles, one of its best and most easily introduced methods of work in theological colleges, and it suggested to the S.V.M.U. in 1903 that missionary campaign work in the Churches should be placed under a special committee appointed jointly by the Theological College Department and S.V.M.U. Executives. The proposal was gladly accepted by the S.V.M.U.

This committee issued in the summer of 1903 two pamphlets for circulation in the Churches, explaining the student missionary campaign, its ideals and methods. Its object " is an organized effort by the students of our British colleges to plead for a very great advance in the foreign missionary policy of the Churches. It is the outgrowth of the more extensive movement among students which recent years have witnessed in this country and throughout the world." The S.V.M.U. with 2000 students who had signed its declaration, 800 of whom were already working as missionaries, was described, and then the pamphlet told how " while working primarily in the colleges this Union has been forced to seek a wider field. The lofty ideal of its Watchword is one which it feels impelled to communicate to others. Throughout the kingdom, wherever a number of students have become imbued with this Watchword, they have yielded to this compulsion to preach it in the Churches." [1]

Some Student Volunteers formed about this period a " Business Men's Missionary Volunteer Union." This

[1] *The Student Missionary Campaign.*

was a forerunner of the Laymen's Missionary Movement of later years, which owed its inspiration to forces set in motion by the Student Movement. In 1904 the Girls' Auxiliary was started by two Student Movement leaders in the United Free Church of Scotland, in the interest of foreign missions; beginning as a missionary movement it broadened its scope later.

The Movement followed the first pamphlet almost immediately with one also entitled *The Student Missionary Campaign*, in which the ideals of the students for campaign were set out at greater length.

> The campaign gives expression to the ideals of the Student Volunteer Missionary Union. It seeks for a wider acceptance of its Watchword, and for the promotion of systematic methods of missionary study. The success of the latter is largely dependent on the inspiration supplied by the former.

The Watchword is expounded in this pamphlet on the same lines as in the Memorial to the Churches seven years before. There is an advance, however, in that the case for missionary study is now clearly put. Before enthusiasm for the ideal of the Watchword can be generated there must be a great increase in missionary knowledge.

> It is idle for a man to profess any great affection for an acquaintance whom he constantly avoids. Communion in any real sense, whether of friendship or love, is dependent upon mutual knowledge. . . . Before we can be sufficiently interested in native churches to pray for them and to help in their support, there must be a basis of knowledge, and if Christians had as much interest in the progress of the Kingdom of God as the ordinary Englishman has in the welfare of the Empire, missionary information would be devoured with as much avidity as the latest news from the seat of war.

The point is pressed home that the kind of enthusiasm which is needed can only be aroused by really good missionary study, that it will not last unless it is " dependent not on sentiment but on knowledge."

The newly appointed Campaign Committee made a comparative study of all the existing campaigns and found that they might be divided roughly into two classes, those which aim at giving definite information about missionary work, and those which seek to get the Churches to acquire this information for themselves. The leaders of all the campaigns were agreed that " the recognition of missions by the average Church and Church member is inadequate, the facts are not faced— they are not even known—and as to provision for meeting them it is far to seek."

The student leaders, having studied the two types of campaign, decided to use their influence to get all the campaigns to " emphasize the Church's duty to solve the problem for herself and make their special subject study, methods for sustaining interest and activity in the home Church." They thought that students had neither the necessary knowledge of missionary work, nor the time to acquire it, to fit them for informing the Churches adequately as to the needs of the mission field, and that this work of direct education was not really within the province of students. What they did think they could and ought to do was to start ordinary Church members studying missions for themselves. " Having ascertained the best methods for our own use, we can suggest their adoption in the Churches, and further, in doing this we gain an opportunity of presenting the Watchword for consideration."

By this time there were five " campaigns " in England; each was organized and undertook work in connection with a particular Church,—the Church of England, Wesleyan, Baptist, Congregational and Friends. There was also the Christian Endeavour Campaign. All these campaigns carried on their work during vacations, the total number of students working through them being about a hundred. There was some campaign work carried on during the term, notably by students in Bristol, Nottingham and the London theological colleges.

R

In Ireland the Irish Presbyterian campaign, which was one of the oldest established, was well developed.

It has its whole field mapped out, and is in touch with all its theological men and all its Student Volunteers. A man is set apart by the Church to devote his whole time to its organization. The work includes the giving of lectures, the preparation of sets of lantern slides, the publication of literature, the visitation of Sunday-schools, preaching, addresses, the organization of conferences, and the convening of committees for the perfecting of missionary organization throughout the Irish Presbyterian Church.

Some deputation work by students was carried on in connection with the Church of Ireland.

In Scotland, while Edinburgh continued its caravan work, the Glasgow students were regarded as being more up-to-date in their methods. Their campaign was controlled by an intercollegiate committee of Student Volunteers. Students visited religious meetings of all kinds for the purpose of addressing them on missionary subjects and managed one campaign which had a national field, namely, a missionary student campaign in the Y.M.C.A., with which the Y.M.C.A. authorities co-operated. In the case of the United Free Churches in Glasgow the missionary authorities of the Church advised and co-operated with the students.

In Wales campaign work initiated from Bala College had by this time been extended to Aberystwyth, Bangor and Trevecca; the work in these places was in co-operation with the Welsh Presbyterian Church. The Welsh Baptist and Congregational Churches were worked through the corresponding campaigns in England.

This sums up the situation in the autumn of 1903, but the work did not stand still. This autumn medical and arts students in the London colleges decided not to leave campaigns to the theologicals, as hitherto, and started a caravan, visiting the villages of Surrey during the summer vacation. The following year they went to Hertfordshire. The same year Cambridge University conducted its first campaign, in Huddersfield. In 1905

Oxford University made a start with a Church of England campaign in and around Bristol. The first women students' campaign was in March 1905, when a group of six women graduates went to Bedford for a week and conducted thirty-one meetings under a variety of circumstances with success.[1]

Campaign work was not without its anxieties and complications from the point of view of the leaders of the Movement. One example, perhaps, may be given. In 1906 the Student Movement was at a critical period in its approach to Anglican theological colleges, and especially to the High Church element in the Church of England. One sunny May day two enthusiastic campaigners in charge of the London caravan, one a Free Churchman and the other V. H. Starr, then a student at King's College, London, who afterwards lost his life at the hands of frontier tribesmen in India, walked into my office to talk about campaign. It emerged that they were proposing to go that summer into some of the villages of Oxfordshire, taking a mixed party of Anglicans and Free Churchmen. They were quite unaware of any of the denominational difficulties that might be involved, but on a preparatory visit to the Oxford diocese had been asked by one or two clergy whether they were coming with the Bishop of Oxford's [2] sanction and blessing. This question had surprised the two students, but what should hinder them from writing to the Bishop? It was his refusal to give his approval that brought them to see me, in pained surprise. What I thought about it is best told in a letter which I wrote to Malcolm Spencer. After describing the facts, the letter proceeds :

May 7th, 1906.

Now the apple-cart is going to be upset entirely for us in a good many quarters if every student who arranges a campaign is going to write to the bishop of the diocese he would enter. If we could ensure that those who wrote were Churchmen and only asked the bishop's blessing for

[1] *The Student Movement,* vol. vii. p. 165.　　[2] Dr Francis Paget.

Church of England work, it would not matter much, but it really is a serious thing for us if men who are not Churchmen are going to ask various bishops to give their blessing to interdenominational work done in connection with the Student Movement.

Think how carefully we angle for bishops, with what care we approach them and explain to them what we are trying to do. Our usual way of approach is to get their approval for some distinctively Church piece of work, or else we get them to a conference. We should not dream of letting our first attack upon them be a request to them to give their blessing to an interdenominational campaign conducted by men about whom they knew nothing whatever. It was simply madness to have written to the Bishop of Oxford. I do not see how he could have done anything else but refuse his blessing.

These students don't seem to realize that a bishop is a marked man, that everything he says and does is criticized with the greatest possible vigour by all the Church papers, and that he has to be infinitely careful as to what he gives his blessing, and it is unthinkable that he would give his blessing to work of which he knew little or nothing. I should think that the net result of this episode with the Bishop of Oxford will be that it has made it about fifty per cent. more difficult for us to get in touch with Cuddesdon College than it was before. Starr is a Churchman, but evidently has not studied the Anglican position—may the saints forgive him! The man who actually wrote to the Bishop of Oxford, holy Moses, is a Plymouth Brother. O Malcolm, these wild young friends of ours will upset the blessed apple-cart altogether if they go and do this kind of thing all over the country.

The Movement was not only at a critical stage as regards its relation to the Church of England, but it was also full of hope as to the possibilities of the conservation of the results of campaign work in the Churches.

A turning-point came in the autumn of 1905. Malcolm Spencer became travelling secretary of the Theological College Department, and having done much for the Student Missionary Campaign while at college, it was much to his taste that the body for which he now worked had campaign work as part of its policy. I was still in

J. H. OLDHAM   S. K. DATTA   MALCOLM SPENCER
WILLIAM PATON   EDITH E. OVERTON   MARTYN TRAFFORD
NEVILLE S. TALBOT   LESLIE S. HUNTER   WINIFRED M. SEDGWICK

charge of the missionary study work of the Movement and a member of its Campaign Committee in addition to being general secretary. Spencer was feeling his way in relation to the missionary societies with a view to getting missionary study adopted as part of their official policy. We made common cause.

It was obviously desirable that the burden of providing missionary study text-books and accompanying literature which the student campaigners required for their work in the Churches should not continue to fall upon the Student Movement but should become the care of the societies. About this time E. J. Wigney, assistant manager of a City bank, who was an enthusiast for the Student Movement study scheme, became secretary of the Young Christians' Missionary Union (re-named the British Young People's Missionary Movement in 1907 [1]), which grew out of the campaign work of the Student Movement, and which had the promotion of missionary study in the young people's societies of the Free Churches as its chief object. Spencer was a member of the committee of this organization.

Spencer introduced me to Wigney, and in 1906 the three of us proceeded to create a group to work at the question of missionary study in the Churches. Stanley Sowton of the Wesleyan Methodist Missionary Society and H. L. Hemmens of the Baptist Missionary Society were drawn in. G. T. Manley and T. R. W. Lunt, both old Student Movement men who had recently been appointed to the staff of the C.M.S., and J. H. Oldham, mission study secretary of the United Free Church of Scotland, joined us. We tackled a double task, the work of relating the missionary study circles started by the campaigns to the young people's work of the societies, and the introduction of missionary study to the missionary societies.

It was not so easy as it might seem. The senior

[1] This organization became, after a year or two, the Free Churches Sectional Committee of the United Council for Missionary Education, and was merged in the Council after the war.

secretaries of the great missionary societies were heavily burdened men. The missionary study method was something which needed time and attention from anyone promoting it. It meant reading a text-book and all the literature describing the formation and conduct of missionary study circles, and unless a man had been in a missionary study circle he felt it difficult to commend the method. This was all rather difficult from the point of view of an elderly and busy secretary, and while the missionary society secretaries who were in touch with the Student Movement and came to its quadrennial missionary conferences spoke with general approval of the enthusiasm of the students and their methods of missionary study, there was not much likelihood of getting them to do anything about it. But, on the other hand, as junior men who had been in Student Movement study circles were appointed to assistant secretaryships in the missionary societies, men who understood the method were available as helpers inside the societies.

The group used to meet at first at the Student Movement offices. While its inspiration came from the Movement, much practical help came from America. The missionary study movement there was flourishing at this time and we adopted their text-books, re-editing them for Great Britain. Our procedure was to offer a chosen text-book in advance to each of the societies represented in the group through the group member from that society. As the text-books were suitable and cheap, and a big discount was offered for orders in advance, and the imprint of the society ordering was put on the title-page of the copies ordered, the group's work flourished. It retained a small profit to defray the cost of editing the following year's text-book.

The group published its first book in 1907, *The Uplift of China*, by A. H. Smith, and sold 10,000 copies to the Missionary Societies. The book was a success, but it nearly lost us an important recruit to our group, Canon Charles H. Robinson, editorial secretary of the

S.P.G. I had been asked to secure Robinson and I did so, but a few days after he had agreed to join—and before he had met the group—a copy of *The Uplift of China* was sent to him; he read it and wrote an indignant letter withdrawing his name—the S.P.G. was not mentioned in the book! Although the references to particular missions were slight, owing to its small size, it was a blunder that the important work of the S.P.G. in China was not named. I pleaded with Canon Robinson that it was to prevent just such blunders in our text-books that we wanted to make our group representative, and he relented and joined us. He made the condition that the group should remain a private one and not publish the names of its members, otherwise, as a S.P.G. official, he could not continue in it, as that society did not have relationships with any but Anglican organizations.

In the spring of 1907 Mr C. A. Flint, as one of the numerous services he has rendered the Student Movement, offered a sum of £250 a year for three years to enable the Student Movement to employ a secretary for campaigns. The man chosen for this work was Alan W. Stevens of Wadham and Mansfield Colleges, Oxford. The appointment was a success and Stevens worked with discretion and zeal. He promoted innumerable campaigns, collected students from all over the country, visited towns and villages arranging for the reception of the campaigners, and when the campaigns were over spent much time in training suitable people who had come forward as leaders of missionary study circles. He also did a good deal of work on literature, helped to prepare missionary study outlines, compiled suitable lists of books and pamphlets for sale at campaigns, and wrote some of the best campaign literature that has been produced at any time in connection with campaigns. He worked very closely in touch with the Young People's Missionary Movement, for which he was practically travelling secretary at one time.

Stevens himself thought that the most important part of his work was to follow up campaigns by training those who had signified their willingness to lead missionary study circles.

" The missionary study movement," he wrote, " is doomed to failure unless efficient leaders can be found. The campaigners do not seek to start study circles straight away, but to get the names of those who are willing to take part in them, and especially those who are willing to lead them. . . . Shortly after the close of a campaign the Student Movement sends to the centre one of the expert secretaries of the Young People's Missionary Movement, who will give a short course of training to leaders."

The person almost always sent was Stevens himself.

It must be one of the regrets we have in the Movement that we did not build up a fund, while Stevens was secretary, to enable the Movement to appoint a successor when his term of office, and the gift which made it possible, came to an end. That this was not done was chiefly due to the fact that those in the Student Movement who might have tackled this were borne down with far more work than they could carry throughout this entire period. In November 1910 Alan Stevens concluded his term of office as campaign secretary, and became minister of Burslem Congregational Church.

Soon after Stevens started work the group arranged a conference on missionary education at Baslow (May 1908), at which almost all the secretaries employed on young people's work by the missionary societies were present. The S.V.M.U. delegates were : S. K. Datta, J. Macleod Campbell, Malcolm Spencer and T. Tatlow. This conference strengthened the work of the group, and it decided that in future it should be known as the United Council for Missionary Education. It was not, however, until 1909 that a constitution was adopted which formally related it to the missionary societies. This is the story of how missionary study became a regular part of the work of the missionary societies of the Churches in Great Britain.

As for Canon Robinson's desire for privacy, the S.P.G. had by this time decided to join in the preparations for the World Missionary Conference, Edinburgh, 1910, which was on an interdenominational basis, so that there was no longer any difficulty about its being related to an interdenominational body—the United Council for Missionary Education.

While all this critical business of establishing the missionary study method at the missionary societies' headquarters was taking place, the students continued campaigning. Scotland was very much to the fore.

Three successful student campaigns in Galashiels, Perth and Inverness encouraged campaign leaders in Scotland to undertake a bolder enterprise, and after a year's preparation, 150 students from the universities and theological colleges of Scotland visited Aberdeen under the leadership of Stanley Nairne and W. P. Young, occupying on Sunday, March 28th 1909, practically every pulpit in Aberdeen, and during the following week holding meetings with the workers and young people in nearly every Church—Presbyterian, Free Church and Episcopalian.

The campaign closed with a public meeting, when Prof. Sir William Ramsay, Prof. W. P. Paterson and Mr William Watson, a former chairman of the S.V.M.U., were the speakers. Prof. David S. Cairns, writing in *The Missionary Record of the United Free Church of Scotland*, said :

That which must, I think, have struck most of us was the strength of the Student Movement, which, when summoned to the help of the Church, could put so strong a body of men at her disposal. Few people outside university circles have any idea of the strength of this Movement ; it has avoided the leprosy of advertisement ; and has preferred to go its own way and follow its own ideals. But it is growing to be one of the most powerful influences for good of the age.

This Aberdeen campaign reflected in an interesting way how quickly and easily thought among students is transferred through them to the Churches. The Student Movement had been concerned for some time about the state of society at home. A new social consciousness had grown up in the Student Movement, and this had influenced campaigns, so that while the campaigners were still talking about the Watchword and were more careful than ever in the methods they used to promote missionary study through campaigns, the new social note influencing the Student Movement was apparent in their addresses. As Dr Cairns wrote :

> The aim of the addresses given was to show that alike at home and abroad the social and missionary problems were more and more coming to the front ; that if the Churches were to meet the new conditions they must produce a new type of character, new belief in prayer, and a new standard of giving.

The text-books which were used in the demonstration circles conducted before full audiences at the United Free Church Club on two nights of the campaign were Dr Datta's *Desire of India* and Mr Spencer's *Social Degradation*.

" As I understand the matter," wrote Dr Cairns, " what we are witnessing in the Student Movement and in its offshoot, the missionary and social study movement, is the appearance of what we may call a new religious protoplasm. I mean, that I think we are seeing in these movements the rise of a new religious ideal and way of looking at things which should be of the deepest interest to every Christian teacher and preacher. That idea was, I think, somewhat crudely expressed in what is known as the Watchword of the Student Movement, ' The evangelization of the world in this generation.' What lies behind this expression, however, is the general idea that the tragedy of human sin and sorrow is preventible ; that it is not part of the fixed order of things ; that we have to be up and doing to sweep it away into the abyss ; that above all, to faith all things are possible. The ideal which is appealing to our young men and maidens is that of a Christianized world with a juster and nobler order of society. If I am right, the Church which recognizes this is the Church which holds the keys of the future." [1]

It would be wearisome to comment on more campaigns. In 1910 there were elaborate campaign programmes in Scotland and Wales, while in England campaigns took place at Bath, Croydon, Cambridge, Darwen, Leeds and Southampton.

The preparation of the students for campaigns received increasing attention. A *Campaign Handbook* was produced, which, although only a good sized pamphlet, was the outcome of considerable experience. It also contained a great deal of wisdom. The leaders had no doubt about their call.

Inspiration is needed ; it comes from the ideal of the Watchword humbly accepted. Knowledge is needed ; the missionary study movement, originated in the student world, has proved God-willed and God-guided. . . . Greater possibilities are contained in mission study than anyone can at present forecast. A wiser strategy, a more scientific selection of men to occupy particular posts, the raising up of a type of native Christian fitted to be in his turn the most effective evangelizer of regions beyond his own —all this, and much more, may be the result to the Church of her combined intelligence consecrated to her great task. Campaign has its part to play in bringing about this consummation. . . . The rank and file of the Church, absorbed in detail work, are likely to lose sight of that which the student is bound to keep in view, namely, the connection of the missionary problem with every other question, political, international, philosophic, religious. The isolation of foreign missions is, or should be, the first victim of the student campaign.

Much attention was given in the *Handbook* to the kind of appeal which it is desirable campaigners should make when face to face with audiences : the need of the world, the need for knowledge, the possibilities of the mission study circle, what it is and what it can achieve. Careful advice was given about the need for personal service.

[1] *The Missionary Record of the United Free Church of Scotland*, May 1909.

It will be emphasized, though with great carefulness ; personal service will be shown to be not the prerogative only of the man who goes abroad ; the effectiveness of the service of intercession will be pleaded.   It will be shown that intercession is a toil and a burden for every Christian —a definite and fruitful service.   The importance of sound and enthusiastic committee work can be brought before the audience—the personal service of some may be in that direction.   No indiscriminate appeal for foreign service can possibly be made.   If this appeal is mentioned at all it will be with the most stringent reservations.   It is worthy of note here, however, that in some audiences the opportunity for Christian service in the life of a business man abroad may be a new and valuable thought.

The Study Movement in the Churches grew in extent until the World War and continued to be closely related to the campaigns undertaken on behalf of foreign missions by students.   Some universities and colleges developed their own campaigns, but it was all related to the Student Movement, and the Theological Department Committee in particular was unceasing in its attention to the work of the campaigns, both in helping to extend them and make their work more effective.   A few months before the war broke out the Movement planned to give more attention to Student Missionary campaigns in the Churches, and having felt the need of a campaign secretary since Alan Stevens left, retained the services of E. Murray Page, who had been a travelling secretary in the theological college, as campaign secretary.

When the War came most of the campaigns arranged for the autumn of 1914 were cancelled.   One or two attempted to carry on, but lighting restrictions spoilt the attendance at evening meetings.   Before long most of the people who would under normal circumstances be on campaigns were either soldiers or war workers with the Y.M.C.A.

This halt was not, however, the end of student campaigns, as we shall see.

CHAPTER XIV

THE YEARS 1905–1907

EARLY in 1905 John Mott came to England, and among his other interests at this time was the collection of information about the supply of university men as candidates for the Christian Ministry. He came into the office one day and expressed the desire for an interview on the subject with the Archbishop of Canterbury (Dr Davidson), and he wanted the interview at once. This was at a time when we were unaccustomed in Student Movement circles to mixing with high ecclesiastics, and none of us had ever been inside the walls of Lambeth Palace. Mott, however, was insistent, so I rang up Bishop Montgomery, the secretary of the S.P.G., and asked his help. He happened to be just about to start for Lambeth, so promised to see whether he could arrange an interview. The result was that next day Mott and I set out on what was for each of us our first visit to Lambeth.

While our hansom careered down the Embankment towards the Palace, Mott laid his plans.

You don't know this man?

No.

Will he be sympathetic?

I don't really know; he's a very busy man and probably knows very little about the Student Movement. He'll very probably not want to become involved in a new interest, so is most likely, unless you really interest him, to attempt to be polite and yet get rid of us as quickly as possible.

Well, I'll introduce the subject of securing young men for the Ministry at once, and if his attention is not immediately caught, then I'll break off and begin to interest him about the Federation, and we'll start again on the Ministry when we have caught him.

Yes.

Now, we have got to interest him. I'll tell him about the students in the Far East and carry him round the world, and the minute I stop speaking you cut right in and pick up any points that you think I have missed. Don't give him a chance, don't let him say anything, we must interest him.

All right, I'll do what I can.

By the way, what do I call this man—my Lord?

No, you call him your Grace, but don't say it too often.

On arrival at Lambeth we were greeted by a chaplain and within a few minutes were in the Archbishop's presence. I recall the scene vividly. The Archbishop shook hands, motioned us to a couch where we sat side by side, and seated himself at his writing-table, across which he looked at us. He wasted no time, but immediately asked that we should state our business. Mott explained that he was making an inquiry on the subject of recruiting the ablest young men for the Ministry and was anxious to have the opinion of the Archbishop on the subject. The Archbishop interrupted him to explain that he had just appointed a committee on this very subject, and that until the committee had reported he felt it was impossible for him to say anything official on the subject. The interview showed every sign of an early end, but Mott's prearranged strategy was put relentlessly into operation.

Excuse me, your Grace, but I should like to tell you something about the work of the Student Christian Movement among young men.

Then without a pause Mott started with Japan and began describing his meetings in the University of Tokyo. I looked anxiously at the Archbishop to see how he would take it. As soon as Mott began to speak he lent back in his chair with a resigned look upon his face, as much as to say, " Alas ! I am evidently in for it with this troublesome American." But as Mott spoke

on, addressing the Archbishop exactly as if he was a
public meeting, his Grace's interest began to be aroused
and within about five minutes he had his face in his
hands with both his elbows on the table, and his gaze
fixed on Mott in a concentrated frown of interest.
Mott, having found an attentive auditor and a very
important man rolled into one, was in his element, and
with emphasis, eagerness and gesticulation, he proceeded with his address to the fascinated Archbishop.
He must have spoken for at least half an hour, when
suddenly without any warning he swung round to me,
remarking, " Now my friend, Mr Tatlow, has many
more interesting things to say to your Grace." By
this time the Archbishop was as putty in our hands and
looked responsively at me to see what I had to say.
Knowing Mott's ways and how carefully he stuck to his
programme, I was ready, and cleared up one or two
points in Mott's speech which by watching the Archbishop's face I had noticed had raised questions in his
mind. After a few minutes the conversation became
general between the three of us, and at the end of about
two hours the Archbishop suddenly said, " I don't often
meet two men who know their own minds as thoroughly
as you two do ; what do you want me to do about this
subject of the Ministry."

The upshot of the interview was that it was arranged
that when Mott returned a week later from Holland,
which he was just about to visit, there should be a
specially called meeting of the Archbishop's committee
to meet us and discuss the whole question. This was a
committee presided over by the Bishop of Hereford
(Dr Percival) with the Rev. S. A. Donaldson as secretary.
We had an extremely interesting meeting with the committee, the Archbishop himself attending. Mott made
a speech on the subject of recruiting for the Ministry
and then cross-questioned the committee, eliciting an
amount of very interesting information from those
present.

I took careful notes for Mott of what was said, which

was put in the form of a memorandum for him. But Mott was not satisfied, he had not got what he wanted. What he wanted was a letter on the subject from the Archbishop which he could use as propaganda, to draw attention to the importance in different countries of the question of recruiting for the Ministry, and he mourned that he had nothing in writing from the Archbishop. I felt that his Grace had been so kind and interested that there was no reason why Mott should not write and ask him for a letter. Mott, however, was very timid about doing this, but egged on by me he wrote, and as I expected, received in response just the kind of letter he wanted. " Oh my, isn't this just fine," he said, as he displayed the letter; " I tell you, this will weigh a ton in some of the countries in which I shall use it."

From this time onwards I became a regular visitor at Lambeth and came before long to have the privilege of the Archbishop's friendship, as well as his help and advice in relation to the work of the Movement to the end of his life.

The World's Student Christian Federation met at Zeist in Holland in 1905 and took a step long looked for by the Movement in Great Britain by creating a women's committee and appointing Miss Ruth Rouse as its first woman secretary. Our Movement had secured the recognition of women as having the right to be members of the Federation, but women students had no representative on either its committee or staff for the first ten years.

At this time we incorporated a new clause in the Constitution of our own Movement which restated its aim :

> The aim of this Movement is to lead students in British Universities and colleges to become disciples of Jesus Christ ; to unite them in seeking a fuller spiritual life ; to promote among them regular habits of prayer and Bible Study ; to keep before them the importance and urgency of the evangelization of the world, the Christian solution

of social problems, and the permeation of public life with Christian ideals, and to enlist them in whole-hearted service of these objects.

The story of the Movement is difficult to tell with directness because three vigorous Executive Committees were at work side by side, each developing different aspects of the work of the Movement. The General College Department Executive had the founding and development of Christian Unions in hand. This, with the promotion of Bible and social study, evangelistic work, conferences of all kinds and the provision of study text-books kept it busy. The S.V.M.U. Executive was occupied with missionary study, securing student volunteers, promoting student missionary campaigns and arranging large missionary conferences every fourth year. The Theological College Department was extending its influence in the theological colleges, hammering out its policy in relation to these colleges, steadily winning its way into the Church of England colleges and incidentally working out an interdenominational policy for the whole Movement. The General Committee kept all together, and undertook the discussion of major questions, such as the aim, basis and staffing of the Movement. It organized the summer conferences and provided finance for itself and the general and theological departments—the S.V.M.U. was self-supporting.

The four committees held a united conference in September to train new members in the work of the Movement and discuss major questions; each then met in succession for two to three days. Meetings at Christmas and Easter, and a business meeting at the summer conference amounted to four weeks a year spent in committee apart from sub-committees.

The leadership was primarily in the hands of the committees and secondarily with the secretaries. It is worth recording this, since during the World War primacy of leadership passed to the secretaries and has

S

never been regained by the committees of the Movement. The committees now advise secretaries and shape their ideas rather than produce creative work.

The Executive of the General College Department made inquiries in many quarters to see if it could find Bible Study text-books suitable for undergraduates, but without result, and many text-books were planned at this period by them and written to order, chiefly by former leaders of the Movement.

The problem of finding an adequate supply of student leaders in the colleges became acute, and in December 1905 I raised on committee the question for the first time: What steps can be taken to train leaders with the help of senior men? One result was the bringing of seniors to the summer conference to study what was needed in different parts of the college field. The leadership of Bible circles was obviously a considerable piece of work when we remember that there were 675 Bible Study circles at work under the auspices of the Movement, with 4800 students in them, of whom 1100 were not members of any Christian Union.

Bible Study was not the only concern of some of us at this time. I had not forgotten the intellectual hostility to Christianity which I had come in contact with among engineering and science students, when I was a travelling secretary visiting the new university colleges in England. Nor had Stephen Band's plea for intellectual help been forgotten by some of us.

It was not an easy period for the Christian who used his mind. The scientific movement which was based on a mechanistic view of nature that regarded the world as a closed system of a material order, moved by mechanical and mathematical laws, held the field. Herbert Spencer had just died and his influence was still potent; T. H. Huxley and Tyndall were constantly quoted. Haeckel's *Riddle of the Universe* was being spread broadcast in a sixpenny edition by the Rationalist Press Association, and, while some notable scientific men like Sir Gabriel Stokes (who died in 1903) and

Lord Kelvin, were Christians, the average demon-
strator one met in the college laboratories thought that
the theory of evolution explained the universe and left
no room for God.   Science students as a rule thought
that they could not be true to their studies and believe
in Christianity.   " I am an evolutionist, so I can't be a
Christian," said more than one man to me of those
who drifted into Christian Union meetings because they
had seen on the notice board that the speaker was an
engineering student.

The Churches were nervous and often defended
positions they ought not to have desired to defend.
They tried to show that the science of the Old Testament could be squared with the science of the day, and
theological students were taught Paley's *Evidences*!   I
had bought and read a good many books on the relation of religion and science as an undergraduate, and
when I returned to the Movement after a second period
at Trinity College, Dublin, I was anxious that the
Movement should lay itself out to help the large body
of men and women who thought that if they accepted
the teachings of modern science they could not at the
same time become honest Christians.

I continued to raise on the committee the question
of dealing with the difficulties of science students, but
without result.   The suggestion that we should have
lectures on religion and science at the summer conference was rejected again and again on the ground
that if we turned men's thoughts to the consideration
of intellectual questions we should deflect them from
more fundamental matters, such as conversion and
consecration.

I talked with individuals in the colleges and at summer
conferences for several years off and on, and then a
group of women Fine Art students in London asked
me to meet with them regularly, give them talks on
apologetic lines and discuss these with them.   The
Rev. Alexander Connell, a friend of mine, then minister
of Regent Square Presbyterian Church in West Central

London, lent me his dining-room in the autumn of 1905, and I asked the group to select and invite thirty students who could come regularly. The numbers never could be kept down to thirty. We carried on week after week in a room packed to suffocation. I dealt with doctrinal questions more than with apologetics, speaking for half an hour and then discussing for one and a half hours. The group was eager and live-minded, and a need was so obviously being met that the committee asked me to speak on " Christian Evidences " at the next summer conference at a series of sectional meetings. The meetings were crammed and the Bible readings parallel to them deserted ; this convinced the committee that this new element must be added to the programme at the summer conference. No summer conference since that day has been without addresses dealing with Christian apologetics or doctrine.

The London Women's Committee arranged for me to continue to lead an apologetic and doctrinal study group the following winter, but were not deflected by this from their interest in Bible Study, as some feared they would be. They convened a conference of Bible Study leaders at Westcliff-on-Sea from November 24th to 26th, 1906. This conference dealt with such topics as individual Bible Study, how to face difficulties about the Bible, the use and abuse of text-books and commentaries, the function of a Bible-circle, difficulties in the conduct of a circle, the responsibilities and preparation of leaders. This Bible School turned the minds of its promotors to the need for a more thorough and scholarly presentation of the Bible at the summer conferences to supplement the usual devotional Bible readings. The question of the Movement's attitude to Biblical scholarship was faced, and in the end the Movement decided to adopt frankly the modern position about the Bible.

In the meantime, former members on the mission field took a great deal of interest in the Bible Study books being issued by the Movement. Foremost

among these was Henry T. Hodgkin, by now working
in China, who wrote :

Friends' Mission,
Chentu,
4th August 1906.

My dear T.,
    There is a point I have been thinking about a good deal
lately, in reference to the Bible Study department of the
S.C.M. I am afraid I may not make it quite clear as I
cannot talk it over with you. It seems to me that the
Movement has practically developed a new method of
Bible Study, or at least has made a very real contribution
towards the practical working out of a new method of
study. There is something in our text-books that one
looks for in vain elsewhere. They have a combination of
scholarliness and devotion that is very rare, and the way
in which the individual is made to think things out himself is most valuable ; and I certainly know of no other
series that succeeds so well in meeting a need that I think
is much wider than our own constituency. I have been
thinking that there rests on the Movement a certain responsibility in this respect, both to our own members who
have left college, and to others who have been introduced
in various ways to the S.C.M. text-books, and who feel
that they have opened to them a new vista of the possibilities of Bible Study. I had this moral pointed out to
me the other day by receiving a letter of very warm thanks
for my *Hebrews*, which the writer said had given her quite
a new idea of Bible Study, and she went on to say that
after having been through it she was at a loss to know
what to do next, in order to carry on study on the same
lines. . . . I have been feeling that the S.C.M. might be
doing the right thing if it were to put its hand to the carrying through of the work it has begun in preparing these
text-books, especially in two ways. In the first place, I
think that you might look to the publication from time to
time of new books, and make ultimately a complete series
of text-books on the Bible on the same lines as those
already published, and in the second place, I think there is
a wide field open to the Movement in the direction of
applying the same method to topical studies. . . . I am
coming to think more and more that the Movement must
be prepared to take a rather larger place in the religious
life of the country as time goes on. There are an increasing

number of men who have drawn their religious inspiration and ideals largely from the Movement, and we are beginning, whether we will or no, to be looked up to by these and others as standing for a particular set of ideas which they cannot see adequately represented elsewhere. This and other things force us to accept a wider sphere of usefulness than that which is strictly represented by the field which we have chosen for ourselves. I think one needs to get away from the Movement for a bit to realize this. . . .

Yours affectionately,

HENRY T. HODGKIN.

While some wanted books, written in untechnical language, which presented the best that Biblical scholarship could offer, others wanted the Movement to produce very simple books to assist devotional study without making any intellectual demand. This was not in the interests of obscurantism, but came from medicals, who pleaded " no time," and training-college students, whose slender intellectual background and crowded course made serious study difficult. Garfield Williams, St Bartholomew's Hospital Medical School, made an onslaught on the text-books the Movement had produced and led those who asked for simpler books with a lesser intellectual element in them. Finding that Miss Warner, the chairman of the Bible sub-committee of the Executive, tended to take the same line, I entered the field on the other side, writing :

93 Chancery Lane,
E.C.

Dear Miss Warner,

You and Mr Williams both seem to desire to eliminate the intellectual grind in Bible Study and substitute for it the finding of " best thoughts " and emotional appeal, with a view to securing that students shall go out to their day's work with hearts spiritually warmed by their Bible study. Now there are days when Bible Study alone will spiritually warm the heart, and I admit that there is an element of real value in the type of Bible Study which gives one a " best thought " for the day, which is the very centre of

Mr Williams' position—that is the thing he always talks about—but I do not feel that I really believe in this kind of Bible Study.   It simply tends to produce the C.I.C.C.U. type, what Dr Forsyth is never tired of talking of as " the Christian Endeavour type of Christianity."   This type of Bible Study tends to make people keen and sentimental. I want to make people keen and intellectual.   There is a revolt in our day against theology as such, but I do not think we can get on without theology, and you cannot have theology without a certain amount of dryness and intellectual grind, and I believe that the best kind of Bible Study is the kind which in itself may be the least heart-warming spiritually at the time.   The man who studies the Bible thoroughly may find nothing to move him for many days, but he is laying down a base, he is building up a solid structure and in the long run he will be a stronger man spiritually than the man who always wants to get a " best thought " for the day and is satisfied when he gets it.

Yours very sincerely,

T. Tatlow.

The intellectual element in the study work of the Movement was steadily strengthened, while we tried to meet the need of the simpler folk in the colleges.

The work was growing rapidly at headquarters, and the Executive appointed Miss Margaret Bretherton, who had been a successful travelling secretary, as my first assistant secretary, in September 1905, and a year later, when she left, appointed her sister, Miss Gladys Bretherton, as my first private secretary. Miss Bretherton remained in this post until 1914, when she resigned to become one of the secretaries of the World's Y.W.C.A. As she had the kind of gifts needed for the post, plenty of brains, and was methodical and industrious, she became a pillar of strength at headquarters.   She acted as sub-editor of *The Student Movement*, dealt with corre-spondence, the preparation of most of the literature for the Press, and kept the records of the Movement.   She also talked with the growing body of secretaries as they came in and out of the office and became invaluable to them, as to me.

The sub-editing of *The Student Movement* involved correspondence with editors of localized editions of it. The first special edition of *The Student Movement* was issued by the Art Students' Christian Union, and the first university which produced its own supplement was St Andrews University. Edinburgh and Oxford followed this example at once and others soon followed.

The Annual Meeting of the Movement in London continued to be appreciated by members and friends and drew a thousand people. The Christian Unions were developing an increasing initiative and finding new methods of their own. St Andrews University was the first Union to hold a week-end conference during term. This was in 1904. The next year there were such conferences at University College, Aberystwyth; Alexandra College, Dublin; Armstrong College, Newcastle, and at Cambridge and Dublin Universities; and a couple of years later the method had been copied by several of the new university colleges in England, with good results.

The difficulty of finding a meeting-place for study circles and a centre where the Christian Union library could be kept and committee meetings held was very acute in the case of all the non-residential colleges, and W. W. Seton [1] gave a great deal of time and thought to this question. The large buildings erected by the Student Department of the Y.M.C.A. in American universities interested a number of Student Movement visitors to America. Seton thought that the time would come when British non-residential universities would have their own S.C.M. buildings.

With this question arose that of having a man to devote all his time as a Student Movement secretary in a university. Whether the secretary or the building should come first gave rise to a great deal of discussion. In the end, the sub-committee which Seton convened advised that the secretary should come first, and that

[1] Afterwards Dr Walter W. Seton, Secretary of University College, London.

while a Christian Union building was an idea to keep
in mind for the future, it would need more money
than could readily be secured, but in the meantime " it
would be a wise policy for the committee to suggest to
strong Christian Unions, which did not already possess
premises in or near college, the propriety of taking steps
to secure a room." The sub-committee pointed out
that Edinburgh University Christian Union had its own
rooms, University College, London, had a room in
Gower Street, while the Christian Unions at Owens
College, Manchester, and University College, Reading,
had been given rooms in college, and University College,
Leeds, had been promised a room in college.

The places the sub-committee reported as needing
local secretaries urgently were : Liverpool, Manchester,
University College and King's College, London, Cambridge, Edinburgh and Glasgow Universities; and in
the women's colleges, London, Manchester and Edinburgh. London was regarded as the most urgent need
among the women. There were sixteen affiliated
women's Christian Unions in London and six or seven
unaffiliated Unions, with a great deal of administrative
work arising from the activities of the London Women
Students' Committee. In Edinburgh a woman graduate, Miss Mackenzie, was doing the work of a general
secretary in an honorary capacity.

The immediate result of this report was a move in
Liverpool University to have a secretary. The leaders
asked my help, and I raised in Liverpool most of the
money required for the first three years. H. E. Dallimore, a graduate of the university, was appointed as
whole-time secretary at Liverpool in the autumn of
1907, being paid by the Liverpool Christian Union,
which handled the money that had been raised. My
first idea was to create a committee of senior men, but
it was ascertained privately from the Vice-Chancellor,
Dr Alfred Dale, that although he was strongly in favour
of the Christian Union having a secretary, he did not
wish senior men in Liverpool to be associated with

an undergraduate university society. So a Board of Control of the Liverpool Secretary Fund was formed, consisting of the Vice-Chancellor, Professor Gonner and three students. Thus Liverpool was the first of the modern English universities to have a whole-time paid S.C.M. secretary. Dallimore made the office a success.

It was the growth of the Christian Union which necessitated the services of a man giving all his time to it. While a union was small and undeveloped it was possible for an undergraduate to act as secretary without his college studies being unduly interfered with, but as study circles—Bible, missionary and social—multiplied in number, general meetings, prayer-meetings, and committee meetings increased, more elaborate printing connected with programmes and membership was needed, more efforts to reach freshmen had to be made, more visits of Student Movement secretaries arranged, more delegations for conferences worked up, it became impossible for an undergraduate to do anything like all that was needed, together with his college work, without being hopelessly overburdened. Christian Union secretaries, even in the residential universities, felt the pressure of what had to be done. It was much more serious in a non-residential university, where the officers of the Christian Union often had to spend much time in travelling from where they lived to the university, and had to attend far more lectures than was required in one of the ancient universities.

When, therefore, it was proposed to secure the services of a young graduate to give his whole time to the work of the Christian Union, live within easy reach of the university, undertake many of the duties which had hitherto fallen to an undergraduate secretary, and, above all, lay himself out to become personally acquainted with students, study their needs, and be prepared to initiate advance in new directions, the proposal was received with enthusiasm, and other places soon followed the lead given by Liverpool.

Perhaps it is worth interjecting a word about the

sense in which the Student Movement has always used the word "secretary." If anyone thinks of a secretary in the Student Movement sense of the word as a person primarily concerned with business and routine, he is entirely mistaken. Whether the word has been used to describe workers in the colleges or on the staff of the Movement, it has been the designation of those whose primary function was spiritual leadership. If the Student Movement used the word "pastor" or "chaplain" to describe its secretaries, such description would give a more accurate idea of the work of a Student Movement secretary to people outside the colleges. While local secretaries have always had a certain amount of business to transact, their primary function has been spiritual leadership. None of us realized when these secretaryships were first instituted the amount of individual and intimate help and guidance those who held them would give. This side of the work has varied with the personality of the secretary, but whenever he could rise to it (and the majority of them have risen to it), he became the moral and spiritual counsellor of a considerable body of students. In a modern university there is no one, as in the ancient universities, whose business it is to devote himself to the moral and spiritual needs of the students, and as soon as the Movement began to institute these secretary-ships, undergraduates who had not known to whom to go for help and advice now found the helper and friend they wanted in the intercollegiate secretary.

Many have been the problems that have come to these intercollegiate secretaries. Was gambling becoming a serious problem in the University Union? It seemed natural to turn to the intercollegiate secretary for help and advice. Did drunkenness show itself at college functions? Again, what was more natural than that the help of the Student Movement secretary should be solicited. And so these secretaries came to have an acquaintanceship and an influence far beyond the bound-aries of the Christian Union, and received support and help from vice-chancellors and other university authorities as cordial as any friend of the Movement would wish.

University authorities have not been slow to recognize the value of the presence of a carefully selected man, living among the students as one of themselves and only a year or two senior to them, whose whole time and strength is devoted to helping them, and the Movement's foremost helpers in raising funds have been vice-chancellors in the modern universities.

Walter Seton, being one of the most competent people on the committee in relation to college matters, was asked to prepare a report on the colleges unentered by the Student Movement, and a document which he presented in December, 1906, guided the committee and secretaries for a number of years. He raised the whole question of the principles on which Christian Unions had been admitted to affiliation, pointing out that these principles had never been formulated, that the committee had been guided by a general idea and precedents based on individual instances.

Seton unearthed one or two interesting things from the past. For example, in January, 1896, the committee had decided not to admit " the Y.M.C.A. Bible-reading Unions into affiliation with the Movement " and at the same time to admit no Christian Unions in colleges that had only evening classes. In 1897 the National Health Society and Sanitary Institute had applied for affiliation but was not admitted. The committee, however, at this time decided that naval and military colleges should be induced to affiliate Christian Unions and that an attempt should be made to enter training-colleges and art schools. In 1898 the Movement decided not to admit pupil teacher centres nor to admit law students, except where they were students attending lectures in universities or colleges. In 1905 it decided against schools of cookery and physical training colleges [1] but in favour of veterinary colleges.

[1] Christian Unions in Domestic Science and physical training colleges were first admitted to the S.C.M. in 1920.

Seton prepared a complete list of universities and university colleges, agriculture, art, architecture, dental, engineering, law, medical, military, music, naval, technical and training colleges, indicating those that he regarded as eligible for affiliation and offering explanations where any college should, in his judgment, not be regarded as eligible. This report concluded with a list of twenty-six colleges of all kinds which the Movement had not entered and which he regarded as eligible. The report was adopted with one proviso, and that was that Tom Inskip,[1] a former member of the Movement, should be asked to investigate the situation with regard to law students and report to the committee, which he did. Seton's list was carried by travelling secretaries for many years and a number of the colleges in it ultimately entered by the Movement. Some of the colleges, as time went by, disappeared or were amalgamated with other institutions.

The rapid growth of the Movement and equally rapid change in personnel among the leaders led to the decision to create a Senior Advisory Committee, composed of former secretaries and committee members. The object of the committee was: to discuss questions referred to it by the General Committee of the Movement, to offer suggestions as to the general policy of the Movement, to administer any trust funds committed to it by the General Committee, and to undertake any executive work which might be entrusted to it by the General Committee. In order to qualify them for their work, the members of the Senior Advisory Committee were asked to read the Minutes of the General Committee and the three departments of the Movement, to attend the summer conference and the executive conference in the autumn: the committee to meet not less than once a year, after the autumn meetings of the General Committee and before the Christmas meetings. The first committee appointed at the end of 1906 consisted of Frank Lenwood, A. W. Davies, J. H. Oldham, Ruth

[1] Afterwards the Right Hon. Sir Thomas W. H. Inskip.

Rouse, Lilian Stevenson, with R. L. Barclay and T. Tatlow as *ex-officio* members.

During this period the most important activity of the S.V.M.U. was missionary study. The Union printed a table in the Annual Report, presented July 1906, showing the progress of missionary study during the previous six years. I give the table, adding one more year so that it shows statistically what happened during the seven years I added the responsibilities of a study secretary to my other duties for the Movement. The table is instructive. The Movement published no missionary study statistics for 1899 to 1900, but missionary study had dwindled to very small proportions after Douglas Thornton went to Cairo in 1898. The Report of 1900-1 says that twenty-eight colleges began to study missions for the first time. Next year there was a further rise, then a drop—I had taken up work in a busy London parish and gave much less time to interviews and letters about study. I returned to full-time work for the Student Movement in the summer of 1903 and immediately there was an increase in the amount of study. Study must be promoted.

	Number of colleges having study.			Number of study bands or meetings.			Number studying.		
	Men.	Women.	Total.	Men.	Women.	Total.	Men.	Women.	Total.
1900-1	24	34	58	31	38	69	290	486	776
1901-2	16	37	53	30	41	71	400	610	1010
1902-3	11	31	42	15	35	50	300	630	930
1903-4	25	34	59	40	72	112	546	914	1460
1904-5	24	38	62	39	86	125	590	1002	1592
1905-6	21	34	55	61	113	174	727	1015	1742
1906-7	22	46	68	72	139	211	740	1338	2078

When the period covered by this table began, the Executive was in the depths of despair because the number of students signing the Volunteer declaration had fallen to 92. During these years there had been an increase each year in the number of Student Volunteers until at its close the number joining annually had more than doubled. We had again proved the truth of

Douglas Thornton's dictum that the way to get Student
Volunteers was to promote missionary study.

Our attention was drawn in a new direction. The
majority of the women leaving the colleges went into
the teaching profession, and we were constantly being
told of the spiritual needs of these women and their
sense of isolation in many of the schools in which they
found themselves. The Union of Students for Work
among Schoolgirls[1] and the Movement were concerned
with this question, and wanted to bring together schoolmistresses interested in religious work among schoolgirls. Accordingly they decided to combine and hold a
conference for women teachers in secondary schools.
This took place in Crossfield Road School in Hampstead
from January 7th to 12th, 1907; 187 delegates attended,
of whom 135 were teachers, representing 91 schools.
The remaining 52 persons were representatives of
different forms of Christian work in schools, together
with some of the secretaries and committee members of
the Student Movement. The conference was organized
by Elsie Stevens, Somerville College, Oxford. She had
to sail for India, however, to take up missionary work
there three months before the conference, and Mrs
Tatlow took her place as secretary of it.

The chair of the conference was occupied by Miss
Douglas of the Godolphin School, Salisbury, one of the
outstanding schoolmistresses of the day, while the
speakers included, the Rev. the Hon Edward Lyttelton,
headmaster of Eton, Canon G. H. S. Walpole, the Rev.
W. B. Selbie, John Lewis Paton, headmaster of the
Manchester Grammar School, Miss Maynard, mistress
of Westfield College, Miss Staveley of Bristol University
and several secretaries of the Student Movement. The
level of speaking was high, and the outcome was a
decision to enlarge the Union of Students for Work
among Schoolgirls to include mistresses in secondary

[1] This Union was founded by S.C.M. members in 1899 and
subsequently became the Federation of University Women's
" Camps " for Schoolgirls—a valued ally of the Movement.

schools and develop its policy for the benefit of both elements—mistresses and schoolgirls. In the event the development did not take place, but we profited in the Movement by a better understanding of the help needed by those preparing for the teaching profession.

This spring some time and thought had to be given to the question of the comprehensiveness of the Movement. R. P. Wilder was doing good service in connection with the Movement's approach to High Churchmen. The man most loved and trusted by the Evangelicals was a *persona grata* in High Church circles. Neville Talbot was also working hard on behalf of the Movement. Its comprehensiveness was attracting sympathetic attention in religious circles in England.

The comprehensiveness of the Student Movement was neither achieved, nor is it maintained, without difficulty. It has often been claimed by those who disliked its growing comprehensiveness that it was ultra-evangelical at its start, but while this is partly true, it was always more comprehensive than a great many people have recognized. For the first decade it was unrepresentative of the Church of England, none of its leaders, and hardly any of its members, coming from any except the evangelical school of thought. In Scotland it was representative of one of the great Presbyterian Churches in Scotland, the United Free Church. In practice this meant that there was always a strong liberal element in the Movement in relation to Biblical scholarship; from the first there were men in its leadership who appreciated the great movement of the Spirit manifested in the work of Biblical scholarship, technically known as Higher Criticism, and who realized that it was the Higher Criticism which prevented many thoughtful men from putting the Bible upon the shelf.

In England there were similar thinkers among Free Churchmen in the Movement; the Anglicans, however, had most of them been brought up in an extremely conservative school, especially in relation to the Bible, and while it was a school of thought that insisted on a competent knowledge of the contents of the Bible, it taught a very narrow view of inspiration.

The senior friends of the Movement in England in its early days were almost all from this conservative school of thought ; but the desire for comprehensiveness was there from the first, and we had the double task of thrashing out with one another our views, especially on Biblical questions, and at the same time of explaining and justifying our policy of comprehensiveness to some of our best friends. This was not easy. The evangelical school of thought in the Church of England was beginning to be divided sharply on the question of the Bible, but this tendency was only in its beginning and it was often not easy for the student leaders to know where individual men stood. Some, like Dr Eugene Stock, were conservative themselves but sure that God was with the Student Movement, and ready to see it invite to its platform Presbyterians who were Higher Critics ; other evangelicals were very uncompromising; their attitude may perhaps best be indicated by giving a letter from Prebendary Webb-Peploe, one of the leading evangelicals of the day, who had accepted an invitation to attend the Conishead Conference of 1907 :

Onslow Square,
S.W.

My dear Mr Tatlow,

It always pains me to appear doubtful as to my duty, but sometimes one is placed in a position which demands action. I have been twice informed during the last few days, to my great astonishment and distress, (1) that at your Conishead Conference I shall not only find present brethren of the Protestant Evangelical and Keswick school of thought, but higher critics from many parts (England and Scotland) who will be allowed to stand up and teach their opinions, and (2) that though you have given me the sole place of speaker at the evening meeting, I am almost sure to find myself on the Tuesday and Wednesday mornings appointed to teach in one place while another man of different views will be teaching elsewhere at the same time.

T

May I ask if these reports are true, or whether (as at Keswick) all the speakers will, D.V., be of " one mind, heart and mouth," and whether I shall have the whole conference (*i.e.* if they choose to come) present with me on Tuesday and Wednesday mornings ? I am compelled to say, plainly, that the reports which have reached me have upset all my views of your gathering (if true) and they would make me totally out of sympathy, I fear, with your gatherings. I can face no conference where " the house is divided against itself " and where I am to pit my teaching against a rival of another school. Forgive plain speaking for the matter is awfully solemn to me and I need complete guarantee before I can offer my services. Every man has a full right to his own opinion and I am in no sense my brother's judge ; but my duty is to my mind absolutely clear—only to co-operate with men whom I believe heartily to be of one mind upon God's Book, from Genesis to Revelation inclusive. Pray pardon me for writing thus plainly and believe me,

Yours very sincerely,

H. W. WEBB-PEPLOE.

P.S.—It is for the young Christian's sake that I express myself so strongly. May I ask for the names of your other speakers ?

I replied to Prebendary Webb-Peploe saying that the conference had been planned on the same lines as usual, that its great feature had been the wonderful spirit of unity throughout. " We are all of us much in prayer that it may be so again this year, and we are certainly not conscious of having made any plans likely to jeopardize such a spirit of unity in Christ as we have realized in the past." I explained that simultaneous Bible readings would be given by the Rev. E. S. Woods, Vice-Principal of Ridley Hall, and Canon Kempthorne,[1] Rector of Liverpool, but that they were in no sense to be regarded as rivals to him ; it would give a choice of subjects to the students and also lessen the strain involved in listening as one of a large audience in a

[1] Afterwards Bishop of Lichfield.

tent. In the end the Prebendary came to the conference. He did well on the whole, but could not resist
a whack at the Higher Critical views of some of his
fellow-speakers. It was the only occasion in thirty-
nine years' attendance at Student Movement summer
conferences that I have ever heard a speaker attack the
views of some of his fellow-speakers.

If we had our critics from without it was very
encouraging to get a letter from W. E. S. Holland
after the conference, saying: "Were you and the
Executive happy over the conference? I told you
what a revelation it was to me. Since our days *magna
fecit Dominus*. It is wonderful in our eyes." Little did
Gairdner, Holland, Donald Fraser, J. H. Maclean and
other of the early leaders realize what a help it was
to some of us in those difficult years of developing
relationships to find them happy at our summer conferences and rejoicing in what seemed to them wonderful
progress.

During the early summer good news came from the
East. The World's Student Christian Federation car-
ried out its intention, delayed by the Russian-Japanese
War, of meeting in the Far East. It arranged a conference, associated with the meeting of the General
Committee of the Federation, at Tokyo, April 3rd to
7th, 1907. There were 627 delegates from twenty-five
countries, of whom 184 came from outside Japan.
This was the first international gathering of any kind
held in the Far East and the interest taken in it by the
Japanese people was widespread. Viscount Hayashi,
Minister of Foreign Affairs, gave a reception to the
delegates at his official residence; there were numerous
other receptions by notables; King Edward VII sent
a message expressing his " earnest hope that the conference now being held at Tokyo may prove a
great success." The King of Norway and President
Theodore Roosevelt also sent greetings, and the
Marquis Ito gave the Federation £1000. The Press
was uniformly sympathetic. Nor was the purpose

of the gathering lost sight of, for, wrote Frank Lenwood :

> The first aim, that of the presentation of the fact of Christianity, has been accomplished here in as complete a way as could be wished. The evangelization, not of individuals, but of the corporate life of Tokyo, has been partially effected—of this the newspapers are sufficient proof. Great political leaders, groups of men who direct the commercial policy of the country, have entertained us as if we had been so many dukes.[1]

The delegates of our Movement were : Professor Sir Alexander Simpson, Edinburgh University ; Professor Alexander Macalister, Professor of Anatomy, Cambridge University ; Frank Lenwood, Mrs Lenwood (*née* G. M. Wilson), a former travelling secretary ; A. W. Davies ; Basil H. Backhouse, an undergraduate at Cambridge ; H. Garfield Williams and Una M. Saunders, travelling secretary.

The conference marked a new stage in bringing to the Federation the effective co-operation of Oriental student leaders.

[1] *The Student Movement*, vol. ix. p. 197.

CHAPTER XV

THE WORK OF THE MOVEMENT IN LONDON, INCLUDING THE RISE OF THE ART STUDENTS' CHRISTIAN UNION

THE work of the Movement in London occupied our attention a good deal round about the opening of this century. When the B.C.C.U. began work in London most of the colleges were virgin soil except the medical schools attached to the great hospitals, most of which had branches of the Medical Prayer Union.

The Medical Prayer Union was inaugurated in 1874 and from that date had carried on its work uninterruptedly. Its object was " the promotion of spiritual life, Christian work and missionary interest among the members and students of the medical profession." It consisted of two sections : the junior section for students, with branches at the various medical schools, and a senior section for qualified men and women. Its activities were, an annual general meeting held in January, when addresses were given on the Christian life, an annual medical missionary breakfast held in May, occasional conferences and special meetings, while its branches devoted themselves to " the study of the Scriptures, prayer and evangelistic efforts among students."

A year or two after the foundation of the British College Christian Union, which at first hardly touched London, the Medical Prayer Union " was anxious for some mind and hand to move among the members of the junior section, to infuse fresh interest and start newer methods of work, but was unable to secure such a man." When the B.C.C.U. began to concern itself with the problem of religious work in London, it did not organize apart from the Medical Prayer Union. A branch of this organization was almost invariably the nucleus of the Christian Union, which under the influence of the B.C.C.U. began to form in each of the Medical schools. The Executive of the B.C.C.U. conferred with delegates from the Medical Prayer Union in 1898, and as an outcome it was thought desirable that a joint appointment should be made of a man to act as secretary for London, whose chief duties would be to invigorate the Christian work in all the colleges and to found Christian Unions in those in which none as yet existed. By this means it was felt that the two Unions might mutually assist one another and, at the same time, the work in London would be extended and strengthened. A third of the salary of the London secretary was provided by the Medical Prayer Union, and H. W. Oldham of the Central Technical College began his work in October 1898 as the first occupant of this new post.

In the course of time the work of the London secretary created fresh energy, and soon began to create a generation of students who looked for leadership to the B.C.C.U. rather than to the Medical Prayer Union. After various private conferences it was agreed in 1906 by the two organizations that a change in their relationships should take place. The Medical Prayer Union decided to reconstitute itself as a union composed solely of qualified medical men and women, agreeing that its junior section should be disbanded, the members being already in the Christian Unions affiliated to the Student Movement. The Student Movement, on its part, undertook to bring the existence of the Medical Prayer Union to the knowledge of its members as they were about to qualify, and to recruit them for membership in the senior section on qualification. The Medical Prayer Union Committee met at Exeter Hall, Strand, W.C., on March 17th, 1906, and agreed to this arrangement. The actual handing over of the junior section to the Student Movement took place on September 5th, 1906, by a resolution proposed by Albert Carless, M.S., F.R.C.S., seconded by W. Macadam Eccles, M.S., F.R.C.S.

The man who carried the negotiations through was C. W. G. Taylor, London secretary, 1905-1906. When he took office London was suffering not only from the fact that there had been no London secretary for a year, but that H. W. Oldham, J. Percival Barnes—who qualified immediately before he took office—and Tom Jays, a man who had qualified at St Thomas's Hospital after a term of service on the mission field, had each of them been in office for one year only, a period just long enough, in a complicated and scattered field such as London, to make a start. Taylor had gained experience as a travelling secretary for the Movement before be became London secretary, and he not only carried through this reorganization, which greatly simplified machinery—an improvement pleasing to the busy medical student—but he did good work in promoting the spiritual objects of the Movement. There were college missions in University College and in St Bartholomew's Hospital Medical School, and a meeting on the message of the Movement at the Guildhall, presided over by the Bishop of London and addressed by Frank Lenwood, was attended by over one thousand London students, men and women. This meeting was followed by the first conference of men and women students in London on March 9th and 10th, 1906, at Morley Hall, Hanover Square. There had been a conference of 150 men the previous year. The women were much earlier in the field, having held their first conference in 1895.

Robert Wilder, who had returned to England from India, had become a member of the staff of the Student Movement the previous year, and he was invited to succeed Taylor in London, a small committee being formed to help him in his work. This was the genesis of the London Council. The London students elected it at the summer conference by desire of the Movement, whose general secretary was made an *ex-officio* member of it.

The following year a memorandum, signed by Walter W. Seton (chairman) and Garfield Williams (London secretary), was adopted by the London committee on September 18th, 1907, and forwarded to the Student Movement. It consisted of a scheme for the constitution of a London Intercollegiate Christian Union composed of all Christian Unions in non-theological men's colleges in London affiliated to the Movement, the Union to be controlled by an Executive Committee of fourteen members elected at the summer conference of the Movement. The affiliated Unions and the retiring Executive to have the right of nomination to this Executive.

It was proposed that this committee should take the place of the Advisory Committee to the London secretary appointed by the Movement in 1904, because " the time seems to have arrived for the London Christian Unions to constitute an Intercollegiate Union which will be possessed of financial and administrative autonomy, and which will be governed by a committee or executive which will be elected by the London men students themselves." The memorandum said that it was hoped to raise in London the necessary funds to pay a London secretary and carry on the work of the Movement in the men's colleges in London. The General Committee approved of this proposal and agreed that the grant contributed by the Medical Prayer Union towards the salary of the London secretary should be transferred to the committee of the new Intercollegiate Christian Union.

The new London Intercollegiate Christian Union was composed of Christian Unions affiliated to the S.C.M.; its committee was autonomous and had no defined relationship to the committee of the Movement. Robert Wilder, who had been London secretary, directed by the General College Department Committee and assisted by an informal committee of London students, became evangelistic secretary of the Movement, and the London Intercollegiate Christian Union Committee appointed S. H. Wood as secretary.

The L.I.C.C.U. launched a big programme which included a mission to London students by John R. Mott in the spring of 1908. It began with a meeting in the Albert Hall for students and their friends. It was attended by about 10,000 people, with the Bishop of London in the chair, and Mott gave a striking address on the "Crisis in the Far East." This address was ultimately printed and had an enormous circulation. This meeting was followed up by a series of four evangelistic meetings for men students in St James's Hall at 5.30 each evening; 500 men attended the first night and from 700 to 800 the other three evenings. During the mission there was a prayer-meeting each day at 8 a.m. in the Caxton Hall and at the same time a celebration of Holy Communion in Westminster Abbey, when there was special prayer for the mission. Students attending Caxton Hall and the Abbey breakfasted together at an A.B.C. near Big Ben daily. The mission made a deep impression upon the London student field.

The following year the chief corporate activity of the L.I.C.C.U. was a series of lectures in St James's Hall by the Rev. William Temple, Fellow of Queen's College, Oxford, on "The Faith and Modern Thought."[1] In 1911 a missionary conference in the Great Hall of King's College in the New Year and a social study conference at Easter were events in London student life.

The next year the L.I.C.C.U. was asked to arrange the Annual Meeting of the Movement. This was held on February 6th, 1912, in the Queen's Hall, which was nearly full. I was in the chair, and the speakers were the Bishop of Winchester (Dr Talbot), Mrs Creighton, Mr Mott, and the London secretary, K. E. Kirk. A custom had grown up of having a meeting in the autumn for London Freshmen, organized by the S.C.M.,

---

[1] The lectures were subsequently published under this title. The volume was one of Dr Temple's first books.

in the Mansion House; the first was in 1905. This year the Bishop of London was in the chair and he and Robert Wilder addressed 500 men. As the work in London grew, more and more attention was paid to the needs of students from the Orient, and Kenneth E. Kirk was appointed Foreign Student secretary. The first hostel for these students in London was opened in Ealing, under the care of the L.I.C.C.U.; later it was transferred to Hampstead.

The L.I.C.C.U. initiated an entirely new piece of work at this time. Some members of the Movement who were in the first camp of the London Corps of the Officers' Training Corps on Salisbury Plain in 1909 suggested to the L.I.C.C.U. that they should take some steps to meet the spiritual needs of the students in camp. Major Capper, the commanding officer, gave permission, and a marquee was provided in 1910, fitted up as a reading and writing tent, and liberally supplied with chairs and tables, writing materials, papers, magazines and games. Prayers were said in the tent daily and services conducted on the first Sunday by the Rev. Douglas Carey, chaplain at Sandhurst, an old Cambridge S.C.M. man, and the second Sunday by the Rev. N. S. Talbot, chaplain of the Junior O.T.C (Public School contingent). The Principal of London University visited the marquee and made a speech of appreciation. The tent was crowded whenever the men were at leisure, and many who were not members of the Movement took an active part in the management of the tent, some of whom were drawn into the Movement in London later. Members of the Movement in different colleges were brought in touch with one another, and the Christian witness of the tent and what it stood for was recognized as a spiritual asset in the life of the camp. The responsible committee " felt that the majority of men in camp were in sympathy with the tent and its- purpose." Major D. S. Capper wrote to the Movement very appreciatively, when the camp was over, about the value of the tent.

The next year improvements were made. There were 600 men in camp and there was universal approval of the action of the L.I.C.C.U. in providing the marquee.

Kenneth Kirk, with his London experience, raised the question of the relation of these camps to the Movement as a whole, the matter was taken up by the General Committee, and by 1914 the Movement had extended its work to the Scottish camp at Stobs, where students from Durham, Reading and Aberystwyth, as well as from Edinburgh, Glasgow and St Andrews, were in the same camp. Major J. Gough, V.C., commanding officer, thanked the Movement publicly for its services to the 800 men in camp.

Thus for half a dozen years the work in London was developed with great vigour under the guidance of the L.I.C.C.U., which found able men for its staff, amongst them S. H. Wood, L. S. Kempthorne, K. E. Kirk, F. M. Cheshire, M. S. Lawson and G. H. C. Angus.

Student Movement activity in London among women students had a different beginning, and it is now time to turn back a few years and see what was happening among them.

Two women students, one from the Royal Academy School and the other from the Royal College of Art, South Kensington, were stirred to activity as a result of a visit to the Keswick Convention in 1889. They arranged various meetings for Fine Art students and in 1890 their work resulted in the formation of the Art Students' Christian Union for South Kensington women students. The meetings of the Union were attended by art and music students, and also by Bedford College students until a Christian Union was formed there.

Fortnightly Bible readings were held, the leader being Miss Mayers, the South Kensington student referred to, who was secretary until 1894. Her successor, Miss Best, arranged for the affiliation of the Union to the British College Christian Union on April 9th, 1896. Miss Lilian Stevenson, a student at the Slade School of

Art who was interested in the South Kensington Union, became editor of *The Student Volunteer* in 1896, and discussed with Temple Gairdner, who was a keen musician, the best method of relating fine art students to the B.C.C.U. They sought to enlist the sympathy of G. F. Watts, R.A., the most famous painter of the day. Gairdner was received by Watts, who expressed his sympathy with the project of a Union for all art students and related to the Student Movement, but he felt too old to come from his retirement to share in the formation of the Union.

On November 27th, 1897, some sixty students from the Royal Academy, Slade, Herkomer, South Kensington, Bloomsbury, Lambeth, Blackheath and Crystal Palace Schools of Arts met at 8 Seamore Place, at the invitation of Blanche, Countess of Rosslyn. Gairdner described to them the B.C.C.U. and its work, and Lilian Stevenson spoke as an art student of the bond of common study and the bond of a deep-rooted need " which even the fulfilment of our most cherished ideals in art would fail to satisfy." Isolation and misunderstanding are the lot of the art student.

> The very nature of our work is isolating. . . . We are misunderstood, and what are in our eyes huge necessities, and mighty realities in the realm of art, are to our friends mere fads and artistic fancies. . . . There is an intense loneliness in the struggle for the expression of our very souls, beaten back ever and anon by the material of our vehicle of utterance, by our inability to bridge the gulf which separates the vision which floats before our eyes from the crude creation of our hands in which *we* can see so much and others—nothing.

The indefiniteness of the length of time a student must study, his days of inspiration alternating with long stretches of dull hard work, the demand upon his emotions with the consequent vacillation between morbid depreciation and jealous pride in his talents were skilfully set forth.

Lilian Stevenson spoke of the impossibility of men

and women created of God satisfying their souls in the beauty of the outward, and told of the deep underlying thirst for God.

She stated the case for an Art Students' Christian Union. " We must bring Christ to him, and to him *as an art student*," for the art student tends to stand aloof from Church organizations.

> As he sees the width and depth of the study to which he is giving his life, as he grasps new ideas of the principles of art, ideas which he feels are inexplicable to the outsider, the truths of the spiritual life to which he has hitherto given an unquestioning assent seem to him to have become part of that outer world which cannot enter into the inner sanctuary of art. He will follow art for art's sake, and let the rest of the world go their way. If they have found a Teacher, so has he. As for a Saviour, he will not think of that need yet awhile. The average art student, then, does not willingly put himself in the way of learning of Christ. We must bring Christ to him, and to him *as an art student*.

With deep understanding Lilian Stevenson spoke of how the art student lived in a world of his own, a little out of sympathy with the joys and sorrows of other people. The contrast between the squalid greyness of a dreary back street and the golden mist of sunset framed between narrow walls meant beauty to the artist, but his ears were often dull to the grim realities of the lives of men who dwelt in squalor. And more—the artist was tempted to think in the same way of God and Christ and the Christian life ; " ideas to be dreamed over and expressed by brush and chisel, but not facts to be lived out in our daily lives."

The address touched all present and most of the students gave their names as ready to share in the extension of the work of the Student Movement into art schools. Four months later the Art Students' Christian Union was founded and affiliated to the Student Movement. Its objects, as stated in its Constitution, were :

> (*a*) To bring the claims of Jesus Christ before every art student.

(*b*) To deepen spiritual life and promote Christian activity among the art students of Great Britain.

(*c*) To unite the Christian Unions already in existence among art students.

(*d*) To establish branches in art schools where none exist.

All art students, whether at schools of art or studying in private studios, were eligible for membership.

Unions were formed in the Royal Academy, Royal College of Art, Slade, Central School of Arts and Crafts, Royal College of Music and Alexandra Hall, Trinity College of Music, the Royal Academy of Music and the Guildhall School of Music—all in London. Also in the Schools of Art in Edinburgh, Glasgow, Dublin, Manchester, Liverpool, Nottingham, Sheffield, Leeds, Birmingham and Bristol.

Considerable interest in foreign missions was aroused and a scheme started for helping the missionary societies with illustrations for magazines and missionary books, and a great deal was done to give practical help in providing diagrams, cartoons and posters for exhibits both at the S.V.M.U. missionary conferences and at missionary exhibitions.

The expansion in various directions was largely due to the indefatigable work of Lilian Stevenson. She kept up continuous personal correspondence with the branch secretaries and with individuals. She was succeeded by Emily Scott (Mrs Tatlow) of the Dublin Metropolitan School of Art and the Royal College of Art, South Kensington, who was followed by Zoë Fairfield of the Slade School of Art, while on the men's side N. D. Davis and George Murray of the Royal Academy of Art, A. W. Pope, J. M. Woodroffe and Stanley Mitchell, all of the Royal College of Art, were successive secretaries.

In addition to her work for art students, Lilian Stevenson edited *The Student Volunteer* and later *The Student Movement* for six years, was the leader for several years of the whole women's side of the Move-

ment, edited *Students and the Missionary Problem*, and
was the life and soul of the women's delegation at the
summer conference on both its business and its religious
side. This gifted Irishwoman threw herself heart and
soul into whatever she had in hand, and her influence
lives on in the Movement to this day. She was asked
to revise the register of Student Volunteers, and she
not only did so, but devised a system whereby it is
possible to see at a glance how many volunteers have
joined and what has happened to them since joining.
No one has ever felt the system she devised can be
improved.

Miss Fairfield did all that her predecessors had done
for art students and more. Her circular letters to the
members of the Art Students' Christian Union did
much to inspire them. Here is one, typical of many :

St Normans,

Ewell, Surrey,

Sept. 1902.

Dear Fellow-students,

There was a sentence in the closing address at the Summer
Conference which struck me as being particularly true—
" When we leave the Conference we sometimes feel
superior to others *because we have been close to great ideals* . . .
the test of our renewed consecration is to come." To see
great ideals is something ; to make them living realities
in our lives is everything ! We need vision and we need
reality.

A good many of you to whom this letter will come have
been at the Conference yourselves (there were 20 women
from 6 Art Schools, and 6 men from 3 Art Schools at
Matlock). I wonder how far your impressions coincide
with mine ? I felt all the time that one's *vision* of the
meaning of life, and of its possibilities ; of the true relation
between God and every department of the world's life ;
of every individual soul to God—was being enlarged
and intensified, but that through it all this thought stood
out strongly—" *be real—do not dream.*" Face facts—do not
hold the truth at long range—if your faith be false you

are bound to change it ; if it be real you are bound to live and die for it—what sort of grip has it got of you ?   Are you living for it so intensely that if all others did the same, the Kingdom of God would come and His will be done ? Strong emphasis was laid from the first on the *reality* of sin—of temptation—of our weakness—of the difficulty of swimming against the stream and not with it—of our proneness to dally with temptation—" to turn it over, to look at the pleasant side."   Mr Mott told us in speaking of " a spiritual awakening " that one thing absolutely necessary was a *revival of reality*—in speech, in thinking, in battling with temptation, in possessing what we profess.   On the second evening the Russian delegate spoke a few words to us.   Speaking of their last Conference he said, " Our former Conference had been pleasant and helpful—at this we saw spiritual conflict."   If we would win men for Christ *we must cease to be indifferent*, we must prove that our religion carries us to the point of self-sacrifice.

During the last days we heard a great deal of the possibilities of a life of bondservice to Jesus Christ ; that sin is practically self-will, self-love, self-indulgence—rebellion against the will of God, shutting out the love of God, refusal to give all to Him Who gave all for us.   Bondservice to Jesus Christ is the essential condition on which our life reaches its true and best development :—it is the secret of unwasted years.   Left to ourselves we see ideals and fail to reach them,—we aspire and our aspirations vanish away like dreams ;—but there is absolute correspondence between Christ's ideals for us and His power to realize them in us.   Victory, not defeat, is surely our Lord's will for us, and victory is a gift to the faith that enthrones Christ in the heart—Christ Who has overcome on our behalf.

Probably the secret of most of our failure lies in the region of everyday life—in neglect of prayer and Bible study.   We see visions, and want to realize them ; we see difficulties, and long to overcome—but we do not go to God for strength.   " How extraordinarily hard it is to read the Bible—and to pray ! "   Life is so busy and fascinating—everyday duties are so real and so obvious— *but* life is first of all an opportunity for making character, somehow or other we must learn to be the masters of our circumstances, not their slaves.

We art students went to the Conference this year hoping for special help in our own special problem—the question of religion and art : and I think we found it, or at any rate, we were put in the way of finding it. [Here a number of practical matters were dealt with.]

Believe me,

Yours most sincerely,

ZOË FAIRFIELD.

About this time the Art Students' Christian Union stated the questions the art student had to face, in a leaflet explaining the Union, its objects and work, in these terms :

1. Where Art, in its widest sense, is divided from religion and ethics, and it is said that there is no relation between character and work, it is possible that art *may* not suffer, it is almost certain that the artist *must*. Some very great artists have been very bad men. The human soul is the supreme reality in human life, and art does not gain when it is ignored and character neglected. The pursuit of art in any of its forms makes such large demands upon the personality of the student that there is no room for any second claim : unless Christ is Lord of the whole life, including the work to which it is given, His Lordship will be nominal, or denied altogether.

2. When Art is put in the place of religion, and beauty or any other created thing is made the supreme object of worship, the result is something very like idolatry, which must in the long run tend to the degradation of both life and art ; while the acceptance of Christ's authority will mean at least this, that the artist's work will express nothing that is disloyal to our Great Master and His teaching. Whatever may be thought of the right of art to teach, no one can deny its power to influence, nor that there are tendencies in much brilliant modern art which need correction.

3. An artist is in no way exempt from the needs and the responsibilities common to humanity ; he has indeed the additional responsibility of a gift held in trust from the Giver for the service of men. He has the same need of God as other men, and the same need of help in his everyday life ; to him, no less than to others, Jesus Christ is the supreme revelation of God, at once His Image and our Ideal.

U

In 1904 a course of lectures was arranged by the committee of the Art Students' Christian Union—two at Leighton House, Kensington, and two at University College—on the relation of religion to art. They were delivered by Mr George Hare Leonard, Dr P. T. Forsyth, Mr T. Stirling Lee and Mr Alfred U. Soord, the last two being artists, and were attended by about two hundred students, who much appreciated them. Zoë Fairfield, who was the moving spirit in arranging the lectures, wrote afterwards :

> We certainly feel much more sure of ourselves [in the A.S.C.U.], more ready to go forward, convinced that we have a message with reason and history and truth on its side ; that artists and art students need the spirit of Jesus Christ to sanctify and bring to their best uses their work and themselves.[1]

Similar courses arranged from time to time have invariably been well attended by fine art students.

This year the Union also began the production of a four-page supplement to *The Student Movement*. The first number of the supplement gives a good deal of information about the Union, showing that it was very much alive, had a variety of activities and was financially solvent, a balance-sheet being published which showed that the expenditure of the Union during the year had been £112, 2s. 10d. It had helped its members with summer conference fees to the amount of £17, and had sent a donation of £20 to the Student Movement, closing its account with a balance of 8s. 8d. in hand.

The Union continued its work until 1910, when it was disbanded in order that the Christian Unions which composed it might take their full share in the national and district councils which were being organized by the Student Movement, of which more will be said later.

The art student is not a good administrator, not

[1] *The Student Movement*, vol. vi. p. 167.

because he has not the ability (he often has considerable ability in this direction) but because his energies are absorbed, and ought to be absorbed, by his work if it is to be good work. Art students have never organized themselves to any extent in their colleges, and never will; but if someone comes along whose work is less absorbing than that of the artist, and organizes lectures, discussions and the like, the art student will gladly respond.

While the Art Students' Christian Union carried on its work independently of what was happening among London students generally, the development among the men students, referred to earlier in this chapter, led the women students' committee, which was working in close co-operation with the Movement, to appoint a sub-committee consisting of Maida Lenwood, Zoë Fairfield and Marian Neatby. They reviewed the work in the London colleges and requested the Executive of the Movement, in April, 1907, to empower the London women to appoint a secretary, make a grant of £40 towards her salary, and provide her with a room at the offices of the Movement, 22 Warwick Lane, E.C. The committee asked at the same time that if a secretary was appointed, London should not be removed from the field of the women travelling secretaries of the Movement, who should visit it as heretofore.

In reviewing the claims of the London field the sub-committee pointed out that the London women's sub-committee had been formed in 1898, when there were three affiliated Christian Unions in London women's colleges, and at a time when the Art Students' Christian Union had just been formed to work among fine art and music students. When the London committee was formed it found very little contact existing between the women's Christian Unions. The only joint activity was an occasional meeting for London women students. There were also two meetings a year for men and women who were members of the S.V.M.U.

By 1907 the number of women students had considerably increased. Apart from fine art students it was estimated that there were 3000 women students in London. Among these there were now twelve affiliated Christian Unions and four others which it was hoped would soon be affiliated, while three more colleges were about to start Christian Unions. There was a conference in October, held for the purpose of interesting new students in the Movement, at which the attendance had risen steadily year by year, about three hundred women attending at the time of the report; a Whitsuntide conference for students who were unable to attend the summer conference; a conference for Bible circle leaders towards the end of the first term; and two joint conferences between the men and women London committees.

Since 1901 there had been corporate observance of the Universal Day of Prayer for students, the men having joined with the women. The first service in church for London students was on the Day of Prayer in February, 1904, when I preached at St Barnabas Church, Kensington, to a congregation of several hundred students. This church had been chosen as it was where I had served my year's curacy, and students knew the church; the vicar, the Rev. G. R. Thornton, an uncle of Douglas Thornton, was sympathetic. By 1907 this service had been moved to a more central church, Holy Trinity, Marylebone.

The London women's committee had grown. In 1898 it consisted of three students, of whom Miss Fairfield was one. In 1901 the B.C.C.U. General Committee added to it the travelling secretary for women's colleges and made it a grant of £3 for expenses. The committee was increased in size more than once, and a good deal of help given it by Miss Fairfield and one or two other people whose college work was completed; but when the women came to the General Committee of the Movement in 1907 asking for a secretary there was so much growth that the need for the full services of a secretary was urgent. On the other hand, the Student Movement committee was feeling the difficulties caused by expansion and was very short of funds. It made the London women a grant of £8, and appointed a sub-committee to look into the matter further. The London women realized that this meant delay, and as they were not to be daunted, they found an honorary secretary. Miss E. S. Bryan-Brown, London School of Medicine for Women, wrote as their chairman on September 22nd, 1907, that the London committee had appointed Helen Coomber as its secretary. She was a graduate who was able to give most of her time to the work of the committee in an honorary capacity.

It was not until 1912 that the salary of a full-time secretary for London was provided by the Movement, when Helen Squire was appointed. The women's committee in London set itself to build up the work of the Movement inside each London college; it had few corporate activities. The policy was successful, and the Women's Christian Unions grew steadily in size and influence in the colleges.

We must return to the situation among the men. The London student field contained one-third of the entire student population of the British Isles, and it was growing rapidly. An autonomous committee administering so large a section of the student field naturally became preoccupied by the immensity of its own task and tended to be forgetful of the rest of the Movement. The General Committee of the Movement, however, has always been a vigorous policy-making body, and it desired that its policy should influence the work in London. London students read its literature and came to its conferences. This resulted in the creation of a body of students in London who wanted to keep in step with the Movement's policy, while the London committee, without any hostility to the Movement's policy, was preoccupied with its own. Accordingly there tended to be two Student Movement policies for London. The absence of any formal link between the autonomous London committee and the General Committee was a source of weakness, the gravity of which became increasingly apparent. If it had not been for close personal friendship between myself, as general secretary, and the leaders of the work in London, the Movement would have known a great deal less than it did about the policy of the London committee, and the situation would have broken down sooner than it did.

There were also difficulties emerging from a different quarter. The women's colleges in London had organized years before the men and independently of them. The London women's committee was virtually a sub-committee of the Movement, with the result that its policy was closely in line with the general policy of the Movement. There were never wanting people to point out that this arrangement worked better than did the men's organization. While most of the London colleges had separate Christian Unions for men and women, there was a certain interchange of views between Christian Union leaders in co-educational colleges and an occasional joint meeting (the days of joint Christian Unions were yet to come), and as a result of this there was fairly constant suggestion that the London Men's Committee ought to shape its policy more definitely on the policy of the whole Movement. The women were critical of the London Men's Committee and many of the men were sensitive about this criticism.

As the London committee developed its work rapidly and came in time to employ not only a London secretary but an assistant, and a special secretary for work among foreign students, adding to this a hostel for them, the question of continuity became important. The work was too extensive for one student committee to pass on to another student committee, also the committee found that it needed an office and a financial policy which it could only have if there was continuity, which constantly changing London secretaries could not provide. This led, in practice, to Walter Seton, who had become a member of staff at University College, taking charge of the policy of the London committee. He was its chairman and worked with great ability and devotion, built up its finances and made himself indispensable to the work in London. He was not, however, a man who found it easy to share his ideas with younger people and accept theirs.

There is a subtle distinction between being a dictator and a leader. The leader of any group so democratic in its sentiments as that composed of British students must be clear that it is necessary to carry them with him whole-heartedly. To do this he must often sink his own ideas and must always be quite sure that he has a sympathetic understanding of the ideas of the younger group with which he is working. This Seton, with all his gifts, was not able to do and he tended to be a dictator rather than a leader. Kenneth Kirk, who became London secretary in 1910, saw this difficulty and strove to help Seton to adjust himself to the realities of the situation, but without avail. This ultimately led to Kirk's resignation before he had completed what was intended to be a long term of office with the Movement in London.

After Kirk left the tension between Seton and some of the younger men grew, with the result that he ultimately retired from the leadership of the London Intercollegiate Christian Union. Those who were left found the machine which had been built up in London wa. too heavy for them to carry. The foreign student hostel was too small, and in consequence did not pay, and no one had Seton's skill in securing and maintaining a body of subscribers. Then came the War, which aggravated all the difficulties of the situation. I had kept in close touch all through this period with Seton, Kirk and later G. H. C. Angus, who was the chief London secretary of this period, and the day came when he visited me, not simply in his private capacity, but on behalf of the London committee, saying that they were overwhelmed with their difficulties and asked formally for help and advice from the general secretary of the Movement.

It seemed wise to deal with the situation root and branch. The type of autonomous organization which had been built up in London had not proved itself well suited to the realities of the situation, while the inter-collegiate unions in Ireland, Scotland and Wales were working well. Accordingly I advised that a meeting should be called of S.C.M. representatives from all London colleges, both men and women, that they should be told quite simply, without going into detail, that the men found reorganization in London was essential for them, and that after a brief statement on these lines the proposal to form a London Intercollegiate Christian Union for men and women, to include theological students, administered by a committee on the model of the Welsh, Irish and Scottish committees, should be made.

This proposal was accepted *con amore* by the men. I had ascertained that the women would support the proposal, and when we held our joint meeting it was carried through without a hitch. Thus the London Intercollegiate Christian Union took its place beside those of Ireland, Scotland and Wales as an advisory committee of the Movement, with powers delegated to it by the General Committee. These powers have been enlarged in the post-war years. The sad thing was that the London committee had incurred debts to the amount of £800. There was nothing for it but for the General Committee to pay these debts and give the work in London a new start, which it did.

CHAPTER XVI

A NEW RELATIONSHIP TO INDIA AND A QUADRENNIAL CONFERENCE

THE Summer Conference, Conishead, 1907, was an eventful one in the life of the Movement. The Executive, reporting a year later, said of it :

The Movement has received no stronger proof of the blessing of God than the spirit maintained through the days we were together. The sense of unity was complete. The harmony of different faculties and the interweaving of the different points of view tended to draw together, and not to divide, the members of the conference. Above all, there was manifest a great working of the power of the Spirit of God both in the individual and the mass. In the meetings, in the recreation in the afternoons, in the moments of deep communion with one another, and in the secret worship of the heart, there was felt to be deep spiritual power. . . . An intense spirit of prayer united and sustained the conference, and created the sense of a great spiritual entity, to be used for the extension of the Kingdom of God.[1]

The meeting for intercession one day was devoted to India and S. K. Datta spoke on the claims of India to the greater love and sympathy of us all. Datta was an Indian who, after graduation at the Punjab University, studied at Edinburgh University, where he qualified in medicine the year before. He had spent a year travelling in the colleges with marked success, and already showed those gifts of insight and statesmanship which years later were to result in his becoming a member of the Legislative Assembly of India and a member of the Round Table Conference on India in

[1] *Annual Report*, S.C.M., 1907-8.

London, 1931-32. Mr John Morley had recently made some of his great speeches on the Indian question and it was Datta who read them with avidity and explained to us who worked at the Movement's centre the significance of these utterances. His address at Conishead made a deep impression on the conference and led to earnest intercession for India. The following day a totally unexpected cable was received from Calcutta addressed to the conference, which read :

> India's students her greatest peril and highest hope. Our Movement appeals to yours for leaders.—Azariah, Andrews, Carter.

The juxtaposition of Datta's address, the prayer which followed it and this telegram made a profound impression on the conference. The men who signed it were known to many. V. S. Azariah [1] was one of the leaders of the Student Christian Association of India, Burma and Ceylon, and was connected with the newly formed Indian National Missionary Society. The Rev. C. F. Andrews had come into touch with the Movement as a don at Pembroke, been a member of the round-table conference which discussed the relationship of the Movement to the Church of England, and later, as a member of the Cambridge Mission to Delhi, had become a regular contributor to *The Student Movement*. E. C. Carter was a graduate of Harvard University, a leader at one time in the Student Christian Movement in America, he signed the cable as General Secretary of the Student Y.M.C.A. of India. When the cable was read to the conference, those present, by a unanimous vote, authorized the committee to send a reply signifying willingness to help, and the following cable was despatched to India :

> Cable found British students already deeply stirred in sympathy and prayer for India. We will help you, God willing. Tell us how.—Tatlow, Davies.

[1] Afterwards Bishop of Dornakal.

These signatories being the secretary of the conference and Arthur W. Davies, University College, Oxford, its chairman.

The same day these cables were received and despatched, cards printed during the afternoon were distributed at the evening meeting, bearing the following words :—

A CALL TO PRAYER FROM INDIA

To the Student Christian Movement. India's students her greatest peril and highest hope. Our Movement appeals to yours for leaders.—Azariah, Andrews, Carter. Calcutta.

Let us thank God for this call to prayer and service.

Let us pray that God may show us clearly how we may help our brothers in India.

Let us pray that our people may meet the aspirations of India in the Spirit of Christ.

Let us pray for the people of India, and for the students that they may now be led into the truth of the Gospel and be the means of bringing to their fellow-countrymen the unsearchable riches of Christ.

Conishead,
26th July 1907.

That day there was set in motion influences which have drawn hundreds of members of the Student Christian Movement to India and have resulted in the maintenance of a sympathetic and understanding attitude towards India on the part of the Movement. This book cannot do more than indicate the far-reaching influence of the Movement in relation to India. The tie which has bound the Student Christian Association of India and our Movement together is a very close one. The seas divide us, but we have interchanged ideas and workers, and the names of V. S. Azariah, Lilavati Singh, S. K. Rudra, S. K. Datta, Kuruvilla Zacharia, K. T. Paul, John Matthai, R. Rallia Ram, Paul Ranganadhan, J. S. Aiman, Ariam Williams, Appadurai Aaron and A. Ralla Ram are names of Indians who have not only visited British colleges or worked as officers under the auspices of the Student Movement, but have been the close personal friends of many of the Movement's leaders.

The conference was also notable for the effective way in which that of the previous year had been followed up in relation to the Church of England. The committee felt it was of prime importance at this stage that it should secure the attendance of a representative group of Anglican dons, and as a result there were present the Rev. B. K. Cunningham, Head of Bishop's Hostel, Farnham; the Rev. Canon Johnston, Principal of Cuddesdon College; the Rev. S. A. Donaldson, Master of Magdalene College, Cambridge; the Rev. T. C. Fitzpatrick, President of Queens' College, Cambridge; the Rev. A. J. Tait, Principal of St Aidan's College, Birkenhead; the Rev. W. J. Conybeare, Head of Cambridge House; and Canon Scott Holland, who paid his first visit to a Student Movement conference and addressed an evening meeting on "Christianity and the Social Problem."

There was no one in the least like Canon Scott Holland. He was best known as a keen Christian social reformer, but although he spoke for the Movement on social questions on his first visit, it was his Bible Readings which became famous amongst us. He had never been before and promised to come and speak one evening, but said he must get off the next day. The address made a great impression. I was very busy with the conference as its secretary, and did not notice that Scott Holland did not go the next day, as he said he must. I only realized the last day that he was still there. I can see his big, burly form, round smiling face and arms swinging like a windmill as I met him between camp and Priory. "I thought you had to go after you had spoken," said I. "Dear old thing, I couldn't go, I loved it so," was his reply.

He came again and again—a great teacher and a great Christian. It was only when painful illness made it almost impossible for him to speak in public that he ceased coming.

Besides the clerical dons named above, we had with us Canon G. H. S. Walpole,[1] the Rev. H. P. Cronshaw, Dr Hugh Barbour of Edinburgh University and Mr A. L. Smith of Balliol College, Oxford, afterwards its distinguished Master. It was John Macleod Campbell who secured the attendance of A. L. Smith, an attendance which surprised people as he was not thought, at that time, to have any great sympathy for Christian activities. As a matter of fact, this conference played a bigger part in Mr Smith's life than anyone knew at the time except myself. He wrote immediately after the conference :

Balliol College,
Oxford,
July 26th, 1907.

Dear Mr Tatlow,

I beg to send a small donation which if you approve might go two-thirds to the Movement, one-third towards your conference expenses. Of all the hundreds there, no one can have been more impressed than I was by the wonderful spirit of the gathering and by its potentialities. It was the most interesting three days I ever spent ; not to mention the pleasure of meeting so many old friends. To yourself and all your committee who were so kind to me I beg to return through you my most sincere thanks, to congratulate you all on the success of your Movement and to express my deepest wishes for its continuance and increase.

Yours most sincerely,

ARTHUR L. SMITH.

The conference was undoubtedly a turning-point with him. I saw a good deal of him from time to time during the rest of his life. He became a whole-hearted friend of the Movement. One day, walking with him in Oxford, he suddenly stopped, turned round on the pavement and faced me, saying, "I like your Movement, Tatlow. I like it well." "I know you do,

[1] Afterwards Bishop of Edinburgh.

Master," I said.   " But tell me why."   " It is sound education.   Dons in my college sometimes complain to me that it occupies men's time too much with brown paper and string, but I tell them that it is not true.   It widens men's minds and helps them to think."

There were a number of representative Presbyterian and Free Church speakers at Conishead, pre-eminent among whom were : Professor James Denney, Dr R. F. Horton and the Rev. W. B. Selbie.   Miss Annie Small was not, I think, a speaker, but exerted no small influence on the conference in relation to Indian questions. Evangelicals had a prominent place on the programme and were represented by Prebendary H. W. Webb-Peploe and the Rev. Harrington C. Lees.[1]   An unusually large number of old Student Movement leaders were also present.   Louis Byrde, A. G. Fraser, Mrs A. G. Fraser (Beatrice Glass), Ruth Massie, Lucy Harris were all there, back from the mission field and most of them speaking.

The Federation meeting, which lasted two hours, is described as having been " crammed with interest." Baron Nicolai told of the difficult situation in Russia. We greeted Mr H. C. Rutgers as a man about to become general secretary of the Student Movement in Holland, and there were student speakers from Sweden, Norway, Hungary and Germany.

We were reminded of the Student Movement in South Africa by the fact that we took farewell of Oswin Bull of Jesus College, Cambridge, who had accepted an invitation to go to South Africa for two years to act as travelling secretary of the Student Christian Association. He has found a life-work in South Africa.

The conference provided a trying experience at the office in that the fees officer deposited £110 camp fees with the manager of the Priory in a safe, and forgot all about it.   I spent two months trying to find out how the money had been lost and then, as a last resort, communicated with the manager to see if he had any light

[1] Afterwards Archbishop of Melbourne.

to throw upon the loss. He turned out his safe and found the envelope with the £110 intact !

In the autumn much discussion took place on the committee as to the special call from India which had come to the summer conference. Correspondence ensued with the Bishop of Lahore (Dr Lefroy), the Rev. H. M. M. Waller,[1] the Rev. A. B. Wann and Mr J. N. Farquhar. These and a number of others were consulted as to the best way in which the Movement could respond to the request from India for help. Our first idea was to send a deputation from the Student Movement on a tour of visitation to the Indian colleges, and some of our correspondents were in favour of this, but on the whole the weight of considered missionary advice was that the real need of India was an increase in the number of first-class men and women who would devote their lives to missionary work in the country. A lead was given by the chairman of the conference, A. W. Davies, who decided as a result of the Indian cable to undertake missionary service in India.

An immediate practical outcome of the interchange of cables was the starting of what is known as " The Short Service Scheme." C. F. Andrews wrote emphasizing the sore need of permanent workers. " But," he said, " there is an immediate need, and this immediate need is pressing." The student class throughout India is under the influence of a wave of nationalism which tends increasingly to take up a position of hostility to all that is Western, and to Christianity, inasmuch as Christianity is in their minds identified with what is Western. The force which can check this movement more effectively than any other is beyond question personal touch between Indian students and Englishmen who are themselves in touch with Jesus Christ. " Personal influence ! personal influence ! that is what we are crying out for day by day."

Mr Rudra, the Principal of St Stephen's College, Delhi, had often said to Andrews, " Why don't men

[1] Afterwards Bishop of Madras.

come out here for part of their preparation and serve an apprenticeship first, and try their armour and find its weak spots?" Andrews quoted him to this effect, and in a letter of February 9th, 1908, wrote:

> Rudra has suggested more than once this very scheme which I am proposing . . . let us have a reinforcement of good men, who can come out immediately for two years (while preparing for their future vocation) and work *inside* our colleges and hostels as temporary members of the staff; let them have time to read and prepare, while giving their personal help to us.

What made Andrews act on Rudra's suggestion was a letter from A. W. Davies asking whether it would be possible for him to go to St Stephen's College for a term and bring four ordination candidates with him.

The short-service men were to be allocated to one of the colleges or hostels in India, to live among the students, give lectures in English, " probably teach Tennyson or Shakespeare, and take part in the games and social life of the college. It will be a real student movement from students to students; it will be really the students' gift to India, and it is the Christian student spirit from England that we ask for, it is that fresh, glorious enthusiasm of men that we need to bring in touch with the young rising life of India and to bring that touch on the spiritual, personal side."

A number of educational missionaries were consulted on the scheme and it met with their approval. The General Committee of the Student Christian Movement in Great Britain asked one of its members, John McLeod Campbell,[1] Balliol College, Oxford, " to investigate the practical possibilities, and if possible to initiate the experiment." Under this scheme, which is still operative in connection with the C.M.S., S.P.G. and L.M.S., a number of men have gone to India, many of them at the end of their two years having formed the purpose to make missionary service in India their life work.

[1] Afterwards Principal of Trinity College, Kandy, Ceylon.

We must now turn back to the fourth quadrennial missionary conference which we prepared all the previous year and carried through in the opening days of January 1908 at Liverpool.

A quadrennial conference of the Movement is not born in a day. J. W. Woodhouse records how, in March 1907, a small bundle arrived at his lodgings in Oxford which, on opening, he found to be Prayer Calls for the Liverpool Conference. " Ten months to pray for one week ! " he remarked, and when the conference was over we find him emphasizing in the pages of *The Student Movement* this fact of ten months of prayer in preparation for a week of conference as of no small value in having made the conference what it was. Prayer-meetings all over the college field and the prayers of a great body of individuals were all a definite part of the conference itself.

The business side of these conferences was never discussed on the committee of the Movement. The minutes say that it was decided " that Mr Tatlow should go forward at present with local arrangements and finance." This meant that after the committee had decided to hold the conference in the Philharmonic Hall, Liverpool, all the business of securing hospitality for the delegates, building up a local organization, making arrangements in Liverpool of all kinds, securing finance, was left in my hands. My wisest advisers in days before I had become expert in organizing conferences were three general secretaries of the Y.M.C.A., Mr Whitwell, Y.M.C.A. secretary at Birmingham, Mr J. H. Putterill of the Y.M.C.A., who had his office at Exeter Hall, and Mr Jameson, general secretary in Liverpool. There was no use in discussing these questions on student committees because students knew nothing whatever about the organization of a big conference.

What students have always done for the quadrennial conference is to concentrate upon the main lines of the programme. The final programme was the result of nearly two years' work, when a sub-committee, then the

x

whole committee and finally a conference committee thrashed out the main lines of thought which the conference should attempt to express, and broke it up into topics, choosing speakers for these.

I found that Liverpool people had not forgotten the conference of 1896, and everyone was very kind. The Vice-Chancellor lent the S.V.M.U. a room in the University as an office, which was used for several months until we transferred to the Y.M.C.A. a few days before the conference. The Lord Mayor with many leading citizens, the Bishop of Liverpool and the Free Church leaders all threw themselves into the arrangements with cordiality. We were provided with all the hospitality for delegates and all the money for expenses that was needed, so that when the conference promised £1818 spread over five years, with £757 available within a few months, it was possible to reserve it for future work.

Some of the preliminary literature was translated and printed in French, Norwegian and German, and John McLeod Campbell and H. C. Rutgers visited a number of the universities on the Continent to work up delegations. Steps were taken to secure the attendance of the missionary societies, all of which readily agreed to send official representatives appointed by their committees.

The S.P.G. alone was not at first approached, having been the only society without a representative at the previous conference. This does not mean that S.P.G. people were not at the conferences and among the speakers, but they came in their private capacity. We had, however, by this time developed our relationships in Church of England circles and the Movement's platform and membership was representative of all types of Anglicans, and I felt the time had come to bring in the S.P.G. In this frame of mind I visited Oxford, and while there was questioned rather searchingly by some students as to the attitude of the S.P.G. to the Movement. They were men who were thinking of missionary service and who would offer to the S.P.G.

if they decided to go abroad.   Friends had asked them
to sign the S.V.M.U. Declaration, "It is my purpose,
if God permit, to become a foreign missionary."   Not
unnaturally, they wanted to know whether, if they came
into the Movement, the society in the Church with
which they had affinities was sympathetic to it.   I told
them that Bishop Montgomery, the secretary of the
S.P.G., had come in his personal capacity to the last of
our missionary conferences, that a number of S.P.G.
missionaries had spoken and that I hoped the S.P.G.
would be represented officially at our next conference,
although I could not be certain that it would.

When I returned to London I went to S.P.G. House,
saw Bishop Montgomery, and asked him to request the
Standing Committee of S.P.G. to appoint a delegate to
our forthcoming quadrennial conference.   He replied
that he intended to come to the conference and hoped
I would be satisfied with this, as he was not sure that
the Standing Committee would appoint an official
representative to a conference that was not exclusively
Church of England ;   as there might be opposition on
the committee he did not want to raise the question.

I was not satisfied, and proceeded to state my case
in detail, pointing out that the S.P.G. had received
most sympathetically a deputation at the time of the
S.V.M.U.'s approach to the Churches ten years before,
that three Archbishops of Canterbury had expressed
their sympathy with the Movement, that its platform
and membership were representative of all parties in the
Church, that the S.P.G. wanted us to help in securing candidates for it from the universities, and, therefore, that it was only reasonable that we should ask
for the formal approval of the Society.   I told him
about the Oxford incident, and said that students who
hoped to go out under the S.P.G. could not be expected
to join the S.V.M.U. if the S.P.G. was not openly in
sympathy with it.   I reminded him that the whole
missionary propaganda was weakened, especially in
universities like Oxford and Cambridge, if the High

Churchmen stood aloof because the chief society which had their sympathy in the Church did not support the Union.

Just as I had finished stating the case and Bishop Montgomery was looking very troubled, the door opened and Mr Pascoe, the keeper of the records of the S.P.G., came in. As it happened, I had recently discovered for Mr Pascoe the words of a poetical quotation which he had been unable to find and he was in a grateful mood. When he saw who it was, he at once said :

" Ah, Mr Tissington Tatlow, how nice to see you here; I hope you are going to get plenty of Student Volunteers for the S.P.G."

" I am going to do nothing of the kind," I said. " The S.P.G. will not perform a friendly act by the Student Movement, and I am just telling Bishop Montgomery that as far as the Student Movement is concerned I am going to wash my hands of the S.P.G."

Mr Pascoe looked horrified and Bishop Montgomery remained silent, so I thought I had better seize the opportunity and let Mr Pascoe hear our case and rub it in to Bishop Montgomery by restating it, which I did as vigorously as I could. It was awkward for Mr Pascoe, with his chief present, and muttering expressions of sympathy and sorrow he withdrew in some confusion from the room, leaving me alone with the Bishop, who said : " Put it in writing, Tatlow, and I will see what can be done." I shook hands at once, and we parted.

I went upstairs to find Canon Charles Robinson, the editorial secretary, with whom I was on very friendly terms. I repeated to him the incident which had just taken place in the room below. He chuckled, in his gruff way, and said : " I am very glad to hear you have done that. I hope you will succeed." It was obvious that he was heartily in sympathy with what I was after. I went home hopeful.

After an interval I received a letter from Bishop

Montgomery, telling me that the S.P.G. had appointed official delegates to the Liverpool Conference.

A year later, when I was one of a small group discussing with the Archbishop of Canterbury (Dr Davidson) the scheme for a conference of missionary societies to be held at Edinburgh in 1910, one of the group said that it was hoped the S.P.G. would take part in the arrangements for the Edinburgh Conference in view of the nature of its basis, questions of faith and order being excluded from its purview. The Archbishop said: "But I am afraid they cannot take part in a conference not exclusively Anglican. I believe there is something in their charter which prevents them." I said: "I succeeded last year in getting an official delegation to represent the society at our S.V.M.U. conference so that their charter cannot prove an insurmountable object." I remember the eager way in which the Archbishop swung round towards me and said: "You had them officially at your conference? I am profoundly thankful to hear it. I am profoundly thankful to hear it."

Do not let me leave any impression of unfriendliness towards Bishop Montgomery. Officially he was in a difficult position. As for himself, he was a warm friend of the S.V.M.U. A few months later he wrote in *The East and the West*: [1] "It is becoming one of our sheet-anchors, since it is bringing to our ranks hundreds of university men, Churchmen, who are the very material we need." It was just because he was a real friend and a warm-hearted fellow-countryman of mine that I found it possible to get him to take the Standing Committee of the S.P.G. in hand.

On January 2nd, 1908, the conference began. The arrival of the special train at Lime Street Station was a sight not soon to be forgotten. The railway stewards, who were men from Liverpool University, worked hard giving directions. Foreign delegates struggled for their baggage with bewildered porters, and quickly

[1] *The East and the West*, October 1908, p. 364.

the whole company was surging out of the station to find their hosts, and return in time for the first meeting at the Philharmonic Hall.   There were many happy reunions at the conference, students from different colleges who had met at past summer conferences meeting again and introducing new-comers, who were greatly in the majority.

In the body of the hall the majority of students were seated.   They looked up towards the platform, where there were a host of green labelled missionaries, representatives of missionary societies, and a number of members of staff of colleges throughout the British Isles, all guests of the conference.   There were 1640 delegates present.   While waiting, many turned over the leaves of their handbook, reading the list of names, asking a neighbour if he could tell who was sitting outside on the left or inside on the right.   There were many men and women whose names were well known to the students.   The Principals of Cuddesdon, Wycliffe Hall, Farnham, Ripon, Lichfield, Wells, Salisbury, and the Director of the House of the Sacred Mission, Kelham, were all there.   Oxford and Cambridge men recognized well-known dons, the Master of Selwyn, the Deans of Trinity and of Queens'.   Dr Karl Fries of Sweden, chairman of the World's Student Christian Federation, and Mr John R. Mott, its general secretary, were both present.   Jack Woodhouse wrote afterwards in *The Student Movement* :

> The impression we got was that there was scarcely a religious body or movement unrepresented.   This gave us an encouragement which it is hard to describe.   We could not speak to all these people.   We might never be introduced to them all our lives, but it did us students good that they were there.   We thank them for coming. It encouraged us.   The foreign delegates sat in the first five rows before the platform : 145 foreign delegates, men and women, from America, Australia, Belgium, Bohemia, China, Denmark, Finland, France, Germany, Holland, Hungary, India, Japan, New Zealand, Norway, Russia, Sweden and Switzerland.   There is never any

applause at Student Movement conferences except when
we welcome the delegates who have come from overseas.
Then cheer after cheer rises as the names of members from
each country are read out and the delegates stand on their
chairs to exhibit themselves. The conference comes thus
face to face with the World's Student Christian Federation.

Facing the audience was the Watchword, adopted in
Liverpool in 1896 : " The evangelization of the world
in this generation," and at the end of the hall the motto
of the Federation : *Ut omnes unum sint*.
The united meetings were in the Philharmonic Hall
in the morning and evening, presided over by R. K.
Evans, Merton College, Oxford, who was chairman.
The afternoons were devoted to sectional meetings by
countries, by societies and such like.

The general tide of the conference was felt in the main
hall, but some of the sectional meetings were of great
interest and importance. One day the conference was
faced with the choice of a visit, so to speak, to China, India,
Japan and Korea, Africa, South America, Mohammedan
lands or to the Jews. Another afternoon the denominational missionary societies held meetings. On yet another,
medical, educational, evangelistic work were dealt with.
A conversazione for professors, lecturers and tutors was
an occasion when the leaders of the Movement had an
opportunity of meeting this element of the conference, and
the Rev. E. J. Palmer,[1] chaplain of Balliol College, Oxford,
spoke with wisdom and boldness on the place of dons in
the Movement, showing how much good they can do by
sympathy and support and how much harm by taking the
leadership and initiative out of the hands of the students
themselves.[2]

The mornings were devoted exclusively to missionary topics, while the essentials of the Christian
faith were dealt with in the evening. The conference
was probably the last occasion on which the Watchword
made an impression upon students.
A feature of the conference was Mott's address dealing

[1] Afterwards Bishop of Bombay.
[2] *The Student Movement*, vol. x. p. 99.

with the situation in the Far East.   The great Asiatic renaissance had begun.   " We saw out there in the Far East ' Japan leading the Orient, but whither ? ' We realized with him the awful danger of the Eastern awakening if it was not met with Christ, not gradually but immediately.   The next ten or fifteen years is the most critical in the world's history."

Last came Dr Horton's address.

> It made prayer a more real thing to many of us than it had ever been before.   A spiritual moment was reached when he said, " Let us intercede for the world."   We all knelt down and found ourselves in a real passion of inter- cession for countries we had never seen and people we shall never know.   We then sang, *For all the saints who from their labours rest*, ending with the lines :
>
> > From earth's wide bounds, from ocean's farthest coast
> > Through gates of pearl streams in the countless host,
> > Singing to Father, Son and Holy Ghost,
> > Alleluia.
>
> By the next evening the delegates were scattered.   The conference had given an object in life ; we can take no lesser ideal than " The evangelization of the world in this generation."   Mr Tatlow's address on the Watchword will not be forgotten.[1]

There was an exhibition of photographs from all parts of the world ; charts showing past progress and future needs, stalls organized by the different mission- ary societies, model libraries of many kinds and a large exhibit of books.

The Lord Mayor gave a reception on the afternoon on which the conference opened, and each day a different Liverpool citizen entertained the foreign delegates to lunch and tea in the Hope Hall.   The conference was unusually well reported, as Walter W. Seton agreed to take this in hand and secured the personal interest and help of Mr Robbins of the Press Association.   The standard then set has not been departed from.

The conference was one upon which the leaders of

---

[1] *The Student Movement*, vol. x. p. 99.

the Movement looked back with deep thankfulness, and it bore fruit in every department of the life of the Movement in the ensuing year. It was the last quadrennial conference to be organized exclusively by the Student Volunteer Missionary Union.

Although Jack Woodhouse in reporting the conference had said the address on the Watchword would not be forgotten, the Watchword was never again the subject of a speech at a quadrennial conference.

The Watchword of the S.V.M.U. adopted at the Liverpool Conference, 1896, was in constant use for about seven years, during which time it would have been regarded almost as sacrilege for student volunteers to criticize it. Frank Lenwood, however, soon after he came into the Movement made it clear that he was critical of the words " in this generation," and in 1903 J. H. Oldham gave an address at the summer conference on the Watchword, taking a line of interpretation which, as Henry Hodgkin said to the S.V.M.U. Executive at its September meeting, " was opposed to that taken by Mr Mott in his book.[1] The one considered the Watchword was impossible, the others affirmed that it was entirely possible." Hodgkin asked the Executive

to consider very seriously their attitude to the Watchword and their definition of it. . . . He felt that we lowered our ground in discussing the Watchword when we entered into the question of its possibility . . . but held that in so far as the Church makes her plans for anything less than evangelizing the world in this generation she is culpable. It is not ours to say whether it is possible or impossible.[2]

For the next half-dozen years there was constant discussion of the Watchword, not only among the leaders of the S.V.M.U., for the discussion quickly spread to members of the Committees of other departments of the Movement. Everyone was talking about the value to be set upon the Watchword and about its

[1] See page 111.   [2] S.V.M.U. Minutes, September 1903.

proper interpretation.   Criticism of the Watchword was to some extent lulled by a moving and powerful address on it at the Edinburgh Conference, 1904, by John Mott, but the discussion waxed more and more vigorous as another quadrennial Conference approached, and the S.V.M.U. Executive arranged a special meeting to discuss it.

This meeting was held on December 22nd, 1906, and the attendance of all the former leaders available was invited.   R. K. Evans was in the chair, and there were twenty people present, among them R. P. Wilder, C. Kingsley Williams, Frank Lenwood, C. W. G. Taylor, Malcolm Spencer, W. G. Hardie, Walter W. Seton, J. McLeod Campbell, S. K. Datta, Louis Byrde, Lilian Stevenson, Una Saunders and Ruth Rouse. Some who could not attend sent letters—J. H. Oldham, A. G. Fraser, H. T. Silcock and G. T. Manley. Different points of view were expounded to the meeting and vigorously discussed.   Oldham was not able to be present, but in two letters stated what everyone agreed were the points at issue; his letters were the basis of our discussion.

Oldham had no doubts about the immense effect the adoption of the Watchword had exerted, not simply upon the Student Movement, but upon the missionary work of the Church throughout the British Isles.

> What the Watchword has done for the Movement has been to keep before it the note of urgency.   The traditional attitude of the Church before the Watchword appeared on the horizon was one of recognition of the missionary obligation and a determination to execute it. But people were apt to consider that they were doing all that was possible and looked forward with a certain complacency of mind to the realization of their aim at some period several hundred years hence.   The Watchword came as a sort of thunderbolt, and substituted for the " several hundred years hence " an imperative *now*.   Therein lies its power.[1]

[1] This and following quotations from two letters (Nov. 6th and Dec. 20th, 1906) by J. H. Oldham to T. Tatlow.

PAST AND PRESENT COMMITTEE MEMBERS AND SECRETARIES, CONISHEAD, 1907

Back Row:—G. Kingsley Williams, A. C. Grant, H. T. Silcock, W. W. Seton, M. S. Lawson, Alan Stevens, J. W. Woodhouse, . ., Margaret Bretherton, S. F. Hawkes, Dorothy E. Brown, Mary Saxelby (Mrs Simon), N. S. Talbot, Cyril Knott, T. H. Robinson, Malcolm Spencer, Garfield Williams, E. S. Woods, A. G. Fraser.

Second Row:—H. G. Wood, Dorothea Warner, Nancy Borrow, Ethel Mackenzie, A. W. Davies, J. M'Leod Campbell, Una Saunders, Mrs A. G. Fraser, Mrs Lenwood, Jocelyn Smyly.

Front Row:—H. E. Dallimore Winifred Sedgwick, Tom Jays, S. K. Datta T. Tatlow, . ., Josephine Woods, Lucy Harris.

He thought, however, that we must face the fact that while it was important that "the power of that tre-mendous appeal" should not be weakened "by any profitless and abstract discussion regarding the distinc-tion between a prophecy and a purpose," yet this was exactly what had been happening for the past seven years.

The Watchword was adopted as the expression of a purpose and not as a prophecy, but experience had shown that

> the distinction between a prophecy and a purpose is one which even intelligent people find it exceedingly difficult to grasp. . . . The crux of the whole matter lies in the word "evangelization," or to be more exact, the seeming neces-sity for defining the word "evangelization" imposed by the words "in this generation." If you hold strictly to the view that the Watchword is the expression of a purpose and not a prophecy, there is no necessity for defining "evangelization."

Mott had asked for one missionary for every fifty thousand people as being what evangelization meant. "But against any such precise definition and consequent weakening, emasculation and distortion of the word the whole soul of men like Warneck rises in indignant protest."

Oldham went on to speak of the difficulty of making evangelization effective, of the inadequate command of the vernacular on the part of missionaries, their use of modes of Western thought, the prejudices of the people who steel their hearts against the foreigner, with the consequent closing of their minds against his message, the terms he has to employ to convey that message so filled with a non-Christian content that whatever he may mean something different is suggested to his hearers. All these things he urged as of fundamental importance in the view of those who have looked deeply into what the problem of evangelization really means.

If the S.V.M.U. could remain at the standpoint of

purpose and refuse to define evangelization the Watchword was defensible, but some would discuss it in terms of the number of missionaries, and this stirred others to raise all the difficulties in the way of effective evangelization. The phraseology of the Watchword seems to be responsible for the fact that the majority of people do not remain at the standpoint of purpose, but pass to the discussion of definitions of evangelization.

> The result is that the Watchword has " exercised an injurious as well as a beneficial influence on the S.V.M.U. . . . it has led people both on the Executive and in the colleges to spend an unnecessary amount of time in discussing purely abstract questions, in hunting for definitions and in fighting unreal battles, which might have been spent with much greater advantage in trying to secure men for the mission field."

Oldham, however, felt the force of the reason which prevented the S.V.M.U. from abandoning the Watchword, closing the letter quoted with these words :

> On the other hand—and this is quite as important as anything I have written—it is essential to the very life of the S.V.M.U. that no change of attitude with regard to the Watchword should be taken which would lessen the pressing and overwhelming urgency of the missionary appeal.

A year later, at the quadrennial S.V.M.U. conference, Liverpool, 1908, I was chosen by the S.V.M.U. Executive as their spokesman on the subject of the Watchword. This was the last occasion on which the Watchword was presented formally to students on the platform of the S.V.M.U. The address, however, was printed and circulated for several years to every new member of the Union.

Frank Lenwood continued to press that something should be said in public about the criticisms of the Watchword. Discussion had hitherto taken place in committee only. I sought and obtained the consent of my colleagues to publish an article by him in *The*

Student Movement, and there he analysed at some length the objections to the Watchword. " A phrase which is capable of several meanings is not for use in the fighting line " ; the words " in this generation," explained as having a different meaning for each person, were unsatisfactory in that evangelization was not the duty of each person but the duty of the Church as a whole. " What then for the Church does ' in this generation ' mean ? If we may not accept the idea of thirty-three years from the date of acceptance I question whether there is an answer." Having expounded these points at some length he then tackled, as so many had done in private, the question of what exactly was meant by the word evangelization.

The article closed with an interesting section criticizing the Watchword for its implied conception of the Gospel.

> It does less than justice to the Gospel; for its whole theory is based upon a static Gospel, and it leaves out of account that the Gospel is something infinitely greater than our present understanding of it, something into which we shall only enter with the aid of nations spiritually yet unborn. Suppose that the Church among the Kaffirs were in a position to evangelize the whole world, we should all be filled with the deepest misgivings, for we should feel the wide presentation of a crude form of Christianity to be a calamity of the most far-reaching kind. Yet when we look seriously into the condition of our British religion in the light of our Master's requirements, can we put ourselves on a much higher plane ? Do we wish that the faith to which we have attained should be thrust upon the whole world and dominate its future religious history ? [1]

This idea was further developed at some length and the article closed with a call for a new Watchword which " should be in the nature of an advance and not of a retreat."

From this time the history of the Watchword became

[1] *The Student Movement*; art. : " Concerning the Watchword of the Student Volunteer Missionary Union," Frank Lenwood, vol. xi. p. 55.

rather ignoble. The men it had inspired were gone
and it did not grip the new generation. Discussions
about it flared up again and again on the S.V.M.U.
Executive without any decision being reached, while
the phrase steadily dropped out of use. A. W. Stevens
in March 1909 told the Executive that very few students
going on student missionary campaigns wanted to refer
to the Watchword in their addresses. Thus the motto
which had been a tremendous inspiration to the leaders
of the Movement at the time of the Liverpool Conference, 1896, and which had won the sympathy of Dr
Temple, the Archbishop of Canterbury, and Dr Eugene
Stock for the Movement and made a great impression
on the missionary societies, fell into disuse.

In 1912 a new S.V.M.U. Executive revived the discussion of the Watchword and wrote to about twenty
former student volunteers in different parts of the
mission field asking their opinion of the Watchword in
the light of their experience. There was no consensus
of opinion in the replies and again the Executive took
no decision.

The Watchword was forgotten during the war, but
at its close the S.V.M.U. Executive noted in its minute-
book " that the Watchword needed revision." In 1921
leaders who knew nothing about the history of the past,
for the war had completely obliterated knowledge of it
and, like all the post-war leaders, they knew nothing
of what had gone before in the Movement except
the scraps of information they picked up from me,
found that the S.V.M.U. had this unused Watchword,
" The evangelization of the world in this generation."
William Paton, the secretary of the S.V.M.U., reported
that he had had correspondence of an indecisive kind
on the subject with the colleges. The general feeling
of the committee was that the Watchword " was dead,
though a certain sentiment still clung to it." [1]

It was clear that the Watchword of the S.V.M.U.
would never be revived. In former years it had not

[1] S.V.M.U. Minute-book, April 1921.

been abandoned, because everyone was convinced that it could not be abandoned until a better Watchword was found. With the passage of time, however, watchwords and mottoes of all kinds had gone out of fashion. Students no longer put framed texts and mottoes on the walls of their rooms in college, as their predecessors had done. The committee decided that in the redrafting of the Constitution then taking place the Watchword should be omitted. When constitutional changes were presented to the business meeting at the summer conference in July 1922, we explained to the assembled students that the Watchword had been omitted. No one made any comment. Thus it disappeared with an old Constitution and its appearance was without comment outside, as well as inside, the Student Movement.

CHAPTER XVII

THE COMMISSION OF 1908

THE year ushered in by the fourth quadrennial missionary conference brought great encouragement. It also brought a number of important matters to be dealt with. The Movement consisted of 137 affiliated Christian Unions [1] (60 men's and 77 women's) in the universities and colleges, with 5526 members and 45 associated theological colleges.

News from almost every college was good. A few items may be selected as typical. Aberystwyth University College Christian Union (Women) reported in the term before Christmas 22 Bible Study circles, with 173 members, all studying *The Teaching of Jesus*, by J. H. Oldham, the most successful text-book hitherto published by the Movement. After Christmas the Union had 8 missionary study circles, with 60 members, studying *The Uplift of China*.

Edinburgh University Christian Union (Men) had 200 members and reported that one-third of the whole body of students in the university was attending Dr Kelman's Sunday night services held under its auspices in the Operetta House.

Aberdeen University Christian Union held Sunday evening services jointly with the Students' Representative Council and reported that the general body of students "manifest a very keen interest in these meetings."

On Ash Wednesday London medical students assembled at Lambeth Palace by the invitation of the

---

[1] All the co-educational modern universities and university colleges had separate Christian Unions for men and women up to the War.

Archbishop of Canterbury, conveyed through the Movement. The Archbishop addressed 150 men who crammed the chapel and overflowed into the organ-loft.

The Christian Union at the Royal Normal College for the Blind at Norwood provided *The Student Movement* regularly in Braille for its members.

The Annual Report said :

An attempt has also been made to grapple more definitely with intellectual difficulties. Dr James Hope Moulton lectured on New Testament criticism to the women student leaders at Manchester ; Mr Tatlow gave a course of apologetic lectures in London, and Christian Evidence circles were held in Oxford University, Cambridge University, Newnham College and the Cambridge Training College.

Evangelistic missions were held in London, Glasgow, Oxford and Cambridge by John R. Mott, and in Dublin, Belfast, Birmingham, Bristol, Manchester and Cardiff by Robert P. Wilder. Missions to women students were organized for the first time and Miss Rouse conducted these in Edinburgh, Glasgow and St Andrews. " We confidently believe," reported the Executive of the Movement, " that there has never been a time when the spiritual tide in these universities has risen so high and so many undergraduates have felt the imperial sway of the rule of Jesus Christ." [1]   It was an encouraging period.

On the other hand there were anxieties. The tide of questioning was rising in the modern universities. More students than ever before were interested in religion, but more wanted to be helped to relate their religion to the thought of the day than ever before. The General Committee was aware of the need for more work on the whole question of Christian thought and the relation of this to Bible Study, and it was increasingly concerned by the growing insistence of social questions. It was also anxious to see the results of the Liverpool Conference conserved.

[1] *Annual Report*, S.C.M., July 1908-9, p. 20.

Y

Students were more inclined to study social questions and less ready to join Bible Study circles. They wanted to pick and choose more and did not so readily agree to use the Bible Study books provided by the Movement, especially text-books on the Old Testament.

The advice of a number of senior men was sought, especially with a view to discovering how far they thought the Movement's tendency to concentrate on the New Testament was wise or not.   Miss Fairfield and I lunched with Canon Scott Holland at his house in Amen Court and discussed this matter with him at length. He was very emphatic that the New Testament has its roots in the Old, and that the study of the Old must not be neglected by the Movement. " How can you understand *Romans* apart from the Old Testament? " We discussed possible speakers at the summer conferences, and he wrote later:

> I feel more and more since our talk how good an element George Adam Smith would be in the particular direction we spoke of. I cannot help thinking that the day has come which will close the reaction against the Old Testament and will bring the book out in an entirely new light as one of the most interesting and thrilling opportunities of study. Poor Miss Fairfield, she seemed quite sad at this prospect, especially with the *Epistle to the Romans* to follow. But she was very good and helpful about it all.

The increasing number of students who found no answer to their difficulties at Bible circles, and the tendency of the Movement to develop a variety of activities, began to have an effect upon the number of students joining Bible circles.   In the summer of 1908 the committee said that there had been a decrease of 100 Bible Study circles during the year.   The membership of Bible Study circles was reported as 4607 as against 4955 the previous year.   The student leaders in the colleges were helpless in face of the situation, and while there were a few apologetic study groups as already mentioned, very little work of this kind was being done anywhere else in the field.   As one of the travelling secretaries said: "Apologetic study is very rare, hardly anything being done to help those in difficulties." The following year the committee reported to its constituency as it might have done this year:

It must be regretfully admitted that in the life of many thoughtful students to-day the Bible is losing its centrality. Men and women no longer look to it so instinctively and so habitually as before, as the natural and sole guide to all life. Bible Study circles are often shunned, either because they are supposed to demand the prior acceptance of questioned hypotheses, or else for fear that it will be impossible to take honest part in them without giving uncalled for pain to some people's beliefs.[1]

By this time we were in new offices. The growth of the Movement led to a need for larger offices, and just before the Liverpool Conference we moved from 22 Warwick Lane, E.C., to 93-4 Chancery Lane, W.C. The new offices were on the first floor of a building on the south side of Chancery Lane, and were situated over an old-established firm of tailors and robe-makers, Messrs Ede, Son & Ravenscroft, who were our landlords.

Mounting a rather narrow staircase, there was a small room at the top, which a secretary occupied. A winding passage to the right led to a group of rooms, the largest of which overlooked Chancery Lane and was used as a book-room. If instead of turning to the right at the top of the staircase a left turn was made and the staircase to the second floor was passed, the passage was blocked by a door erected by the Student Movement. Behind this door were a set of four rooms occupied by the general and assistant secretaries and the stenographers. Most of these rooms were rather dark. They were overshadowed by an enormous plane-tree which always seemed to be in leaf! Offices in the City for an organization that needed as many as ten rooms were very difficult to find at that time.

[1] *Annual Report, S.C.M.*, 1910, p. 14.

S. K. Datta and I wandered round most of West Central London before we found these.

With the change of office came a new determination to tackle new problems. The Committee recognized that a new day had come in the life of the Movement and that some older men must be retained in its councils to help to bear its growing responsibilities. It was the responsibility of the modern university work that was chiefly felt. The Movement's work was growing rapidly there, and the students leading it were restive at the inadequacy of their representation on the committees of the Movement. The women students also felt they were under-represented. Both complaints were justified.

The General Committee decided at Easter 1908 to appoint a commission " to wait upon God to know His will regarding the Movement " and to review its policy and methods of work.

The question of retaining a senior element in the Movement it decided to tackle at once; J. H. Oldham was invited to become Missionary Study Secretary, and I was invited to become " permanent General Secretary." Hitherto I had been appointed for short terms. As to Joe Oldham, he had been General Secretary from 1895-96, spent a period in India doing missionary work until health forced him to retire, and had then studied at New College, Edinburgh. While at Edinburgh he had been chairman of the Theological College Department Executive, 1904-6. When he was asked to rejoin the staff as Missionary Study Secretary of the S.V.M.U., he had already undertaken to be responsible for missionary study work in the United Free Church of Scotland; an arrangement was ultimately made whereby part of his time was given to the Movement.

The committee sought to relieve the pressure on me by arranging that Malcolm Spencer, who was travelling secretary of the Theological College Department, should give part of his time to helping me.

Finance was a great anxiety, and Wilder was asked to cancel part of his college visitation and undertake money

raising. This he did with success. A little later a
finance committee with some senior men on it was
created, but never produced much money. A circular
to the colleges produced £105 and John Mott spoke at
a financial breakfast in the winter, securing £336 at it.
A big effort was made by members of the General
Committee. Walter Seton and Robert Wilder undertook to secure £300 which was needed for the World's
Student Christian Federation Conference, which was
coming to England, and the other members promised
to raise an additional £207. J. Harry Miller[1] agreed to
start a local association in Glasgow to help to finance
the Movement, and it was decided to try and arrange
drawing-room meetings with the secretaries of the Movement as speakers. All this was financial work in new
directions.

As I have already indicated, the rapid growth of the
Movement in the new universities and also in Wales,
together with the fact that its leadership still remained
chiefly with men at either Oxford, Cambridge, or the
Scottish universities, was causing uneasiness. The
university colleges of Bangor and Aberystwyth passed
a resolution asking for regular representation on the
General Committee, while Manchester forwarded the
following letter to the committee :

The University,
Manchester,
May 13*th*, 1908.

Dear Tatlow,
    This letter is to express the strong feeling held by the
undersigned leaders of the Movement in Manchester concerning the need for increased representation on the
Executive of the Northern and Midland Universities.
    Having carefully drawn up the following statement of
the case, we desire to preface it by a word as to the spirit
in which it was written and in which we trust the Executive
will consider it.

[1] Afterwards the Very Rev. J. Harry Miller, D.D., Moderator
of the United Free Church of Scotland.

We desire it to be understood that we have taken this step without consultation with the rank and file of our membership, for we felt that to do so might have engendered dissension where none is yet articulate. We trust that this letter will be taken to imply no disloyalty, for it is almost unnecessary to state that none whatsoever exists. We have written frankly for we feel that a matter affecting the fundamental policy of the Movement is best brought up in this form and with as little commotion as possible.

We write merely as leaders in Manchester and do not speak for the other universities involved, but we believe that the same opinions would be forthcoming if the Executive were to enquire of them.

We feel the need of increased representation of these universities to be very real because—

1. Intimate acquaintance with the, in many ways, unique conditions of life in these universities is essential to the true solution of present problems and formation of future policy. This intimate acquaintance is not sufficiently secured either by the visits of travelling secretaries or by the conferences. It can only be attained on Executive through representation both direct and adequate. This we feel does not yet exist.

2. These universities contain a total of upwards of 6000 (day) students, distributed as follows (1906-7) :

Durham	.	.	.	c. 800
Manchester	.	.	.	1408
Liverpool	.	.	.	1003
Leeds	.	.	.	1116
Birmingham	.	.	.	850
Sheffield	.	.	.	674
Nottingham College	.	.		400
				————
				6251

3. Not only is the number of these students large, but their relation with the life of the country is close and intimate. Situated in the chief commercial and manufacturing centres of the empire, these universities are more and more attracting the future leaders of industry and also a large number of foreign students.

They are in very close touch with the pressing social problems of populous districts ; they train a very large number of school teachers ; they exist in the midst of

fierce denominational controversy which is the more felt
owing to the non-residential character of the universities.

They therefore constitute both a large field and one of
potent possibilities for the influence of the Movement on
the mass of people.

4. During the last six years a large number of Campaigns
have been officered and partly manned by students from
these universities. The study of social problems has been
brought to the fore and a successful conference was held
in this university last November. The Free Church Theological Colleges have their own committee, and regular
united meetings are held during each session.

In addition to this, the study of foreign missions has
and is receiving the special consideration of the local
leaders of the Movement. Already, the knowledge and
experience gained is being made use of by groups of
Churches in the North and Midlands. The missionary
Summer Schools are also benefiting from the work of the
Movement through the attendance at those schools of
members of the Student Movement of these parts as leaders
of study classes and speakers.

The result of this participation in the work and life of
the Churches has been to increase the power and ability
of the members of the Student Movement in these universities, fitting them for a fuller share in the control of the
national interests of the Movement.

5. The citizens of the great commercial centres in which
are situated the universities in question have, for these
latter, a high regard, great interest, and devotion. It may
be safely said that these universities, as long as they prove
to be of value to the commercial interests of the different
communities, will not be handicapped for want of financial
support. This fact is of importance, for it indicates the
action that must be taken by the Movement if it is to secure
the pecuniary assistance of this part of the British Isles.
Let the Movement establish itself so thoroughly in the
life of these universities as to become, and be regarded as,
part of the university life and the appeal for financial
support will not fall on deaf ears.

6. The life of these universities is in some ways unique,
giving rise to problems that require special knowledge and
experience for their solution.

These universities are very largely non-residential, with
the result that the main work of the Christian Unions has
to be done during the mid-week. This makes it necessary

for the Movement to formulate special policies for bringing the non-resident student into closer touch.

At present the members of the Christian Unions are largely drawn from those who have been and are still engaged in Church work.

Again, men and women attend the same lectures, take the same examinations, and share common interests and rights in the university life. This means that at and about the age of decision young men and women intermingle for the purposes of study, which coming together, however, creates great possibilities for good and evil. This is another important factor which must be taken into consideration in formulating the policy of the Movement.

In view, therefore, of the reasons above stated we think that one representative on each Executive Committee at least is necessary for the proper growth and development of the Movement in this group of universities. We feel that in the choice of the representatives sex need not be considered, for the problems of the men's and women's unions are practically parallel.

> Believe us,
>
> Yours very sincerely,
>
> W. H. Kauntze.
> Cyril W. Knott.
> Samuel Spicer Harman.
> MacEwan S. Lawson.
> Margaret C. Paull.
> E. Mary Saxelby.
> A. Gordon Simon.

I was able to reply at once to this letter by telling the signatories of the decision to appoint a Commission which would, among other matters, consider the question they raised, and also that Mary Saxelby and M'Ewan Lawson, two of their number, had been appointed members of the Commission. This brought from Cyril Knott, on behalf of the Manchester signatories, an assurance that they were more than satisfied with the action that was being taken. Knott added, "I think there are few people who love the Movement so deeply as some of the Midland university leaders, to whom it has meant more than anything else in life."

The summer conference intervened before the Commission could get to work. We would have been glad to return to Conishead Priory for the summer conference, but its summer business was improving, and the manager, not anxious to disturb it by a student conference, wanted to put up prices. Miss E. F. Fox (now Mrs Hall) undertook to search Derbyshire for a suitable village to hold the conference. On her advice we selected Baslow and engaged every available bedroom in the villages of Baslow, Curbar, Calver, Edensor and Eyam, for women students, and secured permission from the Duke of Devonshire to set up the men's camp in Chatsworth Park.

It was a big business. We had to drive the whole conference—over 1000 people—from Bakewell station, four miles away, using horse vehicles of all kinds. The women were driven daily, morning and evening, from the outlying villages to Baslow. The village institute was the central office for women, and the meeting marquee was set up in the park, near the men's camp. Everything had to be thought out. An entire camp with sleeping, feeding, kitchen and sanitary accommodation had to be set up. The Duke of Devonshire had no available water, so an elaborate piece of plumbing was needed to bring it from the Duke of Rutland's estate.

This year the women students dined in the middle of the day in a large hall attached to one of the hotels in Baslow, but as this did not prove very satisfactory next year a marquee was set up not far from the meeting marquee in camp, and they were provided for from the same kitchen as the men at both lunch and tea, an arrangement which proved satisfactory and economical. We had all our meat sent up from London, contracting for quantities of legs and shoulders. The women said that they had never been better fed, yet we dined them at a cost of fourpence per head per day. I had to organize the camp and make the contracts. Miss Nellie Salt, the vicar of Curbar's daughter, was a splendid helper and dealt with all the local landladies.

We remained at Baslow by the permission of the Duke of Devonshire, who was very kind, until we moved to Swanwick.

All this time we were preparing for the Commission. The time was ripe for an examination of the policy and methods of work of the Movement, for no survey had been undertaken for ten years. The last occasion of any review had been in 1898, when the Theological College Department was formed and the British College Christian Union and the Student Volunteer Missionary Union brought together to form with it the Student Christian Movement.

The Commission met at the Grand Hotel, Baslow, Derbyshire, from October 29th to November 4th, 1908, and consisted of: J. H. Oldham (chairman), Tissington Tatlow (secretary), Idris Davies, University College, Cardiff; F. W. Henderson, New College, Edinburgh; MacEwan Lawson, Manchester University; Frank Lenwood, Mansfield College, Oxford; R. L. Pelly, Clare College, Cambridge; Ruth Rouse, secretary, World's Student Christian Federation; Una M. Saunders, Somerville College, Oxford; Mary Saxelby, Manchester University; Malcolm Spencer, Corpus Christi College, Oxford; Dorothea L. Warner, Froebel Institute, London; and J. W. Woodhouse, University College, Oxford. A number of memoranda were prepared by individuals and groups for the use of the Commission, dealing with all the more important aspects of the Movement's work, which the members had in advance for their information. The Commission worked very hard, being in session for eight hours a day, " part of the time—on some days a large part—was spent in prayer." It was found impossible to cover all the Movement's work, but the major matters were tackled.

The Commission's Report opened with a statement on the *raison d'être* of the Movement :

> The justification of a Christian Movement concerning itself especially with students is to be found, not in any ideals or religious ideas which are its special and exclusive

property, but in the peculiar conditions of student life. College years are the extraordinary years of life, the years in which ideals are established and in which decisions are made. Students share in a common life and are brought into intimate relationships with one another in ways that make men and women at college peculiarly accessible to influence by their fellow-students. The student class is composed of those who have their lives before them and are free to dedicate these lives to the service of Christ and of humanity. The exceptional conditions of student life and the unique opportunities of the student class demand the existence of the Student Christian Movement.

The Commission advised the restriction of the Movement's work, to ensure effectiveness, to universities, university colleges, theological colleges, training colleges and medical schools. This advice influenced in a restrictive direction the policy of the Movement for a number of years in relation to the colleges from which it would accept Christian Unions for affiliation.

A reference to the academic side of the student's life, with its duties and responsibilities, appears in an official document of the Movement for the first time, the Commission saying : " The greatest care must be taken not to multiply the activities of a Christian Union in such a way that they will impose on officers or members a burden that is incompatible with the proper discharge of college duties." The Movement was advised not to ask students to attempt too much, but to have as its aim " to produce in students the right *attitude* towards the ideals for which it stands."

A clear statement as to what should be the Movement's policy in relation to the Christian Church appears for the first time. Hitherto, while the Movement had been anxious to draw in all Christian students, whatever their Church connection, it had said very little to students about the Church. It was a new note, therefore, the Report struck when it said :

It cannot be too clearly stated that the Movement, so far from attempting to usurp the functions of the Christian Church in regard to its members, seeks rather to emphasize the allegiance they owe to the Church. It expects its members, on the one hand, to respect the ecclesiastical position of their fellow-members and to refrain from using the Movement to attack or undermine that position, and, on the other hand, for their own part, to suppress or compromise nothing which they believe to be a part of Divine truth. The truth of Christ is to be found, not in a bare residuum of common opinion, but in the rich comprehension of many types of thought, feeling and experience. The ideal of the Movement is not a weak and colourless undenominationalism, but an interdenominational fellowship that will help to prepare the way for ultimate unity in the Christian Church.

The heading of another section of the Report is " The danger of becoming an institution."

Since the life of the Movement lies in the ideas by which it is inspired, the fundamental requirement is that these ideas should be fresh and living, and should represent the conviction and aspiration of the living generation of students. If the Movement becomes an organization directed by older men working among students, it will lose its fundamental character. It is vital that the men and women actually in college should have a large share in determining the policy of the Movement. There is a serious danger that the Movement should become a mere institution, and lose the freedom and spontaneity of its life. On the other hand, it seems to be impossible for the Movement, any more than for an individual, to escape the dangers which come as the result of growth. The presence of senior men in the Movement must be accepted as necessary to bear the burden of the increased complexities and responsibilities of the work.

The chief safeguards against the danger of institutionalism which the Commission saw were :

1. That the senior men in the Movement should regard it as the first of their duties to be in sympathy with all new movements in the colleges, and to esteem the views of the younger men as being as worthy of consideration as their own.
2. That the Movement should be kept living and free by a deep prayer-life and earnest seeking to know the will

of God, and by a constant attempt to advance in thought and life to new views of Christian responsibility.

3. That while the secretaries should often be appointed, or reappointed for a term of years, the Executive Committee should always repudiate any expectation of permanence, and should not retain a secretary beyond the point justified by his ability to sympathize with younger men and to understand newer movements of thought.

The Commission was deeply convinced of the importance of evangelistic work. " The primary aim of the Movement is evangelistic, namely, to bring all students to accept the personal attitude to Jesus Christ expressed in our Basis," and there is no satisfactory evangelistic policy until the committee, each Christian Union, " and each member is consciously committed to the carrying out of this aim as both a corporate and individual responsibility involved in personal loyalty to Jesus Christ." The Commission thought that there was a tendency to allow other activities of the Movement to crowd out its evangelistic work and that the Committee should make it plain to all committee members and officers " that their appointment to the service of the Movement commits them to its evangelistic aim." It advised that committee members and officers should take a share as far as practicable in evangelistic work in the colleges themselves, and that travelling secretaries should be helped " through reading and by association with the work of others who have a richer experience in leading students to Christ." Turning to the colleges it analysed the situation there, and as far as the Christian Unions were concerned, said that :

There is a lack of sustained and uniform endeavour throughout the colleges to grapple with the situation. During the year 1907-8, out of 60 men's Christian Unions, only 37 claimed to have made some effort along evangelistic lines either by meetings, missions, or individual work. Out of 70 women's Christian Unions only 30 claimed to have made some effort along one or other of the same lines to win students for Christ. All the Christian Union leaders who have studied the problem are agreed that their great chance lies with the freshmen. It is probably not an exaggeration to say that in most Unions 90 per cent. of the members have been recruited in their freshmen year ; and many of these were at the time won for Christ. The majority of unions say that they never win a hostile man after freshmen days.

The difficulty of doing effective work in the non-residential colleges was felt rather strongly, the more so probably since most of the members of the Commission had been educated at residential colleges. They had much less hope of effective evangelistic work in the modern universities than have later generations of Student Movement leaders.

The Commission remarked that the colleges regarded the summer conference " as the most important evangelistic agency of the Movement." Much stress is laid upon the importance of work among freshmen. The commissioners returned to it more than once in their Report :

> The Committee of the Movement should do more than is done at present to help colleges to plan freshmen's campaigns. . . . It ought to recognize more fully than at present how important a month October is, and should press every available helper into the service for that month, so as to help the Christian unions to reach the freshmen. Where Christian unions are weak, travelling secretaries should spend time in the summer term planning with them the freshmen's campaign. Travelling secretaries ought to give far more time to this in the summer months than they do at present.

The section of the Report dealing with the policy of the Movement in relation to social problems is in more general terms than the rest of the document. This was owing to the fact that the problems of society seemed to be so serious that the Commission did not attempt to deal with the subject in detail ; but there was agreement that a grave state of affairs existed in the country, and it is significant in view of subsequent experience that the chairman of the Commission should in a brief

introduction to its Report have written, "In the consideration of the social problem the Commission was conscious in a special way of the leading of God's Spirit."
The Report said :

It is a fact, the significance of which we can scarcely exaggerate, that a large number of our fellow-men are born and are compelled to live under conditions which seem practically to deny them their share in the Fatherhood of God. . . . It is terrible enough that such degradation should be possible, but it is surely more terrible that society should acquiesce in its existence. . . . It is impossible to ignore the reaction of this problem upon the faith of our whole country. While in our industrial enterprises a growing number of men are conscious of the iniquity of this state of affairs, and are listening for some clear, strong note of social reconstruction, others, who are equally convinced, bow to accept the yoke at the cost of sincerity and honour ; others, again, who have been called to positions of industrial and commercial responsibility, express openly to one another the awful conclusion that Christian principles cannot be realized in practice ; and yet a fourth class, especially among the working men, draw from our failure to apply our Christianity the inference that the Church is radically insincere, while the spread of the Gospel abroad is hindered by the reports of misery and immorality which filter out to the great non-Christian lands. In these and in many other ways we begin to realize the responsibility which Christians are called to face.

The Commission thought that the Movement was called to a new step in its history in relation to society and its problems, and that students should be summoned to service which would express itself in two ways—" in the work of rescue and in the work of reform."
It recommended " that a conference for the purpose of prayer should be called as early as possible, probably at the Easter of 1909," when those should be summoned " who felt upon their hearts the burden of the problem of modern society, to come apart to intercede with God for guidance." It suggested that while there should be some addresses to guide the prayers of those

who came, no names of speakers should be published, nor should any details of the programme be given, lest the purpose of the gathering be obscured—" that of intercession for the guidance of the Movement in face of human suffering and alienation from God." " This Conference," said the Commission, " probably not a large one, would be the starting-place for our future policy." How fully this prophecy was realized will be told later.

The Report concluded with a number of recommendations to the committee regarding the general work of the Movement : more intercollegiate secretaries to be appointed in the university towns, travelling secretaries to be retained for more than a year—three, if possible, Scottish and Welsh secretaries to be appointed, a Bible Study secretary to be appointed for a term of years, the chairman of the General Committee to hold office for at least two years, a meeting to be held for training newly appointed officers in September, a permanent site to be secured for the summer conference, and " that the summer conference had grown too large and should be limited to 600, other conferences being provided." It is surely a matter of great interest that every one of these recommendations was carried out during the next few years !

The Commission resulted in still more work for the General Secretary, but Malcolm Spencer found it impossible to find time to help me in the office: visitation of theological colleges, social study and student missionary campaign arrangements more than filled his time. An inexperienced helper would have been little use. We were puzzled what to do. Then Spencer suggested that Zoë Fairfield should be invited to become assistant to the General Secretary.

Miss Fairfield accepted the invitation and began work at headquarters in September, 1909. She had already had ten years' experience of the Movement, as a student at the Slade School of Art, as honorary secretary of the Art Students' Christian Union, alternately chairman and secretary of the London Women Students' Committee, and chief officer on several occasions of the women's side of the summer conferences. She was, at the time of her appointment, secretary of the Guild of Helpers of the Y.W.C.A. People thought of Miss Fairfield at first as someone who was going to help to bear the burden of day-to-day business in the office, and she certainly bore this burden year after year, but soon people realized that a first-class mind was being brought to bear on the problems of the Movement. There is no side of its thought and work in which she did not share at one time or another; and no man or woman who has served the Movement has been her equal in combining range of thought, independence of judgment and creative capacity, with the single exception of Douglas Thornton.

CHAPTER XVIII

THE RISE OF THE SOCIAL CONSCIOUSNESS

WHILE the Movement led both within and without the universities in regard to the missionary enterprise, the story in relation to the rise of a social consciousness is a different one. In the Student Movement the evils and disorders of society and their cause were never mentioned during the first seven or eight years of its history. As a S.V.M.U. travelling secretary I recall a Welsh theological student asking what I thought of the Fabian Society, and I am ashamed to say I had never heard of the Fabians. It was from outside that the influences came which caused the Movement to turn its attention to the question of society and its problems.

The undergraduates at the older universities who founded the Movement, were not in touch with the small body of those who were interested in the settlement movement or those who were in the tradition of Dickens, Kingsley and F. D. Maurice, and were thinking out the relation of society as it was to the idea of the Kingdom of God. The Kingdom of God meant another world to the men in the Movement, and they thought of their task as being to preach the Gospel of individual salvation so that men might be saved through Christ, and passing through this world as strangers and pilgrims might reach heaven.

The Evangelicals were a deal better than their theology in fact, for they were active in the service of all in need, but because they despaired of the world, which they regarded as irredeemably evil, their social service tended to be of the palliative description. If men were suffering from poverty or bad housing, or were tempted to drink,

338

it was sure to be because of their own sin. So the cure for all evils was to preach individual salvation. Save men's souls and they would become prosperous and social evils would disappear.

There were a few who saw deeper, chiefly among theological students. The Higher Criticism was beginning to have a beneficial effect. The study of the Old Testament prophets was making some think deeply about society. The writings of Professor A. B. Davidson and Professor George Adam Smith, especially the latter's volumes on *Isaiah* in the *Expositor's Bible*, stirred men to think about God and His relation to the world.

There was one man who by his personal charm, experience as a social worker, and gifts as a speaker won the attention of a number of students at Oxford. These suggested that Mr George Hare Leonard of the Broad Plain House, Clifton, should be a summer conference speaker. The women added the suggestion that Miss A. W. Richardson, a lecturer at Westfield College, and one of the ablest and most convincing speakers of the day on temperance questions, should also be invited. Their visit made a great impression at the Matlock Summer Conference in July, 1900, and in the account of the conference in *The Student Movement* it was said that :

> The subject of work for the poor at home has perhaps been rather neglected hitherto by the Union (B.C.C.U.), but at Matlock this was rectified. The keen interest in social work felt by many of the delegates was shown as much by the constant discussion of its problems with Mr Leonard and Miss Richardson in conversation, as by close attention to their addresses on the subject.[1]

Several leaders went straight from Matlock to the Conference of the World's Student Christian Federation, associated with the meeting of its General Committee, at Versailles. There the two representatives of the Dutch Student Movement, L. E. Brandt and J. A. L. Hovy, presented to the gathering a statement which dealt with

[1] *The Student Movement*, vol. iii. p. 5.

a correspondence which had taken place with our Movement on the subject of the South African War,[1] and then
proceeded to appeal to the Federation not only to deal
with the spiritual life, meditation, prayer, the Holy
Spirit and such topics, but also to recognize that " it is
to be our calling as disciples of Jesus to examine the
different questions of our social and political life, praying
that He may give us the answer." [2]

They stated their case with frankness, earnestness
and ability and made a great impression upon us, both
because of what they said and because it came after a
reconciliation with the Dutch concerning differences in
relation to the war.   The British delegates were J. A. P.
Barnes, H. T. Hodgkin, Frank Lenwood, C. W. G.
Taylor, Stanley Wright and myself, and we brought
back to our Movement with conviction the Dutch
message : " It is not merely for ourselves that we are
saved, not only to preach a set of doctrines—but that
the very life of Christ may through us permeate the
whole fabric of our social and civic life."

The following winter *The Student Movement* provided
a series of seven papers on " Social Questions."   The
subject received increasing attention from the General
College Department.   The Theological College Department Executive was anxious to get students to study
the subject and asked me, in the autumn, to write some
studies on social questions for the guidance of those
who wanted to form social study circles, and as a result
I produced the first publication of the Movement bearing
on the relation of Christianity to society, entitled *Outline
Studies in Social Problems*.   The pamphlet contained nine
studies suggesting outlines of papers with appropriate
readings on poverty, employment, sweating and housing.   I was asked to prepare the studies because of the
success attending my missionary study outlines.

I knew nothing about social questions, but the advantage of being young is that one plunges in unaware of

---

[1] See p. 186.
[2] *Report of W.S.C.F. Conference, Versailles, France*, pp. 71-75.

one's ignorance and the results are often better than one deserves! I sought advice in university circles, read a number of books, and the studies served their purpose. They were used very little in the theological colleges, but study circles worked through them in London and the university colleges in England.

When the committee of the Movement presented its annual report at the summer conference literally all it could find to say about social questions was to refer to the conference a year before and remark : " The subject of work for the poor in the slums of our great cities was brought prominently forward, as well as the claims which Christ has upon us for work in the foreign field." [1] It was characteristic of the period that the committee should have thought it necessary, in the single sentence written about social questions, to drag in a reference to foreign missions.

Another year went by and very little thought was given to social questions, but in January 1903 a striking article in *The Student Movement* by Dr J. H. Adriani of Holland attracted attention. He took up the matter from where the Dutch delegation had carried it at the Versailles Conference in August 1900. He was not only critical of us, but of the whole Federation.

"When we study," he wrote, "the literature of the World's Student Federation and the different national Movements, we generally receive the impression that for us a social and political life does not exist. This is the more surprising when we consider that the importance of the Student Movement is confirmed by the fact that students are destined, in later life, to occupy prominent positions in social and political circles." [2]

He complained that no one acquainted with the life of the Movement would think that its members did anything but attend Bible circles and conferences, read books on missions, and live in an entirely spiritual world. He asked : " Dare we know the world fully,

[1] British College Christian Union, *Annual Report*, 1900-1, p. 1.
[2] *The Student Movement*, vol. v. p. 87.

and dare we feel how the world opposes itself to our faith ? " He suggested that we should enter the world and question people.

Our relations in life are based on commerce and industry. Ask the merchant. He will tell you that he approves of your going to Church and reading the Bible ; he will offer you a gift for missions, but at the same time he will tell you that it would be ridiculous to apply the teachings of Christianity to commerce. . . . Ask the manufacturer. His answer will be, " I know many influences in my department, but those of Christianity are out of place there." Ask the lawyer, " Can you apply the laws of the Gospel in your profession ? " He will look at you in amazement and say that it is useless to discuss the matter with one who apparently has so little knowledge of the world. Ask the politician and he will tell you that in his sphere the laws of evolution are in force, and their moral is that the great nations are destined to rule the small, to plunder and exterminate them. You will say that you do not believe that God respects the great and mighty of the earth, and you read to him Isaiah ii. 11-18. He will look at you pityingly and say, " That is good for your Bible-circle, but do not enter the world with it, because it would be ridiculous. Meanwhile, when my conquering army goes out to plunder and destroy (for such is war) I will allow you to do Y.M.C.A. work amongst the soldiers. I think I shall then have answered all reasonable demands." [1]

Dr Adriani concluded his paper by urging that we should proclaim freely the Kingdom of God even when its principles " condemn our society." *The Student Movement* editorial comment was that what Dr Adriani had said was well worth thinking about, and that " we might become more intimately acquainted with the social and political life of our country. Those whose life work is to lie at home might realize that they have a part to play in the combating of evils in our national and social life." The hope was expressed that the paper would promote discussion and lead men to view the Student Movement from the national standpoint.

Dr Adriani's article arrested attention. While the

[1] *The Student Movement*, vol. v. p. 88.

kind of thing he wrote became commonplace twenty years later, it was novel in Student Movement circles at this period. The hope of the redemption of society was yet to come, all we thought of was to snatch men's souls as brands plucked from the burning, or to ameliorate the lot of the poor and outcast. We never thought that society as a whole needed to be changed.

The Executive reverted to the question from time to time, some being concerned about the whole subject, some afraid lest the direct spiritual work of the Movement be hindered, others afraid that too much attention to home needs would divert students from considering the claims of the mission field. Henry Hodgkin, the chairman of the S.V.M.U., was a valuable influence. He was an effective leader, his missionary keenness was unquestioned, and he saw that the need of the world was a unity. The fact that he believed the Movement ought to give its mind to the study of society helped to keep us together. The Executive's report presented at the business meeting at the summer conference, 1903, said that special attention had been paid to the subject of social problems; that although the Christian Unions were not doing much about the matter the Executive "feel strongly that in view of the present situation in this country, the alarming alienation of the masses from the Church, and the widespread agitation for social reform, the subject must have an increasing share in the attention of Christian Union members." The idea of social reform as a bait was uppermost in the mind of the Executive. "We must seek to reach and influence that wide class of students who are already interested in questions of social reform, and to whom Christianity appeals chiefly along such lines."

The new note in the Movement found a response from the men and women in the new university colleges, for then, as now, it was in these that the students closest to the realities of life were to be found, and here too were the students preparing for an industrial career.

Oxford and Cambridge men at this time usually went into the professions. Belfast, Glasgow and the new university colleges and theological colleges in England provided the majority of those who undertook social study. The man who did most to promote thought and action was Stephen Band of University College, Liverpool. He urged that relieving occasional cases of distress did not exhaust the command of our Lord to give alms.

> It can only be obeyed by enquiring into the causes of distress, and in addition to individual treatment, there must be careful diagnosis of social evils, wise legislation, and efficient administration by borough and city councils. Hence Christ's command has special reference to modern forms of municipal service.[1]

The feature of the summer conference at Matlock, 1903, was a discussion that took place on the relation of the Movement to social problems. There was a recognition " that many students who are profoundly interested in the matter have scarcely been touched by our local unions," and that " for some years past it has been apparent that if the Student Movement is to be a true expression of essential Christianity we can no longer put off the consideration of social evils," and, most important of all, what emerged was felt to be the call of God.

> Those who have watched the growth of the Movement have been very conscious of God's guidance in each fresh development, and it is with gratitude that we acknowledge the hand of God in this the latest development of all. . . . The unity of the work of Christ's Kingdom at home and abroad has been recognized and emphasized in an unmistakable fashion. Not a few of those who spoke most strongly on the urgency of facing home problems were men who were looking forward to foreign service.[2]

This uprise of the social consciousness at the summer conference did not take all the leaders of the Movement

[1] *The Student Movement*, vol. v. p. 158.
[2] *Ibid.*, vol. vi. p. 25.

by surprise. The Executive of the General College Department had given much thought to the subject during the year, and they were ready with recommendations, Stephen Band being their spokesman.

> Educational circles should be formed for the study of social questions and a library of suitable books should be collected for the use of members. . . . Students should visit settlements during vacations, and where possible take part in settlement work during term time.

The following year the Movement was absorbed in growing evangelistic work. " The duty of social service and of the study of social problems is slowly but surely winning its way into the ideals and life of the Movement, but this sphere of our work is as yet almost in its infancy," is the note struck the year after, although the Christian Unions were making attempts to tackle the subject. The Executive, however, said that " these attempts are more valuable as signs of an awakening conscience upon the subject than for their own intrinsic worth." [1]

Study and social service steadily increased, and in 1908 a three days' conference on social problems, organized by the combined Christian Unions in Manchester, and a course of four lectures on " Poverty," arranged by the Christian Union at University College and attended by a large body of students from all the London colleges, attracted much attention in the Movement.

The situation was ripening for what was to come as a result of the Commission [2] which reviewed the work in the autumn. This Commission, recognizing the inadequacy of its findings in relation to the Movement and social questions, said :

> We recommend that the Executive should arrange a meeting of four days' duration, and that they should summon those who feel upon their hearts the burden of the problems of modern society, to come apart to intercede with God

[1] *Annual Report*, 1905-6. [2] See p. 335.

for guidance. While we recommend that addresses should be given to guide prayer, names of speakers should not be published, nor should any details of the programme be given which would tend to obscure the central issue—that of intercession for the guidance of the Movement in face of human suffering and alienation from God.

The General Committee took this advice and issued an invitation in *The Student Movement* in January, 1909, to a gathering for united intercession in relation to the Student Christian Movement and social problems. The invitation referred to the burden of the problems of modern society as having been for some years laid upon members of the Movement with an ever increasing sense of gravity.

> Many, however, must have felt a lack of definiteness in statement and appeal which made it unlikely that results would follow on a scale at all proportioned to the real warmth of feeling aroused. The Student Christian Movement needs a more definite purpose in relation to the social problem. Such a purpose can only be formed, if the past experience of the Movement goes for anything, at the footstool of God. The Executive have, therefore, decided to summon a conference for the purpose of prayer, in the full assurance that in the atmosphere of prayer, and there alone, will the Movement obtain the guidance it needs. They call any who feel the awful magnitude of human degradation, and the impotence of any power but that of Jesus Christ to heal the many diseases of which it is but the symptom, to come apart just after Easter and give themselves to meditation, communion and intercession.

No programme or list of speakers was given.

The conference which assembled in response numbered one hundred persons, about an equal number of men and women. The meetings were held in the Congregational Church School-room, Matlock, from April 16th to 20th, 1909, the men living at Jackson's Hydro and the women at Dalefield. Frank Lenwood was chairman and the speaking and leading of intercessions was shared by C. F. Angus, Kenneth Maclennan, W. Pelham, William Temple, Malcolm Spencer, T. Tatlow, W. M.

Cargin, Una Saunders, Dorothea Warner, Ruth Wilson, W. W. Longford, H. G. Wood and S. H. Wood.

The addresses were all followed by an opportunity for a further contribution of thought; there was much prayer and much silence. The first evening and next day were spent in considering actual social conditions. The next subject was "The World Defying Christ." The Church is on her trial—she professes to know the way of salvation, yet on the whole it is not the Church which is in earnest about human brotherhood. A night later we heard an address on "The Factor of Individual Sin in the Problem." This address was followed by a meeting without a chairman or any human guidance.

> The meeting was a venture, made with but small faith, but the sense of the Presence of God working quietly in our midst was so plain, that we knew we had come to the central point of our conference. We were there, not that we might learn from speakers what the aims of the Student Movement were, but that we might learn from God what they ought to be. The time was spent in giving expression to the ways in which the question was coming home to us, and in which we felt that God was leading us, and in prayer. There was an extraordinary sense of unity and of corporate guidance, greater than any presence of personal and individual problems.[1]

This evening was the high-water mark of the conference. "Many spoke, many prayed, and speech and prayer alike gave new impetus to the united movement of our thought. From one and another came, in different words, and born of different experience, the same simple claim for discipleship."

At Matlock the lesson learned was that the social problem neighboured more closely upon each of us than the wisest had suspected. The essential message

---

[1] *The Student Movement. An Impression of the Gathering for United Intercession in connection with the Social Problem*, vol. xi. p. 188.

of this gathering to those who were present lay in the words, " we are the social problem."

Till then, for most of us, " social problems " had always roused the thought of a slum, with its penury and degradation ; but then it was revealed to us that the spiritual problem is found in germ wherever men cast off the yoke of Christ. In want of sympathy between members of one family, even when it arises from a difference in moral ideals, in the contemptuous patronage of a class which we consider to be beneath our own, in any superior aloofness towards the unpopular man in college, in all sweeping and careless judgments of men or groups or nations, in all malice and uncharitableness, in short, *in all denial of the law of love there lies the root of evil from which all the trouble has grown*.[1]

To a later generation words like these may seem to convey familiar thoughts, but they were not familiar at this period, and it was this conference that discovered them not only for the Student Movement, but for a wider circle. Many of those who shared in this gathering went from it to be among those who, during the following quarter of a century, became leaders of much of the social thinking in the different branches of the Christian Church. The chairman of the Conference on Politics, Economics and Citizenship (C.O.P.E.C.), held at Birmingham, 1924, Dr William Temple, himself a member of the Matlock Conference, was undoubtedly right in saying of that gathering that it had its roots in the Matlock Conference of 1909.

The conference was deeply moved as it turned its thought and imagination to the amount of suffering and degradation in contemporary life.

When all is said in mitigation how grim the suffering is ! They live in houses where family life, to say nothing of thought or worship, is possible only for the victorious few ; many find their livelihood from early youth in casual and

---

[1] *Discipleship and the Social Problem*, a pamphlet embodying the message of the conference. The subsequent quotations in this section are from the same source.

unskilled labour that unfits them to serve their own or the national interests ; there must be millions, not starving indeed, but stunted in body and mind by a regular insufficiency of decent food ; their education, even if they have the stamina to assimilate it, is wooden, theoretic, and so incomplete that often no traces of its influence are to be discerned ; their scanty natural pleasures are eked out by the attractions of the music-hall in youth and of the public-house in manhood.

The main body of Christian people at this time thought of themselves as aloof from " the lower orders," among whom they deplored much degradation and sin, usually setting down as the cause either idleness or drink. They did not think of themselves as implicated. One of the convictions brought home by the Matlock Conference was the extent to which we are all implicated. It was a new note to find the conference saying :

> We profit to some extent by the system which produces, or at least allows, this wretchedness. That a man is an undergraduate of any university is proof sufficient that he belongs to a privileged class. The money which unlocks to him the glorious opportunities of a modern student would not come to him but for the labour of working men. This being understood, let us go on to consider it in the light of the statement that there is no such thing as clean money, even though we earn it cleanly ourselves.

We also realized at Matlock that we were implicated in the sense that " the corporate faith of Great Britain is lowered and impoverished because Christians have cared so little to make society Christian, and, though perhaps we may not know it, the faith of each of us is lowered and impoverished too."

There was talk about the outward means of deliverance, the duty of legislative action. " It is certain that some such action will be taken, and that, in whatever manner, a new basis will be found for our society." Here was something quite new. We had never before thought of the re-ordering of society. Up to this we had been concerned with improving the existing society and providing palliatives for the benefit of those who suffered from its defects. It was an entirely new idea to think of a new basis for society. There was some reference to the system of Karl Marx and the " horrible thing " that it was probably possible to found society, as he suggested, on a readjustment of self-interest. We thought of putting away " sweating," uplifting the standards of education, and crushing financial interests that batten on human degradation. " We must express in the law of our land the principle that property should count for less and human souls for more."

We should not be satisfied with the statute book. There was thought about existing laws " wise enough and strong enough to remove many of the worst evils," but laws which were unknown or neglected in administration. We needed a new type of public official who would use the weapons the law provided.

The duty of the individual, as a citizen, was considered. He should avoid the use of shops and articles which seem to encourage sweating, and he should try to keep a personal relation with those who serve him, and refuse to make money from unhealthy conditions of labour. The Christian citizen should help " to cast out the demon of greed from the community by deliberately living at a scale below that which he can afford."

The last means of outward deliverance considered was the work of rescue. Men and women in the grip of poverty, who men see as a social problem, God sees as needy men and women who He loves one by one.

If the conference had much to say about the outward means of deliverance, it had still more to say about the spirit behind this means.

> If it be true that we are the social problem, if from our hearts issue all the elements of evil, then from our hearts too must rise the generative force of good. If we are to serve our brethren, we must be fit to serve. The Kingdom of God, if it is to exist at all, must be within us.

Two of the Beatitudes were constantly quoted at Matlock and seemed to be brought home with power in a remarkable way to the hearts of all present. " Blessed are the poor in spirit," and " Blessed are the meek." If we were to contribute service of the smallest value we must rediscover the meaning of discipleship.

This discipleship must be a very costly thing, and day by day the price will be paid. . . . It will mean a slow and painful surrender of self-will and a daily attempt to walk in humility before God and men. Expenditure, pleasure, the choice of our life's work, and, above all, speech and thought as they touch those around us, must all be modified. . . . We are called to be meek. Since no quality is further from the practice and respect of our country, we shall do well to count the cost.

The conference asked itself whether the Movement had lost some of the passion of those to whom it owed its birth.

The wider the sympathy, the more certain the need for a burning fire within. . . . We who were at Matlock believe that we have found in this call to discipleship a new Puritanism which by God's grace will give the hardness and detachment from the world needful to those enlisted in a great spiritual campaign.

The campaign was to be a campaign to bring home to all in the Movement the need for discipleship in every sphere of life.

Perhaps it will help some to catch the spirit of this conference, from which so much came, if I quote a letter to E. S. Woods, written the day after the conference closed :

> 93, Chancery Lane,
> W.C.,
> 21st April 1909.

My dear Edward,

I have just come back from the social gathering at Matlock, where we have had a most remarkable time together, and where High Churchman, Nonconformist, and member of the Salvation Army have been holding intimate spiritual communion with one another. I wish it were possible to write for you a complete description of our days together. I think what happened, in a word, was this, that we began by thinking about various aspects of social need, concentrating our attention chiefly upon the poor, and seeing mental pictures of slums, but were gradually forced back upon the thought that if anything was to be done, the Church must learn to re-interpret what it means not only in theory, but in practice, to be a disciple of Christ, and to feel that it is sinful for a disciple of Christ not to love his enemies, to be self-assertive, to seek for a career in that spirit which is a contradiction of forsaking all to follow Christ. When we feel these things are as serious as when a Christian lies or steals, then the disciples of Christ will really become as salt in the earth, and will exercise a seasoning influence upon society they do not now exercise.

The days we had together were, I think, taken all round, more remarkable than any I have known in my experience of the Movement. We had with us 100 people extraordinarily diverse in every way, and yet as we waited upon God during our four days together, we were welded together into a united whole, and when on the third night we felt it right to have what was practically a Quaker meeting and give up a chairman, waiting for the Spirit of God to lead us, we reached the highest point of the conference.

There was no confusion. Some spoke to us, some led in prayer, but it was felt that what everybody did was a real contribution to the gathering, and that in literal fact, we realized what it was to be led as a body by the Spirit. There will unquestionably be practical outcomes of the gathering, because not only were the hundred people gripped with the idea that an entirely new spirit is needed among Christians, but also with the idea that this spirit would produce fruitage in action, both personal, commercial and political.

A special meeting of the General Committee is to be summoned for June, and our next step will be to work and pray that the lessons of our days together may be communicated to the summer conference. You will have an opportunity of reading, later, an account of our time together, as we have arranged to publish an " Impression " of the Conference. I know you will have been praying for us as we were together, and now you may certainly give thanks for us, but much prayer is needed for the Executive, upon whom great responsibilities lie, in order that the spirit and message of our time together may be conserved and transmitted to the whole Movement.

Yours affectionately,

TISSINGTON TATLOW.

Students were ready to pay attention to the message of the Matlock Conference; 1139 students had been in social study bands or reading unions during the winter, and there was a great deal of social service being undertaken.

The work done is of every possible kind—settlement work is the most common, but in some places services are held regularly in the wards of Hospitals and Poorhouses, and in St Andrews the Christian Union has taken over two country missions. As far as possible social study is complemented by practical work or by tours of inspection, and conferences on the social problem have been held in Glasgow and Leeds; in Birmingham the women students arranged a vacation school for social study.[1]

The Movement strengthened its social study committee, adding to it among others the Rev. William Temple. This sub-committee spent a good deal of time working out the right aim and policy of the Student Christian Movement in relation to society. This it defined as follows :

Aim :
> To urge upon students the necessity of learning the will of Christ, and following it in every department of life.

Policy :
> 1. To draw attention to the grave conditions of modern life, and to the duty of the disciples of Jesus Christ in the face of these conditions.
> 2. To emphasize the Christian function of home, business and professional life, and to claim men and women for the service of Christ therein.

[1] *Annual Report*, *S.C.M.*, 1909, p. 21.

2 A

3. To direct thought to the discovery of those forms of social life which are the fit expression of the Spirit of Christ.

4. To recover the hope of the redemption of society.

Malcolm Spencer had a large share in the formulation of this statement. He also presented a memorandum on methods of work.

Later the " Aim " of the Movement in relation to society was altered to read :

To call the colleges to the study of the will of God for modern life,
to the hope of the redemption of society,
and to the discipleship of Jesus Christ in every department of conduct.

Next year the committee reported that " the new call to discipleship which came to the Movement at the Matlock Conference on Social Questions, 1909, was being heard with evergrowing obedience," and they also make the significant remark, " that realization of its meaning is gradually growing." [1]

[1] *Annual Report, S.C.M.*, 1910.

CHAPTER XIX

MARTYN TRAFFORD AND NEW LIFE IN THE THEOLOGICAL DEPARTMENT

IN the autumn of 1908 Martyn Trafford became secretary of the Theological College Department. It was an appointment made with hesitation; the committee saw no one else but was uncertain about his being the right man, while he was oppressed by his own sense of limitations. Nevertheless, Trafford was to prove the ablest and most successful of all the leaders of the Theological College Department. He worked quietly for six months and then his influence began to tell. "I feel I know more about the Movement," he wrote, "and its place in the life of the theological colleges, and I know what it ought to mean to the colleges I visit."

Martyn Trafford was a Baptist, and the son of a Baptist missionary who had been Principal of Serampore College, India, for twenty-six years. He was educated at Mill Hill School and Glasgow University, where he gained prizes in moral philosophy and logic, graduating with second class honours in philosophy. On graduation he became Eglinton Fellow at Glasgow, lecturing on Berkeley and Lotze, until he went to Mansfield College, Oxford. It was from Mansfield that he joined the Student Movement staff. Like many sensitive men he was slow in finding himself, and this tended to rob him of ease in contact with various types of men, and also to make him morbid at times. While at Mansfield he wrote :

I fear I lack the gift and sense of humour in its highest sense; for humour, as a Christian grace, can belong only to him whose heart is pure, whose defence is strong, and who is not afraid. It is only the man of faith who can touch life with a light hand. The man who is conscious of his own weakness, who is haunted by the horror of his sin, whose skin is sore with the wounds of recent conflict, may not do so, cannot do so. He shrinks from even a caress, he hears a rebuke even in the word that was meant to encourage.

But for all his criticism of himself his growth in strength of character was rapid. He had hung in his study as the motto of his life the words, " He set his face steadfastly to go to Jerusalem," and it was often referred to by his friends as characteristic of his dedicated spirit.

Martyn was a small, dark man, with a pallid face, sensitive mouth, and eyes that sparkled and glowed as he warmed in his talk. Dr Cairns, to whom he loved to talk about his work, summed him up well as " the brave, merry, keen-witted comrade who had the heart of a soldier and the face and speech of a boy." He showed a rare combination of mental and spiritual qualities, was clear and trenchant in his judgments, and passionately earnest in his desire for the noblest spiritual ends.

As a friend he excelled. When he died in August 1910, after two years' service in the Movement, one of his friends wrote, " It is not Martyn's work that I admire most in his life, it is his capacity as a friend." The tenderness, sensitiveness and intensity of his nature made his love of a very fine quality. Two quotations from his letters on the subject of friendship will help to reveal him.

At the new year I wrote down one or two resolves or rather ideals. One of these ran thus—" Never to claim the gratitude or respect or love of men as my right ; always to regard them as a gift."

Many times he repeats in different ways that love is a gift. He knew the difference between liking a man and loving him.

I am inclined to say, because I cannot be friends in the highest sense with this or that man, I won't have anything to do with them at all. This is wrong; it is a tendency which must be overcome. . . . It is only selfishness and narrowness which tries to live in the Holy of Holies where love can be seen in all its wonder, and refuses to come out into the outer world to fight for and bear witness to that love which is so often scorned and misunderstood or even unknown. To love is something like prayer; it is not a luxury, nor is it something which having found we are to keep to ourselves for our own enjoyment. It should be an inspiration which drives us out to do great and difficult things for God and the Kingdom of Heaven.

Trafford played a many-sided part in the life of the Movement. College visitation, the oversight of missionary study in both the theological and non-theological colleges, the promotion of missionary campaigns and social study, work on the summer conference programmes and on special committees—he was a good committee man—made him a force. Two pieces of work, however, will always be especially associated with his name. One was the initiation of theological retreats and the other the revision and clarifying of the policy of the Theological College Department.

After he had been at work for a year, Trafford produced a memorandum on theological retreats. The object he had in view was to help towards " the development of a wider catholic outlook, and the deepening of the prayer life in Nonconformist and Presbyterian theological colleges." His idea was quite a simple one: that each retreat should be for three days and limited to ten selected men, carefully chosen from Anglican, Nonconformist and Presbyterian colleges, with one senior man as leader—he named in his memorandum as suitable leaders William Temple, W. W. Longford, Neville Talbot, E. K. Talbot, and J. H. Oldham. A good deal of time was to be given to corporate prayer and intercession, " with hours when men could be alone "; the afternoon should be free and the evening devoted to discussion on fundamental questions.

The first of these retreats was held at Calver, Derbyshire, January 10th to 14th, 1910.   Eight men were present, representing Kelham, Mirfield, Ridley Hall, Handsworth, Richmond, Lancashire, and Mansfield Colleges.   The time-table for each day was as follows :

9.30 a.m. to 9.50 a.m. Morning Prayers.
10 a.m. to 10.45 a.m. Intercession.
    The subjects taken were : the World Missionary Conference ; theologicals and the unity of the Church.
5 p.m. to 6.30 p.m. Conference.
    The topics were : a missionary Church ; the grounds of our belief ; the demand on the Christian ministry in the face of modern doubt ; and the function of the S.C.M. in theological colleges.
8 p.m. to 9.30 p.m. Conference.
    The subjects were : the prayer life of a theological student ; what do we mean by the Church ?
9.30 p.m. to 10 p.m. Evening Prayers.

Trafford, reporting afterwards, wrote :

The rule of silence was observed pretty strictly in the mornings up to 1 p.m.   A book was read aloud at breakfast, men taking it in turns to do this. . . . The experience of the rule of silence was new to at least half the men, but it is worth reporting that we were all unanimous at the end that it had been most helpful.

Of the daily conferences he said :

One of the most prominent characteristics of these conferences lay in the fact that they were much more of the nature of talks.   There was very little debating of points at issue.   It was much more a process of exchanging ideas and ideals than a discussion of problems.   We made no attempt to arrive at any agreement or even sum up conclusions.   Each man stated his own position with the utmost frankness, and the discussion was useful in so far as it helped us to understand our differences and points of agreement more clearly. . . . On the last evening we had no fixed subject but each man said anything that was in his mind.   It was certainly the most remarkable of all the meetings.

Martyn himself was the leader of this retreat.

The second retreat was held at Overhaddon, Derbyshire, three months later. Ten men were present from Kelham, Egerton Hall, Mansfield, Lancashire, Didsbury, Hartley and Manchester Baptist Colleges. The leader was the Rev. William Temple, Fellow of Queen's College, Oxford, Trafford again being present. Of this retreat he wrote :

> The success of a retreat depends very largely upon the leader. We were fortunate in securing Temple. He was splendid ! We forgot that he was a don, he became one of ourselves, kept us on the right lines, and was the life and soul of the party. He struck the right note on the first evening, and this did much to make the retreat the great time it certainly was. We were reminded that we had come to Overhaddon not to meet one another, but to meet with God. We were not going to have debates or even discussions, but were just going to throw our ideas into a common pool as it were and each man could draw out what he thought of value to himself.

A number of similar retreats were held in England from 1910 to 1914, and several also took place in Scotland. They probably did more than anything else the Student Movement has ever done towards promoting a spirit of unity and educating men in the point of view of Churches other than their own. A number of the men who appeared as representatives of British Churches at the World Conference on Faith and Order at Lausanne in 1927 received their initial impetus to work for unity, and their first training in understanding the questions at issue, at these theological retreats.

The success of these retreats emboldened Martyn in the lead he was giving to the Theological College Department. He undertook the first survey of the history and records of the Department made since its formation in 1898, added the results of his own observation in the colleges and constructed a clear and coherent policy for the Department which was adopted by its committee.

Under his inspiration the aim of the Department was defined :

1. To link the theological colleges together so that what is best in the life and tradition of each may be shared by all the rest, and more especially through the development of this intercollegiate fellowship to work for—
The cultivation of the missionary spirit.
The Christian interpretation of social duty.
The strengthening of the devotional life.
The fuller understanding of Christian truth, and
The promotion of the spirit of unity.

2. To enable theological students to take their share in the world-wide Student Movement, receiving its inspiration, and making their own special contribution to it.

It will be noticed that the old hesitation about creating a union of theological colleges had disappeared and in its place was a frank statement of purpose to draw the colleges together and help them to share one another's good things.

Trafford's special contribution to this statement of aim was twofold—" The fuller understanding of Christian truth " and " the promotion of the spirit of unity." He elaborated his contribution in two memoranda of unusual interest.

He was the first leader of the Theological College Department who invited it in its corporate capacity to consider the question of truth. He pointed out that the leadership of the Movement was alive to the intellectual awakening which was stirring men's thoughts and unsettling their faith, but that the theological colleges were behindhand in realizing its importance. " The following facts," he wrote, " are of serious and special significance " :

1. Systematic theology as taught in the majority of our colleges is lifeless and has little or no relation to the problems and difficulties which are perplexing the minds of men in the colleges and in the Church.

2. There are a large number of individual students, especially in the stronger Free Church colleges, who are feeling the pressure of theological difficulties in their

acutest form, and who are doing splendid work in their endeavour to think their way through to a more adequate statement of Christian truth, but for the most part they are working alone, and in many colleges they receive little encouragement or help from their professors or tutors.

3. A very large proportion of the students are not really awake to the situation. The theological colleges are isolated. The men, for example, do not come into personal touch with the scepticism of non-Christian students, nor do they know the difficulties which are perplexing the minds of the thinking men among the laymen. This is possibly especially true of the Anglican colleges, where men do not even have the opportunities which preaching engagements afford. . . .

Then come his reasons, summarized in almost his own words, for holding that the Theological College Department was intimately concerned with the whole matter:

1. It is the duty of theological students as students to study truth, and it is their privilege as belonging to the Student Movement to study it together.

2. The ferment of theological unrest is spreading right through the Movement, and theological students ought in large numbers to be helping to meet the difficulties of men in other faculties.

3. The theological colleges ought to be turning out men who, because they have come through the storm themselves, or at least are fighting their way through it fearlessly, can effectively help by word and pen those who are being beaten down by it. If our theological colleges had been doing their work effectively in this direction, there would be any number of men whom we could ask to speak for us at conferences or deliver lectures or write text-books dealing with the intellectual difficulties of students. As it is there are very few.

4. Some of the strongest men in the colleges are deeply concerned about this matter, and they have held aloof from the Movement because they have felt they were not welcome, and that we did not share their interests and ideals.

Trafford viewed without dismay the pressure of intellectual questions.

"We may well believe," he said, "that the intellectual awakening which is everywhere stirring men's thoughts and unsettling their faith is part of God's plan for leading us into a fuller and richer knowledge of Himself. The interest which is aroused may well be symbolic of growth, indeed there are many who have come through it, under a sure sense of the guidance of God, into a larger faith."

He was convinced that because it was a time of reconstruction, it was a time of opportunity. "There is such a thing as enthusiasm for truth. We must stand for this . . . we must emphasize the fact that we are not merely theological students, but students of theology."

It was his lead which resulted in the conference on the Problem of Truth which was held in 1911.

The other item in the new aim of the Department which was especially his own was " The promotion of the spirit of unity." He recognized the fact that the question of Church unity had been kept deliberately in the background in order that the Student Movement might avoid the entanglements of ecclesiastical controversy, and he accepted the limitations of an inter-denominational movement. " In the realm of practice we cannot go a step in advance of the ecclesiastical bodies to which the students connected with the Movement belong." But the theological retreats, though not exclusively concerned with the question of unity, had stirred all those who took part on this subject, and he felt strongly that the Department ought to state emphatically that it was working definitely for the unity of the Church. The function of the Department is " to stimulate thought " on the problem of unity.

There is urgent need for this to be done. (a) The problem of the unity of the Church is ultimately a problem of truth. It is our duty as theological students to study truth, and it is our privilege as belonging to the Student Movement to study it together. (b) Not many men have yet realized the central importance of this problem. The theological curriculum does not, in the majority of colleges, bring them face to face with this question. In Nonconformist colleges men study the doctrine of the Atonement and the doctrine of the Person of Christ, etc. They are not instructed in the doctrine of the Church or led to give serious thought to ecclesiastical questions. (c) In consequence of this, and also in consequence of the fact that the Theological Department does not declare its interest in the question of unity, men do not appreciate the significance of the work of the Movement in this matter. They rest content with the unity of feeling and spirit which is found at camp. The delight of discovering what jolly good fellows High Churchmen and Baptists can be obliterates all thought of the differences which separate them. This may be all very well for ordinary students, but theologicals need to strike deeper. The new-found sympathy and friendship should set them thinking and searching for a deeper unity. It is our concern to see that this happens. It will not happen as a rule unless we declare our purpose and our concern more emphatically.

Martyn Trafford left the whole Movement enriched by his faith and insight, and he left it a force in the theological colleges. His death on the eve of sailing for India was wholly unexpected and a cause of deep grief to us all.

CHAPTER XX

DEVELOPMENTS IN WALES, IRELAND AND SCOTLAND, AND CONTROVERSY IN ENGLAND

THE honour of having conceived and organized the first of the National Councils of the Movement belongs to Wales. The Welsh delegation at the Liverpool Conference, 1908, decided that if the Movement was to appeal as it ought to Welsh students, it must have a Welsh National Council. The delegation led by E. L. Roberts, Bala College, drafted a constitution for a Welsh Intercollegiate Christian Union, and referred this to the meeting of the Welsh delegation at the summer conference. The Union was to be composed of all the Christian Unions in Wales affiliated to the Movement, but was to be autonomous, with its own secretary and finance. The plan broke down because the Welsh students did not see how they could finance committee meetings, literature and a secretary. I heard of the breakdown and asked a Welsh group to meet me. We discussed the matter at considerable length and I advised them to propose a Welsh Intercollegiate Christian Union with a Council, which should be an advisory council to the General Committee, to ask the General Committee to recognize this as part of the machinery of the Movement and to bear the necessary cost.

The General Committee accepted the plan in December, 1908, and the first meeting of the Welsh Council was held on February 20th, 1909, at Shrewsbury. Those present were: Idris Davies, University College, Cardiff; B. F. Armitage, University College, Bangor; Illtyd Jones, University College, Aberystwyth; G. W. Griffith,

Bala College, and T. B. Wheeler, University College, Aberystwyth. The representatives of the General Committee were : Walter W. Seton, Malcolm Spencer and H. M. Trafford. Oliver Thomas, Aberystwyth University College, was nominated as the first Welsh national secretary and appointed by the General Committee. It was a good appointment. Oliver Thomas had gifts of imagination and industry. He was liked by the staff of the whole Movement and, as a Welsh speaking student, commended himself to the students of Wales, not excepting the many English students who are always to be found studying in Welsh colleges.

The idea of an Irish Intercollegiate Christian Union was discussed by the Irish students at Baslow, 1909. The idea was carried by them to Ireland. A conference had been arranged in Dublin by an intercollegiate committee, representing Trinity College, the Royal College of Surgeons, the Royal College of Science, the Metropolitan School of Art, Alexandra College and the Church of Ireland Training College, for January 21st to 24th, 1910. This conference received sympathetically the suggestion of an Irish Intercollegiate Christian Union as part of the Movement. The Union was organized by Jocelyn Smyly, Trinity College, Dublin; W. M. Cargin, Trinity College, Dublin, and T. M. Barker, Queen's College, Belfast; and the first meeting of the committee of the Irish Intercollegiate Christian Union, which came to be known as the Irish Council, was held in Dublin, September 10th to 12th, 1910. Those present were : W. M. Cargin, Trinity College, Dublin, who was elected chairman ; J. Smyly, Trinity College, Dublin ; Miss Dobbin, E. M. Norton and Miss Revington (T.C.D.), W. S. Lynd, T. M. Barker and Miss Robb (Belfast), F. Lewis (Galway), G. H. Mahony (Cork) and Miss Kyle (Londonderry).

Cargin wrote to me on September 13th :

We have done really solid work, and whatever our inexperience, it is something for which we ought to thank God from the bottom of our hearts. It cost a great deal of time and thought to Smyly, Barker and myself, but the results were far beyond everything . . . the whole thing was wonderful. God took us and led us all from the cloudiness and pessimism of our first meeting to a fuller knowledge of His way and to a quiet confidence in His power.

Much time was devoted at this meeting to formulating the aim of the new Irish Union. That ultimately decided upon was as follows :

To call Irish students to the knowledge of God in Jesus Christ and His discipleship in every department of conduct, that, united in Him, they may study the will of God for modern life, and may hope and strive for the redemption of Ireland, seeking to realize her mission in the Kingdom of God on earth.

One further extract from the minutes of this meeting is worth recording. Under the general heading, " The Presentation of the Gospel in Irish Colleges," the first paragraph reads as follows : " Recognizing that prayer is the greatest practical force in the presentation of the Gospel, the committee gave considerable time to the discussion of this matter." Then follows a long series of suggestions concerning individual and corporate prayer.

It was not possible to find a man as Irish secretary immediately on the formation of the Council, but there was unanimity that Tom Barker of Belfast was the man who was wanted as soon as his college course was finished. He was asked to act as honorary secretary of the Council this first year, and in May 1911 he became the first full-time Irish secretary of the Movement.

Up to this time the work of the Christian Unions in Ireland had nothing that was characteristically Irish about them. Almost no social study had been undertaken. Meetings dealt with the fundamentals of the Christian Gospel. Missionary study flourished as Irish students considered the needs of the non-Christian world, and all the Unions had Bible circles. Almost all the members of the Student Movement belonged either

to the Church of Ireland or to the Presbyterian Church.
They were all Protestants, and racially either Anglo-
Irish or Scotto-Irish.

Traditionally the body of Protestant students had
always been Unionist, and thus the strongest political
tradition amongst them was opposed to the idea of
Home Rule, especially as it had taken shape in the
proposed legislation of Mr Gladstone in the 'eighties.
Most of these students had never learned Irish history.
The history they had been taught was the history of
England. Consequently, they knew very little about
Ireland's past and did not think very much about
Ireland's future. Their main desire was that the Celtic-
Irish, who were most of them Roman Catholics and
Home Rulers, should not come into political ascendency.
There was little or no contact between Roman Catholic
and Protestant students, and there were very few Roman
Catholics in Queen's College, Belfast, or Trinity College,
Dublin. The only places where Protestant and Roman
Catholic students met were in the University Colleges
of Cork and Galway, which were mainly Roman Catholic,
though each had a small group of Protestant students.
University College, Dublin, was a wholly Roman Catholic
institution, with no Protestant students.

It is not surprising that a considerable number of the
most vigorous personalities among the students looked
forward to a life-work outside Ireland. The Indian
Civil Service, the Colonial Service, the Army and the
Ministry of the Church of England drew from Ireland
each year a large proportion of the best of the graduates
from Trinity College, Dublin. It hardly occurred to
the average Irish Protestant to think seriously and con-
structively about Irish life and problems.

Tom Barker was a Protestant, a Presbyterian and an
enthusiastic Irishman, but unlike the average Irish
student he thought they should be taught to think and
work in a new spirit and in a new way for Ireland. He
carried Cargin with him, for it was to these two men
the Irish Conference of 1913 was due, and they planned

a conference dealing with Irish questions, which was such a conference as had never before been held in Ireland.

There had been numerous Student Movement conferences in Ireland, but this was the first arranged by the new Irish Council. There were two hundred and seventy students and some fifty guests present, the latter including a number of members of staff. Tom Barker was chairman, and in his opening address stated the nature and purpose of the conference. "This is the first conference on record in which Irish students, as Irishmen and Christian Irishmen, have attempted a comprehensive study of the conditions of our own land."

After speaking of the formation of the Irish Intercollegiate Christian Union and its aim, he spoke of the conference as part of the policy through which the Union was attempting to fulfil it.

> With the knowledge of God is inextricably interwoven the brotherhood of man. This is the first problem which meets the Christian Irishman. Why is it in our land we have failed to realize that brotherhood—are failing to realize it to-day—and are closing from ourselves as a people this avenue to God? . . . We all know that our country suffers from intolerance of other men's notions, carelessness for other men's welfare, hatred of other men's creeds.[1]

The conference was, he said, an attempt to fulfil the first duty of students—to study the facts—the facts both of the past and the present, in the light of the knowledge that the solution of all questions lies with the God we seek to know.

> The salvation of Ireland, no matter at what price, and our share in the work, are the objects of our quest. . . . We have to ask ourselves, "Is Jesus Christ sufficient for the needs of Ireland to-day?" . . . It is these two things —the love of country and the love of Christ—that have in God's providence called this conference together. We

[1] *The Student Movement*, vol. xv. p. 108.

have a country whose ancient glory and present shame demand the very best our youth can give. We have a power in the Christian gospel that can use that best to bring again the ancient glory and turn even our failures into triumphs. . . . We are weary of the storm and stress of present-day disputes, and we cannot get away from the belief that behind them all there must be some state more permanent, some force more stable, some truth more true.

The first two days were given to the study of different aspects of Irish social problems—capital and industry, education and citizenship, emigration, intemperance, housing, national sins, political bitterness and religious intolerance. Among the speakers were the Revs. R. M. Gwynn, Canon J. O. Hannay, R. W. Hamilton, and A. W. Barton,[1] also Mr E. J. Gwynn [2] of Trinity College, Dublin.

The conference later dealt with the relation of Ireland to the world, telling of Ireland's missionaries, religion in the East to-day, the problem of Islam, and Ireland and the missionary ideal. Among the speakers on these topics were the Revs. J. A. Murray, D. S. Cairns, and Professor R. M. Henry.

The relation of the Irish Intercollegiate Christian Union as part of the Student Christian Movement to the subjects of the conference were dealt with by Bolton C. Waller, T. Tatlow, Miss G. Revington and Miss Cunningham.

The conference made a profound impression, and its report, *Ireland's Hope*, was used in many study circles.

We all anticipated that there would be a great outcry in Ireland that the Student Movement had become political because of some of the topics with which it dealt. Although there was protest from some quarters, in the main the conference passed off with less hostile comment than was anticipated. This was to some extent due to the fact that the extreme Unionists had overreached themselves. Many of them regretted the

[1] Afterwards Bishop of Kilmore, Elphin and Ardagh.
[2] Afterwards Provost of Trinity College, Dublin.

2 B

establishment of Ulster Day and the Ulster Covenant, subsequent to the introduction of Mr Asquith's Home Rule Bill the previous year.   By the time of the conference there were the beginnings of sympathy with Home Rule ideals in some student Protestant circles.

Scotland had for some time been causing the General Committee of the Movement anxiety.   While Irish students were grappling in a new way with Irish questions, and there was rapid progress in the English universities, the Christian Unions in Scotland were not growing in influence.   The travelling secretaries, with a field comprising the entire British Isles, were able to give only a very limited amount of time to visitation in Scotland; also, the post of travelling secretary had been filled by a succession of Oxford and Cambridge men to whom the Scottish situation was unfamiliar.   Their influence in the Scottish universities was inconsiderable. In September 1909 the General Committee discussed the possibility of appointing a Scottish secretary but took no action.

Some of us hoped that Scotland would quickly follow the example of Wales and Ireland and form a Scottish Intercollegiate Christian Union.   As no movement had been made by the summer conference of 1910, I began to wonder whether someone outside Scotland would not have to act, and asked Professor D. S. Cairns whether he thought I dare invite the Scotsmen to meet and consider the matter.   His advice was against my doing this.   He thought that in view of the independent character of the Scot there might be opposition simply because the idea had come from outside Scotland. Matthew White, the president of the Christian Union in Glasgow, was also uncertain how the suggestion would be taken.   As the matter hung fire I decided to risk failure.   Accordingly, I invited the Scottish delegation to meet me one afternoon and suggested an Intercollegiate Christian Union for Scotland.   The proposal was received with enthusiasm, and a committee appointed to take steps for the formation of the union.

This committee asked me to draft a constitution and to propose it on its behalf at the Scottish Colleges Conference, Edinburgh, March 22nd to 24th 1911.

The conference was a great occasion. There were nearly 600 students present. The note of patriotism was struck powerfully and used by Professor Cairns to a high end. He was ably seconded by Dr Kelman on the opening night, and J. H. Oldham on the closing night. Dr Cairns drew a vivid picture of the spiritual crisis which had been precipitated by the drawing together of the East and West: "We all find it harder to believe in God because of the existence of the Edinburgh slums. . . . We talk about irreligion at present. It is nothing to what it will be in twenty years if the East goes over to materialism." It was also a time of crisis in Scotland, she had not chosen her vocation. "What are you going to do to help Scotland to find her vocation?" The speaker thought it was a time of great opportunity for the Student Movement.

All the old religious ideals of Scotland are behind you in the Student Movement. Scottish religious life has always stood for the idea of the theocracy—the Kingdom of God. There always have been some, as there are some still, who think solely of the saving of the individual, but such a view was sheer atheism to the old Scots religious leaders. They thought of the individual, but they thought much more of the City of God. . . . In the Student Movement you stand for theocracy. You stand for the Christianizing of the world and of society—for the Kingdom. You have the whole religious history of Scotland behind you.[1]

Scotland has always stood for the visible Church. "I praise God," said Professor Cairns, "for the great free-lances of history; but the conquest of the world will never be won by the free-lances, but by the regular army—the Church."

"Scotland has always loved great thinking in its

[1] *The Student Movement*, vol. xiii. p. 175.

religion." With a tribute to Calvin as a thinker and to Knox for having brought Calvin's contribution to Scotland, Professor Cairns spoke about the humanistic revival of the nineteenth century and the need for it. "But," he continued, "are we not weary to-day of singing the praises of nature and of man? Is there not a deep, impatient yearning in our modern world for God? I believe God is speaking to the youth of the country in a way in which He is not speaking to the older people." The stillness in the hall when Professor Cairns sat down indicated how deeply the audience had been touched. It was so still that with eyes shut it seemed as if none were present but oneself, the speaker and God.

This address touched the imagination of students in Scotland. It was printed and circulated widely and helped to give the Scottish Intercollegiate Christian Union a fine start.

The Scottish Intercollegiate Christian Union was founded by a unanimous vote of the conference, of which Kenneth MacIver [1] was the very efficient secretary. He acted as secretary of the interim committee of the Union until it was fully constituted. The Council held its first meeting on October 27th 1911. There were present: John Stewart, United Free Church College, Aberdeen, chairman; W. M. Christie, New College, Edinburgh; W. Douglas, St Andrews University; G. S. Duncan,[2] Edinburgh University; T. C. Gibson, Glasgow University; A. G. Henderson, Edinburgh University; Andrew Hislop, Edinburgh University; H. Leggatt, Aberdeen University; R. G. Macdonald, Aberdeen University; Hugh Martin, Glasgow University; P. C. Millar, Glasgow University; James L. Smith, Aberdeen University; Matthew White, Glasgow University; T. Tatlow; Miss Carswell, Glasgow University; Mary Cumming, Aberdeen University; E. S. Hendry,

[1] Afterwards the Rev. Kenneth MacIver of Birkenhead.
[2] Afterwards the Rev. Professor G. S. Duncan, St Andrews University.

St Andrews University; Jess Mackintosh, Edinburgh University; W. V. Sayers, Glasgow University. John Stewart[1] was unanimously elected chairman, and George Barclay,[2] Glasgow University, co-opted and appointed treasurer. The first thing the Council did was to discuss its aim. It was a fine discussion, when not only were the needs of Scotland considered, but the work of the Student Movement as a whole reviewed, and the contribution which Scotland should make to it discussed.

The General Committee of the Student Movement was ready with the suggestion that R. G. Macdonald should be appointed Scottish secretary, and he was called to this position by the unanimous vote of the Council. " R. G." threw himself with enthusiasm into the leadership of the work of the Movement in Scotland, and it went ahead by leaps and bounds during the three years that remained before the ruin caused by the World War.

The Councils of the Irish, Scottish and Welsh Intercollegiate Christian Unions were by constitution advisory bodies to the General Committee of the Student Movement, which was the final court of appeal in the Movement throughout the British Isles. The Movement assumed financial responsibility for the work of the Councils, having found by experience that changing student bodies could not conserve finances, and that the continuous work which headquarters alone could give was needed if supporters were to be retained. Thus it came to centre all its funds in London, trying as far as possible to constitute committees in different centres, which would help to collect these funds.

Although the Councils were nominally advisory bodies, actually they did a great deal of executive work. There was provision that immediately at the close of each Council meeting there should be consultation between the Council's secretary and the general secretary of the Movement to see if there was any decision which

[1] Afterwards the Rev. John Stewart of Manchuria.
[2] Afterwards the Rev. George Barclay of Cambridge.

should be reserved for consideration by the General Committee, otherwise the work decided upon was begun at once. The arrangement worked well, and was continued until the reorganization of the Movement in 1929 gave additional powers to the Councils.

Until the Movement began to appoint national secretaries in 1909—if we except London, which had had its own secretary for a decade—all the visitation in England, Scotland, Ireland and Wales in connection with the ordinary work of the Christian Union was done by one man, while a second man travelled on behalf of the S.V.M.U. For many years one woman, and later, two women, covered the same field. Looking back, it is wonderful to realize what these four men and women accomplished. They each visited from sixty to eighty colleges in a year and mediated to the Christian Unions in them the policy of the central committees of the Movement, and brought back to the committees a knowledge of all that was happening in the colleges.

These travelling secretaries had to speak, and often several times, in every place they visited, and varied indeed were the subjects on which students wanted them to talk. " I am engrossed here in Newcastle, taking two days off to write a paper on ' The history, accuracy and consistency of the Four Gospels,' on which Dundee University College has advertised that I will speak next Friday, without consulting me ! It was rather a staggerer, but I decided not to funk it ! " wrote Howard Houlder in 1909.

The speeches asked for from travelling secretaries dealt with the Student Movement, the World's Student Christian Federation, the policy of the Movement concerning Bible, missionary and social study, and addresses on a variety of devotional, social, missionary, apologetic or doctrinal topics. No wonder that the Movement ransacked the entire university field for the ablest and most devoted men and women it could find for its staff.

The travelling secretary spent a certain amount of time in meeting the Christian Union Committee, and often sub-committees as well. He would usually be invited to visit any study circles that were meeting and take part in their work, sometimes being asked to speak at the close. The different officers of the Christian Union wanted to talk about their work, and over-burdened or discouraged presidents and secretaries looked to the visit of a travelling secretary as an occasion when they would have an opportunity of talking over their difficulties with one who had perhaps met similar difficulties elsewhere and would have something to say. At any rate he would be sympathetic and ready to cheer on these workers. Time was given to occasional meetings with senior friends, and especially to maintaining contacts with sympathetic members of staff. Occasionally public meetings in connection with the Movement were addressed, and above all, there was the work which never ceased, of talking to individual students, often far into the night, and night after night: students who brought every kind of intellectual, moral and spiritual difficulty to the travelling secretary for his help. If there was a student conference or week-end gathering of any kind when the travelling secretary was present, he was likely to find himself on the programme for several speeches. I don't know if anybody has calculated the number of speeches made by a travelling secretary in a term, probably he would make one on most days and sometimes would find himself with as many as five meetings to address in a single day.

What chiefly taxes a travelling secretary is the fact that he is invariably expected to give a lead and to lift a situation on to a higher spiritual plane than that on which he finds it. Again and again secretaries have shown great ingenuity in their methods. Jack Woodhouse, writing from Bangor, which he was visiting as a travelling secretary a few months before he was succeeded by Howard Houlder, said: " Here in Bangor I was advertised for 8.15 p.m. last night. There were two men present at that hour. By 8.30 there were ten all told. It was a lecture on Baslow (summer conference) with a lantern." Jack wanted a decent audience and was not to be daunted. He took counsel with B. F. Armitage, the secretary. They decided to postpone the meeting until 9 p.m. and sent off the ten men, telling them to return at 9 p.m., each with two others.

> " It was Biblical," writes Jack, " and that bore me up. 'Go into the highways and hedges and compel them to come in.' They did. *Daily Mails* were wrenched from their hands, hatless and bootless they were dragged to the meeting—men who had never been to a Christian Union meeting before. By 9 o'clock we had thirty-five men and I fired away."

The World's Student Christian Federation held a meeting of its General Committee at Oxford from July 15th to 19th 1909 on the invitation of the Movement. Thirty countries were represented by 123 men and 55 women; the meetings were held in the hall of Exeter College ; the men had Keble College as their centre, where all meals were taken ; Wadham, Balliol and Trinity provided sleeping accommodation as well as Keble, and the women lived at Somerville College.

One clear impression at the close of the conference was the unexampled rapidity with which university education was increasing throughout the world, the most startling case being China, where the sudden abandonment of the ancient examination system by the Government had driven thousands of students to seek an American or European education and created a demand in China which neither teachers nor institutions were sufficient in numbers to supply. Another noteworthy fact was the great increase of women students in almost every part of the world. In Western Canada university education was being organized with astonishing rapidity, Korea was pressing forward eagerly, and in Mohammedan lands Western education was driving out antiquated systems. The movement was the same everywhere—the modern spirit driving young men and young women to seek the best education obtainable and killing traditional religion in their minds. It was regarded as a time of great peril and opportunity.

The Federation Committee spent much time in reviewing the needs and encouragements in Christian work among students over the entire world. The three methods of work which received most attention were : the development of Bible study, the consideration of what apologetic had been most helpful in leading students into faith in Christ, and how the Student Movements of the world could help in solving the social problems of the time. Papers were read, followed by vigorous discussion. Representatives of each Movement spoke of its ideals, hopes, policies, successes and its doubts, difficulties and failures. The gathering was a council of war. The Federation was not making a demonstration but planning a campaign.

There was very little time for recreation. I remember one incident with amusement. On one of the paths outside the hall at Keble students from several countries were passing the time between meetings one morning by competing with one another in a long jump. A. C. B. Bellerby, president of the athletic union at Cambridge, was standing on one side, looking rather amused. After many countries had competed, I suggested that England should now try what she could do and pushed Bellerby into the competition. None of the men standing round knew that he was a " Blue." He jumped easily nearly twice the distance anybody else had achieved. It was with awe that the men eyed him as the competition slowly broke up and men went off in groups to discuss, in their astonishment, the athletic prowess of the English!

The delegates from other lands were, needless to say, delighted with Oxford. Parties given in the gardens of Magdalen, Lincoln and Christ Church on three afternoons, attended by many senior members of the university, were greatly appreciated. No one was more interested in the conference than the Rev. Prof. William

Sanday, who expressed his intense delight in this revelation of the Federation.

At our summer conference which followed at Baslow a number of changes were made in the Constitution of the Movement. The membership of the S.V.M.U. and General College Department committees was each increased from six to eight, with the requirement that in the case of the S.V.M.U. at least three should be women students.

In the case of the General College Department and the Theological College Department committees half those elected had to be student volunteers, an arrangement made when the S.V.M.U. gave up its complete independence and became part of the whole Movement. It was decided to delete this requirement from the Constitution. It was found in practice that it hampered the committees in the choice of people they needed and did not greatly assist the work of the S.V.M.U.

The increase in the number of secretaries was causing the General Committee difficulties. Hitherto all the secretaries had been by Constitution members of the General Committee, with the exception of intercollegiate secretaries, who, being appointed locally,[1] did not have seats on the committee, even so as the number of S.C.M. secretaries was increasing rapidly it was found that there were too many secretaries on the committee, and with their knowledge of the work of the Movement it was increasingly difficult for the student members to maintain the ascendency which they had hitherto had on Student Movement committees. While, therefore, retaining the clause giving secretaries appointed by the S.V.M.U. and Theological committees full membership, the General Committee inserted a clause in its Constitution that the only *ex-officio* member of the General Committee should be the General Secretary, but that it should have the right to co-opt by standing order " such

[1] There were local secretaries for men at Oxford, Liverpool and Cambridge, for women at Glasgow and Edinburgh, and for men and women in London.

other officers of the Movement as it may feel to be necessary."

In order to secure efficiency and continuity in the Bible study of the Movement and to secure that the meaning of Christian discipleship with reference to social conditions should· receive proper emphasis in the work of the Movement, two standing committees, to be called " The Bible Study Committee " and " The Social Service Committee," were constituted, these committees to be of an advisory character.

These changes in the constitution were passed unanimously at the business meeting at the Baslow Summer Conference, 1909.

A sub-committee was appointed, October 1909, consisting of Frank Lenwood (chairman), R. L. Pelly, M. Trafford, T. Tatlow, Dorothy Brown and Zoë Fairfield (secretary), to draft the programmes for the three summer conferences. Although there had been programme committees on previous occasions, yet owing to the growth of the Movement and the decision to hold three conferences more responsibility than ever before fell upon the sub-committee. The leadership of this sub-committee passed into the hands of Miss Fairfield, and for twenty years she was the chief maker of programmes for summer conferences and had a very large share in deciding who should speak. Some years the programme committee had fresh and original ideas concerning the main lines of the programme, other years it tended to fall back upon the experience of its predecessors. As Miss Fairfield's experience grew, the kind of guidance she was able to give the sub-committee grew in importance, but perhaps her chief service to the summer conferences was in watching that the range of speakers was not limited by the inevitably limited knowledge of people possessed by the members of the sub-committee. A study of lists of speakers while Miss Fairfield was secretary shows how representative was the body of men and women collected year after year to address the summer conferences.

As the committees of the Movement grew in size and agenda lengthened, secretaries found that many questions relating to their work hitherto talked out on committee were crowded out, so the practice arose of having special gatherings of the secretaries. These have been held at different places, but none were happier, more intimate or more useful, than those held for a number of years at Oakenrough, Haslemere, the home of Mrs Tritton Gurney.

The first meeting at Oakenrough was held November 25th to 29th 1909. Mrs Tritton Gurney was a delightful hostess, and the surroundings were among the most beautiful that Surrey can provide. During all the years we went there the staff of secretaries was sufficiently small to be a unity, which meant that even when we adjourned conference for recreation, we did not break up into groups, but either played together in the grounds or sallied forth in a body to walk across the heather.

The groups that used to go to Oakenrough consisted of Student Movement secretaries, retreats of the London Council, college Christian union committees, theological students, fine art students, training college students and Oriental students. A letter from a student who had been at one of the retreats expresses well the thoughts of many who have had the privilege of spending some time at Oakenrough :

> The sun and the birds, the heath and the hills, all seemed in conspiracy to bring us into the presence of God, and I do not think there is one of us who was not influenced by the quiet sense of peace and security that pervaded the whole atmosphere. I think it was a real time of worship for many of us ; I thank God.

Mrs Tritton Gurney died in 1921, but left the house and grounds for retreats and conferences, and it is still used for these.

When the General Committee met at Christmas (1909) it gave much time to its relation to Cambridge University. The Cambridge Intercollegiate Christian

Union, which was founded in 1878, was the strongest Christian society among students during the period before and after the founding of the Movement. It was this union which Robert Wilder used as his base when he organized the S.V.M.U. in 1892. It was one of the foundation Christian Unions a year later, when the Inter-university Christian Union was founded, and gave it a number of its early leaders. It had begun, however, to give anxiety to Douglas Thornton before he went to Cairo in 1898, because of the stagnation of thought which lay behind the lack of sympathy with the policy he, more than any other man, had led the Student Movement to adopt, of trying to draw into its fellowship Christian men of all types and points of view. The C.I.C.C.U. had its roots deep in the Evangelical party of the Church of England. It was hostile to all that savoured of being High Church and, although it was not a Church of England society, it made no attempt to win Nonconformists. Its members tended to have a traditional evangelical theology, which they did not examine very closely yet held with great tenacity. The verbal inspiration of the Bible was one of their most strongly held tenets.

When the Student Movement began to broaden its platform at the beginning of the century by the inclusion of both Churchmen and Nonconformists, whose theology differed from that of the C.I.C.C.U., its uneasiness and suspicion of the Movement's policy grew. As the Movement was represented by it in Cambridge it always secured for its committees some of the C.I.C.C.U. leaders. A succession of C.I.C.C.U. presidents were committee members of the Movement. Almost all these men, coming to understand the Movement from the inside, sought to win the C.I.C.C.U. to cordial support, but there was always a strong element in the C.I.C.C.U. which did not want to change, while at the same time there was a considerable body of old C.I.C.C.U. members whose influence was used to prevent change.

The policy of the Student Movement in relation to its choice of speakers for summer conferences, its relation to Church of England theological colleges and its invitation to younger dons at Oxford and Cambridge, whom it regarded as coming men whose help it wanted for the Movement, led to the building up of a body of friends in Cambridge who were not members of the C.I.C.C.U. These men influenced pupils and friends among the undergraduates to attend the summer conferences. Many of these felt the atmosphere of the C.I.C.C.U. uncongenial and wanted a society in Cambridge representative of the Movement. By 1907 this situation was becoming acute.

The leaders of the Movement thought that the position would right itself by an influx of the Cambridge friends of the Movement into the C.I.C.C.U., but these pointed out that the C.I.C.C.U. was not a democratic society, and they could not hope to influence it. The membership did not elect the controlling committee, which was a self-appointed body. People therefore felt that there was little use their joining the C.I.C.C.U. in the hope that they might have a share at an annual meeting of members, and on similar occasions, of influencing its policy.

In 1907 R. L. Pelly became president of the C.I.C.C.U. and during his office made a big effort to effect a change. The discussions he initiated continued for two years. The feeling of men outside the C.I.C.C.U. was voiced by many in letters to the general secretary. For example, Mr Alex. Wood of Emmanuel College, Cambridge, wrote on August 1st 1908, after he had been at the summer conference :

> I have come back more than ever convinced that it would be an enormous boon if we could broaden the C.I.C.C.U. here so as to include the best elements of the Nonconformist Union. I could not help being struck with the fact that the Student Movement is a much broader thing than the C.I.C.C.U. It is significant that men like C. F. Angus of Trinity Hall, A. M. Smith of Emmanuel,

H. G. Wood [1] of Jesus, J. K. Mozley [2] of Pembroke and many others among the younger generation of fellows and lecturers, who are keen on the Student Movement, should always have been outside the C.I.C.C.U.

In 1909 A. C. B. Bellerby became president and again tried to effect a change. He secured a decision from the C.I.C.C.U. that they should either alter their policy, and among other things have an annual general business meeting at which every member should have a vote, or else, alternatively, they must give up affiliation with the Movement and allow it to create a fresh organization in Cambridge.

I was asked by the General Committee to spend some time in Cambridge and decide whether it seemed wiser to advise the breaking of affiliation or to make a further attempt to bring the C.I.C.C.U. into line with the Student Movement. I spent a good deal of time in Cambridge seeing individuals and attending conferences, and in the end advised disaffiliation. I was influenced chiefly by the fact that there was a group of determined senior men, only a few of whom lived in Cambridge, who exercised continual pressure upon the undergraduates who led the C.I.C.C.U. to maintain it as an organization of Christian men with no other theology than the theology which they favoured.

The great facts upon which the Christian faith is based do not alter, but the history of theology has been the history of man's growing, and therefore inevitably changing, insight into the true interpretation of these facts. Theology is dynamic and not static. The senior men represented a school of theology which had been dominant in the evangelical movement ten to twenty years earlier, but which among thoughtful men was giving place to new theological formulations.

These senior men had seen theological colleges in which they were interested ceasing to teach some of the things which they believed. They felt that heresy

[1] Afterwards Director of Studies at the Selly Oak Colleges.
[2] Afterwards Canon of St Paul's Cathedral.

was growing, that they lived in perilous times and that youth must be kept in the old paths. Their stronghold among students was the C.I.C.C.U. at Cambridge. Once it changed, the source of supply of young university leaders to take their places would be gone. I have seen numerous letters and telegrams from conservative senior men to C.I.C.C.U. presidents, warning them against the Student Movement and begging that they should make no change. The literal, verbal inspiration of the Bible, the penal view of the Atonement, and the near return in physical form to the earth of our Lord were their basic tenets. In their zeal for their point of view, some of them made statements about the Student Movement which were a grave misrepresentation of its position. The most frequently spread rumour from this source was that the Student Movement had given up all belief in the inspiration of the Bible and in the divinity of our Lord.

An attempt was made by a group of junior dons at Cambridge to adjust the whole position. As leaders in the Church Society, the Nonconformist Union and the Societas Trinitatis Confraternitas, they formed a committee composed of a dozen men representing these three organizations, together with the Free Church Devotional Society and the C.I.C.C.U. They made an attempt to devise some scheme whereby people who were interested in the Student Movement could have contact with it without necessitating the Movement's breaking its link with the C.I.C.C.U. While, however, negotiations were going on, the C.I.C.C.U. decided, in March 1910, by seventeen votes to five, to break affiliation with the Student Movement, much to the disappointment of Bellerby, who wrote to me :

> I am now branded as the president of the C.I.C.C.U. during whose office this great step was taken, namely, I am branded as a narrow evangelical and an anti-Student Movement man, whereas I have wasted a whole year fighting for the other side.

Curiously enough, at the meeting at which the C.I.C.C.U. decided to break affiliation, it decided by fifteen votes to seven that it desired "democratic government."

The committee of the Student Movement decided to accept the proposal of the united committee that it should carry on for the present in Cambridge, and that it would not affiliate for a time any fresh organization in the university.

There were about a hundred Student Volunteers at this time in Cambridge, and many of them were very restive about their membership of the S.V.M.U. owing to the break in affiliation with the C.I.C.C.U., of which a large number of them were members, and in the following year fifteen of them resigned from the S.V.M.U.

The dissatisfaction and ultimate severance of the connection of the C.I.C.C.U. with the Movement had various repercussions. The two universities which the English public knew something about, at any rate that section of the public which were interested in the Student Movement, were Oxford and Cambridge. When they spoke of what was happening at the universities they meant what was happening at Oxford and Cambridge. Not only did they not know what was happening at the modern universities where the majority of students were studying, but they hardly realized that there were modern universities. Trouble between the Student Movement and the C.I.C.C.U., and the ultimate severance from it of the C.I.C.C.U., were a source of distress to many senior friends, who feared that the Student Movement "was going off the rails."

I spent a good deal of time both in conversations and by letters trying to explain to some people, whose confidence we valued very highly, what it was we were trying to do in the universities at this period and what was the situation we had to try and meet. One man to whom I shall feel grateful as long as I live for help at this period was Dr Eugene Stock, editorial secretary

2 C

of the Church Missionary Society.   He was himself
one of the ornaments of the evangelical movement.
We never lost his sympathy, and probably no one did
more to interpret us to our evangelical friends at this
period than did Dr Stock.   When Douglas Thornton
was initiating me into the Movement he told me that
the most important man among our senior friends to
keep in touch with was Dr Stock, and from the time I
joined the staff of the Movement in 1897 until he died
at over ninety years of age, I never lost touch with him.
The Student Movement should always hold Dr Stock
in reverent memory as one of its most understanding
friends and most valuable interpreters at a time when
it needed such help.

There was another difficulty with a section of our
senior friends, especially those who were definitely
associated with the evangelical party in the Church of
England, and that was our cultivation of other elements
in the Church of England.   There were plenty of men
who did not beat about the bush, but took me to task
for helping to bring High Churchmen into the Student
Movement.   Some of them first raised the standard
of battle when the Bishop of London (Dr Creighton)
was invited to speak at the quadrennial conference in
London, 1900.   A section of the religious Press kept
up an attack on the Movement for not being adequately
and exclusively Protestant from then onwards.

Father Kelly's cassock at the summer conference, and
the appearance of men like Canon Scott Holland and
Bishop Gore on the platform caused me no little trouble
behind the scenes.   The Student Movement leader who
was my most valiant helper was R. P. Wilder.   He was
trusted by the Evangelicals much more than I was because he was more conservative theologically.   On the
other hand, he was completely at home with the High
Churchmen.   I remember his telling me that there was
no place where he liked to stay more than at Pusey
House, Oxford, with its head, the Rev. V. Stuckey
Coles; and dear old Mr Stuckey Coles—who was a

great saint—used to talk to me in an equally lyrical way about his friend Robert Wilder.

The difficulty of this period was added to by the fact that students are quickly sensitive to movements of thought, and new ideas take root in the universities more rapidly than anywhere else. Their sympathies are always with senior men who are progressive in their thinking, and who are ready for new ideas. They are not interested in men who feel that they are holding the fort against the intrusion of new ideas.

The situation was specially difficult in relation to the summer conference. For a period from 1900 to the outbreak of the war, a series of kindly but very mournful letters were addressed to me by evangelical Churchmen who did not like or understand the interdenominational position of the Movement. They remembered its origin in evangelical circles in England and wanted it to be a stronghold of evangelicalism. They regarded the progressive broadening of its platform with distress, and constantly suggested the inclusion of men representing their point of view as speakers in the programme of the summer conference. I was constantly trying to persuade the student leaders to accept some of these names, but it happened many times that when some man who was urged upon us as suitable for a course of Bible readings or an address at one of the evening meetings, was given the place on the programme suggested for him, he failed to hold the students. More than once, when such a man was billed for a second address, I have had to go round the conference and beg committee members and Student Movement secretaries to come into the tent to provide him with an audience. The students did not want to hear him again.

A common complaint was that the Student Movement was being captured by the High Church party. The truth, of course, was that High Churchmen were in a minority and had to accept a great deal that was strange to them in the practice of the Movement and the conduct of its conferences. All this is ancient

history now.   Although there are parties in the Church
of England that do not love one another to this
day, there is far more harmony, and the great body of
Churchmen who are interested in religious matters in
the universities are, I believe, happy in their acceptance of the Student Movement's cordial welcome to
both Evangelicals and Anglo-Catholics—to give the
High Churchmen their new name.

CHAPTER XXI

THE INTERDENOMINATIONAL POSITION OF THE MOVEMENT AND THE WORLD MISSIONARY CONFERENCE, EDINBURGH, 1910

THE Church of England was by this time taking considerable notice of the Movement. Its theological colleges were joining it, prominent Churchmen of all parties were participating in its summer conferences, and the Church Congress [1] at Manchester in 1908 devoted a session to it. I described the Movement to the Congress, and was followed by Canon Kempthorne, the Rector of Liverpool, who spoke as one " who has been converted from a position of scepticism about the Movement to a whole-hearted belief in its spirit and policy." Bishop Ingham, clerical home secretary of the Church Missionary Society, declared to the Congress—" this Movement has come to stay. It bears the image and superscription of God the Holy Ghost. And it is destined to influence profoundly not only the regions beyond, but the Church life of this home land."

The most important of the set speeches was that of the Warden of St Augustine's College, Canterbury, the Rev. J. O. F. Murray, who spoke " as a responsible college officer," who had been in touch with the Movement since the Liverpool Conference, 1896, which he had attended when Dean of Emmanuel College, Cambridge. He described the nature of his connection with the Movement,[2] and analysed the possible reaction of

[1] *The Official Report of the Church Congress, Manchester*, October 1908, pp. 350-79.
[2] See p. 207.

a Catholic to the Movement and declared that times had changed.

> The old ideal of education was, as far as possible, to shelter students during their period of training from the danger of contact with erroneous opinions behind a hedge of tests and subscriptions. . . . Under the conditions of life in a modern university this ideal is no longer attainable . . . nothing we can do can prevent the freest and most public discussion of the deepest theological problems. . . . It is no doubt a time of searching, fiery trial.

The Warden spoke of the questions raised in the mind of a college dean by the presence of a branch of the Movement in the college for the religious life of which he was responsible. What line should he take " with regard to this independent, interdenominational organization ? It is altogether a new thing, initiated and controlled directly by young men, amenable to influence, but outside the sphere of official discipline."

I listened without anxiety from my seat on the platform for I knew what Mr Murray was going to say and that he was as eager as I was that the sympathy of the congress should be won for the Movement. He continued :

> We cannot fail to find in this Student Christian Movement an instrument prepared by God Himself for our hand, whereby we may, without any sacrifice of principle, as the natural expression of the inherent, though as yet it may be undeveloped, inclusiveness of our inheritance, encourage our pupils to prepare for that corporate reunion for which we pray.

Mr Murray concluded his address by a reaffirmation of his conviction that the Movement was " a veritable extension of the Pentecostal outpouring. It is, indeed, God who is pouring out His Spirit on His servants and His handmaidens in our day. It is He who has opened the eyes of these young men that they may see."

The Bishop of Lahore (Dr Lefroy) then took up the tale.

We stand at one of the great crises, the great epochs, the great turning-points of history—one, as I myself believe, of the greatest the world has ever known. That it is a period of great change, almost of revolution—if, thank God, of more or less peaceful revolution—amongst ourselves here in Western lands, we recognize. Yet, believe me, this is as nothing compared to the upheaval, symptoms of which are patent on every hand, among the great nations of the Far East to-day. I say the *nations*, for I am most anxious that our eyes should not be so exclusively fixed upon India. . . . Unmistakably and beyond all question the changeless East is changing, or already in the commencing throes of change, under our eyes to-day ; the old life is breaking up and passing away, the days that shall be cannot be as those that have been : *some* new life, be it of what kind it may, is coming to the birth, and who can exaggerate what it will mean for the whole civilized world when the change is fully come, when those mighty nations really find themselves, really arrive !

The Bishop went on to say that it seemed to him "mere folly and childishness to look merely with alarmed and pained surprise to what is going on in India." England had been pouring into India for two generations, through numerous agencies, a flood of Western ideas and standards and learning and hopes. It was not a situation to meet with repression. From the religious point of view indifference and stolidity and deadness had given way to a feeling out after some larger, freer, more wholesome form of life. India was not looking consciously and avowedly to the Christian Church for guidance and support, nevertheless "the opening before us is a magnificent one, and the influence which the Church may still exercise on the new life which is thus coming to the birth is immense if only— *if only*—we can supply at this crisis in adequate measure real leaders, men both large-hearted and wise, able to sympathize with all that is best and truest in these large movements which are taking place, and to make their influence felt in their development." Dr Lefroy went on to say : " I have seen enough of the representaives of the S.V.M.U. in India to know that to them, to their home organization, we owe some of those amongst us at the present time who answer to the type I have sketched." Dr Lefroy concluded with whole-hearted commendation of the Union.

The Bishop of Lahore was the last of the set speakers and he had made a notable contribution to the meeting, inspiring it with a vision of the opportunities of the hour in India. And who will say that the hour has yet passed in that land ?

In the discussion, the Rev. A. G. B. West testified, after twelve years in Australia, that the Movement was doing "an admirable and glorious work throughout the whole of Australia." Mr West's speech contained a good deal of information about the Movement in Australia. He had been a speaker at the summer conference there, and also in touch with the social service work which the Australian Student Movement had initiated and was developing, and it suggested the outreach of the Movement that a testimony to it from India was followed by one from Australia. The Bishop of Southwark (Dr E. S. Talbot), who, as will be told later in this chapter, had already been drawn into the preparation of the World Missionary Conference, Edinburgh, said that "No one can come into contact with this interdenominational movement and not feel that there is the direct prompting of the Holy Spirit."

Others took part and all were sympathetic, the debate being concluded by the chairman, the Bishop of Bristol (Dr Forrest Browne), who spoke of "the incalculable good which this Movement is doing," and picked out for special mention the fact that "these Student Volunteers are showing us that in the religious area we can extend our united work "—namely work done jointly by Churchmen and Nonconformists.

This recognition of the Student Movement by the Church Congress, marked by a series of sympathetic speeches from men who obviously understood it, was of great value at this juncture.

The spirit of the time and the way in which the leaders

of the Movement met concrete situations will best be made clear by one episode and its treatment.

One of the Welsh Nonconformist members brought to the notice of the Executive the fact " that a student from a High Church college had tried to exert undue influence over a Welsh delegate and wished that precautions might be taken in future to guard against any such pressure being put upon anyone." [1] There is no doubt that nothing in the least undesirable took place, but suspicion of the High Churchman as a proselytizing person, whose influence was very dangerous, was rife in Free Church circles. The Free Churchmen knew nothing whatever about the High Churchmen and it was really rather ticklish work bringing them together. The men from the High Church colleges were very self-conscious about their churchmanship and many of them nervously anxious to expound their position to all and sundry. They wanted to discuss the whole question of reunion. Happily the day came very quickly when they had their way, and far from their attempts to expound their position being regarded as efforts at proselytism, the Free Churchmen became as anxious to hear what the Anglicans had to say as the Anglicans were to understand the Free Churchmen's point of view.

The two men who were most helpful at this period were Father Kelly, the director of the House of the Sacred Mission at Kelham, and Martyn Trafford, the Baptist travelling secretary of the Movement. No one was more welcome at Kelham than Trafford, and none did more than these two men to get the issues between the Anglican and Free Churches out into the open for discussion. On the committee, however, it was perhaps not unnatural that there should have been a certain amount of nervousness and that everyone was rather frightened at the suggestion of proselytism.

The committee decided to ask Neville Talbot and H. G. Wood to write a joint memorandum on inter-

[1] Minutes of the Theological College Department Committee, September 1908.

denominational relationships.   What actually happened
was that Neville Talbot wrote a long letter affirming the
desirability of interdenominational co-operation and explaining the reasons why he thought that though they
were bound to co-operate, the Movement ought "frankly
to face the fact that—expressed in party terms—the converging tendencies of to-day are likely to play into the
hands of the Church (though the enemy speaks of it
in terms of betrayal and capture)."

H. G. Wood's reply had a very calming effect.

"The Movement," he said, "is calculated to make us
High Churchmen in a broad sense of the term.   It stands
for an ideal of the Church, of a united Church, which
reaches out beyond the achievement of any existing Church,
and makes each Church's interpretation of Christianity
incomplete.   We are looking for a fuller Christianity in a
nobler Church.   Many, perhaps most, will feel with you
that the Church of England, as it stands, comes nearer to
this higher ideal than any other existing Church in England.
I am personally inclined to agree with you that converging
tendencies play into the hands of the Church.   But I also
feel, as perhaps you do too, that the Church has some way
to travel before her expression of the ideal becomes a
basis of reunion.   I take it, however, that the attitude of
the Movement must be, to recognize that we are moving
towards a higher ideal of the Church, to leave men free
to frame their conception of that ideal, but to urge men to
recognize the need of a higher Churchmanship."

Wood went on to say that "there would be offshootings
from one regiment to another" as discussion proceeded,
and the net gains were likely to rest with the Church of
England, but that while recognizing this, the Movement
must continue to discourage proselytism " and I think
individual secessions."

Of course, if anyone is led to feel that he cannot honestly
stay where he is, he must be encouraged to shift.   But the
essence of our Movement is the fostering of a spirit of
unity among the scattered and separated groups of be-
lievers.   To do this it is essential that those who have

caught the wider vision should evangelize their own people. . . . In the interests of the ideal Church, we must be chary of urging men to join, or of allowing ourselves to join, the Church which seems to us to embody that ideal most nearly at present.

Wood wound up his letter by saying : " Beyond this, we must make our members see that it is no crime against interdenominationalism to discuss reunion at Baslow or elsewhere ! " In this last sentence he had certainly hit the nail on the head. His letter had a considerable influence at the time. It caused the Free Churchmen on the Committee to take a line which led people to change their minds and cease regarding Anglicans as dangerous people when they tried to discuss their theory of interdenominationalism and what they thought about unity. The letter also allayed a great deal of nervousness in Student Movement circles lest people should suddenly change their denominations and thus embarrass the Movement, by its suggestion that men were most likely to serve the cause of unity by remaining in the Church in which they found themselves, expounding there the ideal of unity which was beginning to come to them through participation in the Movement.

The Movement had by this time established its position in the eyes of the Christian Church as an interdenominational body. It was a new thing. There was nothing else like it in the country. Through its influence the Churches were about to make an important experiment in interdenominationalism in a World Missionary Conference at Edinburgh, and its preparatory commissions were in full swing. Yet the Movement had never formulated its position in any statement, rather it had been guided to take one practical step after another as it had tried to think and pray and follow the guiding of God. And who can doubt that the Holy Spirit was leading it in ways that would help to bind up some of the wounds of the broken Body of Christ—the Church ?

It is worth while, even at the risk of repetition, to

review what had come to pass. First of all, college men and women who were fired with a passion for the evangelization of the world had bound themselves together to prepare for missionary service and to call fellow-students to join them in winning the world for Christ. Round these missionary-hearted students grew up Christian Unions as they realized the spiritual needs of fellow-students. The pioneers were determined from the first to try and draw into their fellowship and inspire with their missionary zeal all students who professed and called themselves Christian. They found that some of the stronger denominationalists hesitated; some of these were Church of England, some Presbyterian and some Nonconformist; most of them were theological students. They set out to win not only theological students, but to bring all the theological colleges of the United Kingdom into the Movement. Senior men were approached and asked for their co-operation as speakers at conferences. They knew by accepting they would find themselves on the platform with men from whom they differed, possibly on important doctrinal questions and certainly on questions relating to the Church and ministry. They would be associated with men with whom they had never co-operated in spiritual endeavour. Many of those invited refused, but the students were not satisfied to accept refusals and suggested conference with them regarding what they were trying to achieve. Interviews and conferences begat growing sympathy with what the Movement was trying to do. Invitations at one time refused were accepted and the difficulties of some, who feared that they might be expected to adjust what they had to say to the views of people from whom they were divided, were swept away by the request to say all that they believed God had given them to say, without regard to other men's approval. High Churchmen, Evangelical Churchmen and Nonconformists, who had never met or heard each other speak, found themselves sharing a wonderful spiritual fellowship and in many cases forming lasting friendships. Men of different spiritual traditions, different ways of approach to Christ, different methods of maintaining their spiritual life, spoke freely what they had to give and found the result was not chaos, but a rich diversity which emphasized rather than detracted from a deep underlying unity which they had not hitherto known existed. One illustration may be culled from scores which could be given. The Warden of Pusey House, Oxford, the Rev. V. Stuckey Coles, came to the summer conference because he said that one undergraduate he had tried to help without success " had been soundly converted at the previous summer conference," and he wanted to see what kind of gathering it was that had won him. Mr Coles said at the end that he had never before been so conscious of the presence of God, save occasionally at a small Anglican retreat, and he added that the most intimate spiritual fellowship he had had with anyone at the conference was with Henry Hodgkin. It was with surprise that he learned after the conference was over that Hodgkin was a member of the Society of Friends and not a fellow Anglican. Mr Coles' experience was typical.

But all this was not enough for the leaders. Was the Movement really clear about its principles ? Would its work last ? Would the results be found in the end to be good ? Were all its methods wise ? An exchange of prodigiously long and deeply interesting letters took place between Martyn Trafford, a Baptist and travelling secretary for the theological colleges; Kenneth Kirk, an Anglican and London secretary; Leslie Johnston, an Anglican, Fellow of Magdalen College, Oxford, a member of the S.C.M. General Committee; and J. H. Oldham, a Presbyterian and missionary study secretary. The correspondence was copied and circulated to the leaders of the Movement. It arose out of discussions begun on the committee of the Theological College Department as to whether the Movement was right in doing evangelistic work in the colleges.

The High Churchmen had doubts and, with the candour all were accustomed to use in the Movement, expounded those doubts as fully as possible to their Free Church colleagues. Should Churchmen take part in the Movement after all, because it tried to evangelize in the colleges, and ought they to be responsible for men who were not Churchmen evangelizing students when the content of their message might be very inadequate? "The Catholic cannot dissociate himself from the Church. . . . Simple gospel teaching has very little meaning for us," wrote one, "unless it involves implicitly and is intended to lead up to the whole position of the Creeds."

To this his Nonconformist correspondent replied : "In bearing public witness to Christ, and in preaching His gospel in so far as we know it, we are following our duty as individual Christians. But we cannot offer all that is needful for the full development of the Christian life, because there are many things that can only come through the corporate life and fellowship of the Body of Christ, which is the Church." Were they so very far apart after all ?

The correspondents discussed the evangelization of Oriental students, the work of the Y.M.C.A. in the Far East, the question of authority, the relation of the historic Church to the denominations, the way in which reunion would come, the danger of " a Student Movement gospel " being evolved, the desirability of affiliating denominational societies to the Movement, the ministry of prophecy and the order of priesthood.

The General Committee thought a small sub-committee should consider what it was all about and prepare a memorandum which would help the committee to define its interdenominational position and determine its policy. The committee appointed consisted of W. W. Seton (chairman), Zoë Fairfield, MacEwan Lawson, Kingsley Williams, Martyn Trafford, Neville Talbot and T. Tatlow. This group met at Oxford on February 19th and 20th, 1910. After prayer, Seton opened the meeting with a short speech which is worth giving in full. It set the tone of the meeting and revealed a point of view acceptable to all those present.

The ideal of unity which we believe is in the purpose of God for His Church must be based upon the profound realization of the sin of our divisions, and that is where the note of penitence ought to come in, when we realize how often we get into the way of regarding our divisions with complacency, how we settle down to the fact that Christ's ideal for the Church has been shattered by sin, both corporate and individual. I think it is fairly clear that it was the intention of Christ that there should be unity and that that unity was to be the greatest apologetic to those who were outside the Church and the greatest secret of the conquering force of the Church, and so as in an individual case there is need for penitence, so, too, there is a need for the same as an Executive and as individuals. It is time we should get back to a sense of our own insufficiency, it is time we should realize more acutely than ever before that we who are supposed, who have been called, to lead this Movement are not ourselves living near enough to Christ to be able to lead it adequately. There is a danger that the Cross which stands at the beginning of our personal experience should gradually recede into the distance. If we are to see Jesus Christ lifted up, as we so often pray, we shall see Him lifted up on a Cross, and that should call us to our need for forgiveness.

First then there is the danger of self-sufficiency in our work as individuals and in our work as a Movement, and secondly there is the danger of our stereotyping our methods, of our forgetting our need for a progressive and continuous revelation of the will of God, danger of our going on automatically without confession, without penitence, without the divine forgiveness, and so right at the beginning of this time I think we could not do better than spend a short time in confession so that the sin, individual and corporate, may come home to us. I believe that this is the only way in which we shall be able to think aright and plan aright.

After talking for two days the group separated without writing anything down, but asked me to prepare a memorandum for the General Committee on the

basis of their talk. I did so and the group approved
the document. It was revised in a few particulars by
the General Committee and issued to new committee
members and secretaries for twenty-two years under the
title, " The Interdenominational Position of the Student
Christian Movement."

This document defined the interdenominational position in these words :

> The Student Christian Movement is interdenominational,
> in that while it unites persons of different religious de-
> nominations in a single organization for certain definite
> aims and activities, it recognizes their allegiance to any of
> the various Christian Bodies into which the Body of Christ
> is divided. It believes that loyalty to their own denomina-
> tion is the first duty of Christian students and welcomes
> them into the fellowship of the Movement as those whose
> privilege it is to bring into it, as their contribution, all that
> they as members of their own religious body have dis-
> covered or will discover of Christian truth. The Student
> Christian Movement, therefore, while extra-ecclesiastical
> in the sense that it does not concern itself with questions
> of ecclesiastical organization or Church function, is in a
> position to have its life enriched by its members each
> bringing into it as their contribution all the truth for which
> they hold that their own denomination stands.

Having arrived at a definition, the practice of the
Movement came in for consideration. There was no
difficulty in setting down what was expected of speakers
on the Student Movement platform as already scores
of Churchmen had been assured, in response to anxious
enquiries, that they were not expected to take into
consideration the fact that members of other denominations might differ from them, but were to speak fully
and freely all that they believed God would have them
say on the subject allotted to them.

> We consider that it is important that the Movement
> should seek to derive its spiritual life through the religious
> bodies with which its members are connected ; and, when
> at summer conferences or on other occasions, a member
> of any religious body addresses the Student Movement he

should be expected to give his full message, and not to seek to modify it in view of the fact that there may be some in his audience, who, because they are members of other Christian bodies than that to which he himself belongs, may not agree with him.   It is assumed that the aim of all speakers will be to deliver a positive message, and that they will not consciously attempt to proselytize.

Much time had been spent upon deciding on what Christian activities all could unite without compromise of principles.   There was immediate agreement as to the propriety of gathering men to pray together and also to undertake missionary and social study.   More difficulty was felt about evangelistic work, Bible study and the preparation of apologetic literature.   The considerable place which the Movement's Bible study text-books played in guiding the Bible study circles in colleges caused difficulty.   All were agreed that " as a Movement we are right in urging men to read and study the Bible," but the High Churchman felt that elements of truth which have been the occasion of division in the Churches might be slurred over, or even neglected.   The difficulty, however, was in the end recognized as more theoretical than practical, for only one text-book came under criticism in all the discussions, and this criticism was not due to a divergence of view between Churchmen and Nonconformists. The committee finally agreed that Bible study text-books

can and should be fair and objective expositions of the books of the Bible according to the best scholarship, and that such should be acceptable to men of all denominations.   At the same time, we think that there should be no suppression of standpoint on the part of the writer of these books, nor should they handle the material in an un-denominational manner, but rather give a scientific account of the various views which have been held on the passages dealt with.

Apologetic literature came in for the same kind of criticism and the group reached the rather curious

2 D

conclusion that the Movement should not issue any large apologetic work but only pamphlets. These should be written by representative men of different denominations, who should be free to give their own message. The Movement was already making various books of an apologetic character known in the colleges. The suggested pamphlets were partly to supplement what was available, but " also that students may realize that the Movement as a whole is in sympathy with their needs."

The difficulty about evangelistic work had arisen largely because the Student Movement had recently appointed Robert Wilder as evangelistic secretary.[1] There was no desire to hinder the evangelistic work of the Christian Unions or to prevent the travelling secretaries from forwarding it by every means in their power. The committee readily decided to say : " We are unanimous in holding that it is an elementary duty that every Christian man should seek to make Christians of those of his fellow students who may not be committed to the Christian position, and also that students in a college should join together for this purpose." Where the difficulty lay was in the fear that the Movement might build up a staff of its own evangelists who might come to deliver something very like a Student Movement gospel. It was agreed that this must be avoided, but it was added that " this does not preclude the propriety of any Student Movement secretary from time to time bearing his own witness to Christ, he being a member of a Christian body."

The position of Oriental students who were non-Christian came in for some consideration, as did the work of the Y.M.C.A. in the Far East. This organization was prominently in the thought of the Movement at this time, partly because a number of the Movements in the Federation were Student Departments of the Y.M.C.A., and partly because the influence of Mr Mott was being used to secure Student Movement

[1] He became Evangelistic Secretary in September 1908.

leaders for service in the student work of the Y.M.C.A. in the East.

As regards Oriental students the report said that " the Churches are not doing anything for Oriental students in this country, and it seems to us that the Student Movement is only fulfilling its plain duty in seeking to create links between these students and the best life of the Churches."

As regards the Y.M.C.A. it was pointed out that one of its functions in the East was to be a missionary society and that, as such, preferential treatment should not be given to it by the Student Movement, but that it should get " the same facilities that are given to the missionary societies to recruit agents from the colleges."

The committee decided that members of the committees of the Student Movement should be members of some Christian denomination. Long discussions ranged round the question whether denominational societies, especially at Oxford and Cambridge, should be affiliated to the Movement. Leslie Johnston was a very strong advocate of this course. He thought that at Oxford it would strengthen the Christian forces if the various Anglican and Free Church societies were all affiliated to the Movement and some kind of co-operating committee representing each of them created. He did not, however, carry the committee with him. It thought that from the experience it had of denominational societies the result would be that in a changing student constituency it would be almost impossible to bring them into a co-operating relationship with one another. They would tend to continue to develop their own activities separately, and the contact of men of different Churches which the Student Movement achieved would largely come to an end. The committee recognized " that one of the most important things in its history has been that men of all denominations have been brought into its fellowship, and that the strength and richness of its life has been to a large extent dependent upon this fact."

The committee was also convinced that a strong interdenominational movement was more likely to reach men not at present committed to the Christian position than any denominational society or federation of denominational societies, adding that : " Experience goes to show that existing denominational societies partake more of the nature of spiritual clubs for members of particular denominations than anything else." It was decided, however, that while the affiliation of denominational societies was not favoured, the Student Movement " should recognize the propriety of such denominational societies," whose chief work should be to form a link between members of a particular denomination and encourage them to study and understand the ecclesiastical position of their own denomination, but that they ought to encourage their members to join the Movement " for the purpose of giving a united witness for Christ to their fellow students, and for purposes of Bible, missionary and social study and united intercession."

The relation of the Movement to the service of Holy Communion did not, at this stage, call for special discussion. The practice of giving facilities at Student Movement conferences for different Churches to arrange communion services for their own members, and for the Free Churches to hold a united communion service, was a well-established practice.

All this took place while the World Missionary Conference, Edinburgh, 1910, was being prepared. The Movement was very closely related to this conference. This is not the place to describe that gathering ; that has been done by Temple Gairdner,[1] but a good deal of the inner history of the planning of the conference is very closely related to the Movement, and that should be told.

In 1900, what was entitled an " Ecumenical Missionary Conference " was held in New York. It was a great demonstration, with no corporate preparation behind

[1] *Edinburgh*, 1910, by W. H. T. Gairdner.

it so far as the subject-matter of the conference was concerned. It appointed a small continuation committee, the object of which was to keep alive the idea of holding another such conference ten years later. As it had decided the next conference should meet in Edinburgh, the committee it appointed was largely Scottish in composition. The outstanding figure on it was Dr George Robson, well known for his work as translator of Dr Warneck's *History of Missions* and as editor of *The Record of the United Free Church of Scotland.*

The group in Scotland met in 1906, and considered holding another world conference. Later Dr Robson discussed the situation with J. H. Oldham, who was both secretary of the Mission Study Council of the United Free Church of Scotland and study secretary of the Student Christian Movement. They agreed that there was little value in bringing missionary leaders together from all over the world, at great expense of time and money, to make speeches on the missionary enterprise, but that there were many problems which needed careful study, and a conference which was the climax of a period of study would be of great service to Christian missions. They devised a scheme for a series of study commissions to be composed of about two dozen persons each—men and women outstanding in the life of the Church at home, in education and in missionary work. This plan they described in a letter to Mr J. R. Mott, the General Secretary of the World's Student Christian Federation, who was emphatic in his approval, and on whose advice the scheme was adopted by the Edinburgh committee.

The question then arose as to how the committee was to be made representative. The Presbyterian and Free Church societies, also the Church Missionary Society, had men on it, but if the conference was to be a representative one, the Church of England must be represented, not only by the Church Missionary Society, but also by the Society for the Propagation of the Gospel, and outstanding men not actively associated with any of the missionary societies must be secured for the preparatory work. At this stage Dr Robson wrote to me on behalf of the committee, explaining the plan, saying that the representative of the C.M.S. on the committee, the late Rev. H. E. Fox, was so identified with the Evangelical party and its organizations in the Church of England that they did not think that an effective approach to other Church of England groups could be made through him. " Accordingly we want you to join the committee which has to plan the conference, and we want you to bring the Church of England with you."

I remember quite well feeling that Dr Robson could have very little knowledge of the Church of England if he thought that I, who was working for an inter-denominationl society and had no status in the Church of England further than permission to officiate in the Bishop of London's diocese, could bring in the Church of England. I wrote saying that I was interested in the conference and would like to join the committee, but that I was afraid I had extremely little influence in the Church of England. As it turned out, however, the Student Christian Movement had a great deal more influence by this time than I realized. For ten years its interdenominational position had been increasingly understood. It was steadily winning friends, and events were to show that much could be done by its general secretary. The story cannot be told in full. Perhaps some day Dr Oldham will write the history of the Movement which began with the Edinburgh Conference of 1910. I must confine myself here to the connection of the Student Movement with it.

When the British Executive Committee had adopted the plan of preparatory commissions it appointed, in conjunction with committees in America and on the Continent, an international committee of eighteen people. This body met at Wycliffe Hall, Oxford, for four days, planned eight commissions and chose between 150 and 200 men and women as members of them. At one stage while we were at Oxford the members of different Churches and societies were told to meet separately and make a panel of names from their Church from which the committee might select names for each commission. I found myself alone with Prebendary Fox as a sub-committee charged with the responsibility of suggesting a panel of names of members of the Church of England from which people might be selected for the eight commissions. It was a difficult experience. Prebendary Fox was a keen party man, with staunch Evangelical principles, and he drew up a list drawn exclusively from members of his own party. On the other hand I had prepared a list which included men of all sections of the Church; on it were the Bishop of Birmingham (Dr Gore), the Bishop of Southwark (Dr E. S. Talbot), Father Kelly, Director of the House of the Sacred Mission, Kelham, Father Frere, Superior of the Community of the Resurrection, Professor Michael Sadler, Mrs Creighton and the Dean of Westminster (Dr Armitage Robinson). Prebendary Fox did not approve, and we contended in one of the bedrooms in Wycliffe Hall for a long time on the subject, but I held to my point that we must try and make the commissions representative of the Church of England and not of any one party in it. In the end he said, " Have your way," but he would not propose the names, and he made me spokesman when we appeared before the International Committee with our suggestions. This committee was fully in favour of the more representative names, and looking back from this distance it is clear that representative people were chosen.

After the Oxford conference came the difficult task of securing the co-operation of the men we had chosen for the work of the commissions. The Bishops of Southwark and Birmingham, Father Frere, the Dean of Westminster and some others had not hitherto co-operated with Free Churchmen on missionary or similar matters. The committee left the approach to them to

Mr Oldham, who had by this time been released by the Student Christian Movement to become secretary of the conference. He came to me saying that as he was a Scotsman and a Presbyterian he must have help in approaching men in the Church of England. We decided that if we could get two or three key men, the others would probably follow their example and we should get the lot. We conned the matter over and decided to begin with Dr Armitage Robinson, who was then Dean of Westminster. He had been at the summer conference of the S.C.M., where his speaking had aroused the deepest interest among the students, and he had been warm in his appreciation of the conference. I agreed to see him, and on writing for an interview was bidden to tea at the Deanery.

The Dean was in one of his whimsical and charming moods. He opened the conversation by saying, " I have been discussing the revision of the Prayer Book all day and am in a very bad temper." I explained to him about the conference and the Commissions. He agreed readily to become a member of the Commission on " Co-operation and the Promotion of Unity." I remember a sense of keen delight at feeling the first ditch was safely crossed and a key man secured. As the conversation went on, however, it became clear that I had not been sufficiently explicit in my explanation as to the body that was holding the conference, and that the Dean thought it was a Student Movement conference. It became necessary, therefore, to explain this to him:

But, Mr Dean, it is not a Student Movement Conference. Then whose conference is it ? said the Dean sharply.

The Missionary Societies are co-operating in its organization.

Oh, I don't want to have anything to do with that sort of conference. I don't want to work for a conference of the Missionary Societies. I thought you wanted me to do something for the Student Movement. I am not going to have anything to do with it.

I was dismayed, but I was determined to get my man, and after arguing with the Dean for a long time that a really good thing was being planned, he at last agreed that he would serve and I departed in triumph.

The next man we determined to approach was Dr Talbot, the Bishop of Southwark, and Oldham joined in a visit to him.   He was chosen because his son, Neville, was a member of the Student Movement at Oxford and had, we knew, interested him in it. Neither of us knew him personally, and we were both a little afraid that he might be a difficult man to secure, but we felt we had a link with him because of Neville. I remember a sense of dismay as he stumped into the room followed by Father Frere, who, unknown to us, was staying with him.   It was bad enough to have to face the Bishop, quite dreadful to have to meet the combination of him and the Superior of the Community of the Resurrection !

Father Frere was very non-committal, but the Bishop was very friendly, asked a number of questions, referred very sympathetically to the interdenominational position of the S.C.M., which was to be the basis of the conference, and said that he would think very carefully over our invitation.   In the end both he and Father Frere accepted membership of Commissions.

A. G. Fraser, at home on furlough, was pressed into the service to approach Dr Gore, who was then Bishop of Birmingham, and paved the way for Oldham, who secured him.   Shortly after this a group of us visited the Archbishop of Canterbury, to ask that if the conference plan worked out successfully he would give public expression to his approval of it, a request cordially granted.

On all these occasions there were numerous references to the Student Movement and its interdenominational platform ; and it was repeated again and again that the interdenominational principle which respected the differences of men who were members of different Christian bodies would be the position of the conference.   The

Bishop of Southwark and a number of others made no secret of it that it was the Student Movement which had converted them to a belief in the interdenominational position. At a luncheon in Dr Alexander Whyte's house in Edinburgh during the conference, when a group of Scottish divines were invited to meet him and several other Anglicans, he said across the luncheon table, " We "—meaning by this the group in the Church of which he was a distinguished representative—" would not have been here in this conference had it not been for the Student Christian Movement."

A great deal of work for the conference was done from the S.C.M. office in London in the early stages. I was secretary of the commission on " The Training of Missionaries," as well as being a member of the British Executive Committee. The Student Movement had asked for the commission on the Training of Missionaries. It was very difficult to secure places at the conference, and in the end it was decided that the Student Movement should be given the privilege of providing all the stewards and thus enable a number of students to hear the debates in the Assembly Hall. The Movement was also given fifty seats to be occupied by students in the Synod Hall, where additional meetings were held.

The official representation of the Student Volunteer Missionary Union was, of course, a small one. Those chosen to fill the two places allotted were R. P. Wilder and myself. Miss Una Saunders and Miss Rouse were appointed as " special delegates " by the British Executive Committee. The Student Movement influence in the conference was considerable. It gave to the conference its chairman, Mr John R. Mott, its secretary, Mr J. H. Oldham, and its historian, the Rev. W. H. Temple Gairdner. Old Student Movement members took a considerable share in the debates of the conference, and the reports of the Commissions are full of quotations from memoranda supplied by them. Years after the Conference Dr Temple wrote that " Members of the Movement ought to know that without their movement there never could have been held the Edinburgh Conference, which was the greatest event in the life of the Church for a generation." [1]

Familiar faces met one at every door since the Movement provided the stewards. These included William Temple, N. S. Talbot, H. G. Wood, J. R. S. Taylor, William Paton, K. E. Kirk, E. Murray Page, W. P. Young and William Manson. Leslie Johnston, Mac Lawson, Howard Houlder and Kingsley Williams might be observed daily at the big iron gates demanding to see delegates' tickets. R. L. Pelly and J. Mcleod Campbell haunted the doors to the gallery behind the speaker's chair; Neville Talbot loomed up in the gallery; Oliver Thomas sat daily writing letters to his Welsh S.C.M. constituency and stewarding at the speakers' entrance; W. H. Parr spent his time turning bishops and peers of the realm off benches in front which he was trying to reserve for members of the Commission whose report was being presented.

It is a matter of ancient history that the conference was an immense success. It owed its success to J. H. Oldham more than to any other one person. He had originally only been lent by the Student Movement to the conference committee, and up to the end of the conference we hoped that he would return to his place on the staff of the Movement as missionary study secretary. The conference, however, proved so important and he was so obviously at the heart of it, that when a continuation committee was appointed, one of its first acts was to approach the Student Movement and ask it to agree that Oldham be permanently released from his Student Movement secretaryship to become the first secretary of the Continuation Committee of the Edinburgh Missionary Conference, 1910. Out of this continuation committee has grown the British Conference of Missionary Societies centred in Edinburgh House, the *International Review of Missions*, and the International Missionary Council.

[1] *The Student Movement*, vol. xvii. p. 96.

Immediately after the conference Mott wrote *The Decisive Hour of Christian Missions* for use as a missionary study text-book.   We had 328 missionary study circles, with 2185 men and women in them—over 300 of the circles in the colleges used this book during the winter following the Edinburgh Conference.

CHAPTER XXII

THE FEDERATION AT CONSTANTINOPLE AND WIDER UNITY

NOW that we had firmly established interdenominational practice in the Student Movement, had threshed out the principles on which this practice was based and seen it not only working satisfactorily in the Movement but influencing the life of the Churches, we turned our attention to the World's Student Christian Federation and its policy in relation to the Churches. The Federation announced its intention to have a meeting of its General Committee followed by a conference at Constantinople in the spring of 1911.

We were ready to make our contribution. The General Committee minuted, in April 1910: "The interdenominational position of the Movement having been considered and a new memorandum drafted, it was decided that at the next meeting of the Federation the British Movement should make its interdenominational position clear. It was thought that this would help the Federation."

The year in which the Federation met at Constantinople was a great year for it. It was already a strong international body, being a federation of national Student Christian Movements in North America; Great Britain and Ireland; Belgium, the Netherlands and Switzerland; France and Italy; Germany; Norway, Sweden, Denmark and Finland; Australia and New Zealand; India and Ceylon; China and Korea; Japan; and a number of Christian Unions in different countries without national movements, grouped together for admission to the Federation. The grouping given represents the way in which Movements were grouped together for admission to the Federation.   This was done to keep down the size of the General Committee, each group having one or two people to represent it on the committee.

The aims of the Federation at this time as stated in its Constitution were:

> To unite Student Christian Movements or organizations throughout the world and promote mutual relations among them; to collect information regarding the religious condition of the students of all lands; and to promote the following lines of activity, namely, to lead students to become disciples of Jesus Christ as only Saviour and as God, to deepen the spiritual life of students and to enlist students in the work of extending the Kingdom of Christ throughout the whole world.

The total number of individual Unions or associations in the federated national movements was 2196, with a membership of 148,500 students and professors.

John R. Mott and Ruth Rouse were at the zenith of their pioneering activities.   We learnt to know something of what students in Serbia, Bulgaria, Roumania and Greece were thinking.   The Russian Student Christian Movement was growing steadily under the leadership of Baron Nicolay.   Switzerland was the most cosmopolitan student field in the world and the Movement seemed well established in it.   Student leaders in France were tackling vigorously the free-thought movement in that country and keenly interested in the conflict between Church and State, while a gallant fight was being put up by a rather struggling Movement in Italy.

The Movements of Scandinavia, Germany and Holland invariably sent strong delegations to our own conferences.   We had a close link with South Africa through Oswin Bull, a Cambridge man, whom we had sent to South Africa as a Student Movement Secretary.

Australia seemed less far off as Henry K. Archdall,[1]

[1] Chairman of the Swanwick Summer Conference, 1912.   Now headmaster of King's College, Auckland, New Zealand.

B. B. Chapman and Miss Holden, three of its leaders, had come to study in England, and the first two of these were taking an active part in our Movement. In addition to this William Temple had recently returned from a visit to the Australian Student Movement. We had never forgotten the link between the Quadrennial at Liverpool, 1896, and our Movement, and it was extraordinarily encouraging to hear from Temple that of all the marvels in Australia " the greatest marvel of all is the Australian Student Christian Movement."

He told us how the three universities were founded at a time when the keenest intellects thought that the day of Christianity was over and that, at first, the tone of the universities was hostile rather than neutral in relation to Christianity ; that at one of the universities Mott was not admitted to the university to speak, but, he said, all was changed.

> In all the centres one heard of the change in the whole life and outlook of the university that has come since the work of the Christian Union began. The achievement of the Christian Union, in spite of very serious obstacles, is very great. Its membership is good; but its influence on the general university life is even greater than the number of its members would lead one to expect. Everywhere there is an intense eagerness to hear about the Christian belief, to learn what it really is, and to find its relation to contemporary problems, both practical and theoretical. And senior members of the universities are ready to state with confidence that this, and also a marked change in the whole tone of university life, is due to the work of the Christian Union.[1]

The continual coming and going of Student Volunteers at work in Africa, China, Japan and India kept Africa and the Far East before us, while America, the largest Student Christian Movement in the world, poured news and literature upon us. Almost the only country about which we heard little was South America,

[1] *The Student Movement*; art. : " Impressions of Australia," Rev. Wm. Temple, vol. xiii. p. 54.

and even from there cheering little bits of news came from time to time.

Mott made a prolonged tour in preparation for the Federation meeting.   Early in the year he was in Egypt, holding meetings for students in the Abbas Theatre in Cairo ; 2000 students were present at each meeting, and the third day a cordon of police was necessary to restrain the mass of students who desired to press into the theatre three hours before the advertised time.

A few days later he was at Beirut, conducting a six-days' mission among the students, with an average attendance of 650.   A brief visit to Alexandria drew 1500 students to hear him at the Alhambra Theatre, while the Bishop of the Greek Orthodox Church at Smyrna sent out runners and brought together a meeting of 500 of the most influential Greeks in the district. He passed from there to Greece, and started a branch of the Movement in the University of Athens.

Miss Rouse had also been visiting in Europe preparing the way for the Federation meeting and seeking suitable delegates in Belgrade, Bucharest, Sofia and Constantinople itself.

When we arrived at Constantinople the whole place was stirred.   It was a beautiful city, whether one wandered through the narrow lanes of Stamboul, sailed out on the Bosphorus to look back at its hills covered with irregularly beautiful buildings, or visited the glorious St Sophia, the many mosques, the museum and the ancient hippodrome with its relics of Constantine the Great.   Standing on the Galata bridge one could watch men of almost every nation crossing—all men, hardly any women—and see the old and new in juxtaposition as the crowds parted for a motor-car, followed by a buffalo team and then perchance a camel.

Constantinople had recently passed through a revolution.   There were beginnings of liberty in the Turkish Empire.   Overturned sentry-boxes showed the end of the reign of espionage, newspapers were freely sold, a

CONFERENCE OF THE WORLD'S STUDENT CHRISTIAN FEDERATION, CONSTANTINOPLE, 1911

Attended by representatives of some thirty denominations, including the Armenian, Bulgarian, Coptic
Greek Orthodox, Maronite, Roman Catholic and Syrian Churches

few women appeared in the streets unveiled, political discussions were to be heard everywhere.

There was no racial centre quite like Constantinople. In Pera, the European quarter, every European language was to be heard. In the streets of Stamboul every Asiatic race and type might be seen—Persians, Hindus, Arabs, men from Turkestan, Bokhara and Kashgar, Georgians, Caucasians and Mongols of every kind. The African was not absent, while Turks, Greeks, Roumanians and Bulgarians abounded. Constantinople was the ecclesiastical centre of both the Mohammedan and Orthodox Church world. It was the city of the Sultan, and also, of the Ecumenical Patriarch of the Greek Orthodox Church, the Patriarch of the Armenian Church and the Exarch of the Orthodox Church of Bulgaria.

Two hundred and forty delegates from nearly thirty-three countries took part in the Federation Conference. The outstanding speakers were Professor Nathan Söderblom,[1] Professor D. S. Cairns and Mr Michael Sadler,[2] in a gathering where the speaking was on a high level. A new element at a conference of the Federation was the presence of a large group of members of the Orthodox Church. They came from the Orthodox Churches of Greece, Turkey, Asia Minor, Bulgaria, Servia, Roumania and Russia. There were also members of the Gregorian, Nestorian, Coptic and Maronite Churches and from the Jacobite Syrian Church of Travancore. These two groups were deeply interested, for such a conference was a novel experience to nearly all of them.

We did not meet in Constantinople itself, but at Robert College, a short sail down the Bosphorus. The delegates lived in Constantinople, and in one or two villages near the college, and the leaders were in the college itself.

The reason we met in Constantinople was to demonstrate to the student population of South-Eastern Europe,

[1] Afterwards Archbishop of Uppsala.
[2] Afterwards Sir Michael Sadler.

where scepticism was rampant, that a great body of students in all lands believed in God and in the Christian view of the world. Public meetings were held in Constantinople in connection with the conference which were attended by 10,000 people. We came partly to demonstrate and we were successful.

John Mott opened the conference with a speech which left no doubt regarding our purpose. "We meet," he said, " to make attractive, compelling, visible, the fact of the World's Student Christian Federation. We cannot make this great ideal real in any way save by bringing delegates together from all the world."

He claimed that from the ecclesiastical point of view the conference was the most widely representative which had assembled since the Ecumenical Councils of the early Church. He was right, and thus the Student Movement paved the way for the Christian Church, for the Church reaped the fruit of the seed sown at Constantinople when it met for the World Conference on Faith and Order at Lausanne sixteen years later.

But if the conference was interesting and useful, real importance centred in the meeting of the General Committee of the Federation which was held on the Island of Prinkipo in the Sea of Marmora from April 20th to 24th, 1911, just before the full conference. It was there we had an opportunity of supporting Mott and Baron Nicolay of Russia in an effort to make the Federation representative of Catholics, Orthodox and Protestants. The opportunity arose over the question of the conditions under which national Student Movements admitted members. Some Movements only admitted to membership students who were members of Evangelical Churches ; in America, for example, a Roman Catholic or a member of the Russian Orthodox Church was excluded from full membership. Some were asking for a resolution which would bring pressure on all Movements in the Federation to open their membership to members of all Christian Churches. We were helped by one of the German delegates who said, " From history and practice it is clear that we are a Protestant Movement." This gave us an opportunity to state our deep-seated opposition to this point of view. Baron Nicolay said that if the Federation called itself Protestant it "would deal a death-blow to the Movement in Russia," and I said it would lose us much hardly won ground in England.

The Federation was in fact a Protestant movement in its origin, but it never shut the door to non-Protestants. Douglas Thornton was probably the first British leader consciously to work and pray for the day when members of Protestant, Catholic and Orthodox Churches would all share in its fellowship. John Mott's visit to Russia at the end of the last century and his close contact with the interdenominational developments in the Movement in Great Britain, which brought him into personal relationship with some of the finest types of Anglican Catholics, had stirred in him the desire for a wider fellowship than a Protestant student federation. The Federation is still predominantly Protestant as regards numbers, but the Orthodox Church influence is a strong one in it, while there are a number of Roman Catholic members in several of the Movements affiliated to the Federation. The battle for this comprehensiveness was won at Prinkipo, when after days of debate and explanation to one another of the vital importance of the issue, we passed unanimously the resolution :

> The General Committee puts on record its opinion that it is desirable that no student, to whatever branch of the Christian Church he may belong, should be excluded from full membership in any national movements within the Federation if he is prepared to accept the basis of the Federation or whatever equivalent test is approved by the Federation.[1]
>
> The committee requests such National Movements as may be affected by this resolution to consider the possibility of making their basis conform to this principle.

[1] Minutes of the W.S.C.F. General Committee held in Prinkipo and Bebek, Constantinople, April 20th to 27th, 1911.

This resolution has been quoted more frequently at W.S.C.F. committee meetings than any other it has passed. Its importance has always been recognized, and having passed it the Federation set itself to draw into its ranks members of all the confessions of Christendom.

The Student Christian Movement of Great Britain and Ireland was represented on the Federation General Committee at Prinkipo by William Paton, Winifred Sedgwick and myself. At the conference at Robert College we were joined by Rena Carswell, Zoë Fairfield, MacEwan Lawson, W. W. Seton, Edward S. Woods, Professor Michael Sadler and Professor D. S. Cairns.

While we were at Constantinople Walter Seton invited me to join him in a visit to the Ecumenical Patriarch, Joachim III, to pay our respects to him as English Churchmen visiting Constantinople. It was quite an adventure. Seton had asked a Greek student at the conference to come and act as interpreter. We came up from Robert College on a Bosphorus steamer and had an early lunch in Constantinople in a café overhanging the Golden Horn and at the end of the longest and darkest passage I've ever traversed. I had been hearing about long passages and slides at the end down which the Sultan hurried his enemies in sacks which slid weighted into the Bosphorus. It was a creepy place that restaurant where we lunched.

After lunch we clambered down to the shore below, and after much gesticulation and with the aid of the young Greek we got into a tiny rowing boat. Seton and I sat in the stern, the Greek at our feet and a villainous looking Kurd plied the oars. We were a strange crew. It was a blazing hot day, and I was in grey flannels, but Seton was dressed for the occasion in one of the tallest and narrowest chimney-pot hats I have ever seen, which he had brought all the way from London for the occasion.

We landed in about half an hour on the beach at Phanar and were quickly shown into the presence of the Patriarch, who knew we were coming. He was a tall, handsome, old man of very impressive appearance. He asked all about the Federation Conference and then said to us : " Many people come to me to talk about reunion, but I do not find the discussion of this topic very profitable, but you come to ask our young men to join your young men in working for the extension of Christ's Kingdom, and that I think is very good." Seton was delighted with the visit and kissed his hand like an adept. It was my first visit to a distinguished Greek Church ecclesiastic. I, too, have learned how to kiss an ecclesiastical hand as the years have gone by.

Joachim III had been very kind to Miss Rouse when she was preparing the conference, and had told her to see the Bishop of Stravopolis, who lived in Pera, as he was a good English scholar. Miss Rouse relates how she went to see him and attempted to explain the Federation with no result until she produced a pamphlet descriptive of the Movement she had written for us, and known as " The Green Rouse." As soon as he saw it he said, " Oh ! now I know what you are talking about; I've been at Conishead."

The Bishop, who was a young man, had a few years before been sent to St Andrews to study under the care of the late Professor Kay. The Professor had been a missionary to the Jews under the Church of Scotland in Constantinople, and had made friends in the Greek Church, so when the authorities wanted to send one of their students—Christopher Kneetes—abroad, they sent him to St Andrews University, where Dr Kay had become a professor.

Dr Kay sent Kneetes on to Oxford University, and at the same time asked me to draw him into the S.C.M. and get him to a summer conference. This I did, and after the Conishead Conference of 1906 Kneetes wrote me a long and grateful letter saying that the conference had been a wonderful spiritual experience for him. Shortly afterwards he returned home, was soon consecrated a Bishop, and was an immense help at the time of the Federation Conference at Constantinople. He and a row of long-haired and long-bearded ecclesiastics sat in the front at all the meetings. The contacts then made have been followed up since in various ways. As for Christopher Kneetes, the last I heard of him was that he had become an Archbishop.

After the conference at Constantinople was over deputations visited a number of student centres in Hungary, Roumania, Servia, Bulgaria, Greece, Asia Minor and Egypt. Mott was invited to visit the seminary on the Island of Halki where the priests of the Greek Orthodox Church are trained. The students there pressed two questions upon him : " How can we learn to preach so as to influence men's lives spiritually ? " and, " How can we develop our own spiritual lives ? "

The strongest deputations were sent to the Universities of South-Eastern Europe, especially Bulgaria, Roumania and Serbia. In these countries the majority of students were members of the Orthodox Church, though many of them adhered more for political than religious reasons. In Bulgaria they regarded the Church as their bulwark against the Turk. The Church was unready to help students. It had not related its message to the modern intellectual world. The majority of its priests received very little education, while the students were to be found in institutions organized on a secular foundation, after the pattern of the universities of Western Europe. We heard a great deal about the divorce between learning and religion in South-Eastern Europe. And the remark of the Serbian student who said that in his university students no more believed that Christianity was true than they believed that the world was flat, was constantly quoted as typical of the attitude of the student class. It was among students with an outlook of this kind that the Constantinople conference helped to plant the Federation. It is still a small plant, but it is alive.

After the Constantinople Conference we came home to grapple with the question of truth, realizing that it was not only for the sake of our Movement, but for that of the Federation, with its vast problem of unbelief among students in Central and South-Eastern Europe, that it needed to be tackled.

CHAPTER XXIII

THE PROBLEM OF TRUTH

THE phrase " the search for truth " was perhaps the one most frequently used among the leaders of the Movement at this time. It is impossible to give any adequate account of the immense change which was taking place in the thought of the whole student class. It filled some people with hope and others with despair. To some it seemed that a study of the nature of the change which was taking place, and the causes for it, would be of great value. I must stick closely to the situation as we saw it from the angle of the Student Movement. During the first decade of the Movement's existence there was no demand for apologetics. A small group of students, most of them coming from Christian homes where they had received a careful religious training, composed the Christian Unions. They won a small number of their friends from the great body of students. The majority of students were apparently unconcerned about their personal religious position. Probably most of them went to church because that was the custom in the homes from which they came. Few of them ever said anything to suggest that they had any doubts about the truth of Christianity. Many of them in their more serious moments would imply, and some of them would even go so far as to say, that they expected to yield to the demands of Christ when they got older, but they regarded personal religion as something rather repressive and they wanted to have a good time.

Then there was a very small group of thoughtful people in the colleges who were not organized in any way, who believed that modern science had made the

Christian view of the world untenable. Most of these, as I met them, were sad about it, but felt it was a matter of truth and that the new materialistic view of the universe must be accepted. Very occasionally one came across men who were militant on behalf of materialism, feeling that this was in the interest of truth. I can recollect very few such men among undergraduates. Most people whom I can now recall as having talked with about religion and science in those days were members of staff, chiefly junior demonstrators in science laboratories.

As we entered the second decade of the Movement's life things began to change very rapidly and the doubts and difficulties confined to the few began to spread to the many. More and more students studied science. None of them were prepared intellectually for this study. Many of them had never heard the word evolution mentioned until they came to college, and discovered with a shock that there were some among their teachers who believed that evolution, which was made so much of by teachers of science at this period, cut at the roots of Christianity.

The Church was unready to meet the new situation. Its ministry was recruited from men trained in a variety of subjects, arts, philosophy, history, classics, with a longer or shorter theological course according to their denomination, but seldom in science.

Such apologetic literature as was available was of little or no use to the science student; a great deal of it would be apt to increase rather than diminish his difficulties. Religious writers dealing with the question of evolution were apt to expend their energy on suggesting that there were gaps in the sequence of evolution, and when they had found, as they had thought, a gap, triumphantly explain that this was where God came in. As the gaps were constantly being filled up by the work of scientific research, God was being steadily squeezed out. An apologetic that took cognizance of the development of modern science was obviously badly needed, and there were signs that psychology would need before long to be thought about, although it was in a very embryonic state.

Senior friends were often unhelpful in relation to all this. There were, of course, a few scholars amongst them who were thinking hard about the new problems being raised, but others, who valued the Student Movement for its religious influence on students and because it was recruiting men and women for missionary service, were distressed by the questions students raised, and when these questions were taken notice of in an occasional article in *The Student Movement* or in an address at a summer conference, the average senior friend deplored our dealing with such questions and wanted us to stick to an exclusively spiritual message.

It was really the Student Movement's attempt to present the fundamentals of Christianity in this new intellectual setting that had caused the breach already referred to between it and the Cambridge Intercollegiate Christian Union.

There were great discussions on the committee about this whole matter. Some of the members were distressed at the amount of turmoil, but not so others, who felt that there were reasons for great encouragement, that the doubts and difficulties of students meant that they were thinking about the Faith, and that the whole situation was an enormous improvement upon a previous decade, when among students generally there seemed to be a lack of interest in religion.

Howard Houlder, who, as travelling secretary, had more insight than some into what was going on, wrote :

Not only are a freer-minded lot entering the Christian Unions than before, but in the minds of the students at large earnest religion and earnest thinking are tending to mingle their streams, progressively more and more. The result is a type of religion acutely conscious of all the precariousnesses of the Christian faith, and deferential to a point of timidity of upholding Christianity in the open. However, the process of thinking is bound to bring men to the truth, and there are signs that students are now coming through their throes to a certain grasp of their faith which will be stronger than ever. This means that looking below the surface into the future we have great cause to be thankful. There is slowly appearing a body of potential evangelizers in the colleges who are like previous generations of students in their devotion to Christ, but *unlike* previous generations (broadly speaking) of Christian students in their grasp of what Christianity means in relation to the real needs as against the imaginary needs of the sons of men to-day.

He said that in Oxford, Cambridge, Scotland, Manchester, and among the leaders of the Welsh and Irish Christian Unions were people in whom were to be seen the beginnings of a new and living evangelism.

Much thought still centred in the question of how to get students to study the Bible, and Houlder considered that the way to begin the assault on people was by putting the Bible forward as an interesting and valuable book, subsequently aiming at bringing men to understand its spiritual power. In childhood students had heard the study of the Bible commended on grounds of religious duty. " If the present generation of religiously ill brought up students are to be persuaded to study the Bible, they have to be approached by an appeal that means something to them." He wrote a successful study book himself on Christian discipleship and social questions [1] which was studied all over the field and helped many students.

The women students were the first among undergraduates to be concerned with intellectual questions. As questions arose among the women they were passed on by them to the men in the co-educational universities. The quotations about apologetics which are made in the annual reports of the General Committee at this period are almost all quotations taken from women's Christian Union reports. It was in the women's colleges that the first study circles on apologetic subjects were started,

[1] *Christian Discipleship and Social Life*, H. F. Houlder.

and women students asked for the first course of
apologetic lectures given under the auspices of the
Movement.

It was when it was realized, however, that doubts and
difficulties were becoming urgent among theological
students that Spencer suggested that the Movement
should arrange a conference on the " Problem of Truth."
The curriculum of most of the theological colleges was
constructed on traditional lines and underwent very
little change from year to year ; one result of this was
that many of the more alert minds among the theological
students were deeply concerned at finding that there
seemed to be little connection between the questions
laymen were asking and the kind of training they were
receiving in college.   And the secretaries of the Student
Movement were even more concerned to find how out
of touch was both the study and the thinking of the
majority of the theological students with what was going
on in other student circles.   Probably no men in the
country had a better chance of comparing tendencies of
thought in the universities among the abler students and
junior dons with thought in the theological colleges.
The contrast was painful and caused growing concern to
the leaders of the Student Movement.   Spencer's suggestion, therefore, of a conference which would examine
the doubts and difficulties of thoughtful men in the light
of the work being done in theological colleges, was
readily agreed to and steps taken to call it together.

It is possible to give an account of the conference as
Mr B. H. Streeter wrote a pamphlet [1] of some twenty
thousand words descriptive of it.   This was printed for
private circulation and issued to Student Movement
secretaries.

The first step in the preparation of the conference
was to send a paper containing three questions to a
number of well-known clergy and ministers of various

[1] *Doubts and Difficulties* : a personal impression of the conclusions
of a conference of theological teachers and Student Christian
Movement leaders, Swanwick, July 4th to 7th, 1911.

denominations, to some members of the staff of theological colleges, to a few doctors and other professional
men, to one Labour M.P., and to a number of students
in theological and other colleges who were likely to have
a special knowledge of the difficulties and doubts of
their fellows.

These questions were as follows :

(a) What do you find to be the prevailing difficulties regarding the Christian faith, and the Christian interpretation of life, whether outspoken in explicit doubt
or implied in religious indifference ?

(b) To what vital questions affecting the truth of Christianity does it seem difficult to give an answer which
is convincing to the modern mind ?

(c) In what ways is the influence of the modern temper
upon Christian faith and character giving rise to an
impaired apprehension and experience of God ?

A mass of interesting letters and memoranda was
the result. Some of it was summarized and some of it
transcribed and supplied to a group of people invited
to discuss the questions which had been sent out on
the basis of the evidence collected. In addition to the
memoranda already referred to, four men who we had
hoped would have been present sent memoranda, Professor John Oman of Westminster College, Cambridge,
the Rev. A. E. J. Rawlinson of Keble College, Oxford,
the Rev. C. Kingsley Williams, Chaplain of the Leys
School, Cambridge and Mr H. G. Wood, who was on
the staff of the Woodbrooke Settlement.

Eighteen people came together at Swanwick from
July 4th to 7th, 1911, to confer. The Revs. Professor
D. S. Cairns, Dr Vernon Bartlet, J. R. Darbyshire, H. H.
Kelly, B. H. Streeter, N. S. Talbot, J. R. S. Taylor,
David Phillips and David Williams were members of
staff teaching theology. Leslie Mannering was a mem-
ber of the Cambridge Pastorate, and Leslie Johnston
was a don at New College, Oxford. Two students
were included to put the student point of view—H. K.
Archdall of Cambridge and George Ewen of Edinburgh.

The Student Movement sent three secretaries, Malcolm Spencer, Oliver Thomas and myself, and two members of the Theological College Department Committee, E. Murray Page and William Paton.

We recognized at the outset that many of the difficulties were as old as Christianity itself, but we were there to consider how we could best help students to realize the real nature of the difficulties, and to indicate such solutions as we had found most satisfactory both to our own minds and to others with whom we had to deal. A short preliminary discussion soon made it clear that the greater number of difficulties grouped themselves round a comparatively small number of vital issues, and that experience had shown that where light could be brought to the mind of an inquirer on these vital questions, minor difficulties and some which might at first be classed as major difficulties, tended to sink into a position of comparative unimportance.

The questions in which discussion centred were the following : the practical problem of how best to assist the individual doubter in his many varying types ; the fundamental question of the existence of a supernatural sphere at all, in view of the prevalence of naturalistic theories of the universe ; how effectively and clearly to present to the modern mind the three great Christian doctrines of God, Christ, and a future life ; the question of the value and place of authority in religion.

The discussion was marked by that spirit of frankness and courteous consideration for the point of view of other people which has always marked Student Movement discussions.

We had to try and distinguish people's real difficulties in the midst of a great deal of vagueness. " A point which was brought out in nearly every one of the answers received was, that in the majority of cases the doubts felt were of a general, vague and indefinite kind." The doubts of a specific kind had to do with the problem of evil, the difficulty caused by the fact that the lives of Christians seem in general no better than the lives of other people ; and the purely intellectual difficulties, the challenge to a belief in the existence of God by scientific materialism, and doctrinal difficulties connected especially with the Incarnation and the Atonement. Many said that vague difficulties " were materially increased by the fact that much of the traditional terminology of Christian doctrine was felt to be unintelligible and remote from modern life. Several witnesses also emphasized as a cause of doubt a prevailing ignorance as to what Christian beliefs really are —an ignorance partly due to inadequate and even misleading instruction in the Sunday-school or from the pulpit."

In addition difficulties connected with the Bible, the future life, prayer, free will, miracles, the Holy Spirit and the Trinity were spoken about in the memoranda sent to the committee.

When we came to consider the memoranda dealing with the problem of evil, there was a good deal about the difficulties caused in the minds of many by social injustice. One wrote :

Among working people the supreme difficulty is the injustice of our industrial system : they are subject to petty tyrannies ; they see others profiting both by their labours and their ideals ; they find life both hard and difficult, and cannot reconcile the evils of life with the goodness of God.

The writer of one memorandum said : " Wherever I go men question me about the person of Christ, His incarnation, His resurrection. Often in past years I have been asked such questions by non-Christians, but now Christians are perplexed about these things as they were not before." This statement points to where the great change had taken place. It was the perplexity of men both inside and outside the Student Movement who reckoned themselves definitely as Christians which gave much concern.

There were many more questions about the Incarnation,

and also a number about the Atonement in the evidence presented to the group.

The Bible was a source of a good deal of difficulty. " Men have got it into their heads that Christianity stands or falls with a theory of the verbal inspiration of the Bible. ' Who can believe in the falling of the walls of Jericho, etc. ? ' *ergo*, Christianity is false."

Most of the questions about prayer centred round whether it was any good to pray in face of the uniformity of nature.

The main causes of doubt the group had to deal with did not differ to any great extent from the causes to-day. " Has not Christianity failed after two thousand years in winning the world or in bringing human love and happiness ? " This has a very modern ring about it, as also has what was said to us about the ignorance of the nature of Christianity. " Most of the troubles seem to me to be due to sheer ignorance," and again, " Many of us (ministers) have taken too much for granted in dealing with our people. Most of them are painfully ignorant of even the main drift of Bible history, and have never done an hour's solid thinking on religious subjects. We have ourselves to create the interest which we try to satisfy."

Misunderstanding of theological terminology was referred to by many as a cause of difficulty. " The forms of the orthodox creed are not so much unconvincing, as unintelligible to many educated people to-day." Or, again, " Slipshod and unexplained use of the traditional terminology, which seems to remove religion far from the life of the street and the workshop," and " Men are turned away from the Church's hard and fast definitions."

There was much evidence of doubts and difficulties concerning religious experience. " The modern mind has no longer any meaning for such words as ' apprehension and experience of God.' Religious experience is explained away as an interesting psychological phenomenon."

The main body of the Report was, of course, concerned with estimating the importance of the different kinds of doubts and difficulties and making suggestions for dealing with them. The line of thought in the document is on the whole such as would be followed to-day, though where natural science is touched upon there is often the note of hesitation although no doubt the right line is suggested. Take, for example, the following: "Another important reflection is that the fact of the uniformity of Nature and the reign of law ought not to be regarded as something which is altogether disadvantageous or hostile to man." To-day we should hardly include the word "altogether" in this sentence.

If there is not space to summarize the kind of answers that the group offered to people's difficulties, answers which were spread abroad in the colleges by Student Movement secretaries as they travelled in the course of their work, a summary may be given of a few practical suggestions with which the document closes.

The first suggestion asks for better teaching in Sunday-schools "as to what is the real teaching of Christianity." It is urged that no small part of the difficulty, even among professing Christians, was due to ignorance, not because they had not been taught Christianity, but because of the kind of teaching they had received at school and Sunday-school which left them with many things to unlearn about the nature of inspiration, untenable conceptions of the manner and circumstances of a future life, rigid claims to a merely external authority and false antithesis between reason and faith. "To unteach is far harder than to teach."

The second suggestion was that theologians of different denominations should meet from time to time and seek to attain a deeper interpretation of truth, and as they found it they should state it in a way that avoided "the technical terminology of theologians."

The group declared that Christianity would "have small hope of recovering its hold upon the working

2 F

classes until the Church as a whole realizes and makes a conspicuous and intelligent effort to Christianize not merely the individual but the social life." It is not enough to sympathize with people on whom the evils of society press. " The life of Christianity consists in its taking up a positive and aggressive attitude to evil whenever and wherever detected."

A rather colourless paragraph says that lives of Christians ought to show tact, courtesy, consideration in the smallest trifles, while another urges that an increase in the individual and corporate devotional life in the Churches was a prime necessity.

The last suggestion is really an earnest plea that the Churches should face the fact that " the problem of how to meet the intellectual doubts of the age is the hardest and most vital of all the problems which the Churches have to face to-day." The group thought that the Churches did not realize the situation. " Not unnaturally," they write, " partly from shyness, partly from a feeling of courtesy, the layman hesitates to tell the minister that he half suspects that the whole system the minister stands for is an edifice built on sand." The group did not think the situation was likely to become better in the immediate future, because students in the theological colleges as a whole were not being sufficiently helped to realize the exact nature and importance of the problem, nor were they being trained to deal with it.

One result of the work of this group and the issue of *Doubts and Difficulties* to the secretaries of the Movement was to strengthen the apologetic and doctrinal parts of the programme at summer conferences. In the twenty years that have elapsed since this document was in circulation many of the more prominent theological thinkers of the day have given of their best in courses of addresses at summer conferences and the discussion of what they have said and the suggestions they have made, both of new ideas and of literature, have put hundreds of students on to new lines of thought.

The Movement had already appointed an apologetic sub-committee. This it strengthened as a result of the work of this group. Among those who took most part in the work of the sub-committee were: William Temple, Leslie Johnston, MacEwan S. Lawson, Zoë Fairfield and C. K. Williams. The sub-committee projected a good many books and pamphlets which were never written, the reason, I think, being that it is a very slow business getting fresh apologetic literature prepared. When new ground has to be broken up in the sphere of thought there has to be a preliminary process of getting people together to talk about the difficulties to be dealt with. Then they need plenty of time to read and think. It has often happened that half a dozen years have lapsed after the Student Movement set out to secure the preparation of a book on a particular subject before that book has been on sale. Some of the composite books which Canon Streeter has been responsible for editing in later years had their genesis in the group of which I write.

What the apologetic sub-committee did at this period was to study existing literature and suggest suitable books for use in study circles in the colleges. Among those which were recommended at this period and widely used in the universities were: *The Fact of Christ*, P. Carnegie Simpson; *Studies in the Character of Christ*, Charles H. Robinson; *The Faith and Modern Thought*, William Temple; *Christianity, its Nature and its Truth*, A. S. Peake; *Ecce Homo*, Sir John Seeley; *In Relief of Doubt*, R. E. Welsh; *The Incarnation of the Son of God*, Charles Gore; *Thoughts on Religion*, Romanes; and *Christus Futurus*.

This last book was published anonymously at first, but later it became known that the author was Miss Lily Dougall, who published more than one book with the Student Movement and became our friend and benefactor in many ways. She was a woman of learning, with an original and sympathetic mind. She found herself thoroughly at home in the atmosphere of Student

Movement conferences and might invariably be seen
with a group of students round her, discussing all kinds
of theological questions. A memory cherished by
Student Movement secretaries in office at the time was
a secretaries' meeting lasting for several days, held at
her beautiful house at Cumnor.

CHAPTER XXIV

THE MOVEMENT HOLDS TWO SUMMER AND A QUADRENNIAL CONFERENCE, AND FOUNDS SWANWICK

IMMEDIATELY after the Edinburgh Conference we had plunged into our first experience of two general conferences in the summer in the place of the single conference which had taken place annually since 1893. There was also the officers' conference. All three took place at Baslow. The total attendance at these conferences was 1630 persons, of whom 938 were men and 692 women.

Mr T. R. Glover of St John's College, Cambridge, was on the programme for the first time, also the Bishop of Birmingham (Dr Charles Gore). The list of speakers was a distinguished one and included : the Bishop of Durham (Dr Handley Moule), Canon Scott Holland, the Rev. Harrington C. Lees, the Rev. R. F. Horton, Dr John Kelman, the Rev. F. B. Meyer, Prof. A. S. Peake, Miss Gertrude Tuckwell, the Rev. W. J. Conybeare, the Rev. D. Macfadyen, the Rev. Newport J. D. White, Canon B. K. Cunningham, the Rev. Ivor Roberton, the Rev. A. J. Tait, the Rev. Elvet Lewis, Prof. D. S. Cairns, the Rev. V. S. Azariah, the Rev. G. H. Bondfield, the Rev. J. E. Watts Ditchfield, the Rev. E. S. Woods and Mr Sherwood Eddy, the hostesses being Lady Reichel, Mrs Alexander Whyte and Mrs Temple (widow of the late Archbishop of Canterbury).

Sports day in camp was by this time well established. Pillow fighting on the pole for the world's championship, an international potato race, Jack Woodhouse at his best at the prize giving and Father Kelly well to the fore, were features of the occasion.

Charles W. Gilkey, Harvard, concluded an interesting visitor's impression of Baslow:

> But the real heart of Baslow beats not in the rare good fellowship that so truly pervades the camp, and is so delightfully concentrated in the continuous merriment of the afternoon given over to " sports "; not in the conferences with all their vigorous grappling with living issues; not even in the general addresses with all their vision and power. The deeper source of Baslow's life and inspiration lies in the personal contact and communion with the life of God, which men and women there are seeking and finding through private and united devotion and prayer. . . . Baslow is a place of prayer; and its delegation meetings, its daily periods of united intercession, and most of all the devotion of many there who spend much time alone in prayer, are the hidden springs of the spiritual power which it is exerting in the life of British universities, and on every individual student who there comes into closer touch with the realities and forces of the unseen and eternal world.

I quote this because it is typical of a great deal that is said round about this time. The spirit of prayer was very much alive in the Movement in these pre-war years.

The autumn began with a new start in the missionary side of the Movement's work. The sense of disappointment which had been felt at the beginning of the century that the S.V.M.U. was not flooding the missionary societies with offers of service had died down for some years, but it welled up again at this period. At Christmas the Executive of the S.V.M.U. had held a two days' meeting " for the purpose of waiting upon God, seeking His strength and guidance and a revelation of His will." Time was set aside for both prayer and conference and between the periods of conference silence was kept.

The chairman of the S.V.M.U. Executive, C. Kingsley Williams, wrote an account of this meeting in *The Student Movement*:

> No Student Volunteer can seriously maintain that our success—wonderful and undeserved as it has been in many ways—is at all commensurate with our ambition, which

is nothing less than this : to call men and women in
adequate numbers and of adequate ability to serve God on
the foreign field. . . . To persuade men to be missionaries
must always be our first aim. . . . If history is the scroll
on which God writes His purpose, and not the veil with
which He hides His will, then it is certain that the will of
God is that the S.V.M.U. should be the instrument in His
hands for bringing the colleges to see what their share of
the burden of Christendom is.[1]

When the Executive of the S.V.M.U. presented its
report to the Union in the summer, it said of the same
meeting :

The sense of weakness and penitence for our lack of
faith, which first impelled us to wait upon God, was profoundly deepened during those days, and we would call
on the whole Union to share in this acknowledgment of
our failure—of the true inadequacy of our puny efforts in
the past. . . . We became overwhelmingly convinced that
the impending conflict and collision between Christianity
and the opposing forces of the world was a call to the
Church to gird herself anew, and in the power of the Lord
to strive and to prevail. There could be no uncertainty
as to the issue on the Divine side, for God is all powerful
and all loving. But God uses men. . . . Men are the
conditions and the appointed instruments of victory. So
we were brought to understand and believe that it is the
will of God to claim men and women in the colleges for
work abroad, in greater numbers than we had ventured to
contemplate before—men and women of the greatest gifts.[2]

One outcome of this gathering was a decision to
strengthen the secretariat by the addition of a central
volunteer secretary for men and another for women.
It was desired that both these officers should have seen
service on the mission field and should hold their office
" for prolonged periods."
We hardly realized the immense difficulty of finding
the people needed for such secretaryships. If they were
to be effective in the colleges they must still be young

[1] *The Student Movement*, vol. xii. p. 113.
[2] *Annual Report*, *S.C.M.*, 1909-10, p. 10.

and vigorous, but such people did not leave the mission field. The first of the posts filled was that of the central volunteer secretaryship for women. Agnes de Sélincourt was appointed. She had had a distinguished academic career at Cambridge, served on the Executive of the S.V.M.U. in 1895-96, had been for a number of years principal of the Lady Muir Memorial College, Allahabad, and had returned to England owing to the state of her mother's health. She began work in the summer of 1910.

Agnes de Sélincourt was a very able woman with a keen intellect, vivacious manner and attractive personality. She was a small and slightly built woman with a dark complexion and somewhat pronounced features. One was attracted at once by her eyes, sparkling, dark brown eyes which never seemed to lose their glint, were always kindly and gave one a sense of a vigorous personality behind them. She was a good speaker and committee member; further, she had the capacity not only for producing ideas, but for carrying them into action. Suave, courteous and persuasive, she held to her purpose with immense tenacity, and in consequence had a great power of achievement. She served the Movement for three years, always hoping that she could return to India. Her health proved a difficulty, however, and when she was quite sure that the medical verdict against her return to India was final, she accepted the principalship of Westfield College, which had been offered to her.

"One of the great joys of my new work," she wrote, "is that it will be closely linked with the Student Movement to which I have owed more of inspiration than can easily be told. It is nice that, geographically even, Annandale and Westfield are near together. Our college has the proud distinction of being the nearest of any to S.C.M. headquarters, has it not? That is, I feel, a good omen for the future."

All her friends felt that a good choice had been made by Westfield and that the college had found someone who would serve it with both ability and devotion. It was a great sorrow to a wide circle of friends that an accident should have terminated her life. A fall from a bicycle coming down a steep hill in Yorkshire, after she had been principal four years, led to injuries which proved fatal. She left a cottage and a small sum of money for its upkeep, to be used by Student Movement secretaries who wanted a haven of peace. Its distance from London, however, and the increased cost of travelling owing to the war, made it of little value for the purpose she had in mind. It was accordingly sold and de Sélincourt bursaries provided from the proceeds. These are given to Student Movement secretaries in turn, to be used by them in seeking rest and recuperation in the middle of their period of work.

It was not until the year following Miss de Sélincourt's appointment that the Movement was able to find a man for the central volunteer secretaryship for men. The first occupant of the post was William Paton, Pembroke College, Oxford, and Westminster College, Cambridge. He began work in September 1911 and for ten years played a prominent part in the work of the Movement. Beginning as central volunteer secretary, he later became assistant secretary, was given leave of absence towards the end of the war to serve with the Army Y.M.C.A. in India, and returned at the time of the Armistice as missionary secretary. While occupying this post he took a large share in the leadership of the Movement as a whole, being one of the small group who helped to remake it immediately after the war.

With Agnes de Sélincourt and Bill Paton in charge of its missionary activities the Movement pushed forward this aspect of its work with vigour in preparation for another quadrennial conference which was now in prospect.

The Liverpool Conference, 1912, the fifth quadrennial conference held by the Movement, had its roots in both the social conference, Matlock, 1909, and the World

Missionary Conference, Edinburgh, 1910. It was inevitable that the Matlock Conference with its immense influence on the outlook of the Student Movement should have a profound effect upon the programme to be placed before the students at Liverpool. In September 1909 the social service committee of the Movement, resolved " to inform the S.V.M.U. Executive that this committee is unanimously of opinion that a joint conference on the home and foreign work of the Church is desirable in view of the identity of the problem, and to ask them to allow us to confer with them as to the possibilities of holding such a conference." This was a startling proposal to many, but others were ready for it.

When the Student Movement, with its strong missionary outlook, first began to pay attention to the problems of society in Great Britain, it thought of work at home and abroad as unrelated. Adherents of each of these interests tended to regard one another as rivals in the attempt to win the attention of students. It was with some surprise that the leaders of the Movement found that somehow interest in social questions had been greatly stimulated and helped as a result of the missionary conference at Liverpool in 1908. It was said by many that the genesis of the conference at Matlock, April 1909, which came as a call to the Student Movement for a new attitude and a new discipleship in relation to the social problem, was the Liverpool conference. As soon as the next quadrennial came in sight people began to say that it must show marks of the Matlock conference in its programme. " The S.V.M.U. could not now produce a programme which did not take into consideration the social problem."

The conception of the unity of the problem of the extension of Christ's Kingdom at home and abroad had been steadily growing upon the Movement. The solution of the problem was one and the same, truer discipleship. Further, there were many students, " and not the worst type, who will not hear of foreign missions except along the line of their interest in the social health of the body politic." There were also some subjects, such as the Christianization of international relationships, which had not hitherto been tackled by the S.V.M.U., which were proper to a conference dealing with home and foreign matters. There were those who said that the function of the S.V.M.U. conference was to secure missionaries, but to this Malcolm Spencer, whom we have been quoting, replied:

> The function of the S.V.M.U. conference is not and never has been primarily to secure immediate decisions for foreign service, but to give such a comprehensive, penetrating and arresting survey of the problem that men will inevitably consider the relation of their own lives to it in the spirit of Christian service.

The Social Service Committee secured the support of both the Theological College Department and General College Department committee for its proposal, but the S.V.M.U. committee debated at length whether or not it would hold any conference in 1912. It did not reach a decision for seven months, and then decided to hold a conference on home and foreign work.

The World Missionary Conference, Edinburgh, had issued a message to the Church in Christian lands, saying:

> The next ten years will in all probability constitute a turning-point in human history, and may be of more critical importance in determining the spiritual evolution of mankind than many centuries of ordinary experience. If those years are wasted, havoc may be wrought that centuries are not able to repair. On the other hand, if they are rightly used, they may be among the most glorious in Christian history.

This call obviously affected students and gave importance to their conference at Liverpool. The Movement knew that many in the Churches and some in the colleges would be opposed to the idea of a conference not exclusively missionary, so it prepared and circulated a pamphlet which was an *apologia* for a joint conference. It recounted the call of the Edinburgh Conference to missionary service, spoke of the denial of Christ in Christendom, quoted the Edinburgh gathering as showing " the unity of the foreign missionary and social problems," and then stated the fundamental issue.

A consideration of the need of the non-Christian world and of the condition of society in Christendom itself drives us to ask whether there exists any solution for the problems that confront us, and whether we may dare to face them in a spirit of confident optimism. Is Jesus Christ able to furnish an adequate solution for these problems ? Is He the final and completely satisfying word of God to man ? Is He the Saviour of all men, the inaugurator and creator of a new social order, the Light and Life of the world ? This, surely, is the most central, crucial and vital of all questions. The conference in Liverpool will achieve much if it helps to focus the attention of the present generation of students upon this supreme and fundamental issue.

The Church is confident that the answer to the question is beyond doubt. And yet somehow the testimony of the Church does not seem in practice to be sufficiently convincing. It will probably be generally admitted that in its present spiritual condition the Church is not equal to the task to which it is called. This fact was stated with great emphasis at the World Missionary Conference. For example, one prominent speaker said :

" We are frank to concede that it is futile to talk about making Christ known to the world in this generation or any generation unless there be a great expansion of vitality in the members of the Churches of Christendom."

And another :

" *Something must happen to the Church at home* if it is going even to look at the work which has been put on it by this conference."

" What is it that must happen to the Church? Surely it is that we should see with fresh eyes the things that we profess to believe, that they should hold us with the power of supreme conviction and be realized as possessing transcendent worth. Suppose that a group of men were to believe in the depths of their souls, as the early disciples believed, *that God revealed in Christ is light and that in Him is no darkness at all*, what might they not do ? If they should come to know God as a God full of compassion and gracious, plenteous in mercy, forgiving iniquity and transgression and sin, as the infinite Father present and active in the world that He has made, longing to put an end to all misery, sorrow and sin, and hindered from accomplishing that purpose only by human unbelief, would they not feel that they had an utterly satisfying Gospel for the world? If God should completely fill their vision as the living and sovereign ruler of the universe and disposer of events, could they be stayed by any difficulties or regard any task as beyond the power of achievement? Our fundamental need is beyond doubt a rediscovery of God. Not that we have to wait for some strange and mystical experience; the word that unlocks the treasure-house is near at hand. We need only to see more clearly and to grasp more firmly the spiritual realities revealed in Jesus Christ and laid bare for us in the pages of the New Testament.

The pamphlet concluded with a series of suggestions of subjects and books for study in preparation for Liverpool.

Liverpool entertained the conference with the same kindness and generosity it had shown in 1896 and 1908. The conference was again in the Philharmonic Hall and was the largest of the kind yet held. The total number of delegates was 2093, made up of 856 men and 691 women students, 151 foreign delegates and nearly 400 guests, including " dons " of every kind and either sex and the representatives of fifty missionary societies. A meeting for teachers was attended by 170 dons, schoolmasters and schoolmistresses, guests of the conference. An exhibit consisting of Courts of Religions and a Social Exhibit were highly regarded by experts, and were a feature of the conference.

There was a new significance in the foreign delegations. It was not only that some came from countries unrepresented four years before—Austria, Bulgaria, Roumania, Russia and Turkey—but the meaning of their presence was better understood. The Rev. Alex. Connell, speaking for the churches of Liverpool the first night, bade us lose no opportunity of advancing the supreme interest of international peace. Later the chairman in welcoming them said : " Your presence here is indispensable. The social problem is an international problem, and the evangelization of the world too great a task for any one nation." Recent events made war with Germany seem no remote possibility,

> and successive speakers showed how fatal to the hopes of the conference would be such a sin and a calamity as a European war . . . one lesson at least that we have learned during this week together is that among the objects for which our Student Movement works and prays international peace must henceforth be included.[1]

The conference faced the fact of the situation abroad in four addresses : " Coming religious changes in the Far East," by Professor D. S. Cairns, " Christ and Indian unrest," by Mr A. G. Fraser, " The Problem of Islam," by Herr Missionsinspektor Axenfeld of Germany, and " The Backward Races," by Dr Wardlaw Thompson.

> The addresses on the facts at home traced " the problems of drunkenness, ' social vice ' and ' destitution ' back, through the conditions of sweating, overcrowding and unemployment, and the methods of competition to the belief in money and denial of brotherhood, to the selfishness, in short, of average respectable people, *like ourselves*. Just as, Mr T. R. Glover told us, it was the ordinary impulses of practical people that led Christ to the Cross, so, Mr Temple showed, it is the combined action of millions of people no better than we are that crucifies Him afresh to-day and puts Him to an open shame. And, further, as Mr N. S. Talbot insisted, the spirit that makes outcasts in the world is none other than the spirit in us which term after term makes outsiders in our colleges. ' The racial and social problems exist in *us*,' in the lovelessness and unbrotherliness of you and me." [2]

The conference was merciless in its exposure of the impotence of man. " We can't achieve brotherliness by being frantically brotherly ; " " we can't build the

---

[1] *Christ and Human Need.* Liverpool, 1912, p. 10.
[2] *Ibid.*, p. 12.

Kingdom of God upon the arts of successful self-assertion . . . we are morally bankrupt," " with men it is impossible." And so convinced of sin and helplessness, the conference turned to the revelation of God reconciling the world to Himself in Christ, and in the consideration of His life and character, His death and rising again to dwell within men, the centre and climax of the conference was reached. The Christian Gospel came with power to those present.

During the conference a telegram was received from the German Student Christian Movement which read :

> We pray and believe that the Holy Spirit will bless your conference for the whole world, and give peace between the Christian people as a testimony for the non-Christians. *Ut omnes unum sint.*
> Deutsche Christliche Studentenbewegung,
>
> Graf PUECKLER, *Chairman.*
> Dr NIEDERMEYER, *Secretary.*

Students were not thinking about relations between Germany and her neighbours, but some of us were alive to the strength of the militarist party in that country, and had been concerned over the sending of the German gunboat *Panther* the previous July to Agadir. J. H. Oldham was chairman of the conference and he collected a group of leaders with a few senior friends, and we composed the following reply, which was approved by the conference and sent in its name to the German Student Movement :

> We, the members of the Student Conference on Foreign Missions and Social Problems assembled at Liverpool, January 2-8, 1912, and composed of 1680 Principals, Professors, Tutors and Students from 165 British Universities and Colleges, desire to express our deep appreciation of the friendly greeting sent to the conference by the German Student Christian Movement. We feel very deep and anxious concern at the differences of opinion which have arisen on questions of national policy between the Governments of Germany and Great Britain, and we earnestly

pray that a way may be found for the removal of any ground of misunderstanding or estrangement between the two nations. Upon the preservation of the peace of Europe, and in a special degree upon the friendly and intimate co-operation of the peoples of Germany and Great Britain, depends the realization of those plans of Christian service for the fulfilment of which we pray, and the furtherance of which we desire with God's help to make the chief purpose of our lives. The preaching of the Gospel to non-Christian people, the removal of terrible evils in the condition of the poor and destitute in our own country, and the deepening of the sense of human fellow-ship in industrial life—duties which we believe to have a paramount claim at this time upon Christian men and women—would be set back for a generation by an out-break of European war. From the immeasurable evils of such a disastrous fratricidal conflict we pray that Christ-endom may be preserved.

J. H. OLDHAM, *Chairman.*
TISSINGTON TATLOW, *Secretary.*

It was a matter of both thankfulness and relief to the leaders of the Movement that the conference was a success, and the S.V.M.U. recorded in its minutes their unanimous conviction that they had been led of God in their decision to combine missionary and social ques-tions at the conference. " The possibilities of failure had been great, but criticisms might be considered trifl-ing, and it was felt that God's guiding hand had been very manifest in all the organizing and carrying through of the conference." [1]

It was an experiment not without anxiety, for some of the best friends of the Movement in the missionary societies had been extremely nervous about the results of the decision to combine home and foreign questions. Mr C. C. B. Bardsley,[2] the honorary secretary of the C.M.S., whose knowledge of the Movement extended over many years and whose sympathy for it was un-questioned, expressed in the gravest manner to me his fears lest the value of the conference to the non-Christian

[1] S.V.M.U. Minute, January 1912.
[2] Afterwards Bishop of Leicester.

world should be seriously impaired by combining a consideration of home and foreign questions ; and he was not alone in feeling this among friendly missionary society secretaries. There is no doubt, however, that the leaders of the Movement were in touch with the temper of mind of the college field at the time, and all fears were set at rest during the conference. Mr Bardsley came to me in the speakers' room before the conference was half over, saying that he was more than satisfied that the right thing had been done.

The committee was determined to publish a report, but those of previous conferences had led to a loss, so I determined to bring it out at once, believing that this would materially influence the sale. I discussed the matter with the manager of the Botolph Printing Works and he promised to have the report ready within ten days. Some of the papers were collected from speakers in advance, others were transcribed during the conference, and by sitting up at night and working on the report and sending speeches to the printers as they were delivered, it was actually possible to get the report into the hands of people who had ordered it at the conference within a week.

As I expected, the promise of the report so quickly affected the sales, and a good edition had already been sold before the conference closed ; 6500 copies of *Christ and Human Need* were sold, and a number of the addresses were also published and sold in pamphlet form.

The most important outcome of the conference, as far as the policy of the Movement was concerned, was a decision that the whole Movement must obviously and unequivocally in the eyes of the college field be committed as much to the foreign as to the home side of the work. The S.V.M.U. sent the following resolution to the General Committee :

That in the interest of the missionary work of the Movement, this Executive recommends that the General Committee should appoint a missionary committee which

2 G

shall be composed of members of the Student Volunteer Missionary Union Executive, plus some additional members to be appointed by the General Committee, and that such ought to become the missionary sub-committee of the General Committee.

The Union decided, however, that it ought not to involve itself in general questions concerned with the relation of foreign missions and social problems, but should restrict itself to the recruiting of men and women for the work of the missionary societies and of helping those recruited to prepare for their work.

This decision left the responsibility of presenting the comprehensive ideal of the service of the Kingdom of God at home and abroad to students, to the General Committee guided by a sub-committee. A year later, however, the S.V.M.U. committee decided that the missionary sub-committee had been a mistake and that it was the General Committee itself which ought to take the lead in missionary matters, and so it asked the General Committee, instead of leaving missions to a sub-committee, to agree to devote an entire day, when it held its three-day committee meetings, to foreign missions. This was done for a time, but pressure of business soon reduced the period from a day at each meeting to two or three hours.

We were all beginning to be excited about the prospect of a permanent home for summer conferences. Such a development had been in my mind since I saw the splendid conference sites in the United States of America on a visit in 1901. Frank Lenwood was the student leader who responded most warmly to the idea, and he and I raised the matter for discussion several times. Then the committee asked me to take steps in the matter. I called a conference at the S.C.M. offices of the secretaries of a number of societies, told them about the American sites and asked if they did not feel the need for something similar in England. All agreed, and all said their organization would use one if it was secured. But when it came to the question of finance, all said that their societies were so pressed that they could do nothing about money.

I told the S.C.M. committee that there never would be a conference site in Great Britain unless we promoted it. The committee said, " Go ahead." Ultimately we secured the part services of Erskine Crossley, Clare College, Cambridge, and a few of us were appointed to help him to form a company, secure finance, purchase a property and plan suitable buildings. It all took time, but on April 1st, 1909, Crossley laid before the General Committee a proposed form of prospectus for a company to promote a permanent site for conferences. It was a plan to float a company with an authorized capital of £120,000, to purchase an estate on Lake Windermere, and erect buildings to hold 500 persons. The committee discussed the whole thing at great length and approved the proposal, the suggestion being that a small syndicate of friends of the Student Movement be formed who should purchase the estate and then become the vendors of it to a limited liability company.

The committee, as student committees do when they are dealing with something which is outside their field of knowledge, indulged in a long discussion. The man who had hitherto shown most perspicacity about a permanent site was Frank Lenwood, and he was absent. I demurred at the large sum for which the company was to be capitalized, feeling quite convinced that no site with this amount of capital sunk in it could be made to pay, but Crossley was convinced of his figures and all the others were out of their depth, so I left the matter, but a few days later went to Oxford to see Frank Lenwood and tell him how the land lay.

We went through Crossley's figures, mutually agreed that the proposal was an impossible one and mapped out the general lines on which we thought a practical proposal could be drafted. I then had to make a run for my train, promising Lenwood to work out figures for our scheme on the way up to London. This I did, allowing £30,000 for the purchase of an estate, erection of buildings and furnishing. After some difficulty Crossley was got to accept this scheme, which among other things meant giving up Lake Windermere, which from the first several of us had doubts about, not only because of its expense, but because it was placed so far north that we feared it could not hope to secure the custom which would come to a more central site.

By October Crossley had found another site, Edge Farm, Crich, Derbyshire, and this the General Committee authorized Crossley, Walter Seton, Walter Saunders and myself to purchase and then take the necessary steps to register a limited liability company to take over the estate, erect buildings and carry out the whole scheme. This was duly done.

The First Conference Estate was incorporated on May 11th 1910, with an authorized share capital of £30,000, divided into shares of £1 each. The first directors of the company were : Robert Armitage, Esq., M.P., R. L. Barclay, Esq., M.A., Erskine A. Crossley, Esq., B.A., Sir William J. Crossley, Bart., M.P., Sir Andrew H. L. Fraser, K.C.S.I., Walter W. Seton, Esq., M.A., and the Rev. Tissington Tatlow, M.A.

We all thought that building would begin in the autumn of 1910 and the place would be ready for the summer conference of 1911. I went for August to Maresfield, in Sussex, very tired after the work of the year concluding with the largest summer conference we ever held at Baslow, and was sitting in the garden one day when my wife came out and said : " Mr Cecil Harris has turned up and is full of a new place for conferences he has found. Come in and see him."

Sure enough, Mr Harris, who was an old friend of ours in the Movement and who knew all about the plans for developing the property at Crich, was full of the superior suitability of The Hayes, Swanwick, owned by Mr Wright. He wanted me to go off then and there and see the property. I remember feeling, as one does when one has got to a holiday spot after a long spell of conference, that nothing would induce me to go and see anything, least of all to revise a plan which had taken two years to complete and which was shortly to be put into execution.

Harris told me that R. L. Barclay, our treasurer, was going to Scotland almost at once. Accordingly I got in touch with him and asked him whether he would go and see the site. He did so and pronounced it as a much more suitable one than Crich.

Fifty thousand pounds had been spent in building The Hayes, Swanwick. It was a substantial house of Derbyshire stone. There were roomy hunting stables, the grounds were laid out in a very substantial manner as regards surface of roads and paths and the quality of railings, etc. As the years had gone by there had been encroachments of coal-mining and the iron industry upon the estate. This had depreciated its value. At the same time, when the Wright family learned the purpose for which the place was required they offered it at about one-fifth of what it had cost.

Crossley sold the Crich Estate without any difficulty, and before Christmas the company had purchased The Hayes, Swanwick, for £11,500 and had begun building operations. The chief changes made were to erect a hostel near the house to hold 200 people, to build a dining hall for 300 persons by the side of the kitchen wall of the original house, to turn the hunting stables into an attractive quadrangle containing 50 bedrooms, and to build a conference hall for 600 persons in the grounds near the house. The house itself was left practically untouched. The most important later addition was the building of a winter garden connecting the original conservatory and the dining hall.

A very large proportion of the shares of the company was taken up by former members of the Student Movement and their friends. The Student Movement took 500 management shares of £1 each as vendors to the company. I always thought this was very generous on the part of the Movement, but students are generous people. If we had been a committee of business men we would have taken at least what the promotion of the company had cost, which was far more than £500. The Movement also acquired the right to have first choice of dates for conferences and to appoint a proportion of the Board of Directors.   In all other respects it took its place as one of the ordinary customers of the company.

Crossley pushed on the work with almost incredible speed, and we held our conferences for the first time at Swanwick during July 1912.

CHAPTER XXV

BIBLE STUDY, EVANGELISTIC WORK AND A NEW GRAPPLING WITH THE MOVEMENT'S TASK

THE leaders of the Movement settled down to their work with new confidence after the conference on the problem of truth, and not having forgotten the suggestion of the Commission of 1908 that the Movement should have a Bible study secretary, made a search for a man. R. L. Pelly accepted the post and entered upon his work on October 1st 1911, as the first Bible study secretary of the Movement.

He found that while many of the best men in the Movement believed in the importance of Bible study, " enthusiasm is conspicuously absent."

> Our Bible study department is nothing like the power station it ought to be. It ought to be giving men such a realization of God and such a vision of Christ as would electrify all other departments. This simply is not happening, and probably the most important thing we have to do is to recover the belief in the possibility of great results through associated Bible study.

Dick Pelly organized Bible schools and wrote interesting and invigorating memoranda to guide the travelling secretaries in promoting Bible study. He contributed regular notes for the guidance of the Christian Union leaders in *The Student Movement*. He was a first-class honours man and handled his department with competence. The result was a marked improvement in the quality of Bible study.

During the year that followed 4017 students (1294 men and 2723 women) were enrolled in 476 Bible study circles.   College reports showed that Bible study was the central activity of most Christian Unions and the chief recruiting agency for membership of the Movement.   Cardiff University College may be quoted as typical :

> We regard this phase (Bible study) of Christian Union work as of the utmost importance, and all the men who show keen interest in the Christian Union are those who join Bible study circles in the first term.

The Bible study circle was also regarded by many as the most successful evangelistic method.   The circle provided a favourable atmosphere in which friendship grew.   Intimate topics could be discussed.   Friendships were formed with students outside the circles, and friend led friend to Christ.   " Several colleges reported real spiritual awakening as the result of the Bible study work."

In August 1911 a training school for women was held at Swanwick, and at Easter 1912 there was a conference of Student Movement officers with a group of about 60 senior friends, both men and women, who met to discuss the best methods of training leaders for Bible circles.   The appointment of R. L. Pelly had borne fruit.   His advice and help was sought from all over the field.   He conducted a number of leaders' retreats and helped with the thinking out and preparation of literature for use in the promotion of Bible study.

The changed conditions under which the work of the Movement was carried on and which led to the Commission of 1908 continued to exercise the mind of the leaders of the Movement.   That Commission had been an unquestioned success, not least in having pointed explicitly to a number of practical things which the Movement ought to do and which the Movement had found it could do, and do successfully.   Within three years the Movement had held the Matlock conference on social questions ; developed student interest in social work and study ; appointed a social service secretary and a social service committee; formed a Bible study committee and appointed a Bible study secretary; developed and enlarged the Officers' Conference; established the practice of having two general conferences each summer at Swanwick; organized the Welsh, Irish and Scottish Intercollegiate Christian Unions and appointed national secretaries; appointed two Student Volunteer secretaries and planned the consolidation and development of the policy of the S.V.M.U.

In spite of all this growth and improvement of machinery, the situation in the colleges grew increasingly difficult to handle. The Christian Unions seemed to be touching chiefly the well-disposed, but, to some extent at any rate, leaving outside the first-class thinkers in the colleges and also the virile, unspeculative, natural man. There was the new phenomenon of leaders, and faithful leaders too, of the Christian Unions expressing doubt about the central doctrines of the Christian faith. "Instead of black and white we find grey," said one of the leaders of the Movement.

There was a revolt from the religious phraseology of the past and a lack of strong spiritual life. Students asked that their intellectual difficulties might be answered, and they demanded a Christianity which worked.

The General Committee became concerned regarding the increase of machinery and activity, feared that it overburdened the Christian Unions, and believed that if they could find a way of lightening the ship the result would be an increase of effectiveness in evangelistic work and with this a solution of the problems of many students. Remembering the success of the Commission of 1908, it decided at its meeting in April 1911 to appoint another commission to review the whole situation;

> The general feeling was that the Christian Unions were being overloaded with a variety of Student Movement interests which had to be kept going in the colleges, and that this was very disturbing to the true spirit of Christianity.[1]

[1] Minutes of General Committee, 1911.

At its meeting the following October the Committee chose the Commission and decided that its terms of reference should be:

> To consider the present constitution of the Movement and its suitability for present circumstances, especially in view of the recent development of national intercollegiate unions, and to discuss possible co-ordination in the work of the Movement.

Another approaching quadrennial conference was now absorbing the attention of the leaders and the Commission did not meet until June 1912. In the meantime Manchester University Christian Union, under the leadership of R. H. Lomas, developed a new kind of circle after "Liverpool." It was not a circle formed to study a doctrinal or Bible study text-book, but to discuss people's difficulties about Christianity. The Manchester experiment was widely copied throughout the Movement.

The demand for these circles arose because of the growing number of students who were not convinced Christians, had received very little religious instruction before entering college, but who, while unready to join a Bible study circle which was taking some such subject as the *Epistle to the Philippians*, were ready to join a circle where they could air their difficulties and possibly find some answer to their questions. These circles needed competent leaders. Good work was done where the leadership was in the hands of well-instructed students, but there grew to be a great deal of vague talk at many of such circles, and this continued until after the war, when George Cockin took the situation in hand and succeeded in getting a great deal of useful doctrinal and apologetic study work done.

The new Commission met from June 22nd to 25th 1912. Its members were: MacEwan S. Lawson (chairman), W. Paton, R. L. Pelly, Winifred M. Sedgwick, Malcolm Spencer, Oliver Thomas, with Zoë Fairfield and Tissington Tatlow as joint secretaries.

The Commission reviewed the Movement, and stated as its main conviction the "need for a richer spiritual life."

> We lack the spiritual momentum necessary for the accomplishment of our task. There is no strength to bring forth, not better organization, nor fresh ideas, nor even a stronger apologetic, but simply a richer spiritual experience is felt by the Commission to be our supreme need at the present time.

The Commission made a variety of suggestions, the most important of which were : that the General College Department, while remaining as a nominal department, should be merged as far as its control and work were concerned, into the General Committee ; that the Bible Study and Social Service standing committees should be disbanded ; and that the programme of the summer conference should as far as possible be simplified. All these proposals were with a view to reducing machinery and achieving co-ordination and economy of effort, that energy saved might find spiritual channels. On the whole this Commission did not have any very important bearing upon the life of the Movement except in one particular, it helped to stimulate the committee and officers to promote evangelistic work, and the fact that so much evangelistic work was done during the college year 1912-1913 was, largely, the outcome of its work.

It is doubtful whether the decision to abolish the committee of the General College Department was a wise one. This committee was not concerned, as was the General Committee, with questions of constitution, finance, outside relationships, the co-ordination of Student Movement interests and the planning of corporate activities such as the summer conference. What it did was to review what was actually happening in the college field, often taking the universities and colleges one by one under the guidance of the travelling secretaries in charge of S.C.M. work in them. It considered the spiritual situation revealed—Was the Christian Union paying adequate attention to building up the spiritual life of its members, what was its Bible Study work like, what was its relation to the rest of the college, had there been an evangelistic mission in recent years, was the situation ripe once more for something of the kind? In this way the policy of the department in relation to the Christian Unions was built up and communicated—usually through the travelling secretaries—to particular universities and colleges.

It was work of careful and thorough spiritual direction. The travelling secretaries prepared reports about every college visited. These reports were transcribed in the office and issued to every member of the committee, so that all were in constant touch with what the secretaries were doing in the colleges. In no sense did the direction of the work lie with the secretaries. Members of the committee often took a more leading part in making decisions regarding policy than did the secretaries.

The two things which stand out in the Minutes was the amount of time and attention given to promoting evangelistic work and Bible study. In the case of Bible study a great deal of the preoccupation of the committee was planning Bible study text-books, Bible schools and local and central training for the leaders of Bible study circles. These two main concerns of the committee were closely related to the summer conference, much time being given by the committee to considering how the summer conference could best be used to extend Christ's Kingdom in the colleges and to build up in the Christian faith, specially through the study of the Bible, the men and women who came—not necessarily through membership—under the influence of the Movement.

The amount of evangelistic work that was done during this period was considerable. Almost all the members of the Movement and a considerable body of students who were not members joined Bible circles.

Many Christian Unions regarded Bible study circles as their best method of evangelization. These Bible study circles, the effort of members of the Movement to reach their friends through personal work, the evangelistic campaigns held frequently all over the college field and the strong evangelistic influence of the summer conference, where scores of students were brought by their friends in the hope that they would make the Christian decision, led a large body of students every year to the decision to become disciples of Jesus Christ.

It should be added that there was constant attention to how best to help students in the prayer life. The importance of private and corporate prayer was continually emphasized. The *Terminal Intercession Paper* issued during this period had a wide circulation. The subject was dealt with regularly at the summer conferences which were probably the most potent influence in helping students to regard prayer as one of the real things in life.

The Book of Prayer for Students was planned on the recommendation of the Theological College Department Committee at this time, though its publication was later. Leslie Johnston wrote the daily services in it, Malcolm Spencer and I compiled from various sources most of the prayers, Philip Loyd wrote those for the Movement, and the whole was put into shape by Hugh Martin. A large edition was printed with the belief it would take several years to sell, but 5000 copies were sold in a few months. The book was revised and since then has passed through several revisions and editions.

The evangelistic movement, which the committee so greatly desired, and which sought to reach the man who was not a Christian, came during the academic year 1912-13, and by the middle of November R. L. Pelly, who was in general charge of the arrangements for evangelistic work, circularized the committee with reports which he described as " wonderfully encouraging." R. P. Wilder at King's College, London ; Dr T. R. Glover, T. Tatlow and Miss Muriel Harris at University

College, Reading; R. P. Wilder, Winifred Sedgwick and Dr Tom Jays at University College, Cardiff; T. Tatlow at East London College; Dr Kelman at Edinburgh University and a series of Sunday evening meetings at Glasgow all reported large and successful gatherings. The field was certainly ripe.

Several people had the kind of experience that came to me at East London College. I choose it because the experience was typical and because I can describe it more accurately than others in which I did not share personally. I had accepted an invitation from the Christian Union to give a series of three addresses to students at 5 o'clock in St Benet's Church Hall, next the College. Although they were called apologetic lectures, there was quite as much exposition of the Gospel and treatment of Christian experience as of apologetic in them. I was surprised, as were the Christian Union leaders, by the large attendance at the first address. I said at the conclusion of it, just before 6 o'clock, that I would be glad to remain and meet any who wanted to talk. At once a man came to the platform to talk to me. After a few minutes I looked up to find that most of the rest of the audience had formed itself into a queue of waiting people. Realizing that if I stayed all night I could not talk individually to everybody, I asked the audience to sit down, saying that we would have a general talk. A few people went away, but almost everybody stayed and they went on staying too, for at 8.45 p.m. I broke the meeting up, saying that I simply must go as I had someone waiting for me at my house that night! For me this was the beginning of the practice of discussing the address at its conclusion with one's audience. Hitherto I had always talked to individuals after speaking at general meetings in college, but I had never talked with an audience, but from that night, over twenty years ago, the majority of general meetings which I have addressed have been followed by questions from the audience, and I believe that this has been a common experience of Student Movement secretaries for many years. The questioning is always of the frankest kind and constantly deals with great questions relating to God and man and the world.

After the series of addresses were over, I was asked whether I would come again and speak on agnosticism, as there was an agnostic group whose leader said that if I would talk about agnosticism and have discussion afterwards, he would bring his group, so we had a tremendous evening of discussion on agnosticism. Then some of the Jews, of whom there were many in the college, hearing the discussions that went on in the Common Room throughout the week, sent a message to say that they would like to hear what I had to say about the person of Jesus Christ. An address on the divinity of our Lord produced a remarkable discussion which lasted for hours. Others reported similar results in a number of colleges.

It was this year that the Anglican Fellowship was founded. Spencer had started the Free Church Fellowship chiefly for those who had been drawn together in the Movement. He spoke much of its success and its value to the Free Churches. I suggested an Anglican Fellowship to Neville Talbot at the summer conference, 1911, and asked him to start it, but he hit me a blow in the chest I still remember and said : " You are the man to do it : call us together." We had a meeting in the S.C.M. office in Chancery Lane on April 25th, 1912. Those present were : Revs. William Temple, B. H. Streeter, J. R. S. Taylor, John McLeod Campbell, R. G. Parsons,[1] Howard F. Houlder, T. R. W. Lunt, J. Leslie Johnston, Edwyn Bevan and myself. We decided to found the Anglican Fellowship. It was a fellowship to promote thought, prayer, fellowship and service among members of the Church of England and definitely planned to be non-party. Unlike the Free Church Fellowship it was open to women as well as men from its foundation. I acted as secretary for a short time, but as I was going to America in 1913, on the suggestion

[1] Afterwards Bishop of Southwark.

of H. K. Archdall, I secured A. C. Turner, Fellow of
Trinity College, Cambridge, as secretary and passed to
the chairmanship. Turner's death during the war was
a severe loss. He had begun to make the Fellowship
a power.

We were all greatly cheered by the reference which
the Archbishop of Canterbury made to the Movement in
his second charge which he delivered to the Diocese of
Canterbury in February 1912. He recounted in one
section of the charge sources of encouragement in the
religious outlook in England and instanced the Movement as one of these.

> Or what again of the Student Christian Movement, a
> movement which in its spontaneity, its buoyancy, its inter-
> national character, and its quiet force, seems to me to be
> one of the most remarkable organizations—if organization
> is not too rigid or prosaic a word—which any part of
> Christendom at any time or place has seen ?
> I cannot dwell upon all these, though I should like to do
> so. Let me take the last-named only. Most of those who
> are here probably know the facts in outline, but perhaps
> you have not fully realized their significance. They furnish,
> as it seems to me, an almost unchallengeable reply to the
> weak-hearted. Let me remind you of what has actually
> been happening.

There follows an outline of the work of the Movement. He has more to say about it, for after quoting
some statistics he proceeds :

> My point, however, is not the mere numerical growth of
> the Movement, but the richness of its life and interests. No
> department of Church work, whether in Great Britain or
> abroad, lies outside its range. It is not undenominational
> but it is interdenominational. There is markedly and
> emphatically no sinking or ignoring of denominational
> differences, and we have it on the authority of men like
> the Bishop of Winchester and Dr Frere that the care taken
> in this respect, and the thought devoted to the matter, have
> rendered possible not these conferences only, but other
> gatherings such as the Edinburgh Conference of 1910, in
> which different Christian leaders took part without the

smallest loss of denominational distinctiveness, or even what is sometimes called " the sinking of differences." [1]

The offices of the Movement in 93 Chancery Lane had become inadequate for their purpose. New secretaries had been added to the staff, the Publication Department had grown and more storage space was needed, and some of the secretaries were complaining that the offices were so dark, dirty and congested that they could not do their work satisfactorily. It was Mrs Fairfield who drew attention to a house—Annandale—standing in an acre of ground near the tube station at Golders Green, and suggested it should be purchased as offices for the Movement. Five of the secretaries already lived in Golders Green, the saving in rental would be considerable, and the number of non-student callers at Chancery Lane were occupying so much time that relief in this direction was needed. A large number of the callers were student volunteers on furlough, who, visiting the different missionary societies' buildings nearby, dropped in to hear how the Movement was faring and to be brought up to date. It was difficult to refuse to settle down for an adequate talk with somebody who turned up smiling, saying he had been in Central China for five years, and yet the drain on time and strength was very severe.

It was decided to leave the Publication Department in 93 Chancery Lane, to purchase Annandale and make it the secretarial headquarters of the Movement. This decision was one which was never regretted. We all had more time for our work, the house was cheaper than the office in the City, we could lunch together and have guests, there was less daily travelling to and fro, and the conditions were more healthy.

Agnes de Sélincourt organized a conference of schoolmistresses on Education in the Far East, in Oxford, September 1912. It was attended by about one hundred

[1] *The Character and Call of the Church of England*, by Randall Thomas Davidson, Archbishop of Canterbury, pp. 76, 78.

2 H

and fifty university women engaged in teaching. It brought much missionary knowledge to the schools and took some teachers abroad.

The paucity of medical student volunteers gave rise to an inquiry which revealed the fact that while the Movement as a whole had made marked progress, Christian work among medical students had in some places been at a complete standstill, while in others there had been actual retrogression. Although Christian work in London medical schools dated back many more years than in the majority of non-medical colleges, the proportion of medical students belonging to the Movement was only nine per cent. as contrasted with an average of fourteen per cent. of the students in other London colleges.

The question of leadership is a difficult one, especially in the London medical schools. The senior students, who provide the leadership in other colleges, tend among medicals, as they become senior, to take less and less part in the work of the Christian Union. The medical student during the second period of his training, which is in both the hospital wards and the medical school, works under great pressure. It is hard to find time for corporate activities, church attendance is difficult, and his inner religious life tends to weaken as it ceases to find outward expression. The junior men are often discouraged that their natural leaders seem not only too busy, but also to have lost interest.

There was criticism of the methods of the Movement in relation to medical students. Study circles, with the necessity for careful preparation, involved more time than medical students felt they could give, and it was only the exceptional man who found what he wanted at the summer conferences. " The kind of addresses given at summer conferences are far too theological and speculative," said the medical committee, " for a type of man whose thoughts hardly ever run in a philosophical groove, and who is mainly concerned with difficulties of a moral and scientific nature."

The sub-committee suggested the appointment of a special medical secretary and a re-examination of Student Movement methods with a view to adapting them to meet the needs of medical students, such as the arrangement of sectional meetings for medical students at the summer conference, the organizing of special evangelistic and apologetic meetings in medical schools, the provision of a medical missionary study text-book and the substitution in the hospital medical schools of Bible readings, for Bible circles, by men who could make Bible study both spiritually effective and attractive.

The Movement made valiant efforts to respond, and meetings for medicals at the summer conference resulted, but medical students are as different from the rest of the student body as theological students, and need a department of their own with a committee and staff which will study their needs and the best way of helping them. In the early days of the Movement there was strong Christian leadership from within the medical faculty, this has ceased, and both before and since the conclusion of the World War medicals have looked outside their ranks for help and leadership.

The rapid expansion of the Student Movement had for several years caused the General Committee financial embarrassment. An attempt made some years earlier to enlist the Christian Unions in systematic contribution to the Movement had proved a failure. The one group that took its full share in the support of the Movement was the body of students who came to summer conferences. The financial sessions held year after year at these conferences yielded annually sums totalling five to six hundred pounds, but while the rank and file contributed to their local branches, most of them did nothing for the Movement as a whole.

Brooding one evening at home over the question of how students' help could be enlisted, I came to the conclusion that the methods we had tried on previous occasions had been too cumbersome for a rapidly changing constituency, and that what was wanted was a plan which everyone could easily understand, and regarding which there would be no doubt as to what was expected of one. Thus thinking, the idea of holding a Finance Week occurred to me. I put the proposal before the General Committee, who told me to go ahead. The first Finance Week was held from February 8th to 15th 1913.

We had made up our minds to regard Finance Week as a success if anything over £250 was raised. The amount actually contributed by the colleges was £773. A large number of collecting cards were used, and they showed that the way money had been raised was by the sale of sketches, flowers, coffee, biscuits, sweets, second-hand books, crochet, blotting paper, photographs. Money had been made by painting on bags, blouse-making, darning, doing own washing, cleaning bicycle, coaching, making table-centre, boot cleaning, cushion making, cleaning kid gloves and satin slippers, washing dishes, sewing on buttons, cleaning candlestick, washing hair, washing brushes, bed-making, ironing, giving dancing lessons, sale of jewellery. Self-denial was practised by doing without flowers, fruit, cream, sugar, groceries, tobacco, newspapers, taxis, theatres and concerts. There were a certain number of entries which had the distinction of being unique, such as : " bus fares and teas saved by having influenza," " saved owing to training " (this came from a member of the Cambridge University Boat) and " earned by casual labour in the kitchen."

There was no question but that Finance Week had been a success. Not only did it bring a substantial sum of money into the coffers of the Movement, but it created fresh interest in the colleges in it. The Movement had never quite found itself in the matter of finance. Many suggestions had been made from time to time by the General Committee regarding the giving and collecting of money, but they had been received, as a rule, with hesitation, diffidence and some grumbling. Here, however, was something which the colleges appreciated. It seemed to suit their genius, for as an intercollegiate secretary wrote : " The idea has caught on tremendously." People felt they were asked to do something which they could do and they responded willingly. Many of the colleges said that it had helped them in relations with non-members who, observing enthusiastic finance week efforts being carried out in college, displayed a new interest in discovering exactly what it was for which the Student Movement stood.

The largest contributions came from Queen Margaret College, Glasgow (£33, 9s.) and Oxford University (£32, 2s. 1d.). The Slade School of Art, London, Westfield College, London School of Medicine for Women, Bedford College, and Newnham College, Cambridge, all contributed amounts between £25 and £30. The women have always led in generosity during finance week.

CHAPTER XXVI

THE BASIS OF THE MOVEMENT IS ALTERED A SECOND TIME

THE Movement altered its basis at its annual business meeting in 1913, but for three years before that the subject had been under constant discussion. It was a very serious matter for the change involved giving up a personal basis accepted by each individual member of the Movement.

To understand all that was involved it is necessary to recall that at the Matlock summer conference, 1902, the Movement had decided that every voting member of a college Christian Union must accept the basis then adopted : " I desire in joining this Union to declare my faith in Jesus Christ as my Saviour, my Lord and my God." The Committee hoped that within a student generation its decision would be accepted by every affiliated Christian Union.

In 1906 the situation was reviewed by the senior advisory committee, which advised the General Committee to make an inquiry as to the position of every affiliated union in relation to the basis ; and to follow this with an attempt to secure the adoption of the basis by colleges still without it. This committee recommended that in the case of colleges " which might in the future break affiliation on account of the basis, it was inadvisable to stop the visits of travelling secretaries, and forbid such colleges to send delegates to the conferences, as this would only result in their getting out of touch with the Movement and making reaffiliation more difficult."

A sub-committee of the General Committee, consisting of S. K. Datta, T. Tatlow and Miss Una M.

Saunders, approved of the advice of the senior advisory committee, but added that Dr Datta dissented from the view that colleges affiliated prior to 1901 should be pressed to take the basis. This was significant. Dr Datta was a graduate of Edinburgh University, and knew that Scottish sentiment had always been strongly opposed to a personal basis. The previous year the Women's Christian Union at St Andrews University had adopted the basis by the casting vote of the President, but after a year's trial had abandoned it. The Rev. John Kelman, whose student services at Edinburgh University were the most largely attended in the United Kingdom, was strongly averse to a personal basis and so was Dr Hugh Barbour, a distinguished member of the Faculty of Medicine in Edinburgh University, a friend of Professor Henry Drummond, and a man who had been for over twenty years in personal touch with the Edinburgh University Christian Union, and was then its president.

A little later the basis was considered by the Christian Union at Aberdeen University and a long correspondence ensued between its representative, John Stewart (how well we all loved " the people's John " !) and the general secretary, but the basis was not adopted.

There were signs that the basis was regarded as a difficulty in different parts of England. Armstrong College, Newcastle, adopted an associate membership for those who did not accept the basis, but did not, in practice, differentiate between members and associate members. Manchester University had an associate membership, about which it was increasingly uneasy, finding that some of the most effective Christian men in college became associate members to avoid accepting the basis, while in Cardiff there was a heresy hunt in relation to the basis and the attitude of one of the leaders of the Christian Union to it.

All this was closely connected with the fact that the Movement was rapidly strengthening its position in the modern universities and university colleges in England.

The Christian Unions had passed from the stage of being small groups of people who came from Christian homes, and associated themselves with the Christian Union with a view to finding fellowship and sustaining faith in the midst of student life which they did not expect to influence to any great extent. The constant emphasis on evangelistic work had borne fruit. Men and women, who had come to college uncommitted to the Christian life, were being reached, and, under the influence of the Movement, were coming to have some real religion of their own. These, however, were uninstructed in the Faith, and each year almost every Christian Union found itself in contact with more and more students who had doubts and difficulties to be dealt with. The thing had been coming for some years, but it came in full tide between 1908 and 1912.

They were rather breathless days for leaders whose age was just under, or just over, twenty years. The rapid expansion of the Movement's work as a whole, leading out from the Commission of 1908, the coming into the unions of considerable numbers of students with no previous training in Christian doctrine (it should be remembered that most of the early leaders of the Movement had had a tremendous grinding in the old evangelical theology: they knew their Bibles and a great deal of Christian doctrine), and the rather considerable unsettlement in theology in the country at large with much talk of the new theology, restatement in theology, etc., laid a considerable burden upon the committee and secretaries of the Movement, of the weight of which they were very conscious.

The Executive was nervous about the attitude, in many places, to the basis, and this nervousness is reflected in the report of a " Commission on the Basis of the Student Christian Movement," which was appointed in September 1910. The members were: Kenneth E. Kirk, chairman; MacEwan S. Lawson, Oliver Thomas, R. P. Wilder, T. Tatlow, Ruth Rouse and Winifred Sedgwick. The term of reference was: " To consider the basis of the Student Christian Movement both in its wording and in its application." The first question which the Commission considered was whether the Movement should have a personal basis of membership. It reported : " We are of opinion that every body such as the Student Movement in which the control is in the hands of its members, must have a definite membership. . . . The actual control of the Movement is vested in the ordinary members who have the right of election of the Executive. . . . It becomes perfectly obvious that the membership of the Movement must be a definite thing. . . . It is evident that on ordinary constitutional grounds the Student Movement must have a basis of membership, and this basis must be applied personally."

The second question considered was : " What should be the qualifications for membership of the Student Movement ? " This was discussed at great length, and the reply the report gives is by no means simple and direct in its line of thought. First arose the question : " Are we to regard the Student Movement as a body of men with a definite message to give to their fellow-students, which message is concentrated in the Gospel of Christ, or as a body of seekers, either looking for the foundation of true religion, or examining the Christian position in the hope that they may find it to be the satisfactory one ? " The answer is : " We have always regarded ourselves as having something definite to offer, as being called to evangelize and not simply to seek." There is an admission, however, that while this was the intention of the original founders, the policy of other Student Movements and the wish of most of the colleges, there were exceptions at the present time, and that some who were members of the Movement were concerned with seeking. The Commission thought, however, that the seekers were provided for by the fact that it had always been the policy of the Movement to throw open its activities to all students, non-members as well as members.

There is a reference to the fact that the Scottish
colleges found difficulty in accepting " so definite a
basis," but, they add : " This is due mainly to the fact
that the Scotch would have difficulty in giving individual
assent to any basis whatever, however mild."

The commissioners then adopt a different line, and
proceed to say that there is " a large section of the
student community which objects to anything of a
theological or credal character for their basis ; they
wish the basis to express an attitude and not a belief."
This is related to early days, since when a basis was first
adopted " it was stated that it was not a theological
statement but an expression of faith." " But people see
differently now and are inclined to think that an expression of faith is invariably bound up with a theological
position." The inevitability of this position having been
argued, the report then goes on to say :

> It is often the case that a man's power of expression or
> articulation is so slight that he cannot state in theological
> terms what his attitude is, and it is therefore necessary that
> the basis of membership should not be too theological, for
> otherwise it would exclude those who are genuinely con-
> verted, but have not sufficiently thought out their position
> to enable them to subscribe to it.

This section of the report, which is a long one, is
concluded by a paragraph which, though intended as a
summary of the position of the Commission, was hardly
a summary of all it had discussed :

> This commission agrees that the Student Christian Move-
> ment has a definite Gospel, the central point of that Gospel
> being that God was Incarnate in Jesus Christ His only Son
> our Lord; and that for our evangelization work to be a
> success, or indeed to continue at all, it is necessary that the
> basis of membership of the Student Christian Movement
> should be such as definitely to assert this faith in the
> Incarnation.

The report then proceeds to discuss what should be
the wording of the basis. Having agreed that the
present wording was not entirely satisfactory, it said

that " the question of expediency comes in here very strongly." If the basis were to be altered, or even publicly discussed, it would be thought in many quarters that the Movement was vacillating in its standpoint ; that many of the colleges would be " extremely surprised and disturbed " ; and that in any case it was doubtful whether a more satisfactory formula could be found. To these considerations the Commission added this paragraph :

It is also true that if a basis discussion is aroused, men's minds, whilst they will certainly be led to do some valuable and necessary theological thinking, will be turned away from their personal relation to Christ, and consequently all our evangelical and missionary activities will be retarded. We should meet with an unfruitful period, during which our central belief would be in the melting-pot, and consequently our wills would lack stability. The question has also a side wider even than that of its effect on British colleges. We have a large and important duty towards foreign Student Movements, and in the case of almost all of them the basis has for some time been a point of discussion and debate. The Dutch Movement has just come out of a basis discussion. Denmark is in the midst of one. France is strengthening its application of the basis. Switzerland is reviving its basis (largely as a result of the presence of English delegates at their conference). Japan is very shaky on this point, and even America is troubled with its basis problem.

This report was issued to the committee and discussed at its meeting at Christmas 1910 ; a variety of points of view was revealed, and three groups were invited to prepare memoranda explaining their position. There was a good deal of tension, rather more than we were accustomed to in the Movement ; some thought that their orthodoxy was unfairly suspected, but there was no breach of fellowship, and the discussion was a perfectly friendly one.

One group asked to prepare a document consisted of E. Murray Page, William Paton, C. Kingsley Williams and MacEwan S. Lawson. These met in February 1911 and produced a memorandum of great interest. It examined the situation in the colleges, and laid bare the fact that the Commission had not adequately faced the difficulties of the Movement in relation to the basis. After speaking of the increased interest in theology which had marked the last few years and left its impression upon the colleges, as well as the theological unrest in many parts of the college field, the group declared that there was a situation which must be dealt with, and that it was " no time for a wise passiveness." They urged that what was of real importance was to keep in view the standpoint of the freshman.

> The whole point of this memorandum is to insist emphatically on the wide difference in theological outlook that sunders the ordinary man, who is asked to sign the basis in his first year, from those who at present constitute the General Committee, which is called to legislate or suggest legislation in this matter for him. Our plea is for the little child—the little child at any rate who is just beginning his theological thinking ; who has, it may be, accepted in simple uninquiring thoughtfulness the theology of his Church and home only to find himself plunged in his first year into the tossing currents of modern thought.

They spoke of the approach of some as being Johannine, and others as Pauline, but urged that very frequently the approach of many students was almost altogether untheological. " They know that Christ makes all the difference ; that He alone is worthy of their allegiance—an allegiance which it would be absurd to share with another ; they find God in Christ as they find Him nowhere else." The discovery stimulates them not only to a great devotion, but to keen theological labour, and " when the vastness of the modern intellectual problem dawns on them they find themselves, theologically, at sea."

The group went on to analyse the position of those they were thinking of at considerable length, reiterating again and again that the students they had in mind were aware of a relation to Christ, and knew this meant everything in their lives, but, they said, it is one thing to know a person and another thing to have a theory of personality, and of knowledge, and of their relation.

The memorandum spoke of their agreement with the point of view that the Movement must have a basis of membership applied personally. " The idea that a basis can be enshrined in the archives of the Movement in Chancery Lane and held in trust by the Executive (or, perhaps, by the General Secretary, as the only element of permanence in a vanishing world !) does not commend itself to our further reflection." They agreed that the Movement was called to evangelize and not merely to seek, but at this point showed some of the confusion of mind as to what should be done, which the Basis Commission had shown. They turned again to a diagnosis of the situation in the colleges, and went on to claim that the original promoters of the basis had insisted that it was not to be taken theologically, and were consequently kindred spirits with themselves. They agreed that the Commission was right in thinking that the promoters of the basis were wrong in the supposition that it was not theological. " It certainly is theological—very theological ; that is precisely our main count against it." They felt that the interpretation of the basis by the Commission had enhanced the difficulty of the situation because of the Commission's insistence " on belief in the Incarnation as a necessary element present explicitly in the consciousness of the regenerate man." They urged that this was not true of all who were living in an attitude of faith towards Christ. They affirmed, however, lest they should be misunderstood, that they themselves believed " that faith in the uniqueness and absoluteness of the revelation of God in Christ is of the *esse* of Christianity. But in our experience the interpretation put by the Commission upon that uniqueness is often reached only after many years of theological thought."

The memorandum then proceeded to a long examination of the group's objections to the basis as worded.

They criticized it as being uncatholic to state absolutely and without qualification " Jesus Christ is my God," with no reference to God the Father.   They thought it contained too mature a Christology for the freshman ; that it was more an intellectual test than a statement of faith, and that if it was to be regarded primarily as a test of orthodoxy, it should be remembered that no test of orthodoxy was likely to be more than partially successful in the unusual circumstances that are normal in Christian Unions.

> The difficulty is this : a man comes from a pious home ; he has accepted, a little listlessly perhaps, the creed of his fathers ; and he thinks that the doctrine of the Incarnation and its expression in the Basis of the S.C.M. is a correct representation of his attitude to Christ.   He signs it.   Next year the trouble begins ; he may be wrong in thinking that it is very theological ; but he does think so : he may be wrong in thinking at a later stage in his thought that it is theologically unsound ; but he does think so.   And yet as long as he is in sympathy with the aims of the Movement, as he may very well be all through this period, he will not and should not resign.   And so it comes about that in spite of all your tests there are men in the government of the Christian Unions who are at least dissatisfied with the Basis.

After examining what should be the nature of the ideal basis, they suggested for the Movement's consideration the following : " I desire in joining this Union to surrender my life to God through Jesus Christ my Lord and Saviour."

The group closed the document with a few pungent paragraphs on the question of expediency as referred to by the Commission : " We confess to a feeling of something like horror at some of the arguments from expediency which the Commission has put forward."   They wound up by saying that our Movement has a duty to Movements in the Federation : " to show them that evangelistic fervour is not the same as timid orthodoxy, and that a converted man need not wear his head in a theological sack."

The first result of this memorandum was to bring Neville Talbot, a member of the General Committee, into the field with the memorandum he had promised. He writes from Balliol College that he must get something written, although " I have been living like a cork in a cataract."

He begins by stating his position under three headings : First, that he wants the Movement as a whole to stand for full Christianity, namely, the truth of the Incarnation and of the Trinity, adding that he himself has been " through a good many phases of Christianity which one may call less-than-full Christianity." Secondly, apologizing for his Oxonian manner, he expresses the greatest sympathy with inquiry by students :

> Old Plato was perfectly right when he said that young men when they learn things are like puppies who tear everything up. It is good for the puppies' teeth. Students, as students, ought to inquire, yes, and to find also, though many a man will find fully only in his post-student days. But he ought to inquire, for it is in *his* heart and mind that the Gospel is renewed and refashioned for his generation.

He notes that Christianity is now in process of being forged anew.

> But the forging won't take place in the old buffers, it will take place, if at all, in the minds of students as they realize that they are of the same generation. If it does not take place a jolly good revolt will come instead.

Talbot's third point is elaborated at some length as he points out how creeds both hold before a student full Christianity and also leave him free to inquire about it.

> For a creed is the profession of faith—the witness to the Truth—of the whole family. The family has been the family for a long time. It has had its creed for a long time. The younger son or daughter, when born into the family, finds it there. They find all the old buffers reciting it. Perhaps some old buffer will try to bash the younger son or daughter over the head with it. This may happen ; it has happened often enough. But it need not happen necessarily. The fact that it is there means that the younger son

is not responsible for it *qua* younger son. What he is responsible for is the effort to make it his own. He is free to do this if he will only use his freedom. The truth will not perish because of his doubts. But, by jingo, the witness to it will perish if he will not dare to inquire, for the old buffers will die, and what then?

I do not mean in the least to say that because a student finds the church's creed *there*, in the possession of the whole family, therefore that that creed as so expressed will go on descending through the generations with a sort of mechanical infallibility. No, the creed that the student finds already there, is the expression of the heart religion of his fathers, and it will die and become a mere obsolete formula unless he can find in it an expression of his heart religion.

I have no doubt at all that if student generations are faithful to this, their primary duty, details of the old historic expressions of faith will have to be altered. My contribution to this question is not that of cast-iron devotion to formulas, imperishable, unchanging, and as full of spikes as prickly pears; it is the contribution of the conviction that there is freedom for the student within the creed of the family of which he is the young, and *ex-hypothesi*, squeaking member.

He then goes on to express the desire that the Movement should hold before its members an expression of what full Christianity is, seeking their conversion but recognizing that the conversion of the whole man is often only brought about by contact with life, when student days are over. If we were not in such " an awful Church muddle," the holding the faith before the eyes of students ought to be done by the adult members of the body and the burden of it should not be thrown upon students. We need to shift some of this burden from students' shoulders to the shoulders of the Church. " I ask, therefore, can we not make Church membership a test of membership in the Student Movement? " Hitherto the Movement has had, as its practical theological basis, Bible-truth. At the beginning it had much affinity with this, the attitude of undenominationalism, but it has also shown that corporate membership in the Body of Christ is vitally connected with the individual's grasp upon Christian Truth and Life. We would make interdenominationalism more real and vital if our basis difficulties were used as " an opportunity for strengthening our dependence on the Church—I mean, for our purposes, the Churches."

Talbot saw objections himself to this proposal. " The Churches are far away from college horizons and student minds " ; and a Church membership requirement would not provide an expression of personal allegiance to our Lord, and therefore it would not concentrate and consolidate aggressive and striking forces, but he hoped that each Christian Union would be " a cylinder with definite enclosing walls getting up steam pressure." The Christian Unions must secure " that there is leaven inside the dough." And in spite of objections he put forward, as he said, tentatively, the suggestion that Church membership should become the qualification for full membership of the Movement.

These two memoranda were discussed by the General Committee of the Movement, April 1911. The members were puzzled : how were they to maintain a certain standard of orthodoxy without laying too heavy a theological burden upon the man whose views were in a state of solution ? This must be done so that " the Movement as a whole should not be asked to stand merely for the position which the man in solution was able to reach." Neville Talbot's suggestion of a Church membership basis raised the difficulty that if the Movement adopted this solution it would be called upon to provide a list of bodies which were to be regarded as Churches. It was felt that to attempt this would raise more difficulties than it would solve, while at the same time " it would not ensure personal allegiance to Jesus Christ," and would mean that " mere intellectual assenters " might be admitted to the Movement. No conclusion was arrived at at this meeting. Members agreed that they understood one another better than at Christmas and decided to postpone the matter until the autumn.

2 I

In the autumn they had no further light on the situation and decided to seek Dr Mott's help. Dr Mott discussed the matter at length with the committee and suggested that a group of senior friends should be invited to meet a group of members of the General Committee representing different points of view, to talk over their difficulties with regard to the basis and try to arrive at a solution of the problem. This suggestion was acted upon and the committee invited the following senior friends to meet them : the Bishop of Liverpool (Dr F. J. Chavasse), the Bishop of Winchester (Dr E. S. Talbot), the Rev. Professor James Hope Moulton, the Rev. Principal Adeney, the Rev. Professor H. R. Mackintosh and the Rev. A. B. Macaulay, together with MacEwan Lawson, William Paton, Kingsley Williams, J. R. S. Taylor, Neville Talbot and Tissington Tatlow. This combined group met on June 21st 1912. It was an extremely interesting meeting. The senior men were most of them strangers to one another, but they were all eminent men, known to each other by fame, and one of the features of the meeting was that the seniors were rather thrilled to meet one another !

All the memoranda hitherto prepared, together with a historical statement of the acts of the Movement in relation to its basis, had been sent in advance to the seniors, and when they arrived they had obviously studied carefully everything sent them. The meeting plunged very quickly into a frank, friendly and extremely interesting discussion. The result was the help for which the committee looked. The seniors were united in saying that a personal basis was advisable ; but they pointed out that it was unsatisfactory to have a single form of words which was used both to declare the theological position of the Movement, and also to be presented as a statement of personal faith to freshmen entering the Movement which they should be asked to accept. They advised that the Movement should formulate two statements, one indicating its theological position, and the other a basis of membership which should be an expression of personal faith which a Christian student could accept, even though he had not thought out his theological position.

The Movement already had an article in its Constitution entitled " Object," which ran :

> The aim of this Movement is to lead students in British universities and colleges to become disciples of Jesus Christ ; to unite them in seeking a fuller spiritual life ; to promote among them regular habits of prayer and Bible study : to keep before them the importance and urgency of the evangelization of the world, the Christian solution of social problems, and the permeation of public life with Christian ideals, and to enlist them in the whole-hearted service of these objects.

It was suggested that the first part of this statement should be altered to include a statement of the theological position of the Movement. The group suggested in addition an amended " basis of membership."

These proposals were submitted to the General Committee in September and the new principle of division was immediately approved. The wording proposed, however, by the seniors was the target of a great deal of criticism on the ground that there was very little difference in the wording suggested by them for the new " object " and the new " basis of membership." The General Committee broke up, recognizing that the seniors had given them the new principle for which they were looking, but deferred decision as to the actual wording.

At the Christmas meeting the General Secretary proposed a form of words which was adopted as the Aim of the Movement as follows :

> Article II.—Aim and Basis.—The aim of this Movement is to lead students in British universities and colleges into full acceptance of the Christian Faith in God—Father, Son and Holy Spirit ; to promote among them regular habits of prayer and Bible study ; to keep before them the importance and urgency of the evangelization of the world, the Christian solution of social problems, and the permeation of public

life with Christian ideals ; and to lead them into the fellowship and service of the Christian Church. Any Christian
Union becoming affiliated shall incorporate in its Constitution the following clause : " The corporate activities of this
Christian Union shall be in harmony with the Aim of the
Student Christian Movement, which is to lead students,"
etc., as above.

This proposal having been adopted, the company
discussed at much greater length what should be the
wording of the basis of membership, and had far more
difficulty in arriving at a conclusion. Ultimately, the
following form of words was agreed upon unanimously :

Article III.—Declaration of membership.
" In joining this Union I declare my faith in God, through
Jesus Christ, to whom, as Saviour and Lord, I desire to
surrender my life." Any student in becoming a voting
member of an affiliated Christian Union, or in signing the
Declaration of the Student Volunteer Missionary Union,
shall be understood thereby to express this acceptance of
the above. Those theological colleges may be associated
which are recognized colleges of denominations whose principles are in harmony with the Aim of the Movement.

These two forms of words were submitted to the
seniors, who were unanimous and cordial in accepting them as being better than those they had
suggested.
It was decided to put these proposals before the annual
business meeting of the Movement to be held at the
second Swanwick Conference, July 1913. A preliminary
discussion, however, took place at the first conference
at Swanwick. No vote was taken, but it was apparent
that while the proposed aim was generally acceptable,
there was a good deal of opposition to the proposed
wording of the basis of membership. It was the word
" surrender " which the students did not like. A meeting of the General Committee was held when the
conference was over, and before the second began ;
as a result, it decided to advise the business meeting
to support an amendment proposed by Miss A. R.

Carmichael of Edinburgh University, and seconded by Miss E. Ross of Dublin University, as follows :

> That instead of the first three lines of Article III, the following words be inserted : " In joining this Union I declare my faith in God through Jesus Christ, whom as Saviour and Lord I desire to serve."

When the business meeting came on Monday, July 28th, it had before it a certain number of constitutional changes of a not very important character which it dealt with, and then proceeded to discuss the proposed aim and basis changes. The General Secretary was called upon to speak for the committee, and told the story of the difficulties with which it was trying to deal, the negotiations with senior friends, and the reasons why it put forward the particular form of words. He pointed out that the Movement's doctrinal position had never been, and was not now, in question, but it was not desirable that in order to safeguard its doctrinal position, freshmen should be forced to accept a statement which many of them did not fully understand, and therefore were not ready to accept. What was of vital importance was that its policy should be in harmony with the truth of the Christian Gospel, that at Christian Union meetings, in its literature, at its conferences, the teaching given should be full Christian teaching. This would be secured by the proposed " aim and basis " by which the nature of this teaching must be determined.

> " Further," said the General Secretary, " the Christian Church is round about the Movement, which is not a Church, but which draws its life from the Christian Church. To the objector, who would say that the declaration of membership does not contain a statement of the Godhead of Jesus *as a doctrine*, the committee would reply that this is perfectly true, that it is not intended to contain it, but that it does contain that attitude towards Jesus Christ out of which the belief in His Godhead, as a doctrine, springs. This is what we desire of those who join the Christian Unions— not that they should have arrived at full Christian maturity

before joining, but that they should have the right attitude towards Jesus Christ, and that they should be willing to place themselves in the hands of, and have a share in, a Movement which states it as its explicit aim to lead them ' into full acceptance of the Christian faith in God—Father, Son and Holy Spirit.'"

After the General Secretary's statement, a resolution was considered, proposed by W. W. Seton, University College, London, and seconded by Dr Tom Jays, St Thomas's Hospital, London : " That inasmuch as the new basis proposed by the committee does not adequately safeguard the doctrine of the Deity of our Lord, and on other grounds, the basis at present in use be maintained." After a long debate this amendment was put to the meeting and was lost by a large majority, only twenty-eight voting for it. The meeting had been in session for five hours and was then adjourned.

At the adjourned meetings on July 30th A. H. Wilkinson,[1] Manchester University, moved that the *status quo* be maintained for a year to give the colleges further time to consider the matter. The motion was seconded, but after a short discussion was lost by a large majority. The meeting then discussed the amendment, supported by the General Committee, and eventually the two articles of the Constitution under debate were put to it; a vote was taken by ballot, with the result that 364 members voted in favour of the proposals, 28 voted against, while a few abstained from voting.

The Movement now had an aim and basis (see p. 483) and also a declaration of membership—" In joining this Union I declare my faith in God through Jesus Christ, whom as Saviour and Lord I desire to serve."

[1] Afterwards Secretary of the British and Foreign Bible Society.

CHAPTER XXVII

A FEDERATION CONFERENCE: WINIFRED SEDGWICK AND TRAINING COLLEGES

I SAILED with my wife for the United States on April 13th 1913 to undertake a tour of visitation under the auspices of the Student Christian Movement (technically the Student Department of the Y.M.C.A.), the purpose of my visit being to see whether the theological colleges of the Episcopal Church could be brought into the Movement. I was to attend, at the end of my visit, the biennial meeting of the General Committee of the World's Student Christian Federation at Princeton.

Shortly after I arrived in America I attended, in the Hotel Astoria in New York, a joint meeting of the different committees working for the promotion of a World Conference on Faith and Order. The leaders asked advice as to how the same interest could be aroused in the Free Churches in England which had been shown by the Church of England. I pointed out that an influential deputation had visited the Church of England, been received by the two Archbishops and several diocesan bishops, and that it was at the instance of this deputation that a representative Archbishops' Committee had been appointed to keep in touch with the preparations for a world conference, and that if the same action were taken in relation to the Free Churches I had no doubt but that the results would be equally satisfactory. With true American promptitude the gathering decided then and there to send a deputation to England. They invited me to make plans for the visit and act as adviser while in England. This I agreed to do, and it was as a result of the link through my person between this deputation and the Free Churches, on the one hand, and the Church of England Committee, of which I was secretary, on the other, that it ultimately proved possible to bring together the representatives of the Church of England and the Free Churches in a joint conference at the Jerusalem Chamber, Westminster Abbey.   This meeting led to a representative commission of Anglicans and Nonconformists being appointed to consider questions of faith and order, which issued two reports under the title *Towards Christian Unity*,[1] which had the largest circulation of any of the numerous documents which have appeared in the last twenty years in connection with the movement for unity, and paved the way for the " Appeal to All Christian People," issued by the Lambeth Conference of 1920.

This is not the place to tell the story of the Faith and Order Movement, but its relevance to the Student Christian Movement is that my place in it kept the Movement in close touch with all that was happening in both the Anglican and Free Churches in relation to Christian unity, and this helped to keep alive in the Movement in the difficult post-war years the interest in Christian unity which was so marked a feature of the years before the war.

The General Committee of the Federation met at Princeton University for five days at the end of May.   The British representatives were : William Paton, T. Tatlow and Winifred Sedgwick.   The Student Christian Movement of Russia was admitted to the Federation at this meeting.   Another matter of interest was a change in the article of the Constitution containing the basis of the Federation.   Hitherto this had read " to lead students to become disciples of Jesus Christ as only Saviour and God."   President Ibuka, one of the Japanese delegates, had, however, seen the words used in the Constitution of our Movement and was very urgent that they should be substituted for the existing ones in the

[1] *Documents Bearing on the Problem of Christian Unity and Fellowship*, 1916-20, pp. 4-14.

THE OLD "ANNANDALE": S.C.M. HEADQUARTERS, 1912-1928

basis of the Federation.   They were : " To lead students to accept the Christian faith in God—Father, Son and Holy Spirit."   He urged that in some countries students had no conception of the Christian God, and that in view of this the phrase used as its basis by the Federation was inadequate.

While President Ibuka pressed this point, Baron Nicolai was extremely anxious that there should be a reference to the Bible in the basis of the Federation since his experience in Russia had shown him that there were large numbers of people claiming the name Christian who were ignorant of the Bible.   Accordingly the basis of the Federation was revised to read : " To lead students to accept the Christian faith in God—Father, Son and Holy Spirit, according to the Scriptures, and to live as true disciples of Jesus Christ."

This is, of course, not all that happened at the meeting.   An immense amount of work was done and the Federation was revealed as growing both extensively and intensively.   Its membership had increased to 156,071 students.

From Princeton we went to Lake Mohonk, from June 2nd to 8th, for the Federation Conference.   There were 320 delegates from 42 countries.   It was a great demonstration of the strength of the Federation.[1]   The Student Christian Movement of Great Britain and Ireland was represented by Constance Garside, Muriel Harris, Helena Lowenfeld, Philip Loyd,[2] R. G. Macdonald, Catherine Mackinnon, Hugh Martin, William Paton, R. L. Pelly, Ronald Rees, Winifred Sedgwick, Ida Southall, Amelia Stephens, T. Tatlow, Mrs Tatlow, Bolton Waller and Professor D. S. Cairns.

The delegation was not only large but strong in its personalities.   I think the delegate of whom we were proudest was Winifred Sedgwick, her strength, dignity and spiritual gifts made her one of the outstanding figures of the conference.

[1] See *Lake Mohonk Conference*, 1913, pp. 500.
[2] Afterwards Bishop of Nasik.

She served for eleven years as a Student Movement secretary. When she left the Movement her chief work was as warden of the first Y.W.C.A. Training Centre in London. Then came long illness and she died at the age of forty-two years in August 1922.

Winifred Sedgwick took a prominent place in the life of the Movement. Her able mind and devoted spirit fitted her for leadership. She was a good committee member, clear and definite in discussion, with a competent knowledge of theology and the Bible, and a firm hold on experimental religion. Sympathetic, tenacious and conciliatory, she could hold her own in any debate. Men and women both liked her and she always had something useful to contribute when consulted. She was one of the three or four ablest and most effective women leaders the Movement has had, and I think the best speaker of all its women secretaries and committee members.

Winifred was of medium height, slightly round-shouldered, and she held herself well. She had an oval face, what she often joked about as " my Wellington nose," large brown eyes and a head of wonderful golden brown hair. She was pleasing and interesting looking, but two things about her were beautiful—her voice and her hands. Both in speaking and singing her voice was rich and musical. It was not strong, but rather low-toned, with a lovely, satisfying quality. Her hands were beautifully shaped, very white, sensitive and restless.

One's first impression of Winifred was likely to be that she was making a mental analysis of you. She had an incisive, analytical mind and was not easily deflected by side issues, but went at once to the heart of the matter upon which her mind was at work. She was immensely interested in people, watched them, considered their motives, and tried to find the principles, good or bad, on which they lived. Some found her critical mind a barrier, but her love of people was deep and true, she had a wealth of kindliness and sympathy, and students in need sought her help in large numbers.[1]

In the early summer of 1903 the Student Movement invited her to become a travelling secretary, and this so exercised her mind that it included a bad spell of sleeplessness, which she used to say cost her a " First." Nevertheless, she had a first-class mind, and was the intellectual equal of the many students who, having won first-class honours at the university, joined the staff of the Movement.

After two years as travelling secretary, during which period she and Margaret Bretherton shared the oversight of the Movement's work in the women's colleges throughout the British Isles, she was sent by the World's Student Christian Federation first to Geneva to work as a pioneer among the foreign students in that university, then the most cosmopolitan in the world, and afterwards went to help to build up the Movement in the University of Moscow. In 1909 she returned to our Movement as evangelistic and general travelling secretary, which post she held for five years.

She was the first Student Movement secretary who made a special appeal to music students, and co-operated with the Art Students' Christian Union in bringing many of them into the Movement and in founding several branches of it in music colleges.

In all her work among these students she sought to bring them face to face with two facts. " We, as music students, are faced by two facts. The fact of our gift, and its demand upon our life. The fact of Christ, and His demand upon our life."

What she had to say about music never failed to appeal to many music students.

> There is the fact of our gift . . . the power of gathering up sound and making it *beauty*. More than that ; the power to perceive, draw out, express the hidden meaning, the thought, the idea behind the sound.
>
> The measure of the gift differs with each of us. Some of

---

[1] Cf. *The Student Movement*, vol. xxv. p. 26.

us have the power of making music in this way the vehicle of our own thoughts, ideas, emotions—of putting ourselves into it.   But for most of us our gift is rather the power of gathering up, passing on, and interpreting to others the meaning which those before us have put into music.   Ours is to interpret rather than to create.   But in whatever degree we possess it, this gift makes great demands upon our life.   For while it is a gift, we can only enter into full possession of it by patient, unremitting toil.   Toil which demands the best of our thought, our energy, our time.

She used to speak of the demands which music made upon personality, of the self-surrendering sympathy with the composer which almost comes to be absorption in his personality, and of the loneliness of the musician : " To acquire an insight into music we must be alone with it.   The life of the musician is almost inevitably one of isolation."

The fact of Christ she presented with equally direct simplicity.

Here is Christ, the Master of men, demanding that our whole life shall be spent in His service, reminding us that we are not our own.   Christ who demands the surrender of our personality to Himself, that by His Spirit He may express Himself through us to the world.   Christ who calls us to look on the realities of life, sin and death, righteousness and judgment, from His point of view.   Christ whose example was anything but a life of isolation.   Who, though unique and alone because of His great gifts which lifted Him beyond the comprehension and sympathy of other men, yet gave Himself to men, and sought to make His gifts a way into the hearts of men, not a barrier between Him and them.

Her conclusion was always an appeal to music students to " trust God with our art."   This would inevitably mean limitation.   The musician would refuse to yield himself to express in music any influence or thought which was not according to the will of God, but if there was consecration of the gift in the service of the giver, a full use would be made of the gift.

Although Winifred was an excellent speaker, expressing herself with simplicity and clarity, she always declared that she could express herself better through music than in any other way. She liked nothing better than combining music and talk. After playing Chopin, Bach, Grieg or Schubert, she would swing round on the piano seat and begin talking about the Cross, or inspiration, or faith or grace, and then quite abruptly would begin to play or sing again.

The one musician she would never play was Wagner, always declaring that he made her feel wicked. In singing she seldom attempted the interpretation of elaborate music. The simpler song always appealed to her most. Who ever heard it will forget her singing of:

Little lamb, who made thee?

or the songs with words from R. L. Stevenson's *A Child's Garden of Verses*.

I saw you toss the kites on high,
And blow the birds about the sky;
And all around I heard you pass,
Like ladies' skirts across the grass—
O wind, a-blowing all day long,
O wind, that sings so loud a song!

Sometimes she would sing an old ballad and then a rollicking Irish song. The committee's favourite was "The Fluter's Ball," in which everyone used to delight.

A new tune was always a joy to her, and when Dr Vaughan Williams wrote his tune *Sine Nomine* to the hymn

For all the Saints who from their labours rest,

she soon established it as a Student Movement favourite.
An older woman wrote after her death:

Winifred had not a big voice, its charm was in its quality. It was one of the most moving and satisfying voices I have ever heard. A friend writes of it as "her supreme gift through which she revealed her real self. I never heard singing just like Winifred's; so much went into it, the voice was lovely, a haunting voice, the only voice I ever heard which I can hear again at will simply by withdrawing from other sounds.   The charm of execution was its perfect simplicity, she took her hearers into her confidence and talked to us ; the choice of songs, and the union of her song—e.g. *Little Lamb*, or *The Wind*—with her inner self, were so perfect that her song was, as I have always felt, Winifred's true message.   All her friends must have memories of the inevitable long silence after she had sung, expressive not only of the delight she had offered to our senses, but of the uplift she had offered to our souls."

The friendship she gave to her friends was stimulating and bracing. She gave her friendship freely to both men and women. She hated sentimentality and detested being adored ; " I can't abide the calf love of some of these young women," she remarked more than once ; but she had all the qualities needed for friendship at its best—steadfastness, insight, candour, patience and tenderness. Perhaps her chief characteristic as a friend was to stimulate.   " I always feel as if I had had my head shampooed when I have seen Winifred Sedgwick," remarked one woman, in speaking of her. This gift never failed her, it was partly due to the quality of her mind, and partly to her vivid interest in everything about her.

She could write very well, but did not care for writing. Under pressure from the leaders of the Movement she produced a study text-book, *Christ the Teacher*. This was written for students in training colleges, and was later translated into Italian, but that with two or three articles in *The Student Movement* was all she ever wrote. She was constantly pressed to write, but her medium of expression was music, and she always felt she could not express herself satisfactorily in writing. Some of her friends put this down to the artistic temperament, while others used to admonish her for being desultory. Certainly when she came to the Student Movement headquarters full of the purpose of writing reports and bringing her correspondence up to date, it often ended in talk. No doubt we all tempted her. Who would not have desired to talk with one who, of all Student

Movement secretaries, probably had the best right to be described as a brilliant conversationalist?

When a day planned for writing was spent in talk she used to repent with much contrition. This happened often, and she wrote to me more than once about what her critics described as desultoriness. I cull a sentence from one letter.

> To me it is a huge comfort that God intends my perfection and does not adapt His standard to mine. It is the sternness of it which is good for a slack creature like me.

She probably tried harder to acquire method than most of us realized, but very likely it did not matter much, for as one of her friends said, " Winifred made people rather than did things."

A marked quality of Winifred was her daring and courage. Her work for the Federation in Geneva and Russia needed courage. In 1905 the Geneva student field was very different from what it is at present. Winifred reported that she believed about 400 women were attending lectures at the university. She wrote:

> The large majority are Russians, the larger proportion of whom are Jewesses. The Russian universities are closed entirely to Jews, so they are driven to seek their education elsewhere. Then there are Poles, Armenians and Germans, with a sprinkling of French and Americans. I have not yet found a Swiss woman student . . . it is the Slav that one sees everywhere, under one variety of type or another. By far the greater number of these women are very poor. They either have a room and take meals at restaurants, or at the club for Russian students, or live under worse conditions still, such as have earned for the Russian students as a class a bad reputation among the Swiss.

It was with these students she began to make friends, getting to know them one by one, and taking classes herself at the university to enable her to do so. Religious conditions were especially difficult, as the professors in the university were largely materialistic in outlook and tended to be propagandist as regards their views.

A few months after Winifred had been in Geneva she shared in an act of great courage. The Café Brasserie Handwerck, in Geneva, was a centre of demonstrations of an anti-Christian character. There were only sixteen Christian Union members in the university. Three of these, stirred by their sense of impotence and yet desirous to speak for Christ, sent out an invitation to the university to come on a given night to the café and hear them speak on *Our Faith*. One-third of the university packed the café, and the three men and Winifred Sedgwick stated quite simply and directly what Jesus Christ meant to them. One who was present wrote : " You had to look at the audience to understand the courage it took." After they had spoken there was a brief interval and then discussion.

The storm they had awaited burst, man after man sent up his name to speak ; each rose with a smile of contempt, glorying in the opportunity of annihilating the Christians, and poured forth the fiercest, bitterest attacks on the speakers, on Christianity, and on Christ Himself. They were greeted with shouts of applause.

But the object aimed at was gained ; the cause of Christ was brought before the university, interested students were found, and more meetings for the discussion of religious subjects arranged. This work later grew into the important Foyer work which gave a lead to many countries.

When she went to Russia in 1908 her task was an even more difficult one. The Russian prisons were full of students suffering for their political opinions or acts, the police were specially afraid of the women students, and some of these were ruthless in the extreme, sticking at nothing, not even murder, to attain their ends.

In Moscow she made Bible study work her chief activity, reporting in a short time four study circles with about thirty members studying St Mark's Gospel. This work was begun in French, but she studied Russian, and before she left Moscow was beginning to use it in her personal intercourse with students.

When serious illness made her an invalid during the last three years of her life, it was her sense of humour which prevented her giving way to invalidism, as many people would have done years before she even admitted she was ill.

On a committee she saw the funny side of things, while never failing to take her full share in its work. A sense of humour and a love of truth are invariably linked, and it was her love of truth that was the outstanding trait in her character. It was because she loved truth that she loved God. While her knowledge of theology was considerable, for she had read widely and to good purpose, her chief interest was in experimental religion. Experimental religion did not mean to her primarily personal spiritual experiment. It meant the experience of the grace of God. She was always restless when people spoke of imitating Jesus and invariably burst out in protest : " Christianity is more than that. It is not what we do, but God in Christ doing for us and with us what we could never do of ourselves." The great catholic words faith, grace, atonement, redemption were full of content for her, and she loved to use them and to explore their meaning.

One naturally passes from Winifred Sedgwick to training colleges, for she gave much thought to them and to their students.

The influence of the Student Christian Movement in the colleges for the training of elementary school teachers had been considerable, but it is not at all easy to describe. There is no class of college where improvement in the quality of staff, teaching and students is more obvious during the last quarter of a century. The Student Movement is by no means the only cause of this improvement, but it has been an important factor. The opportunity it has given to elementary training college students to share in its conferences, councils and committees with students of all kinds, the large number of teachers in training colleges who have received their first training in leadership as officers of university Student Christian Movement branches, and the close attention given by the training college committee of the Movement (on which many well-known educationalists have served) to the improvement of its work in training colleges, have all been important factors in the improvement of these colleges throughout the British Isles.

Although there had been Christian Unions among training college students for more than ten years, it was not until 1907 that the Movement began to give its serious attention to the needs of those training to be teachers in elementary schools. There were at this time sixty-four training colleges in England and Wales, with 8330 students.

The members of committee and secretaries of the Movement were all university men and women, ignorant of training colleges and their students, but with a desire to include all students in the Movement. Applications from individuals or groups in a number of these colleges had led to the formation of Christian Unions. These were visited by the travelling secretaries, who promoted the kind of activities in them which they were accustomed to in the universities, they also helped training college students to come to summer conferences, which these did in considerable numbers.

The travelling secretaries were often baffled and distressed by what they found in the training colleges, and they knew that the Movement was not giving the kind of help they needed.

The first step towards help for these students was the circulation of a memorandum on training colleges prepared by Miss Dorothea Warner, a student at the Froebel Educational Institute. Two years later training college students present at the Baslow summer conference passed a series of resolutions asking the Executive of the Movement to develop its work in training colleges and to appoint a normal training college sub-committee. This sub-committee was appointed in

the autumn and began both the education of the leadership of the Movement on the subject of training colleges
and a study of what the Movement could do to help
students in them. It arranged for the preparation of
several study text-books on Bible and social subjects,
suitable for use in training colleges. It gave advice
about general meetings, summer conference delegations
and how to choose the right kind of people as officers
and committee members of Christian Unions in the
training colleges. This work led to the preparation
of a memorandum on the policy of the Student Movement in training colleges in May 1912, signed by several
members of the General Committee, secretaries and some
members of the teaching staff in training colleges.

In March 1914 a group met to prepare the first conference of students from training colleges. This group
of twenty persons consisted of Student Movement
secretaries, teachers in training colleges, a care committee worker, an elementary school teacher, and one
of His Majesty's Inspectors of Schools.

This group discussed the ethics of the existing educational system, the status of teachers, their vocation,
belief and Bible study, relation to foreign missions, the
contribution of the Student Christian Movement to
training colleges and the contribution of these colleges
to the Movement.

The training colleges for preparing elementary school
teachers constituted in 1914 a large and growing number
of institutions. They varied considerably. " A typical
training college for teachers in elementary schools does
not exist," said the Board of Education. There were
three main groups in England and Wales : (1) The
residential denominational colleges, thirty belonging to
the Church of England, seven to the Church of Rome
and two to the Wesleyan Methodist Church. (2) Residential colleges on an undenominational basis, five
belonging to the British and Foreign School Society,
council colleges and day training colleges, but with
nearly all their students living in hostels. (3) Non-

residential undenominational colleges. These were either the training departments of the new universities or university colleges or council training colleges. There were some hostels in connection with the colleges in this group.

In Ireland the Church of Ireland had a training college in Dublin, and Marlborough Street Training College, " which," wrote a Student Movement secretary, " is like nothing on earth." It was remarkable for its method of dealing with the sectarian problem, and for its rigid system of supervision and discipline.

The Scottish training colleges, with one exception, were of unmanageable size—700 to 800 students—and a hostel system partially developed. " Routine, rule of thumb, fulfilling the time-table, passing your examinations, and putting in your two years of durance vile— these are the features of the large Scottish training colleges."

The students in all these colleges followed a two-year course, with the exception of a small minority of students reading for a degree. They came to college after a rather unideal education, with fewer opportunities of mental development than the university fresher, and less training in leadership or organization. They came, also, without much consciousness of a deliberate choice or acceptance of their life work ; usually circumstances have pointed to it and at sixteen they have had to decide. The time-table was crowded as an enormous amount of general education and professional training had to be crammed into their course. There was a strong corporate life in the residential colleges and the students tended to do everything *en masse*, this affecting their attendance at religious meetings as well as in other ways.

The Anglican colleges had chapel services with compulsory attendance, and gave a certain amount of religious instruction, though only a few provided lectures on the teaching of Scripture. In some there was considerable missionary interest, official arrangements being made for visitation by missionaries.

In the undenominational residential colleges there was a non-sectarian religious element, represented by morning prayers, the vitality of which depended on the taste of the Principal. As official religion was limited, the staff were often glad to help in an unofficial voluntary society such as the Christian Union. In the non-residential undenominational colleges any corporate religious life there was centred in the Christian Union.

In the early days of the Movement, little thought was given to this type of college as such, but as the social consciousness of the Movement became better informed, it began to dawn upon the secretaries that students in the training colleges were to have the education of the greater number of the children of the nation. This gave the elementary training college student a new importance in the eyes of the Movement, and it brought its leaders face to face with the vital problems of national education.

> It is evident that the ideals of the Movement—the hope of the redemption of society through a deeper and more rational faith, an increase of fellowship and service, and a wider vision of the Kingdom of God—are largely dependent for their realization on the work of education.[1]

The first conference for students from training colleges for elementary school teachers was held at Swanwick, parallel with the officers' conference. The addresses and discussions dealt with the preparation of training college students for teaching the Bible, how to help them to learn what the best biblical scholarship had to give, and how to guide them to study the Bible for inspiration and help in personal life. The relation of these colleges to missionary work, and to the social side of the teacher's work, and to the problems of society were also dealt with. The Rev. William Temple, Miss Winifred Mercier,[2] Miss Winifred Sedgwick, Miss Fairfield and Mr S. H. Wood[3] were the leaders of the conference, which

[1] *Training Colleges and the S.C.M.*, a memorandum written to guide the travelling secretaries.
[2] Afterwards Principal of Whitelands College.
[3] Afterwards of the Board of Education.

consisted of 150 men and women. The influence of the
Student Movement had already counted for far more
in the women's than in the men's training colleges of
the country, and there were more women than men at
the conference. This is probably due to several causes :
some of the best women in education are on the teaching
staffs of these colleges, the greater scope society offers
men than women has meant that the human material the
training colleges have had to deal with has been better
in the case of the women's than the men's colleges, and
more women than men want to teach, with the result
that there has always been a higher sense of vocation in
the women's than the men's colleges. For these reasons
the Movement has appealed more to the women's
than to the men's training colleges.

Meetings of the S.C.M. training college sub-committee became a regular feature of the Movement's life,
and a conference at Annandale for a week-end in the
spring of 1916 on " Christian Education and Citizenship "
was followed by one in Edinburgh in November on the
same subject. Interest in education became general
among the leaders of the Movement. Lorna Southwell [1]
reviewed the results of this work at the desire of the
Committee, in a pamphlet privately printed, to take the
place of the original memorandum prepared to guide
the secretaries as to the Movement's policy. The
policy of the Movement concentrated attention upon
improving the ethics of the educational system, raising
the status of the teacher in public estimation, developing
a sense of vocation in those to become teachers, dealing
with difficulties of belief, and specially with difficulties
about the Bible, and creating interest in citizenship and
in foreign missions.

The ethics of the elementary school system came in
for constant discussion—the problems of teachers who
know good methods but are hindered or forced to give
way by inspectors, education committees, head teachers ;

[1] Afterwards Headmistress of St George's School, Clarens,
Switzerland.

the stress laid on marks, prizes, places, showing off
in examinations, and minding-your-own-business ; the
general rule that each child works at the same task for
his own end and his own good, co-operation being forbidden and self-help the keynote, not service of others ;
and the classes of fifty and sixty which force teachers to
adopt methods which are unintelligent, short-sighted and
false to the principles of true education. The chief intellectual difficulties of the students were connected with
the Bible. These arose from general uncertainty as to
the validity and importance of various parts of the Bible,
and confusion as to the nature of inspiration. There
were difficulties over evolution, creation, miracles, Jonah,
the unjust steward, apocalyptic, etc. Most of the undenominational colleges provided no lectures on Scripture, and the lectures given in Church colleges seemed
seldom to appeal to the students. " From the point of
view of the future teacher, the subjects dealt with are
often both useless and boring."

The general religious difficulties were those raised
by rationalistic attacks on Christianity, the " defects in
the lives of Christians," and the " one gets so sickened
with the formality of religion in college." The most
advanced intellectual difficulties were those raised by
the study of psychology. This was usually a new subject to the students and raised questions about the validity
of religious experience, prayer, and the place of auto-
suggestion in religion, and sometimes produced a state
of mind which was a kind of scientific fatalism.

The Movement was fully convinced of the importance
of these colleges.

We hear a great deal of the unbelief of the working-
classes. Have any of us, has the Church, in the least realized
the necessity of giving all possible help to the teachers in
elementary schools ? In spite of the limiting conditions of
" religious education," an immense amount can be done
through existing channels ; and in particular it would seem
that the denominational training colleges should turn their
attention to the problem, and give the students a training

which would equip them more adequately for the work of laying the foundations of religious faith in this country.[1]

The Movement recognized the value of corporate religious life in the colleges when their foundations made this possible, and advised its travelling secretaries accordingly :

The training-college student being younger than the average student is often at a more transitional stage of life. He is passing from the stage of external rule and immaturity in religion to a greater freedom and sense of personal responsibility.   Hence some of the revolt against compulsory chapels and organized religion, and hence some of the hopefulness and the dangers of a spontaneous religion in the Christian Union.   It may tend to divide the college into sheep and goats, it may encourage people to be goodygoody, or emotional, or priggish ; these are real dangers. But with well-chosen leaders and the wise co-operation of the staff it may be the means of using the opportunity for development and growth in faith in a most practical way. In this way the Christian Union may also lead people to appreciate college chapel, and find it (as one student said) "a work of love, really, when you analyse it." [2]

We saw that most of the things we desired to see accomplished were not for the Christian Unions, such as giving students a satisfactory knowledge of the Christian faith and the Bible, or altering conditions in the elementary schools.   But we increased our contacts with others concerned, we constantly sought to interest university students in education reform, and we tried to do our own work better.   Text-books for Bible study in training colleges were published, notably *Christ the Teacher*, by Winifred Sedgwick, which was widely studied.   *The Day School Teacher and Foreign Missions* pointed to " what could be done in the schools by giving children a right attitude to other races, and awakening interest and enthusiasm for missionary work." The ordinary methods of study circles, visitation and meetings were used.

Nor was there failure to recognize the contribution of

[1] *Training Colleges and the S.C.M.*, p. 16.   [2] *Ibid.*, p. 18.

the training colleges to the whole Movement. " They brought valuable reinforcements to our body of ' senior friends ' in members of their staff."

The mere fact that the training colleges include students of a different type from the university colleges makes them of value to the Student Movement—not through an excess of broad-mindedness, or a desire to have every specimen in our museum, but because of the enrichment of fellowship which comes from this diversity and the wider power of service for the Kingdom of God.[1]

" The Training Colleges bring into the Movement a fresh body of experience in close touch with the life of the nation. ' The training colleges are the executors of your social service policy.' " [2]

The study of the training colleges at this time quickened the interest of the whole Movement in the problems of national education and it decided to revise and enlarge its training-college sub-committee and rename it " The Education Committee."

All this concern for education grew during the last two years of the World War and was a valuable factor in the life of the Movement. When the universities and colleges were filled to overflowing after the war much of this particular interest was lost in the tide of new problems.

[1] *Training Colleges and the S.C.M.*, p. 20.   [2] *Ibid.*, p. 20.

CHAPTER XXVIII

THE OUTBREAK OF THE WORLD WAR AND THE MOVEMENT

IT is a curious thing how blind people can be even when they are recognized leaders. In the years prior to 1914 we lived in a world where naval and military establishments were being continually strengthened and the element of competition in increasing armaments was growing more and more pronounced, yet hardly anyone in the Movement thought about the relation of all this to Christianity. In 1912 we had been startled by the possibility of war with Germany and exchanged messages with the German Student Movement, but that was an incident. The Officers' Training Corps flourished in the universities and we had our tents, with services of various kinds, in their Brigade Camps in the summer, taking all military preparations as inevitable. There were peace societies in existence, but none of us in the Student Movement knew anything about them, and whether the impression that they were run chiefly by cranks was true, or not, I do not know. The war took us by surprise, few of us had thought about the question of Christianity and war.

In 1914 the last summer conference at Swanwick was begun on July 23rd, and thus synchronized with the date of the ultimatum of the Austrian Government to Serbia which precipitated the World War. The weather was beautiful, the conference of 697 people very successful, and war was something which seemed utterly remote. None of the students or secretaries of the Movement paid any attention to the war clouds in Europe, only some senior friends at the conference shook their heads anxiously. I remember feeling surprised at their anxiety, and then putting the whole thing out of my mind. Within ten days, however, none of us were thinking of anything save war and what it was likely to mean.

When war was declared I was on holiday at Aldeburgh, Suffolk, with my family, and Dr T. R. Glover was staying with us. Long and anxious were the discussions which took place as we sat on the beach, looking out to the North Sea, and wondered what the war would mean. My holiday house soon became a busy office as letters poured in from secretaries, committee members, student and senior friends, announcing decisions and seeking information and advice. Fortunately Miss Gladys Bretherton, my secretary, was with us and we both got to work. I wrote a circular at once to the staff and committees, advising that " for the moment we should watch and pray." As it was vacation no immediate action was needed so far as work in the colleges was concerned. There was constant speculation on all hands as to how long the war would last, the general impression was that it would not last long. " It will be over in three months," said many people, but some heeded Lord Kitchener, who said that it would be a long war.

Soldiers appeared, guarding post offices and bridges in the quiet country. A moratorium was a novelty that we did not fully understand, but it made one feel very sober, and the banks withheld the gold which we needed for everyday use.

Before I left Aldeburgh I sent the following letter to a body of people, both inside and outside the Movement, to whom I had for long sent requests for prayer. It is, perhaps, of interest as being written after two weeks of war and the perusal of a flood of letters asking for advice:

Aldeburgh, Suffolk,
18th August 1914.

Dear Prayer Helpers,

My last letter to you was written before our summer conferences. We looked forward to them with great hopes, and we were not disappointed ; 1890 people came, and we had wonderful conferences ; a constant sense of the Presence of God throughout, inspiring addresses, and daily testimony to blessing upon individuals. Experienced people went about saying, "surely the Movement has never held better conferences than these "—and none of us wished to deny that they were right. The Federation meetings were good too—how we loved all the foreign delegates, including the Austrians and the Germans !

And now—No ! I am not going to write, " Its promise has all vanished." God was with us then and is with us still. Our British Movement is His work, so are the other Movements of the Federation.

And now—we have to do our work and bear our witness under conditions harder than we had expected. But we must go on. This awful tragedy is a not unnatural outcome of the national policies of our own and other nations. Until men refuse to put their ultimate trust in physical force, and let the law of love govern their relationships, sooner or later the hideous crime of war must occur. It is inconceivable that the path of peace should be through national preparation for war. Psychology and common-sense are against it as surely as are the laws of God. Surely now men will listen to the voice of God. Is not now the time to call men with renewed earnestness and hope to seek His will for national and international life ? Must we not together seek anew to take hold of the living God, that He may come to the world again in a new manifestation of His almighty grace and power. Will not men now be ready to hear Him say, " Look unto Me, and be ye saved, all the ends of the earth ? "

We are in the hands of the unchanging God. In the Student Movement throughout the world He has been working in a new way. May it not be that it has come to the Kingdom for such a time as this ? We have seen a vision, we have received a call. If the hour is dark there is all the more need that we should have faith and " Cling Heaven by the hems." Let us remember " Faith is always a going against appearances." Let him who has not seen the vision or heard the call turn back, but to those who have we say—" on." And to those who go on surely our Master will say, " According to your faith be it unto you."

Pray for the Executive and Officers of the British Move-ment that they may have faith, courage, and sound judg-ment at the present time.

Pray for the Continental Movements, especially for France, Belgium, Austria, Hungary, Germany and Serbia. Some of us know and love their leaders as well as our own ; men like Grauss (France), the two Nyegaards (Belgium), Phildius, Rose and King (Austria), Victor (Hungary), Niedermeyer, Mann, Le Seur, Miss Baart de la Faille (Germany), Lecco (Serbia). Pray that whatever comes we may be true to the call God has given our Federation to unite the students of the world to work for Him. Pray that we may all be prepared to make sacrifices. We shall lose a great deal of financial support, and although we have no debts we have no reserves. It will be a real struggle to keep our work going and we are not going to be able to do it without sacrifices on the part of those who give and those who receive. Together with your prayers for us all, combine financial help by gift or collection if you can.

If you feel moved to write and express your goodwill or offer advice I shall be glad. One of the great things about the Student Movement has always been that it is a society of friends, and we rejoice to have seen drawn into this fellowship many who have never been students, and others whose college days are long past. Let us stand together more than ever for the sake of one another, and for the sake of the Kingdom of God.

" The Lord of peace Himself give you peace always by all means."

I am,

Your fellow-servant,

T. TATLOW.

The Y.M.C.A., which had gained much experience in Territorial Army camps, started work at once in four hundred centres where troops were being trained, and appealed to us for workers. We found one hundred student workers in a few weeks, forerunners of many hundreds. When the Theological College Department Committee met it decided to write to the principals of all the theological colleges and ask that groups of students, working in relays, be allowed to give a month's service each during the winter; such permission was given in most colleges. The Movement's literature was appreciated by the large body of educated men in training, and there was much demand for it.   The S.C.M. men introduced it into the Y.M.C.A. huts.

It became clear that we could not wait for the usual committee meetings the last week in September, so on September 1st the Reference Committee met.   The chief question was : To what extent is the war likely to hit the Movement, especially financially ?   The war was regarded by us at this stage as an affair of the professional army and navy.   We did not know that within a few weeks it would absorb thousands of students and challenge the very existence of the universities and colleges.

We issued a letter to the Christian Unions, saying that the Movement's ideals " were never more needed by the world than in this hour when the falseness of the ideals which the nominally Christian nations have pursued stand revealed through this awful horror of a fratricidal war."   The letter offered a number of practical suggestions for the work of the Christian Unions, and asked for the support of all in sympathy, prayer and financial help of the Movement.   The committee decided, also, to abandon the autumn Executive Conference for all the committees and secretaries of the Movement, which was to have been held at Swanwick.

We lost at this time the valuable services of Miss Gladys Bretherton who, as my private secretary for seven years, had been in close contact with all that was happening in the Movement, and whose room was the haunt of a constant stream of secretaries and others wanting information or advice.   Miss Bretherton left us to become corresponding secretary of the World's Young Women's Christian Association.   Her departure was a great loss to me, the staff and the whole Movement.   She believed whole-heartedly in it, was very industrious and accurate, and brought a high degree of intelligence to her work.   In addition to the mass of work she shared with the general secretary, she paid special attention to the files and records of the Movement, and this history owes much to her.   She first began to collect material with a view to its being written.

By the time the committee assembled, S. R. Hepper and S. Harris, of the Annandale staff, had joined the King's Royal Rifles and 19th Hussars respectively. Harris was killed in action, happily Mr Hepper returned and is now the Movement's chief accountant. Cordy Wheeler (Keble College, Oxford), coming into office as travelling secretary in England, and J. Dudley Whyte, London secretary, received commissions in Kitchener's Army. W. G. F. Smith (St Aidan's College, Birkenhead) resigned his place on the Theological Department Committee on taking a commission, and the Rev. A. E. J. Rawlinson [1] (Christ Church, Oxford) was co-opted in his place. Gerald Smith was killed in action.

The committee decided it must retrench. Howard Partington's (Manchester University) appointment as intercollegiate secretary at Birmingham was cancelled, Dr S. K. Datta coming from India to serve the Movement was cabled to defer his visit, the post of S.V.M.U. travelling secretary was left vacant and has been vacant ever since. R. P. Wilder was given a year's leave of absence, on his own suggestion. Secretaries and clerks had offered a reduction in their salaries of over £800 to help to meet the committee's financial anxiety. It was an important offer and was accepted. The total budget of the Movement at this time was only about £5000. I had raised a guarantee fund of £2500 from friends of the Movement, to be drawn upon in case of need. The committee abandoned plans for a Bible school after Christmas, and preparations for a quadrennial missionary conference, January 1916, were suspended. It was not held until 1921. The issue of Scottish, Welsh, Irish and London editions of *The Student Movement*, with insets containing news and special articles for each group of colleges, was suspended and they have never been revived. The General Committee did these practical things, but its mood was troubled, and not the less that thousands of students were looking to it for guidance.

[1] Afterwards Archdeacon of Auckland.

The conscience of the nation was deeply stirred by the violation of the treaty protecting Belgium and by the ruthlessness of the German attack, and there were very few to whom the duty of Great Britain did not seem perfectly clear. But if it would have been wrong to refuse to do what we had covenanted by treaty to do, was war ever right? Very few of us had ever given any thought to the subject of war. After a long discussion the General Committee decided " to hold a retreat to seek from God further light on the whole subject of Christianity and war." But long before the gathering could assemble, which it did three months later, the Movement had to determine its policy in relation to the war.

It was a new experience for students to find themselves faced with responsibilities to the nation. The State needed them, indeed they had suddenly become among her most valuable members. Hundreds responded to the call to arms, content to leave the responsibility for that call to the State, hundreds more responded without a thought for themselves, but deeply perplexed as to the right or wrong of it all, while some stood questioning as to what they ought to do.

The Student Christian Movement was appealed to for guidance from all sides: " What does the Movement think about it?" In the Movement's leadership and its membership alike two views were held. The majority felt that the violation by Germany of the treaty which should have protected Belgium made it impossible for England to repudiate her treaty obligations and see Belgian liberties disregarded, her land and cities laid waste and her people put to the sword. Men volunteered in thousands, not from any desire to kill, but in response to the call to defend liberty, justice and honour, and it hardly seemed the time to choose to tell them that the noblest thing many had ever done was wrong.

The other view, held by a small minority, was that under no circumstances should a follower of Christ take part in war.

Discussion raged on such subjects as compromise, the use of force, the Christian morality of making treaties that might involve a country in war, the duty of an individual to the state of which he was a member. Most students had never thought about these subjects, the word pacifism was unknown to them. On the other hand, to refuse to respond to the call " Your king and country need you " seemed to most the evasion of a plain duty.

It was not long before this attitude towards the war, together with the call " Your king and country need you," brought to an end the early stage when we all felt the war was the affair of the professional army. Students began to troop to the recruiting stations. In the first two months of war thousands of students received commissions, for the Officers' Training Corps was strong in the universities and especially in Oxford, Cambridge and the Scottish universities. It was natural that O.T.C. men should volunteer at once, and that those not members should move more slowly.

Members of the Student Christian Movement in some universities went into the army at once almost to a man, everywhere the proportion of members joining was high. In Glasgow University of fifteen members of the Christian Union Committee only two remained when term started. Indeed, R. G. Macdonald, Scottish secretary, wrote that most plans for the winter's work " had been upset by the war owing to the vast numbers of men who have gone." In England there was a movement *en masse* into the army in many places. In Wales the students were slower to move. And in Ireland B. C. Waller, Irish secretary, said that " the war has depleted the men's colleges enormously." Returns from the colleges in November showed that about 60 per cent. of the students in the universities had volunteered, while in the case of members of the Student Movement the rate of volunteering was 10 per cent. higher than the rate for students generally.

The colleges, however, were by no means empty.

2 L

Boys from school continued to enter college all through the war in larger numbers than ever before, there were those who were near the end of their course whom the authorities were helping to finish quickly to free them for the army. In the new universities a large number of students were under age for the army or navy. Then there were the unfit, bodies of students kept to help in making munitions, 13,000 women students and 2000 foreign students.

When the war broke out there were 43,000 (30,000 men and 13,000 women) students in the field occupied by the Movement.

The students who were left in college discussed the war from morning until night, and many sought help in their thinking. Numerous groups were started to study two sets of outline studies which the Movement had ready when term commenced, *Christianity and War* and *The War and Missions*. *Papers for War Time*, a series of pamphlets produced by a group composed for the most part of past and present Student Movement members and senior friends, were recommended to the colleges. The series, which was started by papers by the Rev. William Temple, Professor D. S. Cairns, the Rev. A. H. Gray, Mr Edwyn Bevan and Mrs Luke Paget, was striking and effective and had a wide circulation.

The Movement's senior friends, the most trusted of them, seemed to have much less doubt about the duty of all to support the war than some of the leaders of the Movement. Professor Cairns wrote:

> I am convinced that the judgment of history will say that the immediate responsibility of the war did not rest upon our nation, that we had no alternative in duty and in honour but to stand by the weaker people that was being grievously wronged by her mighty neighbour.[1]

Mr Edwyn Bevan gauged the situation accurately when he wrote that "if we take the religious men of

[1] *The Student Movement*, article, "The Call of God to the Student Movement at this Hour," vol. xvii. p. 3.

the country as a whole, it would appear that, so far from checking the resolution to fight, it is just the religious men, generally speaking, who most compellingly have felt it as a duty." [1] Mr Bevan made it plain that he shared the common feeling of duty but felt uneasy about it as he thought about God.

The Student Movement was urged to become a recruiting agency by some and begged to turn itself into a pacifist society by others. It steadily refused to do either of these things. It stuck to its task in the colleges, and never departed from the attitude reflected in the first Editorial which appeared in *The Student Movement* after the outbreak of war.

Whatever our individual opinions may be upon the ethics of war, or whatever service we feel it right to offer to our country at this time, our obligation as Christians remains what it was before the war, and we must prepare ourselves by every means in our power to solve the problems which will be created by it for the Federation. The most important preparation is the preparation of our spirits. If the bond of national friendship between ourselves and the German, Austrian and Hungarian Student Movements is broken, let us remember that they are bound to us by more than one bond, and that the bond of fellowship in Christ transcends all others and remains unbroken. [2]

All through the course of the war the discussion between student soldiers and pacifists continued. When conscription came, the pacifists stood firm and went to prison. But there was never any breach in fellowship in the ranks of the Movement because of this divided view as to the right course of action. We had it out with one another with complete candour and the result was mutual respect. At the headquarters of the Movement men bid good-bye to one another with affection as one went to the front and the other went to prison, each knowing that the other was honestly trying to do what

[1] *The Student Movement*, art.: "The Idea of God in relation to War," vol. xvii. p. 25.
[2] *Ibid.*, Editorial, Oct. 1914, vol. xvii. p. 2.

he believed was right for him. When the war ended
and soldiers and pacifists alike returned to the service
of the Movement, neither group was favoured above
the other, each had tried to follow the path of duty.

When the seriousness of the war was realized, the
first question the Movement *qua* Movement had to face
was whether it should suspend its work or carry on.
Some, especially those past military age, said that
patriotism demanded that all should join the ranks or
become chaplains or Y.M.C.A. workers, for the Y.M.C.A.
had leaped into the forefront of the picture as the body
ready and able to provide comforts for the troops. But
some thought differently, like Professor D. S. Cairns,
who wrote on August 26th : " I am quite clear that
there should be no slackening but increase of energy
in the ordinary propaganda work. By all means the
Movement must be strengthened and not weakened
this winter. We have to think of the new world beyond
the wreck, and of the men who will have a hand in
shaping it." The question, however, was quickly
settled by the students who had gone into the army and
navy. Their view may be summed up by quoting one
Christian Union leader who, on receiving his commission,
wrote : " The Student Movement is fearfully important
now." The Movement was the embodiment of ideals
which, when they could be realized, would bring war to
an end for ever. So it came about that there were
thousands of men who found they loved the Movement
as they loved nothing else, and khaki-clad men and
letters on Y.M.C.A. training camp paper, and soon
letters in copying-ink pencil written from dug-outs
" somewhere in France " poured into Annandale with
scraps of personal news, requests for news of their
friends, subscriptions, and—without exception—the
command " keep the old Movement going until we
come back."

An immediate effect of the war was increased religious
earnestness in the colleges. One university had three
changes in the secretaryship of the Christian Union and

four changes of treasurer and numerous changes in other posts, all in the first term, and yet carried on its work effectively. In time of peace no Christian Union could have survived so much change without complete demoralization. Freshmen came to meetings in larger numbers than ever before. At Oxford and Cambridge Universities almost the entire body of freshmen attended the meetings planned for them. Prayer-meetings in men's and women's colleges were unusually well attended.

It was feared that absorption with the war would result in foreign missionary work being forgotten; this was not so at first and the number of students who became members of the Student Volunteer Missionary Union in the first term of the war was 112, as against 92 during the autumn term the previous year. Interest in the World's Student Christian Federation and our membership of it was deepened and extended. There was much solicitation for the work of the Movement in Europe, and widespread satisfaction that news was available early in November of the Movements in France, Germany, Austria, Hungary, Holland, Switzerland and Scandinavia, showing that they were carrying on their work vigorously and were " all anxious so to act now that the World's Student Christian Federation shall not be broken by the war."

At the time the war came our relation with the German Student Christian Movement was very friendly, they sent delegates regularly to our conferences and we to theirs. In 1914 there were Germans at Swanwick— we gave a prize to one at the sports " for his grin," he was a jolly-looking lad—and we had appointed delegates to their conference at Wernigerode, to be held in August. The idea of a European Council of the Federation had been proposed by Dr H. C. Rutgers; but Dr Mott, who was nervous about such a council, I think lest it became absorbed in European interests and detracted from the interest European Movements ought to take in the Federation as a whole, sought to limit its scope by suggesting to Rutgers that our Movement should not be represented in it. On learning this, I begged Rutgers to include us and he consulted the Germans. They were emphatic, and their general secretary wrote to him : " When we are going to talk about Student Movement questions in Europe, this I must say that more than any other thing it is of the greatest importance for our German Movement that England co-operates." [1]

The result of this was that we went to the Swanwick summer conference with exceptionally cordial feelings towards the German Student Movement men who wanted us.

The men's Movement in Germany had at this time four full-time secretaries, an annual budget of 60,000 marks, and a monthly circulation of its periodical of 7500 copies. A few weeks after the outbreak of war, Dr Niedermeyer, the German general secretary, sent me some literature through Dr Rutgers, who wrote :

> I hope you will answer Dr Niedermeyer. Especially in this terrible time of war we of the Student Christian Movement ought to show that, even when we fully approve the attitude of our country and believe that the war we are engaged in is a righteous and just one, that even then we can fully keep a Christian and friendly attitude towards our Christian brethren in the opposite nation. Now and in the coming year is the time that the real strength of the brotherhood of our World's Federation will be tested, and God forbid that a war will be able to ruin it.
>
> A few friendly words from the side of the British Movement may do a lot of good now.

I wrote the following letter :

Annandale,
Golders Green, N.W.
1st September 1914.

My dear Dr Niedermeyer,
I have just received from Dr Rutgers *The German White Book* which you have so kindly sent to me, and thank you most cordially for sending it. We are thinking much at this time of the Student Movements in each of the countries

[1] Quoted in letter of Dr Rutgers, July 4th 1914.

which are involved in the war. We can honestly say to one another that war is the enemy of the things which your Movement and our Movement care for most. We are involved in a struggle which is not of our making, and which we heartily wish had not come to pass. We have nothing but the friendliest feeling for you and your colleagues in the German Student Movement, and we shall pray, as we are convinced you will pray, that this war may speedily come to an end, and that we all may be free to give our strength to working together in the World's Student Christian Federation for the coming of the Kingdom of God.

It was a great pleasure to have several German delegates at our summer conference this year. We had looked forward to having our delegates at Wernigerode. I have heard nothing of course, but no doubt the conference was not held. With kindest regards,

Believe me,

Yours very sincerely,

TISSINGTON TATLOW.

The German reply was a letter in German; the translation of it as made in our office is as follows :

Berlin,
17th September 1914.

My dear Reverend Tatlow,

I received your letter of 1st September a few days ago.

I can well understand that you as a Christian look upon the fearful horrors of this war with the deepest emotion, as I also do. Our prayer, like that of thousands of German Christians, is that God may lessen these horrors.

Words fail me to describe the impression produced in Germany that we who were at perfect peace and sympathy with all people, suddenly saw ourselves in great danger through the mobilization of Russia and the invasion of East Prussia which threatened our homes and our work. Everyone in Germany who can bear arms now stands under the flag of our beloved and noble Kaiser. This has resulted in an enthusiasm such as has never been known, whose worth lies not in the numerical strength of those who have rallied to the flag, but in the knowledge that they are protecting the peaceful homes of Germany.

My position in this war is shown in the Revelation of

St John vi.   There is no German nor German Christian who is not ready to give his life blood and all his possessions for this just war.   Sixty per cent. of our members are already fighting.

God has at all times spoken most powerfully to the consciences and hearts of men through war, and at the end of all time, until the new Heaven and the New Earth appear, there will still be wars and rumours of wars.

Therefore, my dear brother, my first wish is not that God should at once give us peace (although we desire it), but that His justice should be made known and His Will be done.   In these times one can no longer hold to one's desires and wishes, but only to the Cross of Golgotha.   We will throw ourselves upon God's grace.

Dr Fries wrote me in his last letter : " how powerfully God is speaking to the peoples !   But what is to become of our Student World Movement ? "

The answer to that question I do not know.   Something different must come out of it.   How often have I been grieved to read in the organ of the French Union of the War of Revenge against Germany.   I have also read, not without anxiety, of the tendencies of the Slavophile articles in your most important paper.   For a long time something terrible has been in the air and now it has forced itself even into our Christian circle.   Therefore something very different must come out of it.

In the belief and in the love of Christ I, as a converted Christian, can overcome the power of hate and the coldness of contempt for your people which is filling the hearts of our people in the hour when England has betrayed the white race for the Mongolian, and I can stretch out to you the hand of brotherhood and beg you to pray with me : " Thy Will be done, O God ! "

With friendly Christian greeting,

Yours, etc.

GERHARD NIEDERMEYER.

This letter is written with the entire approval of the President of the Committee of Management of the D.C.S.V.,[1] Dr G. Michaelis.

Dr Rutgers came to England more than once during the war and brought us news about Germany.   On the

[1] Deutsche Christliche Studenten Vereinigung.

last occasion I sent him off early in the day from my house and about 9 p.m. was sitting before the fire—it was bitterly cold—when a ring came at the front door and a minute later I heard Dr Rutgers' voice in the hall, saying to my wife in calm tones, " Well ! here I am again." His ship had been torpedoed in the Channel, and he had been in an open boat for some hours. He was frozen. We wrapped him up before the fire and thawed him with hot drinks. Although the railway carried him back to London, all comforts such as heated trains and refreshment rooms afford were only memories. We often laugh at him still for the calm way in which he calculated how long it would take to get the boats out, and that it would give him time to go to the cabin and secure his suit-case. He lost nothing, not even his umbrella !

Herman Rutgers rendered valuable and courageous service during the war in keeping us in touch with student affairs in Germany and the Central Powers ; he was a reliable medium of communication. Sometimes he infuriated us by his defence of the German conduct of the war, but we learned later that he defended us to the Germans. In the end, his activities were too much for our Intelligence Department at the War Office and his visits to England were prohibited, but he always behaved as a gentleman and a Christian.

The war made the leaders of the Movement in the countries involved anxious to share experiences and to try to safeguard the future of the Federation. Miss Michi Kawai wrote from Japan : " I wonder what that band of Christian Union workers in Paris is doing now especially for the soldiers and for the country, and what sort of prayers the students of Great Britain are offering when they come together."

Baron Nicolay, the leader of the Movement in Russia, wrote of the strictness of the military censorship in St Petersburg, which forbade public advertisement of meetings, so that only Bible circles for members were possible. " What an ocean of hatred," he added,

" there will be among the nations for a long while to come, and what social misery and upheavals."

In Paris all the men members of the Movement had been called to the Army before the end of November, except one. Yet the women carried on the work and wrote constant letters to all their members in the trenches, not simply news but letters full of thought and spiritual help. They wrote to say that they read *The Student Movement* and saw there that the difficulties that we encountered were theirs. They told us of their fears for the Federation.

> We are very deeply troubled over the work of the Federation. To what extent can it continue its forward movement for the conquest of the world for the gospel ? . . . We should be very glad to know a little in detail what you are doing in England. Please say to the English students that we are thinking much of them, that we pray for them and that we ask them to pray for us.

The war had a remarkable effect in drawing out the loyalty to the Movement of all its parts. For example, the Christian Unions flooded us with news of their doings in a way we had never before experienced, and all through the war the " News from the Colleges " section of *The Student Movement* was exceptionally well supplied with news. The stream of letters already referred to as coming from student soldiers never ceased throughout the entire war.

In November the invitation to the conference on Christianity and War appeared in *The Student Movement* and described thus the purpose of the gathering :

> The call to action and to sacrifice is ringing in our ears, and the splendid response made by the colleges to the country's call for service indicates that for large numbers of men their immediate duty is clear, and we hope to do all we can as a Movement to help and support those who have joined the Army. This does not, however, alter the fact that all the while men's hearts and consciences are deeply touched by the War, and they do not cease to ask insistently—What does this great human catastrophe mean in the light of Christianity ?

The programme was planned with a limited number of speeches and considerable periods for conference and for prayer. And the following document was sent to all who applied for membership of the conference :—

Retreat on Christianity and the War

To all who are Coming

" If there is therefore any comfort in Christ, if any consolation of love, if any fellowship of the Spirit, if any tender mercies and compassions, fulfil ye my joy, that ye be of one mind : doing nothing through faction or through vainglory, but in lowliness of mind each esteeming other better than himself : not looking each of you on his own things, but each of you also on the things of others."

It must at least appear to us all that we meet at this retreat in circumstances which are in one sense different from any in which we have met before. We are in the midst of war, and this must give to our meeting together a sense of immediate and tragic urgency. Probably this urgency is not really any greater than that which surrounds a missionary conference or a social conference at any other time. War is in fact going on around us at all our meetings, but it is brought home to us now as it has probably never been brought home to us before.

There are things, also, which may easily tend to make this conference difficult. The processes of our minds have been hurried and our opinions hardened into decision by the pressing question of personal duty which has come to most at least of the men, and less directly also to the women, who are to meet together. Added to this a strange sense of impotence hangs over many of us. Our minds are still numb. In face of the tragic realities of the time we shrink involuntarily from the travail of thought. There is a temptation that we should keep near the surface, that we should argue on behalf of and defend our own convictions as far as they go, though we all admit that they end, most of them, in mists and darkness. We are surrounded by a strange tangle of influences. We hardly know how much our own will is behind what we believe or how much is reaction in one direction or another from what is going on around us.

This letter is being sent to you all to ask you most solemnly to come to this conference with spirits prepared and disciplined. We shall need to keep a constant watch over ourselves lest we sin against one another and shut our souls to the light. We meet not so much to seek light which shall show our own views to be right or wrong, though we hope we may find light; nor do we come that some of our own difficulties may be cleared away, though we hope that they may; but we meet to seek a revelation of the Will of God with reference to the service which He requires of us and of our generation. That Will may be revealed to us in clouds and darkness. His Will for us just now may be that we should realize our spiritual blindness, our incapacity and unworthiness to prepare the way of the Lord.

Therefore we meet together to watch and pray and to seek a clearer understanding of what God's Will for us is as individuals and as members of the World's Student Christian Federation, to find out how best we may witness to and hasten the coming of His Kingdom.

If evil is much at work just now, certainly God is also at work in the world. We come together to understand, if we may, what He is doing, and to hear what He will say to us. To reach, in the circumstances of our time, the openness of mind and singleness of heart to which alone the vision of God is given, will call for all the sincerity of prayer of which we are capable.

WILLIAM TEMPLE
TISSINGTON TATLOW.

About 120 men and women assembled at the Grand Hotel, Baslow, from January 4th to 8th 1915. William Temple was in the Chair and Canon Scott Holland opened our conference with an address on "Faith in God." The subjects (with introducers) which were on the programme for discussion were: "The Church and the Kingdom of God" (W. Temple), "The use of force," "The working out of Christianity in national and international life"—which Mr A. L. Smith, Senior Fellow of Balliol, introduced, "The claim of the nation and the Church on the individual" (Nathaniel Micklem), "The World's Student Christian Federation and the war," "The meaning of the Cross" (William Paton), "The war and foreign missions" (J. H. Oldham), "Practical considerations with refer-

ence to the future " (Mary Pelham), " A discussion
of the conditions of settlement " (J. St G. Heath), and
" The Divine purpose." Intercessions were led by the
Bishop of Winchester (Dr E. S. Talbot), Professor D. S.
Cairns, Malcolm Spencer, C. F. Angus, Edwyn Bevan,
Ronald Rees and Rena Carswell.

Some of our senior friends expressed the wish to
join us in conference and some were invited. They
all came readily, saying they needed help, that the
Student Movement " had created a new temper and a
new aspiration," and they wanted at this crisis to meet
in its atmosphere and share its fellowship. It was a
tribute which drew our hearts wonderfully to our
seniors.

In addition to the speakers already named there came
to the gathering the Bishop of Derby (Dr Abraham);
Cyril Bailey, Fellow of Balliol College, Oxford; Mrs
Cyril Bailey; Ernest Barker, Fellow of New College,
Oxford; H. F. Houlder; the Rev. A. E. Laurie, Rector
of Old St Paul's, Edinburgh; the Rev. S. D. Morris,
Wellington College Mission; W. Piercy, Lecturer at the
London School of Economics; the Rev. A. E. J.
Rawlinson; F. R. Salter, Fellow of Magdalene College,
Cambridge; the Rev. B. H. Streeter, Fellow of Queen's
College, Oxford; R. H. Soltau, Lecturer at Bristol
University; Dr H. H. Swinnerton, Lecturer at Univer-
sity College, Nottingham; Marcus Tod, Fellow of Oriel
College, Oxford; Miss Abernethy, Mistress at St
Leonard's School, St Andrews; Miss G. B. Ayre, Miss
G. E. Bretherton, Mrs Creighton, Miss Lucy Gardner,
Miss Dora Ivens, Lecturer at Girton College, Cambridge;
Miss Winifred Mercier, Vice-Principal, The Training
College, Leeds; Miss M. M. Mills, Miss Edith E.
Overton, the Hon. Mrs Talbot and Miss Irene Whit-
worth. Among the Student Movement secretaries and
students present were : W. H. Dyson, L. K. Elmhirst
Geoffrey Hoyland, L. S. Hunter, R. G. Macdonald,
Hugh Martin, A. Victor Murray, R. D. Whitehorn,
P. N. Whitley, Freda Barrie, Jean K. Borland, Zoë

Fairfield, Madge Lowenfeld, Grace M'Aulay (Mrs L. S. Hunter), Osythe M. Potts, Lettice M. Shann, Alice Smith, Lorna Southwell, A. Stephens, Edith W. Thornton and Nora Wynne.

" The discussion," wrote William Temple, " ranged over large fields, and there was much difference of opinion, but from the first there was perfect unity of spirit.   As regards the nature and function of the Church in relation both to the nations of the world and to the Kingdom of God, there was a good deal of perplexity ; but one thing stood out clearly—that the Church is a paradox, a combination of the heavenly and the earthly, a society of Divine origin and authority, yet consisting of men and women who are also members of the world and of their own nation.   Similarly, with regard to the use of force there remained a definite and honourable difference of opinion, though it seemed that it was but the slightest touch which inclined the balance this way or that. Certainly all were agreed, whether or not they were convinced, that war could never be lightly entered into by a nation, that taken as a whole it was ' the devil's work.' The great spiritual unity which the Federation had created was recognized as an illustration of what the Church of Christ must become for all its members." [1]

The message of the conference to the Movement was, however, in another direction. " It was in a new sense of personal responsibility, a new discovery of the meaning of the Cross, a new experience of the power of the Resurrection." Again, as at Matlock in 1909, the conference was a revelation of our sin. As at Matlock the Student Movement learnt that " We are the social problem," so at Baslow we learnt that " We are the war." It is what happens when some millions of people very much like ourselves live together in the world. The war is the issue of conflicting selfishness, and all our selfishness had gone to help to make it. It is the working out of our type of character.

It was not this of which our minds were full when we went to Baslow. German militarism seemed to most of us the real cause of the war. At Baslow we

[1] *The Student Movement*, vol. xvii. p. 95.

were taken a stage further than at Matlock. There we had been confronted chiefly with the Sermon on the Mount; at Baslow we were led to the Cross. The Cross was set before us as the revelation of what is God's nature and method. He is Love which will bear any wound and any insult. And yet this anguish over sin is the expression of His antagonism to it, He forgives only at unimaginable cost. Love, too, is His method which by its own sacrifice of itself wins back answering love. We too must take the sin and sorrow of the war and of international conflict into our own hearts, and the love which makes us so to take it will be able also to transmute it.

The message of Baslow was that the Cross and Resurrection of Christ reveal the nature of God and His method. That nature we can share; that method we can follow, and so become His instruments for conquering war. The conference did not answer all our questions or resolve all our difficulties, but it brought us " to a wonderfully vivid realization of the spirit in which we were to live, if we would play our part in healing the hurt of the world." It also closed the period of hesitation and perplexity as to the vocation of the Movement in time of war; after it we settled down to peg away at the work of the Movement during the duration of the World War.

CHAPTER XXIX

WAR TIME PROBLEMS AND FRESH ACTIVITY

THE second year of the war was the most trying
for students. There was a widespread feeling that
there ought not to be any men in the universities
and that it would do no harm if they were closed until
the war was over. We came to have a form of compulsion much less satisfactory than compulsion by the
State. Employers, dons, clergy, ministers and women
were all found taking a hand in amateur recruiting. On
the other hand, there was a large body of students in the
universities and colleges—over thirty thousand—half of
whom were men. The men were under age, unfit or
studying chemistry or engineering, such being retained
in college in considerable numbers in connection with
the production of munitions. There were many men in
the medical, training and theological colleges, and two
thousand foreign students. The women numbered
fifteen thousand.

Long before the summer of 1915 came, a decision had
to be reached as to whether or not the Swanwick conferences were to be continued. The decision was
determined by the attitude of Student Movement men
in the army. There were so many members of the
Movement in the army that Student Movement news
circulated in military circles with surprising rapidity.
The rumour went round that the General Committee
was thinking of abandoning Swanwick on account of
the war, and at once representations, by letter and by
men on leave who came to Annandale, were made in
very urgent terms, that Swanwick should be continued.

Many men said that if they could arrange their leave they would come to Swanwick, and, as a matter of fact, all through the war there were a number of men in khaki at the conferences.

The conferences were never more needed. Students were young, the senior men had gone and much help with local leadership had to devolve on Student Movement secretaries, none of whom have ever had to work harder than those who served the Movement during the war. The Movement would not have survived the cessation of its conferences. There was opposition to holding it from the heads of some of the theological colleges. The head of a Church of England theological college wrote : " I think that the existence of the summer camp this year, unless you invite recruiting sergeants to it, is a disgrace to Christianity," and the principal of a Free Church theological college wrote : " It does seem to me highly undesirable to say the least to assemble hundreds of young men of military age in holiday camp at Swanwick or anywhere else under present circumstances. For the credit of the Student Movement I wish the conference had been cancelled." But we got all the support we needed from senior friends, as the list of speakers shows.

The academic work of many students was being ruined at this time by the constant suggestion that the colleges were full of shirkers, and the authorities were troubled and anxious. I found myself consulted by all kinds of people ; students naturally asked for advice. The authorities wanted to know what the Germans were doing about keeping their universities open and about recruiting different classes of students, and came to me for information. The Archbishop of Canterbury sent for me several times, both to find out what was being thought in the colleges and to give me advice. Vice-chancellors and professors, torn between the desire to maintain their universities as effective, though for the time being limited, educational institutions, and to help to find every available man for the army, wrote

2 M

for information as to what was happening in other places.

It was obvious that some move must be made to try and get things on a better basis, so I wrote to Dr Michael Sadler, Vice-Chancellor of Leeds University :

Annandale,
Golders Green, London.
2nd June 1915.

My dear Sadler,

As I am possibly the only man in England whose work brings him into direct touch with every university and college in the British Isles, a good deal of information comes my way, and gives me a chance of co-ordinating impressions and making generalizations of a reasonably accurate character as to what is going on in the British student world, to say nothing of information coming from other countries, which keeps me in touch with what is happening in college circles in other countries.   At the present time I am getting a number of questions addressed to me, both by students and university professors, bearing upon the question of military service for students in this and other countries, and these questions have caused me to wonder whether there is any body of men in the British Isles giving attention to the best handling of the student class at the present time with an eye to the military needs of the hour and with an eye to preserving the universities, professional schools, and other institutions of higher learning in such a reasonable degree of efficiency as to enable them to continue an uninterrupted, even though it may be a diminished, contribution to the best life of the nation.

I do not think things are working out for the best at the present time.   We should have been much better off if we had had some form of compulsory service.   The voluntary system is all right for dealing with a situation on a small scale, but the scale had been too large and the voluntary system has really broken down, although it may be too late now to make any change.   I say the voluntary system has broken down, not because it has not produced large numbers of men.   In that sense it has done splendidly, but it has broken down because in actual fact we no longer really have a voluntary system.   With employers, professors, and many other persons in authority, bringing systematic pressure to bear upon those over whom they have authority to join the army or navy, we have got a form of compulsion of a much less satisfactory character than compulsion on the part of the State. There is no use in crying over spilt milk, but we have all got to do the best we can, first and foremost to bring the war to a victorious close, and then to see that we do not let irreparable harm, which can be avoided, come to any department of our national life.

Now what is the situation in the universities ? In the majority of them a large proportion of men have joined the army. They are the best men. In the case of some universities, probably far too many have joined. It would have really served the nation better in the long run if a smaller proportion of men had been taken for the army, and if they had been taken on some system which would not have resulted in the departure of all the best.

What is going to happen in the immediate future ? Are we still going on with a policy of drift ? Supposing the Government decides on some form of national service, it seems to me to be really important that educationists should be ready to make their voices heard, and to point out that we are none too keen on education as a nation ; that our system is full of defects as it is ; that university traditions take a long time to grow, and that any form of conscription which would clear out the rest of the men from the universities, and take every freshman next October who is over eighteen years of age, would be to do something which would be not of very great value to the military forces of the nation, but which would be a tremendously serious blow to the nation at a place where she is very weak—*i.e.* in the matter of the higher education of her sons.

If, on the other hand, we do not have any form of compulsion, I think the state of affairs on the whole will become worse. Steady pressure will be put on everyone to seek a commission or enlist, and the men who remain will be very poor material for the educationist through their uneasiness, and even misery, as a result partly of the fact that they are probably being constantly asked why they are not soldiers, and partly because they themselves suffer from a greater or less degree of bad conscience. Either we ought to take everybody, or else we ought to fix a proportion of its undergraduate members for a university to supply to the army, and when once the required proportion has been provided the remaining men in the university should be told to go on with their work in all good conscience, that for the time being to do so and thus prepare themselves for the future was the best service they could render to the State. Perhaps no one knows better than I do the miserable state of masses of students who have not volunteered for one reason or another, good, bad, or indifferent, and who are not hopelessly unfit medically.

You may tell me, of course, that work on this problem is going on behind the scenes, and that sooner or later the educationists of the country, in agreement with the Government, will issue some kind of statement. If, on the other hand, nothing is happening, cannot we make something happen ? Cannot we be wise before it is too late ?

We are in a much worse case than other belligerent countries. Take the case of Russia, for example ; no student in Russia, even at the present moment, is required to go on active military service until he has taken his degree. Men are being allowed to volunteer and a certain proportion have done so, but if the numbers become unduly large, I understand a stop would be put to it, the idea being that under no circumstances can the State afford to cease having a section of the best of her youth undergoing the training of a higher education.

In Germany the universities are all open, with the exception of three in Prussia, and, I understand, there are from twenty-five thousand to thirty thousand students still left in the German universities. I believe there are all kinds of exemptions made with a view to seeing that men are continuing their preparation in adequate numbers for leadership in all departments of German life. Also I am told that the conscription is of such a character as to ensure that German families are not wiped out—eldest sons and only sons are not taken. Also the religious interests of the nation are guarded. Theological students are not only exempt from conscription, but are not allowed to volunteer for the army unless they change their faculty. As long as they remain theological students they are ineligible.

I have less accurate information as regards France save that I know that most of the French universities are open. I have reports of Christian Union work going on in Bordeaux, Lyon, Marseilles, Montauban, Montpellier and Paris. I believe, though I cannot be absolutely certain, that the only French universities which are closed are Lille and Nancy. I think there is a real danger that when this war is over we may find that, through not having taken sufficient thought, we have allowed things to happen which are ruinous to the educational institutions of the nation. What are we to do about it ?

Ever yours sincerely,

TISSINGTON TATLOW.

The Vice-Chancellor replied at once :

The University,
Leeds,
5th June 1915.

My dear Tatlow,

Your important letter, dated 2nd June, has reached me this morning. In the midst of emergencies, I reply (as best I can) at once.

I have come to the conclusion that national service should now be imposed on all—not military service necessarily but some form of public service. The population should be classified and registered. Each case should then be dealt with (locally, but on lines laid down by the Government) on its merits. The right men could then be assigned to the right work, and the wise exceptions made.

I realize the enormous difficulty, but am sure it could be surmounted.

In the meantime, we here are dealing with each case individually. The medical students, the teachers in training, the chemists, the technologists, the agriculturists are all in different positions and need separate (and individual) consideration.

With regard to a committee or conference, it would be wise to have one if the Government institute national service—or if the Government plan, when disclosed, seems to fit imperfectly the needs of students. Until the Government policy is announced, I don't think a conference would end in more than talk.

Yours very sincerely,

MICHAEL SADLER.

Shortly afterwards correspondence ensued with others to whom he had showed my letter.

In the autumn there was public discussion about the medical students. No class of student went to the recruiting-stations with more alacrity than the medicals when the call for recruits was sounded by Lord Kitchener.

After some months the paucity of junior medical students—the senior men hurried to qualify and get into the army as doctors—began to cause anxiety. Sir Donald MacAlister, Principal of Glasgow University and President of the General Medical Council, called attention to the serious shortage of doctors—and to the threat to the future supply through so many medical students taking combatant commissions.

As a result of this medical students were advised to return to college, and the army authorities gave facilities for them to do so. But on returning to college many medicals complained that both professors and others told them they ought to be in khaki. Some could not stand this and returned to the army.

The matter was taken up by The Times,[1] and while disclaiming any intention of coming between a man and his conscience on the subject of his becoming a soldier, it stated a strong case for an adequate supply of medical students. The Times dealt with the shortage of doctors before the war, the serious increase of this shortage as a result of the war, and criticized the action of the War Office in that, having released medical students, it later issued a statement saying that while fourth and fifth year students should complete their course " it is not advisable to suggest that junior medical students should not accept combatant commissions." The result was that many enlisted, and many more were so torn by the uncertainty as to where duty lay that their medical studies were seriously interfered with.

Students retained in connection with munition making, agriculture, the large numbers under military age and the medically unfit, as well as the medicals, were sensitive to the bullying attitude of older people, who constantly talked at them about their duty, so that even those whose clear duty it was to be in college were rendered chronically uncomfortable.

We consulted a considerable number of the heads of universities and colleges about the position of students

[1] The Times Educational Supplement, September 7th, 1915.

in relation to the war, and asked their opinion about our policy of carrying on as long as there were students. The response was immediate and emphatic. They said the number of shirkers was negligible, and as for the Movement's work, it must go on. We took up the cudgels for the students in *The Student Movement*, analysed the situation, said that " People who have leisure to look for shirkers will find more scope for their energies elsewhere than in the college field," and declared :

> The best advice we can offer to those who are rightly in college is to try and settle down to their work, and to the preservation of all the good traditions and features of college life.[1]

As for the advice of the heads of colleges, it was given without a dissentient voice. The letter of one Vice-Chancellor, Sir Alfred Dale, of Liverpool University, may be quoted as typical, and Dale was a cautious man :

> Whatever may be the number of those who are left, I have no doubt that it is our duty to keep the Christian Union going. Two reasons have weight with me : (1) The needs of those who remain, which will be greater, not less, than in ordinary times. (2) The difficulty of starting again what it is comparatively easy to continue. We cannot afford to scrap what we have built up, or to break the tradition that has developed during the last few years.

The position of everyone was simplified when the Government introduced compulsory military service for all unmarried men under forty, and tribunals assumed responsibility for deciding whether men should go into the army or were more needed elsewhere.

Before the autumn brought this to pass and decided many questions, the summer saw us in conference at Swanwick. As the Movement did not expect more men to attend than one summer conference could provide for, it was decided to precede it with a Bible school

---

[1] *The Student Movement*, Editorial " Students and National Duty," vol. xviii. p. 2.

for women. Professor M'Fadyen lectured on the utterances of Isaiah of Jerusalem and Professor James Moffatt on the parables of the Gospel during the mornings, a period of study following. After tea came discussion circles, with three lectures by Dr W. B. Selbie, in the hour before dinner, on the nature and message of the Bible. The evening meetings dealt with revelation in its historical aspects, followed by two on personal religion, Dr P. Carnegie Simpson and Miss Sedgwick being the speakers. The school was guided by Leslie Hunter, the Bible study secretary, who had become a force in the leadership of the Movement. The school enriched the knowledge of God of those present, and it also convicted the members of much ignorance. It did much to awaken a desire for more thorough Bible study in the Movement, a desire which Leslie Hunter fostered with success.

At the general conference which followed, an interesting feature was the Continental students' conference carried on parallel with it. The fifty-four members were most of them students who had been driven out of the universities of Belgium and Northern France by the war—Belgians, Russians, Poles, Jews, Greeks, Italians, French, Czech, Galicians, Lithuanians and Swiss. Four of the students were technically alien enemies, a fact which caused much searching of heart to the local police, one of whom, never before having had to tackle the racial problems of Austria-Hungary, was overheard to say that for his part he hoped the war would soon be over!

For this Continental conference we secured M. de Rougemont, the General Secretary of the Swiss Student Movement, as chairman, and Professor Henri Bois of Montauban, a much-loved senior friend of the French Movement, as chief speaker. Most of this conference was in French, and most of the students were at least a-Christian, never having come into touch with vital Christianity before. They all entered with zest into the life of the conference. One recalls a picture of them grouped before the camera, singing their various national anthems simultaneously while British students helped them to be photographed by addressing to them such remarks as " *Regardez le* dicky-bird ! " and " *Etes vous* fed-up ? "

Including the Continental students, we totalled 798 persons with men in the majority.   The conference was sustained by hope.   The Federation meeting gave us a picture of the nations, with their varied gifts, uniting in Christ for the service of humanity.   France, Denmark, Norway, Holland, Switzerland, New Zealand, India and Russia were the countries represented by the speakers.   Hope, too, shone for us in an address by Dr Cairns on the Resurrection, and in another by the Bishop of Oxford (Dr Charles Gore) on the Redemption of Society, and a letter from Neville Talbot—its chairman the previous year—read to the conference was in tune with this message of hope.

3rd Bn. Rifle Brigade,
6th Division,
7th July 1915.

Dear T [2],

I write to you from " Wipers " with a great longing for your prayers.   I do this perhaps with a pardonable selfishness, for here we await the arrival of the phalanx, which, now or never, is to blast a way through us to Calais.   But I do so I think more eagerly because of my belief, of which I will not let go, that the decisive factors in this long agony are not only howitzers and high explosives, but spiritual weapons.   Right and wrong do not neatly coincide with the Allies and with the Germans, yet there is a great main spiritual issue between the two sides in this war of ideals. The Allies need the moral stamina and mutual loyalty to go on, until, through failure, the mind in which Germany has made war is changed.   How are minds changed— whence comes conversion ?   Not by might, nor by power, but by My Spirit, saith the Lord.   Pray then, knowing our own needs.   Pray like any set of Publicans.

Secondly, I write with a strong belief that the lessons learnt and the visions seen by the Student Movement are not obliterated by the war.   The phrase which best sums up the lessons and visions is the Kingdom of God—the sovereignty of the Living God—the reign of His love and faithful purpose, rooted in vital personal and inward religion and embracing all the world.

We come to a summer conference, each with a great desire for our own immediate and individual contact with God.   You will be meeting this year overshadowed by a great darkness.   Once more may God shine out of darkness and in each one of your hearts to give the light of the knowledge of Himself in the face of Jesus Christ.   Only, leap beyond the narrow circle of your own soul's needs and walk abroad in that light, for it is the light not only of God's love towards me, towards you and the next man, but the light of the faithful Will and purpose of God, which held on its way in our human flesh and blood and through suffering and death, to change the world.   Hold to the Cross of the Risen Christ not only as assuring to your own soul God's love and forgiveness, but as the banner of God's Kingdom which marches onward through all the press of human history.   Drink in eagerly this teaching, which, through the historical re-understanding of God's revelation to the Jews, of Christ's relation to the faith and expectation of Israel, of His teaching about the Kingdom and of His apocalyptic vision, throws into relief one thing— God at work in His world.   And pray that the Holy Spirit may take of the things of Christ—things of God's Fatherhood and our brotherhood—and show them to the divided and captive Church and to the nations which rage together.

God is working out His judgments in this His awful day. He recalls the world to the forgotten things of His Kingdom and Righteousness.

Ever yours,

NEVILLE S. TALBOT.

The S.C.M. was very active in the colleges during the first year of war.   The freshers' meetings in the autumn were well attended ; 500 women attended the London Freshers' meeting.   There was a packed audience when in the hall of Queen's College, Oxford, a joint freshman's meeting for men and women was held for the first time in that university, and Lorna Southwell and I expounded the S.C.M.

There were " an unprecedented number of Christian

Union committee retreats in Scotland," according to
Donald Grant.   At St Andrews University only four
women were absent from the opening S.C.M. meeting
of the term.   St David's College, Lampeter, with little
more than a hundred students, had seven study circles,
Bible, missionary and social, with 77 members.   In
Leeds University 106 women were Christian Union
members out of 168 students.

Ireland ran two Bible schools.   Bangor Training
College (Men) had twelve study circles, and Queen
Margaret College, Glasgow, fourteen prayer circles, with
from five to sixteen members in each, meeting weekly.
The annual meeting of the S.V.M.U. in Cambridge was
attended by 400 undergraduates—nearly half the university at this time.   Such are some of the doings of the
time culled at random from records from 1914-15.

The war not only stimulated activity in the Christian
Unions, but intensified the tides of questioning and
desire which always keep the student world in a state
of ferment.   If undergraduates seldom lack gaiety and
high spirits, neither do they often lack tremendous
seriousness.   There was not only no general relaxation
of intense preoccupation with great questions concerning
God and man and the world so long as the war lasted,
but during no period in the forty years of the Student
Christian Movement has there been an equal degree of
intensity in thought and action.

The reports, minutes and other documents of the
Movement all through the war are full of the subject of
students and the Church.   The Churches were the subject of incessant discussion and criticism.   It mattered not
whether students were Anglican, Presbyterian or Nonconformist, their criticisms were the same.   The Churches
had a deep hold upon the student class, almost all the
members of the Student Movement, and many who were
not, were Church members and a very large proportion
of them were Church workers, especially Sunday-school
teachers.   The criticism of the Churches began with
disappointment that they had nothing commanding to

say about the war and seemed content to second the demands of the State. Student opinion declared " that it is the business of the Church, at all costs, to uphold the ideal of the Kingdom of God, and they consider that the Church has put the major part of her strength into upholding national ideals." They were disappointed that " she did not make her influence felt as a powerful factor at the time among the nations." [1]

While the tendency in the Churches was to feel that they must encourage and hearten those who were doing their duty in a righteous cause, the tendency among students was to question this taking of sides by the Christian Church. Ought she not to remain above the battle ? Ought she not to be able to say to both sides, " Sirs, ye are brethren ? " Many clergy, ministers and theological professors in all the countries at war were foremost in expressions of hatred ; they seemed to many students eager to believe the worst of the enemy and readier than the soldiers to inflame feeling against the foe. There was little to choose between the Churches in Great Britain and in Germany, and the student class was deeply shocked.

Once the confidence of students in the Churches was shaken criticism of them grew ; a page of quotations of Christian Union reports embedded in the Annual Report of the Movement is typical of this period :

A few quotations will indicate the prevailing attitude in the colleges : " The Church is criticized most about the hollowness of its fellowship, and its failure in meeting the intellectual needs of its members, except in rare individual cases." " The clergy do not seem to be able to attract students and are more criticized than any other class." " The following are roughly the criticisms of Church life : (1) The unreality of Christianity and remoteness from life as exemplified in Church services, etc. (2) The conservatism of the Churches, who seem always to hang behind the nation instead of leading it, and the lack of essential Christianity in Church life, for example, love and unity. (3) Dissatisfaction with regard to the position of

[1] *Annual Report, S.C.M.*, 1914-15.

women in the Churches." " Most students seem very much alive to the shortcomings of their Church and are full of criticism. They complain of dullness, lack of real life; also of formalism and convention."

Another college summarizes students' criticisms as follows : " (1) Church services are so ' busy ' that there is no time in Church for silence and meditation. (2) The minister has so much to give, and of the student no contribution is asked. (3) There is lack of sympathy with the student's point of view. He finds no one ready to think with him. (4) The Christian Union seems to supplant the Church for some by its wideness of outlook, its democratic ideals, its insistence on spirituality and clear thought, and its ideal of fellowship. (5) The Church is afraid of missionary and social questions as they are, and offers no adequate explanation of the Christian attitude to war." These are quite representative quotations, and the startling thing about them is that it does not seem to occur to any of the writers that students should have any other attitude than that of criticism.[1]

On the other hand, the World's Student Christian Federation was a great bulwark for thousands of students, here and on the Continent, against the flood of hatred that was poured out in Europe. The bonds of affection and fellowship in the Federation were strong and made it easier for students than it was for many others to withstand this evil and keep their spirits free of hatred.

The missionary societies showed up as the finest groups the Churches possessed. Their leaders were cheerful and determined. They remembered the faith of their founders; for the London Missionary Society, the Baptist Missionary Society, the Church Missionary Society and the British and Foreign Bible Society had all been founded between 1792 and 1804, a period during which twenty years of desperate war was draining the resources of the country, so much so that at one point during this period the Bank of England suspended payment. Yet the missionaries went forth, and their supporters kept them going with funds. We took heart from the

[1] *Annual Report, S.C.M.*, 1917-18, p. 15.

missionary societies, and felt we too had something to say to our Student Volunteers.

The Annual Reports of the Movement during the war years are full of interesting descriptions of the effect of the war on the life and thought of the colleges. The first year of war produced the discussion of pacifism which has been referred to ; at the same time members of the Movement felt " the need for greater reality and sincerity in personal religion."

> This is producing much searching of heart and mental striving and also the need for a vital Gospel with regenerating power for individuals and for society, but chiefly for society. It is noticeable how eagerly students respond when anyone speaks to them of Christianity as a redeeming force in national and international life, and how they are being gripped by the idea that Christians must go out into life with what they have received as Christians, intending nothing less than to turn the world upside down. The hope of the redemption of society is becoming for many more than a mere phrase. Many students are thinking deeply of their responsibility as members of the Church and are longing for a renewal of the life of organized Christianity.[1]

Evangelistic work by way of college missions became impossible in the men's colleges, though some meetings, singly or in series, were held in the women's colleges, but the committee wrote :

> There has been an unusual amount of thoughtful inquiry concerning the central and essential things in Christianity . . . in committee meetings, retreats, study circles, and discussion groups the question of interpreting Christianity to the whole body of students in college has been seriously discussed. . . . Many Christain Unions have realized as never before that there are large numbers of students who do not know what Christianity is, either as a system of belief or as the experience of a new life, and a systematic attempt is being made in many colleges to help these.[2]

A feature of the war period was the amount and quality of the Bible study that was done throughout the Movement. This was due in no small measure to

[1] *Annual Report, S.C.M.*, 1915-16, p. 5.   [2] *Ibid.*, p. 7.

R. L. Pelly and, following him, L. S. Hunter, two first-
class men who served the Movement in turn as Bible
study secretaries. Dick Pelly set a new standard as to
the quality of the work that Bible circles ought to
attempt and Leslie Hunter developed Bible schools,
bringing to them as lecturers some of the ablest Biblical
scholars in the British Isles.

The turning of one of the summer conferences in 1915
into a Bible school has already been dealt with ; this
was not an isolated effort on behalf of more and better
Bible study; fresh Bible study text-books were published,
the training of circle leaders tackled more systematically,
the colleges more widely canvassed for study circle
members, and Bible schools extended to Wales, Ireland,
Scotland and London.

The Movement stated its policy about Bible study
again and again at this period ; two quotations will indicate what it was.

As to our policy. We are convinced as strongly as ever
of the value of Bible study and are concerned that the habit
of Bible reading should be so much in abeyance even among
religious people. Our aim is to make the Bible a living
book and a source of spiritual strength among our members.
But before it can be living, it must be familiar and intelligible, and to the majority of those coming up to the
colleges only very small portions are either familiar or
intelligible. Their knowledge about the Bible as a whole
is small, and they are unduly worried by doubts and minor
difficulties which ought to have been disposed of in the
Sunday school, the Bible class or the Scripture lesson in
the day school—but they have not.

Our policy is to give students every opportunity of
becoming familiar with the best Biblical scholarship, so that
they may be better qualified to understand the mind and
the message of the Biblical writers, to give them the right
point of view and to liberate them from the tyranny of
small difficulties, and to lead them to a deeper, wiser and
more devotional reading of Scripture. We seek to carry
this policy out through our publications, through study
circles which are urged to work in touch with competent
senior advisers, and by retreats for training circle leaders,

and Bible schools where we are fortunate in securing some of the best scholars in the country as lecturers. And we claim that this policy has been justified by its results. In colleges where it has been adopted there has been a new enthusiasm for Bible study, and what before was often formal and not very profitable has become living and real and has strengthened the religious life of the Christian Union as well as of the individual.[1]

In reporting to the Federation in 1917 the Movement wrote :

It is a well-worn remark to repeat that the chief difficulty in the way of making Bible study alive is a narrow view of the Bible and of the way in which reading it will influence the religious life. Perhaps that is only a clumsy way of saying that we have to combat a narrow view of God and of life and of the relation of God and life, which leads to an unreal distinction between the " sacred " and the " secular." And we are inclined to think that the best way to enlarge and deepen this limited view of the Bible is to bring students to feel the human element in the Bible . . . our aim in discussions and talks this year has been to get the members of Bible circles to realize that the Bible, like our Lord, touches the whole of life, and links it up with God. We need to find in it a revelation of human life and divine guidance : to enter into the mind of the prophet, the piety of the mystic, the doubt of the sufferer, the sincerity of the sceptic, the clash of races, the antagonism of classes, the wisdom of a people, the poetry, pathos and passion of life, the beauty of holiness and the holiness of beauty—all those things which make up the life of men and the glory of the universe, and reveal the character and the love of God shining through all and in all.[2]

A vigorous Bible study policy in the Movement has always resulted in a demand for new text-books, and we issued within a year or two *The Nature and Message of the Bible*, by the Rev. W. B. Selbie ; *The Cross of Job*, by the Rev. H. Wheeler Robinson ; *The Fourth Gospel*, by the Rev. R. H. Strachan ; *St Paul to the Romans*, by R. L. Pelly ; and *According to St Luke*, by Hugh Martin.

[1] *Annual Report, S.C.M.*, 1914-15, pp. 17-18.
[2] *Report of S.C.M. to W.S.C.F.*, 1917.

The publication which had the largest circulation about this time was *The Jesus of History*. This was a series of lectures Dr T. R. Glover delivered in India ; he sent the manuscript from that country. I was travelling to the North the day I received it, and took it with me to read in the train. I realized at once that it was a fresh and interesting approach to the life of Christ. I decided to ask the Archbishop of Canterbury to write an introduction, which he consented to do. He sent it to me with an autographic letter on December 3rd 1916. His chaplain, G. K. A. Bell, also enclosed a note in the envelope, saying, " The Archbishop is really delighted with the book, and is very pleased at having any part in its issue."

A little later the Archbishop told me that he had received a number of letters protesting against his having associated himself with a book which the writers regarded as unorthodox and dangerous. I remember the Archbishop chuckling over this and telling me once again that he thought it was a really useful book.

The prosperity of the Movement's publication department was laid on the basis of this book by Glover and two books by Dr Fosdick, *The Manhood of the Master* and *The Meaning of Prayer*. Edition after edition of these three books was called for ; special cheap editions on which profits were foregone were issued for circulation in the army, but the public also purchased them in large quantities and money flowed in.

We saw the opportunity, knew that books which were first class intellectually, and yet written in untechnical language were needed by the laymen, and we invited theologians accustomed to write learned tomes for each other's perusal also to write in more popular terms for the layman. The Movement thus pioneered a new type of religious book—the kind that a layman, untrained in theological or philosophical language, could read with ease. It has been our pride that we have never published a book, however brief and simple, behind which there was not sound scholarship. We have had many imitators among the publishers in the last fifteen years, and we wish them well.

It is of course obvious, that the Movement had done some publishing from its inception, pamphlets, Bible and missionary study text-books at first, and later social study-text books, and many were purchased by the general public, but we thought of no constituency except our own in the colleges until this time.

Publishing was from early days part of the ordinary routine of the office; the General Secretary acted as editor and publisher-in-chief among other duties, other members of the staff took their share in the work, and the cost of publishing was not separated from the cost of the other work of the Movement. There was a ledger account against which was posted all that the Movement spent on literature of all kinds—bills from printers, paper-makers, binders and for advertisements went into this account, which not only provided for the books and pamphlets which were sold, but for all the literature of the Movement used for free distribution. When the account was balanced at the end of the year, the profit or the loss, as the case might be, was entered in the income and expenditure account of the Movement. On May 31st 1914, there was a surplus on literature, after providing for free literature, of £58, 17s. 4d. The following two years there was a surplus of a few shillings, but on May 31st 1917 there was a surplus of £860, 14s. 7d., on May 31st 1918 a surplus of £2539, 15s. 3d., and on May 31st 1919 a surplus of £2208, 6s. 9d.

The General Committee used most of this surplus on the work of the Movement, but a certain amount was retained to establish its publishing, which has never lost the position that it gained during the war. This is due to the work of Hugh Martin, who had no responsibility at first in connection with the publishing work of the Movement. As, however, this grew, he took more and more responsibility until he ultimately became responsible for all its publishing work.

Hugh Martin joined the staff of the Movement in

1914 as educational secretary. He was to care for the study work of the Movement, see that the Committee's plans for Bible, social and missionary study were mediated to both the Movement's secretaries and the colleges, and undertake the training of leaders for study circles.

Hugh was an experienced S.C.M. leader when he came to headquarters. He had been an officer of one of the most effective Christian Unions in the Movement, that of Glasgow University, and also a member of the Scottish Council of the Movement, his training as an engineer and a theologian was an admirable one for the Movement's work, and he was soon drawn into many activities as well as that of looking after study. He could organize, speak, and write, and the Movement found a speedy use for all his gifts. We have had many a genius on the staff of the Movement and much of the artistic temperament, but it was a joy to welcome a colleague who always kept any promise he made and had no inhibitions about doing what he was asked to do. The complete reliability of Hugh Martin was something quite new, and I rejoiced and do rejoice in it.

Hugh soon added the work of assistant secretary to the study work on which he started. He continued as assistant General Secretary until the time came for him to create the S.C.M. Press of which more later.

It was during the war period that the appearance of our books was improved. For years the General Committee's instructions had been to publish at the lowest possible price in order that books might be accessible to the largest number of students. During the war, however, the revival of interest in the Movement among fine art students, and the reaction on the Movement through their claiming a place for the beautiful in life, led to criticism of the appearance of the Movement's publications, and Leslie Hunter, whose taste was fastidious, urged incessantly that the appearance of the Movement's publications should be improved. The increase in sales made improvement possible without a prohibitive increase of prices, since it gave us more money to handle.

We also began to think about the general public and to realize that while popular books, like those by Glover and Fosdick, which were being widely boomed in the Press, would probably sell irrespective of their appearance, we must make our books more attractive looking if they were to have a good general sale.

The result, of course, was an inevitable increase in the cost of books to students. At first there was some grumbling, and I found myself between two fires—the complaint of travelling secretaries that Student Movement books were getting too expensive for students to afford, and the withering remarks of Leslie Hunter about the poor appearance of the books being produced! As a matter of fact, what solved the problem was the general increase in the cost of everything as the war went on, which resulted in people losing all power of comparing prices.

In a relatively short time we brought up the standard of appearance of our books to that of the best class of publisher, while maintaining the price at a rather lower level than that usually charged for books of the same kind. But this was not until after the war when Hugh Martin, who was joined by Alexander Walker—whom we all know as Johnnie—took the production of Student Movement books in hand.

CHAPTER XXX

WORK AMONG FOREIGN STUDENTS

THE absence of any systematic historical study of the British university field makes accurate generalization impossible, but any available records show that there have been foreign students in our universities as long as they have been in existence.

Since the beginning of the century students have come to Great Britain from an ever-widening area, and the influx of students from the Orient has had far-reaching results in its effect, both upon the thought of our universities and upon Asia, more especially upon its political life.

Most of the students have come with little knowledge of the West, yet with high hopes. We are, however, insular in our ways, there is a good deal of colour prejudice in our midst, and the majority of the Orientals have been left far too much to themselves. The Government has tried to help those from countries in the British Commonwealth, but the help is necessarily of a limited kind, and Indians and Egyptians, the two groups that have come in unusually large numbers, have always been suspicious of government help, suspecting an element of espionage. The tendency has been for students to fight their own battles in loneliness, lack of knowledge of Western ways, and, in the non-residential universities, to have to surmount the difficulty of finding suitable lodgings.

The average British student is not interested in those of another race, also he is as a rule younger than the foreigner and much less sophisticated. He is shy and awkward and seldom realizes the importance of making an effort to get to know men of a different race from his own.   The resultant neglect of the foreigner results in loneliness and bitterness of heart.   Indians, above all foreign students, are anxious to meet English people and get to know them socially, and the history of British relations with India during the last fifteen years might have been infinitely happier if the Indian student generally had been welcomed and given of our best.

The majority of Asiatic students who seek university education abroad are usually enterprising above their fellow-students, and they are always marked men when they return home, many reaching eminence in their own country.   Anyone who has known many Oriental students during two or three decades and watches the foreign page of *The Times*, or the appointments to foreign embassies and legations in London, will find many familiar names.

The Student Movement, with its thought for the extension of Christianity in the East, has always been interested in the Oriental student.   Douglas Thornton, when an undergraduate at Cambridge, did a great deal for the Indian students in that university, and, following him, much good work was carried on at Cambridge under the general supervision and through the personal influence of the Rev. G. T. Manley, who in December 1904 contributed an article to *The Student Movement* on " Oriental Students in England."   The return to the Movement, as a secretary, of Robert P. Wilder in 1905 at once affected the relationship of the Movement to work among foreign students.   Wilder realized the importance, and knew the needs, of these men and, whatever else he was doing, never neglected opportunities of cultivating friendships with them.   His house was always open to foreign students.

In the early winter of 1908 John Mott visited the Movement, and everywhere he went stimulated interest in the Oriental student.   Speaking at a meeting in the Royal Albert Hall on November 21st 1908, which was organized by the London Intercollegiate Christian Union (Men), he asked for a campaign of friendship on behalf of students from India, China, Japan, Korea and Turkey.

> Let them be introduced to Christian homes, to our schools, our philanthropic institutions, our churches, in other words, to the best side of our civilization. Let us make real friends of them, so that when they return to their own countries they will be able to say that when they were in a strange land the people who most interested themselves in their comfort and welfare were the Christians. . . . In my judgment, such a policy carried on with wisdom and conscientious thoroughness during the next few years will mean more than sending hundreds of missionaries, important as that is.[1]

Such words fell upon prepared ground, for two months earlier the Movement had appointed a sub-committee to consider its relation to the presence of foreign students in England, and " to encourage and unify work among foreign students in the provincial towns." This sub-committee found that Glasgow University Christian Union had a special committee for foreign students, and in connection with it some twenty visitors were visiting systematically among the sixty foreign students in Glasgow University. Manchester University Christian Union was doing work on somewhat similar lines. Leeds University was co-operating with the Ripon Diocesan Board of Missions in helping foreign students. And the London Intercollegiate Christian Union (Men) was laying plans to secure a foreign student secretary, which it did later in the person of Kenneth E. Kirk, St John's College, Oxford, who began work on April 1st 1909.

The General Committee, being burdened with work through the rapid expansion of the Movement at this time, felt that it could not give adequate attention to the needs of foreign students, and, after discussion with the committee of the Student Volunteer Missionary Union, decided that, as " the S.V.M.U. was the only one of the three departments which had sufficient time

[1] *Modern World Movements*, by John R. Mott, p. 15.

to give attention to this work," it should take it in hand.

This the S.V.M.U. agreed to do, appointing a committee consisting of John Macleod Campbell, Balliol College, Oxford, chairman; W. M. Cargin, travelling secretary, S.V.M.U.; A. G. Henderson, Glasgow University; Kenneth E. Kirk, foreign secretary of the London Inter-collegiate Christian Union; MacEwan S. Lawson, Manchester University, and R. P. Wilder. It was decided at the same time to ask Miss Fairfield " to watch the interests of Oriental women students and developments among them," and the sub-committee was told to keep in touch with her. The number of Oriental women students being very small, it was not felt necessary to make special provision for them.

The number of these students has always remained small. They have been scattered in a number of different colleges, welcomed by British women students, and, as a rule, have been happy during their time in England. They have never constituted a problem, although individuals from time to time have needed help. The Student Movement has had its attention much more engaged by the needs of groups of Continental women students, studying in England, than by the Oriental students. When Oriental students are spoken of as a problem the reference is always to men.

The new sub-committee sent a circular at once to about a hundred foreign missionary stations, saying that the Movement would be responsible for the welfare of any students who might be reported to them as coming to Great Britain, and a little later Kenneth Kirk was asked to make a survey of the foreign student situation in the British Isles. This survey revealed a total of about 1500 Oriental students in Great Britain. Exactly half of them were Indians, 400 of them were studying in London, 150 in Edinburgh and 100 at Cambridge. Glasgow and Oxford each had between 30 and 40, and the others varied in number from one Indian at Aberdeen University to 10 at Leeds University. Bristol,

Liverpool, Reading and the Agricultural College at Cirencester were the only other places where there were Indians.

The Chinese numbered 300, of whom 200 were in London, 34 in Glasgow, 25 in Edinburgh and 20 in Birmingham, with the remainder were scattered in small groups in Aberdeen, Cambridge, Leeds, Liverpool, Manchester, Oxford and Sheffield.

Of 200 Egyptian students 100 were studying in London. Oxford, Edinburgh and Glasgow had from 25 to 30 each, the remainder being at Bristol, Liverpool, Manchester and Cirencester.

The only other group of any size was the Burmese, who numbered 70, practically all of them being in either London or Cambridge. The remaining students comprised a variety of nationalities in ones and twos, the only group of any size comprised a dozen Cingalese. In the case of African students, only two were discovered.

The Christian Unions at Aberdeen, Birmingham, Bristol, Cambridge, Glasgow, Leeds, Liverpool, Manchester, Newcastle, Oxford, Reading and Sheffield, each had a student looking after foreign students, and some of them did effective work. In Bristol four Egyptians who were Moslems were in a study circle with four Christian ·Englishmen, studying the Koran and New Testament side by side. The president of the Student Movement in Cambridge had founded an East and West Society four years previously, which was doing good work. A number of the younger dons were interested, and the Student Movement organization was in the capable hands of F. M. Cheshire. Mrs Pitt, who had been for some time in India, had fortnightly meetings for Indian students, which were well attended, and she kept open house to Indians for tea on Sunday.

A. G. Henderson, a Glasgow University student, had made it his business to get to know every Oriental student in the university, and was so successful in introducing Orientals and Scotsmen, that not a single Oriental in Glasgow was without a friend. There was a Bible circle for Indians. In all the other universities the Orientals, who were few in number, were befriended by members of the Christian Union.

The only places where the foreign student, and especially the Indian, was regarded as a problem were Edinburgh, Cirencester and London. In Edinburgh the Scottish student body found the Oriental student element of between 300 and 350—more than half of whom were Indian—too large to absorb into their community, and for a long time there had been ill-feeling between Scottish and Indian students; this had been fostered by Colonial students, of whom there were a number in Edinburgh, who were hostile to the coloured student. The swimming club of the university published at this time conditions of membership: "Membership of this club is open to gentlemen of white colour who are, or have been, members of the university." Lord Morley was appealed to about this by the Indians; without giving any definite opinion as he was not fully acquainted with the circumstances of the case, he replied that he considered "That any action that accentuated colour differences in university circles was undesirable from every point of view." The Indians took the matter to the Students' Representative Council, and a motion was carried disapproving of the action of the swimming club by 27 votes to 4, but it did nothing to decrease the ill-feeling which already existed. The Christian Union did little in relation to the problem.

At the Royal Agricultural College at Cirencester there was a large group of foreign students, most of whom were outside the social life of the college. "The situation is rendered more difficult by the fact that there has been a distinctly seditious feeling among the Indians there in the past, and several of them have been expelled on that account."

The most elaborate work undertaken for foreign students was that in London. The London Intercollegiate Christian Union (Men) gave a lead to all work in England for foreign students, London having received its inspiration in relation to foreign students at the quadrennial conference, Liverpool, January 1908. It constituted a Foreign Student Department at the summer conference (Baslow) 1909, and stimulated activity in each of the London Christian Unions, and also arranged corporate work for the whole of the London student field. The most interesting feature of the work in the Christian Unions was the number of non-Christian Indians and Chinese drawn into Bible circles. The general work in London included meeting students at the docks on arrival, finding suitable lodgings, giving much personal assistance, such as getting papers signed for students entering the Inns of Court, providing special entertainments and introducing students into private homes.

The survey made by Kenneth Kirk was the basis of advice which the S.V.M.U.'s sub-committee embodied in a memorandum signed on its behalf by Campbell and Kirk; this guided the main lines of the policy of the Movement until the war brought new problems. The memorandum collected together information as to all the different kinds of work being done. It also stated clearly the objective of the Movement.

> Our object may be stated as twofold : first of all, to win the friendship of Oriental students in our colleges ; and secondly, to bring them in the end to the knowledge of Christ. We wish to make it clear that the first of these must be attained before we can hope to reach the second : but that we shall never be successful in either unless we keep definitely before ourselves the ideal of winning these our brothers for Christ.[1]

Much stress was laid upon the indirect influence on the Oriental of the lives of those around him in relation to winning him. Personal friendship, the work of the Christian Unions and special Bible circles for Orientals were advocated. And the suggestion made that where a Christian Union felt strong enough it should attempt to find good lodgings for Oriental students. The

[1] *Foreign Students in British Universities*, February 1910.

Movement's work for foreign students grew steadily up to the war, while all the time the number of these students was on the increase.

In the autumn of 1913 Mr David Yui, of the Student Department of the Y.M.C.A. of China,[1] visited university centres in Great Britain where Chinese students were studying, and his help and advice strengthened our relations with this group of students. Mr Yui left with us a series of " practical suggestions for co-operation," in written form, the first of which reads : " Avoid the use of the word ' Chinaman ' on account of its sinister association ; use the term ' Chinese.' " It is worth recalling this as so many educated people in England still use the disliked designation. The last of his nine suggestions was : " Always remember the object in view, that is, to lead him, slowly, if necessary, but definitely, to Christ."

The work of the Chinese Students' Christian Union was well led at this time and conversions and baptisms were of regular occurrence. It was in close touch with our Movement.

The war caused a great stir among Oriental students studying in our colleges. The hope was awakened among Indians that the response of India to the call of the Empire for war service would create a sense of obligation towards them in Great Britain which would lead to the realization of their national aspirations. The Chinese were very restless in relation to Japan and greatly disliked the alliance between Great Britain and that country. There was a great deal of tension among Egyptian students, and the extension of British authority in Egypt was very distasteful to them. The Oriental students discussed eagerly the ethics of war, and spoke plainly of their surprise that nations which all professed the Christian religion should engage one another in war.

The work being done for the benefit of foreign

[1] Affiliated to the World's Student Christian Federation as the Student Christian Movement of China.

students was bearing fruit, and many foreign students were beginning to realize that the Student Christian Movement was doing more for them than any other body in the country.

The foreign student secretaries declared that the greatest hindrance of all in the colleges was the undergraduates' " colossal ignorance of foreign affairs." It seemed incredible to Indian students, for example, that British students should know nothing whatever about politics in India, and Mac Lawson (a foreign student secretary shared by the General and London I.C.C.U. Committees) told us that until the colleges understood the political issues in relation to India it was hopeless to think that we could have the right spirit towards India in the colleges. Robert Wilder shared with Mac Lawson the leadership of all discussion on the General Committee at this period about foreign student work. He stressed how extraordinarily difficult it was " to help Orientals to realize the value and greatness of Christianity in face of this terrible war."

We began, under Wilder's leadership, to think sympathetically for the first time about bringing Oriental men in touch with Christian homes where they would meet women. Few had thought, up to this time, of the peculiar sense of isolation and strain produced on one sex by being cut off entirely from the company of the other, and for the first time we realized how tremendously it was appreciated by Oriental students when they were given an opportunity of contact with Christian homes and members of the opposite sex.

Then came a demand of a new kind. Among the flood of refugees which poured across the Channel the first winter of the war were a number of students, and many of these were received into our colleges. There were about three hundred in London ; they came from the Belgian universities and from Nancy and Lille in France. About half of them were Belgians and the rest Russians, Poles and Russian and Polish Jews. They were very lonely, very miserable and very poor.

The Movement formed a committee to help them, under the chairmanship of Dr Crichton Miller, with Rena Carswell as secretary. Miss Carswell was the moving spirit and quickly got work going. A *foyer* for men students was opened at Kingsway Hall, London, on March 8th 1915, the Wesleyan Methodist Trust lending us a room, with J. E. Oldham as leader devoting his time to the students who came to it. In May a *foyer* for women students was opened at 8 Torrington Place, W.C., under the care of Miss Rena Carswell and Miss Margaret Boyle.

At these *foyers* the students could read and talk and secure light refreshments. Later on a programme of lectures and entertainments was arranged. There was hardly any religious conviction among these students, and great efforts were made to help them out of the dull, hopeless unbelief common among them. Mr R. G. Collingwood [1] lectured to them with success, and there were spiritual results. After some months Henri Louis Henriod came from the Swiss Movement to help us and remained with us until the World's Student Christian Federation sought his services. We lent him in the beginning of 1920 to the Federation to help to prepare for its first post-war meeting of the General Committee, and when the committee met at St Beatenberg, Switzerland, the same summer, he was appointed one of its secretaries.

Henriod undertook the first tour ever made of our universities in the interest of foreign students as a whole; hitherto attention had been concentrated on Oriental students. He found students of twenty-two nationalities, very few of whom were in touch with the Movement. At Easter 1916 Henriod became joint foreign student secretary of the Movement with F. A. Cockin, who had spent three years on short service work at Delhi. This strengthening of the staff detailed for this work, together with the prominence of the foreign student owing to the absence of most of the older British men students,

[1] Fellow of Pembroke College, Oxford.

brought the Movement's work for foreign students into prominence. Wilder, who knew the importance of organizing activity if it is to be permanent, started Christian Unions in 1915 among the Indo-Ceylonese, Egyptian and West African students ; the latter collapsed after some months owing to the departure of its leading members, but it was restarted as a Joint Union of West African and West Indian students.

The name of Robert Wilder has often occurred in this book. Perhaps no better place can be found to speak of his contribution to the Movement than in a chapter dealing with its relation to Oriental students. His first visit to Great Britain in 1891-92 led to the establishment of the S.V.M.U. as a national organization. In 1905 we heard that he had to leave India on grounds of health, and we invited him to join our staff. He accepted the invitation, and remained with us until 1916, when he resigned to become once more, after thirty years' work on the mission field and in Europe, the Secretary of the Student Volunteer Movement for Foreign Missions of the U.S.A. and Canada.

Robert Wilder's home was always open to students of all races, and he was respected and loved by all. Whether he was travelling, London, evangelistic or foreign student secretary—he held all these posts at one time or another—there were some things he never neglected. He was a fisher of men who found opportunity everywhere—in railway trains, college rooms and lodgings, and in meetings, large and small. Men were grateful for the definiteness and candour of his approach to them as he urged upon them the joy of whole-hearted surrender to Jesus Christ as Saviour and Lord. He had much of value to say about the cultivation of the spiritual life and the importance of Bible study and prayer. He worked without ceasing on behalf of foreign missions. The cause of Christian unity was near his heart. And he found time for writing, raising money, and attending to matters of organization. When we could spare him he went to one country after another on the same errands, under the guidance of the World's Student Christian Federation.

Those who knew him will not easily forget his piercing blue eyes and friendly smile, nor the patience and persistence with which he pled the cause of Christ. He was a steadfast and loyal disciple. I hope that the Student Movement in Great Britain and throughout the world will never forget the debt they owe this man, who was the founder of the Student Volunteer Movement.

Far more important than organization, however, was the drawing out of the sympathy and the training of the understanding of British students in relation to those from other lands. For some years the need of this had been recognized and much done to promote friendship with and for students from abroad. There was, however, a development of importance at this time, and this was the attempt to make this work co-operative.

> We constantly talk about our work for foreign students, and we naturally tend to think of them as people who need helping and guiding and shepherding in every possible way. Well, that is our British way of looking at things and it is very dangerous. We always tend to regard ourselves as the only really effective people, and our way of doing things as the only really sensible one. That means that we organize things on behalf of other people and then ask them to come in and enjoy the results. Such a method comes dangerously near to patronage—and patronage is the unforgivable sin where foreign students are concerned . . . so long as we regard ourselves as philanthropists working for the good of others, we shall make a mess of things. It is only as we attain to the ideal of genuine co-operation that our efforts will be really fruitful.[1]

What helped to teach us this lesson was trying to set straight relations with some Egyptians. The production of a leaflet which seemed to be without offence to us had given offence to them, and discussion with them brought it home to some amongst us that we must learn to do things *with* them, instead of *for* them. Soon after this we invited Oriental students to join our

[1] *Annual Report, S.C.M.*, 1916-17.

Foreign Student Committee, and advised all the councils of the Movement to make room for foreign students as members or visitors. Later, when Ariam Williams, a Ceylonese, came from India, where he was working, and Warren Scott, an American Negro, joined our staff, they were welcomed into our secretarial fellowship and shared in it on exactly the same terms as did men and women of our own race.

The large increase in Indians studying in London caused Mr E. C. Carter, who had come to London in connection with the work of the Y.M.C.A. in the American army, to suggest that rooms should be taken for the use of Indian students and a representative of the Student Department of the Y.M.C.A of India installed to look after these students. He discussed the question with F. A. Cockin, who brought it to the General Committee as a question of principle was involved. There had been an understanding with the Y.M.C.A since the foundation of the Student Movement in England that the Association would not enter the student field, but would regard it as the sphere of the Student Christian Movement. There was also an understanding in the World's Student Christian Federation that a national Student Movement would not undertake any work in the field of another national Movement, even for its own students, without the permission of the national Movement concerned.

As a result of the pressure of the war the matter was not proceeded with at the time, but at the conclusion of the war K. T. Paul discussed the needs of Indian students with both our Movement and the Y.M.C.A. The result was that the Shakespeare Hut, which had been built for the use of troops on the vacant site behind the British Museum—afterwards acquired for the University of London—was occupied by the Indian Y.M.C.A., who opened it as a club for the use of Indian students, with the cordial approval of our General Committee, which accepted an invitation to be represented upon the management committee.

2 O

Some years later the Indian club was moved to 112 Gower Street, where an Indian Students' Union and Hostel was opened. The Movement has been represented from the first on its management committee.

Our interest in Serbia had been stirred in a special way through the adventures of one of our members, A. W. Blaxall, Keble College, Oxford, who, when Belgrade was overwhelmed, had been advised to make for the mountains and avoid capture and internment. One night, as he was looking for a place to sleep, a Serbian met him and asked him in a mixture of Serbian and English if he was from Great Britain. He then asked him if he had heard of the Student Christian Movement. Delighted to find they were fellow members, for the Serbian was from the S.C.M. of Belgrade, these two read the Bible and starved and froze together, and ultimately reached safety.

About a year later we were approached by Father Nicholai Velimirovic,[1] a priest of the Serbian Orthodox Church, who had come to England to look after the care and education of 400 Serbian students and schoolboys, part of the remnant of the youth of Serbia, who had been rescued when it had been overrun by Austria. We secured the services of Blaxall and put him in charge of work among the Serbians, who were distributed in the universities of Birmingham, Cambridge, Leeds, London, Manchester, Oxford, Reading, Edinburgh and Glasgow.

At a conference at Oakenrough, Haslemere, at Easter 1918, an organization was set up by the Serbians themselves to interest their students and schoolboys in the Y.M.C.A. and in the S.C.M. Later, when Blaxall was called to war work in Salonica, the General Committee appointed to its staff for the first time a member of a branch of the Orthodox Church, Father Damaskin Grdanitchsky. He was a young priest, the same age as most of the S.C.M. secretaries, and worked very happily with us. The Serbian group of students were

[1] Afterwards Bishop of Ochrida.

an important element in the summer conferences of 1918 and 1919.

It was the need of foreign students in London that brought to a head a long-cherished hope of a Student Movement building in London. Temple Gairdner was the first man to speak of a central building in London, as far back as 1898. There are records showing that I discussed the matter with Arthur W. Davies in 1908 and with Walter Seton and Kenneth Kirk a year or two later. Our idea was a central building where the Movement would have its headquarters, where London students could have rooms for meetings and a club, and where foreign students would find a welcome.

During the war the success of the *foyers* for men and women and the fact that their quarters were temporary and far too small, made the question of accommodation an urgent one. It was on the mind of Henriod, and one afternoon he came to urge me to find better quarters for the *foyers*. I told him about our dream of a Student Movement House. It was new to him. He was enthusiastic : " But it is splendid ; you must do it at once." I said it was impossible in war time, and he went away.

It was twilight, I did not turn on the light but threw myself in an armchair in front of the window. " Was it impossible ? " The need was very great. Multitudes of new things were being done by the Movement, perhaps we could do it. Henriod did not let the matter rest, he went and told George Cockin all I had said to him about a Student Movement House, and together they went to Miss Fairfield, and the three of them began to press me to act.

Mr Cecil Harris, one of our senior friends, suggested that we should ask people to provide the House as a memorial to our students who had fallen in the war. The idea made the proposal easier, so I wrote a memorandum advocating the leasing of a house in Central London as a centre for work among London students, foreign students, a place where our publishing work could be developed, and, above all, where members of the Student Movement could meet one another. Enquiries had been made about houses in Central London, and the document included an estimate of the probable cost to the Movement. A few weeks later the General Committee approved the proposal and appointed a committee to carry it into effect, consisting of T. Tatlow (chairman), F. A. Cockin, L. S. Hunter, H. L. Henriod, R. D. Rees, Zoë Fairfield and Lorna Southwell.

We fixed on 32 Russell Square, W.C., prepared a statement concerning the uses to which the House would be devoted, and asked for contributions towards a fund of £5000 to secure the House as a memorial to students who had fallen in the war. The nucleus of the fund was legacies to the Movement by two secretaries and a committee member who had fallen—J. Dudley Whyte, W. H. Dyson and Gerald Furness Smith.

The invitation to contribute to the memorial was backed by forty men and women well known in university and Church life, and gifts began to pour in. The money came in sums varying from one shilling to one hundred pounds, and was sent by soldiers, sailors, lecturers and professors, students, parents of students in the army, and senior friends. Many gifts came from students in Ireland, Wales and Scotland. The project was warmly approved on all hands and hundreds of sympathetic letters received. Contributors were invited to send names for the Roll of Honour to be inscribed on the walls of the House and a long list of names was provided.

We did not delay since success was assured, and part of the house was ready for the September Executive Conference of the Movement. The one thing I recall about that meeting was that one evening when I was in the middle of an address on the Federation for the benefit of new members, and was absorbed in the topic, I became aware that Bill Paton, with a grave face, was coming across the room towards me ; in a moment he

was saying, " There is an air raid just beginning, T."
I then heard the guns for the first time. As many of
those on the committee had never been in an air raid
before some of the London members were afraid they
might be alarmed. So the address came to an abrupt
end, and we repaired to the cellars for what proved to
be one of the most damaging raids experienced in West
Central London.

The House was formally opened and dedicated on
November 26th 1917. The ceremony was in two parts,
first came a meeting over which the Archbishop of
Canterbury presided. I explained the uses proposed
for the House; Miss A. W. Richardson, Vice-Principal
of Westfield College, welcomed the new venture as a
member of staff. The Archbishop then spoke, saying
in the course of his address :

> The wonder, of course, is not that this House should have
> been needed now and set going, but that for twenty-five
> years this Movement should have gone on without it !
> It is a marvellous tribute to the skill of those who have
> carried on the work that they should have been able to get
> on without these premises, which are now so obviously and
> necessarily a part of the work which lies ahead. But in
> spite of the difficulties which lie behind, the work has been
> carried on with the enormous skill with which we are all
> familiar. I always feel when talking about the Student
> Christian Movement, that the difficulty is to get people
> unfamiliar with it to realize either the skill of the effort or
> the range of the far-flung lines of those who are interested
> in it, or the variety of the material upon which and through
> which the work is done. There are very few organizations
> —if that word may be used—in the world which are
> characterized after so short a life by these features in so
> marked a degree, and with so little that is to be found fault
> with or complained of in the carrying on of the work. I
> am sometimes myself bewildered by the various changes
> rung upon words that denote the Movement—Federation,
> Fellowsnip, Union, Association, Movement. I get lost
> sometimes ! But the word that I feel we really like to
> stand by is the word " Movement." It is really character-
> istic of what it has been, a movement on a great scale.
> That is the particular epithet upon which it seems to me

we ought to dwell with the deepest thankfulness and the most complete satisfaction.

After the meeting there was a Service of Dedication in which the Rev. Ivor Roberton, F. A. Cockin and shared, the Archbishop taking the prayer of dedication We sang with full hearts that night,

For all the saints who from their labours rest.

The Quiet Room at the House was beautified by gifts in memory of Student Movement secretaries who had died.

A club committee had already been appointed, and the first warden, Edith E. Overton (Somerville College Oxford), a former travelling secretary, was installed.

Only one change of importance was made soon after the House was opened. We had planned to provide tea only, but other meals were demanded, so the big kitchen was turned into a refectory and the large scullery became the kitchen.

The two *foyers* were moved to the House, and the publication department came from 93 Chancery Lane.

The shortage in house accommodation as a result of the cessation of building during the war bore very heavily upon the Oriental students, who found it more and more difficult to secure lodgings in London, and the General Committee authorized Miss Fairfield and Mr Cockin to gather a hospitality committee in London. The committee could not do very much, but later Miss Constance Grant was appointed for work among foreign students, and gave a great deal of time to trying to place them in suitable lodgings and homes, using the Student Movement House as her base.

There are many names associated in the minds of students all over the world with the Student Movement House—Edith Overton, Maud Atkinson (Mrs David Adams), Louise Royaards (Mrs Alexander Walker), J. W. Parkes, C. W. Warner, Mrs Brants, Nell Latham Josephine Currie, and a host more too numerous to name but each remembered by some as "the best person who ever worked in the House." Certainly the House and its membership has had the deep devotion and untiring service of a fine band of men and women.

The House has seen various improvements but no considerable change since it was opened. Edith Overton set the pace from the start and it has been maintained ever since. There is always something going on, and anyone who attends the activities of the House for a few years will hear many of the leading clergy, ministers, actors, economists, professors, writers, poets, musicians and publicists in England expound in lectures and discussions or exemplify in song, by reading or by playing that aspect of British culture for which they are famed. And from time to time the different aspects of the culture of other races are displayed for the delight and education of British students. The House's membership is in constant flux, but in a full year 1200 students of over 50 nations have been found using it.

The value of the House to the student from overseas is incalculable, and thousands who used to pass from college lecture halls to poorly chosen theatres and cinemas and then to dingy lodgings, and knew no more than that of England, now gain a very fair idea of the general range of our national culture. More than that, the House is the place where hundreds of friendships begin between members of different races. In every university group I have met where I have been in recent years—Austria, Germany, France, Denmark or Switzerland—there have been affectionate inquiries for a well-loved spot—the Student Movement House.

The various Christian Unions of students from abroad came to the House for their meetings. The Chinese Christian Union used it as its official headquarters, and an impetus was given to all the work of the Movement for students from other lands by its foundation. So it came about that the most thorough study the Movement has made on the subject of foreign students in British universities was undertaken in the autumn of 1917, when a small commission, led by George Cockin, investigated the subject, reporting after five months' work. The Commission included John Matthai, an able Indian; J. J. Poon, a Chinese with long experience in Great Britain; Olive Moberly, who knew India; A. W. Blaxall and J. E. Oldham, who knew Serbia and Germany respectively; Ted Holtby, who was a foreign student secretary; and some of us who knew the Movement and the history of its various contacts with those from other countries.

This Commission both studied the situation and surveyed the bodies at work, which included reference to twenty-nine societies and clubs whose object was to meet the need of Indian students. It also provided a study of the India Office Department for Indian students created as the result of a commission appointed by Lord Morley, which sat from 1907-1908. The department was ably served at the time by Dr T. W. Arnold.

The report of this Commission was printed and issued to the secretaries. It is worth looking at its suggestions as presumably being those still regarded by the Movement as right, for no more recent study has been issued. In regard to the aim of our work the Commission said:

> The foundation of our work is a Christian one. We are a Christian Movement, membership of which is taken to imply a conviction of the essential value of Christian life and belief—still more of Christ himself—for every individual and for mankind as a whole. Our aim must therefore be to set before those among whom we work that which we believe to be not only the highest attainable standard of human life, and the source of power for its attainment, but also the one effective solution of all human problems, individual and social, and—at the back of all—the one wholly satisfying explanation of God and His relation to the world.[1]

The more difficult question of how this aim could best be achieved is then discussed:

> We have got to take into consideration many factors which may at first sight seem irrelevant; to take precau-

[1] *Report on the Foreign Student Work of the S.C.M.*, p. 20.

tions and to exercise a self-restraint which may expose us
to the charge of cowardice ; to busy ourselves with many
odd jobs which may seem to take up time that might be
better spent in more directly " spiritual " work. We must
envisage as a whole the condition of the people we are
trying to help ; we must understand their needs, material
as well as spiritual, and we must meet those needs in the
most simple and natural way that we know. There is
abundant evidence of the effectiveness of these methods.
. . . What is needed first is action not speech, life not
preaching. . . . If our Christian message is to be with
power, it must be the message which is carried by love and
gentleness, by sympathy and patience, by unfailing courtesy
and unselfish service.[1]

Of our special responsibility to Christian foreign
students, the Commission wrote that more should be
done for them.

For these whose fate here is often the saddest and most
disastrous of all, everything must be done to foster and
develop the Christian life and character. Only too often
they find little enough in the life of professing Christians
which encourages them to stand fast in their belief—or to
witness for it to others. They need our special care. We
must try to understand the religious milieu in which they
have lived at home ; to appreciate the contrast between
that, and the environment in which they find themselves
here in England ; to see how that reacts upon their religious
thought and practice ; in a word, to approach them at the
point of need. We must think out very carefully the kind
of thing that is most likely to help them : our English
methods of Bible study and prayer may not be the most
suitable methods for them : our English services are often
not congenial : some of them are afraid of attempts being
made to divert them from their own traditional forms of
worship : almost all are struck by the apparently narrow
line which divides the real Christian from the professing
Christian, and our Church services do not seem to emphasize
or add reality to the distinction." [2]

As to the methods of work, the Commission did not
advocate anything new, but made a useful summary of
all the different ways through which attempts had been

[1] *Ibid.*, p. 21.   [2] *Ibid.*, pp. 21 and 22.

made in the Movement to assist foreign students—
provision of lodgings in term-time and vacation, private
hospitality, international clubs and East and West
Societies in the colleges to provide social life, lectures,
entertainments, the provision of religious work in the
form of lectures, discussion groups and personal talks,
the work which Christian Unions could do through
inviting foreign students to such of their activities as
careful selection would suggest to be suitable, and
through assistance to Student Christian Unions composed of nationals from one country.

The Student Movement opened a *foyer* in Glasgow
for foreign students in 1918. It was not in a position
to pay a whole-time secretary to work in the *foyer*. A
student committee worked satisfactorily for a time, but
then some students began to introduce undesirable
people, drink was brought in and some of the students
started gambling. Various Student Movement secretaries and members of the committee visited the place
fairly frequently, tidied up the situation once or twice, and
had promises from the student committee in charge that
they would turn out the offenders, but the evils recurred
and the Movement had no choice but to close the *foyer*,
having learned the lesson that when a club is open for
students of all races and anyone may join so long as he
is a student, it is essential that a responsible person be
placed on the premises to give all his time to work in
the club. The trouble is not that the majority of the
students are not well behaved, for they are, but there
is always a minority given to licence, and the only way
to keep this minority in check is the presence of a
responsible worker.

The links of the Movement with students from other
lands were never more varied than during the year
before, and the year after, the war. In addition to the
contacts named, there was close connection with
Roumania and the Anglo-Roumanian Society in London,
with the Czechoslovakian Republic through the daughter
of President Masaryk, a member of the Student Move-

ment in England, with Poland through Mr W. J. Rose, with Belgium through Miss Sneyers, one of the most interesting and able of the refugee students, with Bulgaria through Miss Dimitrieff, a Bulgarian student caught in England by the war who completed her course at King's College and then joined the clerical staff of the Movement, and with Russia through Dr Harold Williams. Every one of these contacts was being used to render some service to the students of the country named—service in the country as well as to its students in Great Britain.

To complete the picture, it should be added that we saw a great deal of some of the leaders of the Student Movement in Australia, New Zealand and the United States of America. They were soldiers in the case of the former two countries and Y.M.C.A. workers in the case of the latter. The American Y.M.C.A. men we saw were graduates who were engaged in prisoners of war camps and, later, among their own fellow-students when the United States sent a large body of its students into British universities immediately on their demobilization.

CHAPTER XXXI

THE WAR CONTINUES AND
THE MOVEMENT FINDS MORE TO DO

THE committee of the Student Volunteer Missionary Union felt keenly the challenge of the war. The Movement had been growing in size, but for several years the numbers joining the S.V.M.U. had been stationary. Various reasons were given, the increasing realization among students of the social need in Great Britain, an increased knowledge of the results of the comparative study of religion. Such study revealed stages of religious achievement and this, coupled with the effect of the all-pervading idea of evolution and progress, had resulted in drift by many into a position where they did not really believe in the final and universal message of the Gospel of Jesus Christ.

Then came the war, with its apparent mockery of schemes for world evangelization, and its stern reminder that if the kingdoms of the world are to be won for Christ, the winning of them was going to be a stiffer business than any of us had thought. In this mood depleted colleges, crippled missionary funds, universal absorption in another and more engrossing matter, made the task of missions seem very hard. The committee decided to meet in retreat at Swanwick from January 3rd to 7th 1916, and to invite others to join them, up to the number of sixty, who " had the missionary situation deeply on their hearts."

This invitation was made through *The Student Movement*, and in response seventy people, most of them students, came together. There was little set speaking, the greater part of the time being given to quiet thought, conference and prayer. It was a wonderful experience which more than any had asked or thought possible revealed God to them.

We carried away from the retreat the conviction that God has again spoken to us as a Movement; at first in answer to the particular problems that were troubling us, and then in a fresh revelation of His Gospel that is for all time.[1]

The retreat had hardly begun when those present saw, over against the idea of religion mainly as a matter of " experience," dependent upon man's capacity and goodwill, the fact of God at work in the world. God became, for all present, the great reality. We sought how to apprehend such reality and we were brought to an awareness of Christ. Christ, unique in His consciousness of God, unique in His view of men, seeing in them potential saints, unique in His view of sin, which did not introduce a new catalogue of sins, but brought into the world a new conscience. And thence we came to the Cross.

We measure life and conduct with reference to its effects upon ourselves and upon humanity; Christ referred it directly to God, and revealed thereby the exceeding sinfulness of sin. He had to save men at all costs.

The cost to love was the Cross.

Here was a message worth taking to the world—the assurance of God's unconquerable purpose of love which rested not upon man's feelings, but upon the fact of what God is.

There is nothing new in this, and there are no new words in which to present it afresh; yet to most of us it came with altogether new force, this deep sense of the uniqueness of Jesus Christ and the supreme value of the Christian Gospel.

The members of the retreat then dwelt on the needs of the non-Christian nations and on what the fulfilment

[1] This and subsequent quotations are from *Foreign Missions and the Gospel : an Impression of the Student Volunteer Missionary Union Retreat*, Swanwick, 1916.

of the Christian hope might mean in the world as we
know it.

That sense of the *present* need and sin of the non-Christian
nations, and that hope of the possibilities before them,
constitute a motive for missionary effort as strong as any
fear for the future fate of souls who have not known the
Gospel.

To meet the need power is wanted.

Christ, with His power and His grace, is there: but we
ourselves are the trouble. In order to have power we
must learn what it means to die . . . our little private,
limited, individual selves must die. That self which is
entrenched in the centre of our beings must be supplanted
by the living Christ. . . . It will mean readiness to brave
apparent failure and loss and waste. . . . We shrink dismayed . . . let us turn to Christ for light. Was He
morose, morbid, unnatural? Did not the children run to
Him? Did He not rejoice in the field flowers and the
sunset sky? Was not His life supremely sane and balanced,
and full of joy and power? Yet from the deeps of His
own experience He said, " Whosoever would save his life
shall lose it, and whosoever would lose his life for My sake
and the Gospel's shall save it " . . . in this life of self-
abandonment men and women throughout the ages have
found, as Jesus Christ Himself found, a joy more radiant
and satisfying than anything the world can give.

The retreat was a new call to the Student Movement
to know Christ.

We are called to a bolder search for the realities of the
Christian faith—in study of the Bible, in the ways of everyday life, in the times set apart for private communion with
God; and the retreat showed us again the hope that is in
fellowship.

It is not fear of sacrifice that holds men back, it is
doubt; men are ready to fling away their lives for a cause,
if only that cause is highly valued. What greater cause
than a vision of what Jesus Christ and His kingdom
can give the world.

The retreat set high once again in the scale of relative
urgency for the Movement the cause of foreign missions.

It was a truly remarkable result for it to achieve in the middle of a world war.

Soon after the retreat the Student Movement held its first public annual meeting for senior friends in Scotland; Dr George Freeland Barbour presided in the University Union, Edinburgh, over a well-filled hall, and Professor James Moffatt, Donald Grant and I spoke. We decided it must be an annual event.

Finance Week received attention at this time of year, and Neville Talbot, asked if he had anything to say to the Movement, wrote from Flanders:

Ypres,
January 13th, 1916.

Dear Student Movement,

I have been asked to send you a few words from Flanders about the S.C.M. Finance Week.

I know from people's common experience out here which they express by saying, " After all, I'd rather be out here than anywhere else," that to stick at the work of the Movement and of the Christian Unions must be a tough job. You must be tempted to think that what you are at does not count.

But you are working at the only things which can at all redeem this vast tragedy—namely, the future and the new things which it holds within it.

The Student Movement in its young way has been prophetic that in the deep things of the spirit—things religious, moral, social, international—the world has been at a crisis. The war does not overthrow the objects of the Movement's aspirations. Rather, in the glare of war's conflagrations we see those objects more clearly—living, candid, personal religion, membership of all conditions of men in a righteous social order, the bringing of all nations into their inheritance in Christ and the fulfilment of national gifts in one fellowship in Christ. The World's Student Christian Federation was—is—the most catholic thing in the world —however small its beginnings. It has at least a hold upon all that this war has challenged and found wanting, and all that the war's sacrifice and sufferings will heighten in value and consecrate.

I dread most of all that whether through littleness and perplexity of faith, or through tiredness or preoccupation in the immediate fortunes of war, or through blindness and hardness of heart, Armageddon may come and go and teach us little. This shall not be, so far as you are concerned, if by *sacrifice*—matching the soldier's sacrifice—you maintain and keep ready for expansion those bands of disciples or learners from Christ which we call Christian Unions.

Yours ever,

NEVILLE S. TALBOT.

Finance Week produced £746, a little more than the year before the war broke out, a symptom of the earnestness of everyone in depleted colleges. The amount was doubled in 1917, when £1480 was given.

Student Movement finances were interesting at this time; with a small decrease in 1917-18, subscriptions and donations remained constant, but our publishing, on which we expected to lose money, produced a surplus. We foresaw this year the need for immediate expansion of staff when the war ended, and began to collect a post-war fund.

We lost heavily in subscriptions through young professional men with families being reduced to army pay, but we gained through hundreds of keen student-soldiers, who, when on a college allowance could only afford 5s., now found it possible as army officers to send £5. Alas! how many sent only one £5; the mortality was terrible.

At Easter came the Dublin rebellion. This and its aftermath had a deeply depressing effect on Irish student life. The pessimism among students, right on until the Free State was established, made a visit to the Irish student field a sad experience.

The theological element in the Movement gained attention in the summer. Some months before the war the Theological Committee had reviewed its work with the help of some senior friends, including the Rev. E. P. Swain,[1] the Rev. John Skinner, Principal of Westminster College, the Rev. W. B. Selbie, and the Rev. F. C. N. Hicks. The suggestion was made by the Student Move-

[1] Afterwards Bishop of Burnley.

ment men that the Movement should assemble a conference of teachers in theological colleges, it being pointed out that it was really the only body which could invite teachers in Anglican, Presbyterian and Nonconformist colleges to such a conference.

We wanted to get the Anglicans to realize that many of their colleges were far behind those of the Presbyterian and Free Churches in the intellectual training they gave their men, and *vice versa* to have the Presbyterians and Free Churchmen realize how little they did to help their students in the cultivation of the spiritual life in comparison with the careful training and discipline of the Anglican colleges. We talked over the project with half a dozen heads of theological colleges without disguising our aim, and secured their names, which were appended as approving, to a tactful letter of invitation. The result was that between sixty and seventy teachers, from all the universities having theological faculties and from forty theological colleges, came together in conference at Queens' College, Cambridge, from June 28th to July 1st 1916.

The programme provided for addresses on different types of theological education, the teaching of theology in view of modern needs, the spiritual life of a theological college, foreign missions, social questions, and the work of the Movement in theological colleges. Speeches were limited in length and there was plenty of time for discussion. I was chairman of the conference, and recall it as a happy and interesting occasion. The chosen speakers were Chancellor J. O. Johnston (late Cuddesdon), Principals Blomfield (Rawdon), Selbie (Mansfield), J. B. Seaton (Cuddesdon), B. K. Cunningham (Farnham), Professors H. A. A. Kennedy (New, Edinburgh), David Williams (Aberystwyth), with William Paton and Malcolm Spencer. Most of those present took part in the discussion, and as we had barred all students, a self-denying ordinance for members of the theological committee, it was candid. We certainly achieved our object in demonstrating how much the different types of colleges had to learn from each other.   The conference promoted the desire for Christian unity.   I do not think it wrought important changes in any of the colleges represented, though one or two introduced lectures on social questions as a result of it.   At the last session the Rev. Newport J. D. White of Trinity College, Dublin, moved a resolution asking the Movement to call a similar conference within three years; this was seconded by Principal P. T. Forsyth of Hackney College, and carried unanimously.

Shortly after the Theological Dons' Conference Bertie Dyson, who had been theological college travelling secretary during the first year of the war, died in France of wounds received in obeying instructions to make a sortie into the German trenches and capture prisoners to get information.   His colonel reported that he secured the information for which he was sent out, and the men with him spoke of " his immense courage and gallant leadership."   We loved him and felt his loss deeply.

W. H. Dyson was educated at the Leys School and King's College, Cambridge, where he was a prize-man and exhibitioner who studied history and theology.   He was a man of wide interests, which included the University Musical, the China, the Wesley (he was an enthusiastic Wesleyan) Societies, and the Student Movement.   It was the element of friendship in the Movement which appealed in a special way to him; in his addresses in the theological colleges he spoke of it frankly, and unaffectedly, as something which was very precious to him.

A slight, erect, neat figure, shapely head well thrown back, auburn hair carefully brushed, rather small features finely chiselled and sensitive, a deliberate and musical drawl—a regular King's drawl as his Cambridge friends said—marked the outward man.   There was almost always something droll about the way he spoke, and this was enhanced by the use he made of his pipe, whether he kept it between his teeth or waved it in his small artistic-looking hand as he used it to emphasize a point in discussion, or a joke. He was not casual and awkward, as some students are, but well-mannered, courteous, pleasant and dignified.

There he went—a radiant soul, bubbling over with humour, salting his speech with quaint and often pungent sayings, never pushing himself forward, never failing in good temper, always ready to play his part for the common good in whatever company he found himself, drawing out the love both of men and women—he had many women friends—and making men want him and want to be like him wherever he went, quite unspoilt by universal popularity. He scarcely ever talked about himself, and did not very often talk about the great things in life which held his secret. His reserve was deep. If, however, the source of his strength was hidden, there flowed from it a stream of purposeful, generous, joyous life which was plain for all to behold. The man had character, with fibre in it.

Although Dyson was a convinced Christian when he attended his first Student Movement Conference at Swanwick in 1913, it helped him very much. He started there a diary of his spiritual life and it opens with the significant entry : " July 14th, Promised Jesus Christ to devote half an hour every day to prayer and Bible study." There is definite evidence that he fulfilled this promise in all possible circumstances until the morning, exactly three years later, on which he died.

His interest was in experimental religion, and theology attracted him not so much for its own sake as for its relation to life. He assimilated thoroughly the different interests of the Movement, and all found adequate and balanced expression in his addresses in the theological colleges—foreign missions, social questions, unity, the value of interdenominational fellowship, the search for truth, the importance of a living theology and the appeal of the World's Student Christian Federation. But the personal note was never lacking, and probably no Student Movement secretary has ever spoken more directly or more courageously to theological students about their personal lives, and especially about the need of a vital prayer life.

He promoted week-end gatherings of theologicals with medicals and students of other faculties. " Now's the time," he said, " for us to learn to understand one another, before we buy our reversible collars and the medicals buy their stethoscopes."

A quotation or two from his reports will help to reveal him.

> I arrived to find that the secretary had forgotten my visit, and had arranged for the whole college to spend the after-noon and evening at another college. Horrid blow ! However, remembering something about clouds and silver linings, I decided to go up to Gilgal and prosper. It felt œcumenical eating tinned pears with a Baptist on one side and a Congregationalist on the other . . . we had recita-tions—the genuine article, with pistols and blood and moonlight, also card tricks, while all one's old chestnuts were worked hard. It gave splendid opportunities for getting to know people. We talked to one another for the good of our souls for hours when we got back.

He wrote of one Church of England college where " several men have a carefully nurtured detestation of dissenters. We had an informal meeting in the common room. One had the impression of being received with fixed bayonets." He enjoyed visiting St Augustine's College, Canterbury, and commented upon every one's interest in " Swanwick." Bishop Knight asked him for summer conference dates that he might arrange term accordingly. Dyson comments : " I always thought bishops had good hearts under their gaiters."

Reporting to the committee on a theological retreat where Dr T. R. Glover was taking part, he wrote :

> Having commenced our ascetic retirement with a heavy meal, I escorted T. R. Glover to his chamber with a view to his preparing an opening address. The first thing he did was to fall asleep—the old dear ! But the address was most incisive and arresting and brought us straight up

against the fact of Christ. . . . After intercessions each day we kept two hours " as a quiet time for devotional reading, etc." Glover was horrified when he saw it on the programme, and thought it meant " sitting still in a room with eight other people looking on to see you did not take your eyes off the Bible ! " We explained this was not the case and he was reassured.

Dyson's humour was all-pervading, it never failed him, and it never jarred, was always free from malice, and never degenerated into flippancy. It was full of the quality of spiritual insight and strength. He could penetrate to the heart of a situation and use his humour to bring its inwardness to light.

Needless to say, he loved children and they delighted in him. More than once he turned up at Annandale, looking somewhat rumpled, to remark with satisfaction, " We've been having a glorious time playing ' tendy bears,' " which was my daughter Pat's version of Teddy bears. The game consisted of Dyson's jumping about under the table in the dining-room for an incredibly long time, making appropriate noises, while the small lady for whose edification he performed, danced round the table shrieking with delight.

Some reference to Dyson and the war will not only help to reveal him, but will also be a very good index of what others like him were thinking about it. He had accepted office as a Student Movement secretary before the war, but before he could start travelling it had broken out. He wrote to me :

I cannot forget that somewhere in my top drawer lies a " Certificate A." It denotes at any rate a small modicum of military knowledge acquired through some six years' service in the Officers' Training Corps. I have changed my views on war a great deal since I joined the O.T.C., and really left it a year ago largely because I did not know whether it was the right thing. One cannot help feeling, however, that what little knowledge one has is held in trust for the service of the country, and it is at any rate a question to be considered seriously whether one should volunteer for military service.

His letter went on to say there were two questions which he must settle : " 1. Whether it is right to fight at all. 2. Whether it is right for me to fight." With regard to the first of these questions, he said :

> I feel that war in the abstract is immoral and unchristian, but in the present situation the position is not so clear. We seem to be fighting a life and death struggle with a barbarous militarism which would be nothing short of appalling were it to overcome Europe. We stand to gain nothing for ourselves but safety through the war. If it is ever right to go to war I think it is right now. It is either a use of force or a leaving our weak ones undefended.

Soon after this he decided to join the army if the war continued, writing :

> I have at last been able to satisfy that delicate piece of human mechanism which we call conscience. I think we agree in our views on this war generally. It is the rightest thing we can do under the circumstances.

This was in August 1914, while the opinion prevailed that war could only last a few months and that the professional soldiers would settle it. He was keen to serve the Student Movement, and a friend in the War Office advised him to get on with his work in it, while being ready to lay it down if the call for officers became urgent. He completed his year's work as theological travelling secretary, and was gazetted second lieutenant of the third battalion, Queen's Westminster Rifles, on August 10th, 1915. He came from a training camp in Winchester to the autumn conference of the committees of the Movement in uniform, and spoke about the theological colleges, beginning by saying we must not think only of him " as falling over his sword in the midst of a brutal and licentious soldiery," but as still keen about the Movement's work.

He soon went to France, whence he wrote constantly about the Movement, and remembering the questioning about holding the Swanwick Conferences during the first year of war, wrote urging us to get every available man to attend.

> Don't stand any nonsense from people who say that there ought not to be any " Swanwick " in war time and all that sort of bish bosh.   Out here things are very much of the earth earthy.   You have only to feel the seat of your trousers when you come in from a working party in a support trench at 3 o'clock in the morning to be convinced of that.   I don't say there is not a subtle something beneath it all, but all the more reason for people being of the spirit, spiritual at home.

He wrote to me at length, in June 1916, about the Theological Dons' Conference which he had helped to plan, concluding :

> It is only the real, deep spirituality of men who are daily digging deeper into the life of the Spirit which they preach will avail to bring the Kingdom a whit nearer, and if a group of such men as you coming together can speak of these things in a spirit of prayer for a while, there is every reason to suppose great things will be revealed to all.
>
> No time for a proper letter.   No peace for the orderly officer.   I dare you to take " Bumbo " [1] on the " Backs " in a Canadian canoe.

The Swanwick Conferences began with a Women's Bible school.   Again we had first-class Biblical scholars in charge, Professor Wheeler Robinson, Professor James Moffatt, Canon Streeter, and again there was great enthusiasm for Bible study with the usual lament :

> It is nothing short of a tragedy that the way the Bible is taught in the majority of schools, elementary and secondary, is sufficient to implant in the scholars a distaste and dislike, from which many are never delivered. . . . Once get your delegate to the school, and all illusions of Biblical dullness will vanish for ever. [2]

The first Welsh Bible school was held a few weeks later and was hailed with equal enthusiasm.

After the Bible school came the general conference,

---

[1] The Rev. F. C. N. Hicks, now Bishop of Lincoln.
[2] *The Student Movement*, vol. xix. p. 7.

with a total of 627 people. Special war intercessions preceded each evening meeting, in which we prayed for soldiers and sailors, the nations and the world, and the accomplishing of the will of God in peace.

There were separate series of meetings again for Continental students and also for Indians. We had men from the army with us, and we were cheered to hear that the Dutch Government had temporarily released seven interned British soldier-students to attend the summer conference of the Dutch Movement.

A good deal of attention was given to the National Mission of Repentance and Hope undertaken by the Church of England. The General Committee was asked to provide a memorandum on evangelistic work for young people based on our experience in the Movement, and the Archbishop of Canterbury appointed me a special Archbishop's Messenger to the colleges on behalf of the Mission.

More discussion about the Church was stimulated. Many desired the mission to succeed, but there was no enthusiasm, and the reason is told pretty plainly in a letter about the Church written by a student, which appeared in the correspondence column of *The Student Movement*, and was endorsed by the editor as " very representative of student opinion at the present time."

The writer asked for more opportunity for women in the Church, more sympathy with labour questions and the reorganization of society, and then quoted a fellow-student as saying " that the saddest thing he had ever seen was the bellicose attitude of the Churches at this time." The writer continued :

> Our clergy have preached recruiting sermons, tirades against Germany, and harsh and bitter ones at that have been heard from the pulpits, and all the time a crucifix has been hanging on the wall, silently pointing out the way of Love, and without a word contradicting the words of His professed follower and ordained Priest. We know that Germany has sinned, but are we free from sin ? Should it not be in the Churches at least that we get away from bitterness and hate ? There is enough bitterness and hate

in the world, we do not need it in our Churches. Now that we are in the midst of war, surely the duty of the Church is to urge upon its members the need for purging their own hearts from petty feelings of jealousy and dislike and hate—the sum of which produces wars—not only war between nations, but economic war.

And again, I know that people are always ready to talk about and criticize the clergy, and set up a much higher standard for them than for themselves. There is, nevertheless, great room for improvement. The clergy—certain of them, there are exceptions of course—seem to lose all sympathy with the younger people, and get so " stodgy." They go on in the same grooves, the same ideas, and lose inspiration. Surely in Christ is continual inspiration and power.[1]

The letter closed, however, with an appeal to students not to leave the Church. " We must consecrate all our youth, enthusiasm and loyalty to the rejuvenating of the Church which holds so much for us, and has given so much and will give."

The Movement's secretaries found that their work grew more and more strenuous, in that the instruction in its ideals and methods, which in normal times was given to newcomers in the men's colleges by senior students, had to be given by them. We were able to keep our staff because most of them happened to be ordained men. The letters from the army continued to urge us, to quote one soldier, to " keep things going as strongly as possible, in order that when at last peace is with us again, those who return may be able to take up the thread, thin though it may have grown, and continue the work."

The committees were competent and spiritually alert in 1916, and the Movement showed its vitality by creating at Swanwick two new councils, on the model of the Irish, Welsh and Scottish, one for the North and the other for the South of England, still leaving London with its own Council.

I was forced in the autumn of 1916 to give a good

---

[1] *The Student Movement*, vol. xix. p. 19.

deal of thought, and spend some time in talks and correspondence with senior people, about the presence of conscientious objectors to war in the Movement. The country was in a jumpy state, and several highly respected senior friends, theological professors, wrote complaining that the Student Movement was being accused of encouraging shirkers and employing pacifists on its staff. I prepared a memorandum in the autumn of 1916 for my own guidance in dealing with the subject. Here it is.

NOTES ON PACIFISM

In the group of men and women on whom the responsibility for the leadership of the Movement rests the anti-pacifists are in an overwhelming majority.

The pacifist movement among students has not had its centre in the Student Movement, but in the Nonconformist theological colleges. Any movement in the colleges must of course affect the Student Movement; this fact is unquestionable.

In the case of the secretaries who are pacifists and whom the Movement had in its employment before the war, would anyone suggest that they should have been dismissed on the ground that a religious society had no room for men who believed that the principles of Jesus Christ precluded their taking part in war ? If any of them used their position in the Movement to propagate pacifist views there would be ground for the Movement taking action. With a single exception any pacifists in the service of the Movement are ordained men. No Church has deprived of their work clergy or ministers for holding pacifist views ; ought the Student Movement to do what the Church has not done ?

The fact that there are some in the Movement who hold pacifist views is well known to members of the Student Movement in the army and navy, not one single protest has reached the Executive from these Student Movement men who are serving ; past and present Student Movement men in army and navy must number at the lowest computation 10,000. I believe that if anyone was dismissed because of believing a Christian may not fight that this action would be viewed with dismay by large numbers of our men in the army, and that we should be overwhelmed with protests.

A number of men in the army have said to me that they were glad there were some pacifists in the Movement, always saying something like this about them: " I couldn't adopt their views, and I think that as things are they are wrong, but they see the ideal, and they uphold the ideal, and we can value that although we do not agree with the method whereby they have chosen to uphold the ideal."

It is the greatest possible mistake not to recognize that the term pacifist is one that is used to describe all kinds of men, and while many of them are mere cranks and wreckers, it would be shutting one's eyes to plain facts to fail to recognize that, however much we may disagree with them, there are pacifists who are men of the highest possible ideals and of ardent patriotism. It is always difficult for the idealist and the practical man to agree as to what the next step should be in an hour of crisis, but that does not mean that the idealist may not have a contribution, both because he has ideals, and because of his own high character. The type of pacifist we have in the Student Movement is not the crank type or the type that uses pacifism to cover the spirit of a shirker; some of them are men who up to the verge of the war everyone would have picked out as the very best men in the colleges. They have not changed, and we need to pause and reflect before reversing too completely our judgment of them because we differ from them in our interpretation of duty in the light of the New Testament.

I have come across one or two cases of men in the army who up to the war were developing splendidly as fine Christian men. They felt themselves led towards pacifist views when the war broke out, but under pressure from their seniors and their friends they stifled these views and joined the army. This acting against conscience has been absolutely ruinous in the effect upon the men's character. If we coerced pacifists into fighting when their conscience is against it, we might gain a few soldiers but we should lose some upright, independent characters. Let us reason with these men by all means and seek to secure a change of mind, but do not let us coerce them. It seems to me that many men who ought to know better in the churches, clergy and ministers, have overlooked this aspect of the case. I am much more impressed by the judgment and balance of mind the Student Movement has shown in its attitude towards pacifists in its ranks than I am by the attitude of the churches to the pacifists in their ranks.

When all is said and done, it should be remembered that the number of pacifists in the Student Movement is very small; I don't think there can be more than 5 per cent. who are pacifists, the other 95 per cent. being anti-pacifists.

This phenomenon of pacifism among the younger generation is apparent in every country in Europe. It has nothing directly to do with the Student Movement, it is, speaking generally, a movement among younger people of all classes, and it is found in enemy countries (*e.g.* in Germany) and in neutral countries (*e.g.* Holland and Switzerland), just as it is found in the countries of the Allies (*e.g.* Russia and Great Britain).

For all the contumely the pacifists had to face during the war, it is their point of view which gained ground. Conscience was awakened among Christian people generally, and war as a right method of settling disputes between nations was arraigned as wrong. A definite advance in Christian ethics was made, and the advance is in the main due to the pacifists—younger men and women who saw the war as a great sin rather than an inevitable duty.

A letter reached me at this time that contained the suggestion of a project in which the Movement came to have a part:

20 Braidburn Crescent,
Edinburgh,
November 9th, 1916.

My dear Tatlow,

. . . I am planning, with the approval of Carter, an investigation into the religious mind of the new armies. If we can really get at that, if there is such a common mind, and if we can strike it, it seems to me we have the basis laid for a true advance in getting ahead with the youth of the country as a whole afterwards.

If one could get a little group of Student Movement men together on the business that is what I should like. Neville is the man I think first of—then there is Woods. Can you suggest any more of first-hand experience of soldiers, and with the vital mind? And what do you think of the design? It has haunted me for a while. We could use all the antennæ of the Huts throughout all the new armies, and I think we could get at most of the chaplains who matter in a thing of the kind. I don't know whether the thing is practicable, but Oldham and Carter seem to fancy the idea. What do you think of it? Meantime it is quite private. If Donald Hankey were only still with us! . . .

Affectionately yours,

D. S. CAIRNS.

We discussed the project at Annandale, and as a result I took in hand the assembling of a group, while the Y.M.C.A. agreed to bear the cost, which was considerable. A couple of years ago Bishop Talbot said to me reflectively, " I wonder how I came to be chairman of the Army and Religion Enquiry during the war? " I knew, for at an informal talk with Dr Cairns, Mr E. C. Carter and Canon Streeter at the Y.M.C.A., with which I was in close touch as a member of its War Emergency Committee, they had said, " You take the thing in hand."

The links of the Student Movement were such that there was no difficulty in securing from among its members and friends a representative group, and the first man I approached was the Bishop of Winchester, with the request that he would be our chairman. He threw himself whole-heartedly into the project, and was the friend of every one of the twenty-seven people responsible for the volume [1] of over 400 pages published by Messrs Macmillan in the spring of 1919.

The group was representative, and one is tempted to reminiscence! The patience of Dr Cairns when we came to the drafting stage and pulled his sheets of printed matter to pieces! He was draftsman and rewrote the report more than once. The efforts of the chairman to follow Dr John Oman in his elusive and elaborate lines of reasoning. Professor A. S. Peake's tremendous speeches which began in Jeremiah or the Book of Job and ended up with the British army. The perspicacity of Baron von Hügel as, guided by Miss Fairfield, whose

[1] *The Army and Religion: An Enquiry and its Bearing upon the Religious Life of the Nation.*

notes for him made as the debate went on he watched like a terrier does a rat-hole, pouncing as a point he was interested in appeared (the Baron, being deaf, heard nothing), and his marvellous command of slang! But I must desist.

The group held several meetings, each of some days' duration—at Hatfield House, Lady Margaret Hall, Farnham Castle, and in London. Annandale was filled with memoranda and letters from army cooks and generals, all intervening ranks being represented. Miss Thornton sorted and filed thousands of documents, and we supplied mountainous bundles of typescript to each member before the meetings. When the volume appeared the Press gave it a cordial reception, but I am bound to say that I don't think the Churches ever took it very seriously or profited by it as they might have done.

As the war dragged on and the number of German prisoners in England increased, service of one kind or another was rendered to them. Henriod visited the camps, and a group of members of the Danish Student Movement sent folios of religious pictures to the Movement for distribution amongst them. We sent books to our own prisoners interned at Ruhleben in Germany.

Wilder and I worked on the Religious Work Committee of the Y.M.C.A. This committee was responsible for the conduct of missions in between 200 and 250 huts in the south-east district of England, with remarkably good results.

The need of workers in India, Mesopotamia and France became increasingly urgent. At one period eighty men were wanted at once for important posts outside England, and this at a time when the difficulty of securing workers, owing to the calling up of men under Lord Derby's Scheme, was greatly increased. The Movement redoubled its efforts to find workers. The women were called upon for more and more help as work on the land became a national necessity. The Y.W.C.A. were as active as the Y.M.C.A., and we co-operated with them in securing women students as hut workers in flax-pickers' camps, and numerous other activities.

The General Committee ended its year's work by holding at its Christmas meeting its first "National Day." The rebellion in Dublin in the spring made Ireland the obvious country to choose. Mr R. S. Dickie, of Londonderry, Mrs Scott (Rita Low) and Miss Eleanor Cargin were present as visitors. J. T. Anderson, one of the Irish students on the committee, opened with a survey of the Irish college field; Mrs Scott dealt with Irish movements, agricultural, literary and technical; R. S. Dickie dealt with the political situation from the Unionist, and Miss Cargin with the situation from the Nationalist, point of view. To an Irishman domiciled in England, it was interesting to observe the almost complete novelty information about Irish life was to the members of the General Committee. The addresses were greatly appreciated, and certainly helped the Committee to understand more of the background of Irish student life.

CHAPTER XXXII

SOCIAL, EDUCATIONAL AND FINE ART DEVELOPMENTS, AND THE END OF THE WAR

THE thought of the Movement on social questions had been increasingly thorough since the Matlock Conference, 1909, and the war helped rather than hindered this process. The fellowship in the army of all sorts and conditions of men threw into relief, which could not be ignored, the strife at home. Employees and employers ranged against one another, employers' associations against trade unions, federations of employers' associations against federations of trade unions. There was a " triple alliance " of railwaymen, transport workers and miners. In the three or four years before the war there was a coal strike, a railway strike, a series of transport strikes, while a bitter building trade lock-out was in being when the war came. The war suspended that and other disputes, but it did not change the conditions out of which they arose.

In November 1915 the Social Service Committee of the Movement met its Education and Training College Committee to consider the social policy of the Movement. A diagnosis of the situation brought three things into prominence, first, that while the war had roused a spirit of sacrifice, and there were signs of deeper understanding and sympathy, yet evil conditions remained, and would be more bitterly felt when the war was over, and reaction and readjustment began. Second, the problem of our national life was not the problem of the destitute, but " of the life of the bulk of our people, the great mass of men, women and children living on round about 30s. a week." Third, the need for an educational

THE NEW "ANNANDALE," AS REBUILT IN 1928

revolution, a revolution which would give every one a
new view of the nature and obligations of citizenship,
and which must be the result of education. Education
in citizenship must become part of the education of all,
from schoolboy or schoolgirl to student.

The conference which resulted in this emphasis on
citizenship set before the Movement the importance of
studying the subject, and of " making real friendship
with people of another social class." It was decided to
ask university and college authorities to provide lectures
on citizenship. At Leeds University, Mr Michael Sadler
responded to the request and arranged a course of
lectures.

The prophets were very busy during the war as to
what would happen after it, and we had every kind of
prophecy, from the threat that the war would lead to
social chaos to the assurance that it would usher in
something like the Kingdom of Heaven. The Movement kept going its study of social questions of all
kinds, and the pages of *The Student Movement* reveal the
range of its interest.

Malcolm Spencer remained the leading thinker of the
Movement on its social questions side. He taught that
while the economic future was incalculable, we had more
data as to the future on the psychological and spiritual
side of the problem, yet we might be sure if it was
peace and plenty for a few it would be peace and penury
for the many. He thought that the leaders would " patch
up our society again sufficiently for it to go about its
business," but that it would be done in the light of their
own philosophy of life, " the philosophy of the generation whose works are evident in this war." To the
younger generation would be left the problem of
" changing the social outlook of the nation." The
elements in the situation which would make for con-
tention and strife would be a return to material misery
for many, and the desire of others to relax and recoup
themselves for the tension of the war.

Spencer thought that the hope of the future lay with

2 Q

the few " whose lives have been put out to the high usury which God pays upon all heroic spiritual investment in times of intense living like the present." Many had had lessons in the social meaning of life, men now saw that virtue might resist violence, but had no value as a constructive agent. Light, too, had fallen upon another realm of social action.

> The power and possibility of collective action organized by the state. . . . It is clear at any rate that the nation, acting together, is not impotent to deal with a crisis . . . our notions of the legitimate sphere of collective action must have widened considerably during the war.

But he was very uneasy about our disunity.

> We are damned by our disunity. . . . The Churches, and the political parties and the various classes of society, have each got hold of a bit of the true notion of how society should be ordered, but there is no fusion of their wisdom into an effective programme.

He urged us to " fling ourselves into all the movements both within and without the Churches which make for fellowship and education." [1]

Students were responsive to this lead, for the outstanding feature of the second half of the war was a rising tide of social interest and enthusiasm. There were 185 social study circles with 1513 members in the colleges in 1916-17, and 210 study circles with 1646 members in 1917-18, an increase on the two previous years in spite of the fact that distractions seemed to make the period a very difficult one in which to study.

In all the colleges in the country only twenty-one possessed any society dealing with social matters other than their Christian Union. Eighteen out of the twenty-one societies were reported as " working in more or less close co-operation with the Christian Union." The main business of the S.C.M. was study, though many Christian Unions also helped in a large number of social service activities—play centres, babies' welcomes and

[1] *The Student Movement*, art. : " After the War," vol. xviii. p. 121.

other infant welfare work, girls' clubs, services in infirmaries and poorhouses, meetings for fisherfolk, college settlements, etc.

While the General Committee realized its privilege in being allowed to arouse and guide the social interest of the colleges, it felt acutely that the task was beyond the powers of any student society.

> We look forward to the time when some training in citizenship shall form part of the college course of every student. We believe that the training of all professional men and women should include instruction on their place in the national life, and the opportunities and obligations of service presented to them by their calling.[1]

Students thought more and more about the implications of Christianity for national and international life.

> There was impatience with those in the Churches " who consider that their full social duty has been performed when they have looked after the welfare of those who have been wounded or broken in the social strife. Students recognize that the Churches have done magnificent remedial work of this kind, and none of them wish to see such work stopped, but they feel that such palliative measures touch only the surface of the difficulty. We must be ready to undertake the revaluation of all our values, to challenge the whole social system of our day by the fearless application to it of the true social principles of respect for human personality, and of the duty and privilege of service which underlie the Christian Gospel. Society is laying itself in ruins to-day because it has forgotten Jesus Christ. Only His redeeming power can save it. We are called to go forth in His strength to help to rebuild the world in the light of His teaching and example." [2]

Women students were as eager as any of the men to see changes in the ordering of society. They had seen great changes in the position in society of their own sex. This is not the place to attempt any description of the revolution in the position of women as a result of the war. When war came the situation was deplorable,

[1] Report to World's Student Christian Federation, 1916-1917.
[2] *Ibid.*

the movement for women's suffrage was before the public in militant guise, and acts of violence followed by prison and forcible feeding of women was occupying public attention, and distressing every one who had a high sense of the value of human dignity.   The fight by women for a full share in the life and work of the community had gone on for many years, hope deferred had made the hearts of many women sick and the conflict had made many men stubborn.   The contest is not one of which men have any cause to feel proud. In the Student Movement the sexes were on good terms, we were so accustomed to working together that we found it difficult at times to understand the antagonism. Before the war the subject of the position of women had occupied our attention, and Miss Fairfield completed for publication early in the war a book, *Some Aspects of the Woman Movement*, which was a collection of essays, two of which she wrote, the remainder being contributed by different university dons.   The book was well received, and many study circles formed on it in the women's colleges.

The war opened a multitude of new avenues of activity for women, and offered them a host of ways in which they could help the nation.   When opportunity was offered, women proved as eager and as competent to take it as men, their position was revolutionized and their freedom won, a freedom of which the franchise granted to them at this period was the symbol.   In the women's colleges the war had a stimulating effect on a large number of people.

> There is more open-mindedness about questions which used to be dealt with dogmatically, questions of religion, politics, the conventions and social matters.   There is a marked unwillingness to accept anything on the basis of either authority, history or established custom.[1]

Everywhere there was a desire for radical change and a readiness for action.   "What can we do to make

[1] *Annual Report*, S.C.M., 1916-17, p. 5.

things better ? " was a frequent question. Neither the colleges nor the Movement ever became wholly pre-occupied with the war. The future was always kept in view. One result of this was great interest in every kind of corporate relationship, whether it was the relationship between capital and labour or between nations, and always we came back to the question of education.

The Movement's Committee on work in training colleges had stirred our minds not merely upon its work in these colleges but upon the whole subject of education. The Theological Dons' Conference had been concerned with what was a question of education, the problems of society raised the same issue, and so did revived interest in the relation of art to life. The result was that we began to look in a new way on edu-cation and the educational value of what the Movement was trying to do.

Education had never been popular in England. The upper and middle classes have never had a very high appreciation of their own education, and the children of the working-classes were almost all removed from school just before the age at which they might most fully profit by school life.

And now, to crown all, our civilization has been thrown into chaos by the nation which prides itself upon being the best educated in the world. There is a real danger that we miss our way more than ever. Some feel that Germany has simply emphasized the danger of being over-educated. After all, however, what they have really demonstrated is that education is a great power, but since it may be of the wrong kind, it may be a great power for evil. The con-verse is true. If it is of the right kind it may be a great power for good.[1]

We decided we must try to play a wise part in the Movement in relation to education.

As a Student Movement the whole question is one which concerns us deeply. As students . . . because many of

[1] *The Student Movement*, Editorial, vol. xviii. p. 26.

us will become teachers in every variety of educational institution. More than all, it concerns us because the true end of education is intimately connected with the ideals to which as a Movement we are committed. The training of character, the inculcation of great principles, the opening of the mind to fundamental realities, the setting free of the human spirit, the production in man of that goodwill which will lead him to right relationships, both human and divine, are essential parts of true education.

It was a constant source of distress to us, especially to those who had been educated at one of the older universities in England, Ireland or Scotland, that in the new universities, university and training colleges, students seemed to be studying under serious disadvantages.

> The predominant practice is still to teach a large number of facts, and to do so in a way which leaves the mind tired, over-crowded, confused, and unawakened . . . Our great secular universities may be a gigantic blunder! Some of our training colleges may be entirely unsuited for producing the kind of people best fitted to train the children of the nation.

We knew the value of the Movement's work, because of the large body of ex-students who said " that the Christian Union just saved the situation for them when they were at college." Still more were we " grateful for the support we receive from an ever-growing body of teachers," who agreed with us " that the things which the Christian Union stands for are vital, and should have full recognition in the life of every educational institution." We resolved " that the future should find us absorbed with the whole question of education. We do not say with religious education, for all education, if it is to be true, should be religious." [1]

A memorandum printed privately for the guidance of Student Movement secretaries and committees at this period contains an interesting and stimulating review of education and educational institutions in Great Britain

[1] *The Student Movement*, Editorial, vol. xviii. p. 27.

and Ireland, a searching examination of the aims of British education, a sketch of the ideal university, and, after summarizing the work of the Movement in connection with education, closes with a series of suggestions. The document is far too long to quote in full, but the first four of its suggestions to the Movement were as follows :

1. The Student Movement should put all the force of its inspiration and interest behind college work—study. The influence of a really Christian member of staff is nearly always seen in the love of his or her students for their subject—history, science, or whatever it may be. We need more conviction that work is in the centre of the Christian life, and not an incident or interruption. Students should be encouraged to use everything good in their college curriculum, and to aim less at numbers of " activities " and more at real knowledge.

2. People with a vital belief in Christianity should be encouraged to be dons. All the fundamental things come up, and can be discussed freely in the course of ordinary college work with greater thoroughness and more knowledge than in the average study-circle.

3. A number of intercollegiate secretaries are needed for all the large university centres.

4. More study secretaries are needed at once, so that the study work of the Movement may be thorough and up to a good standard : they would also help the intercollegiate secretaries with study work in the different centres.

Our declarations about education and articles in *The Student Movement* brought a sympathetic response from many quarters. We hoped for a national lead on the subject since the topic was in the public mind, but the Government had nothing positive to say about education, while the London County Council introduced education economies. Whenever public economies are introduced in England expenditure on education is invariably reduced. Encouragement, however, came from France. The French Minister of Education issued a stirring memorandum on the subject of education, to which we gave what publicity we could.

The French Minister asked for no eligible man to

be spared from military service, nevertheless he urged that the fires of education be kept burning.

> But whatever the difficulties, not only the permanence, but also the vitality of higher education must be ensured during this year. This is necessary for our country's own sake, for other nations, and for the future.
>
> For the sake of the students not of military age, or whose physical condition debars them from the field of battle, for the sake of those who return wounded and wish to continue their studies, for the sake of the young women who wish to be initiated into the methods of higher learning in order that, later, they may carry the devotion of womanly co-operation to the highest national tasks; the intellectual fires of our country must not be allowed to go out.
>
> They must be kept burning for the sake of our foreign guests, for those students of neutral countries who even now during the war are coming to seek our culture and learning, and who will come to our universities in ever greater numbers on account of the sentiments which the odious deeds of German culture have awakened throughout the world. They must be kept burning, because after the war the universities must make an immense effort to make higher learning the guide and leader of a renewed national economic activity, and of the vast movement for the renewal of chemical and physical industries which will necessarily follow a victorious peace.[1]

A reference above to the revived interest in work among fine art students should have further elaboration. The conjunction of Dorothy M'William, Zoë Fairfield and Leslie Hunter in the Movement at this time led to the revival of its Fine Art Sub-committee. This committee thought about art and life, and also planned ways in which what it was thinking might find expression. Leslie Hunter wrote a book, *The Artist and Religion*, which stirred thought in a wider circle than the fine art colleges and music schools. A great deal of interest was also aroused by a series of lectures planned by the sub-committee and worked out by Miss Fairfield. Three lectures of the series were given at University College,

[1] Translated from the French Minister of Education's circular in *Le Journal Officiel de la République Française*, September 11th 1915.

Gower Street, and two at Queen Alexandra's House, Kensington Gore.

The lectures dealt with the value of art to the community, the relation of art and national life, the relation of art and religion and the personal life of the artist. One of the lecturers was Mr A. Clutton Brock, who was well known through his work for *The Times*, and with whom we had made great friends in the Movement. Alas, that death took his fine spirit from us at an early age! How he loved to talk, and what good talk it was! Once, at Muriel Harris' house at Lye Green, he paced up and down the garden alone after breakfast. Two or three of us were indoors struggling with correspondence. Clutton Brock bore it for a little, and then in came his head at the door. " I say, do come out and talk; how can you bear not to talk when we've got so much to say?"

Other lecturers were Mr Geoffrey Shaw, H.M. Inspector of Music, Mr Will Rothenstein,[1] Mr G. K. Chesterton and Miss Lena Ashwell. Among the chairmen were Mr John Hassall, the shyest man I ever piloted into the chair at a lecture, Mr George Clausen[2] and Rev. William Temple. William Temple took the chair for Chesterton. I got them on the platform and they sat down in chairs side by side. The audience hushed for the meeting to begin. Temple looked round at Chesterton as he was about to rise, but suddenly fell back into his chair, remarking in a loud voice, " I don't know if this is a joke on the part of the Student Movement, but we do look extraordinarily like Tweedle-Dum and Tweedle-Dee." Then he began to laugh. Temple's laugh is the most infectious in the kingdom. The audience roared in sympathy, while Temple and Chesterton sat in their chairs side by side shaking with laughter, until I thought there would be no lecture!

The following year another course was arranged, and an audience which averaged two hundred fine art

[1] Afterwards Sir William Rothenstein.
[2] Afterwards Sir George Clausen, R.A.

students attended a series of lectures in the Physiological Theatre, University College, London, arranged by the Movement. Lecturers and subjects were: A. Clutton Brock, "What is good art?"; Professor G. H. Leonard, of Bristol University, "The artist as citizen"; Professor W. R. Lethaby, of the Royal College of Art, "Work and the worker"; Canon Streeter, "Æstheticism, ugliness and art"; and Dr H. Walford Davies,[1] "Art and worship." On this occasion there was discussion after each of the lectures.

These two courses, followed by lectures to fine art students in other parts of the country—Clutton Brock went for us to Scotland—and discussions and study circles, did much to bring art into its true place in the life of the Movement at this time, as well as to help many art students.

Two main ideas were emphasized. One was the necessity for reality—as opposed to conventionality, insincerity, ecclesiasticism—in art, life and religion.

> The other was the conviction that if the feeling of separation between the artistic community and the community as a whole, and in particular the religious group, was to be overcome, a considerable change must take place, not only among artists, but throughout the rest of the community. The Church must again make clear its need of the artist, it must trust him more, it must give him not only greater scope, but greater freedom to express the truth in ways which are alive and real to the mind of his day. And if art is not only expression, but also is "work well done," then the community must repent of the hideous travesty of art as work well done which is to be found in every city and every industry to-day, and must hear again what the artist has to say. The vital connection between the work of artists and social reform is a subject which merits the study of all members of the Student Movement.[2]

At the summer conference, 1917, the first serious attempt made by the Movement to improve the singing was undertaken. Leslie Hunter suggested that Mr

[1] Afterwards Sir H. Walford Davies.
[2] *Annual Report, S.C.M.*, 1915-16, p. 34.

Geoffrey Shaw and his brother, Mr Martin Shaw, should be invited to come to Swanwick and take the music in hand. They accepted the committee's invitation, and were given opportunities of speaking about music and training a choir.

The singing at summer conferences had always been lusty but very poor as music. The effect of the work of the brothers Shaw was to raise the standard in so marked a way that the improvement was obvious to all. It became a tradition, which has not been departed from since, that an expert musician should set to work at once when a summer conference assembles and pick and train a choir to lead the singing.

Music was thus given a new place in the life of the summer conference, and it was not long before a regular place was provided on the programme for an hour's music each day. The daily concerts vary somewhat in quality from year to year, according to the performers available, but there is always some really good vocal and instrumental music every summer at Swanwick during the conference. In recent years Miss Trevelyan's fame as the creator in a night of madrigal parties, the maker of concerts in an hour, the leader of the jolliest of sing-songs, is world-wide.

The presence of the Archbishop of Canterbury for four days the same summer as we reformed our singing was an event. I had on several occasions suggested to his Grace that he should come to a summer conference, because he only knew the Movement through literature, one or two of its leaders, and the medical students whom he entertained every Ash Wednesday at Lambeth. I felt sure that he would be immensely interested if he were to see the Movement in being at a summer conference.

In the spring of 1917 I saw him at Lambeth and urged that he should come that year. He agreed and made the condition that he should not be one of the speakers at the conference, explaining that he would feel much freer to enjoy it if he was not burdened with the responsibility of speeches.

When the students knew he was to be one of the guests his visit was anticipated with the liveliest interest. It was well known in Student Movement circles that he was a friend. Most of the students had never seen him. There were numerous inquiries as to what he was like, whether he would be very stiff and aloof and prelatical. The men wanted to know whether he would visit them in camp, what they were to call him, would it be right to address him as " Your Holiness," and so on. The conference was in full swing when he and Mrs Davidson arrived. Needless to say, they both of them went everywhere and talked to everybody, and it would be no exaggeration to say that the Movement never had a visitor who so came up to expectations as did the Archbishop.

He did not escape without speaking, as the students were determined that he should address them, which he did at a specially convened meeting. It was a very simple speech, in which he talked about what seemed to him to be the potentialities of the Movement. He was obviously deeply moved, as he referred to the anxieties and sorrows of the war, how it had broken traditions and damaged many good causes, and how heartening it was to meet a body of young people who cared for the Kingdom of God, and who would be ready to take a share in the spiritual leadership of the future.

As he was about to step into the motor that was to carry him to Ambergate station, he turned to me and said : " Well, upon my word, Tatlow, with all the opportunities I have had and all that I have seen in life, I did not think anybody could give me a new experience in connection with a religious gathering, but all I can say is, that I have never been at anything in the least like this conference and I am profoundly thankful for it." Within a day or two came a letter from G. K. A. Bell,[1] one of his chaplains, an old member of the Movement who was greatly interested in the visit, saying that he was delighted to find it had been such a

[1] Afterwards Bishop of Chichester.

success and that the Archbishop had enjoyed it so much.
He added that his Grace "feels more than ever the importance of the Movement to the whole life of the nation."

It has been touching to observe how to the end of
Archbishop Davidson's life the knowledge of his love
for the S.C.M. was passed on in the student committees.
Scores of student leaders who never saw him have felt
their fellowship in the S.C.M. enriched by his friendship.
His name for many years was never mentioned without
there being a sense of reverence attached to it.   Students
have a sure instinct in discerning their friends, and they
made no mistake in being sure of Lord Davidson's deep
friendship for the Student Movement.

This year the General Committee elected a woman
for the first time as its chairman, Dora Ivens,[1] Girton
College, Cambridge.   The Rev. L. W. Grensted, Egerton Hall, Manchester, was elected vice-chairman and
M'Murray Cole as second vice-chairman.   These extra
elections were unusual and a sign of the uncertainty
of anyone's attendance.   As a matter of fact, Miss Ivens
was working with the Y.M.C.A. in France when the
General Committee met in September, but she was back
at Christmas 1917 to serve as chairman.

A new responsibility came to the Movement when
term opened.   Sir Joseph Maclay [2] had offered to secure
two houses opposite the University of Glasgow and
present them as a hall of residence for women students
if the Movement would accept the gift and undertake
the management.   There were 900 women students in
Glasgow and only one hostel was available.   The donor
expressed the wish that the house should be run at as
economical a charge as possible to make it available
for poor students, and that it should also be used as
a centre for Student Movement work among women
students.   The General Committee decided to accept
the offer with gratitude.   Thus South Park House,
Glasgow, fully equipped and ready for occupation by
thirty-four students, came into its possession.   It is the

[1] Afterwards Mrs T. W. Pym.   [2] Afterwards Lord Maclay.

one student hostel owned by the Movement. Miss Hitchcock, the women's intercollegiate secretary for Glasgow, was appointed as the first warden and a management committee was chosen to act under the direction of the General Committee. Mrs Dempster, who was already well known in Student Movement circles through the fine work for Oriental students she was doing in her home together with her husband, the Rev. J. Dempster, became honorary secretary of this management committee. The house was opened in October 1917 by Miss Melville, Principal of Queen Margaret College.

As the war continued more and more women entered the universities and colleges, the increase in women medical students being most marked. Special provision was made for them at several hospitals in London, where they were admitted as medical students, and Edinburgh University made them full members in the autumn of 1916. The joint fresher social at Edinburgh of the men's and women's Christian Unions had a large number of medicals of both sexes among the 500 students who attended it. A considerable proportion of the women who commenced medical courses were unprepared, and some unsuited, for the intellectual, moral and spiritual strain of qualifying in medicine. The Movement brought help to many through the appointment to its staff a year later of a qualified woman doctor as a travelling secretary. Dr Mollie Hemingway began work on May 1st 1918 and Dr Elsie Towers succeeded her after a year.

Some of the best thinking that has been done in relation to medical students, and the things for which the Movement stands, was done under the guidance of Ronald Rees before he joined the Royal Horse Artillery, to which a series of articles by him in *The Student Movement* [1] bears witness.

The Movement had never ceased giving time and

[1] *The Student Movement*, " Medical Students and the S.C.M.," vol. xx. pp. 21, 37, 53.

thought to India, where so many of its former leaders were at work. This meant the promotion of knowledge, both missionary and political. India received renewed attention as peace approached, for two reasons. One was the appearance at midsummer, 1918, of *The Report on Indian Constitutional Reforms*, which is popularly known as the Montagu-Chelmsford Report. The scheme contained in the Report was intended to carry into effect the pledge made by the Secretary of State for India in the House of Commons on August 20th 1917, that the policy of Great Britain in India is henceforth to be " the gradual development of self-governing institutions, with a view to the progressive realization of responsible government in India as an integral part of the British Empire." Mr Ernest Barker, Fellow of New College, Oxford, hailed this in *The Student Movement* as " a very fundamental announcement, almost of the nature of a Magna Carta for India."

The other reason for new interest in India was the return from there of Bill Paton. He had been given leave of absence a year before to undertake special service for the Y.M.C.A. in India. The Movement told him to use the opportunity afforded by the visit to study the missionary situation, and thus qualify himself to present both Indian and missionary questions to the colleges when he returned. The General Committee wisely decided to relieve Paton of his duties as assistant secretary on his return in order that he might devote himself to the missionary work of the Movement. Paton had used his time in India to good effect, made many friendships in Indian circles, and returned to be the best qualified missionary secretary the Movement has ever had.

Although many missionaries who had been student volunteers had served the Movement when on furlough, we learnt that to send a man, whom the colleges knew and who knew the colleges, to study at first hand some of the more urgent missionary questions, has an effectiveness no other arrangement can equal.

The sorest blow of the war to the Federation came six weeks before the Armistice. Charles Grauss, the general secretary of the French Student Christian Movement, was killed. We knew him well, he was at our quadrennial conference at Liverpool, 1908, and had also been at summer conferences. He was a man of high courage, outstanding ability and deep devotion. I should like to enshrine his memory in this record of our British Movement. He was one of the men who made the Federation " live " for us.

A man of middle stature, with large blue eyes and heavy lids, an oval face, firm mouth and fair hair parted in the middle, falling in two points on to his forehead. He proved himself a real leader during the thirteen years he was general secretary of the French Student Movement. He often had to face great opposition, the French student field is not an easy one in which to lead a Student Christian Movement. To see him square his shoulders, and throw back his head, as he faced an audience, was to realize that here was a man accustomed to meet and overcome difficulties. He found time while in the French trenches, just before he was made a Chevalier de la Legion d'Honneur, to write an historical account of the development of the policy of the French Student Movement for *The Student Movement*.

" Starting with a strong tendency to individualism," he wrote, " we were gradually led to feel a great yearning to make the Gospel known, and we realized that we were responsible for the spiritual welfare of the students of our university. . . . Then we began to think of French national life, till our sense of responsibility extended to all the universities in the world, and weighed with special force on our minds with regard to those countries where Latin influence is most felt. . . . We longed ardently to reconcile the intellectual expression of our faith with the new problems arising from modern thinking, either philosophical, moral or social.

He was at the front from August 2nd 1914 to August 29th 1918, when he was wounded in the attack on Juvigny, dying the same day.

His care for the Movement never relaxed.   More than one noble message came from his pen addressed to the students left in the French universities, and whenever he had leave he always made his way to the headquarters of the Movement in Paris.   His optimism was of a fine quality.   " We are just as optimistic as ever," he wrote from the trenches.   This optimism was rooted in faith in God and in God's purpose for the Movement.

" The more brutal the war," he wrote, " the more we feel our need of God ; as hatred grows, the beauty of love is felt to be ever more irresistibly attractive.   We feel that national loss can only be compensated by spiritual enrich-ment, and it is only by basing its social, moral, religious, economic and international institutions on the sacred foun-dations of justice that the world can be so enriched.   Does it not seem as if God's hour was drawing near ?   No demands for sacrifices will find us unprepared. . . . We want Christian ideals to permeate our whole life ; Christian principles to be carried to their last consequences ; nothing and no one shall stand in our way ; we want to live a full realization of our faith.   And that is only encouraged by remembrances of the past, trusting more than ever in the immortal genius of our country, with the glory of our fallen friends shining on us, in faith toward God we dare to face serenely the days to come, ready, as we are, to die for France and for the world." [1]

A few months after the Armistice a little group of us, led by the chairman of the French Movement, Professor Raoul Allier, of Paris University, made our way through smashed, torn, ravaged, desolate Northern France, to his grave, and there thanked God for this noble man, and pledged ourselves afresh to God and to one another in and through the work of the Student Movements of France and England.   It was a day of grief and anguish of heart, and yet of hope.

The ordinary work of the Christian Unions in Great Britain, as well as the central activities of the Movement,

[1] *The Student Movement*, art. : " The Period of Growth in the French Student Christian Movement," Chas. Grauss, LL.D., vol. xx. p. 57.

were carried on all through the war. There were never less than 24,500 students in the colleges—that was the number in them the term it ended. Twenty-four per cent. of these were members of the Movement. This membership was unusually high, and in addition, many students not members joined in the activities of the Christian Unions. Six hundred freshmen in a very depleted field attended the London freshmen's meeting in 1917, and that was typical.

Nine conferences and Bible schools were organized by the Movement in 1917-18. Those at Swanwick were Bible and missionary study schools held at the same time, a general conference followed by an officers' conference, parallel to which was a training college conference. Seven hundred and eighty-six persons in all were present.

The labours of Victor Murray, who visited the Christian Unions of the British Isles, were herculean, and George Cockin added the care of London men's Christian Unions to his work as foreign student secretary. They were the only men left at work for the Movement in the field at one time, with Henriod to look after the foreign students. A fine group of women worked with unflagging vigour in every sphere of the Movement's work, while Hugh Martin and I moved constantly between the colleges and Annandale as we laboured in a day of opportunity. Miss Fairfield stuck to headquarters, and was the leader of most of the committees of the time—education, conference, fine art, social, auxiliary. Every one worked at top speed.

The strain of the war was tremendous. The suspense, the loss of relatives and friends, the sufferings of the refugees, the stories of atrocities embellished by the less reputable Press, the constant propaganda rendering all news unreliable, the knowledge of homes, indeed whole towns, in utter ruins, the destruction of ancient churches, Gothic buildings famous throughout the world for their memories and beauty, the flood-tide of ill-will and hate, the suppressed excitement. As the war became more ruthless, there was the huge loss in torpedoed ships, air raids on London night after night with the accompanying racket of our own guns' defence—how well able we became to distinguish the sound of the German tauber from that of our own aeroplanes—the shriek of shells, the clatter of shrapnel on the asphalte roads, the scarcity of food to eat and paper to write or print on, the difficulty of travel. And always the telegraph boys with those distinctive coloured envelopes it was an agony to tear open.

The talk about a better world was omnipresent and gained in volume as the war proceeded. One heard it in the colleges and out of them. It was a favourite theme in the Press, it was on the lips of politicians. It was also deep in men's hearts at home and in the trenches ; in France, in Mesopotamia, and on the seas men said that if they came through the war they would do all they knew to make a better world. In the Movement we shared this hope with the rest, but we knew it meant tremendous effort.

We shall not achieve a better world without a vast social reconstruction. There are not many signs that the number of people who realize how fundamental this reconstruction will need to be are very numerous . . . all are aware of the existence of social problems, but that does not carry us very far. . . . Very few see what needs to be done if England is to become a Christian country—politicians do not see it, the leaders of the Churches do not see it. Numbers of them are interested in social questions, but they are all occupied with palliatives. . . . We need a change of heart on a great scale as a nation. . . . It will mean a revolution, a constructive revolution, and this will require great intellectual and moral qualities.[1]

We worked with an eye to the future. A group to prepare for the coming of peace came into being in 1918, with several S.C.M. secretaries on it. The Hayes, Swanwick, was kept available for conferences, with the

[1] *The Student Movement*, Editorial, vol. xix. p. 137.

help of the Archbishop of Canterbury, and prisoners of war were interned elsewhere.

Old ideas had taken on a new meaning. " We are members one of another." " The world is a unity," Indian and African troops fighting in a European war ! Places we knew nothing of providing soldiers—pictures of Annamese in the papers ! Japan in arms for the Allies ! Questions of race and international relationships had gained a new significance. The frankness and directness of the call for service, " Your King and Country need you," put to shame our hesitating and apologetic recruiting of student volunteers for missionary service. Above all, there was the uncovering in ordinary men of the virtues of courage, self-sacrifice, devotion and heroism, and the reflection that the Christian warfare called for just these qualities—that it might use them to bring not death, but life.

There were signs that the war was drawing to a conclusion as I wrote on November 1st 1918 to tell members of the General Committee of the arrangements for our Christmas meeting. This account of the war began with the first letter I wrote on its outbreak; let it close with the last I sent to the committee before it ended.

> Everything in the Movement seems very lively and all the secretaries are very busy. The need for more men secretaries to work in the colleges is very great. We are thinking here (Annandale) about a big extension policy to be brought before Christmas Executives involving much more staff, more hostels, and needing more money. I think we ought to pray these times that the Student Movement may have vision to see its possibilities as regards the future; that it may have a mind and heart open towards God, and that He will give it the gifts needed to enable it to fulfil its vocation; that means gifts of men and money and gifts of new spiritual power to us all. We are none of us up to our task these days. It is all too big for us. We must turn back again and again to God; the more so, the more we realize the bigness of the task and what spiritual shrimps we all are.

CHAPTER XXXIII

THE POST-WAR MISSIONARY COMMISSION AND A NEW BASIS

THERE was a great change in the Movement between the spring and autumn of 1918. A revolt against orthodoxy in general, and the Churches in particular, grew in strength during the last period of the war. The students tended to say, as one group expressed it, " the Churches are useless and have no decided views about anything." This attitude led to theological unrest, and there were times when it seemed as if a vague pantheism was taking the place, even in some Student Movement circles, of the Christian faith. We were very anxious about this during the spring and early summer.

When we met in the autumn, however, the General Committee, which was a good deal changed in personnel, had taken on a new lease of spiritual life. There was also a more hopeful atmosphere due to signs that the war was drawing to an end. The after-war stage of the Movement's life really began at this meeting. Mrs Pym, our chairman, opened the meeting with an address on " our Gospel," and the discussion which followed centred round the experience of Christianity as a working force, tested and purified by the experiences of men and women in France and in England. J. H. Oldham and W. E. S. Holland—the latter called back from India by the Archbishop of Canterbury to lead a recruiting crusade —put before us the necessity of facing anew the responsibility of Christ's disciples towards the life of the whole world. We talked about the aim and basis; the Scottish Council held at St Andrews at Easter had voiced a desire for a change. The meeting concluded with a visit from

Baron Frederick Von Hügel, who spoke on "Institutional Christianity" for an hour and a quarter, and was listened to with rapt attention even though it was after three days' very strenuous work.

It was at this stage that the Movement appointed its third commission. Two and a half years—nearly a student generation—had passed since the missionary retreat which had done so much towards helping the Movement to maintain its missionary interest in spite of the absorption of every one in the war, and the subject needed fresh attention.

The committee of the Student Volunteer Missionary Union took the lead and in a tremendous discussion gave expression to anxiety, dissatisfaction and determination to stem the ebbing tide of missionary interest in the colleges. It is not surprising that the years of the war were difficult ones for the S.V.M.U. It had been very difficult to secure recruits for the mission field. Students' minds were engrossed with the war, with home claims, and with the future of society in the British Isles. Knowledge and interest in regard to non-Christian lands had tended to diminish. Nevertheless, 560 students signed during the war the declaration: "It is my purpose, if God permit, to become a foreign missionary." Missionary study had been undertaken by over 4500 students, some of the study being really good, a missionary study conference carried through with success, and keen missionary leadership had not failed all through the war.

The S.V.M.U. Committee wanted to see a big missionary push made when the war was over, and was very sensitive to the amount of criticism aroused in the colleges by efforts to interest students in the missionary enterprise.

The S.V.M.U. carried its "concern" to the General Committee and suggested it should appoint a commission to consider the missionary work of the Movement in all its bearings, and should send a questionnaire to the Councils to make sure the data it had before it was adequate. The Commission was agreed to, as was the questionnaire to the Councils. The questions asked were as follows :

1. Have the students in your college any place in their ideals for reconstruction in other lands ?
2. If so, what practical demands do they feel this makes on them ?
3. Do they feel that Christianity is the essential element in helping to work out new national ideals ?
4. Do they feel that they have any message about God to carry to other nations ?
5. How far are students prepared to make their contribution through the missionary societies ?
6. What is the opinion of your Council as to the value of the S.V.M.U. ?

These questions were passed on by the Councils to the college Christian Unions and " caused a great ferment in the colleges." The replies were studied by the Councils and a series of memoranda prepared on them for the Commission. The one thing that was clear was the widespread interest of students in the idea of a League of Nations which was before the world for consideration, but which had not yet been formed at the time of the Commission. Students generally thought that all should try to make an effective League of Nations, and that this was better than missionary work. Some asked if there could be some connection between making a League of Nations and carrying on missionary work ?

Bill Paton came back from India just before the Commission held its first meeting on November 27th, 1918, and his influence on behalf of Christian missions from the moment he returned made itself felt throughout the colleges of the British Isles.

The members of the Commission were : F. A. Cockin, Zoë Fairfield, Grace M'Aulay, Olive Moberly, William Paton, Dora Pym, Mary Anderson Scott, Lettice Shann, Tissington Tatlow, together with the following senior friends and former members : Miss G. A. Gollock, assistant editor, *The International Review of Missions*; the

Rev. W. E. S. Holland, C.M.S. missionary, Calcutta; Miss Florence Mackenzie, head of the Women's Missionary College, Edinburgh; and Mr J. H. Oldham, editor, *The International Review of Missions*.

The Report,[1] which was ready by the end of March 1919, diagnosed the situation, and after touching on temporary difficulties, indicated that some radical ones must be faced seriously :

> Such as grave criticism of the Churches and dissatisfaction with organized Christianity ; unwillingness to perpetuate denominational differences in other lands ; a considerable amount of criticism of the missionary societies, somewhat vague, but concerned with such matters as training, salaries, furlough allowances, the position of women, and theological teaching ; ignorance of the work actually carried on by the missionary societies, and of the growth and needs of the young Churches in the non-Christian world ; a growing belief that other religions contain much that is true and are better adapted than any imported religion could be to the needs of the countries in which they are found—a belief due partly to the presence of students from these lands in many of the colleges, and to the growth of interest in the comparative study of religion.

These did not, however, " touch the heart of the matter."

> Deeper and more important by far is the great question as to whether there is a message—Good News about God —which is distinctively Christian, and which is the gift the Christian missionary has to carry to other peoples ; a revelation which is given us in Christ and which is true for the whole world ; something, moreover, which may be verified in life and experience, whether racial, national, or individual.

Diagnosing the situation in the colleges, the Commission said :

> Perhaps the most striking fact is the widespread and increasing doubt as to whether there is any distinctive

[1] *Report of the third Commission appointed by the Executive of the Student Christian Movement in September* 1918 *to consider the missionary work of the Movement.*

Christian message at all.   This is largely due to ignorance
of Christianity itself, and to half-knowledge of the non-
Christian faiths.

In this state of mind students asked of Christianity,
" Will it work ? "

The Commission devoted considerable space to a
study of the Christian message.

To a world which had been made by God, but had lost
the way, came Jesus of Nazareth, calling men to repentance and proclaiming the nearness of the Kingdom of
God.   To our own as to every age He comes again with
the same message : that the work of the Church which is
called by His name is to transform the kingdoms of this
world into the Kingdom of God. . . . Progress has been
slow because men themselves have been slow to recognize
and carry out His will.

We have, in Christ Jesus, the true expression of the
character of God.   Does God care ?   Look to Christ.

In Him we come to know that the power at the heart of
all things is love : that love is the supreme force, all wise,
all powerful, all pervading.   That is the fact, from which
we start in all our enquiry and investigation, on which
we build all our interpretation of the universe, of human
life and destiny.

The Commission dealt with the meaning of the Cross
and the Resurrection ; with the revelation in Jesus
Christ of the possibilities of human nature, which possibilities can be realized in personal relation with Him.

It is an integral part of the revelation of the Father given
by Jesus Christ to the world, that fellowship with God,
loving, personal and gracious, is possible for man. . . .
Some will think of this power as coming through a mystical
union of the soul with God ; others will think of it as the
effect of one personality upon another.   The essential truth
is the same in either case.

The report dealt at some length with the " cardinal
importance " of the uniqueness of the Christian message,
disclaiming the idea that it means that " while Christianity is true, all other religions are false," or that " other

faiths owe their truth to contact with Christianity." The uniqueness of Christianity was defined as meaning :

> That in the revelation of God, given in Jesus Christ, we have the one perfect, flawless and whole revelation ever given. Compared to this all others are faulty or incomplete, in greater or less degree . . . it follows that this revelation is ultimate, in the sense that it cannot be superseded. . . . In this sense we have in His teaching and life the answer to every question and problem. In them lies the germ of all truth, and as we enter deeper into the understanding of the root principles on which they are based, we find the lines on which we can work out the solution of our own difficulties. . . . It means that no *truth* about God can be discovered which is not consistent with (because ultimately implicit in) the truth as revealed by Jesus. The Christian revelation is the criterion, the norm, by which all others must be judged.

The Commission made many suggestions for missionary education, reading and study circles on broader lines, urged more conferences between the leaders of the missionary societies and of the Movement, and recommended the development of missionary campaigns by students. It advised that the Auxiliary should co-operate in maintaining contact in the interest of missionary work with students who had become teachers, and it recommended a missionary conference in January 1921.

The report drew attention to the effect of the presence of large numbers of Oriental students on the missionary outlook in the colleges.

> There is no doubt that the presence of students from other lands in our colleges has a stimulating effect upon our own students. East and West societies, debates upon international subjects, personal acquaintance and friendship with individuals, have all helped to awaken a new interest in the history, present conditions, and future development of other races, especially the races of Africa and the East.
>
> This is all to the good. But there is one feature in the situation which gives some ground for anxiety. The fact that a man happens to belong to a particular country does

not of itself constitute him a reliable source of information on any subject connected with it. The ordinary British student rather easily tends to lose sight of this fact; and there is no question that in some cases quite misleading impressions are conveyed by foreigners of the conditions existing in their own countries. When it is further remembered that many of these men are non-Christians, with a strong bias against missionary work, it is not difficult to imagine the amount of harm that may be done by them, especially in view of the fact that their word often counts for more than the evidence of experienced missionaries.

Friendship with foreign students by student volunteers was advocated, as was the use of " very carefully selected " Oriental students invited to speak about their countries.

The Commission, in dealing with the relation of the Movement and the missionary societies, reminded the General Committee " of the very great responsibility which rests upon it, and upon the whole Student Movement, in the matter of missionary recruitment."

The missionary societies do not, except in the theological colleges and the few universities where denominational societies are vigorous, themselves attempt to recruit in the colleges. They leave this task to the Movement. Their representatives, when they visit the colleges, do so almost always at the request and under the auspices of the Student Movement. It is highly desirable that this arrangement should continue, and that a single missionary appeal should be made to the university world; but we have no right to expect that the societies, especially in the desperate need for volunteers which the war has created, should continue to observe this arrangement, unless we are doing all in our power to make the most effective appeal possible and to enlist the recruits whom the societies so urgently need.

The " striking challenge " which comes from the history of the S.V.M.U. was dwelt upon.

Men and women of wide experience in the mission field, and the home secretariat of the missionary societies, tell us that they have found in the men and women who have gone out from the S.V.M.U. the qualities of sympathy, progressiveness of spirit, and zeal for co-operation in an unusual degree. These things are not recorded as matters for boasting, but rather that we may see into what a heritage we have entered.

The position of women received attention in a section of the report. This was due to the fact that some of the most pungent student criticism came from women. " Women do not occupy in the secretariat or on the boards of the societies the position which they hold in most spheres to-day, and of the women who do occupy any position very few are university women," and the Commission tactfully expressed its sense of the urgency and importance of the societies dealing with this situation. Women, too, specially criticized furlough pay and allowances. Students had shown in the war sacrifice which placed beyond cavil that they were not personally selfish, but—

There is, for instance, a growing feeling of professional solidarity among university women, which makes them unwilling to support a system which they conceive to be defective in principle, though they might raise no objection as individuals on their own behalf.

The theological tests of the societies were said to need scrutiny.

In a region where generalization is unsafe, it will not perhaps be wrong to say that the present generation of students, on the whole, comes slowly to theological definition, and that theological tests which are designed to discover their fitness for missionary service should be framed with this fact in view.

A section of the report deals at length with the S.V.M.U., its nature and future.

The question has been raised whether a separate union is necessary for intending missionaries, and if it is maintained, why it should not be opened to all who go abroad in any capacity, but with a " missionary purpose," desiring to build the City of God. . . . Against the dissatisfaction which exists (which it would ascribe, in part at least, to the inanition from which the S.V.M.U. is suffering) they would put the wealth of testimony from members of the

S.V.M.U. all over the world to the value of the Union and of the declaration. There is universal testimony to the strengthening of purpose and crystallizing of decision which men and women have experienced through signing the declaration. It is beyond doubt that many, including some of the most prominent, missionaries would never have gone abroad but for the S.V.M.U., and it is a dangerous thing to dispense with a spiritual weapon of proved worth.

" The Commission is of the opinion that the existence of a Union is required by the clear facts of the case." It set out at length two considerations which in conclusion it summarized in these words :

The justification of the S.V.M.U. lies in this double circumstance, that the work of the missionary is peculiar and important, and that it is remote from the attention of people in this country.

The report made a study of the declaration, which led ultimately to its being altered to read : " It is my purpose, if God permit, to devote my life to missionary service abroad."

The Commissioners thought that the missionary expansion of the whole Movement made it desirable to dissolve the S.V.M.U. Committee and to transfer its work to the General Committee, which should appoint a missionary sub-committee on which " some expert senior friends should be invited to sit." The Commission said that if the recommendation to dissolve the S.V.M.U. Committee was accepted, it " ventured to remind the General Committee of the very great responsibility which would rest upon it, and of the importance of choosing a really efficient missionary sub-committee."

The Commission considered " associate membership " of the S.V.M.U., " but thinks that the best results will be obtained from strengthening the Auxiliary, enlisting in its membership more of those students who go abroad in government and other services, and developing its activities so that it may mean more to its members."

The members advised that the watchword[1] be discontinued.

They feel that the arguments for and against it are now virtually rendered obsolete by the fact that the watchword is in truth dead, so far as the present generation of students goes. They consider it impossible to revive it, believing that it is nearly always futile to attempt to galvanize a phrase into life.

They recommended, however, that the aim and basis of the Movement " be so strengthened as to afford the rallying-cry for the whole Movement which the S.V.M.U. watchword once was for the S.V.M.U."

The report closed with a vigorous statement about the need for more staff.

The whole work of the Commission points to the necessity for an adequate missionary staff. Missionary education, the interpretation of the missionary message, relations with the societies, relations with foreign students, personal touch with volunteers—all this points to an adequate staff. The Commission feel that nothing of what has been sketched can be carried out unless the missionary department of the Movement is sufficiently staffed. They recommend the following as, in their opinion, the appointments necessary :

1. A man, to act as director of the missionary department, to keep in touch with the societies and maintain close relations with student volunteers.
2. A woman, to maintain the same society and volunteer relationships, on the women's side.
(Both the above to spend some time in the colleges.)
3. A missionary education secretary.
4. Two missionaries, probably on furlough, to travel in the colleges, speak at meetings and spread missionary information and enthusiasm.
5. Part of the time of an assistant secretary, to arrange tours, etc.
6. Part of the time of an Auxiliary secretary, to help with gone-down student volunteers.

The Commission met three times, spending eight days on its report in addition to time spent by indi-

[1] See pp. 313-319.

vidual members in drafting. Its first meeting was on
November 27th 1918, and its last on March 19th 1919.

Its recommendations all received attention, and its
practical suggestions have been acted upon except in the
matter of staff. One man and one woman has been all
the missionary staff the Movement has been able to
afford.

One recommendation that has proved of doubtful
value has been that the S.V.M.U. Committee should be
dissolved and the General Committee made solely
responsible for the missionary work of the Movement,
and for the S.V.M.U. It is an anomalous position to
have an S.V.M.U. with a large membership, an annual
business meeting and yet no committee of its members.
The loss through not having a committee of the
same standing and authority as the committee of the
Theological College Department, and composed of
people all expecting to be missionaries, has been considerable. The General Committee decided when it
dissolved the S.V.M.U. Committee to devote a full day
at each of its three sessions in the year to missionary
matters. Except on rare occasions it has never done
so, its agenda is too long for it to be able to devote so
much time to one aspect of its work. When the
S.V.M.U. Committee and its income went into the
General Committee's pool, the hope of an adequate
staff on the Movement's missionary side was gone until
the day when far more money is given for the Movement's work.

It is undoubtedly right that the General Committee,
as representing the whole Movement, should recognize
its responsibility for Christian missions, and it is desirable that activities such as a quadrennial conference
should be the direct concern of the General Committee,
but the Missionary Sub-committee has never been a
success and the S.V.M.U. Committee used to exert far
more influence on the General Committee. In my
judgment the loss of an autonomous committee with
an income to spend on its work and composed of people

who had all definitely made up their minds to be missionaries has been a serious blow to the missionary effectiveness of the Movement.   This problem still needs attention and coupled with it there remains the need of an adequate missionary staff.   The cause of missions is still unquestionably at the heart of the Movement, but more needs to be done, for the missionary responsibilities of the Movement are great—very great.

We had no sooner set the Movement's house in order in relation to foreign missions than we had to tackle the question of the aim and basis and declaration of membership.   Prior to 1913 a single basis clause in the Constitution served as aim and basis, and also as declaration of membership.   In that year the Movement divided the basis clause into two parts —an aim and basis for the whole Movement, and a declaration of membership to be accepted by each voting member.   In adopting the particular formula that was chosen the attempt was made to avoid a theological test and to provide a simple statement of personal faith.   The words chosen were : " In joining this Union I declare my faith in God through Jesus Christ, whom as Saviour and Lord I desire to serve."

It soon became apparent, however, that this membership qualification required too much of students and that it would not long remain unaltered.   It was the incidence of the war that postponed the change until 1919.   Students came to college in large numbers without having thought out their religious position. When the Student Movement brought them face to face with an essentially personal religious issue, all that many felt they could say with absolute truth was : " I want to be of your fellowship, I cannot affirm anything very definite at the present time, but take me with you, I want to go your way."   This applied to many who had been confirmed in the Church of England or were members of Free Churches.   In being confirmed or in joining the Church, senior people had suggested to them the step then taken, and it had been taken in all seriousness. But more than one big change may take place during adolescence, and to be confirmed while at school is no guarantee that the great change to college, with new intellectual environment, new freedom and greater responsibility will not produce a state of mind in which the student's attitude to the Christian faith has to be faced as if it had never before been seriously considered.

The universities and colleges have been full of people for the last twenty years, who have begun either for the first time, or *de novo*, to think out their position during their first year at college. These are some of the best people. What should the Movement say to them? Hitherto it had said to such : " You cannot be of us until you are able to affirm what we hold is a minimum of faith."

The General Committee had also to take cognizance of the fact that an increasing number of Christian Unions ignored the declaration of membership in accepting members, and these were not feeble and ineffective Unions, but the strongest in the Movement. Those which had a living message which changed men's lives were the Unions which felt they were not prepared to exclude from their membership any students of serious Christian purpose, who understood what the aim of the Christian Union was and who wanted to join it, even if they would make no religious declaration. They were not afraid of these students ; they did not regard men and women thinking their way towards the articulation of their personal faith as a source of danger to the Christian position of their Union, far from it ; they were convinced that these were the very people with whom they wanted to be in closest touch.

The General Committee discussed this situation just before the end of the war and decided to make no constitutional change until all the men had returned from the army to the colleges. After the Armistice, however, as the men poured back, they combined with

2 S

the women and the travelling secretaries in demanding immediate change. The need for a change in the declaration of membership having opened up the whole question of the Constitution, some of the leaders, who had felt for some time that the aim and basis could be greatly improved, led us to examine it at the same time. It was criticized because of its omissions, and by medical, science and fine art students because of the technical language of its first clause. They declared that it must be rewritten in untechnical language, so that it would make an appeal to a wider range of students who did not understand the present wording. The aim and basis under discussion read :

> The aim of the Movement is to lead students in British universities and colleges into full acceptance of the Christian Faith in God—Father, Son and Holy Spirit ; to promote among them regular habits of prayer and Bible study ; to keep before them the importance and urgency of the evangelization of the world, the Christian solution of social problems, and the permeation of public life with Christian ideals ; and to lead them into the fellowship and service of the Christian Church.

We decided that the abandonment of the old declaration of membership would make some fuller reference to Jesus Christ in the aim and basis necessary, and that it was desirable to find a new form of words which the Christian Unions could use with satisfaction when they were approaching new students on behalf of the Movement.

There was no desire on the Councils or the General Committee to change the theological or doctrinal position of the Movement, nor in providing a fuller statement did the Student Movement intend to write a creed.

> It is not the function of the Student Movement to attempt to say what Christianity is—that is the function of the Church. All a Movement like ours can rightly attempt to do is to make clear that the Christian Church of the ages is

its foundation, and then set out some of the things it has seen and wants to help others to see.[1]

At Christmas 1918 the General Committee agreed it must deal with this situation at once. The Constitution, however, required that notice of any proposed change must be given to the Christian Unions in February if it was to be voted upon at the business meeting of the Movement in July at Swanwick. A basis question could not be threshed out and decided then and there, and the committee could not meet again until Easter. The solution agreed on was to circularize the Christian Unions and see if they would be willing to support a resolution at Swanwick, suspending the clause in the Constitution requiring notice in February of any notice of motion to change the Constitution. If they were agreed, the General Committee decided it must be ready with a new aim and basis, and declaration of membership by the summer term. The colleges were practically unanimous in their replies desiring that the matter be dealt with as suggested.

The General Committee had appointed a Basis Subcommittee in anticipation of the need for immediate action. It consisted of Mrs T. W. Pym, Zoë Fairfield, Muriel Wood, Hugh Martin, F. A. Cockin, William Paton, E. F. Griffith, Norman Capener, Victor Murray and T. Tatlow. The advice of senior friends was sought, including the Bishop of Winchester (Dr E. S. Talbot), Canon B. K. Cunningham, Canon E. A. Burroughs, the Rev. W. B. Selbie, the Rev. W. R. Maltby and Mr Maxwell Garnett. From these much valuable criticism and help was received.

New wording was suggested by the Basis Committee, commented upon by the National Councils, discussed by the General Committee, rewritten several times by the Basis Committee, and finally the General Committee

[1] *The Student Movement*, art.: " The Revision of the Constitution of the Movement," vol. xxii. p. 4.

approved the following wording, which was ultimately adopted :

AIM AND BASIS

The Student Christian Movement of Great Britain and Ireland is a fellowship of students who desire to understand the Christian faith and to live the Christian life.

The Movement seeks to set forth Jesus Christ as the supreme revelation of God and of the true nature of man.

It sees in Him the one sure guide for all mankind in every sphere of thought and conduct, in art and industry, in politics and the professions, in science and education ; the source of power for the overthrow of evil and the renewal of all human life.

The Movement challenges students to recognize the urgent need of the whole world for Christ, without limit of race or nation, and to respond by dedicating their lives to His service as He may guide them.

It calls them to explore His teaching and to follow the guidance of His Spirit in the pursuit of truth, beauty and righteousness ; to prepare themselves by study, discipline and prayer for the tasks of the future ; joyfully to accept God's gift of deliverance and life for themselves ; and to enter the fellowship of worship, thought and service which is the heritage of the Christian Church.

MEMBERSHIP

The membership of Affiliated Christian Unions and of the Student Volunteer Missionary Union shall be open to students who, having considered the aim and basis, desire to enter the fellowship of the Student Christian Movement. Those theological colleges may be associated which are recognized colleges of denominations whose principles are in harmony with its aim and basis.

When the business meeting came, several amendments of wording were proposed and all of them rejected. It was clear that the General Committee's proposals were to the mind of the meeting, and when the final vote came, the new declaration of membership was passed with two dissentients, and the new aim and basis with four dissentients, in a meeting of two hundred and eighty representatives of Christian Unions and associated theological colleges.

It was at the same business meeting that the new wording of the declaration of membership of the S.V.M.U. suggested by the Missionary Commission was inserted in the Constitution, " It is my purpose, if God permit, to devote my life to missionary service abroad."

The General Committee issued an official exposition of the new aim and basis, and as this had a wide circulation in the colleges and was the basis of hundreds of addresses by Student Movement secretaries, it is worth some attention. It indicates the main lines of the Movement's message at this period if taken together with what it had to say about international, missionary and social questions.

The pamphlet began by saying that in the new statement of its aim and basis, " the Student Christian Movement has endeavoured to set forth the beliefs about God, about Jesus Christ, and about human life, which it has tested in its corporate experience and has found true. It is in no sense a creed, but an attempt to state those aspects of the Christian faith which for the purposes of the Movement seem to need emphasizing." [1]

The Movement believed that God had shown it the right road, and its message " is not a piece of kindly instruction and advice, but a summons to a common adventure." This adventure was God's call, and the ground of the Movement's conviction was Christ, who led men along the road that takes them straight to the heart of reality.

> For in Him we see the answer to the age-long question of humanity—What is God like ? In Jesus we see the very nature of God as He is, no mere illustration, or demonstration, or copy, but the actual reality—God Himself. And the God Whom Jesus has revealed is love— love that is strong and daring as well as patient and gentle ; love that is invincible, because it will not let itself be overcome by evil. That is the meaning of the Incarnation.

[1] *The Aim and Basis of the Student Christian Movement*, 1919. The following quotations are all from this pamphlet.

Jesus has also shown us in Himself the true nature of man. "He has shown us what human nature can attain to when it is true to what God meant it to be." This makes a profound difference to our whole view of life. "It shows God's plan and any attempt to shape our life, our social system, or international relationships, on any plan which is inconsistent with His, can only end in absolute disaster." That is why the Movement holds that Jesus is the one sure guide in every sphere of thought and conduct.

> Think what this means. Industry and commerce must be established on a basis which embodies His values; science and medicine must take into account His insistence on the supremacy of spirit, in working out their conception of the nature of the universe and the meaning of life. And every one of us must re-examine every detail of our daily living in the light of His demands.

This cannot be done by copying Jesus, but by intercourse "achieving closer understanding and communion with another who, though far beyond Him, is yet so near that intercourse with Him is the most real experience in life. . . . Those who are His disciples can know the meaning of living friendship with Him. This is the true gift of His Spirit."

This is true for the world as well as for us. How is this programme going to be carried out? By the power of God working in men's lives, but "God's power never can and never will infringe our personal freedom. Our wills are ours, and it is our business to make them His." It means going into hard training and never coming out of it again.

> We are up against the fact of sin, and "it is only as we see on Calvary the price of suffering paid day by day by God Himself for all human sin, that we can enter into the experience of true penitence and forgiveness which sets us free to embark upon a wholly new way of life, not in our own strength, but in His. This is the meaning of the Atonement. This is the gift of deliverance and life which He offers freely to all who are willing to receive it."

This is the experience the Student Movement calls men to share and the task it summons them to undertake. " As we respond we enter the fellowship, not of a small group of students, an insignificant minority of a few thousands, but of the great company of those who down the ages have formed the Church of Christ."

Students were reminded that this aim was more than the expression of the belief of an individual student and more than he could do. It was the corporate faith of the whole Movement. The individual was asked to study it that he might understand the aim of the fellowship, and if, having considered it, he was ready to say, " I'm not sure that I can accept more than a little of all you say as my own faith, but I want the thing you seem to be after, I'd like to come in and take my share, and learn more from inside "—then he was to join the Movement by becoming a member of his college Christian Union.

This new aim, basis and declaration of membership was quickly adopted and used by almost all the Christian Unions.

CHAPTER XXXIV

THE PRIMARY AIM OF THE MOVEMENT

THERE is no purpose which the Student Christian Movement has pursued more consistently during its course than the presentation to students of the Christian view of the world, including the redemptive purpose of God and the claims of Jesus Christ upon their lives. Before the war ended a new and a wider call had come to the Movement through the Oxford Auxiliary Conference.[1] It was a call to reach men and women inside and outside the colleges. It was the old call which had stirred the imagination and thrilled the hearts of students from the Movement's earliest beginnings—the call to win men for Christ.

At the Oxford Conference no words had made a deeper impression than those of Dr Cairns :

> The young manhood of our nation, and, to a large extent, its young womanhood, are not only out of touch with Christianity, but their conception of Christianity is of the most confused kind, a kind of dim, broken theism with incomparable Christian qualities in it. . . . We are called to take part in a practical way in retrieving the whole formidable situation.

The issue of the conference was " the call to a great crusade . . . to go out to win the youth of the country to Christ."

The war was at its height and the Movement greatly reduced in numbers. In a few months came the Armistice, and soon a flood of men began to enter the colleges. The Movement increased its staff of secretaries at once and began to plan for summer conferences at Swanwick, which would be a reunion of many who

[1] See p. 732.

had been parted by the war, and which would give a good start to the winter's work. The General Committee set itself to bring together as speakers and guests as notable a body of old friends of the Movement as possible, and some new ones—the Rev. W. R. Maltby came for the first time. There were 1500 persons present, and the conferences were impressive occasions.

In September the Movement's committees and staff went to Swanwick for a conference and committee meetings prior to the winter's work. Seventy-five people were present. " Fears that the large staff would monopolize the talk and over-weight the students were not realized. Rarely has the student element at these conferences been so assertive and independent." [1]

A new sign of the moving of the Spirit was apparent in a message which was issued to the Movement.

> There bubbled up, as it were time and time again, a feeling that we were experiencing something together which we ought to express and try to share with others. . . . That feeling became so compelling, that . . . it was decided to ask five of our number to meet and see whether what we were feeling could be expressed in words. . . . On the last day of the committee a draft prepared was read and received with an approval that was remarkable. It was a message we wanted to express and to give to our fellow students, and the men and women of our generation. . . . Before the draft was finally accepted there was a time of quietness and prayer which none of us are likely to forget.

A CALL TO BATTLE

The world is at a crisis when we believe Christians must attack or fail.

Society has to be re-ordered.

Through Christ men have the power to do it.

The foundations of society are wrong, because the relations between man and man are wrong. We have failed to be Christians. Jesus told us to love one another, but as a plain matter of fact, we do not love one another.

[1] *The Student Movement*, " The Autumn Meeting of the Executive," vol. xxii. p. 30.

If we did, war would be at once condemned, and certain social conditions would not be tolerated.

We are convinced that if men practise looking at society with the eyes of Jesus, they must make great changes in its structure. Would He tolerate the system under which our fellows live and work—a system which robs so many of their birthright of joy and freedom ? We must study and think out these problems, and at any cost act on what we believe to be right.

We are finding that obedience to Jesus Christ gives the power to live a life which is brimful of reality, purpose and hope. Nothing less can satisfy us now. We know that the spiritual power of Jesus Christ in us is greater than the power of evil, and therefore we believe that the Kingdom of God is coming in our world. We stand with Him and with all who serve Him down the centuries in the battle for His Kingdom.

We have found in working with students of other nations and races a unity in Christ which overcomes prejudice and enriches the common life. Before God and in Christ we are all one. We are convinced that this unity is the only sure hope of peace and of the true development of nations. Now is the time to do all in our power to create a public opinion that shall constrain statesmen to act on this belief.

We feel that the divisions of the Church in our country are no longer tolerable, because they obscure that unity in Christ which we know to be more real than our differences. We ask for instant and courageous action. We want to serve a Church which stands as one in fearless love of truth.

The issue before us is a straight fight with the power of evil. Only in and through human lives can the power of God become effective. We are called to face sacrifice, apparent failure, and distress of body and soul, for the joy of the triumph of Jesus Christ in the lives of our fellow men and women.

We ask you to search out the truth, and in obedience to it to take your side in the battle.

A message from a Conference of the Committee and Secretaries of the Student Christian Movement of Great Britain and Ireland. Autumn Meeting, 1919.

Signed—

J. N. ANDERSON, New College, Edinburgh.
FREDA BARRIE, Queen Margaret College, Glasgow.
A. J. BOYD, Glasgow University.

T. F. BOYD, University College, Nottingham.
DAVID BRADLEY, Leeds University.
J. R. COATES, Peterhouse, Cambridge.
F. A. COCKIN, University College, Oxford.
CICELY CREWDSON, Westfield College, London.
JANET EDMINSON, Newnham College, Cambridge.
ZOË FAIRFIELD, Slade School of Art, London.
A. J. GAILEY, Queen's University, Belfast.
MARY GELL, Sheffield University.
CONSTANCE GRANT, Newnham College, Cambridge.
E. F. GRIFFITH, St Mary's Hospital, London.
OWEN GRIFFITH, Memorial College, Brecon.
HILDA GRIFFITHS, University College, Aberystwyth.
R. O. HALL, Brasenose College, Oxford.
KATHLEEN HARNETT, Lady Margaret Hall, Oxford.
HARRY HASTINGS, Edinburgh University.
ELIZABETH HEWAT, Edinburgh University.
H. L. HENRIOD, Neuchatel University.
ADA HODGSON, Training College, Leeds.
A. E. HOWARD, Queen's College, Oxford.
R. W. HOWARD, St Aidan's College, Birkenhead.
L. S. HUNTER, New College, Oxford.
E. C. H. JONES, University College, Aberystwyth.
A. C. KENNEDY, Edinburgh University.
T. H. KIRK, School of Medicine, Newcastle-on-Tyne.
KITTY LEWIS, University College, Aberystwyth.
R. G. MACDONALD, Aberdeen University.
HUGH MARTIN, Glasgow University.
H. A. MESS, London University.
J. B. MIDDLEBROOK, Rawdon College, Leeds.
OLIVE M. MOBERLY, Lady Margaret Hall, Oxford.
A. V. MURRAY, Magdalen College, Oxford.
EDITH OVERTON, Somerville College, Oxford.
GWEN OWENS, Newnham College, Cambridge.
W. PATON, Pembroke College, Oxford.
MARY PORTER, Queen's University, Belfast.
R. D. REES, Trinity College, Oxford.
LOUISE ROYAARDS, Somerville College, Oxford.
ALFRED SCHOFIELD, Gonville and Caius College, Cambridge.
M. BEATRICE SELKIRK, Queen Margaret College, Glasgow.
MURIEL TASKER, Girton College, Cambridge.
T. TATLOW, Trinity College, Dublin.
PHYLLIS TAUNTON, Westfield College, London.

ELSIE TOWERS, Birmingham University.

ALEXANDER WALKER, Business Secretary.

HESTER WATSON, Trinity College, Dublin.

L. K. M. WELCH, Clapham High School Training Department.

R. D. WHITEHORN, Westminster College, Cambridge.

DAVID WILLIAMS, Calvinistic Methodist College, Aberystwyth.

E. ARIAM WILLIAMS, Serampore College, Calcutta.

JOHN WILLIAMS, Liverpool University.

KATHLEEN WITZ, Alexandra College, Dublin.

E. S. WOODS, Trinity College, Cambridge.

W. P. YOUNG, New College, Edinburgh.

STUDENT CHRISTIAN MOVEMENT,
    ANNANDALE,
        HAMPSTEAD, N.W.3.

Ten thousand copies were circulated in the colleges, and it was reproduced in a considerable part of the religious Press. The rest of the Press took little notice of it. This message was read and discussed with sympathy by students, and helped to integrate the Movement as it emerged from the war.

As a result of the appointment of a large staff for the winter's work, the budget leaped from £9000 to £16,000. We were able to face a budget of this size for this reason. We had a post-war fund of £3000, and as we debated a few months earlier what was possible financially, the tide was turned in favour of a bold policy by Janet Maclay,[1] who passed round the room to me a slip of paper on which was written: "Father agrees secretaries are more important than hostels. He will give £5000 to start off financial campaign. Sorry not to have given definite reply about hostels before.— J. MACLAY."

She had told me before Christmas 1918 that Sir Joseph Maclay was contemplating a gift to the Student Movement of money earmarked for the building of hostels (he had already given us South Park House),

[1] Afterwards the Hon. Mrs Inskip.

and I had asked her to persuade him to make his gift to the general work of the Movement instead, as the greater need at this period was that of more secretaries. It was the most timely gift the Movement has ever received, and the rapid rebuilding of its work in the post-war world was made possible by it.

We increased the staff of secretaries in 1919-20 from seventeen to twenty-eight. The new appointments were: London secretary (man), Scottish secretary (man), Welsh secretary (man), missionary secretary (man), literary secretary (man), social service secretary (man), theological secretary (man), travelling secretary (man), Indian secretary (man), foreign student secretary (woman), and business secretary (man).

Only one of the eleven new secretaries came straight from college, the others had all had experience of some kind, either the ministry, teaching, settlement, war work abroad, or the army; two had previously been Student Movement secretaries, Ronald Rees and R. G. Macdonald. The secretary straight from college was Kathleen Harnett, who came from Oxford with a first-class honours degree, and would have added distinction to any staff. Two of the secretaries were already known as experts in the work they were to do for the Movement, John R. Coates, Bible study secretary, and Henry A. Mess, social study secretary. The strengthening of the study staff by adding these two men was a carefully considered step. As William Paton, Hugh Martin, F. A. Cockin and Leslie Hunter were already members of the Movement's staff, and Kathleen Harnett joined it to become missionary study secretary, it was exceptionally strong in people who believed in the study work of the Movement and were well qualified to further it. The Student Movement has always been at its best when it had competent leaders for its thought life and its study work. Travelling and intercollegiate secretaries need a strong study team to help them to do their best work.

A big fight began at once to maintain this staff of

secretaries. While we now had a post-war fund of £8000 in the bank, and were able to increase our staff because of this, it would have been futile to spend it at once. My aim was to keep it intact as a reserve as long as possible, so I asked the secretaries in December 1919, before the General Committee met, for their consent to a proposal I wanted to make to that committee, that the following term we would all suspend our work in the colleges for four weeks, and devote it to a money-raising campaign.

The secretaries approved, the General Committee agreed. I collected the secretaries in January and told them all I knew about money-raising, and we set to work in February, taking every opportunity we could make of speaking in drawing-rooms, halls, churches, and to individuals. We raised £6000 in a month.

The cost of living was rising rapidly and the Movement's budget rose with it. For several years the secretaries continued to raise considerable sums, but it became more and more difficult to get large contributions, and it was an effort keeping the staff up to this financial work. It was novel to almost all of them, the more experienced of them always raised most money, and as they left the staff, and it became younger on the average, it became harder and harder both to enthuse them and help them to do this kind of work. Nevertheless the effect of what was done was to increase permanently the regular income of the Movement.

The students on the General Committee were rather dazed by our financial policy, but backed us up. The following year a budget of £22,130 was presented at the annual business meeting at Swanwick, while the Movement's income was estimated at £14,500. Some of the students took fright at a deficit of £7630 to be raised, and moved a resolution instructing the General Committee to cut expenditure by the amount of the deficit. This would have meant the ruin of the Movement as an organization. After a long debate the meeting was persuaded to accept the budget and to promise to support the committee and staff in an effort to raise it. We secured nearly half the required amount, and had to draw on our reserve fund for the first time.

For the next two years, by special appeals and with the help of most of the staff, we kept the Movement's head above the financial waves. But it needed courage, and the size of the deficit that had to be tackled when the budget was passed at Easter each year used to lead to huge debates. Some thought it could not be done, and year after year some of us had to put up strenuous resistance to the cutting down of the staff.

I had to bear the burden in the main, and had a clear idea as to what I was doing. The war had been a shattering experience for a changing movement of youth, and I knew that the longer I could keep together a strong team of secretaries, the quicker would be the recovery of the Movement from the war-time experience. Each year it was getting stronger and better able to face having a smaller and less experienced staff. So I set myself to fend off retrenchment as long as possible.

Once during this period I was ill in bed when the committee was meeting, the financial issue was raised, and the committee took fright and decided to reduce the budget heavily, a colleague arrived at my house, having dashed along from Annandale a mile away, and told me what had happened. I jumped out of bed, huddled on my clothes, and arrived half an hour before the committee was due to disband to all parts of the country, not to meet again for three months. I plunged into the breach, persuaded them to reverse their decision, and crept back to bed limp, but triumphant!

In 1923, however, reductions were obviously necessary if we were not to run into debt, a thing we had never done, and we began sadly to let our study secretaries go. They were senior men with families to care for and educate, so they received higher salaries than the rest of the staff. But it was a bad business, for the Movement, as I have already said, has always been at its best when it has had a strong team of study secretaries.

They enrich its thought life. They turn the readiness of students to meet and discuss into a purpose to study and compare the results of their study. They provide ideas for the travelling and intercollegiate secretaries to carry into the colleges. They write in *The Student Movement*, and strengthen its contribution to the moulding of the thought of the student body.

When we began to cut down our study staff and specialist secretaries—those who led Bible, doctrinal, social, missionary and international study, and those who worked among students preparing to be engineers or teachers—we did it for two reasons. One was that we had to cut somewhere, and as we spent practically all our money on staff we had to cut secretaries ; the other was that we cut the study secretaries partly because they were the more expensive group, and partly because the pressure from the colleges was in the direction of our increasing the number of resident secretaries in the larger student centres.

Our cutting down was inevitable, but to cut study secretaries was bad policy. Subsequent experience points to the conclusion that travelling and intercollegiate, or resident, secretaries are dependent upon the help of a strong group, guiding the study work in the Christian Unions. Students have always discussed and will continue to do so. The value of the Movement's work depends upon its ability to use this desire to discuss to good purpose. Its study work has always been its backbone. Let this decline permanently and the Movement's day will be over. It was a great misfortune that it could not retain its study leaders.

Pressure from the colleges will probably always tend to obscure the issue. A single university which wants a resident secretary can state a definite case and one which student members of the committee understand. They will back a proposal for such a secretary against a proposal for a study secretary who may be needed by the weaker branches of the Movement, yet who have no representative present to state their case, and they have not sufficient experience to apprise the real value of a study secretary to the whole Movement.

The autumn term, 1919, began with crowded colleges and the meetings to introduce freshmen to the Student Christian Movement were remarkable for exuberance and numbers; 600 attended at Leeds University, 400 at Liverpool University and 200 at Birmingham.

This is perhaps an appropriate place to pause and say something about the student field during the three to four years the ex-service men were in the universities and colleges.

When the Armistice relaxed the strain of war at one stroke, the subsequent excitement resulted in little college work being done. Broadly speaking, students gave up working and for months took to dancing—yes, even at 11 o'clock in the morning and day after day. After Christmas a severe influenza epidemic was another disturbing factor. All the time demobilization was taking place and men were pouring back to the universities. College societies of all kinds were revived and many new ones started. Skeleton Christian Unions had been maintained almost everywhere and in Oxford, Cambridge, Edinburgh and Glasgow, and some other places to which some old Student Movement men returned, rebuilding of the work was rapid. In places where no former members ready to lead were found, progress was slower. In the co-educational universities much assistance came from the women, who retired themselves and put the men into positions of leadership.

By the autumn of 1919 the overcrowding of all the universities and colleges was a problem. The Government provided about thirty thousand scholarships for men from the army and navy. The result was the largest and, financially, the richest student body ever assembled in the universities and colleges of Great Britain and Ireland. The number of students was about sixty thousand men and twenty thousand women. There was a good deal of drinking in some places, but on the whole the ex-service men worked hard, being anxious to finish their education and get to their work in life as quickly as possible.

It was not an easy time.   Classrooms and laboratories overflowed, three men to a microscope was not good for work or nerves ; new societies, new clubs and the revival of old ones made student life strenuous. The men were restless, critical of anything they felt antiquated or unreal, wanting change, eager for a better world, uncertain which road to take and with few leaders in their ranks.

The women showed more signs of fatigue and reaction than the men. The majority of them were in co-educational colleges where the return of the men, the restarting of college societies, the endless activity and the overcrowding brought a new kind of strain after that of the war. The men were optimistic on the whole, while the women were pessimistic, unsettled and dissatisfied. This phase lasted for a year and then disappeared.

While the war lasted there was much expectation of a better world. But a year of life in the post-war world began to usher in a vast amount of disillusionment. The world had been dipped in hell, which is not a good preparation for finding the Kingdom of God. Young men and women were looking for direction, asking the real meaning of life. The Church, which might have helped them, was disunited, worried, uncertain, and the spiritual background of the life of youth underwent a great change. If in earlier days there was a section of the student field sensitive to the deterministic and material views which dominated many of the leaders in scientific research and uncertain about spiritual values, the larger body of students was in touch with the Christian Church. If a minority of these were convinced Christians, the majority accepted the truth of Christianity and thought, with uneasiness of conscience, about their carelessness of Christ's claims upon them. They accepted the Christian view of the world and one day they would pay serious attention to what the

Christian Church had to say, for the Church stood as a great rock under whose shadow they meant to shelter in the day of their need. Now this was changed; the great rock seemed rather insecure and showed signs of crumbling. Anyhow, it was not much practical use in the world, and when one came to think about it : what was the purpose of life ?

This attitude of uncertainty and distrust of organized Christianity affected the Christian Unions, and an enormous amount of time and energy was spent on criticism and diagnosis. The ex-service Student Movement leaders were an interesting body of men. They had all had considerable responsibility during the war, most of them as officers, a few had held important posts as chaplains or Y.M.C.A. leaders. Brigade majors, adjutants and the like abounded. They were accustomed to have authority and to act. They had had a wide experience of men ; they knew the meaning of anxiety and of death. On the other hand, however, they knew nothing of history and cared less, their experience was limited, and they were curiously ignorant of many things that, had life been normal, they would have known. The consequence was that some of them had more self-confidence than wisdom. They made their mistakes more confidently and were therefore harder to help than their pre-war prototypes.

The spiritual temperature was considerably lowered as a result of the war and this affected the Movement. Signs of this began to show a year before the war came to an end and continued for a few years after it was over. There was more talk and less prayer. Extempore prayer almost died out. Some have suggested that the Student Movement largely lost its hold on personal religious experience and concentrated on the social implications of Christianity. That, however, was never the case. A study of the immediate attention to college missions with the clear purpose of converting men and women, and the unceasing attention to evangelism ever since the war, as well as the development of quiet days and the like, make it clear that the Movement never abandoned one of its life-long purposes—that of winning men for Christ and building them up in Him.

The evangelistic missions of the post-war period have been on a far greater scale than in pre-war days. The first mission was at Cambridge. The leaders of undergraduate religious life in the university began in the summer of 1919 to make plans for a mission in February 1920, and Oxford followed suit. The Cambridge Mission stirred the university to its depths. Twelve hundred men and women packed the Guildhall on the first Sunday night, thereafter two thousand undergraduates attended each night, the attendances reaching two thousand five hundred on the last Sunday night.

> Throughout the week there was a most amazing " atmosphere," the mission seemed to have got into the air, and many felt that it was the only possible subject of conversation in the lecture-room, on the football ground or the towpath. Above all, there was an all pervading spirit of prayer . . . all who were in any way interested in the mission felt impelled to pray privately and in little groups as they had never prayed before.[1]

It was the first college mission where there was more than one platform. The missioners were the Bishop of Peterborough (Dr T. F. Woods), Bishop Gore, Revs. Dr Herbert Gray and Barclay F. Buxton. While it was the S.C.M. which inspired and led the movement for the mission, it was organized by a special committee representative of most of the religious societies in the university.

Oxford concluded its first " Religion and Life Week " the day the Cambridge Mission began. It had the same relation to the Student Movement as the Cambridge Mission, but was less explicitly evangelistic. Ten speakers were chosen to state the world's need of Christ and challenge men to meet it, and as Neville Talbot wrote, " that statement and challenge turned most powerfully into personal appeal. The whole world's salvation focusses

[1] *The Student Movement*, vol. xxii. p. 92.

down in the end to the dealings of Christ with the individuals who close with Him." [1]

The missions at Oxford and Cambridge proclaimed a more comprehensive message than similar efforts in pre-war days. Then the message was intensely, and often exclusively, personal. The speakers as a rule assumed the hearers' conviction of the truth of Christianity and aimed solely at a change of heart. Now at Cambridge :

> Taking the Kingdom of God as their starting-point, it was natural that the missioners should lay stress rather upon social duty and corporate righteousness than upon personal conversion and individual salvation. The personal side was never absent; but it was never made the ground of their appeal. [2]

Again the missioners sought to teach a reasonable faith.

> None of the missioners made any attempt to force us to an immediate decision : if they could convince us of the reasonableness and practicability of the faith, then we might be trusted to be honest with it ; sentimentality would only obscure our minds and prevent us from reaching a sincere and lasting judgment. [3]

The whole Movement was stirred and missions followed in the universities of Manchester, Edinburgh, Glasgow, Belfast, Dublin, and in the University Colleges of Nottingham, University College, London, Aberystwyth and Cardiff. Most of these were highly successful, though two were comparative failures. The reason of failure was that the Christian Unions made poor spiritual preparation and depended on the missioner for the success of the mission. Dr Gray, so successful in Cambridge, found Cardiff unfruitful, and no one after the event blamed Dr Gray.

While this was happening in the colleges, some felt

[1] *The Student Movement*, vol. xxii. p. 92.
[2] *The Mission to Cambridge University*. A Report edited by C. E. Raven, B.D., p. 47.
[3] *Ibid.*, p. 43.

impelled to utter their message beyond college walls.
A body of students from the United Free Church
College, Glasgow, after a winter's study of *The Army
and Religion*, " which retold to us what we had found to
be true in our own experience," went to Kilmarnock.
They went to " peal forth the challenge of Christ to
reconstruct our life, individual, social and international,
on His foundation."

At work-gates, in the open air, lodging-houses, halls,
the theatre and the churches, in co-operation with the
Churches, they gave their message during ten days.
The interest shown in the great religious questions and
aspects of the Christian message was very real ; hundreds
of men gathered every day to hear what they said was a
" new way of putting things."

> They felt Christianity had something great, sound and
> practical in it after all, and that it held the solution of the
> problems throbbing in their own minds.[1]

The student missioners issued a series of " recommendations to the Church." They said that as organized
religion does not touch the great masses of labour
itinerant missioners should go to labour ; that cheap
literature " setting forth in plain English, in terms of
modern thought, the great truths of Christianity,"
should be published ; that the ministry should make
known " the modern intelligible view of the Bible " ;
and that the Church should give youth more opportunity
to serve it.

The autumn saw still more and larger plans for
extending the Kingdom. London students carried on
a campaign at Northampton, and sixty Cambridge undergraduates went for the same purpose to Stoke-on-Trent.
Students planned missions for several consecutive days
or special series of meetings, during 1920-21, with
evangelistic purpose in the Universities of Birmingham,
Leeds, Liverpool, Oxford, Aberdeen, Glasgow and

[1] *The Student Movement*, " The Kilmarnock Mission," vol. xxii.
p. 121.

Belfast, in Bangor University College and in several London colleges—St Bartholomew's Hospital, Birkbeck College, Clapham Day Training College, Imperial College of Science, King's College, London School of Medicine for Women and the London School of Economics.

> These all had efforts of a special character, while in "a number of centres where no campaign on a large scale was held, there were series of meetings or local conferences designed to make clear the meaning of Christianity to students in training for different professions, to doctors, to engineers, teachers, scientists, business men, etc." [1]

Edinburgh's special effort was a camp at West Linton to which 137 men came (medicals 53, arts 46, science 35, theologicals 2, law 1), of whom more than half were not Christian Union members, but who "welcomed the opportunity of hearing of and discussing the Christian way of life in such an atmosphere of freedom and good fellowship." In addition to Edinburgh students there were a dozen student delegates and speakers from Glasgow and Aberdeen.

The effort outside the colleges continued, most notable being a fourteen-days' mission to Hamilton, a town of forty thousand inhabitants, and the centre of the coal-mining industry in the Clyde valley. Every Scottish university contributed to the team of one hundred and thirty students, men and women, who undertook the campaign which was prepared for months beforehand in the colleges and in Hamilton's churches.

> Men and women listened . . . seemingly unwearied. . . . It was a wonderful demonstration of the willingness of men and women to listen to the Gospel and an object-lesson of what one campaigner called "the unexploited possibilities of the street-corner." The appeal of the campaign was to all life. Open-air preaching was supported by indoor meetings, individual discussions, socials, smokers, clubs for boys and girls and play centres for children.

[1] *Annual Report*, S.C.M., 1920-21, p. 18.

An evangelistic message that included all these amazed the non-religious.[1]

Dr Cairns saw the importance of what had been begun and sought to reinforce it. He urged " that only a new birth of faith, hope and love in the world would now save civilization from self-destruction." The message the world needed had been rewrought afresh in recent years, beginning with the recovery of the historical Jesus, " the greatest event in the Christian thought of the nineteenth century." There is a common mind as to what constitutes a Christian man, there is a prevailing idea of a Christian family, but there is no common mind or standard as to what constitutes a Christian civilization. " There is no prevailing Christian ideal of nationality, no common mind as to what a Christian nation ought to aim at, or as to the relation of the social classes within it." [2]

What holds any society together is its common mind. Dr Cairns illustrated the truth of this from the experience of the Student Movement. He called again to the Movement :

What can the Student Christian Movement and the Student Christian Federation do here and now to help the Church of Christ and the civilization that has received an ultimatum. I see nowhere in the world to-day any organizations that have in them such potentialities of good for this end as the various international organizations of youth. They can do little or nothing without the weight of the organized Church behind them. But in full and loyal alliance with it their opportunity is unique. If they do not seize and use it history will deride them ! " This generation began to build, and did not know how to finish."

All that they have done hitherto has been to lay the foundations. To me, looking back upon the greater part of its history, it seems to me as if the Student Christian Movement had been called into being by God Himself for precisely this present hour. We have all of us known that God was with us. We have been aware of Him. But we

---

[1] *Annual Report, S.C.M.,* 1920-21, pp. 38-39.

[2] *The Student Movement,* art. : " The Need for a Common Christian Mind," D. S. Cairns, vol. xxiii. p. 130.

did not know the depth of His purpose.   We did not know
the coming baptism in the cloud and in the sea.   We did
not know the coming Calvary.   But now the great design
is becoming clearer.

In the great universities of the world to-day are gathered
the great majority of those who will form the mind of the
Christendom of the next generation.   In almost every one
of these universities the Student Christian Federation has
now its organization, its literature, and its evangelists.
There is no student international organization comparable
with it in numbers, in influence and in resources.   It is
already bound together by countless friendships.   It
believes in the living God.   All this has come into being
without any thought of the present desperate position of
mankind.   The conscious aim of the founders of the
Student Christian Federation was the evangelization of the
world in this generation.   They were not thinking of the
threatening danger of the world in this generation at all.
But they were in the grasp of a mightier, deeper and more
loving Purpose than they knew, and they are in it still !

Beneath all the world's ambitions and hatreds, there is
to-day a great fear at the heart of Christendom, and a great
yearning for deliverance.   Christendom knows that it was
made for nobler and happier things, but it sees no way out.
It is face to face with the truth at last.   There is no Way but
One.   Men have tried to get rid of personal conviction of
sin by shifting the blame on society.   It will serve them
little, for if society has sinned, society will be judged, and
they and their children will be involved in its judgment.
Now if at such a moment as this there came to all the better
mind of the world in its universities a genuine message of
faith and hope and love, of Jesus Christ as the Way, the
Truth and the Life, who shall set limits to the power of
that Gospel ?   It was one of the principles of the old
evangelism that there must be conviction of sin before there
could be conversion.   Is not the nobler mind of the society
of to-day becoming convinced of social and international
sin ?   Ought this not to be the prelude of a conversion that
will lead to the salvation of society, the evangelization of
the world ?   The real hour of opportunity of the Student
Movement has come !   Weak and immature in itself, what
may it not achieve in the hands of the living God, if only it
will draw nearer to Him.[1]

[1] *The Student Movement*, art. : " The Need for a Common Christian
Mind," D. S. Cairns, vol. xxiii. pp. 131-32.

The General Committee responded by securing the help of a good deal of the time of the Rev. W. R. Maltby and Miss Maude Royden as missioners, and obtained, in co-operation with the Auxiliary, the full services of Dr Herbert Gray of the United Free Church of Scotland, with the approval of the General Assembly of the Church.

The following winter (1921-22) there were evangelistic missions, or campaigns as they were now called, in twenty-four college centres, and being better prepared they were more and more successful. The most important mission was that at Edinburgh University, where attendance beginning with four hundred increased to a thousand students the last two nights, and where the results in the lives of men and women were apparent. There were more camps with an evangelistic purpose for Glasgow, Dundee, Bristol, Sheffield and London students. Miss Royden rendered valuable help on the subject of the right kind of relations between men and women; in a good many co-educational institutions the question of the relation of the sexes had become acute.

The General Committee decided at the end of the year that—

> At least once in each student generation every Christian Union should seek to present Christianity to the college as a whole in the special manner which the idea of a campaign implies.

With the passing of the ex-service man from the universities there was a diminution of the number of evangelistic missions, though in 1922-23 eight college centres held missions as well as a "religion and life week" in Oxford and a mission in Cambridge, with two thousand undergraduates attending the last meeting. On the other hand, campaigns by students outside the colleges tended to increase. One at Wigan in 1926, undertaken by students from St Aidan's College (Birkenhead), Rawdon, Bradford and Mirfield Colleges and Leeds University, aroused great interest by the vigour of its social message and the response from the working-class in the town.

In 1926 " the World Call of the Church of England " attracted the attention of students. It originated with Garfield Williams, now back from India and become missionary secretary of the Missionary Council of the National Assembly of the Church of England, with Ruth Rouse as one of his colleagues. A series of surveys had been made of Christian missions in the Moslem world, India, Africa and the Far East, the last under my chairmanship, and when the time drew near for these surveys —each contained in a substantial volume—to be presented to the Church, the Movement was alive to the importance of what was going forward and asked for places at the convention. There were over a hundred students present when two thousand seven hundred delegates, representing the dioceses in England and Wales, met at the Central Hall, Westminster at St Paul's-tide, 1926. The students represented the English universities—these were selected by the Student Movement —the Anglican theological colleges, one or two other student bodies, with a dozen S.C.M. secretaries. The surveys revealed the need for five hundred and fifty-six recruits, men and women, for work overseas. When the diocesan delegations met separately to discuss their plans, the students had their own meeting, when we discussed how to bring the need home to the colleges. The tables had indeed been turned since 1896, when a thousand students asked the Churches to send them !

Not long after the convention a call to meet for corporate prayer in the Jerusalem Chamber, Westminster Abbey, was responded to by some students and, at the suggestion of one of them, a missionary campaign was arranged the following summer by the Missionary Council. The idea caught on, and since then several thousand students have been on these campaigns, a large number of them being members of the Student Movement, and the Movement co-operating by lending the help of several of its secretaries.

The London Council arranged a simultaneous campaign for four days in 1927, beginning February 14th, in forty colleges. The Bishop of Manchester (Dr Temple) led a group of forty missioners, which included the Bishops of St Albans, Lichfield, Barking, Kensington, Kingston and Woolwich; Canons T. W. Pym, C. E. Raven and E. S. Woods[1]; Revs. R. Newton Flew, W. R. Maltby, Francis Underhill,[2] G. A. Studdert Kennedy, A. Herbert Gray, R. G. Parsons,[3] E. K. Talbot, F. R. Barry, A. S. Duncan-Jones,[4] E. Shillito, W. B. Selbie, F. O. T. Hawkes,[5] T. S. Gregory, Bardsley Brash, Dr T. R. Glover, Dr Alex. Wood and Miss Maude Royden.

The campaign was conceived and thought out by Amy Buller. Its preparation lasted for two years. First came a series of questions to the Christian Unions, which made S.C.M. committees in the London colleges think out together what they should expect from the campaign. Quiet days each month for students from all the London colleges helped to direct spiritual preparation, and the speakers were allocated to the different colleges some months in advance and visited the preparing committees. A series of letters from the Bishop of Manchester helped to unify the campaign, and brought home to the colleges that the team of speakers were from the outset as much committed to and interested in the campaign as the students themselves.

An attempt to secure the backing of London churches of all denominations was a comparative failure, and only a few made regular prayer for it. Interest among Christian students everywhere was considerable, and messages from the Irish and Welsh Councils of the Movement and from students in Germany, China and Africa with assurances of constant prayer were deeply appreciated in London.

[1] Afterwards Bishop of Croydon.
[2] Afterwards Dean of Rochester.
[3] Afterwards Bishop of Southwark.
[4] Afterwards Dean of Chichester.
[5] Afterwards Bishop of Kingston-upon-Thames.

The campaign began with a conference of speakers and S.C.M. secretaries at St Dionis Hall, followed by a dedication service at All Hallows, Lombard Street, led by the Bishop of Manchester. Next day the speakers, in forty colleges, simultaneously began meetings at lunch-hour, after tea and in the evening, and talk with groups and individuals filled all the rest of their time. The audiences varied from about forty to three hundred and fifty in each of the different medical schools, training and university colleges. The college most stirred was the Imperial College of Science, where the Bishop of St Albans (Dr Furse) spoke twice daily to crowded audiences. King's and University College mustered over two hundred at every meeting, and in most of the residential training colleges the whole of the staff and students attended. At the closing meeting in the Queen's Hall two thousand five hundred students were present, as well as two hundred members of staff and senior friends. It was a deeply impressive occasion.

The campaign revealed the need for good religious education more than anything else. "The outstanding impression in our minds," wrote Miss Buller on behalf of the four London secretaries who had led the campaign, "is the evidence in the colleges of what does seem like an almost complete breakdown in religious education of students before they come to college." The speakers said the same thing. Mr F. O. T. Hawkes said the students needed "good, clear, thoughtful teaching to help them intellectually." Mr Underhill wrote : "I found that knowledge on religious matters was in most cases vague and ill-informed." On the other hand, the speakers all laid emphasis in their written "impressions" on how vital and central were the questions students asked. The Bishop of Lichfield spoke for all when he said : "The questions asked were good and thoughtful questions." The other main impression of the speakers was how good had been the preparation almost everywhere.

There was great variety in the line taken by the

different speakers, but the object of the campaign was to present Christianity both as a view of God and man and the world to men's minds and as a way of life to be lived in personal relation to God.   At one college, to give an example, during the lunch-hour the subjects were : " The place of doctrine," " The Christian doctrine of God," " God in Christ " and " The doctrine of God and the problem of evil."   These were followed by discussion, and in the evening the subjects were : " Jesus Christ the most knowable Person in the world," " Jesus Christ and the meaning of life," and " Jesus Christ and personal religion."

The results none could tabulate, but it was known that a large body of students were helped to make a first start or a fresh start in the Christian life.

The effect of the campaign on the Student Movement in London, judged by the experience of a year later, was somewhat disappointing.   This was no doubt in some measure due to the fact that the campaign was not well followed up.   The field was too big for the small staff of London secretaries, and the effort somewhat exhausted them.   But the real reason surely was the poor religious education the students had received. Nothing would have availed to garner the seed sown in the mission except careful and systematic teaching of the Faith.   If a staff of study secretaries had been available to train leaders in the summer after the campaign and superintend and help them the following winter, a great work begun might have been turned into a great work accomplished.

The same year Glasgow University held a Religion and Life Week, which was an event in the life of the university and noted for the big attendance at midday meetings, when the university union was over-crowded daily and numbers could not get in.   A feature of the meetings was the public answering of questions by the missioners.   " This is evangelization by question and answer," said one of them.   The Society of Catholic Students co-operated, and the midday meetings were addressed on three days by a Presbyterian and on two days by a Roman Catholic speaker.

In 1931 Dr Temple, who was now Archbishop of York, conducted a week's mission in Oxford, which drew the largest audiences ever drawn together day by day in that university. He was assisted by Canon T. W. Pym. The mission was prepared by an *ad hoc* committee, of which the Student Movement's Oxford secretary, Harry Baines, was secretary. The addresses of the Archbishop were published in book form[1] by the Student Movement after the mission, and the demand was so considerable that the volume became a " best seller."

Glasgow University had another successful Religion and Life Week about the same time. And in the following year Manchester University held a Religion and Life Week. Both these were initiated by the Movement.

It must not be thought that the university and college missions recorded here were the only ones held : they were the most notable.

In trying to gather up for the guidance of the ex-service men the experience of the Movement in relation to evangelistic work I wrote :

> Some lessons are clearly taught by the successful campaigns. First, it is clear that the success of a campaign does not primarily depend upon the speakers, although of course they are an important element. It is where there is a committee in charge of the campaign whose members are possessed by a daring and triumphant faith in the goodness and power of God that results are secured.
>
> Second, there is no record of a successful attempt to present the meaning and claims of Christianity apart from prayer.
>
> Third, results are not achieved apart from hard work. The drafting of advertisements, the making of suitable arrangements as regards halls and speakers, and the interesting of men by letter and by conversation, the effort to clear other college engagements out of the way, are all important, and all take time and energy. In the case of

[1] *The Christian Faith and Life*, S.C.M. Press.

successful campaigns the leaders have not been content simply to provide halls, choose speakers, and hold prayer-meetings, but they have used every endeavour by letter and by conversation to secure the co-operation of every man in the university concerned who made any profession of caring about the Kingdom of God.   Notices on the walls and in college magazines do not make a great impression if Christian Union members are silent; it is the conversation about a college event which awakens interest.   When men in their rooms, in common rooms and elsewhere, talk about a coming event and discuss it, interest is awakened.   A Christian Union is not ready for a campaign until it can be quite certain that all its members will talk about it and attempt to interest their friends in it.

Anyone who travels round the college field must observe that if Christian Unions do not have a conscious purpose to win men for Christ, they become flabby and anæmic. The fact is either the Christian Union is winning men for Christ, or else is being won itself from Him; there is never any standing still.[1]

Now, thirteen years later, what I wrote then is what experience still leads me to want to say about presenting Christ to students.

Campaigns to people outside student life have continued.   The number of students taking part in some kind of effort to extend the Kingdom of God each year, including those going on the World Call Campaigns, has not fallen far short of one thousand.   Probably three-quarters of them have been members of the Student Christian Movement.

It will be noted that on the whole the presentation of Christianity in any particular university or college has been by fits and starts for the last ten years.   The steady winning of students, however, through regular meetings, study groups, the influence of friend with friend, and through the Movement's conferences never ceases.   Year by year hundreds of students take their stand as confessed Christians through the work of the Movement.

[1] *The Student Movement*, Editorial : " Our Primary Aim," vol. xxii. p. 81.

Yet the work of evangelism ought to be continuous, and the reason it is not is because of the diminishing numbers of well-instructed Christian students entering the colleges.

The Student Movement is dependent for its effectiveness on two main factors: first, on men and women who can lead a national Student Movement; second, on these finding enough undergraduates of Christian conviction to lead the work of the Movement in each university and college. This leadership is increasingly difficult to find. From this statement we may exclude Oxford and Cambridge, where the circumstances are different from other places, *e.g.* the religious foundation of the colleges, with chapels and chaplains and the presence of a considerable body of more experienced undergraduates than is found in the new universities.

There is no statement made more frequently in the Annual Reports of the Movement for the last ten years than that the student class, especially in England, enters college deplorably ignorant about Christian truth and about the Bible. The General Committee's report in 1922 says:

It is nothing short of amazing to contemplate the depth of ignorance of Christianity and its doctrines betrayed by men and women who have been brought up in Christian homes, and have passed through Sunday schools and the like. We are led to wonder if the leaders of the Churches are alive to the consequences of the kind of education in religious matters which seems to be provided for the average boy and girl to-day. A very large number of students seem never to have had the Christian faith presented to them, or only presented to them in such a way as to leave a distorted impression.[1]

The following year the General Committee quotes from reports sent to it from the colleges, telling of "complete misunderstanding of Christianity," and "lack of Biblical knowledge."[2] Each year a fresh General

[1] *Annual Report*, S.C.M., 1921-22, p. 15.
[2] *Ibid.*, 1922-23, p. 22.

Committee says the same thing. In 1930 the General Committee quotes as representative the statement of a university college : " There are a large number of men and women in college to-day who are almost without a conception of a spiritual life, or of what Christianity means, except perhaps as a narrow and cramping moral code." [1]

The following year the report harks back to the same theme and quotes an S.C.M. travelling secretary who wrote : " It is no good talking about the *significance* of Christ when perfectly serious and sensible students have either scarcely heard of Him, or question whether He ever existed." [2]

All this does not mean that religion is not of interest to students. When they find fellow students to whom it is a vital matter they are intensely responsive. What it does mean is that the energy of Christian students is taken up in discussion circles in discussing opinions about a faith their fellow students do not know, and are themselves infected with doubts and difficulties with which they cannot cope.

It must not be thought, however, that the Movement has the help of all the Christians in every university. In some of the residential colleges, where its work is much easier by the very fact of residence, it is often able to count on nearly all the Christians in college. In the modern universities, however, where the larger part of the student class is to be found, some of the students are so immersed in the activities of their home churches that they remain outside the ranks of the Movement. During college days the student who is a convinced Christian can find no more fruitful work for God than in seeking to win his fellow students. The best service a student can render to the Church is to uphold the Christian cause in his own university. Clergy and ministers are not wise who use their influence, as many do, to prevent students doing less than they

[1] *Annual Report, S.C.M.*, 1929-30, p. 14.
[2] *Ibid.*, 1930-31, p. 12.

would otherwise do in a particular congregation that they might have time to help the Student Movement in their own college. There are masses of students who are inaccessible to ordinary Church activities, some of whom will occupy positions of responsibility and leadership in our national life, who can only be reached by fellow students. These can be reached by fellow students. The most important " Church-work " a student can do is among his fellow students.

One other matter, the religious training of youth, needs more attention than it is receiving. There is less and less religious training in the homes from which students come, and a great deal of the religious education given in the schools is obviously ineffective as far as schoolboys and schoolgirls who come on to the universities and colleges are concerned. The problem of religious education is the most urgent of any to-day before the Christian Church.

CHAPTER XXXV

POST-WAR ACTIVITIES, 1921-25

WE must now hark back a little and follow some of the other doings of the Movement while it pursued its primary aim of winning students for Christ.

We were cheered by a more hopeful outlook in Ireland. From the outbreak against the British Government in 1916, in Dublin, to the signing of the Anglo-Irish Treaty in December 1921, the situation among students in Dublin might be characterized by the word "pessimism," and in Belfast by the word "anxiety." In Dublin specially it was very hard to make the work of the Movement effective. The Irish student is much more politically minded than the student in England. He and the Welshman are alike in this. Go to a conference of English students, and for a week not more than 5 per cent. of them will trouble to look at a newspaper, and if they do it will be to seek a piece of cricket or football news. Welsh and Irish students, on the other hand, will procure newspapers daily to get political news. The number of foreign students in Ireland has always been small, but they are as a rule much happier than in England. One reason is that they and the Irish have a common interest in politics. I have known South African, Egyptian, Indian and Chinese students, who found Irish student life far more congenial to them than student life in England.

The relationship between the Celt and the Saxon in the Student Christian Movement of Great Britain and Ireland has always been interesting to watch. The Saxon is in the majority on S.C.M. committees, he always talks about S.C.M. work in terms of his own universities and colleges, and if the Irish, Welsh or Scots begin to talk in terms of their student life, he tends to want the matter referred to some other council or committee. The reaction to this of the three races is quite different. The Irishman is tolerant as a rule and rather amused, but he comes of a high-spirited race and may be indignant if a topic about which he feels keenly is pushed on one side. The Welshman is much more sensitive and withdraws into his shell. The recurrent criticism of the Movement in Wales has always been that it is too English. The Scot, if he has something to which he wants the committee to give attention, just goes on until he gets what he wants. Sometimes Irish, Scots and Welsh smile together about " the Celtic fringe " of the S.C.M., knowing that in comparison with the number of English students their compatriots have provided more than their share of the Movement's leaders. After all, what would the Movement have been without J. H. Maclean, O. O. Williams, Donald Fraser, A. T. Roberts, Joe Oldham, Ruth Rouse, Lilian Stevenson, Temple Gairdner, A. G. Fraser, Charlie Taylor, Zoë Fairfield, Oliver Thomas, Herbert Gray, Leslie Hunter, Herbert Morgan, Owen Griffith, Tom Barker, Bill Paton, Bolton Waller, Miall Edwards, R. G. Macdonald, Hugh Martin, John Coates and Robert Mackie? and even I am an Irishman!

But to return to 1921. The Trust Association of the Student Christian Movement of Great Britain and Ireland was incorporated at this time and a body thus constituted, confined to members of the Movement's General Committee, which can hold property of all kinds for its benefit.

William Paton left the Movement this summer after eleven years in its leadership. He served at first on the committee of the Theological Department and then as assistant secretary at headquarters, taking a share in all the different activities of the Movement. After a visit to India he became missionary secretary, and in that position did his greatest work for the Movement. He was a sound theologian, with a lively sense of the importance of keeping one's theology related to life, his churchmanship was vigorous and his judgment to be relied upon. The S.C.M. has had few leaders who possessed such abundant " horse sense "—to use his own phrase—as did Bill Paton. He was universally loved and trusted in the colleges, and no departing secretary ever received such an ovation as was given him at his last " Swanwick " before he returned to India.

Mary Witten joined the staff for 1921-22. She was a trained teacher and she became travelling secretary for training colleges. Her influence was not only felt in the training colleges but throughout the rest of the Movement. She was an interesting speaker, and had a clever pen. She made the problems of the teacher interesting to the committee, and to a wide circle through articles she contributed to *The Student Movement*.

Nearly two hundred training college students were brought together by her efforts in five week-end conferences for students of education in Leeds, Sheffield, Oxford, Bristol and Dublin. Modern educational theory and practice were examined in the light of Christian principles. Courses of lectures on the teaching of Scripture were planned, and college principals asked for their delivery in far more colleges than Miss Witten could visit. She demonstrated how valuable a good training college secretary could be both to students in these colleges and to the cause of education in the Movement as a whole. She prepared a survey of the training colleges, which showed that there was a big movement of change in them. There was an improvement in their government, more freedom for the students, less control of free time and a freer choice of work. Many younger people had been appointed to the staffs of training colleges, and even the over-loaded curriculum had been lightened.

The number of students training to teach grew rapidly. In 1921 there were 15,400 training college students, in 1922 there were 18,500, and in 1923 the total had risen to 19,000. The explanation of the rise was that between 1914 and 1916 monetary inducements were offered to children between the ages of ten and twelve to become teachers. These children were now in college, though many of them had no vocation to teach. The improved salaries under the Burnham scale had also attracted a number of students.

The number of students in the modern universities had also nearly doubled since 1914, and there were more students than formerly giving thought to the nature of the education being offered them by these universities. There was much criticism: the crowded curriculum, the huge lecture time-tables, the lack of personal contact between staff and students, the over-specialized character of the degree courses made a hefty target!

The North and South of England Councils were inadequate to the situation. They were designed to provide policies for the Christian Unions. The students who composed them, however, wanted to turn their meetings into conferences for the discussion of Christianity and of university life and the right relation of the two. The General Committee decided to suspend the councils and try the experiment of holding a Civic Universities Conference, inviting each university Christian Union to appoint two men and one woman to represent them. The first of these conferences was held at Tettenhall College, Wolverhampton, from January 3rd to 7th 1922. Fifty-five people were present. The Movement spent on the conference the sum it would have spent on meetings of the suspended councils, and it arranged successfully a travelling expenses pool, so that the conference cost each student the same, whether he came from near or far.

These conferences were continued, except in the year of a quadrennial conference, until the English Council of the Movement was started as a result of reorganization in 1929. They were quite different from the other conferences of the Movement, and the seven which were held have done much to develop its work in the modern universities.

The enormous pressure of work, consequent on the filling up of the universities after the war, absorbed so much attention that some colleges were neglected by the Movement. This was specially true of the fine art and music schools. The fine art student is an interesting person, full of ideas, and yet the university men and women employed by the Movement have, with a few notable exceptions, been rather timid about tackling fine art colleges, and have generally neglected them unless prodded by Miss Fairfield.

In 1922 the visitation of the colleges by special speakers, notably Miss Royden, interested fine art students. In London A. G. Pite helped the students of the fine art colleges to carry through an interesting exhibition of their work in the Student Movement House for the benefit of the funds of European Student Relief.

Then nothing happened until Elfrida Dorey joined the staff as secretary for fine art colleges in 1924, when study, conference, social and exhibition work was revived by her in a number of cities. Two years later Dr Dearmer opened his house in Chelsea on Sunday evenings for discussions on art and religion, and talks by actors, artists and musicians. This was appreciated. Exhibitions of students' work had been held for three years at Swanwick, and these were continued, as well as all the usual kinds of activities—chiefly discussion groups and conferences.

Kitty Teasdel succeeded Elfrida Dorey as secretary for fine art students in 1927 and carried on the work for a year, but since then all reference to fine art and music students has dropped out of the Movement's reports. Its influence is very small in the artistic community in the colleges, a sad fact.

Fine art students do not organize, and there can be no effective work without a measure of organization. I do not say fine art students cannot organize. I have known many who had first-class organizing capacity, but these have forsaken their art work, temporarily or permanently, when they have undertaken work needing organization. It is very difficult to do creative work and to organize at the same time, and few can combine the two satisfactorily. The Student Movement can have a flourishing fine art section again, as it has had in the past. It needs it for its own sake and for the sake of the influence its members will have later on in the community. Beauty has far too small a place in the life of the modern world. But if the Movement wants the contribution of the fine art student and wants to make its contribution to him, it must not expect him to become an organizer. It must provide staff to do the organizing, he will do the rest.

1922-24 we had a special secretary for technical colleges, E. Y. Scarlett,[1] who opened up an extremely promising piece of work. Scarlett was himself a technical college student, having been educated at the Technical College, Manchester, so he understood the outlook of this type of student.

When Eric Scarlett began visiting the technical colleges to try and start the S.C.M. he found that most of them had no social life.

"The Christian Union's first duty and arduous task," he wrote, "is to create fellowship, to discover for itself, and then to spread abroad the idea that something more is possible than the mere carrying out of a college time-table. . . . In such colleges there is no rival society. . . . A prime duty, then, of the young technical college Christian Union is to encourage, in every way possible, the growth of social life, and to arouse *esprit de corps*. One of the most distressing things about the average technical college student is his entire indifference to his college, its history, its present achievement, and its probable future. It is understandable, but none the less regrettable. Apart from the beneficial effect of a growing corporate sense, the steady presentation of the idea of vocation for Christ would

[1] Sailed for China under L.M.S. in 1924 and six years later shot by bandits.

do much to increase the respect and love of students for the college which was equipping them." [1]

Scarlett deplored the tendency shown by the members of staff of these colleges to lack interest in the college *qua* college.

The technical student had a distinct outlook of his own, with little interest in theology or metaphysics.   He asked : Will Christianity work?

> He demands to see in Christianity a dynamic for his own daily living and for the corporate life of society—for him diagrams of the Kingdom of God must be projected from the here and now, and must show " an engineering job." Nor is this necessarily a lower type of demand or inquiry. The technical college student demands, as do most of his fellow human beings, a Christianity which is relevant to his life, and which promises, and in part realizes, a new world where the wheels revolve with less friction, and the results of which are love, joy and peace, the things which commend themselves to him in his more exalted moments. Again, like most of his fellows, he is attracted by a crusade, the Big Job of service for God and to his fellows captures his imagination (and he is not without the quality), and the promise of hardship but reinforces the appeal.[2]

Scarlett thought that the technical student would be good for the Movement as being an ordinary and simple person who would help it to " achieve an increasingly vital contact with more normal categories of humanity and more commonplace strata of life than are to be found in the cloistral humidity of our more ' rustic ' universities." [3]

He tired at times of the long discussions of a metaphysical character dear to the heart of some Oxford and Cambridge men, hence his jibe at the " rustic " universities.

Scarlett compiled a list of thirty technical colleges in which he hoped to see the Student Christian Movement

---

[1] *The Student Movement*, "The Work of the S.C.M. in Technical Colleges," vol. xxvii. p. 52.

[2] *Ibid.*, p. 74.   [3] *Ibid.*, p. 75.

planted. About half of these had branches by the time he finished his two years' work, some branches he had started, some were older, all he had helped.

The series of articles from which I have quoted begins with a study of the origin of these colleges and is full of useful suggestions. They should be remembered and studied by the next technical secretary the Movement is able to employ. It was a sad waste of a good start that Eric Scarlett's work was left largely to perish for lack of funds with which to provide a successor.

The Indian Student's Union and Hostel at 112 Gower Street was opened on October 6th 1923, and the Student Christian Movement has had a representative on its committee ever since.

This year the Russian Student Christian Movement in Emigration had its rise. It was born at a conference of Russian students at Prerov in Czechoslovakia. It won the support of men like Professor Berdiaeff, Professor Kartashoff, Father Sergius Bulgakoff and Professor Zenkovsky.

A year later Professor Zenkovsky was with us at High Leigh when the Federation General Committee met in England once again after an interval of fifteen years. At the Prerov Conference the Russian Movement, to be so closely related to us in the next few years, expressed its purpose.

> The aim of the Russian Student Christian Movement in Western Europe is the awakening of religious interest among youth, attracting their attention to the questions of faith and strengthening their spiritual life. With these purposes in mind the Movement is trying to bring together and unify youth on the ground of mutual study of the Scriptures, and to deepen as far as possible the Church consciousness in the spirit of Orthodoxy in order to make the Church a vital thing in them and their life.

This Movement has been the one organization that has drawn to its platform Russians of all parties in the Orthodox Church. It has fulfilled its stated purpose with marked success.

The year 1924 opened with news of effective evangelistic work. Dr Gray was busy in Bangor with 340 to 400 students, out of a total of 500, attending his addresses.

The Student Movement House was happy, for it had over a thousand members. Dr W. R. Matthews was arousing great interest by his course of lectures in the House on " The origin and validity of moral ideas."

Liverpool University S.C.M. arranged for some of the staff of the medical department to give a dinner to seventy medicals in the Students' Union. Dr George Hadden spoke about medical missions, and the dinner was voted a huge success.

Sheffield University S.C.M. had promoted a committee of Roman Catholic, Church of England and Free Church members to run a mission. The missioners were Father Hugh Pope, the Rev. J. C. H. Howe and Dr Herbert Gray. There were three simultaneous meetings each night throughout the week, and half the university attended every night. " Students hung round the university—seemed loth to go away." Lunch-hour discussions were well attended, and the missioners were kept busy all day by individuals and groups wanting to talk with them.

The S.C.M. in London began the year with a conference at High Leigh. They were a hundred strong, and for three days Mervyn Haigh [1] steered them with " inspiration, mirth and sanity " ; the Rev. W. R. Maltby and Mr C. F. Angus were the speakers, and there was much discussion about the spiritual life and its maintenance.

We lost a valued friend this spring by the death of Mr A. L. Smith, the Master of Balliol. A few years before the war Leslie Johnston collected about forty heads of colleges and other senior dons in Oxford for me to talk to about the Federation. I was called to speak at 1.30 and warned that every one would want to go at 2 p.m. I stopped at 2 p.m., but most of the company, led by A. L. Smith, adjourned to the combination room to

[1] Afterwards Bishop of Coventry.

ask questions about the Student Movement. I excused myself at 3.45, A. L. Smith came out with me, and as we walked down the High he told me of his abiding sense of the value of the Movement. He came to the conference on " War and Christianity " in 1915 and took part with keenness. He was a true friend to the Movement.

The preparations for a conference on Christian Politics, Economics and Citizenship, which came to be known as " Copec," were watched with great interest by us all. Many streams flowed together to make " Copec." Work and thought associated with the names of Kingsley, Maurice, Westcott, S. A. Barnett, Scott Holland, the work of the Student Christian Movement, various social service bodies in the Churches, the object-lesson of the World Missionary Conference at Edinburgh, 1910, and the value to the missionary enterprise of the study commissions which had preceded it—all these helped to make it. Many Christians keenly interested in social questions were anxious to clear their minds, to discover to what extent they were in agreement, and to see if they could arrive at a statement of the social message of Christianity which they could put before the whole Church, and thus secure for it a greater place in its thought and activity.

Twelve preparatory commissions were formed of men and women with special knowledge of the subjects dealt with. These drew up reports on the basis of material supplied by groups all over the country. The Copec questionnaires were widely used in the colleges, under the guidance of the Movement. In all 150,000 copies of these questionnaires were issued. The reports dealt with " The nature of God and His purpose for the world," " Education," " The social function of the Church," " Politics and citizenship," " Christianity and war," " The relation of the sexes," " The treatment of crime," " Historical illustrations of the social effects of Christianity," " International relations," " Industry and property," " The Home," " Leisure." They are good reading to this day. Old Student Movement members were on all the commissions, and many student groups supplied material for their work.

When the conference came the Student Movement was given fifteen places for delegates. Hugh Martin and I were asked by the General Committee to select its delegation. Those chosen were Amy Buller, Zoë Fairfield, J. T. Edwards, Owen Griffith, J. W. Parkes, A. G. Pite, W. S. A. Robertson and T. Tatlow, all S.C.M. secretaries; and the following students: Janet Lodge (Edinburgh), John Hamilton (Glasgow), Vesey Stone (Oxford), R. H. Slater (Cambridge), Olive Dickinson (Sheffield), L. Irvine (Aberdeen) and Gladys Moss (Dublin). In addition to these Hugh Martin, R. O. Hall, Stephen Neill, H. A. Mess and Dr Herbert Gray attended by virtue of official relation to the conference.

When the conference took place, in April 1924, the influence of former Student Movement men and women was considerable. The officers of the conference were all former members of the Movement—the chairman, the Bishop of Manchester (Dr Temple), the vice-chairman, Dr A. E. Garvie, and one of the secretaries, the Rev. C. E. Raven. The other secretary, Miss Lucy Gardner, very influential in the preparation of the conference would, I think, be glad to be claimed by the Movement for, though not a university woman, she was in constant touch with the thought and activities of the Movement. Her friends were almost all Student Movement men and women, and Hugh Martin was chairman of the Executive which worked with her. Malcolm Spencer and H. A. Mess were in the thick of the whole thing, and I found the names of about five hundred people I had known in the Movement on the list of delegates. How many more there were among the fourteen hundred present I do not know—enough for Dr Temple to say to me during the conference, " If it had not been for the Movement this conference would not have been possible."

As I am only writing about the connection between

" Copec " and the Movement, an attempt to describe the conference would be out of place ; a quotation from Henry Mess, summarising an account of it must suffice.

There can be little doubt that the conference has done its work. A space has been won in the attention of the Christian Churches which will not be lost. The reports of the Commissions constitute a body of Christian social philosophy without parallel for many centuries. The social reformers who have been straggling bands and irregular auxiliaries are being formed at last into an army ; and more than that, the time cannot be far distant when the Christian Churches will both formally and sincerely acknowledge that the redemption of society is a task committed to them by their Lord.[1]

Soon after " Copec " we turned our attention to preparations for the second meeting in Great Britain of the General Committee of the Federation, the first having been at Oxford in 1909. It met at High Leigh, Hoddesdon, from August 7th to 22nd 1924, and the whole party of about a hundred people, representing thirty-six different races, was entertained at the expense of our Movement. The meeting reflected the distracted state of the world, and showed greater divergence in outlook than previous meetings. Some urged that the Student Movements should concentrate their attention on the task of rebuilding human society on the basis of the teaching of Jesus, others that personal religion and right relations with God should be their chief concern. At times the groups from North America and from Central Europe seemed far apart in their thought. The outstanding interpreters of different points of view were George Cockin and Pierre Maury (France). The Russian delegation supplied by Russian students and professors in exile was the strongest Orthodox Church group which had hitherto taken part in a Federation General Committee meeting. It made a spiritual contribution of great value to the gathering.

[1] *The Student Movement*, art. : " C.O.P.E.C.—a Personal Impression," H. A. Mess, vol. xxvi. p. 173.

Miss Ruth Rouse retired from office at this meeting after twenty years' service, which the resolution of the committee thanking her described as " twenty years of abounding, brilliant and most fruitful activity." Her creative gifts, wisdom and devotion had been a source of enrichment to work among students in the sixty countries she had visited, some of them many times.

Our Movement was represented by F. A. Cockin, Zoë Fairfield, R. O. Hall, M. O. Janes and Dorothy Steven. I was present as an *ex-officio* member, being vice-chairman of the Federation.

The Federation meeting was hardly over before Henry Mess announced his resignation as Social Study Secretary on his appointment as a lecturer in social science under the Congregational County Union of Lancashire and Yorkshire. He had only sought this new post because the Movement was in financial straits. It parted with him with great reluctance. In parting with him the Movement parted with the last of the three senior study secretaries it had appointed since the war. It was a sore business. We did not want to lose him. He was scholarly—few could lecture better on Shakespeare—well-balanced, wise. He spoke and wrote well, had creative gifts, understood students and was an expert in his subject. The Movement has needed him every year since he left.

In October two hundred women students attended the first of a series of " quiet days " arranged by the Student Movement in London under the guidance of Amy Buller. These quiet days have been held regularly ever since.

The Manchester Quadrennial Conference came in the first week of January 1925. T. Z. Koo took this conference by storm with a brilliant address on " The New China." China was tackling the task of education and social reconstruction in a way which made T. Z. Koo say to us, " God seems to have breathed on my country and said, ' Let there be life.' "

The rapidity with which the world was changing was

brought out again and again. Africa " is not a dark continent any more, but one bright with hope." In the mornings we looked at the world as it is, and in the evenings turned to the fundamentals of the Christian Faith. There were sixteen hundred people at the conference, twelve hundred of whom were students. Thirty-nine countries were represented. The singing was exceptionally good and was led by Dr Harold Darke. For the first time a closing service of worship and dedication was held in the Cathedral. I prepared a special service for it, which was printed at the last moment for the use of the delegates. I provided similar services for " Liverpool, 1929," and " Edinburgh, 1933."

T. Z. Koo stayed with us in England for some weeks, and before he left spoke to three thousand people in the Central Hall, Westminster, two thousand of whom were students. The Archbishop of Canterbury was in the chair. But far more moving was a meeting in the Archbishop's study at Lambeth. The Archbishops of Canterbury and York were both present, and talked at length with Koo about China and the Christian enterprise in that land, and then Koo rose to go. I stood a little apart and watched the scene. He stood, a slender figure in his Chinese dress of blue, with an archbishop at each side of him, as, reluctant to let him go, they plied him with further questions as to what he thought about many matters relating to the work of Western Christians in China. And as each archbishop shook hands to say good-bye, each thanked him warmly and simply for what he had done during his visit to help English Christians. I was deeply moved by the scene. Behind the trio there rose for me a vision of men of every kindred and tribe and race in one fellowship worshipping God. It was a wonderful tribute to Koo, and it was a tribute also to the humility and sincerity of the two men of God who filled the offices of Primate of All England and Primate of England.

It was at the Manchester Conference we secured Robert Mackie as Scottish secretary of the Movement.

2 X

He had refused office, there were real difficulties in his way, but one night Miss Fairfield and I, and one or two others, sought to take him by assault. He said he was not the man for us, and that it was too difficult in view of obligations he had assumed, but I went to bed assured we should get him. Most of the men who have played a big part in the Movement have been difficult to shepherd into secretaryships; I have always remembered how John Mott refused again and again the invitation to enter student work and how C. K. Ober persisted until he secured him.

Robert Mackie was not a newcomer, he had been for two years a trusted and popular chairman of the General Committee, after a period of membership during which he used to sit silent in a corner at committee meetings looking strangely aloof!

The Student Movement House Club held its first conference in March 1925. It was at High Leigh. The variety of races the seventy members represented, the good programme and fine spirit of it were encouraging. These gatherings continue and are useful.

The General Committee, which usually meets in London, met at Oxford the same year to enable members to take part in the Congress of the National Union of Students of England and Wales, at which six hundred students were present. Toyohiko Kagawa of Japan was with us and was one of us, very simple and friendly. His was the simplicity of greatness.

The tide of interest in the social implications of Christianity which had run strongly in the colleges since the war turned this winter, 1924-25, and moved in the direction of emphasis on personal religion. It was a difficult period. There was a lack of outstanding personalities among students, and in consequence all student societies, including the Christian Unions, suffered.

Norah Inskip started this winter a group for work in East Africa. The idea was to draw into the group men and women who would plan to take up work as teachers, doctors, agriculturists, clergy, some as mis-

R. O. HALL	A. HERBERT GRAY	A. VICTOR MURRAY
F. A. COCKIN	ZOË B. FAIRFIELD	OWEN GRIFFITH
HUGH MARTIN	ROBERT C. MACKIE	HENRI LOUIS HENRIOD

sionaries and some in government service. The members of the group to go to Africa as they were ready, but always to keep in touch by letters, visits and even conferences, in Africa. Her idea has lived and the group holds together, some are at work in Africa and recruits are still joining it.

The increased cost of living, including travel, and the difficulty of raising delegation funds was seriously affecting the attendance of Scottish students at the summer conferences at Swanwick. It cost a student at Aberdeen University over £8 to attend a Swanwick Conference, so to make it more possible for Scottish students to have the help of a summer conference one was held at Dollar, July 28th to August 3rd 1925. It was planned on the same lines as the Swanwick conferences, and at the Federation meeting nationals of India, Sweden, China, Russia and Africa took part, while the S.C.M. leaders there included H. H. G. Macmillan (chairman), Jim Dougall, Alec Boyd, T. Tatlow, Hugh Martin, Dorothy Steven, Ralph Morton, Ella Lindsay, J. O. Dobson and Robert Mackie. One hundred and ninety-nine people were present. Similar conferences were held at Moffat in 1926, 1927, 1928, and then the Scotsmen came back to Swanwick, bagpipes and all, and right welcome they were for their absence had been a sore loss to the conferences.

The next summer the Welsh followed the Scottish example and held a summer conference at Caerleon, with an attendance of one hundred and fourteen. They, too, wanted their conference to be a conference of the Movement held in Wales, and though the majority attending were Welsh, Student Movement leaders and speakers from beyond the Welsh border and nationals from Ceylon, Germany, and Hungary, as well as some English students, were present. It was a good conference and a happy one. I noticed that in the art exhibition—pictures and hand-crafts—the standard of work shown was higher than at a similar exhibition of students' work at Swanwick. Although most of the speaking was in English, the Welsh language was sometimes used on the platform and at meal times, and in small group discussions one constantly heard Welsh spoken.

The Caerleon Conference has been held annually since 1927, and is likely to be a permanent element in the life of the Movement.

CHAPTER XXXVI

THE GROWTH OF AN INTERNATIONAL CONSCIOUSNESS

THE first blow to high hopes came in May 1919 when the terms of the Peace Treaty were revealed.

We of the younger generation had cherished an ardent hope that the idealistic talk of responsible statesmen was real; that bad old ways were to be forsaken and a new road towards a better world entered upon; and that the struggle and sacrifice of the last five years were to be for high ends. We find that it is not so.[1]

We were thankful that the frame-work of the Treaty was of a League of Nations. "But," said *The Student Movement*, "taken as a whole, the document lacks idealism or any traces of the spirit of reconciliation or magnanimity."

We were all the more distressed at the harsh and vindictive terms of the Treaty in that we were re-establishing our links with the other Movements in the Federation—that league of students of all nations. Letters of greetings passed between allies, neutrals and enemies, and we looked forward to an early meeting of the committee of the Federation which had stood the test of the war and remained unbroken.

There was a remarkable turning to the Student Christian Movement in Great Britain for sympathy, advice and help at this period. S. K. Datta wrote to me from Calcutta a long description of the situation in India. He had just completed a tour in which he talked with leaders of all kinds from the Viceroy down.

I wonder whether you cannot help us to do something real for India at the present time, missionaries and money

[1] *The Student Movement*, Editorial, vol. xxi. p. 129.

are small matters as compared with the radical change of heart we desire to see.   Race hatred has become acute . . . my belief is that the only solution lies in vesting authority in India.   Your part of the programme will be to train Englishmen to accept that authority and to work under it. This is true in all departments, whether in the State or in the Church.   There will never be peace in India until Indians are masters in their own house and as such have authority to declare what type of foreigner they will use or refuse.

The Indian Student Christian Movement wanted to send a man to interpret their country and people, and a little later we welcomed their representative, Ariam Williams, a Ceylonese, who had been working in India, as a member of our staff.

John Victor, the general secretary of the Hungarian Student Movement, chafed at restrictions which would not let him visit us.   In March 1919 he wrote : " It was awful, four years and a half ago, to find myself in the position of an ' enemy ' of you and all the other friends in Great Britain, but is it not more awful that I am still counted such a terrible person that I am not allowed to go and meet you ? "   The Home Office was afraid to give a permit.   I was told quite frankly in Whitehall that they feared a question in the House of Commons if they gave it ; so we sent Ronald Rees to the Hague to visit Victor and discuss ways of helping the Hungarian Student Movement.

We had a two days' conference at Annandale between leaders in the Student Movements of the United States of America, Canada, Australia, New Zealand, South Africa and our own Movement.   There were present from the Australian Student Christian Movement : Stanley Addison, general secretary ; Captain F. H. L. Paton, the chairman of the Foreign Service Committee ; Captain F. W. Robinson, late president of the Christian Union in Sydney University ; A. E. Howard, late president Adelaide University Christian Union ; Mrs C. I. McLaren, travelling secretary ; and Captain F. W. Rolland of Melbourne University.   The other countries were equally well represented. Several of the delegates became well known in our Movement, notably Lieutenant T. M. Haslett, Dunedin and Oberlin, travelling secretary; J. McMurray Cole, vice-president Auckland Christian Union; Miss Constance Grant—all of New Zealand; J. J. Rousseau of Cape Town University, Dr J. Ross Stevenson, R. H. Legate, Elizabeth Fox, and Rhoda McCulloch, editor of *The Women's Press*. The military titles are a sign of the war service of the men. Almost all came in military or Y.M.C.A. service uniforms. The conference dealt with the work of our Movements, both in the colleges and for better world relationships.

We also had visits at this time from a number of leaders in the World's Student Christian Federation, including Dr Karl Fries, the chairman of the Federation, Dr Mott, general secretary, and from the vice-chairman of the Federation, Mr C. T. Wang, who was one of the Chinese plenipotentiaries at the Peace Conference at Versailles.

Zoë Fairfield, Henri Louis Henriod and I went to Paris to visit the French Student Movement, and several of their leaders came to our conferences at Swanwick that summer.

Shortly after this we renewed our contact with the German Student Movement. The chairman of the World's Student Christian Federation wrote that Dr Michaelis,[1] the president of the German Student Christian Movement, had told him the leaders of the German Movement " wish to use every opportunity that would be offered for consultation with representatives of Student Movements of enemy countries." The General Committee hearing this decided I should write to Paul Humburg, general secretary of the German S.C.M., saying that we were ready to send two or three men to meet an equal number of them. This invitation was accepted by telegram, and Holland suggested as the country in which to meet.

[1] Dr Michaelis was the last Chancellor of the Kaiser.

Dr Rutgers invited us to the headquarters of the Dutch Student Movement.   After a journey of twenty-six hours, William Paton, W. P. Young and I arrived on New Year's Eve at Kastel Hardenbroek, where we found Paul Humburg and Herr Schiller, a law student, waiting for us.   I had known Humburg for twenty-one years, he had been on the staff of the German Movement, was then a pastor for fifteen years, and had been called back some months before as general secretary of the German Movement.   Schiller had joined the army as a volunteer at the beginning of the war, attained the rank of captain, was adjutant of his regiment, and had won the Iron Cross first class.   He was now the leader of the students on the committee of the German Student Christian Movement, the committee being composed of nine students and nine senior men.

During the time we were together " a spirit of frankness and friendliness was maintained without any effort."[1] Humburg was a Prussian, had a picture of the Kaiser in his pocket, and was a conservative in theology.   Schiller came from South Germany, and was democratic in politics.   The Germans wanted to discuss the war, the blockade and the terms of the peace treaty.

> They were men living very much in the presence of and concerned with the difficulties of life in a country economically ruined, politically more or less in chaos, with the necessaries of life difficult to procure and inordinately expensive.   They made no attempt to put a good face on things, assuming our friendliness at once and telling us . . . of their troubles and difficulties.

Much time was spent in comparing notes about wartime experiences.   When we asked what matters they wished specially to discuss, they propounded six questions all connected with the war.   " What do English Christians think as to the right of asking starving and defeated Germans to sign in the peace treaty that they

[1] This and following quotations are from *Report to General Committee of Conference with Representatives of the German Student Movement*, T. Tatlow.

are solely guilty of the cause of the war?" They thought that the cause of the war was revealed by the peace treaty, namely, an attempt to ruin Germany in order to improve the position of her enemies. They came back to this later when they raised the question of the despoilation of Germany's colonies. The conversation turned to why England came into the war.

> We pointed out that what brought England into the war and produced volunteers on a large scale was the violation of Belgium; that men entered the war because of ideals. They expressed genuine surprise at this, evidently being convinced that Belgium was only an excuse, and that, as they put it, the real aim of the war was apparent when one read the peace treaty. W. P. Young said that they had to face the fact that he personally had joined the army because of Belgium, and that he believed his case to be typical.

This was of great interest to both the Germans, and Schiller explained that he too had been a volunteer and had joined the army to fight for ideals.

The second question referred to what English Christians thought about the decision of the Allies to bring prominent Germans before a tribunal composed of their enemies. It was unjust, they said, and they were greatly concerned as to what would happen, fearing specially French and Belgian influence on the tribunal. We were not enthusiasts for the Lloyd George slogan, "Hang the Kaiser and make the Germans pay," and said so. The fear of this tribunal, though it never came to pass, was very real at this time to the Germans.

Then we passed to the destruction of the work of German foreign missions. Bill Paton provided a lot of information, new to them, about the efforts of English missionary societies to conserve this work, and we said we hoped German missionaries would be allowed to return to their work in the future.

We sympathized with them heartily over their last point, namely, "whether English Christians thought it right to keep Germany uncertain as to how much indemnity she would have to pay?" In the destitute and depressed state of Germany an indemnity which might grow as they rehabilitated their country seemed to us a cruel piece of economic tyranny.

Before we separated some time was spent on comparing notes about the tendencies of thought in our respective Movements. Humburg did not like our new aim and basis, holding that an aim and basis " should be couched in very conservative language." He agreed that the German Student Movement only provided for students whose theological position was very conservative, and that there were many Christian students outside it.

The Federation was a subject of great mutual interest, but when we said we hoped to see the Federation of the future an important factor working for peace and the elimination of war the two men took somewhat different lines. Schiller was cautious but sympathetic. Humburg was suspicious of the idea.

> He made it clear that his theology was quite frankly a theology which despaired of the world. He thought that the Kingdom of God could in no sense come in this world, that it had to do solely with the world to come, that all that could be done was to try and make individual people Christians and prepare them for heaven, that incidentally it would, of course, help human life if people became Christians, but as for war, he said there must always be war in the world, because the Bible said so. When challenged as to whether Christianity could not eradicate war from human life, as it had eradicated slavery, he did not think so. He admitted that we should work against war, " but not optimistically."

One misunderstanding which might have had serious results was cleared up by this meeting. The officers of the Federation had proposed that the first meeting of its General Committee after the war should take place at Wadstena, in Sweden, the birthplace of the Federation. The Germans before we met, while not showing any signs of wanting to withdraw from the Federation, had indicated that it was doubtful if they would be present

at the Wadstena meeting. When we referred to the
meeting soon after arrival in Holland, we saw they
were uneasy about it. I had come to Hardenbroek
determined to try and secure their promise that they
would come, so not having succeeded in this or discovered their difficulty, I returned to the subject the
night before we separated.

I began to put some of the obvious reasons why the
Federation must meet, and in the course of my remarks
said: "I can understand your feeling difficulty about
attending a big Federation conference, but what I cannot
understand is that you do not see that if the Federation is
to go on with its work now, it is essential that the committee
should meet." Humburg sat up, pulled out his watch, and
said dramatically: "Do you tell me that I wait until
10.15 p.m. on the night of January 1st 1920 to discover
that what we are asked to attend is not a jubilee conference
to celebrate the founding of the Federation with rejoicings,
but simply a meeting of the committee?" The trouble
was laid bare, there had been misunderstanding, and when
Humburg found it was not a celebration but a committee
meeting that was proposed he said: "That is quite right, the
committee should meet. I am a member of the committee.
I will attend."

For some reason the Germans had got it into their
heads that there were to be celebrations which they
feared might be rejoicings by those who had won the
war. We reassured them, and later asked the chairman
and secretary of the Federation to set their fears at rest
by giving up the idea of meeting at Wadstena. The
meeting was held the following summer at St Beatenberg, Switzerland.

While we were thus restoring contacts in the Federation as well as expanding the staff of our own Movement
and helping to plan evangelistic work in the colleges,
anxiety amongst us was increasing about conditions on
the Continent. Starvation was being talked about,
and A. E. Zimmern denounced international profiteer-
ing in the pages of *The Student Movement*. Amongst
the profiteers was Great Britain, which was starving and

freezing the Continent by charging huge prices for coal.

> The British people, which is profiteering individually and collectively by the earning of the coal export trade, is as surely responsible for the infantile death-rate in Central Europe and the unemployment to which it is largely due as Herod in the Gospel story was for the murder of the Holy Innocents.[1]

In the same issue Sir Willoughby Dickinson expounded the possibilities of the League of Nations, and appealed to the Student Christian Movement throughout the world to address arguments and appeals on its behalf in the universities and colleges of Europe, Asia, Africa, Australasia and America, to the " tens of thousands of active spirits who in the next dozen years will have become the shapers of the world's destiny." [2]

The Movement had hitherto never considered international questions in terms of relations between the nations, but the bitter experience of the war and the new wealth of relationships that opened up before us caused much thought and discussion. We realized that the Movement had had a long training for taking up the task of helping to guide the thought and purposes of students in relation to international questions. It had grown out of a sense of mission to people of other countries, and during its history 2322 of its members had gone abroad as missionaries. It had always thought of God as the Father of the whole human family ; of Christ as the Saviour of the whole world ; of His Kingdom as universal ; of His Church as catholic ; and of the Holy Spirit as the source of all true life.

It had been a member of the World's Student Christian Federation since its inception, and this had been an international strand woven into all its thinking.

The increase in the number of students in British

---

[1] *The Student Movement*, art. : " International Relations and Economic Policy," A. E. Zimmern, vol. xxii. p. 67.

[2] *Ibid.*, art. : " The League of Nations and the S.C.M.," Sir Willoughby Dickinson, p. 71.

colleges from all over the world, and the Movement's contact with them, had brought the whole question of international knowledge and friendship nearer home.

The Movement itself was international—the Scottish, Irish and Welsh Councils had kept steadily before it the aspirations and problems of their countries.

"The Call to Battle" to the colleges in September 1919 contained a paragraph on international relationships, written out of the Movement's own experience of joy in fellowship.

> We have found in working with students of other nations and races a unity in Christ which overcomes prejudice and enriches the common life. Before God and in Christ we are all one. We are convinced that this unity is the only sure hope of peace and of the true development of nations. Now is the time to do all in our power to create a public opinion that shall constrain statesmen to act on this belief.

The colleges were showing a keen interest in international questions and discussing international problems.

> There is a desire that is often passionate to find some new way of international life, to see new principles applied and a real stand made for a better world. This shows itself in a widespread interest in the League of Nations, in a search for literature on the whole subject, in countless discussions and in a demand for addresses on it from senior friends. Even where students make little profession of Christianity themselves, they often have a real interest in the question of how the principles of Jesus Christ could be applied to international affairs. Many are eager that the World's Student Christian Federation, in which they have great confidence, should discover and make articulate the Christian Gospel to the nations, and call on its members in all the nations to stake their lives on it.[1]

A sub-committee was appointed at Christmas 1919 to consider the relationship of the Movement to international questions, and it advised a threefold educational policy :

1. To consider fundamental Christian principles as they concern international questions.

[1] *Annual Report, S.C.M.*, 1919-20, p. 35.

2. To get actual facts about the international situation known in the colleges.

3. To consider how to apply Christian principles to these facts.

It also made some suggestions for reading in the vacation, and planned a small international conference from May 14th to 17th, at Annandale.

J. H. Oldham had a long talk with me on his return from a visit to America, and urged that the leaders of the British Movement should do all in their power to create a right understanding between Great Britain and America. The state of misunderstanding and misrepresentation was very serious. This talk turned the Movement's attention to the importance of developing its relationships with the S.C.M. in the United States, and led to considerable results.

The Movement held a meeting for London students in the Kingsway Hall, on March 5th 1920, on " Students and the League of Nations." Sir Michael Sadler was in the chair, and Lord Robert Cecil [1] and I spoke to a thousand students, and a little later the suggested conference was held at Annandale. It consisted of senior friends connected with diplomacy, the Press and the League of Nations Union, and considered the duty of the Movement. As a result, the General Committee declared :

> We look forward to giving much thought and effort to this whole subject in the near future ; there is need for clear and fearless thinking, steady educational work, and a strong stand for right standards in relation both to representatives of other nations in our midst and to international questions of all kinds.[2]

Bolton Waller spoke for us all when he declared that the first item in our international programme must be the elimination of war. " It is inconceivable that war could exist in a Christianized world. We are now

---

[1] Afterwards Viscount Cecil of Chelwood.
[2] *Annual Report, S.C.M.,* 1919-20, pp. 35-36.

agreed on the desirability of eliminating war ; the task for this generation is to know how it is to be done." [1]

The next call upon our international sympathies was a practical one, and in a later chapter will be told the story of the share students took in the relief of starving fellow students in Europe. We began to help before the first post-war meeting of the committee of the World's Student Christian Federation. That meeting quickened our desire to do more.

The World's Student Christian Federation General Committee met for the first time since 1913, from July 30th to August 8th 1920, at St Beatenberg, Switzerland. Twenty-four countries were represented, including Germany. A round-table conference of forty-seven students, which included fifteen additional countries, sat in another room, and we mixed between whiles and held several joint sessions. Eighty-nine persons in all were at St Beatenberg. There was much renewing of friendships and the making of many new friends, and " there was the same atmosphere of goodwill, frankness and vital interest in spiritual issues to which we are accustomed in the Student Movement. . . . There was the all-pervading sense that we met in Christ's Name, and that what was going forward would have been impossible but for His presence and leadership." Dr Mott and Miss Rouse had prepared magnificently for the committee, and a survey was made of the guiding principles of the Federation and of the present position of the Christian movement in every student field in the world.

Dr Mott's exposition of the guiding principles of the Federation was accepted by us all, and is worth summarizing :

(1) The recognition of the supremacy of Jesus Christ.
(2) The preservation of the interdenominational principle.
(3) The recognition of the autonomy of each national Movement. (4) The recognition of the interdependence and

[1] *The Student Movement*, art. : " The Federation and International Brotherhood," Bolton C. Waller, vol. xxii. p. 74.

obligations of national Student Movements to one another. (5) The obligation of the Federation as a whole to serve and not to seek to govern national Movements. (6) The maintenance of the non-political character of the Federation. (7) The maintenance of the spirit of true democracy in the constituent parts of the Federation. (8) The determination of all the policy of the Federation from a world point of view.

The General Committee of the Federation decided, on a motion by Great Britain, that in future it would assume entire responsibility for raising and expending the money required for its work, and would ask each national Movement to guarantee a contribution towards the expenses of the Federation. A budget amounting to £8000 was passed, and Great Britain and Ireland guaranteed £1500 of it. Hitherto the secretaries of the Federation had raised money as they could for its work.

The Federation was reorganized so that each national Movement would be directly represented on the General Committee. Hitherto Movements had been grouped and the group of countries given a certain number of places. This had resulted in some countries not being directly represented by one of its nationals on the Federation Committee.

Article II of the Constitution for the Federation was revised. The chief revision was to include a reference to international relationships in the Constitution of the Federation. The following words were added as one of its objects :

> To bring students of all countries into mutual under-standing and sympathy, to lead them to realize that the principles of Jesus Christ should rule in international relationships, and to endeavour by so doing to draw the nations together.

Provision was also made in the Constitution for such an activity as the relief work which had been started, and to this end another clause was added: "To further, either directly or indirectly, those efforts on behalf of the welfare of students in body, mind and spirit, which are in harmony with the Christian purposes."

At this meeting important changes in the leadership of the Federation took place. Dr Fries, who had been chairman since its foundation in 1895, resigned and Dr Mott, having withdrawn from the general secretary-ship, was appointed chairman in his place. Dr W. W. Seton resigned his position as treasurer, and Dr H. C. Rutgers of Holland was appointed in his place. The Hon. C. T. Wang of China and Miss Michi Kawai of Japan were appointed vice-chairmen. An Executive Committee was created for the first time, to meet between the biennial meetings of the General Committee of the Federation. The first Executive of the Federation consisted of the chairman, vice-chairmen and treasurer, *ex-officio*, and Paul Humburg, Germany; Pierre Maury, France; T. Tatlow, Great Britain; S. K. Datta, India; E. Clark, Canada; David Porter, U.S.A.; W. H. P. Mackenzie, Australasia; Mrs Svelmoe-Thomson, Scandinavia; and Leslie Blanchard, U.S.A.

It was at this General Committee that European Student Relief was founded by the Federation.

Another student grouping drew our attention at this period. In connection with French celebrations at Strasbourg and the opening of the French University in November 1919 we learned that " La Confédération Internationale des Etudiants " had been founded. The French National Union of Students proposed this inter-national organization of students. They produced statutes, and a French government official long past student age became its president, M. Jean Gerard. The statutes declared the C.I.E. could be constituted by three national student organizations, and these being forth-coming, since France, Belgium and Czechoslovakia had joined, the new Federation was declared to be in exist-ence. It was immediately joined by Luxembourg, Poland, Spain and Roumania, and invitations were sent to Great Britain, America, Holland, Switzerland, the Scandinavian countries, Yugoslavia, Italy and Greece, inviting their adherence.

A study of the statutes showed that its aims were drawn somewhat vaguely. They were, to bring the students of the countries adhering together, to co-ordinate their action in intellectual matters and to promote intellectual expansion, and to study inter-national questions relative to the moral and material life of students. It was to be independent of politics and religion.

The northern countries, led by Sweden which was Teutonic in its sympathy, fixed their attention on one article in the statutes which excluded from membership the students of the Central Powers until their countries were admitted into the League of Nations. A con-ference was held in Copenhagen in July 1920 by repre-sentative students from Sweden, Norway, Denmark, Holland and Switzerland to discuss the relation of the students of neutral countries to the C.I.E. Their atti-tude was that if the C.I.E. would plan its work on a basis of true internationalism the neutrals ought to join it, but that the article which prevented the students of Germany and Austria joining at once must be deleted from the statutes.

There was a " Conference de Bureau " of the C.I.E. in Brussels in September 1920, when the neutrals, though not yet members, were allowed to take part in the discussions, and as a result the Executive Com-mittee of the C.I.E. agreed to propose to the next congress, to be held in Prague in 1921, that the statute excluding students of the Central Powers be eliminated.

At this stage several universities in England and Scotland became interested, and letters came to the Student Movement from these and also from Student Movement leaders in Holland, Norway and Sweden, asking us to help to get the support of British students who would set the C.I.E. on right lines.

Manchester University Students' Union elected Victor

Murray, the Student Movement secretary there, to be their representative at the C.I.E. Prague Conference, and the General Committee of the Movement decided he should attend and that it would pay his expenses, thinking this would serve the cause of international relationships.   We learned that the suggestion to admit Germans and others was not agreed to at Prague, and that although the C.I.E. was supposed to be independent of politics, the congress spent most of its time on political debates. The idea of a confederation seemed a good one and British and neutral delegates still hoped it would be brought on to sound lines.

The desire on the part of several of the new universities to be able to send properly qualified delegates to the C.I.E. congresses raised the question of the organization on a national basis of their various unions and guilds, and so the National Union of Students of England and Wales came into being. The Student Movement, believing such a union had a useful purpose to serve in university life, provided a place on the programme of the Officers' Conference at Swanwick for the first two years of the life of the N.U.S. to help to make it known to students. A speech about it was made at each of these conferences by a man appointed by the N.U.S.

The doings of the C.I.E. are beyond the scope of this history. Its start was not on good lines, and though Mr Ivison Macadam laboured to make it an effective international student organization, its career has been a chequered one, and its future is still uncertain.

We must now turn back to our own Movement. When the Federation General Committee met at St Beatenberg, plans were already well advanced for our first quadrennial conference after the war. The first four—Liverpool 1896, London 1900, Edinburgh 1904 and Liverpool 1908—had dealt exclusively with foreign missions. The last quadrennial conference before the war, Liverpool 1912, had widened its scope and dealt with " missionary questions and social problems." The first post-war quadrennial conference looked out upon the whole world.

The object of the Glasgow Conference was to bring home to members of the Student Movement the meaning and implications for it of the world outlook.

> All talk of a better world is mere beating of the air unless the world context in which we must seek the Kingdom is understood and taken into consideration. . . . We want to think right about God and man and the world, and we want to apply those ideas to the problems, racial, economic and political, which the world of to-day presents.[1]

Bill Paton had done much already to broaden the missionary message of the Movement and relate it to the international situation, and he was helped in this by Miss Fairfield, who shared with him the making of the programme for " Glasgow 1921."

Bill Paton, in seeking to broaden the missionary message of the Movement, urged—as did leaders twenty-five years before him—that knowledge of the facts is the first essential, but he asked students to seek for much wider knowledge than had been done in the pre-war days.

When the Movement started the people of the mission field, as we called Africa, China, India, were not in the main self-conscious as people. Perhaps the one element in the Orient that was self-conscious was Islam. The Islamic Movement grew in self-consciousness until it seemed to offer a serious menace to the spread of Christianity. Its collapse has been one of the most dramatic episodes in the history of religion. The Movement's leaders who first called for missionary study asked men and women to get to know something of the geography, history and religion of the Orient and, with this slender background, study what Christian missions were doing. The work when studied proved to be evangelistic and educational in the main. It was uncomplicated, for the most part, by political or social movements.

[1] *The Student Movement*, vol. xxiii. p. 17.

A new day, however, had been slowly dawning, and without doubt the Student Movement had had a great deal to do with its appearing. Thousands of university men and women pouring into Africa and the East, carrying with them the social, moral, and religious ideas of their own land and their own religion, were a tremendous force. The ferment of the last thirty years in the Orient, due to the impact of the West upon the East, is due in no small measure to the influence of the keen minds and ardent spirits of the university men and women who, becoming missionaries, mixed more intimately with the people than any other kind of foreigner. " I came not to bring peace but a sword," said Christ. Nowhere has this been more true than in what we call " the mission field," and of no group is it more true than the missionaries. I know of no writer who has yet done justice to the tremendous influence on the social, economic, moral and religious thought of the East exercised by the Christian mission led by the men and women who have come from the ranks of the Student Movements of Great Britain, America and the Continent of Europe. I should not put first, as the man who had been the cause of ferment, either the trader, or the diplomat, but the missionary.

The thing was patent to us all by the end of the war, so Bill Paton wrote :

Knowledge of the actual facts of the world-situation is the first essential. We ought to know something of the meaning of the race-problem—that urgent and perplexing question which greets us wherever we look round the fringes of the Pacific, in India, in Africa, in America, in Great Britain. We ought all of us to know something, and some of us to know a great deal, about the industrial and economic linking up of the world, and the far-reaching effects it has had upon the lives of the peoples of Africa and Asia. Confronted as we are by the great venture which is now being made in Indian Government, we ought to know the main issues which are at stake, and have some idea of the spirit and attitude needed in Britishers who are to be of any real service to the new India. We ought to know something, and some of us to know a good deal, about the great religions which maintain sway over Asia and Africa, and enter into the very fibre of the life of millions of our fellow human beings. I do not pretend that, within limits of our college careers, we can all expect, or should expect, to know very much about these things, but we ought to have enough knowledge to gain the right point of view.[1]

The Glasgow Conference was planned in the light of " the three main issues involved in the relationship of Europe and America with Asia and Africa—the racial, the economic and the political." It was held at St Andrew's Hall, Glasgow, January 4th to 9th 1921, and attended by 2448 delegates ; there was plenty of room in the conference hall for those entertaining delegates, and there were never less than 3000 people at meetings of the full conference, and more than once over 4000 people were present.

A large delegation from the United States of America was a feature of the non-British element : delegates from other lands and foreign students studying in British colleges numbered 398 persons. The conference, described as one " on international and missionary questions," was opened by Viscount Grey, who spoke on the need and possibility of a new world. " You are going to approach," he said to us, " the discussion of political questions from the point of view of Christianity. That is right."

This remark is applicable not merely to the Glasgow Conference, but to the policy of the Movement since. Up to the war, the Movement constantly disclaimed all intention of influencing public policy. It consisted of students *in statu pupillari,* and it conceived its task to be to help them to understand Christianity, to accept it and to study its application in the world, especially in the way of missionary work and social reform. It refused again and again when invited by groups or organizations of senior people to join in meetings, manifestoes and

[1] *The Student Movement,* art. : " A Missionary Policy for the Christian Union," W. Paton, vol. xxii. p. 59.

kindred efforts to move governments, or influence public opinion.

The war changed that attitude ; students found that though they were *in statu pupillari*, they were citizens with responsibility to the State, and changes in the franchise had given parliamentary votes to many who did not have them before the war. The Glasgow Conference programme was the first outward sign of the change that had taken place, not by a vote of its committee, but in the heart and mind of the whole Movement. The programme dealt with public questions with a boldness and vigour unknown at previous Student Movement gatherings. Lord Grey said that one of the signs of civilization was " order and liberty combined, and where you have more disorder and less liberty you have got a set-back in civilization." We wanted to help to stem the tide of reaction, and to do this by a new application of Christianity to common life.

Many of the chief addresses at the conference dealt with public questions. Addresses on India, China, Africa discussed in the main the relation of these countries to the peoples and governments of the West in the light of Christ. It was a missionary conference, so the question, " Is Christendom fit for a world task ? " was on the programme, and produced speeches which were an indictment of the industrial system and of the relations between the nominally Christian nations. The speaking each morning was merciless in its candid examination of the ways of the British people in the world.

The evenings were devoted to a proclamation to the Movement of the Christian Gospel in a series of addresses on a high level; the address of the Rev. W. R. Maltby, on the last night, on " The power of God in human life," being one of the most remarkable addresses ever delivered at a Student Movement conference.

The Report, *Christ and Human Need*, 1921, had a large sale and it is still excellent reading. The Rev. C. E. Raven, in an " impression of the conference," said : " Glasgow

1921 will stand unique among the conferences of the student world," and writing twelve years later I am not inclined to dispute that statement.

The audience helped to make the conference. It was a very remarkable one ; ex-service men, students too young to have fought, student-pacifists from prison, professors, lecturers, schoolmasters, missionaries and all kinds of social workers, with a large contingent of students and Student Movement leaders from thirty-seven countries.

> It was vast and complex ; it was strangely and splendidly one : one in the earnestness of its attention : one in its fearless desire to face facts : one in its appreciation alike of the gravity of the issues and of the source of the power in which they must be met. The memory of that great hall, packed in floor and galleries and platform with tense and responsive faces, will live long for those who saw it.[1]

The most remarkable of the sectional meetings was occupied with a series of addresses on " The Universality of Christ," by Canon William Temple. This was the only occasion on which I have seen hundreds of university men and women running like hares to get into into a religious meeting. The church where Temple spoke was packed daily, and he was at his very best. There is no need to describe the lectures as they are published in book form.[2]

There were a large number of students from the Orient at the conference, including a number of Indians. They had not been brought there without difficulty. They were smarting under the memory of the Amritsar shooting in the Punjab in 1919, and shared the general Indian distrust of British policy in India. If it had not been for the tact in handling a difficult situation some time before the conference displayed by Bill Paton and Ariam Williams, no Indians would have been present.

India had been so prominently in the minds of the leaders, both before and during the conference, that the

---

[1] *Christ and Human Need*, p. xiv.
[2] *The Universality of Christ*, by William Temple.

General Committee decided to send a message to the
Student Christian Association of India, Burma and
Ceylon, telling that Movement that " no subject more
constantly claimed the attention of those present than
the critical and delicate situation in India at the moment,
and throughout the conference the desire for a better
understanding steadily increased." The message spoke
of the intense interest taken by Indian students in the
affairs of their country, and of the extent to which their
minds " must be stirred by the difficulties which confront
her to-day. Further, we recognize that these difficulties
are due in no small measure to the breach in trust and
understanding which has arisen between our two
peoples."

The message referred to the Amritsar shooting, and
" utterly repudiated " the principle that government
primarily rests upon the display of force. " We sympathize with your aspirations for a self-governing India,
and we earnestly hope that the reforms now initiated
may lead surely and rapidly to the attainment of that
goal." It closed with the expression of a desire for a
more genuine friendship with Indian students in Great
Britain and a greeting " as comrades in the service of
mankind who looked to our Lord Jesus Christ for the
power which we need in the struggle against the materialism, race bitterness and militarism which threaten to
destroy human brotherhood."

I believe this was the first message the Movement
sent to another Movement which dealt primarily with
public questions and the relation to such of the Student
Movement. It was a further symptom of the newly
awakened sense of responsibility in relation to international questions in the Movement.

It was a disappointment that the German Student
Movement did not send a delegation to the conference.
While expressing the earnest wish that their absence
should not be interpreted as an unfriendly act towards
the Student Movement in Great Britain, they explained
that the position in which German missions were placed

under the Peace Treaty made it too painful for them to take part in a missionary conference.

The gathering was watched with great interest in religious circles throughout the country, partly for the reason which the Archbishop of Canterbury expressed, in a letter of greeting to the conference, " It is not easy to exaggerate the importance of the position now attained in Christendom by the Movement," and partly because it was very well reported in the Press, led by *The Glasgow Herald*, whose editor, Sir Robert Bruce, was a member of the Advisory Council of the conference. *The Glasgow Herald* provided long summaries of all the principal speeches, as well prepared as the speakers themselves could have done them.

The Glasgow Conference, by the testimony of large numbers, exercised a profound influence on those who were present, and it helped to integrate and consolidate the Movement as it made a fresh start after the war.

The Federation started its first " International Discussion Conference " in 1921. It was held at Hardenbroek, the headquarters of the Dutch Student Movement, and attended by some forty students of twelve nations, including delegates from Great Britain.

The difficulty in persuading the Indians to attend the Glasgow Conference kept our attention not only upon the position of Indians, but upon that of all Oriental students in the universities. We knew they were not welcomed and helped, and were specially anxious to see some other body of people as well as the Student Movement offering them friendship and hospitality. A few of us called together some of the leaders of the missionary societies for an informal talk and put the case to them. The result was the formation of the East and West Friendship Committee. It secured J. O. Dobson as its first secretary, and the Student Movement agreed to give him office accommodation and the status of a Student Movement secretary. Dobson did excellent work, and eventually became missionary secretary of the Student Movement, Kenneth Jardine being appointed his successor by the East and West Friendship Committee. When the latter went to India Lionel Aird was appointed secretary.

Groups of friendly people have been brought together in places like Birmingham, Bristol, Cambridge, London, Leeds, Sheffield and Newcastle-on-Tyne, who have tried to help students from the Orient to find suitable lodgings and some friends. They have initiated holiday parties, and brought students and those ready to entertain them in touch with one another, and in a variety of ways tried to help the Oriental student to make contacts in England which would enhance the value and increase the pleasure of his stay in this country.

In the autumn of 1932 the organization changed its name to the East and West Friendship Council,[1] appointed an executive committee, and added Miss Florence Sutton to its staff, all a sign of expanding work.

In February 1933 a conference took place between Indian and British students under the auspices of the National Union of Students. The British representatives were officers of the student unions in thirteen universities or colleges. The Indians were the officers of the Indian Student's Union in London, or were chosen to represent the Indian students in particular universities. Its purpose was to discuss the difficulties encountered by Indian students while pursuing their studies at British universities. Such topics as the participation of Indian students in athletics, the social activities of union societies, their admission to hospitals for purposes of medical study and the like were discussed and findings drafted. It was decided to transmit these " findings " to the various student unions, with the unanimous request of the conference that their presidents should bring these to the notice of their councils and assist their effective realization in all possible ways.

A successful conference of this nature under the auspices of the National Union of Students betokened

---

[1] When this body was reorganized in 1933 the Earl of Lytton became its chairman.

a great advance towards removing the difficulties of Indian students in British universities and colleges, and absorbing them harmoniously into British student life. Experience, however, suggests that action of this kind needs to be taken in each student generation since, owing to the state of flux in the colleges consequent on the brief duration of a student generation, the good effects of conferences wear off. Students of all nationalities need to be brought together again and again that the international education of each student generation may be a reality.

At a meeting of the committee of the S.C.M. at the close of the Glasgow Conference it was decided to invite Francis Miller,[1] Washington University and Trinity College, Oxford, an American Rhodes scholar, to become the first International Relations secretary of the Movement.

The committee defined his work

> as travelling in the colleges, talking, discussing the question of international relationships with a view to producing right thinking and a right attitude, giving special attention to helping Americans in the colleges, and including regular reference to Anglo-American relations in his addresses, also as paying attention to work among foreign students in colleges where such were studying, and thus helping to mobilize the help of British students for the benefit of work among foreign students.[1]

Before Miller began his work, the committee brought together in one department the training of British students in relation to international study and work for foreign students, the secretaries for the latter being Robert Bewsher and Louise Royaards. Zoë Fairfield was asked to take general oversight of the work of the department. The publication of *Towards the Brotherhood of Nations*, by Bolton Waller (Irish secretary before the war), and many study circles on it, helped to direct

[1] Chairman of the World's Student Christian Federation from 1929.

thought in the Christian Unions on international relationships.

Naturally we gave a good deal of attention to Anglo-American relations while Miller was with us. It was recognized that this would mean study of concrete facts and a refusal simply to be sentimental about one another across the Atlantic.

> We need not only a union of hearts but a union of heads. There are problems well above the horizon which we have to resolve as nations if we are to live at peace. Great Britain and America are to-day the two leading financial, commercial and manufacturing nations of the world, and as such their economic rivalries wax steadily. Most of the quarrels between nations, though nominally concerned with ideals of honour, are actually concerned with material interests like trade and profit. . . . We cannot all tackle these questions, but we can help to raise up men of character and knowledge who will tackle them, and we can all learn to help to create an atmosphere in our nations which will make decisions that are both wise and right possible.[1]

Francis Miller worked for one year, and after an interval of a year was followed by J. W. Parkes, who served for three years as an international study secretary. His work resulted in the promotion of a considerable amount of reading on international affairs and in the formation of numerous international study circles.

The World's Student Christian Federation General Committee met at Peking, China, in April 1922, bringing together one hundred and twenty-nine men and women from thirty-three countries, and in addition six hundred and thirty-five Chinese students. While the committee of the Federation had met at St Beatenberg after the war, this was the first Federation conference since that held at Lake Mohonk, U.S.A., in June 1913. We sent R. O. Hall and Janet Maclay to represent us at Peking. R. O. Hall wrote :

> The Mohonk Conference had broken up in a spirit of great optimism and international goodwill, and its members

[1] *The Student Movement*, Editorial, vol. xxiv. p. 50.

set out as they thought to build a new world at once. Actually they set out to kill each other singing the same hymns, and praying for victory to the same God. The ghastliness of that tragedy haunted us at Peking, for we knew it would happen again unless desperate things were done to make it impossible.

The war issue dominated the conference. There were pacifists and non-pacifists present, and tense discussions took place. In the end those who were concerned more with stamping out the roots of war by revising economic systems than in deciding on the merits of the use of force carried the gathering with them and the conference passed the following resolution :

We consider it our absolute duty to do all in our power to fight the causes leading to war, and war itself as a means of settling international disputes.

As a result of our discussion at the Peking Conference, we declare frankly that we have not succeeded in reaching an agreement as to what our individual attitude ought to be in event of war. Some are convinced that under no circumstances can they as Christians engage in war ; others, that under certain circumstances they ought to take their share in the struggle. We leave, however, with a deep sense of our common determination to follow Jesus Christ, and with fresh confidence in the unity of our purpose and in the power of Christ to show us the way, as we earnestly and penitently seek it in the fellowship of our Federation.

We desire that the different national Movements of the Federation should face fearlessly and frankly, in the light of Jesus' teachings, the whole question of war and of those social and economic forces which tend to issue in war.

These Peking resolutions were spread abroad among the students of the world, and in our own Movement a series of questions dealing with them were issued to the colleges and widely studied, and it was reported later of them as follows :

Representative students were asked to send in answers to enable the Movement to have some idea of the mind of its constituency on international matters. The answers cover a bewildering range, from naïve thoughtlessness to a determined, though puzzled, attempt to face the real difficulties ; from extreme pacifism to a whole-hearted jingoism ; from paralyzed helplessness to a too facile belief that for Christians all problems are easily soluble. There is complete unanimity of opinion that the international problem is the greatest which faces Christians at the present time, and that no life is really a Christian life which is not directed in a measure at least to its solution.

It was a good time to raise again the question of war, as the ex-service men had just left college and the new generation needed a fresh lead to stir their thought on the subject.

The Chinese Press took considerable notice of the conference. It was an event in China. The conference was welcomed to that country by Dr W. W. Yen, Acting Premier and Minister of Foreign Affairs. One result was the starting of an anti-Christian movement which attacked the Federation, saying : " It is opposed to science and its study, and is an obstacle to the free thinking of the people." This anti-Christian attitude caused the merchant class to demonstrate in favour of the Federation, and when the delegates passed through Tientsin, the Chinese Chamber of Commerce and a number of guilds met them with banners and brass bands at the railway station, and they were conducted to a luncheon given by General Li Yuanhung.

The League of Nations Union had come into being, and turned its thoughts to the colleges. Lord Robert Cecil and two of its chief officers met three of us from the Student Movement, and asked us if we would undertake the work of the Union in the universities and colleges, but we suggested that they should organize work themselves as they ought to be able to reach many students who would not join in work planned by a Christian movement, and we promised co-operation. The League of Nations Union developed a university section, and appointed a travelling secretary during the academic year 1923-24.

This year we published *Christianity and the Race Problem*, by Mr J. H. Oldham, on behalf of the United

Council for Missionary Education, and this book was read and studied by many students.

We tried all kinds of experiments in the way of an international council, sometimes with students, then with students and seniors, with the League of Nations Union and with the National Union of Students. We have never, however, made a great success of this.

International study circles have been carried on by some students each year, studying Indo-British questions, disarmament, war and peace. In 1929-30 *Some Aspects of the Indian Situation* was used extensively, but from 1930 to the present time very little systematic study has been carried on under the auspices of the Movement. It needs a study secretary to direct this work, and since James Parkes joined the staff of International Student Service, at the end of the academic year 1925-26, no one has been available for this direction.

Increase in nationalistic sentiment everywhere has been a feature of the post-war world. In the British Isles it has been more marked in Wales than anywhere else, and we may close this chapter by turning back a little and studying nationalism where it is strongest among students in Great Britain. There have always been two criticisms of the Student Movement in Wales. Among the large body of English students which is found especially in Cardiff, Swansea and Aberystwyth, people have said that it was too Welsh, while in the Welsh-speaking group, with its strongholds in Bangor and Aberystwyth, there has always been the complaint that the Movement would never be effective in Wales until it was more definitely Welsh.

The idea of Welsh nationality gained in strength after the war and found expression in a Welsh National Conference, which met from September 6th to 13th 1920 in Aberystwyth. " It will be," said one of its promoters, " a conference for work and not for rapture, for its aim will be to search out what is Welsh nationally and what is to be our attitude as students to it."

Among the general subjects were: The Celtic tradition in Europe; Celtic Wales, its Church and antiquities, arts, crafts and music; the Church of England in Wales; Welsh revivals; the Labour movement; the political life of Wales and Welsh education. These subjects were treated in the mornings, and subjects of a devotional character in the evenings.

It was prepared for by *Cyfle Cymru, students and the service of Wales*, a study book providing questions for discussion and a bibliography. Victor Murray took a leading part in its preparation and was its Editor. The object was to survey the national life as a whole that students might the better appraise their heritage and arrive at a just comprehension of their own age and the tasks which confronted them. Not only were students present but a considerable body of senior friends was collected, among whom were theological professors and ministers, barristers, labour leaders, bards, educationists, historians and literary men. Owen Griffith wrote that—

> This varied character of the conference had raised grave doubts and apprehensions in the minds of several people. Indeed, the whole scheme of the conference had been criticized as having too much of Wales and too little of the Kingdom of God. But any fears we might have had before we met did not survive the second day of the conference, and we had the joy of seeing what we had dared to hope for only during our most sanguine moments become a reality— the fusion of all the different interests in a strong and eager desire to serve Wales, and in so doing serve the interests of the universal Kingdom. We had found in Christ a unity which overcomes prejudices and enriches the common life . . . there was very apparent also a great widening of interest and sympathies, and a genuine desire to understand each other's point of view. . . . Christianity assumed new and bigger dimensions.

The guiding mind in all this development was that of Owen Griffith, who became Welsh Secretary of the Movement in 1919. For thirteen years he strove to use the national spirit in Wales for high ends and considerable results were achieved.

A month later the Student Movement started *Efrydydd* (The Student), a quarterly magazine in the Welsh language, under the editorship of Professor Miall Edwards, which became the official organ of the Student Christian Movement in Wales. It reached a circulation of 3000 copies within six months. It became a monthly in October 1924. Professor Miall Edwards continued as editor until March 1928, when ill health led to his retiring.

A couple of years later the Movement produced a series of pamphlets under the title *Traethodau'r Deyrnas*, which sought to interpret the Gospel of the Kingdom and to apply it to conditions in Wales. These pamphlets were well received and a number of local conferences, as well as the regular work of the Christian Unions, continued to strengthen the Movement among Welsh students.

By 1924 the economic situation had become very acute, and with a younger generation of students in the colleges the Movement begun in the Welsh Conference was more difficult to maintain, while at the same time the nationalist Movement which had begun on literary and cultural lines was tending to flow in a narrower channel that was exclusively political. The Christian Unions, however, were active and took considerable part in the Manchester Conference of 1925.

The Welsh Council and Urdd y Deyrnas decided to combine in holding another Welsh National Conference which would be an attempt to answer the demand for reality in thinking and living made by those students whose lives had been deepened by the challenge of their circumstances, and an attempt to see the actualities of life in Wales and to face courageously all that is involved therein—industry, politics, education and religion—in order to work towards the creation of a communal life in which spiritual values should be formative and supreme. The conference, which was again held at Aberystwyth, achieved all that its promoters hoped for in laying bare the situation in Wales, and it achieved its object for " the greatest result of the conference was a new faith and confidence in Christianity as the only gospel for our age."

Economic need has pressed with increasing intensity upon Welsh student life, and there has been deprivation of the very necessities of life for their friends and their people, and in some cases for themselves, for the past half-dozen years. A self-help movement, inspired by International Student Service, and the institution of a student loan fund became part of Welsh student life in 1928.

The economic difficulties of the country, together with unsettlement of belief due to impatience among some of the best students with the theological conservatism and aloof piety of much Welsh church life, produced impatience among students with all that seemed to savour of orthodox Christianity. This mood seemed to weaken, for the time being, some Christian Unions which had behind them a long and honourable record of work, such as that at University College, Aberystwyth. After a period of discussion this mood changed, and in 1930 the Welsh Council was able to report that " the impatience of a year ago has passed and has given place to a new purposiveness."

The leaders in many of the colleges had re-examined the basis of their faith, with the result that they discovered a deeper meaning in Christianity and a new conviction in their lives. The Welsh Council was sharing at this time in the reconstruction which was taking place throughout the Movement, and students realized anew their responsibility for the work of the Movement in the colleges and showed readiness to take their full share in it. Nevertheless, in a country where 60 per cent. of the students come from working-class homes which have suffered from a long unbroken period of industrial depression, the gaiety and optimism of students is sorely tried.

CHAPTER XXXVII

THE MOVEMENT'S RELATION TO FAMINE RELIEF AND THE DEVELOPMENT OF INTERNATIONAL STUDENT SERVICE

THE Movement played an important part in the relief of starving students in Europe after the war. The first reference to acute need in any publication of the Movement's was an article in *The Student Movement* for November 1919, entitled "The Hungry." It dealt with general relief, and was chiefly an appeal to "save the children." Five months later the Student Christian Movement in Vienna asked for help and the General Committee sent £20. We none of us realized how desperate was the situation. But Donald Grant, Miss Rouse and Miss Iredale were all in Vienna that spring, and we soon began to hear how terrible was the need. The first help of a substantial kind we were able to offer was a gift of one ton of cocoa sent us by Mr George Cadbury. "I should like to send it," he wrote, "as one of the early friends of the Student Christian Movement. . . . I am now in my eighty-first year, and as I grow older increasingly feel the need of brotherliness and of charity towards those from whom we differ in opinion." This was the forerunner of gifts of cocoa from Great Britain amounting to over one hundred tons.

Mrs Creighton wrote to me after Easter suggesting an appeal in the universities. We promised help, but thought the Movement should not launch the appeal. The Archbishop of Canterbury about this time called a conference at the request of the Life and Liberty Movement in the Church of England which resulted in the founding of the Imperial War Relief Fund.

Lord Robert Cecil wrote in connection with this fund

that as the Student Movement had " taken so much interest in the relief of the distressed universities of Europe," he hoped I would come to a meeting at University College, London, on July 7th 1920, to consider how to help students and professors. Sir William Beveridge took the chair at the meeting which was held, and which appointed a provisional committee that got to work to create the necessary machinery.

The next step was the formation of a general council for the universities under the auspices of the Imperial War Relief Fund with an executive committee of twenty persons. The Executive consisted of representatives of staff and students from Oxford, Cambridge and London Universities, it being recognized that other universities farther from London could only be expected to send representatives to the less frequent General Council meetings. In addition to the universities' representatives, Sir Cyril Butler, Mr Owen Hugh Smith, Mrs Buckler, Miss Fry, Miss Rouse and Miss Iredale became members of the Executive, and I was appointed on it as the representative of the Student Christian Movement. The S.C.M. was the only student society, as such, to have a representative on the Executive. Miss Eleanora Iredale was appointed organizing secretary of the committee, which was known as the Universities' Committee of the Imperial War Relief Fund.

Before this committee could begin its work the World's Student Christian Federation General Committee met at St Beatenberg, Switzerland. Miss Rouse and Miss Iredale were present. They not only knew the situation at first hand and had already raised money and provided goods for relief, but had also shared in a relief commission which the officers of the Federation had appointed in preparation for the meeting of the Federation General Committee. This body presented a report based on a very careful investigation of the needs of students in Central Europe.

As this was the first meeting of the Federation after

the war the agenda was very heavy, and it was only towards the end of many days of meetings that we reached the report on the need for student relief. Miss Rouse proposed that a committee under the auspices of the Federation should be set up to collect funds and goods throughout the student world to relieve starving students and professors. There had not been time for all members of the committee to master the contents of the report on the need, and the debate that ensued revealed how little one continent knew another. The Europeans knew the need and were ready to help. The American and Australian students did not dispute that need existed, but they were totally opposed to starting European Student Relief. " Why don't these needy students go to work and earn money ? " These men from far away had it in their heads that European students were too proud to soil their hands with manual work, and that now was the time to force them to throw away their snobbery and work their way through college, as did the American student in numberless cases.

In vain we explained that the students did work when they could get it, and longed for work of any kind. It was a long time before the whole committee realized that the situation was desperate and students were literally dying of cold and hunger. When they did, there was a unanimous vote and European Student Relief was founded. Dr Conrad Hoffmann, an American student leader who had gained experience in prisoner of war camps, was placed in charge. Those who would know the story of how £500,000 in cash and goods was raised and spent should read *Rebuilding Europe*,[1] a volume in which Miss Rouse tells the story of student relief. Here only an outline of its connection with the Student Movement in Great Britain can be given.

The situation in Austria, the Baltic States, Germany, Hungary and Poland was startling. The Allies' blockade

[1] *Rebuilding Europe*, by Ruth Rouse.

during the war, and the subsequent burden of defeat, had produced its results ; food, clothing, fuel, housing, medical aid, books and other student requisites were urgently needed. People were dying of starvation, students among them. The Federation laid down as cardinal principles that wherever possible self-help schemes be initiated or supported ; that relief be administered impartially, without regard to nationality, race or creed ; that both in the securing and the administration of funds co-operation with existing organizations be arranged ; and that each national Student Movement be encouraged to promote in its own country whatever method of procuring help would be most fruitful.

When European Student Relief developed its work in the autumn in Vienna, Innsbruck and Graz, it found the conditions very bad and within two months was feeding 5000 students. It will perhaps give some idea of the intensity of the need if it is recalled that during the months of October and November 1920 twenty-seven tons of flour were distributed for the benefit of students in the three universities named, to say nothing of tons of cocoa, hundreds of cases of milk and large quantities of corned beef, lard, rice, sugar, bacon, biscuits, macaroni, syrup, soap and candles. In the period October 1920 to March 1922 students in Vienna were served with 2,700,000 breakfasts, consisting of a cup of hot cocoa and a slice of bread.

In addition to the need of food was the need of clothing. Many of the students had had no new clothes for five years. Some of the women had no underclothing, and thousands of garments of all kinds were collected and shipped in crates to Central Europe. The problem of heating in the bitter cold of an Austrian winter was met, to some extent, by the provision of firewood, between two and three hundred tons being supplied during the winter.

Medical aid came later as an attempt was made to deal with scourges like rickets, tuberculosis, typhus and the host of other diseases which march in the train of war and famine.

For two years this work went on, increasing all the time, more countries and more students being helped and more students and more countries helping.

In 1922 the first attempt was made to bring together students who were being relieved and representatives of the students who had been giving and collecting money, food and clothing. A conference was held at Turnov, Czechoslovakia, from April 8th to 16th, when students from twenty-nine different nations met and discussed relief and its future. It was a great success. Students of all sorts and kinds made friends and established a tradition of friendship which remains, for this conference was the first of a series that has continued to the present, that of 1933 having been at Brno in Czechoslovakia. What memories are recalled by the names of the places where the conference has met! Turnov, Parad, Elmau, Gex, Karlovci, Schiers, Chartres, Krems, Oxford, Mount Holyoak and Brno.

The Turnov Conference was primarily a business one. It took stock of how relief was collected and administered and of all the methods of self-help which the ingenuity of students had devised. But it was aware that the moral and spiritual results of relief had been far-reaching. One of our delegates was Amy Buller, who wrote: "Closely bound up with all our business resolutions were schemes for a closer co-operation, prepared with a deep sense of international responsibility and a profound longing for world peace."[1]

The students felt that together they had accomplished something, and that they could accomplish greater things. "We had made the plunge, and the spirit which pervaded the whole conference was the spirit of victory—the victory of world student friendship."[1]

The effect of the relief work was striking. Its motive was very simple, to show human sympathy for starving

[1] *The Student Movement*, vol. xxiv. p. 214.

men and women by giving them what they needed to sustain life.   It proceeded as if barriers did not exist; when challenged it refused to recognize them and gave to friend and foe alike, irrespective of religion, nationality or politics.   This has again and again been referred to by all kinds of people as " the spirit of E.S.R.," but those of us who are Christians have never made any secret of the fact that the inspiration of European Student Relief was " the spirit of Jesus."

The effect of the policy was the growth of a widespread conviction that European Student Relief had learned to transcend the bitter turmoil amid which it worked, and was to be trusted.   Help came to it from all quarters and every kind of need was brought to it. Its healing influence became a moral and spiritual force of power and achievement.

This moral and spiritual effect upon the students relieved came as a surprise to us all.   We had not realized the sense of isolation and misery that existed in Central Europe, or that the rallying of students all over the world to help fellow students would have such a tonic effect and bring them moral and spiritual comfort which they remembered long after their physical sufferings had ended.

The work was not carried on without opposition, however, as, for example, when in Vienna students smashed the kitchen because Jews were fed, or when a German taking part in a relief conference found he was challenged to fight several duels for his internationalism. In the end the method of service to all was triumphant. Nothing has done so much to make violent partisans think.

English students were stirred by the breadth of the issues that had been raised, and in the summer vacation a party of undergraduates from Oxford, led by C. P. Blacker, President of the Junior Common Room, Balliol College, Oxford, toured the universities of Austria, Czechoslovakia, Hungary, Poland and Germany, and returned to reveal the need, especially of Germany, and to applaud the work of E.S.R. in Hungary, Poland and Czechoslovakia.

Russia had been much upon the minds of all at Turnov, and Donald Grant had already gone there. An appeal for clothing resulted in seven and a half tons being shipped to Russia. The Russian work was on a huge scale. During the year 1921-22, 900,000 student meals were served monthly, 130,000 garments and 21,700 books and periodicals distributed in Russia. British students sent £33,000 this year to the support of the work of European Student Relief.

A year later a summary of the relief given showed that the students of the world had provided 22,234,345 meals for needy fellow students ; and in addition, nearly half a million of articles of clothing and over seventy thousand books, to say nothing of additional stores of all kinds. It was a great effort !

While Russia was receiving help, attention was turning once again—not without protests from some unwilling to help the chief enemy during the war—to Germany.

In 1923 Miss Iredale visited the universities of Berlin, Leipzig, Tübingen and Munich. She gave a desperate account of the depression and starvation among students resulting from the inflation of the mark, ending her report with these words : " In Germany one feels that one is in a country where civilization is dying and all go about in fear and without joy, in an atmosphere which is tense—so tense that one hardly knows how to describe it."

It needed some courage to advocate that help should be given to Germany. War memories were sore. Eleanor Iredale did not hesitate a moment; she got the *Manchester Guardian* to back her and soon help was forthcoming, and with the immense capacity for self-help of the German student a powerful organization was built up through the co-operation of European Student Relief, German students and the German Government. The German universities were saved and a permanent self-help organization created, which ever since has been a potent factor in German university life.

Some of the members of the Universities Relief Committee desired to bring its work to an end in the summer of 1923, but the European Student Relief workers were opposed to this, urging that relief was still needed for Russian students and for Germany. The General Committee of the Movement was distressed at the idea of relief continuing; they felt that the British universities were exhausted, and the Student Movement, which was in difficulty about its own finance, felt the strain, the more so as a large proportion of the most active collectors of relief in British universities and colleges were provided by it.

The attitude of the General Committee of the Student Movement, however, was deeply affected at this juncture by a visit from Dr Schairer, who met the committee in March 1923, and brought a message of greeting from German students, with their thanks for the help received from the British student field. This was the first visit of a German to the committee since the war. He told us that there were 110,000 students in Germany, 10,000 of these being foreign students, that of the 100,000 German students 60,000 had to earn money working in mines, as stone-breakers, and in numerous other ways, to support themselves during their college courses. Since the collapse of the mark and the occupation of the Ruhr employment had become extremely difficult to secure and from 8000 to 10,000 students were unable to find work and their whole future hung in the balance. Although from 10,000 to 15,000 students were ex-service men, a large proportion of the present student population in Germany had been schoolboys during the war and had suffered in health from the effects of the Blockade, with the result that in a recent medical examination of students in four of the chief universities, 8000 to 10,000 students were found to be tubercular.

The main effect on the students of the present sufferings and privations had been to produce an overwhelming sense of bitterness, loneliness and isolation and an entire loss of the sense of any higher spiritual values. The assistance sent to them by students in other countries had been enormously appreciated and had proved to them the reality of spiritual values. The effect of students working on self-help schemes had brought about a feeling of brotherhood and understanding between the workers and students, who had previously been two distinct classes and quite alienated. Dr Schairer said that if the scheme of self-help could not be carried on he thought from fifteen to twenty universities would have to be closed for lack of students. The State was prepared to subsidize the salaries of professors, but had no means of subsidizing individual students.

The committee's sympathies were moved, they promised to continue to help. This visit gave the relief work a new lease of life in Great Britain.

The following year it became evident that the senior members of the Universities' Relief Committee were decided to conclude their work for student relief. On the other hand, tremendous discussions were going on among the leaders of the World's Student Christian Federation as to what course was to be adopted. There was still a good deal of relief to be done. It was obviously not possible to cease helping students who had not yet finished their academic work, and there was the immensely difficult problem of the thousands of Russian students who were spread all over Europe as a result of the Russian Revolution.

Even more important was the question, what was to happen to all the experience that had been acquired and all the relationships that had been built up in the course of several years' work? There was an immense wealth of experience in the possession of European Student Relief as a result of the variety of different kinds of self-help schemes that had been started, to say nothing of loan funds, medical service, student houses and the like. Then, too, there was all the wealth of human relationships which had been created, and articulate groups of students, such as those in Hungary and Germany, were urgent in their protest that if European Student Relief ceased, they would lose their only contact with the outside world. Some of us knew all this as we discussed with some of the senior men on the Universities Relief Committee the question of how long its work was to continue.

As it became clear that the Universities Relief Committee would not, and indeed ought not, to assume responsibilities which were really those of the Federation, I came to the conclusion that the best thing that could be done was to make the Student Movement in Great Britain responsible for the Universities Relief Committee and its future relationships with the Federation. The General Committee agreed, and I presented a set of proposals to the Universities Relief Committee for its reorganization under the auspices of the Movement.

The essence of this scheme was that the Student Movement should become responsible for keeping the Universities Relief Committee in being and helping it to carry out its work as long as it was needed. The scheme was considered on September 29th 1924 at a meeting held in the Council-room, King's College, Strand, and Mr Ivison Macadam moved a resolution, seconded by Mr Headicar of the London School of Economics : " This committee approves the plan for placing the Universities Relief Committee under the auspices of the Student Christian Movement, proposed by Mr Tatlow on behalf of that organization."

This was accepted and the committee reconstructed, Dr Ernest Barker, who had previously been chairman of the Executive Committee, agreed to continue as chairman of the new committee, Sir William Beveridge was elected vice-chairman and the Hon. Cecil Baring treasurer. The reconstructed Universities Relief Committee was still served by Miss Iredale as its secretary, who devoted half her time to its work. At the same time she became associate finance secretary of the S.C.M.

A tentative policy was necessary from the Student Movement's point of view as discussion continued in Federation circles as to what policy it should pursue in face of the huge piece of work now related to it. We all thought in Great Britain that the Federation would start a social service department which would incorporate European Student Relief. When the General Committee of the Federation met, however, at High Leigh, England, it decided to continue European Student Relief for another year.

In May 1925 European Student Relief met in Geneva, and the name was changed to International Student Service, the French equivalent being Entr'aide Universitaire and the German Weltstudentenwerk. The aims and objects were at the same time revised. The relief of economic distress and the sharing of practical experience in self-help came first, then " the providing of opportunities whenever desired for the discussion of such fundamental problems as : the aim of university education, spiritual questioning and need, the relations between the nations and races."

In March 1926 the General Committee agreed that the Universities Relief Committee should be dissolved, and it asked Miss Iredale to give half her time to raising finance for the Movement and the other half to international educational work in the colleges. It did not reckon with what might be the demands of I.S.S. for financial support, though it knew there might be such.

The decision to dissolve the Universities Relief Committee was in accordance with the desires of its members, and it ceased to exist from May 31st 1926. The Student Movement took over its assets and responsibilities, agreeing that it would conserve as far as possible the work which had been done, and undertaking responsibility for whatever international work the Federation decided upon.

The Universities Relief Committee had been served

by a number of distinguished public men, including Sir Maurice de Bunsen, Lord Emmott, Sir Neil Malcolm, Dr Ernest Barker, Mr Campbell Dodgson, the Hon. Cecil Baring, Professor G. P. Gooch and the Rev. Canon Lock, and gratitude to them was felt for the help they had rendered. The task had been on too big a scale for students to accomplish it unaided.

At this point the scene changes to Nyborg Strand, Denmark. There the future of International Student Service was thrashed out in a series of long debates in the full committee, assisted by a sub-committee which used to sit far into the night. There was a tremendous pull between two opposite points of view on the Federation Committee. One group desired to see such work as had hitherto been done by International Student Service brought to a conclusion in order that the more specifically spiritual work of the Federation might receive exclusive attention. This group was uneasy about work under the auspices of the Federation which was not on an avowedly Christian basis. The other group held the view that the disinterested service which had been rendered to all kinds of students in Europe was one of the most distinctively Christian things about the Federation, that it should not withdraw such service as long as it was needed, and that the wealth of experience acquired should be permanently conserved.

Ultimately a plan was adopted, worked out principally by Dr G. G. Kullmann and Miss Fairfield, whereby International Student Service should become an independent organization incorporated under Swiss law, but having a definite relationship to the World's Student Christian Federation. The object was to provide a new status which would guarantee the impartiality of I.S.S. and its readiness to help students of every race and creed, while maintaining a definite link with the Federation from which it had drawn so much strength. The *modus vivendi* achieved between the two points of view resulted in the Federation retaining responsibility for appointing a majority of the members of the Assembly of International Student Service, giving its general secretary the status of a Federation secretary, and having the right to have the budget of I.S.S. submitted to it annually before it was adopted.

The range of activities decided upon for I.S.S. at Nyborg were defined under four headings :

1. Relief, to provide for emergencies that might arise among students, and help for refugee students of whom the most numerous were Russians.

2. Student Self-help. This covered help in following various methods of earning a living while at the university, and included student kitchens, co-operative shops, employment bureaux, work student service, loan banks, student houses and hostels.

3. An International Student Trust Fund.

4. Foreign Students. Investigation concerning this category of student and his needs, and help for them.

5. Activities. This was a comprehensive heading which was used to cover conferences on social, university and international questions ; student tours abroad ; and the publication of an organ of student opinion, *Vox Studentium*.

"Guiding principles" were laid down for I.S.S. to the effect that it was to offer students its help with impartiality " irrespective of creed, race or nationality " ; it was to confine its work to the lines already indicated ; and " every one is given full freedom to express his own distinctive view-point, it being understood that equal freedom will be given for the expression of the Christian point of view."

Three of those selected by the Federation to serve on the Assembly of I.S.S. were Miss Fairfield, Miss Iredale and myself. At its first meeting I was elected chairman by I.S.S., a position I have occupied since then.

Though not much time was spent at Nyborg on the essential character of International Student Service, this was because time had already been spent on this subject both on the committees of the Federation and on the body guiding I.S.S. As I.S.S. had developed its work, and become far more than a relief agency, many wanted to have some definite connection with it. Many students thought that I.S.S. should become another student society with a membership and committee elected by vote of the members.

The reasons against this course, however, were strong. There were more than enough student societies in several countries, and if I.S.S. became yet another it would compete for the attention of the limited amount of time and energy of students. I.S.S. had already secured the co-operation for its work of numerous student societies, and to start competition with them by working for members and having a programme of work for all would endanger future co-operation. In Great Britain I.S.S. could not have achieved what it did apart from the Student Movement. Members of the Movement were by no means its only supporters, but the Movement's machinery in the colleges was usually at its disposal and of vital importance to it.

Again, it was already apparent that I.S.S. work was often of a technical character which needed experience and knowledge. A democratically elected committee, constantly changing as the committees of student societies change, could not be expected to produce the kind of leaders needed.

Another factor, not without influence on some, was the failure of democracy in many countries at this time. The method was being used for unworthy ends—racial antagonisms, political aims, and even personal ambitions were causing intrigue to secure places in the leadership of some student societies to satisfy ends other than those for which the societies ostensibly existed. Some felt I.S.S. could best be preserved as a body rendering impartial service if it was without a voting membership.

In the end it was decided that I.S.S. should be incorporated as an Assembly of a limited number of people of proved capacity to serve I.S.S. Ever since this time it has been a body partaking of the nature of a corporation or academy, which elects persons qualified to serve its purposes. This decision made the annual conference of increased importance, as the Assembly of I.S.S. recognized that it is its best opportunity to put its programme before a selected body of student leaders from as many countries as possible and secure their co-operation in carrying it out.

The annual conference also provides an occasion when I.S.S. can be criticized, and reminded that it can only hope for support for its programme when that programme is well conceived and promises to be well executed.

At I.S.S. conferences much hard work is done in the different commissions, into which all present are drafted for the study of the different aspects of the programme of work before I.S.S. Eminent men come and speak, and the few platform speeches are often important contributions to the education of all present. And by no means least important are the noisy and cheerful meals and the jolly evenings at cafés, when every conceivable kind of question is discussed with candour, national songs are sung, and those present toast one another, each according to his taste, in every known drink from chocolate to benedictine, and lemon squash to absinth.

International Student Service went ahead after Nyborg with great strides. While its programme of work has varied year by year, and constantly developed and its staff has grown, it has itself only undergone one important constitutional change; that was when the Federation decided at its meeting at Mysore, India, December 1928, to make I.S.S. an independent body. All concerned felt this was the wisest course, for I.S.S. had grown in too many ways for it to be held subject to another organization.

The General Committee of the Student Movement decided to start an International Council, as a result of its experience in connection with I.S.S. and the Federation, the widening of its own international interests and the need for their better co-ordination. This was a direct outcome of the Nyborg Committee meeting.

The services were secured of Dr Ernest Barker, Professor
G. P. Gooch, Mr J. R. M. Butler, Dr Maxwell Garnett,
representatives of the National Union of Students of
England and Wales and of the University League of
Nations Union, as well as Student Movement secretaries
and present students. Its purpose was to be to guide
the General Committee in relation to all its international
responsibilities—I.S.S., the Student Movement House,
the International House, Glasgow, and the international
education of S.C.M. members. It held its first meeting
in King's College, London, on November 6th and 7th
1926. Miss Rouse told the new Council the early
history of European Student Relief, Miss Iredale
described its evolution into I.S.S., and Miss Fairfield
gave an account of Nyborg and reviewed the Council's
immediate task. Professor G. P. Gooch gave a lecture
on "The Background of European Politics." The
Austrian Ambassador in London came in person to
express the appreciation of the Austrian Government
and people for I.S.S. The Council then divided into
three groups to plan work for foreign students, international study and British co-operation with the programme of I.S.S.

The Council started with high hopes, but it has never
been an unqualified success, chiefly because it needed
someone to devote all his time to the leadership of it.
J. W. Parkes, who had done effective work as study
secretary on international affairs, would have led it, but
just before it was created he was made warden of the
Student Movement House, and although he continued
to promote international education at the House, his
duties were too absorbing there for him to take charge
of the new Council. Parkes continued to be warden
for two years, and was then lent to I.S.S., where he
has remained ever since. He has become an authority
on Jewish and Christian relationships in European
history.

The most useful function of the International Council so far has been to turn itself into a round-table

conference from time to time on a particular issue. On more than one occasion it has received visitors like the late K. T. Paul and, as a result, offered useful advice to the General Committee on India or disarmament, or some other urgent international question.

The body which has proved most useful is a small committee convened by Robert Mackie about twice a month to consider all the matters relating to other countries that come to the Movement.

The number of communications relating to almost every country in the world, and dealing with every conceivable kind of question, explains why Student Movement secretaries working at headquarters become well versed in religious, political, cultural, racial questions of all kinds, and happily, too, become the personal friends of the black and brown and white and yellow skinned men who join the Movement, and who, for all their differences externally, are our beloved brethren in the one Lord.

International Student Service has undergone one more change as far as its relationships in Great Britain are concerned. Until 1931 the Student Christian Movement represented its interests in Great Britain. It held its Annual International Conference in July 1930 at St Hugh's College, Oxford, and the occasion was utilized to ventilate the idea of forming an I.S.S. Co-operating Committee for England and Wales. It was not until the autumn of 1931, however, that the Co-operating Committee of International Student Service for England and Wales was constituted. The initiative was taken by Robert Mackie, acting for the Student Christian Movement, with the advice of the leaders of the National Union of Students and the British Universities League of Nations Society.

It is a committee of about twenty people, representative of the student societies creating it, with both senior and junior members of the universities and the British members of the Assembly of I.S.S., Professor Ernest Barker being chairman and Mr Gareth Maufe secretary.

Its object is to promote co-operation with the programme of I.S.S. in England and Wales. A similar committee has been started in Scotland.

The object of International Student Service at the present time, as stated in the last revision of its Constitution, is " to encourage and support all efforts on the part of students, professors and others, to develop the universities and institutions of higher learning as true centres of national culture, intimately bound up with the realities, international, economic and social of the modern world."

The programme through which it attempts to achieve this object is outlined under four headings :

1. The study of and research on university questions ; publications thereon.

2. The development within the universities of friendly relations between students and professors of different nationalities and races, and of their contacts with other social classes, by the organization of lectures, conferences, study, travel, etc.

3. The development of student self-help and creation of student co-operative enterprise.

4. Material help and moral aid for students.

I.S.S. has co-operating committees in the United States of America, Germany, France, Holland and Belgium, as well as in Great Britain, and has related to it as friends of I.S.S. individuals who are interested. Its work remains most considerable on the Continent of Europe, but Wales has a self-help council promoted by it, there has been an I.S.S. Conference in U.S.A., it has rendered many services to Indian students, and has links in both India and China. Its task is a hard one in a world grown intensely nationalistic and bitterly poor, but its influence is wider than that of any other international student body, and for all their nationalism men to-day feel they need a wider outlook, and in that there is hope.

There are many whom the historian of International Student Service will desire to praise. Miss Rouse will always be remembered as the founder of relief work for students by students ; Conrad Hoffmann as the indefatigable leader of European Student Relief in days when the call for help, and yet more help quickly, needed courage, faith and vision concentrated on achieving practical results ; Walter Kotschnig as the leader who conserved what relief and the starting of self-help had done, and who led I.S.S. into the wider field of opportunity to which they had opened the door ; and Eleanora Iredale, as the tireless worker who would dare and succeed while others were still looking at the difficulties. Both European Student Relief and its successful re-birth as International Student Service owe much to her sympathy, courage and imagination.

There may be reverses in store for those who try to promote international co-operation and goodwill, but such can only be temporary, for the world is a unity and mankind is a brotherhood, and God's truth will inevitably win men's allegiance in due time.

CHAPTER XXXVIII

THE AUXILIARY MOVEMENT

THE strengthening of the hold of the Movement upon the colleges and the share it had come to take in moulding the lives of students made many of them loth to sever all connection with it when they left college. Its leaders, too, began to look to former members for more help as the responsibilities of the Movement grew. Several organizations were started with the object both of holding old members together and securing their support for the work of the Union of which they used to be members. We find Mr Clifford Allen[1] circularizing former members of the Movement at Bristol University in January 1909, inviting them to attend what was to be the first of a series of annual reunions. The Manchester University Past Students (Women's) Christian Union and an organization of ex-S.C.M. members at Newnham College, Cambridge, were started, and University College, Nottingham, had a union whose object was to keep former members together and to interest them in missionary work.

The General Committee in October 1911 had before it for the first time a scheme for forming an auxiliary of gone-down students, contained in a memorandum by Rena Carswell and Lilian Stevenson. It had rejected suggestions, made during the past ten years, for the starting of some kind of union to keep together members of the Movement who had left college, and no doubt rightly. Many leaders in the Churches were nervous lest, if the Movement held together members when they left college, the flow of some of the most promising

[1] Now Lord Allen of Hurtwood.

recruits the Churches were getting for service of all kinds should be diminished.

Two facts, however, influenced the Movement in a new way at this stage.   There were an increasing number of people who had no Church contact, and whom the Movement had not had long enough under its influence to bring into Church membership.   These people, who were lost to all kinds of organized Christianity when they left college, might be helped by an organization of gone-down students.   Their numbers were small, and only some of the General Committee saw this as one of the reasons for starting the Auxiliary.

Another fact, and the one which influenced the majority, was the loyalty to the Movement of a number of former members who wanted to form an organization to help it financially.   The new idea was accepted, and a sub-committee consisting of Miss Carswell (convener), Alice Lloyd Williams, Lilian Stevenson, C. E. Squire, Howard Houlder and T. Tatlow was appointed to draw up a constitution and make a plan to start the organization.

In April 1912 the General Committee accepted the report of this sub-committee and decided to found " The Auxiliary of the Student Christian Movement of Great Britain and Ireland."   The announcement said that its aims were twofold :

(a) To unite in a fellowship of intercession and giving former members of the Student Christian Movement.

(b) To assist members to pass into active service in the Christian Church.

Membership was confined to those who had been students and who had taken part while at college in the work of the Movement, or who were in sympathy with its aims, and who were members of a branch of the Christian Church.

The member undertook " to seek loyally to fulfil his obligation to that branch of the Christian Church of which he is a member," and to render it some active service, to pray for the Movement, using the *Terminal Intercession Paper*, and to read regularly the *Annual Report* and *The Student Movement*. The subscription was to be not less than 5s. per annum.

The Auxiliary held its first committee meeting on November 6th 1912. This was appointed by the Student Movement, and consisted of Tissington Tatlow (chairman), H. F. Houlder, Dr H. Crichton Miller, the Rev. Oliver Thomas, Professor E. T. Whittaker, F.R.S., Mrs E. F. Wise, Miss Lilian Stevenson, Miss Jean Macfee and Miss Fairfield, with Mr C. R. Cox, an assistant secretary of the Movement, as its secretary.

Though the Auxiliary thus supplied its members with regular information about the Movement, sought the prayers of members and their gifts, it had no activities except one annual meeting in London when much information about the Movement was given, questions answered and grumbles about the Churches discussed. The Auxiliary grew slowly, its membership being 527 by the outbreak of the war.

Two societies which are still at work grew out of the Movement about this time, the Free Church Fellowship was founded in 1911 under the guidance of Malcolm Spencer, and drew its inspiration and most of its membership from Free Churchmen who had been in the Movement. It was doing useful work in drawing together the forward-looking men in the Free Churches. I had felt for some time that we ought to have a similar organization in the Church of England which would be as representative as was the Movement of the different elements in the Church of England.

We had a meeting in Chancery Lane, decided to found The Anglican Fellowship, and subsequently held the first conference, attended by about eighty men and women, from July 9th to 12th 1913, at Swanwick. Our object was to confer together in order to come to a better understanding of what might be gained for the life of the Church through our contact with the Student Movement. There was nothing else like it in the

Church. We made no attempt to keep it for old Student Movement people, nor did we confine it to men, as was the case at this time in the Free Church Fellowship. All members of the Church of England interested were invited to join.

The Anglican Fellowship is still in existence and holds a conference each summer, but since the death of A. C. Turner, who was killed during the world war, it has done little to recruit younger men and women for its membership.

Other denominational fellowships, among Presbyterians and Wesleyan Methodists, were also started by Student Movement people during this period. The constant reiteration by the leaders of the Student Movement of the duty of Christian students to enter the services of their own churches had the effect of producing a body of students who, on leaving college, sought some opportunity of work for their church which would give them the kind of scope they had found in the Christian Union in college. When these discovered that the churches had little to offer them in the way of opportunities of service they felt that they might find the opportunity they sought with profit to the churches and especially their young people, as well as to young people who might be drawn in, if they started fellowships designed to transmit the best of what they had learned in the Student Movement to their churches. They created the various Fellowships to deal with this situation. It is, however, the fortunes of the Auxiliary as connected with the Student Movement that we must follow.

As the object of the Auxiliary was to help the Student Movement, and it was without activities of its own, its only gathering for a few years was the annual meeting in London. When the war came there came also signs that the keener members of the Auxiliary were anxious to use it as providing a forum where they could discuss some of the numerous questions about Christian thought and action which the war was making more insistent. They represented different denominations and professions and a variety of religious and social organizations, but had in common an outlook and temper of mind which had been the gift to them of the Student Movement. They found in the Auxiliary the only organization whose platform was broad enough to bring them together.

The reports of the Auxiliary's annual meeting in London, which appeared regularly in *The Student Movement*, caused groups of Auxiliary members in several of the big cities to start annual meetings of the same kind. Within a year or two there were Auxiliary groups in Birmingham, Brighton, Bristol, Colchester, Leeds, Liverpool, Manchester, Newcastle, Nottingham, Sheffield, Edinburgh, Dundee, Glasgow and Dublin. These groups with occasional meetings grew in number up to 1918, in which year the General Committee of the Student Movement decided to hold a conference on " Students and the Church."

This conference was the outcome of discussions upon the committees of both the Student Movement and the Auxiliary. It must be remembered that these committees were closely related. The official position of the Auxiliary Committee was that it was a sub-committee of the General Committee of the Student Movement. The Movement, however, appointed only half its members, the other half being elected by the members of the Auxiliary. Discussion had concentrated since the beginning of the war in all the groups and fellowships of younger people in the country upon the Church. The Movement knew that a diminishing proportion of its members were becoming active Church members, and these often gave urgent expression to the difficulties of a young man or woman who wanted to serve the Church and who was, in a very large proportion of cases, offered no further opportunity of service than to teach a Sunday school class. The General Committee of the Student Movement, therefore, decided to call a conference, limited to seventy men and women which it proposed should consist of two members from each of the existing Auxiliary groups, twelve members of the

General Committee, including secretaries of the Movement and a dozen senior friends.

The purpose of the conference was threefold : " To renew our vision of the ideal of the Church ; to discuss with prayer and humility the need and possibility of reform and the part of younger people in such reform ; and to seek to understand in what spirit the difficulties of the situation should be met."

The conference met at Lady Margaret Hall, Oxford, from April 3rd to 8th 1918, and was attended by eighty-three persons. A series of addresses in the evenings dealt with the nature of the Church and its mission in the world, while in the morning and afternoon sessions questions, such as the widespread dissatisfaction with every form of institutional Christianity, the vital necessity of the Church finding out her own mind in relation to social questions and the broken unity of the Body of Christ, were dealt with by competent speakers.

Early in the conference Dr Cairns voiced what many felt to be its central message. He spoke of the Church as a great society divinely designed to be a continuation of the Incarnation, and to do for every land and nation what the human presence of Christ did for His time ; a visible society which should embody His Spirit ; which should be marked out from the world because it bore in itself for all time the principle of the Cross and of the Resurrection. He called the Student Movement through its Auxiliary to go out upon a new crusade to win the youth of the country for Christ and for His Church.

> The thought of the conference was based on the belief that the Church was the deliberate creation, the deliberate intention of our Lord. We are bound to work and pray that out of our broken institutional Christianity of to-day one holy, catholic Church may come. Throughout the conference no one suggested that some new Church might be founded. The Church will rise again ; she will rise out of broken and divided Christendom. The Kingdom is the supreme end of the Church.[1]

[1] *Students and the Church*, S.C.M., p. 3.

The Bishop of Peterborough (Dr F. T. Woods) followed Dr Cairns on the same lines on the second night of the conference, dealing historically with the part the Church had played in England in the shaping of history and of human society. He too dealt with the intentions of the Founder, taking the Sermon on the Mount as the basis of his address. " The fulfilment or non-fulfilment of this intention of the Master constitutes at once the glory and the tragedy of Church history." He spoke of how we were burdened by an evil inheritance from the last two centuries, in which class divisions had been accentuated in a way not known before in English history. The Church had come to be regarded as the religious department of the governing classes.

" The historical causes for the present situation," he said, " are too little realized. The great nobles were created and enriched by the spoils of the Reformation, later the great class of landowners was largely created by the enclosure of common lands. Then came the rise of successful manufacturers, accumulating wealth with extraordinary rapidity, set over against the people, decreasing and overshadowed in the country, increasing in enormous numbers in towns and factories under conditions of labour which ought to make one gasp with astonishment in a so-called Christian land." [1]

" Five years ago there seemed little prospect that the shape society had taken would be radically changed, but the house which had been built is in ruins." There was an opportunity for the Church's message and energy which might not recur for centuries.

What have we to do ? Precisely that which was done so wonderfully in earlier days, to relate men and movements of men to God, to repaint the background, to recapture the ethical view of the whole of life, to teach the sacred significance, the sacramental value, of common life, to re-emphasize the New Testament standard of social values, to force men back on eternal spiritual values, above all, to sound a new call for the superabundant activity of goodness

[1] *Students and the Church*, S.C.M., p. 6.

and love. The situation can only be met through divine, creative power working directly through the consecrated wills of Christ's community.[1]

Frank Lenwood was the speaker on the third night, and dealt with the mission of the Church to the nations, dwelling on the extreme seriousness of the whole international situation, with its tangle of racial relationships and prejudices. He bade us recognize the unity of every economic, commercial and moral problem. As the days of the conference proceeded the consciousness grew that " God has not left the world."

While men have been preparing to destroy, and are even now destroying, the world which is growing old and corrupt, He has been preparing one which is new. It is not surprising, therefore, that the main message of the conference was the call to a great crusade, a crusade in which those who have shared in new movements of the Spirit during the last twenty years should go out to win the youth of the country to Christ, and not the youth of this country alone, but of the whole world.[2]

The Student Movement had passed through a period of preparation, the Church of the coming generation belonged to youth. The call to the Movement was not conceived as a call to work alone. The Movement " is part of a wider preparation of the Spirit. The same spirit was evident in the World Missionary Conference, Edinburgh 1910, and is apparent in the Anglican and Free Church Fellowships, in the Y.M.C.A., the Y.W.C.A., the Labour Movement and the Woman's Movement, and other similar movements."

It was the senior people present who took the lead in expressing this point of view, people like Dr Cairns, the Bishop of Winchester (Dr E. S. Talbot), Dr Frere and Dr W. B. Selbie. Speaking again later in the conference, Dr Cairns elaborated the call to the Student Movement.

Looking back on the years of happy association with the Student Movement, I have felt all along that the thing is

[1] *Students and the Church*, S.C.M., p. 7.   [2] *Ibid.*, p. 15.

a creative work of God, and to-day I am more than ever persuaded that this is so. I feel it also about many other movements that have affinities with the Student Movement. . . . The Student Movement has been led in the twilight to something of which we are going to see the meaning in a day. We shall not get the thing into the proper perspective unless we take it into the depths, unless we see that we have been led by God. Here we have strength unspeakable for what lies before us. Going on on these lines we are in the counsel of God. We can count on the Spirit of God.[1]

It was clear that the Auxiliary was about to enter an entirely new phase. The Student Movement had consistently disapproved of its having any activities because it believed that this was in the best interests of the Churches. The result, as Mr Maltby said, was that the Auxiliary " had been brought up chiefly on slaps." The Bishop of Winchester and Father Frere took the lead in urging that the Christian Church could perfectly well take care of itself and that the Auxiliary would be no rival to it, as some suggested. The Auxiliary, indeed, might be a valuable auxiliary to the Church. While the Student Movement was, no doubt, right in desiring to see each individual student pass into the active service of the Church when he left college, the facts forced us to recognize that he was not always ready for this, and his Church was often unready for him.

The desire for interdenominational fellowship as a step towards reunion found constant expression throughout the conference. " We want to see the fellowship in separated churches in each locality widened into interdenominational fellowship."

Another note of the conference was a growing conviction that the work of the different denominational fellowships and all they stood for must be worked out in relation to local needs. The conference was a call to localize in towns and villages the Auxiliary in the same way that the Student Movement was localized in every university and college in the country.

[1] *Students and the Church*, S.C.M., p. 19.

The Oxford Conference had been carefully planned, and in estimating the attitude of younger people to the Church, its work was based not simply upon the knowledge of those at the conference, for the year before a questionnaire on the subject of ex-students and the Church had been sent out to all Auxiliary members. The replies were carefully studied by Dorothy Brock,[1] who characterized the answers received as "both illuminating and depressing." Her report said that two facts stood out clearly:

> First, that a very considerable number of gone-down Student Movement men and women had honestly and sincerely tried to enter the service of some branch of the Christian Church, that many of them had failed to find that Church a fellowship at all, and that some, in despair, had severed themselves from organized Christianity altogether, while others were grimly sticking to it in spiritual loneliness and depression ; and secondly, that one and all longed for the fellowship they had known in the Movement, some, indeed, looking to the Movement still as the one thing they really trusted.[2]

Miss Brock said that there were some who found what they wanted in the various Fellowships. There were many, however, to whom the Fellowships did not appeal, partly because of their slightly academic spirit and the preponderance in them of the professional element over the laity, and largely because of their denominational character.

The Student Movement was not to be blamed because there was a leakage. It did not have the students long enough under its influence to train them to Church loyalty. Many students had not joined the Movement in their first year, and many more only began to understand what it was all about in their last year in college.

The committee of the Auxiliary decided, after the Oxford Conference, that it must go forward, and it

[1] Afterwards Dr Brock, Headmistress of Mary Datchelor School, and President of the Headmistresses Association, 1933.

[2] *The Student Movement*, vol. xxi., "The Future of the Auxiliary," Dorothy Brock, p. 119.

recommended to the Student Movement the immediate appointment of a full-time secretary for work among gone-down students.

> The main task of such a secretary will be to work up local Auxiliary groups ; to put students, where possible, into touch with fellowships and other collections of like-minded people and with such organizations as the Teachers' Christian Union ; to co-operate with the S.V.M.U. in regard to missionary work ; to give help as occasion may require to such of its members as shall decide to serve the Church and the Kingdom of God, either as missionaries or otherwise ; and to explore the ways in which the Auxiliary itself may help the Student Movement. An important, and not the least difficult, part of the work of this secretary will be to help students to pass into the full service and fellowship of the Christian Church ; to attempt by every means possible to increase understanding between students and the churches, and to bridge those gulfs which we so deeply deplore. This secretary will be a personal link between gone-down students and the Movement, and of the need for some such personal link the daily correspondence at Annandale is sufficient proof.[1]

The Auxiliary Committee was anxious " to annex Miss Fairfield for its sole and permanent use," but she was too deeply involved at this time in the work of the Movement, and it was too much involved in war-time conditions for this to be possible. But the General Committee, under her guidance, encouraged the promotion of local interdenominational fellowships. There was co-operation with the Anglican and Free Church Fellowships, and fifty groups sprang up during the year and brought together " men and women of different churches and different points of view, to discuss together in a spirit of fellowship the problems of the localities in which they live ; the differences between their churches ; the possibilities of co-operation between them ; and the promotion of Christian unity." [2]

In the meantime, the committees of the Auxiliary and

---

[1] *The Student Movement*, vol. xxxi., " The Future of the Auxiliary," Dorothy Brock, p. 119.

[2] *Annual Report*, S.C.M., 1918-19, p. 53.

the Student Movement had been tackling the revision of the Constitution of the Auxiliary, and at the annual meeting of the latter, on May 28th 1919, a new constitution, approved by both bodies, was adopted.

The most important changes were : first, the inclusion of a series of objects which would make the Auxiliary of benefit to its members while retaining their obligation to pray for and give to the Student Movement ; second, the opening of membership to former students whether or not they were members of a branch of the Christian Church. This was an important change and one approved by our senior friends. An increasing number of old members of the Student Movement were being kept out of the Auxiliary because they could only join it if they were Church members. A third change was the decision, which was included in the constitution, to appoint a full-time secretary " for work among gone-down students."

It is worth noting that the first of the objects was " To help its members to see their own circumstances, calling and neighbourhood in the light of the Kingdom of God, and to live and work for the establishment of that Kingdom in all spheres of human life." Notice the word " neighbourhood." From this time on great stress was laid upon the importance of localizing the Auxiliary. We were convinced that the various fellowships, all of which were highly centralized bodies, had achieved all they could by that method of organization, and that what was needed as a further stage in progress was fellowship groups serving the Kingdom of God in the locality where their members lived. A central organization to think and lead was needed, but needed to serve the local groups.

The membership of the Auxiliary at this time was 1462 persons.

The Oxford Conference had become known as " the first Auxiliary Conference." A second was held at Swanwick in April 1921, when one hundred and twenty-five persons attended. The subject of the conference was " Revolutionary Christianity." Two other groups, the Order of the Kingdom—a group which was composed of members of the Auxiliary, some labour friends and some of the secretaries of the Student Movement who had held a series of meetings at Jordans, Baslow and Swanwick—and the Norwood Group—which had come into existence the year before and was drawn from members of the Adult School Movement, the Brotherhood Movement and the Y.M.C.A.—combined with the Auxiliary in planning the programme which dealt with Christianity and its application, ranging from lectures on modern Biblical scholarship to lengthy discussions on bank credit.

This conference passed a resolution asking the Student Movement to widen the Auxiliary " so that all who are in sympathy with its aims may become members." The membership of the Auxiliary had become convinced that a middle-class movement composed of ex-students could not achieve what was wanted. There must be room for members of the Order of the Kingdom and the Norwood Group, both of which included a number of manual workers as well as others who had never been to college. The conference realized that this action might cause great nervousness in the Student Movement, as bringing in people who had never been in it might weaken Auxiliary loyalty to the Movement, a result to be deprecated since the Movement was finding finance a serious difficulty, and a further development of the Auxiliary would mean more expenditure but might not mean more income.

The conference affirmed its loyalty to the obligation of being auxiliary to the Movement, and to testify to its good faith held a financial session, which produced £122 for the work of the Movement, and £275 for the Auxiliary, subject to the General Committee sanctioning a forward movement on the lines of the resolution. In addition there were promises of help for the Federation.

There was a tremendous discussion on the General Committee, when the proposal to extend the Auxiliary to non-students took place. It lasted for upwards of six hours. Some felt that the Auxiliary was becoming so active and vigorous that it might overshadow the Student Movement, and that in any case it seemed increasingly difficult for the Student Movement to be responsible for a movement which was senior to itself. There were also those on the committee of the Student Movement who feared that the Auxiliary would become a serious rival to various young people's societies in the Churches. The upshot of the discussion was that the committee agreed that membership of the Auxiliary should be open to non-students : it also appointed a provisional committee to take the place of the former Auxiliary Committee, with power to co-opt non-students or ex-students and to formulate lines of advance. This committee was instructed to consider releasing the new movement from the control of the General Committee, and to suggest some new relation between it and the Student Movement. It was agreed not to hurry any final decision but to provide a provisional period while the Auxiliary was developed and relationships were discussed.

The Student Movement agreed to the proposal to appoint a full-time Auxiliary secretary, and Margaret Burge, Girton College, Cambridge and the Sorbonne, Paris, was appointed and began work in September 1921.

The Student Movement at this time took the important step of inviting the Rev. A. Herbert Gray to resign his church and become a Student Movement secretary. The proposal originated with Miss Fairfield, who convinced both the committee and Dr Gray that it was a reasonable proposal to make. Dr Gray's appointment had an important bearing upon the development of the Auxiliary, as well as upon the Movement. His work for the Student Movement was of an evangelistic character, and he conducted innumerable college missions during the three years he was on the staff. He was an enthusiastic member of the Auxiliary, and wherever he went for the Student Movement he assisted in developing Auxiliary groups, as well as taking his share in the leadership of the Auxiliary as a member of its committee.

Herbert Gray was absorbed with extraordinary ease into the Student Movement fellowship. He was thirty years and more older than the members of the committee under which he worked. It made no difference! Whether at committee meetings or in the colleges he was as at home with the students, and they with him, as if they were contemporaries. He had had a wide experience as chaplain in the army during the war, and he had a message for students; thousands heard him and hundreds, perhaps thousands, of lives were deeply influenced. He spoke in the language men use in common life; what he had to say was invariably about Christ and he was usually brief. He made religion attractive to men.

The following year the Teachers' Christian Union amalgamated with the Auxiliary, the membership of which was now five hundred and sixty men and one thousand six hundred and twenty women. Local activities had been developed considerably; they included study and service groups on Ireland, India, industry, penal reform, adolescence, civics and unity; hospitality work for foreign students; lectures on education and psychology; public meetings and week-end conferences on the challenge of Christianity, and open-air meetings.

As soon as the Auxiliary was no longer confined to ex-students, people from every rank of life were recruited, and within two years Joyce Powell, who had now become the secretary of the Auxiliary Movement, reported that the Ealing group contained " a barrister, three mothers, two teachers in elementary and three in secondary schools, an engineer, a post-office worker, an art student, two business men, a foreman in an engineer's shop, an official at the Board of Education, a Congregational parson, a lady dispenser, a youthful librarian and an engineer's apprentice." She said a

Brighton group contained "some teachers, a club-worker, a gardener, a lawyer, a domestic servant, a town councillor, a carpenter, a banker, a plumber, a clerk and a social worker." These groups were given as typical of many.

It was decided not to create Auxiliary groups in Scotland as the young people's work in the Scottish Churches was ahead of that in other parts of the British Isles, and members of the Auxiliary found scope in Scotland, as well as inspiration, in summer schools, conferences, study circles, boys' and girls' camps and campaigns in connection with the work of the Churches.

Welsh Auxiliary members held a conference at Caerleon from April 18th to 22nd 1922, at which a provisional constitution for the Auxiliary in Wales was drawn up, a committee appointed and plans laid for future development. A few months later the name Urdd-y-Deyrnas was adopted. It is an autonomous organization which appoints representatives to the General Committee of the Auxiliary Movement. It was closely associated with the S.C.M., as it still is, and shared with the Movement the services of Owen Griffith, who was its secretary from 1922-32. Owen Griffith's leadership was always inspired by a vision of the true place of the Church in the life of Wales.

The Irish Christian Fellowship had been started before the end of the war by former members of the Student Movement, and it was decided by all concerned that such work as the Auxiliary Movement might do in Ireland should be undertaken by this fellowship. The Irish Christian Fellowship greatly strengthened its position in January 1922, when some two hundred and fifty of its members, students and others, attended a conference in Queen's University, Belfast—convened jointly by it and the Student Movement—and studied the need of Ireland for peace and a new way of life.

The Theological College Department had not up to this taken any notice of the Auxiliary, but in September 1922 " there was a long and sympathetic discussion on the Auxiliary Movement. The committee was strongly impressed with the ideals for which the Auxiliary stands, and with the necessity for much closer links between those inside the churches and those outside, not merely for the benefit of the churches, but for the whole outlook for practical religion." [1]

The committee instructed its secretary, when visiting theological colleges, to speak about the Auxiliary and to be prepared to answer questions about it. It also decided to send a letter to men leaving theological colleges, inviting them to join the Auxiliary. A year later it rediscussed the Auxiliary, and arrived at the same decisions.

The Auxiliary Movement has always dated its existence as an independent movement from its conference at Swanwick, April 1921. It was not, however until December 1922 that the General Committee of the Student Christian Movement decided upon a new Constitution for it.

The more interesting features in the new Constitution must now be recorded.

The name was changed to The Auxiliary Movement. A basis was adopted : " a comradeship of men and women who desire to understand the Christian faith, to find the Christian way, and to live the Christian life."

The Constitution defined the aim of the Movement in these words :

> The Auxiliary Movement believes in the coming in this world of the Kingdom proclaimed by Jesus, in the absolute worth of the individual as set forth by Him, and in the coming of the Kingdom by way of fellowship. It therefore seeks to bring people together in fellowship groups, without any limitation or exclusiveness, to seek the Kingdom.

Provision was made for any one in sympathy with the Movement to join as a headquarters' member. There was also provision for group membership. The control of the Movement was vested in a committee of nineteen

[1] Theological College Department Minute, October 1922.

people, eleven of whom were elected at the annual meeting of the Auxiliary Movement, and four co-opted by its committee; the others were representatives of the Irish Christian Fellowship and Urdd-y-Deyrnas, the secretaries of the Auxiliary Movement and the General Secretary of the Student Christian Movement being *ex-officio* members. The relation of this new autonomous Auxiliary Movement to the Student Christian Movement was described in these words :

> The Auxiliary Movement shall maintain a close association with the Student Christian Movement, whose ideals it shares, and shall undertake the responsibility of securing for it a due measure of support, financial and otherwise.

A small joint committee was provided to deal with the matters of mutual interest to both the Auxiliary and the Student Christian Movement. The finances of the two bodies were not completely separated. The Student Movement still did the book-keeping for both bodies, and it was agreed that there should be a joint account, gifts being appropriated " as far as possible in such a manner as shall satisfy the requests of the subscribers."

J. H. Grummitt, A. G. Pite and T. Tatlow were elected as the three representatives of the Student Christian Movement on the joint committee, as provided in the Constitution, to which matters of concern to both Movements should be referred, and to this group, together with the three to be appointed by the Auxiliary Movement, was left the final drafting of the Constitution. This draft was largely the work of Miss Fairfield.

These proposals went to the committee of the Auxiliary Movement for their approval, which was given early the following year, and in March 1923 by the Student Christian Movement General Committee.

Miss Powell was succeeded by Miss Jean Miller as secretary of the Auxiliary Movement in 1923. Miss Miller gave much to the Auxiliary Movement for the six years she was its Secretary. She retired in 1929 to become Warden of the Presbyterian Women's Settlement in East London.

A further stage was reached in relationships between the Student Movement and the Auxiliary Movement in April 1925, as the result of an inquiry by a committee appointed jointly by the Student Movement and the Auxiliary Movement, which was asked to inquire once more into the work and value of the Auxiliary Movement, its possible future development and policy, its relation to the work of the Student Christian Movement in England, Ireland, Scotland and Wales, and, as other Movements in the Federation were developing Auxiliaries, to examine the situation in them and see what guidance they had to offer.

The Commission was appointed because

> some members in the Student Movement leadership did not wish the Student Movement to be responsible to the extent it was for work which its General Committee did not control, and they were doubtful as to the necessity for the Auxiliary in view of the desirability of the development of work among young people's societies in the churches, and its being hampered by the existence of the Auxiliary. The Auxiliary, on the other hand, was disappointed at the small amount of support it received from members of the Student Movement going down from college.[1]

The result of the work of the committee and its subsequent discussion by the General Committee was that the Auxiliary Movement became an autonomous organization with a controlling committee and finances of its own. A memorandum of agreement between it and the Student Movement provided that four pages of *The Student Movement* each month should be edited by the Auxiliary Movement; that every Auxiliary member be provided with a free copy; that the Auxiliary agree to allow the Student Movement to ask Auxiliary members for contributions during Finance Week. The Student Movement, on the other hand, undertook to write to its members leaving college, and invite them to join

[1] Minutes, S.C.M. General Committee, April 1925.

the Auxiliary Movement.   It also agreed to instruct its secretaries to bring the Auxiliary Movement to the attention of S.C.M. members leaving college.   The two Movements each agreed to invite representatives of the other to its General Committee meetings.

The most difficult matter dealt with was that of finance.   Many people were members of the Auxiliary, because they regarded it as the best way of helping the Student Movement and of getting the magazine regularly, and they paid their Auxiliary subscriptions understanding that they went into the coffers of the Movement.   In October 1923 all who paid subscriptions were asked to state in what proportion, if any, they wanted their subscriptions to be divided between the Auxiliary and the Student Christian Movement.   There were 1597 persons on the register of the Auxiliary, and the result was that 1345 of these decided to give £1486 to Auxiliary funds.   As the work of the Auxiliary cost the Movement £1219, the Movement had a balance from the Auxiliary for its own work of £267, in addition to £1273 which Auxiliary members sent directly to the S.C.M.

When the separation had been agreed to it was decided that to share an office and accountant would be an economy to both organizations.   It would also help to eliminate the fear of some people that the two Movements might become rivals.

The frame of mind of younger secretaries and students was reflected in a document prepared by them for the General Committee entitled " To your tents, O Israel," which asked the Movement to turn the Auxiliary into " The Order of the Kingdom," which should be " an order of brothers (men and women) seeking to give their lives to establish the Kingdom of God in their own communities," an order whose members would back one another up in practical Christian living.   The group asked for the whole-hearted backing of the General Committee.

There was vigorous difference of opinion about the

Auxiliary on the General Committee. One section had in mind the large body of people going out of the Movement who seemed unable to find fellowship and friendship in the churches, and who were in danger of being lost to any visible communion of the faithful. The other group had its attention fixed upon the churches, and they feared "there was a danger of promoting in different localities small groups who would feel superior to the churches. The need was for Student Movement members to go into the churches, and to help to make them better through what they had learned in the Movement." All were agreed "that the Auxiliary was not a substitute for the Christian Church." The General Committee was not in a mood for anything striking, and it simply confirmed the agreement between the two organizations.

The memorandum of agreement was put into operation on June 1st 1925, after there had been a joint meeting between the General Committees of the Auxiliary and the Student Movements. This joint meeting was held at New College, Oxford, on April 24th, 1925.

The Auxiliary Movement will no doubt one day have its own historian, who will trace its activities through the years ; here there is only space to speak of S.C.M. relationships.

The Auxiliary Movement has followed the example of the Student Movement in centring its life and work round an annual conference. At its Oxford Conference in 1927 a desire arose to make it a fellowship which committed its members more deeply to one another and itself as one of the bodies, working for the Kingdom of God. An outcome was *The Book of the Fellowship*, which brought together the results of much thought during the previous ten years by those whom the Auxiliary Movement had brought into effective fellowship. It also suggested a programme of work, in relation to education ; politics, economics and citizenship ; service at home and abroad ; study ; work

in country districts ; the Christian Church ; and disarmament, which was based on what had already been
done as well as what it was hoped to do.

It is not unusual for Christians to make statements
which promise more than subsequent performance
would seem to justify, but there has been much in the
life of the Auxiliary Movement which bears witness to
the serious attempt made by many to live up to its
" affirmations."

These affirmations declare belief in the coming in
this world of the Kingdom which Jesus proclaimed ; a
Kingdom which is the will and gift of God, and comes
in the hearts of men and in the organized life of society :
a Kingdom which comes through disinterested service
and recognition of the unique value of the individual, and which sets free the creative power and love
of God through those who, in fellowship, serve its
coming.

In 1929 the Auxiliary Movement achieved its desire
of securing Miss Fairfield as its leader.

In 1933 there are some 3000 people associated with the
Auxiliary Movement. There are fellowships or groups
in some eighty centres in England and a few in Scotland.
The Auxiliary Movement works in contact with the
Urdd-y-Deyrnas in Wales, the Irish Christian Fellowship,
and thirty similar fellowships overseas.

It has two functions. It is a fellowship of men and
women who believe in the coming of the Kingdom of
God in this world. This has resulted in a fellowship
in which the members recognize that the first demand
upon them is that they should seek " to know and love
one another." Mutual giving and receiving is a real
thing in the Auxiliary Movement and is a source of
strength and joy to many who have not known where
else to look for what the Auxiliary Movement has
given them.

Its other function is that it is a fellowship of service.
" Because it is composed of people who are sustained
by one another in a fellowship which has its roots in

faith in God, it is able to look beyond its own borders and undertake definite work for the Kingdom." The projects for which the whole Movement has a measure of responsibility are at present the following :

Education.—Area committees throughout England are helping teachers to tackle the problems that puzzle the younger members of their profession, and the result is that many teachers have been given new courage for their work.

Youth and the Church.—Some successful experiments have been made in bringing young people of different denominations together to find strength in unity, the purpose to promote reunion, and inspiration and insight as to the call of the Church to serve the coming of the Kingdom of God.

Christianity and Industry.—Some of the most baffling problems centre round industry, and the Auxiliary Movement and the Student Movement are co-operating in exploring this subject. Students preparing for industrial careers and business men are together studying the creation of a social order in which industry shall be the servant of all and the master of none.

To all this may be added the activities of the local fellowships and groups—work for the unemployed, for housing, for peace ; and study of all kinds, the New Testament, science and religion, reunion, Russia and communism, economic questions, gambling, etc., etc.

The Auxiliary Movement is still very young, and its future is not to be predicted, but it is full of life, youth and vigour. It is profoundly Christian and at the same time finds room, and room which men find comfortable, for people whose hold on the Christian view of the world is very insecure. It is far from being an " important " society with notable names attached to it, but it can get things done—it has moved town councils to build houses for slum dwellers.

Its interest in " the ordinary person " is not lip service but real in fact, and ordinary people are at home in its fellowship. Class consciousness tends to fade away in Auxiliary Movement circles.

It is a valuable auxiliary to the Student Movement, helping to confirm in men and women the purposes which they have formed in college under its influence.

CHAPTER XXXIX

STUDENTS AND THE CHURCH

IT was inevitable that the Student Movement should give its attention to the relationship of students to the Church in the post-war period. It had recently committed itself more explicitly than ever in its aim and basis to the service of the Church. "It calls them," said the Aim and Basis, "to enter the fellowship of worship, thought and service which is the heritage of the Christian Church." This clause in the Aim and Basis, which was adopted in 1919, was a strengthening of a parallel clause in the discarded Aim and Basis—" to lead them into the fellowship and service of the Christian Church." This new declaration was made at a time when criticism of institutional religion was vocal and insistent throughout the universities and colleges of the country.

The General Committee in the past had "appointed commissions to investigate matters of great importance to its life. In September 1921, owing to its growing concern at the relations between the student body and the churches of this country, it appointed its fourth commission. Its terms of reference, broadly speaking, were to investigate the attitude of students to the Church and to advise as to the future policy of the Student Christian Movement in this matter." [1]

The members of the Commission were: Robert Bewsher, Amy Buller, J. R. Coates, F. A. Cockin, Zoë B. Fairfield, G. C. Glossop, Mrs Glossop, Owen Griffith, Mervyn Haigh,[2] Geoffrey Heawood, Nora

[1] *Students and the Church*, Preface.
[2] Later Bishop of Coventry.

Inskip, J. H. Lewis, Hugh Martin, Miall Edwards, A. G. Pite, Joyce Powell, Malcolm Spencer, Tissington Tatlow, Edith W. Thornton, A. D. Turner and R. D. Whitehorn.

The Commission met on five occasions for long sessions, some of them lasting for several days, and took over a year to complete its report. Although there was a wealth of knowledge of student thought on the Commission its first act was to issue a questionnaire, which was widely circulated in the colleges, seeking student opinion about the Church, asking what hold the churches had upon different types of students and the reasons why so large a number of students refrained from attendance at church services. Questions were also asked about why more men did not enter the Christian ministry, and what the Student Movement could do to help students in their thought about the Church and their duty towards it. There were two questions for women students only, asking their attitude to the Church and to the opportunity for service which the churches offered.

As the Commission proceeded with its work it invited a number of clergy, ministers, laymen and women, representing different churches, to advise and help it.

Although the Commission circulated its questionnaire throughout the British Isles, it found the situation so urgent and difficult in England that it confined its attention almost entirely to that country.

The inquiry was started without any intention of doing more than provide a printed memorandum for private circulation, which might be used by members of the General Committee and the secretaries of the Movement. As the work proceeded, however, the report grew in length and took such shape that, after consultation with the General Committee, it was decided to issue it under the title *Students and the Church*,[1] as one of the publications of the Movement.

[1] *Students and the Church.* The report of a Commission appointed by the General Committee of the Student Christian Movement.

The book was received with attention in the colleges, and a series of questions for study circles upon it were issued and used by some thousands of students. The volume is no longer available, having been out of print for some time, and will not be reprinted because in some respects it is out of date, but as the Movement's thought in relation to the Church in the post-war period has been based upon it, an attempt must be made to summarize its chief contents.

On every hand the churches, one and all, are criticized as being ineffective in providing society with the particular kind of moral and spiritual power that it needs for its present-day development. . . . The Church has become in the minds of many an idea surrounded by doubts and difficulties, instead of an idea offering challenge and inspiration. . . . This situation is found, not created by the Student Christian Movement.

It is impossible, therefore, for the Movement to talk to students about the Church simply on the basis of its interdenominational position. As an interdenominational body it has hitherto based its work upon the Church as it is, taking membership in it as normally meaning membership in some Christian denomination.

" Denominational loyalty is, however, no longer the most effective rallying-point. . . . The Student Movement is therefore bound at this time to say something to students about the nature, purpose and present justification of the Church." This, however, " it cannot do without raising some questions and making some statements about the Church and the denominations which would, till quite recently, have been regarded as outside its province as an ' extra-ecclesiastical ' body."

The Report of the Commission is, therefore, a " quite tentative attempt to provide a rationale of the Church in terms universal enough for all comers without using the specific arguments of the denominations."

While the Commission did not think that the questions it had to answer could be answered without first laying out a broad conception of what the Church really is and

3 C

does, it knew that to attempt to do this meant the possibility of criticism from different quarters.

The detached critic might ask if we cannot cut out this general theorizing and tell him what to make of the Christian congregation of which his family forms part, with its obscurantist parson, its antipathy to its next-door neighbour in the way of churches, and its fear of the new moral issues which social life presents.

The practical " Church worker," with inside knowledge and responsibility for the continuance of the Church as a working institution, might ask if the idealist did not see the inevitable limitations of average people. While the theologians might well ask : " Who are you, anyway, to grapple with such technical questions as these ? "

The answer of the Commissioners was that as spokesmen of the Student Movement, who knew the questions about the Church that students were asking, they thought they should submit for the consideration of students " the line of answer we think it possible to give . . . which we hope criticism will enable us to develop and correct."

No progress can be made by those who want to speak about the nature and purpose of the Church unless they recognize that to the students of to-day the Church is not associated firmly and unmistakably with the ideals of right and truth and progress, and does not stand as the champion of any large constructive social ideal. Students' ideals of social right may not be clear but they are compelling, and they do not find them manifestly honoured by the Church.

Their own standards of truth, naturally, are exacting and insistent, and beside them those of the Church seem sometimes to be tuned to a conservative expediency. To their untried enthusiasms and idealisms the Church seems rather to be giving a tame and slavish obedience to the standards of the past, than to be grappling heroically with the problems of the present and the future. . . . The idea of the Church as a glorious thing is lost in the ingloriousness of the denominations.

We must clear the issue and ask what is the Church for. " The Church exists to proclaim the good news about God and His Kingdom, brought to the world by Jesus, to make all men and all nations His disciples in a fellowship of worship, thought and service." The Church is identical with the best recognized ideals of human and social progress, but goes beyond them in aiming at something deeper, more lasting and more satisfying, and also in providing more unfailing sources of energy for their realization. Its aim is so to touch the springs of human personality that a Christian way of life becomes both desirable and possible to man. " The Church, and the Church alone, confronts the facts of evil and of tragedy with a message of salvation and the disintegration of society with a message of recreative power."

To the critic who would agree that this is the aim of Christianity, but who would question whether the Church as an organized body is needed to realize it, the reply is made that " such an ideal as that of Christianity can only be fitly and adequately embodied in a society of persons. It is too vital to be expressed in anything less than living personalities, and too many-sided to be fully embodied in individual personalities." The society of Christians is not merely an expedient whereby individuals encourage one another in striving for an ideal, but a fellowship of the Spirit of Christ in which the purpose and presence of God are realized, as can never be the case in isolation. Our Lord dwells in the Christian society. Its life and functions are those of Christ Himself, " so that those who are effectually members of the Church are members of the Body of Christ."

The corporate expression of the idea of the Church must take definite and continuous institutional form. In human life anything which is vital creates a society to give it more effective expression, or it passes away. All great achievement is firmly rooted in history, but the average man cannot interrogate the past for himself, or search out those treasures of religious experience and moral attainment which are open to him in the fellowship of the common faith. The Church gives him riches from her store.

The Church calls him to sacrificial service and sacrificial fellowship, " to some regular and central act of corporate worship, which is a symbol of unrestricted fellowship with God and man, of the universality of the Christian fellowship and of the communion of saints." Men chafe at the blemishes in their institutions, but nevertheless they need them.

The historical Church emerged as a sequel to the first Jewish attempt to realize a society in which love and loyalty to God and man should be expressed in stable correlation. The first Christians were in no doubt as to the need of a Christian society.

> Central in the world's history since that time has been the persistent attempt of the Christian society to realize its ideal of a body having at once such fulness of disinterested love, such constancy of Christian aim and purpose, and such vitalized flexibility of mind as to provide the world with a spiritual mainspring for its ordered fellowship.

The Commission recognized the failures and the half-complete success of the Church, discussed the differences of emphasis between the advocates of freedom and the advocates of conformity to type as two ideals for the Church, said that the Church to-day needed to understand the truth in both positions, and declared, " The Church has achieved magnificent things in the transformation of man and society."

The man or woman who would be a Christian is bound by ties of loyalty to all other Christians and to the organized Christian society, but as things are, the individual can " only have communion with his fellow Christians in a mutilated form—regularly and completely with one group, only occasionally and partially with the rest."

The Student Christian Movement has always recognized this situation, and has taken the line that each Christian should find his link with the whole body through loyal participation in the life of that group of Christians which most truly expresses for him the essential life of the Church ; whilst at the same time he owes it to Christ and to the whole Church to take every opportunity for better understanding of those outside his own communion, and such co-operation with them as that loyalty permits.

The fact of dismemberment of the Body of Christ, with its contradiction of the essential unity of the Church and its very considerable failure " to extend the range of Christian social action beyond the sphere of one's family and near acquaintances to the sphere of industry and politics " is a grave defect which strains the loyalty of students. None the less, it is palpably impossible to establish the Christian ideal of fellowship throughout the world if we are cavalier towards the claims of the Christian denominations and lightly break away from them. Religious bodies may delay their support, but it is improbable that anything great will be achieved in the world if it does not ultimately carry the Churches with it. If we are moved by educational or social ideals we should not lose the opportunity of enlisting members of the churches by cutting ourselves off from their fellowship, nor should we risk loss of insight and energy by cutting loose from " sources of moral and spiritual inspiration which have been supremely important in the past history of Christendom." Students should be discouraged from wandering from church to church " attending many, but being in fellowship with none."

Having dealt on these lines with the nature and purpose of the Church, the Commission proceeded to discuss its functions, placing first the worship of the Church.

True worship of God is the essence of religion, and has always been so. . . . With all its emphasis on morality, with all its dealings with politics, philosophy and science, the Christian faith is primarily a relation between God and man, an attitude in the believer of reverence and love, expressing in whatever form his adoration and longing for communion. It is no accident that public worship is the central activity of any body of Christians.

The practice and theory of worship seeming very difficult to many students, the Commission discussed some of the difficulties. The first difficulty is a sense of unreality, yet if man found God easily there would be no problem of religion or Church. It is a fact that many have found Him all through the ages, and to them the discovery has been the greatest thing of all. They never suggest that the way is easy, but despite their incapacities they build their religion on knowledge and faith. The experience of God which comes in worship is dependent upon an adequate conception of God, and it is essential to know the right things about Him and not to acquiesce in ignorance. This is the true corrective to the over-developed critical faculty which is inevitable when students are in the process of being educated.

The new psychology was discussed by the Commission and the need for a knowledge of true faith and true psychology recognized ; also the dangers of a utilitarian standard which current education tended to produce.

Worship does not appear to pay. It takes time ; it requires the cultivation of certain faculties which usually grow but slowly ; its fruits are to be found in unobtrusive forms which do not " take the eye and have the price." Until we regain the conviction that the activities of the human spirit, thought, love, creation, worship are things valuable in and for themselves, and not for the price their products fetch in the open market, worship along with the rest is bound to suffer.

Students must beware of the pace and interest of modern life, remembering that " worship demands at all times peace of mind, concentration and a certain amount of leisure." If this seems a hard way, it only enforces for to-day " the old truth that the things best

worth having are only obtained by discipline. . . .
We cannot have all we would like, and amid so many
wonderful, enthralling and good things, we have ruth-
lessly to cut some away that we may have the best of all."

The Commission thought that instruction in existing
methods of worship missed the heart of the difficulty
of many people.   What was needed was a much fuller
apologetic for Christian worship.   While there is the
moral problem that men refuse to face the demands of
God, yet many students would face the moral decision
if they saw it as such.

> But they are confused by what seems to them insincere
> and shallow thinking. . . . We feel that the first necessity
> is for students to relate their own thinking to Christian
> thinking, to regain that sympathy in the search for truth
> which still exists in our common admiration of goodness
> and in our wonder at the glories of creation.   If they see
> that Christians care for the truth of God, they will be ready
> to learn from them of His holiness and beauty, and as they
> draw near they will come to know themselves, to confess
> and to adore.

A true understanding of what is worship is the first
step towards helping students to understand God and
worship Him themselves.   Worship is the recognition
of worth ; the response of a personality to the discovery
of real value outside itself.   Worship is the personal
response of man to God.   The recognition of worth
is universal and of great variety.   It culminates in terms
of personality.

> Christian worship is communion with God, as known in
> Jesus Christ.   Worship is communion, God showing Him-
> self to man face to face and man responding with a recogni-
> tion of his own unworthiness. . . . This recognition of our
> own unworthiness and the infinite worth of the love of God
> is the beginning and end of Christian worship.

God is always showing Himself but man does not
usually recognize Him.

> In the Cross of Christ God shows Himself most com-
> pletely at the heart of the greatest human problem, the

problem of pain and sin.   Many men first find Him there,
and for all Christians the Cross is the centre of worship. . . .
We cannot expect to grasp completely the nature and purpose
of God, but in worship we endeavour to give ourselves to
the God and Father of our Lord Jesus Christ in thankfulness, in wonder, in love and in adoration.

Christian worship like this needs no further justification.   It is the highest activity of the spirit, but its
effects reach out to all parts of life.   It is a means of
grace as man receives, through his realized intimacy
with his Father, strength and inspiration to do that
Father's will, thus true worship is the basis of true
morality.

It is also a means of truth.   The attainment of truth
is not only a question of argument, discussion, exposition; it finds other means of entrance into the minds,
so prayers, hymns and the proper use of colour, sound
and silence, all that is meant by ceremonial, may help
man to see God in His true beauty and wonder.

How may those who say they have never worshipped
begin ?   The first way is to find what you in fact worship already.   " It may help to examine your own past
experience of love, truth and beauty, to find out what
they mean to you, and whether, after all, God must
not have been speaking in them to you."   The reverence
of the average man for the historical Jesus has in it the
germ of Christian worship, and the response men make
to the best in one another, though incomplete, is a
definite recognition of the eternal values.   Contempla-
tion is a great help in learning.   Let a man take such
passages as 1 Corinthians xiii., or Psalm xxiii., or Psalm
ciii., and see whether they have any relation to himself
or the world as he knows it, and he will begin to grasp
the significance of eternal things.

The other way of beginning is from other people's
worship.   To find God we must be taken out of ourselves, and the worship of the Church offers an opportunity for this.   " Man is taken out of himself by the
glory of God, and this of itself brings him nearer to

STUDENTS AND THE CHURCH

others. . . . Praise and thanksgiving are richer and fuller in true fellowship than alone. Corporate worship may be the means of introducing a man to the experience of God for himself. God in Christ has been and is thus given and received at public worship through the Eucharist, through silence, and through preaching, by countless men and women for the first time and constantly through life."

The Commission suggested a variety of ways in which the Church could help students, especially by meeting the demand for a clear apologetic for worship in general and for services in particular. There was need for bold experiment in the form of services which would weed out bad or obsolete forms, and provide further opportunity for the various denominations to bring their own special contributions to a larger and richer whole.

If public worship is to be sincere and complete, the question of unity cannot be ignored.

> Barriers in worship correspond to no spiritual reality. For man to put them up is felt as a contradiction and by many as a sin. . . . What is needed is a living, loving society, not a heterogeneous congeries of individuals, met to sing and pray together because they live nearby, but who do nothing else together, and have no ties with one another.

The Church must become visible in other ways than through its buildings and ministry, and must not tolerate the dividing forces of classes, money, race, or inequality of education in any part of its life. "This is not a demand for denunciation, but for a visible, living fellowship of all kinds of Christians."

Another need is for corporate action. There is too much attention to individual needs in the Church, and not enough facing " of the necessity for the joint dedication of the whole fellowship to the bringing in of the Kingdom of God." A congregation is responsible to God not only for itself, but for the neighbourhood in which it is placed and for all mankind. The wrongs committed by governments, companies, clubs, trades unions, churches were not done by an individual, and they cannot be set right except by groups tackling them in the power of God's forgiveness. The Church needs to recover a sense of corporate sin and a readiness for corporate sacrifice for the Kingdom.

The Commission reminded students that as they entered the fellowship of the Church they should recognize their need of others who are not students, " the older, the poorer, the simpler, the wiser and the children, to teach them the meaning of Christian fellowship."

Students must remember that worship is not a pleasant experience dropped upon by chance. They must face the demands God makes. The worship of God demands a constant dependence in faith and will.

As the habits of friends and lovers are most inadequate as an account of love or friendship, but are an essential part of its existence and continuance, so communion with God cannot be accurately or completely described. Corporate worship is necessarily symbolic.

The Student Movement calls on students to enter the fellowship of worship which is the heritage of the Christian Church, and in so doing knows it is asking no light thing. " In the worship of God the individual joins himself with all other Christians everywhere, and also in a real sense with the Christians of every age in the highest exercise of the human spirit, the temper of all true knowledge, the key of the mystery of life itself."

The Commission then proceeded to deal with the thought of the Christian Church, frankly acknowledging that " the Church is not adequately discharging its responsibilities," although there is a tendency on the part of students whose main preoccupations are intellectual both to over-estimate the place of the intellectual in religion as a whole, and to ignore the limitations imposed on any minister by the varied demands of a mixed congregation.

It does, however, appear to us on the evidence which comes to us over and over again from the colleges that large numbers of the younger generation are growing up in quite lamentable ignorance of the main principles of Christianity, its conception of God and His relation to the world, its idea of His revelation in Christ and its unique significance, its view of the destiny of the human soul

When students did inquire, too often they found their inquiries met by a use of authority which seemed to them illegitimate, and by an apparent unwillingness to face the real difficulties.

The Commission spoke of a few of the main difficulties, emphatically declaring that it did not believe in a " creedless Christianity " or a broad-mindedness which, in reality, was only being shallow-minded. The Apostles and Nicene Creeds are of the first value as embodying those historical facts on which Christianity is based, and as providing us with a classical attempt to interpret these historical facts in terms of doctrine. The ideas and language, however, were those of the time at which they were written, and the progress of human knowledge had rendered " interpretation " or restatement of at least some of the terms inevitable for all thinking people, but here difficulties began. " How far may this process of interpretation legitimately go ? " If we have " adjusted " our idea of " He descended into Hell," may we similarly " adjust " our ideas of " Born of the Virgin Mary " and " the resurrection of the body ? " What is the right attitude to be adopted to these questions by those who offer themselves as candidates for the ministry ? The duty of finding answers rests with the Church, rather than with the Movement.

The thinking function of the Church is another matter which needs attention. It is usual to speak of " the *teaching* function of the Church," but this presupposes responsibility for articulating and developing the meaning of the faith within its own membership. The phrase, " the teaching function of the Church," is usually construed as the teaching function of the clergy ; and while they have a special teaching function, its value and effectiveness is largely diminished if it is regarded as excluding, or in any way minimising, the responsibility of the rest of the Christian community for taking a share in this process of education. " The ordinary man does not feel that he has a real responsibility for thinking out the meaning of the faith which he professes to hold." This tendency is greatly increased by the readiness of some clergy and ministers to regard themselves as the only people who have a right to handle such questions. This is an attitude which is found among theological students, " most of whom display a measure of irritation, and even contempt, at the bungling efforts of ' mere medicals ' to think out for themselves the meaning of Christian doctrine."

In relation to the thinking function of the Church there are " three points which should be firmly established : one, there is the *thinking* function of the Church as a whole ; two, there is the *teaching* function of those specially trained for the purpose (lay, as well as clerical) ; three, there is the teaching function of the Church as a whole, in relation to the non-Christian world at home and abroad."

The Commission had some interesting things to say about the question of authority, and how no one should be asked to tolerate " the assumption of an abstract and arbitrary authority by one whom they feel to be really unfitted to exercise it."

> The minister, even the theological student, is right in asserting his claim to speak with an authority greater than that of the layman. But his claim will only be acknowledged when it is known to be backed by real authority of thought and study . . . and his authority as a teacher will only be really effective and valuable when it is exercised, *not* as a means of suppressing the thinking of his pupils, but as a means of stimulating and developing it to a higher pitch.

The Commission recognized that the question of the relation of theology to growing modern knowledge, with all its ramifications, was full of perplexity, but gave it as its opinion that the sphere which the thinking of the Church and the teaching of the ministry should cover included the following subjects :

(1) The nature of religion. Its place in the life of man. The history of its development.

(2) The nature of God. His revelation of Himself in history. The peculiar place of the revelation in the Jewish religious experience. Its culmination in Christ.

(3) The significance of Christ. The meaning of His life, death and resurrection. His teaching.

(4) The influence of His teaching upon the life and thought of mankind—especially through the medium of the Christian Church.

(This will include not only " Church History " and " Dogmatic Theology," but also the bearing of Christian thought upon philosophy, science, art, politics, etc., whether in Europe or in the mission field.)

(5) The spiritual life. Its nature, needs and maintenance. The meaning of prayer and worship.

In discussing the methods of discharging the thinking and teaching function of the Church, the Commission confined itself to the specifically educational means, preaching, teaching, study groups and the like, emphasizing the importance of the place of thought in the winning and care of souls.

Distinctions are drawn in too hard and fast a way between true thinking and salvation. The one is regarded as theoretical, the other as a practical matter. Such a distinction, if pressed, is false and dangerous. It is only truth in the message that can have ultimate *saving* power. . . . Evangelization and sound thinking cannot be divorced without disastrous consequences.

This point of view was developed in relation to evangelistic work of all kinds, indoor and outdoor, and to the education of those within the membership of the Church, including the advanced study and instruction required for those who are themselves being trained as teachers.

The Commission ventured some comment on the question, " How far is the Church discharging its responsibility?" based upon information supplied by students. Students said they found it difficult to discover the attitude of the Church towards matters of urgent public importance, and its teaching upon certain difficult questions. They complained, for example, that they could not find out what the Church had to say about compromise in business life, or the claims of spiritualism. More practical moral guidance is needed than seems to be available, while often there is an impression that the spokesmen of the Church lack humility and honesty. The language used in sermons and lectures is a great stumbling-block, and there is need to explain the meaning of terms such as grace, redemption, etc. The complaint was voiced that

> Sermons consist far too much of general exhortations to goodness, or of particular emphasis on details of rule and discipline, *e.g.*, fasting communion. There is far too little straightforward explanation of the essentials of the Christian faith in God and its bearing upon the practical problems of daily life—home difficulties, the use of money, the right use of liberty, etc.

The result of the present state of affairs was that students found difficulty in getting a fair hearing for, or an adequate answer to, their questions, and this tended to alienate the more thoughtful among them from the Church. The impoverishment of thought brought with it an impoverishment of worship and also an impoverishment of the ideal of service.

> Failure to think out progressively the true function of the Church in relation to the growing life of the community produces a conservative inclination to remain content with the old ideals and methods of " Church work." Fresh experiments, especially in the sphere of co-operative social service, are not encouraged since they draw off workers who are needed for " running the machine."

The Commission made some attempt to estimate where the blame lay and suggested some considerations and questions. The burden of administrative routine, especially in Church of England parishes, is heavy and interferes with study and thinking. " How much of it is necessary, how much could the laity do ? " Is the type of ministerial training given at present the best suited to equip men to meet the demands of their work ? How much actual educational training is given, how much differentiation according to special capacity is actual or possible ? Is the sermon the best medium of giving teaching ?

Students were reminded that the minister should not be expected to be an encyclopædia, also that it was an error to suppose that none except the younger generation were doing any thinking, and that they might take the trouble to discover and avail themselves of the opportunities provided by a number of young people's societies. Students were criticized by the Commission for being " lamentably unwilling in many cases to pay the price of hard reading and thinking, without which a real understanding of Christian doctrine is impossible," and those whose interests are primarily intellectual should not under-estimate the value of other aspects of religion. " The elements of worship and faithfulness in small jobs are equally valuable."

The Commission invited the attention of students to the other side of the picture, declaring that " at no time within the last two hundred years has there been so much in the way of experiment and development in the thinking of the Church." The leaders are concerned about these questions, and valuable committee work has been done on the teaching function of the Church in more than one denomination. Young people's departments in several denominations have initiated advance movements since the war, the graded Sunday school movement is doing much to improve the quality of the teaching of children. The missionary study movement and social service unions are doing valuable educational work. It is increasingly common for individual clergy and ministers to devote courses of sermons to the exposition of the main doctrines of Christianity, and the work of Church tutorial classes provides an opportunity for thorough religious study in several dioceses of the Church of England.

The Commission asked for readjustment in the staffing and organization of the Church and for more differentiation of function so that the differing gifts of men might be recognized and their possessors enabled to make their special contribution with less distraction and waste of energy. An intelligence staff is needed, either for the Church as a whole or at least for each denomination, and fuller consideration should be paid to the place of the laity, both men and women.

In the more advanced spheres of specialist study the Church can hardly hope to regain and retain her true place, unless she will avail herself more courageously of the help of those who have devoted their lives to study, especially in those spheres in which theology marches with other realms of knowledge.

The Commission then turned to deal with the Church as a fellowship of service.

The Church does not exist for its own sake. Its outlook should be outward and not inward. Solicitous concern for its own health or wealth save as an agent of the Kingdom is unworthy of its high calling. The Church is here to continue the work of the Incarnation, to be for Christ a Body through which He may now do His will in the world. . . . The field of the Church is the world, its purpose the purification of the entire life of humanity, its end a community truly and completely Christlike.

The Church should unite its members for worship and inspiration, and for the reception of power, whether mainly through the Holy Communion, as some would claim, or through other avenues. It should help its members to work out the meaning of the Christian faith in terms of modern life. It should send them out into the world to claim the whole of life for Christ with its blessing and backing.

Primary in the service of the world by the Church is evangelism and all that this means, but Christianity cannot be expressed, nor the Christian life lived in terms of the individual alone. " The function of the

Church is to save society, and not merely to pluck brands from the burning." The self-sacrificing work of Christians in caring for the social wreckage of our time and similar palliative work is valuable but, " that the present order of society is not yet Christian in some fundamental respects is evident from its results." It is not enough that the Church should rouse itself to protest against abuse.

From generation to generation society offers ever fresh opportunities for the reshaping of its life on higher lines. Christians cannot escape responsibility for translating the values for which Christ stood into actual fact in the world's life.

The Church must insist that Christianity be brought into everyday life. The butcher, the baker, the candlestick-maker must express their religion in their daily life and work.

The primary Christian service of the candlestick-maker should be to make candlesticks to the glory of God, by making them truly for the use and delight of man. No mere subscribing to credal orthodoxy can take the place of living as a Christian in business. . . . Church membership, therefore, should definitely commit men and women to seek the Kingdom of God ; to seek it in the life of their neighbourhood, in their business, in national and international politics. It should band the members together in comradeship in seeking equipment for these tasks and in the doing of them. . . . The Church should be ready to help solicitors or cabmen to realize the higher social possibilities and to grapple with the ethical difficulties of their professions. . . . Christians must examine the structure of society, challenge its evils and inadequacies and ask for their elimination.

In the light of these principles an individual church or congregation should study the needs of its neighbourhood and the world. This would involve a complete revolution in the thinking and working of most congregations.

The work inside an individual congregation, however,

3 D

must not be overlooked. There is usually an outer circle to be won for Christ, and also the fellowship of the congregation to be built up. Fellowship may be born in many ways: in a class for training Sunday school teachers, or in a conference which makes an honest attempt to face the responsibilities of the Church for its neighbourhood. Evangelism must be related to life. Bad housing conditions may obscure the vision of God and make it harder for some to lead the Christian life. The Church should study the well-being of the community. The Commission said it did not advocate the Church hiring playing fields or building houses, or the like, but it should be the concern of its members to inspire and aid the community in meeting these needs. When this cannot be achieved the Church must sometimes be a pioneer, as it has been in the past when it provided medical service or education, before the community as a whole recognized its responsibility.

The existence of separate denominations is a definite hindrance in the way of effective performance of the Church's duty to the community. Interdenominational co-operation was urged wherever possible, but here, again, it should be co-operation to stir the community rather than by the churches as such taking action, for example, creating infant welfare centres.

The educational work of the churches offers students special opportunity. " The work of Sunday school teaching offers scope for the finest qualities of mind and spirit." There is also more advanced work needed in leading the study of Christian doctrine, social, missionary and international questions.

The Commission spoke of the opportunity of student campaigns, remarking that the Church had signally failed to get across what it had to say to the man in the street. The methods employed by young people might arouse attention and win conviction.

Societies in the Churches are often kept going needlessly, and Church machinery should constantly be overhauled. Students ought to be ready to serve the

Church. They cannot expect to be placed in important positions immediately they leave college, but there is scope in most of the denominations in the young people's movements which they ought to back. The Church should not be afraid of making big demands. The trouble often is that its demands are not big enough. " It is the challenge of the Cross we must present. But let us not ask men and women to wear themselves out or bear the Cross for futile or inadequate ends."

The Commission made a strong appeal to the ministry of the churches not so to occupy all the spare time of students, who are attending non-residential colleges, in Church work that they could not help the Student Movement in college; and pled that where a choice has to be made the claims of college should come first. " Each generation of students must be reached by its fellows. The opportunity is unique and brief. These men are the representatives of the Church in their college, and it is there that they can serve the Church best in student days." The Commission saw the value of students maintaining their links with their home church, and asked that a compromise be effected so that they could serve both their home church and the Student Movement in college.

The last section of the Commission's report dealt with students and the ministry of the Church. The case for a full-time ministry was stated briefly and the special needs and difficulties of the time surveyed, such as " the evidence collected for the report on *The Army and Religion*, which makes it plain that by 1914 various causes had produced widespread ignorance of Christianity." Men have too narrow a conception of the Church, and students who have had an opportunity of mixing with different kinds of men and women are needed in the ministry that, among other things, they may help to make it evident " that the Church of Christ, as the instrument of the Kingdom of God, stands for the most liberal application of the highest ideals."

There is also, at the present time, a need for people

who will make new departures and experiments, and not simply regard it as their first duty to keep the system going. The Commission had something to say about credal statements, remarking that " in the opinion of many students it does not seem perfectly honest to make a confession of faith in a phraseology which is not necessarily to be interpreted at its full value."

The Commission thought that many students, especially those from well-to-do homes, " are more or less consciously restrained from going into the ministry on account of the very doubtful financial prospects." This was perhaps due more to parental influence than to students' own thinking, but they recognized that the work of the ministry cannot be done adequately by men in a continual state of financial anxiety. " The remedy for this lies not with the students but with the churches."

The Commission thought that the Movement ought to be able with confidence to guide students in their thinking about the ministry, and ought to win for it some of their best members. The hope is expressed that shortage of candidates should rather lead to the closing of churches and the cutting of activities than " in any lowering of the standard for the ministry."

The report sold rapidly in the colleges, and influenced many in the student generation for which it was provided, and the ideas it contains remain current in the Movement.

CHAPTER XL

CHURCH UNITY IN OUR MOVEMENT AND IN THE FEDERATION

THE subject of Church Unity was very much alive during the war. The army talked about it, and many chaplains vowed to work for it as never before as soon as the war was over.

Two statements relating to points of agreement and questions at issue between the Church of England and the Free Churches were prepared by a Joint Committee and published. They had a huge circulation. The first of these, *Towards Christian Unity: Interim Report*, appeared in February 1916, and the *Second Interim Report* in March 1918.[1] The Joint Committee was appointed at a conference in the Jerusalem Chamber, Westminster Abbey, in 1914, of members of all the committees in England constituted in connection with the Movement to hold a World Conference on Faith and Order. It had among its members some of the most prominent of the leaders of the Churches.

As I was secretary of the Joint Conference all the correspondence relating to it came to Annandale, and I kept the luncheon table there—a meeting-place of the secretaries of considerable importance at this period— informed as to what was happening. The interest in reunion was thus continually being stimulated, for we not only knew what was happening but discussed among ourselves the many and important questions that emerged during the work of the Joint Conference. I may remark in passing that the work of the Joint Conference proved a valuable preparation for the

[1] *Documents bearing on the Problem of Christian Unity and Fellowship*, 1916-20, pp. 5-14.

Lambeth Conference of the Bishops of the Anglican communion in 1920, and its *Interim Reports* influenced to no small degree the *Appeal to all Christian People*[1] issued by it.

The General Committee of the Movement was excited when I was summoned to meet the Committee of the Lambeth Conference on Reunion, and at a meeting held at Swanwick I was instructed to press for a recommendation by the bishops that as a next step the Anglican communion should invite members of the Presbyterian and Free Churches to communicate at a celebration of Holy Communion by an Anglican priest on occasions such as the summer conferences of the Movement, when Anglicans, Presbyterians and Free Churchmen met on an interdenominational platform.

Immediately after the Lambeth Conference I went to Geneva as one of the representatives on the Archbishops of Canterbury and York's Committee in connection with the World Conference on Faith and Order, to discuss at a conference convened from August 12th to 24th the best time and method for holding the World Conference.

The *Appeal to All Christian People*, issued by the Lambeth Conference, had become a famous document by the time we met in the autumn and raised hopes among many students and members of the Auxiliary that the Church of England would make provision whereby Anglicans and members of other Churches could take the Holy Communion together. I was instructed by the General Committee to write to the Bishop of Southwell (Sir Edwyn Hoskyns) and ask if in view of the Lambeth Conference findings he could give permission for a celebration at which members of the Free Churches might be invited to communicate. He replied that the Lambeth Conference findings were only of an advisory character, and that there could be no change in practice until the different Churches composing the Anglican communion had each had an opportunity

---

[1] *Conference of Bishops of the Anglican Communion*, 1920, pp. 26-29.

of considering the Lambeth proposals and carrying through any legislation in relation to them which might seem wise. Accordingly the *status quo* in the Church of England was unaltered.

The committee decided that it must await action by the Church of England, and in the meantime it would maintain the interdenominational position, but it would do what it could to promote study, thought and discussion on the subject of reunion.

As far as the Swanwick conferences were concerned it was decided to continue the practice of asking the senior secretary among the Church of England secretaries and the senior secretary among the Free Church secretaries to make such arrangements for Communion services as would be approved by the authorities of each Church or group of Churches respectively. The committee thought it desirable " that there should be arrangements for members of the Church of England, the Free Churches, the Orthodox Churches and the Church of Rome." I pointed out that it was seldom practicable to arrange for the Liturgy of the Orthodox Church, but that arrangements were always made for members of the other Churches.

The General Committee decided that in the summer conference programme the arrangements for Sunday should be announced under a special heading, and that the exact wording to be used in announcing each service should be decided by the vicar of the parish, the local Roman Catholic authority and the representatives of the Free Churches. And it drafted the following statement which it decided should appear in future on the programmes of its conferences :

Questions of ecclesiastical organization or Church function being equally outside the province of the Student Christian Movement, it does not itself arrange Communion services, or other Church services. It is, however, ready to give opportunity for and to announce such services. While ardently desiring unity, and anxious to promote unity, the Movement recognizes that the way to unity must be found by the Churches. It counsels its members to work steadily and loyally to that end in the Churches to which they belong.

This statement was used from 1921 until 1932, when it was superseded by another statement.

There was a good deal of dissatisfaction in the colleges with what some considered the unduly conservative attitude of the General Committee, and I was asked to write a paper in *The Student Movement* explaining how the Movement had arrived at its interdenominational position. As the last paragraph of the article was a careful statement of the General Committee's attitude at this time, I reproduce it :

There are a certain number of members of the Student Movement who would like to see the General Committee of the Movement arranging a joint Communion service. The General Committee, however, while it ardently desires unity between the Churches, and wishes to do everything it can to promote unity, is not in a position to arrange Communion services, since, the Movement not being a Church, these are outside its province. The only bodies who can arrange Communion services are the Churches, and until the Churches find a way of unity, or agree to recognize one another, and to enter into communion on a wider scale than is the case at present, their disunion will continue to be a painful fact to be reckoned with at Swanwick.

The General Committee does not feel that to take to itself the functions of a Church and to arrange a united Communion service at Swanwick would be of any real service to the cause of unity; and it further recognizes that to take this step would be to turn its back upon the interdenominational policy upon which it has built up its work and its relation to the Churches during the last twenty years. It is convinced that if such a reversal of policy were to take place, it should not be done by the expedient of holding a joint Communion service at Swanwick, but should only be the result of the considered decision of the Movement to enter upon a new path.

The General Committee believes that the work of the Movement is steadily promoting the spirit of unity, and hopes that all members of the Student Movement will work

for unity in their own Churches. It cannot hope to see
within the next few years representatives of all the Churches
joining in a Communion service at Swanwick—the Roman
and Eastern Churches are likely to move slowly in a matter
of this kind—but what it does long to see is a movement
which will place members of the Church of England, the
Presbyterian and Free Churches, in a position to meet
together round the Table of the Lord at Swanwick. This
is an end for which the majority of the members of the
British Movement are in a position to work, but the end
is to be achieved, not by asking the General Committee
of the Student Movement to take action outside its province, but by seeking to move the Churches.[1]

The General Committee was asked in 1922 by
Southampton University College Christian Union and
also by Sheffield University Christian Union to arrange
a Communion service for all at Swanwick, and in 1926
Liverpool University Christian Union asked the General
Committee to change the policy of the Movement
and arrange a Communion service for members of all
Churches at the summer conference. On receipt of
each request the General Committee—with an almost
entirely different membership on each occasion—debated
the subject but reaffirmed its interdenominational position as before.

The meeting of the General Committee of the Federation at Nyborg Strand, Denmark, in the summer of 1926,
was the occasion of prolonged consideration of its
position as an Interconfessional Movement. But before
I say what was decided, some definition of terms is
necessary.

The word "interdenominational," although adopted
from our Movement by the Continent, has come to have
an altered meaning outside Great Britain. It is used to
describe relationships between members of Protestant
Churches only. Interconfessional is used to describe
relations between members of Protestant, Orthodox and
Roman Catholic Churches.

[1] *The Student Movement*, art.: "The Student Movement and
the Eucharist," Tissington Tatlow, vol. xxiii. p. 139.

We met for a fortnight at Nyborg, and among others a " Commission on Interconfessionalism " was appointed. I was chairman of it and Mlle. Susanne Bidgrain, the able Frenchwoman who was for many years one of the secretaries of the Federation and is a trained theologian, was secretary.   There were twenty-five other members ; we represented about seventeen nationalities, and included Slav, Teuton, Anglo-Saxon, Negro and Oriental.   The Anglican, Orthodox, Roman Catholic, Lutheran, Calvinist and various Protestant Evangelical Churches were all represented in our Commission, which met day after day. We used French, German and English.   How much explaining of national background it all required, what an immense amount of educating of one another was accomplished through the hours of talk !   One had the impression of immense variety in experience and out-look, considerable intellectual ability, deep conviction, together with an intense desire on the part of each to understand the point of view of other people and to conserve the contribution of his own heritage.   The differences of culture, with all the complex elements that go to make up a culture, were so great that to understand one another sufficiently to think corporately and suggest a line of action to the Federation was no easy matter.   And yet, with all the differences, we had from first to last a sense of spiritual unity ; in spite of all our differences we were indubitably one in Christ.

We hammered out two documents which, after discussion and revision, were adopted by the General Committee of the Federation.   The first was a statement which set forth the position of the Federation in relation to the Christian Church.

The World's Student Christian Federation in its con-stituent Movements welcomes members of all Christian communions as well as Christian students who do not belong to any communion.   It suffers under the strife which tears the Christian Church and accepts humbly its share of the burden of division ; it cannot adopt an attitude of superiority or indifference to the fact of separation.

The Federation bears grateful witness to God's gift of fellowship in Christ. It knows that its common life is enriched by calling upon all its members to share with one another the spiritual treasures of their Church.

Accepting the task which the gift of this fellowship implies, it asks God to use it to help to prepare the way for unity by the practice of love in such ways as are according to His Holy will. It knows that such obedience to God's will involves struggle and suffering.

The Federation affirms its invincible hope that the day will come when the prayer of our Lord will be fulfilled, " *Ut omnes unum sint.*"

The second statement dealt with the attitude of the Federation to confessional groups. The subject was raised by the representatives of Student Movements in countries where most of the students were members of one of the Orthodox Churches. A leading part in the discussion was taken by members of the Russian Orthodox Church, who held that it was impossible for Orthodox to find spiritual satisfaction in a Student Movement or make their contribution to it as individuals. They must come in as members of the Orthodox Church, living their spiritual life in the Movement in the Church. They begged, therefore, that confessional groups be recognized by the Federation—groups inside the Student Movement composed of members of the Orthodox Church living a full church life, including the Liturgy and ministrations of Orthodox clergy.

The decision reached at Nyborg made this possible, and has worked out extremely well. I have seen much of the Russian students and clergy who have been exiled as a result of the Bolshevist revolution, and while they have developed their Student Christian Movement on their own lines, there has been nothing exclusive about them. They have been eager to learn from non-Orthodox. They have adopted Bible and doctrinal study circle methods and a host of ideas and methods dealing with social service which were novel to them at first. They have been a fine spiritual influence in the Federation, and ready to hold out the right hand of

Christian fellowship to other Christian fellow students, and this not simply to members of the Church of England, with whom they have more in common than with some, but also to members of non-Episcopal Churches.

The decision to admit confessional groups affected, of course, not only the Russians, but other Orthodox, especially student members of the Greek, Bulgarian and Roumanian Churches.

It was not an easy decision for the committee of the Federation to make. The Student Movement had brought us so much enrichment as a result of its inter-confessional fellowship, and was doing so much to unite Christian students and prepare the way for a reunited Church that we were anxious not to take any step which would run the risk of arresting this process. Also, we did not want to see excluded from the fellowship of the Movement any students who, though studying in a country predominantly Orthodox, they were members of a non-Orthodox Church.

The debate was a long and earnest one before we reached a decision, but the Orthodox convinced us in the end not only by their arguments, but by their fine Christian spirit. The resolution passed unanimously was in this form :

> The World's Student Christian Federation, while fully reaffirming its interconfessional principle, and re-emphasiz-ing the need of maintaining locally interconfessional groups, should recognize the existence and approve the formation of confessional groups, and seek to enter into relationship with them, whether as integral parts of a National Move-ment, or in some looser attachment to it. In so doing, it should make it absolutely clear, both in principle and in particular cases, that its aim is to encourage œcumenism, and not to foster an exclusive confessionalism. One of the motives determining this action is the belief that by this means the spiritual riches of a particular confession can be brought into the common life in a different way from that which is attained by individual membership only.

> Recognizing that such a general pronouncement cannot

be of adequate guidance in all particular cases, the staff of the World's Student Christian Federation should ask the National Movements to consult with them whenever such questions arise. By this means the former will be kept in touch with the course of events, and the latter will have the advantage of any experience already gained.

The Nyborg meeting resulted in a friendship between our Movement and the Russian Student Christian Movement in Emigration which has flourished ever since. Nicolas Zernov, one of the Russian students at the Russian Orthodox Church Academy at Paris, and Amy Buller suggested to the other Russian and British members of the committee that we should ask our respective Movements to arrange a conference between Church of England members of the Student Christian Movement in Great Britain and members of the Russian Student Christian Movement in Emigration. Our General Committee recognized that this was an opportunity to act in harmony with the intention of the Nyborg resolution on interconfessionalism, and gladly gave their approval, guaranteeing financial help and appointing representatives on a joint committee of English and Russians to arrange the conference.

The Russians wanted to meet in England and we were glad to have them. It was convenient to choose a place not far from London, and we wanted to have at least one service in a cathedral, so one day Miss Fairfield, Miss Xenia Braikevitch, a member of the Russian Orthodox Church who is on the staff at Annandale, and I motored out to St Albans to take tea with the Bishop of St Albans and discuss the project with him. The result was that we booked the Diocesan Retreat House, with the approval of the Bishop, whose sympathy and help was much appreciated by both Russians and English. He celebrated one morning when we attended Holy Communion in the Cathedral.

The conference met from January 11th to 15th 1927. Its leaders were Bishop Gore, Father Sergius Boulgakov and Professor Besobrazov. A dozen Russian students came from Paris and half a dozen from London. There were twenty-five British students from London, Oxford, Cambridge, Mirfield, Kelham and Cuddesdon, with half a dozen Student Movement secretaries and the same number of senior friends.

Each day began alternately with a celebration of Holy Communion for the Anglicans, or the Liturgy for the Russians, but with the whole conference present on each occasion. The rest of the day was devoted to lectures, talks and discussions, closing with prayers in chapel led alternatively by a Russian or an Englishman.

The programme was planned to help Russians and English to learn what each group believed about the Church and sacraments, and the communion of saints.

The two groups of students met in great ignorance about one another. Most of the English students knew nothing about the Orthodox Church and had never known personally a member of it. The same thing was true of the Russians. Theologically we found we had a great deal in common and some big differences. Spiritually we entered at once with ease and naturalness into close fellowship. One could write a good deal about this : let it suffice to say that we not only liked one another, but we entered into as deep, simple and moving a fellowship with one another in our Lord as I have ever known in all my experience of the Movement.

O. F. Clarke, the S.C.M. secretary at Oxford University, was chairman of the conference. Writing about it he said :

> It was very wonderful to realize how much we shared in common, both in thought and worship . . . but to me the greatest experience of all was something which was entirely unexpected on my part. . . . In England both the mystical and institutional elements (in religion) are insufficiently prized by the majority. Our religion is sternly moral and extremely individualistic in its expression. In our Russian brethren, on the other hand, we found a richness and a vividness of spiritual experience combined with a strong sense of religion which was altogether refreshing

and stimulating. It would not be too much to say that
for some of us the conference opened up a new world. [1]

The Russians were as deeply moved. " It seemed,"
wrote Sonia Zernov, " that the light of Christ's Truth
shone on our path. We, all of us—Children of God—
were building up a way to our common Father, laying
a common track, laying it down in love, in quiet, in
prayer."

Our senior friends present felt about the conference
as did the rest of us. The Rev. J. B. Seaton, Principal
of Cuddesdon College,[2] wrote afterwards :

It is impossible to conclude . . . without expressing
gratitude to Almighty God for the blessing granted to those
who took part in the conference, for the friendships made,
for the better understanding of one another's different
characteristics, for the vision of their blending in a truly
Catholic Church, and for the hopes of such reunion as may
make our full intercommunion possible.

At the second Anglo-Russian Conference, when the
subject was " The Kingdom of God," The Fellowship
of St Alban and St Sergius was founded, the object of
which is to maintain the fellowship which has been
realized at the conferences, especially by prayer, to
promote the exchange of students between Paris and
England, issue a quarterly journal and arrange groups
in England and on the Continent for the continued
study of the two Christian traditions represented in the
Fellowship. It has over three hundred members. The
Bishop of Truro (Dr Frere) is its president. It observes
St Sergius Day (18th July) as a festival on which special
prayer is made for the work of the Fellowship in the
cause of Christian unity.

The Fellowship manages its affairs independently of
the Student Movement, but the Movement continues

[1] *The Student Movement*, art. : " Some Impressions of the
Orthodox and Anglican Conference at St Albans," O. F. Clarke,
vol. xxix. p. 137.
[2] Afterwards Bishop of Wakefield.

to recognize responsibility for the conference, which has become an annual event.

In 1929 the conference was held after Easter at High Leigh. There were one hundred delegates present, and Holy Eucharist was the chief subject.

Arising out of this conference many felt that " Holiness " would be the best subject for the next meeting, so that when the conference assembled at High Leigh in 1930 this formed the main theme of the discussions. In one respect at least this conference was unique, as it was visited by both the Metropolitan Eulogius and the Archbishop of Canterbury (Dr Lang) as an expression of their interest and sympathy.

A few months later the Lambeth Conference met, and its report made us aware of the advance in understanding between the leaders of the Anglican and Orthodox Churches. None regretted more than the leaders of the Student Movement that the Russian Orthodox Church was not represented when Orthodox Church representatives were received at Lambeth. The effect of the Lambeth discussions on the Fellowship was general agreement that " The Church " must be the subject of the conference in April 1931.

The sixth conference was held at Whitelands College, Putney, from March 30th to April 4th 1932, one hundred and twenty persons being present. The Russians have always asked that a few non-Anglicans should be included among the British, and several such have been appreciative members of the conference. Mr Robert T. S. Millar, a member of the Theological College Department Committee, describing the 1932 conference, wrote :

> Into the atmosphere of catholicity engendered it was something rather rich and strange for a sober Scots Presbyterian to be thrown—strange at first, but an experience than which I have known few richer. The devotional spirit was such as I have scarcely seen equalled ; while the depth and sincerity of the testimony to the Christian gospel borne by those other branches of the Church forced me to

realize the power that understanding of alien traditions would have in effecting reunion.[1]

The latest development in connection with our Anglo-Russian relationship was the appointment of Dr Nicolas Zernov, in September 1932, to the staff of the Student Christian Movement, his services being shared with the World's Student Christian Federation and the Fellowship of St Alban and St Sergius.

Nicolas Zernov was the Russian representative at Nyborg in 1926 with whom we first discussed relationships. He was then a student in Paris, later he went to Oxford University, where he took his doctorate in the summer of 1932, and, largely upon the initiative of the Bishop of Truro (Dr Frere), he was appointed to visit the universities and colleges in Great Britain and promote among students knowledge of and friendship for the Orthodox Church. He was received everywhere with sympathy and interest, and has done much to interpret the Holy Orthodox Church to students.

In 1933 the Anglo-Russian Conference took " The Church and the World " as its subject, and 125 students —Russian and English—with a group of Russian and English theologians, considered it from different aspects. For the first time the Conference was followed from June 27th to 29th by a gathering of sixty-one members of the Fellowship of St Alban and St Sergius. The outstanding figure was Father Sergius Boulgakov who, had by now become a much loved and trusted friend of all in the Fellowship.

This annual meeting of English and Russian Churchmen maintains a high level. Its educational and spiritual value to both the Russian Orthodox Church and the Church of England is considerable. It is raising up a body of young men and women who know and understand one another, and who set a high value on this contact between the two great Christian traditions which they represent. And Free Church men are

[1] *The Student Movement*, art.: " The Anglo-Russian Students' Conference," R. T. S. Millar, vol. xxxiv. p. 207.

3 E

not excluded, a few such have always been present, and the Fellowship decided at its 1933 meeting to give them a regular place within it.

Turning back a little, it should be recorded that the Student Movement took a keen interest in the World Conference on Faith and Order held at Lausanne 1927. The Student Movement had its share in preparing the way for this conference. It was an old Student Movement member, Bishop C. H. Brent, who returned to the United States of America from the World Missionary Conference, Edinburgh 1910, convinced that questions of Faith and Order which had been excluded at it should be the subject of a world conference of the Churches. Bishop Brent moved the Protestant Episcopal Church in the United States of America to take the lead in promoting the gathering, for which preparation began in 1912, and which issued in the World Conference on Faith and Order, Lausanne 1927.

As leadership of one of the seven sections into which the conference was divided was entrusted to me—that on " The Church's Common Confession of Faith "—I saw the conference from the inside. The leaders of the sections, with a few others, constituted a small central committee which guided the conference. The majority on this committee were old Student Movement men.

I met at the Lausanne Conference old Student Movement leaders from England, Ireland, Scotland, India, China, Russia, Hungary, Finland, Norway, Sweden, Denmark, France, Germany, Switzerland, Australia and the United States of America. Among them were archbishops, bishops, priests, ministers and professors, and they represented Anglican, Orthodox, Lutheran, Presbyterian, Congregational, Methodist and Baptist Churches, also the Society of Friends. I met none who were not competent and helpful members of the conference.

On the last day Canon H. N. Bate,[1] who was secretary

---

[1] Afterwards Dean of York.

of the Programme Committee, came to me and said :
" You are the proper people to publish the Report.
You are in this thing all over the world," so we pub-
lished the popular report written by Canon E. S. Woods,
Lausanne 1927, and the official *Report of the World
Conference on Faith and Order, Lausanne,* 1927, edited by
Canon Bate.

As a member of the Continuation Committee of the
Conference I was asked in 1930 to bring a Youth group
to the meeting of the Continuation Committee. At
this and the succeeding meeting a group of ten and
then fifteen students from almost as many countries
have shared in the Continuation Committee Conference,
and carried information and keenness for the Faith and
Order Movement back to their colleges. I mention
this as though invitations to join the Youth group have
been given in various quarters, it is the Student Christian
Movements of Europe who have provided most of the
students who have come.

Prior to the quadrennial conference at Liverpool,
1929, a group of students in the Movement at Liverpool
University asked the General Committee to request
the Bishop of Liverpool to arrange a united Communion
service for the members of the quadrennial conference.
The General Committee replied that the arranging of
services of the Church was not the function of the
Student Movement, that for many years the practice of
the General Committee at the time of its conferences
had been to announce from its platform all Church
services that were arranged for members of a conference, that this practice would be followed at Liverpool,
and that it did not propose to approach the Bishop of
Liverpool on the subject.

The Bishop of Liverpool, in the course of an address
of welcome to the conference, however, announced
that he had arranged a special celebration of Holy
Communion in the Cathedral on one morning of the
conference, and invited members of the conference, of
whatever Church, to take part.

The majority of those who were lodged so that it was possible for them to attend the service accepted the invitation. A certain number of Anglo-Catholic members of the Movement disapproved of the action of the Bishop, and some spoke as if the Student Christian Movement was responsible for it. The Student Movement made no statement on the subject, as it was not for it to say whether the Bishop was right or wrong in his action ; the feeling amongst us, however, was that any ordinarily intelligent person had no ground for being other than aware that the Student Movement had no responsibility for the service. It would be unfair to suggest that all Anglo-Catholics regarded the Movement as responsible ; the majority of them, while disturbed by the service, recognized that the Bishop was responsible for it and not the Movement. Anglican students generally appreciated the holding of the service and took part in it.

Concerning Communion services generally, there have been a large number of people, both inside and outside the Movement, who for the last dozen years have kept up continual pressure upon the General Committee to arrange joint Communion services for Anglicans and Free Churchmen. They take the view that the Student Movement ought to give a lead in this matter, and that if it were courageous enough to have joint Communion services it would break down a tradition of exclusiveness which they deplore. The matter has not gone by default in Student Movement circles, and has been discussed again and again on the General Committee. But the Movement has always decided to reaffirm its extra-ecclesiastical and interdenominational position.

The General Committee appointed a commission in 1930 to advise it how it might better carry out that part of its Aim and Basis which declares its members " desire to enter into that fellowship of worship, thought and service which is the heritage of the Christian Church."

This body held a number of meetings but never came

to grips with the main question. It was constantly deflected by discussions bearing on the issues for and against intercommunion and ways in which the Movement might hold the attention of its members to the seriousness of the divided state of the Christian Church. It spent some time on the question of the interdenominational position of the Movement, and offered a revised statement on the subject to the General Committee to take the place of a memorandum prepared in 1911 [1] and issued each year since to Student Movement secretaries for their guidance.

The document, after some revision, was adopted by the General Committee. It is as follows :

THE INTERDENOMINATIONAL POSITION OF THE S.C.M.

BEING PART OF THE WIDER QUESTION OF THE RELATION OF THE MOVEMENT TO THE CHRISTIAN CHURCH

This statement was prepared by a special Commission, and adopted by the General Committee, April 1932. It brings up to date the statement of the Movement's position, the latest previous statement having been issued in 1911.

1. DEFINITION.

The Student Christian Movement is an interdenominational body which includes in its membership those who belong to different communions of the Christian Church, and those who do not belong to any communion. One of the purposes of the Movement, as expressed in its Aim and Basis, is to develop in students the " desire to enter into that fellowship of worship, thought and service which is the heritage of the Christian Church." The policy of the Movement, so long as the Church is divided into a number of separate communions, is to help students to see their loyalty to their own communions in the setting of a wider vision and experience of the Church Catholic and of its task in the world.

2. INTERDENOMINATIONALISM AND UNITY.

" Interdenominationalism " is therefore to be distinguished as a policy from what is commonly known as

[1] See pp. 399-404.

" undenominationalism," namely, the attainment of a measure of unity by the omission of any views distinctive of different denominations. The S.C.M., however, as an interdenominational society, is not concerned to encourage its members merely to emphasize their differences, still less to lead them to accept the continuance of these differences in their present form as either right or inevitable. The Movement desires and looks forward to the effective visible unity of the Church of Christ. It invites its members to show their loyalty to the Church Catholic in their loyalty to their own branch of it, because only so can the fruits of the period of division be gathered, and an ultimate unity be reached, which shall be the richer by the experience as well as the pain of division. The Movement therefore holds to its interdenominational position, not regretfully as an inevitable limitation upon its zeal for unity, but in faith and hope, believing it to be the surest way towards the achievement of real unity in the Church.

3. THE SPIRIT OF AN INTERDENOMINATIONAL FELLOWSHIP.

It is characteristic of the Movement that some of its members acknowledge first their loyalty to one communion of the Christian Church and only secondly to the Movement ; while others put first their loyalty to the Movement and its purposes as set forth in the Aim and Basis, and are less clear concerning their relation to any one of the organized branches of the Christian Church. Neither of these loyalties should be minimized.

Within the fellowship of the Movement the members of communions which have long suffered division and those who are members of no communion are given opportunity of meeting. This should involve for members of the Movement a readiness to learn from those of different traditions and a willingness to search out the central truths and convictions in which they are at one. It means also that they should be eager to share to the limit of their power the distinctive treasures of their heritage.

With regard to differences that are real there must be the recognition that a Movement such as the S.C.M. is only possible if certain limitations are imposed. These limitations will change, but for each generation they exist and must be loyally accepted. They arise in relation to the advocacy of practices and beliefs which one group regards as essential to the Christian life, but upon which another group within the Movement holds different convictions or puts different interpretations. Such differences must in some degree limit the range of our common life and action.

It is essential that the members of the Movement should be able to talk freely, and make well-considered experiments, concerning these matters of difference, but in all such discussions and action fairness of spirit will dictate a forbearance in advocacy and an indication of other views, especially when there is disparity in age and knowledge.

Some people may discover, when they are brought into touch with other communions, that they ought to change their communion ; but, if the Movement is to live as an interdenominational fellowship, proselytizing is ruled out.

The fact that members have entered a Movement, which makes possible the meeting of Christian communions still divided, means that they are done with contempt of one another, willing to take their share in the reproach of division, and believe that division is to be overcome, though the form of a unified Church may not yet be clear.

4. The Service of Holy Communion.

This service is a sacrament of the Christian Church. The Student Christian Movement is not a branch of the Church, though its fellowship is in a particular sense part of the life of the Church. It therefore follows that it is not permissible for the Movement to hold services of Holy Communion. It is, however, its privilege to give facilities to ministers and clergy of any branch of the Church for the announcement and arrangement of such services.

If the officiating minister or priest wishes to extend an invitation to members of other denominations, it is still fitting for the Movement to give these facilities, but in such an event a new situation arises with regard to the nature of any announcement. A service of open Communion presupposes a certain theory of Church order, and in this matter there are wide differences of opinion within the Church. The Movement ardently desires unity and seeks in study and practice to promote it, as is evidenced by the richness of its fellowship both in this country and in the whole world through its affiliation to the World's Student Christian Federation. This interdenominational and interconfessional character of the Movement, however, implies the desire to encourage the growth in churchmanship of the individual member. In the event, therefore, of a service of open Communion being announced there should be added the following statement :—

1. That no member of the Movement is under any obligation to communicate against the dictates of his conscience, or the custom of his church. In this connection it should be remembered that, according to the general usage of the Anglican Church, and the rule of the Roman and Orthodox Churches, their members should receive Communion only from ministers of their own church.

2. That any who feel hesitant may very properly attend without communicating.

The Committee appended to their statement the two statements [1] adopted by the Federation at the Nyborg meeting of its General Committee.

The attention of members of the Movement has been attracted by several happenings in Church life in the last few years. The act of union whereby the United Free Church of Scotland and the Church of Scotland became one Church in October 1929 was observed with thankfulness in Student Movement circles. In an address presented at the Union by Robert Mackie on behalf of the Movement, gratitude was expressed for the help received during forty years from the leaders of the two great Scottish Churches. The address concluded :

This great act of union will encourage and inspire the Student Christian Movement, and the prayer of its members is that God may greatly bless the Church of Scotland for the Christian good of the land, and especially of her four ancient universities and many colleges.

The letter of reply, conveying the thanks of the Church, is one of the Movement's treasures, framed and hung on the walls at Annandale.

The movement working towards a united Church in South India is one in which some of the prominent figures are old members of the Indian, British and American Student Movements, and there was general

[1] See p. 780.

satisfaction when both the Wesleyan Conference and the Lambeth Conference, 1930, expressed approval of the movement.

The Lambeth Conference Report contained several friendly references to the Student Movement, and the report on youth and its vocation said :

> In view of the very special and international work which the Student Christian Movement is doing to present to the students of the world the claims of Christ, and to encourage the serious study of the Faith, we believe that it has a claim upon all the help which the Church can give.

There has been much speculation as to whether one of the Lambeth resolutions [1] on the subject of Holy Communion would lead to a change in policy on the part of the Church of England which would make it possible for Anglicans and Free Churchmen to communicate together at Student Movement conferences. The resolution was to the effect that bishops of the Anglican communion should exercise their discretion in giving permission for baptized communicants and members of churches not in communion with the Anglican Church to communicate in Anglican churches, and *vice versa*, " when the ministrations of their own Church are not available, or in other special or temporary circumstances."

The majority of Anglicans and Free Churchmen in the Movement hope that the passing of this resolution will ultimately make united Communion on special occasions possible. A minority think it would retard the cause of reunion, and for this and more theological reasons is undesirable.

The union which resulted in the Methodist Church has been another movement towards reunion which has been received with thankfulness in the Movement. A resolution passed at the business meeting at Swanwick expressed " our joy at the union which is now being effected. . . . We trust that this union is but a step

---

[1] *Lambeth Conference*, 1930, p. 52.

towards that reunion of all Christendom, the delayed coming of which is a sin before God and a cause of weakness before the world."

We now watch with sympathy the efforts, which are of a promising character, to promote unity among the Free Churches in England.

The Movement has raised up many men in all the denominations devoted to the cause of reunion. There is a variety of points of view amongst us on many of the issues involved, but it is of great significance that a unanimous vote should have been accorded to the Movement's latest official statement bearing on unity (see page 790), which states that " The Movement desires and looks forward to the effective visible unity of the Church of Christ." A resolution looking forward to " effective visible unity " would not have secured a unanimous vote on the General Committee even a few years ago.

The interest in reunion has gradually filtered through from the leadership and the theological colleges into the life of the Movement as a whole. The business meeting at Swanwick in July 1932 gave much time to the subject, and a resolution emanating from the Movement in Manchester University, instructing the General Committee to suggest to the colleges " lines along which further study of the issues involved may most profitably proceed," was evidently much to the mind of the members, who passed it unanimously. The resolution committed the Movement to the statement that reunion is " one of the most pressing problems of the day," as truly it is.

CHAPTER XLI

THEOLOGICAL COLLEGES AND THEN SCHOOLBOYS!

THERE are nearly eighty theological colleges in the British Isles and they differ widely from one another. The Presbyterian and Free Church colleges aim at making men theologians and preachers, and succeed with a good many of their students. In spite of their serving different churches, the training given in them is remarkably homogeneous. The Church of England colleges are more mixed in character. Some are Anglo-Catholic, some Evangelical, and others would prefer to be described simply as Church colleges; few give a thorough theological education. Most of them prepare men for ordination along rather simple, pastoral and devotional lines. There are several which give a careful preparation for ordination to men who have learnt theology at the university. The long courses of the Presbyterian and Free Church colleges tend to make men rather professional, and the preaching which they undertake almost every Sunday, while it helps some men, spoils others, especially if they become interested in trying to get engagements from churches which pay good fees. It is a testing business continuing as a theological student for several years, and all but the best men find it hard not to become " stale."

The Student Movement has to walk delicately. A Student Movement secretary can say a good deal of what he thinks to most students, but it is not easy to do so in a theological college. There are some theological students who want to keep up appearances and do not want the S.C.M. to get behind those appearances to reality ; there are those who are parochial in outlook and prefer to remain so.   The best work of the Movement is done when it can secure the affection of a few good men in a college.   These men absorb whatever it has of value to give and mediate it to the rest of the college.

In the one-year-course Anglican colleges a delegation to the summer conference, the participation of a few men in an occasional retreat-conference with non-Anglicans and an occasional study circle, usually on missionary or social topics, is a common programme in connection with the Movement.   The life of the college may benefit greatly through what some of the men get in this way, and if the college is keen the Movement may have a regular place in its devotions.

In the Presbyterian and Free Church colleges—where the course is longer than in all except a few of the Anglican colleges—the same help is rendered, and sometimes a considerable amount of group-study of doctrinal, social, missionary topics is undertaken.   Participation by students in campaigns increases and decreases from time to time, but taking any decade of the Movement's history the number of men is large who have been on evangelistic or missionary missions in the vacation under the auspices of the Movement or been stirred by the Movement to go on campaigns, such as the World Call of the Church of England.

The Movement has met with much friendship from the members of staff of the theological colleges of the different denominations.   The great majority value the contact with students of all kinds and the world outlook of the Movement.   They frequently assist their students to attend the Student Movement's conferences.

The war brought the work of the Movement in theological colleges to a complete standstill.   The annual business meeting of the Theological College Department decided, on July 21st, 1917, that as most of the theological colleges were closed and the Department had no secretary, a full committee should not be elected, but that one representative each of the Church of

England, Free Church and Presbyterian colleges should be chosen to represent theological interests on the General Committee. Those appointed were : L. W. Grensted,[1] Manchester University ; E. B. Holtby, Hartley College, Manchester ; W. E. Blackburn, United Free Church College, Glasgow.

The next meeting held under the auspices of the Department was not until July 25th 1919, when R. D. Whitehorn, J. B. Middlebrook, W. P. Young, R. W. Howard, Owen Griffith, L. S. Hunter, F. A. Cockin, Hugh Martin, William Paton, A. Walker and T. Tatlow met and elected R. D. Whitehorn, Westminster College, Cambridge, as chairman of the Department, and R. D. Whitehorn, J. B. Middlebrook, R. W. Howard as representatives of the Theological Department Committee on the General Committee. A reconstructed committee for the Department met on September 20th and 21st 1919, and the General Secretary reported that forty-four theological colleges out of the sixty-three colleges associated with the Movement before the war had appointed Student Christian Movement representatives and registered their names with headquarters. All the colleges were told of the revival of the Department now that the war was over.

One of the first acts of the revived Theological College Department Committee, startling to those of us who remembered the general attitude on all questions relating to the women's movement of theological students before the war, was the application and ready admission to the Department of two women's colleges, Carey Hall, Selly Oak, and St Michael's College, Wantage. These colleges were admitted without a sense of anything unusual being done.

The revival of the work of the Movement after the war was longer delayed in the theological colleges than in the universities. There were a number of old Student Movement men who returned to them from the

[1] Afterwards Canon L. W. Grensted, Oriel Professor of the Christian Religion, Oxford University.

army, and many of these made immediate contact with the Movement. The Rev. W. P. Young, D.C.M., M.C., a former member of the Movement in Edinburgh University, who had been for a few years a missionary in Africa and then seen war service, first as combatant and afterwards as chaplain, became travelling secretary in theological colleges in the summer of 1919. Two hundred and thirty-five theological students came to the Swanwick Conferences the following summer, and it looked as if all would be well. The ex-service theologicals were a live-minded body of men, and discussions as to the Christian message and its presentation were endless and keen. Crusades were planned by the students of the United Free Church of Scotland (see p. 646) and their example followed elsewhere. A vivid interest was taken in young people's work in the Church. Here, again, Scotland was to the fore. In all this Student Movement men were leaders.

It was decided to make the Constitution of the Theological College Department more democratic by giving every Union of theological colleges the right to elect representatives to the controlling committee of the Department. To make the arrangement orderly, the committee decided to recognize as properly constituted Unions those at Edinburgh, Cambridge, Bristol, Leeds, London and Manchester—each consisted of several colleges with a committee responsible for a joint programme. The change was made in July 1921. The arrangement was given up in 1927, as it was found the Unions chose a much less effective committee than did the outgoing Theological College Department Committee acting largely on the advice of its travelling secretary. The committee nominated by the Department had to be elected at its business meeting at Swanwick, but this was invariably done without any changes being made.

We thought all was well in 1921 and it seemed the right time to call another Theological Dons' Conference, so after consultation with the heads of a number of

" SWANWICK "

theological colleges we issued an invitation to those engaged in theological training in the different Churches to come and review "the whole question of theological training in the light of modern needs of evangelism."

The conference was held at Newnham College, Cambridge, from June 28th to July 1st 1921. The Rev. Alexander Martin, Principal of New College, Edinburgh, was the chairman. The subjects dealt with were the supply and training of men, the various functions of the minister—education, social service, missionary—and his intellectual and spiritual preparation. The Revs. A. C. Headlam,[1] Wheeler Robinson, W. B. Selbie, H. E. Wynn, Owen Prys, Bernard Horner, A. E. Garvie, W. F. Lofthouse, R. T. Howard and P. Carnegie Simpson were among the appointed speakers. Over sixty men from forty-four theological colleges and theological faculties in the universities, with a few S.C.M. secretaries, took part.

The most lively discussion was when we discussed whether sociology should or should not be part of the curriculum of a theological college. Some thought "yes," and some "no." The men appreciated meeting one another. I don't think the conference had any practical outcome.

As to the work of the Movement in relation to theological students, the promise of these days was not fulfilled. The ex-service men soon finished their courses. The men who came after them were much less enterprising, and because of the economic depression they were poor. This meant they could not afford to come to the Movement's conferences. The number of theological students attending Swanwick had fallen to ninety-seven in 1924. We could not find a successor to W. P. Young who, after serving from 1919-20, had become one of the Movement's Scottish secretaries.

In 1921 George Dryburgh, also a Scotsman, made a gallant start, but his health broke down and again the

[1] Afterwards Bishop of Gloucester.

Movement could not find a suitable man, so that when W. S. A. Robertson started work in 1924 he found that most of the theological colleges knew very little about the Student Movement, and even the students dutifully elected to the Theological College Department Committee by the Theological Unions wanted to know of what use the Movement was to theological students. The brightest spot in the picture was the work of H. A. Mess. As social study secretary he had more than enough to do in the universities, but he saw the importance of the theological student in relation to society and the gospel and visited and stirred a number of these colleges. R. O. Hall was by now at work as missionary secretary, and although he was not able to give as much time to the theological colleges as Mess, his occasional visits to them were of real value.

Algy Robertson started work in January 1924 and his task was a heavy one. He was a keen Anglo-Catholic, a good speaker and a man of spiritual power. He was on the staff for three and a half years and made a valuable contribution to the life of the Movement as a whole, and did much to help the recovery of the Theological College Department as an effective part of the Movement. The most important event of this period was a conference of theological students at Swanwick, April 12th to 17th 1926.

It was twenty years since the last conference of theological students had been held. This one was prepared and worked for with thoroughness. Miss Fairfield, having much fame as a programme maker, was called in to help by the Theological Department Committee. She got on so well with its members that they made her their secretary, and she had a large share in planning the programme for the conference. A series of studies, mainly in the form of questions, were issued on such subjects as " Belief in God," " The Church," " Worship " and " Communism." Groups were formed to study these in a large number of theological colleges, and the two hundred and forty theological students representing most of the theological colleges in the British Isles, who assembled for the conference, were unusually well prepared.

The speaking at the conference was of a high order and the discussions were a success. A carefully selected group of senior friends, clerical and lay—some of the latter labour men—had been brought to help. After an opening evening on " The Challenge of the Times," the subject for the first day was " Belief in God " ; this concluded with a powerful address from Father Kelly in the evening on " The Reality of God and His Purpose for the World." After an opening address each morning, the conference was divided into discussion groups, and the leaders of these groups reported to the whole conference after tea, when their reports were discussed.

The second day was devoted to " The Presentation of the Christian Gospel." Here is the analysis of the topic as it appeared on the programme :

> Relation of doctrine to life : the need for seeing the great affirmations of the faith as interpretations of God's dealings with human life. Its presentation : the task of reaching the mass of men and women. Does Christianity come out into the open ? Can it present a " programme " which will challenge those presented by avowedly " political " agencies? Special difficulties of the present situation. The conflict between " liberal " and " traditional " tendencies, etc.

Again there was a striking address in the evening, this time by Dr G. G. Kullmann, on " Doctrine and Life."

" Worship " and " The Church in Action " were the subjects for the two remaining days of the conference. Dr W. B. Selbie, Dr R. H. Strachan, Miss Maude Royden, Father Jenks, F. R. Barry, Conrad Noel, Malcolm Spencer and A. G. Pite were at their best. Canon J. B. Seaton acted as an inspiring chaplain to the conference, taking morning and evening prayers. The demand for the speeches in print was so great that they were collected in a small volume.[1] The conference

[1] *Theology and Life.*

brought " a new realization of God, and a new realization of the greatness of the task set before the Christian ministry and of our inadequacy in the face of it."

It was a conference that must still be inspiring the ministry of many who were at it, and it regained for the Student Christian Movement its place in many of the theological colleges.

A second post-war theological conference was held at Swanwick, April 1928, when forty-four colleges sent one hundred and twenty students. It was an effective gathering that served its purpose of helping men to face economic, intellectual, racial and international conditions which militate against religious faith.

Algy Robertson was succeeded by Ambrose Reeves in 1927. Ambrose had become a convinced believer in the value of the Movement when he was an undergraduate at Sidney Sussex College, Cambridge. He interpreted it later to his fellow students at the College of the Resurrection, Mirfield, and also to the General Theological Seminary, New York, when he was sent there as an exchange student. He was a man with a tremendous capacity for work ; a good organizer and a good speaker, he made a valuable secretary. He attended to all the different sides of his work in a way which, if emulated by the rest of the staff of the Movement, would enormously increase its effectiveness, *e.g.* he increased the circulation of *The Student Movement*, raised the contribution of the theological colleges to Finance Week by 90 per cent. and sold £100 worth of S.C.M. books in a year—all incidental to his major work.

He saw the value of regular contact between theological students of the different denominations, and strengthened the theological unions created by the Movement in cities or areas where there are several theological colleges, such as London, Oxford, Cambridge, Bristol, the Midlands, Manchester, Leeds, Bangor, Edinburgh, and encouraged these unions to arrange regional conferences. One year, for example, Anglicans of all kinds met members of various Free Church denominations in conferences on " The Church and Youth " in Scotland, " The Gospel in the Present Age " in Manchester, " The Sacraments " in the North Midlands, " The Ministry " in London and " The Church and Sacraments " in the South of England. Thus two hundred and fifty theological students shared in small conferences where thorough discussion was possible and where enduring friendships were formed. These conferences included members of staff as well as students.

The quadrennial conference at Liverpool, 1929, was attended by two hundred and forty theological students from sixty-five colleges, which means that one in every ten of the entire body of theological students in the British Isles—excluding Roman Catholics—was present. Reeves told us that the conference made a profound impression on the theological students everywhere. He knew what he was talking about for this year he visited fifty-two theological colleges.

Other visitors in the last few years whose presence has been appreciated in theological colleges have been Mr Nikitin, a Russian and a member of the Orthodox Church, who was secretary of the Student Christian Movement in Bulgaria, and Dr Visser 't Hooft, who spoke in many colleges on the theology of Karl Barth, a theologian who has had a greater influence on Continental theological students than any other thinker since the war.

It is a curious thing that the World's Student Christian Federation never held a conference for theological students until the year 1931, when it asked our Movement to organize a small conference for a picked group of theological students.

I felt this conference provided a good opportunity to put into effect the suggestion of the Dean of Canterbury (G. K. A. Bell) made to me when I became an honorary Canon of Canterbury Cathedral in 1926, that some day I should bring a Student Movement Conference to

Canterbury. Bell had become Bishop of Chichester, but the new Dean, the Very Rev. H. R. L. Sheppard, and the Chapter welcomed the suggestion, and fifty theological students, representing fourteen countries, spent a week at St Augustine's College as their guests.

The opening service was in the Cathedral, and the Metropolitical Church of Christ, Canterbury, surely never welcomed a more diverse group of students—Orthodox, Anglican, Old Catholic, Lutheran, Evangelical, Presbyterian, Methodist, Congregational and Baptist. I was invited to conduct the service and several members of the Chapter took part. The members of the conference found it difficult to understand one another when talking theology. But they were mutually concerned about questions of international peace and the unity of the Church, and spiritually deeply at one with one another. Amid all the diversity of race and Church the reality of our unity in Christ received recognition from all, as a reference to the many reports of the conference show.

Another theological students' conference met at Basle the following year, in which we took part.

The Canterbury Conference led to the formation of nine groups of theological students in Great Britain, each in touch with a similar group on the Continent, for the study of international peace and having special reference to disarmament. Another result was to stimulate in British theological students the desire to visit German theological students. In 1931 and 1932 parties under the leadership of Donald Dugard—who worked for a year with Ambrose Reeves and when he left in 1931 became his successor—visited Marburg and Bonn, and met professors and students for the discussion of religious and theological questions.

We must now retrace our steps and think of schoolboys ! The Universities' Camps for Public Schoolboys, which ran a number of camps for over twenty years, dwindled to one camp during the years after 1914. The Movement formed a committee in September 1919 " to consider the relation of the Movement to the schools of the country and to any organization working among schoolboys and to report."

Three months later this committee reported that an informal conference had been called by the Universities' Camps for Public Schoolboys, with representatives of the Student Christian Movement, the Free Church Camps, Canon David [1] of Rugby and Mr W. W. Vaughan of Wellington, to consider the situation.

This conference passed a number of resolutions which asked for more co-operation and co-ordination between the bodies working among schoolboys, and for co-operation on such lines " as might prepare them for ultimate participation in the life and activities of such a movement as the Student Christian Movement."

A committee was formed under the title of the Committee for Schools' Camps and Conferences, with the Rev. Canon E. A. Burroughs [2] as chairman, and the Headmaster of Westminster as vice-chairman. It was, however, on a wider basis than the old Universities' Camps Committee, as the Free Church Camps started by Frank Lenwood some years before, and the Student Movement joined in it. Most people in the three groups were old S.C.M. men. Camps were restarted, and in September 1921 a conference for senior boys was arranged at Oxford.

A Welsh Camp movement was started in 1921 by E. C. H. Jones, an old S.C.M. man from Aberystwyth University College, with Professor C. H. Dodd of Mansfield College as chairman. This has since developed in friendly contact with the Movement.

The committee for Schools' Camps and Conferences was served by S. E. Swann,[3] a Cambridge rowing Blue, but as it only had a share of his time its work did not develop, and Ronald Rees and A. G. Pite, who represented

[1] Afterwards Bishop of Liverpool.
[2] Afterwards Bishop of Ripon.
[3] Archdeacon in Egypt, 1928-32; Vicar of Leighton Buzzard from 1932.

the Movement on it, said it needed a whole-time secretary; so in April 1922 we debated the situation at length, and the Movement decided it ought to undertake work among schoolboys. We had often been asked to start work by schoolmasters, we felt the need of work which would reach boys before they entered the university, and we were constantly reminded that many Movements in the Federation were fed by work among schoolboys, notably the Dutch Student Christian Movement.

When the committee for Schools' Camps and Conferences found that the Student Movement was ready to make itself responsible for work among schoolboys, it handed over its work to the Movement. Ronald D. Rees was appointed convener of a preliminary committee, and J. H. Grummitt of Caius College, Cambridge, already an experienced camp leader, invited to become secretary. "Grum" accepted the invitation, and the following year, 1923, became secretary of " The Schools Department of the Student Christian Movement." The Universities' Camps for Public Schoolboys had by now ceased to function, and it decided to hand over its assets to the Student Movement. These consisted of about £150 and some camp equipment.

The Federation of University Women's "Camps" for Schoolgirls applied for affiliation to the Schools Department of the Movement in December 1923. The leaders of the Movement replied that they had no constitutional means of making such an affiliation, but allotted the Federation two places on the Schools Council which it had formed.

The Federation of University Women's "Camps" for Schoolgirls was started by members of the Student Movement, which had reaped the benefit of its work for many years, some of the best of the Movement's leaders in the women's colleges having received their first impetus towards such work at the schoolgirls' camps. A member of the General Committee has for many years been appointed to sit on the Federation of University Women's " Camps " for Schoolgirls Committee as a liaison officer between the two organizations.

The Schools Department also gave the Welsh Schools Camp Movement two places on the Council. This Council was a very imposing body, with bishops, headmasters and parents on it, but it faded away in time as it had no very definite work to do.

The chief activities of the Schools Department have been camps in the summer and winter sports' parties in Switzerland in the winter, cruising parties on the Broads, golfing and reading parties at Easter, and visits to continental countries. The activities of the Department have been designed not only to provide wholesome and delightful holidays, but " to do much more than that : to introduce boys to a Christian community of their own generation and of those but little senior to them— and this the most Christian home can seldom do—and to connect Christianity with the jolliest of times and the best and friendliest of people."[1]

A number of books have been prepared under the guidance of the Schools Department and published by the Movement.

In 1928 the title of the " Camps " for Schoolboys was changed to "Universities and Schools Camps Club, S.C.M.," and as a result of economic necessity " Grum " retired from the work as a full-time officer. He has, nevertheless, while a master at Ipswich School, and afterwards as a house-master at Epsom College, maintained a varied programme. Holland, Germany, Austria have at different times been included in camps or tours abroad. In 1929 a mixed camp was held at Brigels in Switzerland in conjunction with the schoolgirls organization. There have been gatherings for assistant masters, when the discussion of the presentation of Christianity to boys has been of great interest.

I have no complete list of the schools from which boys have come to attend the various " Camps," but I know

[1] *S.C.M. Report*, 1923-24, p. 38.

that in 1925-26 boys came to camp from the following
schools : Ackworth, Ardingly, Battersea Secondary,
Bedford, Bedford Modern, Bishop's Stortford, Bootham,
Bradfield, Brighton, Bromsgrove, Charterhouse, Chel-
tenham, Christ's Hospital, City of London, City of
Oxford, Clifton, Cranleigh, Dean Close, Dulwich, East-
bourne, Eltham, Eton, Felsted, Fettes, Great Ayton,
Haberdashers, Haileybury, Harrow, Hulme, Ipswich,
King's Canterbury, King's College School, King Edward
VI Birmingham, King Edward VI Southampton,
Kingswood, Lancing, Leighton Park, Leys, Malvern,
Marlborough, Mill Hill, Monkton Combe, Newport
Grammar, Oundle, Radley, Repton, Rossall, Royal
Naval College Dartmouth, Rugby, Sedbergh, Shrews-
bury, Southdown, Stowe, Tonbridge, University College
School, Walsall, Warwick, Wellington, West Ham
Secondary, Westminster, Whitgift and Wolverhampton.

It was only possible to carry on the work with an
honorary secretary, because he knew and was known in
the schools from which boys come. When he was a
full-time officer, Grummitt visited widely and acquired
a large acquaintance among schoolmasters.

All this work has been carried on in the vacations.
From time to time headmasters have asked whether
the Movement would start or affiliate already existing
schoolboy religious societies in their schools. In 1930
it became possible to secure part of the time of E. A.
Willis, at one time a student at the Imperial College of
Science, South Kensington, and for long associated with
the St Paul's School meetings. The public schools with
chapels were asked to make it financially possible for
the Movement to start work for boys in secondary day
schools. There was an excellent response, and Willis
became secretary, and the Schoolboys Christian Association started under the auspices of the Movement in
1931. The Archbishop of York is its president, the vice-
presidents being the Headmasters of Eton, Harrow,
Westminster, Alleyn's, Liverpool College, Mill Hill and
University College School, together with the Rev. M. E.

Aubrey, the Rev. P. B. Clayton, the Rev. H. R. L. Sheppard and the Rev. Leslie Weatherhead.

The aim of the Association is to give boys opportunity for the best religious teaching and influence and the help of Christian fellowship. The decline of church-going has involved the parents of the secondary day schoolboy on a considerable scale, and there are a great number of boys who are under practically no religious influence, either at home or by the church. There are very few churches which provide the kind of fellowship and instruction the secondary schoolboy needs. Willis has started a number of groups and branches in schools, and at Easter, 1933, the General Committee arranged to secure his whole time for the development of the Association.

CHAPTER XLII

THE AIM AND BASIS WITH CONDITION OF MEMBERSHIP AGAIN CHANGED

IN a later chapter an attempt will be made to say something about the life and thought of the Movement from 1925 to the present time—the spring of 1933. But before doing so, a long period of discussion which ended in giving the Movement a new Aim and Basis, and imposed a new condition of admission to the Movement, must be described. Although the change was not effected until the middle of 1929, this is the right place to tell of it as the frame of mind out of which the discussion arose belonged to the immediate post-war period. It is doubtful if students to-day would have asked for the change. They have shown very little interest since 1929 in the Aim and Basis, nor do they discuss the kind of questions that led to a desire for a new Aim and Basis. Parallel with this change in the Aim and Basis were study and discussion which issued in reorganization of the Movement and a change of leadership. This topic may also be treated before turning to the thought, life and other activities of recent years.

When the ex-service generation of students rewrote the Aim and Basis of the Movement after the war, they rewrote it in untechnical language. The alteration was in words not in contents, no doctrinal change being intended. The fact of a change, however, led some to think that the Movement had really altered its theological position, and in order to make it clear that this was not the case, the General Committee at Easter 1922 decided that the position would be made clear if the basis clause from the Federation Constitution—with which its own

Constitution must be in harmony by virtue of its membership of the Federation—was appended to the Aim and
Basis. The result was that after the Aim and Basis (see
p. 628) these words were added :

> This Aim and Basis must be interpreted in harmony with
> the object of the World's Student Christian Federation, of
> which the Movement is a part, namely : " To lead students
> to accept the Christian faith in God—Father, Son and Holy
> Spirit according to the Scriptures, and to live as true
> disciples of Jesus Christ."

This action of the General Committee remained un-
challenged for about three years, but then questionings
arose on the staff and in the colleges. Some of the
leaders were uneasy because of an increasing tendency
not to enrol members in the Christian Unions. Some
warmly defended this policy, declaring that a Christian
Union should offer its programme to all who would
avail themselves of it and that membership did not
matter. Wiser folk, however, realized that this was
bound to have unsatisfactory results. The committee
and officers of every Christian Union are elected annually.
Who would elect in a Union with no definite membership ? The Christian Unions had always stood for a
definite purpose to win students who were uncertain,
indifferent, hostile. Could an amorphous body, with
an indefinite membership, be expected to have a sense
of mission ?

It was a difficult period. The influence of the science
student was predominant. No one seemed to have any
interest in history. Authority of all kinds except that
of natural science was suspected, the authority of the
theologian was held as of little account. Students who
would only listen to first-class scientific authorities when
a scientific subject was under discussion, would listen to
any one's opinions about Christian doctrine. There
was, however, much concern about religion, students
were eager to discuss religious questions and anxious
to promote fellowship based on Christian ideas. But
when it came to the study of Christian truth, they felt

that everything was so uncertain that a religious fellow-ship ought not to have any doctrines. It was a time when those leaders of the Movement who valued philosophy and theology became rather tired of the narrow-minded assumptions of the science student.

It was at this period that some fastened on the Federation basis clause appended to the Aim and Basis, and asked why the Movement wanted to concentrate attention on the doctrine of the Trinity above all other Christian doctrines.

Closer inquiry of the Christian Unions on the subject of membership showed that there was constant misunderstanding in the colleges as to the condition of membership of the Movement. It was assumed that only those could join who found in the Aim and Basis an expression of their own beliefs at the time of joining. Yet this was not so. The Aim and Basis was the expression of the definite Christian position for which the Movement stood and to which it sought to bring students. What was required of those joining was that they should know what the Movement stood for, and the nature of the influence under which they placed themselves when they joined it. The membership clause in the Movement's Constitution which had this in view was, however, much too subtle—though this was unintentional—for the general body of students. As it was incorporated in the Constitution of a college Christian Union, what was presented to a student was : " The membership of the Christian Union shall be open to all students of the college who, having considered its Aim and Basis, desire to enter the fellowship of the Student Christian Movement." This was printed on membership forms immediately beneath the Aim and Basis. Students tended to concentrate attention on the Aim and Basis and, not taking the words of the membership clause at their face value, concluded they were being asked to commit themselves to the Aim and Basis.

The result was that the Aim and Basis fell into disuse ;

membership rolls were not kept in many places, and as a result a good many Christian Union leaders became uneasy about the situation that had arisen.

In March 1926 the General Committee appointed a sub-committee on the Aim and Basis, but nothing was done until the following September, when a discussion on the General Committee revealed on that body the same confusion of mind that existed in the colleges, and those of us who had been through previous discussions were told that the doctrine of the Trinity was an unsuitable one to single out and to present to freshers for their acceptance! There were some to whom it was in vain that we tried to explain the true state of affairs.

Further confusion was caused by the existence of a standing order passed in 1914, and still in operation, which required that all who accepted office should be reminded that doing so committed them to the obligation to endeavour to administer the Movement in harmony with the Aim and Basis. There were students in the modern universities ready to share in the leadership of the Christian Unions who were regarded by their fellow students as well fitted by their spiritual earnestness so to lead, but who had had no training in Christian doctrine, and these were anxious lest they should place themselves in a false position in view of uncertainty as to how far the constitutional requirements committed them to a doctrinal position which they had not thought out.

Discussion on the General Committee centred for a time on the question whether the Student Movement could be " a home for those who were seeking God and remain a movement of those who believed they had already discovered the truth about God which they wished to proclaim in the universities and colleges."

The sub-committee, of which F. A. Cockin was chairman, worked for two and a half years. It produced voluminous documents diagnosing the position in the colleges and giving the views of a large number of student leaders. It invited a number of leaders of different groups in the Churches, Anglo-Catholic, Liberal, Evangelical, from the Church of England, and equally diverse points of view in the Free Churches, to meet and advise it. At one time it looked as if the divergence between those who had their attention fixed on people slowly thinking out their position, and those who had a Gospel they wanted to proclaim, was so great that the Basis Committee would not be able to agree. As one reads now the long series of memoranda addressed to the committee and the innumerable letters to George Cockin,[1] one marvels that even after two and a half years' patient conference an agreement was reached which all felt they could accept. It is obvious that during the course of the discussions some learnt a good deal of theology, while the endless patience of George and his consideration for every one's convictions were factors of vital importance.

The first matter that was cleared up was what should be expected of any student on joining the Movement. The membership clause was clarified and strengthened to the satisfaction of all. It is the one now in use and reads :

> *Condition of Membership.*—The Student Christian Movement is a fellowship of students who desire to understand the Christian faith and to live the Christian life. This desire is the only condition of membership.

The next step was to deal with the question of the Basis of the Federation which had been appended to the Aim and Basis three years after it was adopted. It was agreed that the Aim and Basis chosen in 1919 had proved unsatisfactory. The root of the trouble lay in the fact that the Movement, having attempted to express its faith in simple and untechnical terms, appended later to its statement the clause from the Basis of the Federation, on which when challenged as to the doctrinal implications of its own statement, it seemed to fall back

[1] The Rev. F. A. Cockin was nicknamed George when at Marlborough, and so we always called him.

as on some kind of external authority. Agreement was reached that this was unsatisfactory and that any new Aim and Basis must contain all that the Movement wanted to affirm and must stand on its own authority.

The most difficult stage had now been reached. What should be the content of the new Aim and Basis ? The sub-committee was not an easy one to bring to agreement. The General Committee had followed its invariable practice of making its sub-committee as representative as possible of different points of view. At times the differences were so great that the prospect of agreement seemed almost hopeless. Some wanted a statement so general that any one who was a theist could accept it, while the majority wanted a definite Christian statement. As the discussions proceeded, however, the group found itself gradually drawn together in a growing desire to state plainly and unequivocally those cardinal points which it believed had been, or ought to be, the message, the gospel of the Movement.

> "And in doing so," to quote George Cockin, "we realized that a double responsibility was laid upon us, the responsibility of meeting the actual needs of students ; of saying something which they would recognize as *relevant* to their difficulties and aspirations ; and along with this the responsibility of loyalty to the traditions of the Movement, the inherited experience and truth, which we owe not only to ourselves, nor even only to our own past, but to the whole continuous life of the Christian Church, and to the corporate life of the Federation in which we share."

The result of a long process was a more theological statement than the one discarded. The statement prepared by the sub-committee was discussed and revised by the whole General Committee more than once.

The opinion was sought of the Bishop of Manchester (Dr Temple) and Professor H. R. Mackintosh, also of a group consisting of the Rev. Canons Spanton and E. S. Woods, the Revs. J. R. Coates, David Jenks, R. H. Moberly and Ryder Smith. These friends were all asked whether they agreed that the Aim and Basis proposed expressed in untechnical language the essential Christian position. To this question they replied that in their opinion it was a specifically Christian document, expressing a gospel which the Movement could go into the colleges to preach and teach. They were also asked whether they agreed that the statement by itself was sufficiently adequate to justify the disuse of any other statement or formula. In reply to this, they said that, although they could imagine that it would be found inadequate by some, yet for them and, they believed, for most other people it would be an adequate statement and did not need the incorporation in it of any further statement.

In order to make the issue perfectly clear they were asked whether they felt the recommendation of the committee would justify a decision by the Student Movement that in future any body of students or any individual student, having considered the Aim and Basis and having expressed the desire to work in harmony with it, such body or individual should not be excluded from membership because of using the name of Free Christian, Unitarian, or any other title.

Again, the advisers of the Movement said unanimously and definitely that in their opinion the statement was a sufficiently adequate setting forth of a definitely Christian position to make acceptance of its principles on the part of any group or individual a sufficient basis for their entering the Movement. If such a group or individual, having considered the Aim and Basis, desired to work in co-operation with the Movement and in harmony with the Aim and Basis, they felt that the Movement had no right to exclude them. This point was elaborated with regard to speakers at the Movement's conferences, and its secretaries, and the association of theological colleges, and on all three points the same opinion was expressed. This question was raised because the issues had been confused at one stage by interminable discussion as to whether some ought or ought not to be eligible for membership of the S.C.M., because they called themselves by some particular title.

The long process was now finished as far as the General Committee was concerned and was referred to the colleges. The Christian Unions had the proposals before them for five months, and after a long discussion at the business meeting at Swanwick, July 1929, when many amendments were disposed of and two accepted, the Movement adopted the following Aim and Basis, two hundred and twenty-seven voting for it and four against it. One of the accepted amendments was proposed by the Christian Union at Barry Training College. Its representatives made the useful proposal that the words Aim and Basis should have an explanatory sentence added to them, viz., "being an expression of the convictions which guide the thought and life of the Student Christian Movement," so that when the sub-committee's proposed Aim and Basis was finally adopted as Article III of the Constitution, it read :

AIM AND BASIS—*being an expression of the convictions which guide the thought and life of the Student Christian Movement as a whole :*

As a Christian Movement we affirm our faith in God, our Father, whose nature is creative love and power.

God is made known to us in Jesus Christ, in whom we see the true expression of His being and the true nature of man.

Through His life and triumphant death, and through the living energy of the Spirit, we share in the redeeming love which overcomes evil, and find forgiveness, freedom and eternal life.

Faced with the need and perplexity of the world, we desire to give ourselves to Christ and to follow Him wherever He may call us.

We seek the Kingdom of God, the recreation of all mankind into one family, without distinction of race or nation, class or capacity.

We desire to enter into that fellowship of worship, thought and service which is the heritage of the Christian Church.

The Basis Sub-committee and General Committee had both agreed without any difficulty that instead of appending

3 G

a single extract from the Basis of the Federation to our Aim and Basis, the whole " Objects " clause of the Federation, which contains its Basis, should be inserted in the Constitution of the Movement, thus bringing out the true relationship of the two bodies and their respective statements to one another. This was approved by the business meeting. This meant that instead of Article XVIII of the Movement's Constitution reading, " The Student Christian Movement of Great Britain and Ireland shall be affiliated to the World's Student Christian Federation," it was altered to read :

> The Student Christian Movement of Great Britain and Ireland shall be affiliated to the World's Student Christian Federation, the objects of which are :
>
> (1) To unite students' Christian movements or organizations throughout the world, and to promote mutual relations among them.
>
> (2) To collect and distribute information about the conditions of students in all lands from the religious and other points of view.
>
> (3) To promote the following lines of activity :
>
> (a) To lead students to accept the Christian Faith in God—Father, Son and Holy Spirit according to the Scriptures and to live as true disciples of Jesus Christ.
>
> (b) To deepen the spiritual life of students and to promote earnest study of the Scriptures among them.
>
> (c) To influence students to devote themselves to the extension of the Kingdom of God in their own nation and throughout the world.
>
> (d) To bring students of all countries into mutual understanding and sympathy, to lead them to realize that the principles of Jesus Christ should rule in international relationships, and to endeavour by so doing to draw the nations together.
>
> (e) To further either directly or indirectly, the efforts on behalf of the welfare of students in body, mind and spirit which are in harmony with the Christian purpose.

The business meeting also decided to abandon the use of the name " Christian Union " to describe the autonomous college societies which, together with the associated theological colleges and members of the S.V.M.U., compose the Student Christian Movement.

A certain number of students in every generation had for the past twenty years expressed dislike of the title. More than once the suggestion to change it had been made on the General Committee, but there was opposition from some of the older Christian Unions or Associations which were proud of their traditions. They were much older than the Movement, and jealous of their independence, which they felt might be jeopardized if they became merely " branches " of the S.C.M. The traditions of the Scottish Christian Unions, where these sentiments were strongest, were lost during the war, and opposition to change from this quarter ceased. On the other hand, objection to the title had grown in strength, because many students in joining a college Christian Union failed to realize that they had become members of the Student Christian Movement. The vote to abandon the title was passed *nemine contradicente* and " XYZ University (or College) Christian Union " became "the Student Christian Movement in XYZ University (or College.)"

CHAPTER XLIII

THE REORGANIZATION OF THE MOVEMENT

PARALLEL with the consideration of the Aim and Basis another group in the Movement was occupied with its reorganization.

The post-war period brought the Movement some pressing administrative problems to solve. Although every affiliated Christian Union was an autonomous body working out its policy on its own lines, yet the Movement was highly centralized. Its councils in London, England (North and South), Wales, Scotland and Ireland were advisory bodies and executive only in so far as the General Committee gave them power. Three of the six had not been started until during the war, and now that it was over were producing a great deal of work at the centre. The staff of the Movement had grown, causing a great increase of work of all kinds for the General Secretary. It had become an important publishing body. Its finances were on a much greater scale, while, most important of all, the Christian Unions were more active, and, with broader policies than before the war, were making big demands upon the Movement's headquarters for help of all kinds. It was desirable to decentralize, yet we must keep the Movement a unity in the British Isles. It was also necessary to tackle the question of how to distribute responsibility at headquarters where there was a centralization of the administration of the Movement in two people, the general secretary and assistant general secretary. Most important of all was the question how and when to secure younger leadership.

The General Committee was a problem in itself. By constitution secretaries of the Movement were *ex-officio* members of it ; an arrangement quite satisfactory when the staff was small, but the largely increased staff when added to the elected members of the General Committee made it an unwieldy body. The result was that it was not possible in the time available for everyone to contribute to the discussion of the Movement's policy, necessary business dealing with publications, finance, conference arrangements, choice of secretaries and the like took a great deal of time, and the student members were often restive because there was insufficient opportunity to discuss at length the Movement's message and how to present it effectively in the universities and colleges. Welsh and Scottish members found their fields received scant attention, and were specially restive.

In the autumn of 1923 I prepared a memorandum on the organization of the Movement,[1] which was the first of a series which, when collected, make a large bundle of documents. The discussion which ensued at the Christmas meeting opened the question on the General Committee. The next year we were occupied with the quadrennial conference at Manchester, January 1925, but during its course a reorganization sub-committee was appointed which was to start work when it was over. Its terms of reference were :

> To inquire into the organization of the Student Movement in all its aspects and to report to the General Committee what changes, if any, it would advise in the organization of the Movement as a whole or in any of its departments, with a view to making the machinery of the Movement a more satisfactory vehicle of its spiritual message.

The report of this committee led to the starting of a reading party for secretaries at the end of each summer, which was initiated and led very effectively by George Cockin as long as he remained with the Movement. Another result was that a General Council, larger than the General Committee, was created for discussion of

[1] *Organization of the Movement*, T. Tatlow.

policy, and the Reference Committee, already an executive committee in a small way, was enlarged and recognized as responsible for preparing all the regular business of the Movement and doing a great deal of it. The reason this reorganization committee did not achieve more was that the Movement was feeling the effect of the rise in the cost of living, the slump after the brief period of post-war prosperity, and had not yet been able to devise a way of securing the funds it needed. Reorganization required a rising and not a falling income.

The General Committee, however, was trying to tackle the financial problem. It appointed R. D. Whitehorn, in 1921, as assistant secretary with special care for finance, and when he passed to a secretaryship for London in 1923, A. G. Pite was secured in his place. The income of the Movement from regular sources was steadily increased during this period, and Pite undertook a thorough reorganization of the files and records of the finance department at Annandale. Nevertheless, in 1925, after four years' work by a special financial secretary, while the annual expenditure had been reduced by £1200, the deficit had increased by £750 and the post-war reserve fund had been used. Over against these facts we all recognized that the most significant section in the report of the Reorganization Committee was the table it gave of secretaryships once occupied in the Movement, now vacant. Here it is:

Intercollegiate secretaryships vacant

Aberdeen	Newcastle
Edinburgh	Manchester (Women)
Glasgow	Cambridge
Edinburgh (Women)	

National secretaryships vacant

Scottish	Irish

Special secretaryships vacant

Missionary Study	Edinburgh Foreign Students
Bible Study	S.V.M.U. Travelling
Social Study	Foreign Students Travelling
Evangelistic	Manchester Foreign Students
Medical Travelling (Women)	
Training Colleges (Women)	
Technical Colleges	

This situation was due to conditions over which the
Movement had no control. And it was really much
worse than it looked, for the income of the Movement
had been maintained for several years by securing large
gifts by special appeals, and such gifts were becoming
fewer and smaller each year. The Movement could not
hope to finance its regular work on financial windfalls.
New ways of increasing the Movement's income must
be found. Miss Rouse suggested to me that we should
secure Miss Iredale's help. She had been a member of
the Movement, believed in it and had proved in connection with student relief that she had a remarkable
gift for securing financial help for a cause in which she
believed. She became Associate Finance Secretary in
the autumn of 1924, while still responsible for the Universities Relief Committee.

I gave no further lead in relation to reorganization
at this period because the discussions on the subject
had convinced me that reorganization was bound
to increase expenditure, also the conviction was growing in my mind that when reorganization was completed, my long term as general secretary should come
to an end, and it seemed to me impossible to contemplate leaving my post until the Movement had some
reserves and was in a better position as regards income.

Miss Iredale at first concentrated her attention mainly
on conserving the work of the Universities Relief Committee. In 1925 she began to turn her attention to the
finances of the Movement and worked out plans for
raising a National Appeal Fund. She set her heart
on having as trustees of it Mr Baldwin (then Prime

Minister), Sir Robert Kindersley and the Provost of
Eton (Dr Montague James).   I sought the help of the
Archbishop of Canterbury and explained to him, as I
assisted him to robe in his private room in the House
of Lords, why I thought Miss Iredale would succeed
and why he should ask Mr Baldwin to be a trustee.   He
secured Mr Baldwin for us.   The Bishop of Manchester
(Dr Temple) secured Sir Robert Kindersley, and the
Provost of Eton, already a good friend to the Movement,
promised me to act.

The following year Miss Iredale began to secure considerable sums of money from men who had not hitherto
given to the Movement.   There is no complete record
of all she raised because, like the rest of us, she paid
money secured for income into the current account of
the Movement under the name of the person from
whom it was secured.   The National Appeal Fund,
however, she raised single-handed, and it reached a total
of £65,849.

The Movement has never been served by any secretary
with the same genius for securing finance as Eleanora
Iredale.   She paid very little attention to machinery and
methods and had no interest in finance as such, or in
account-keeping.   It was because she believed whole-
heartedly that the Student Movement was a national
asset in that it was helping to make students the kind
of men and women a Christian nation needs, that she
presented with great conviction the request for money
to help it to do its work.

The National Appeal Fund was raised from a small
group of men in Liverpool, London and Glasgow, each
of whom contributed from £1000 to £5000.   She
sought out men who could afford to give liberally to
work in which they believed, and set herself to produce
in them the conviction she herself had concerning the
value of the work of the Movement.   Her strength lay
in her refusal to ask for a penny for anything unless she
was herself deeply convinced of the worth of the cause
she was presenting.   It was also the reason for her

untiring persistence in relation to those whom she
approached. If she did not despise the assistance that
a becoming hat or a friendly introduction would give
in getting access to people, no one gave her money for
irrelevant reasons. What she brought to the Movement was given by men to whom she had laid bare its
heart and thus convinced of the importance and privilege
of sharing in work the chief value of which is that
it helps to build up the character of the students of
the nation in harmony with the Christian view of the
world.

The appeal of the Movement, when made in this way,
was met by extraordinary generosity, and we were all
deeply grateful to those who helped us to maintain and
develop the work of the Movement at a time when
many good causes were crippled for lack of funds.
The National Appeal Fund enabled the Student Movement to provide an adequate headquarters for its work,
some endowment for the Student Movement House in
Russell Square, a capital sum of £3000 for the World's
Student Christian Federation, which literally saved it
from financial collapse, a reserve fund of several thousand
pounds for our own Movement, and some income to
carry on during a period of world depression when even
old-established organizations with considerable reserves
have found themselves in grave difficulties. The problem of an adequate annual income remains unsolved.
The Movement still has far less money than it needs to
carry on its work financially, but Miss Iredale's work met
urgent capital needs and dealt with them satisfactorily,
and what she has been able to raise for income tided
over a period which might otherwise have been disastrous. The fund was closed in 1932.

To return to reorganization, it was when Miss Iredale
began to raise large sums of money that the way seemed
clear for us to begin again the study of the question.
Another happening affected the situation; in June
1926 the Archbishop of Canterbury offered me an
honorary Canonry in Canterbury Cathedral, and this

was followed by an invitation from the Dean and Chapter of Canterbury to become Rector of All Hallows, Lombard Street, London, E.C., with a view to making this church a spiritual centre for London students. I had thus an additional responsibility committed to me, but at the same time my future had been provided for in a way which would allow of my gradually drawing out of the Movement, instead of my having to leave it at once to take up new work when a change was made.

Next spring, therefore, we took up again the question of reorganization, and decided that as a reorganized Movement needed a suitable headquarters, and as Miss Iredale was finding the money, we were in a position to rebuild Annandale. This house was originally held by us on a short lease, but in 1922 we had bought the original lease from the builder of Annandale, thus acquiring a long lease from the Ecclesiastical Commissioners. At this time we owned two houses across the road from Annandale—St Cloud and Etruria. An office in three houses on two sides of a busy main road is difficult to manage! Annandale stood on an acre of land, so in March 1927 we decided to rebuild it. The General Committee chose a Cambridge member of the Movement, Mr William Lord, as architect.

A new reorganization committee reviewed what its predecessor had advised and found that while the enlarged Reference Committee had been a success, the General Council was too large and its functions too indefinite.

The Reorganization Committee not having had time to precipitate its study of the Movement sufficiently to make practical proposals about its chief committee, and yet some change in the General Council being urgently needed, I sat down one day and wrote a document [1] in which I worked out a plan for a General Committee of twenty-seven (students and secretaries), and suggested that it should be tried as an experiment by passing a

[1] *Proposed Administrative Experiment.*

resolution at Swanwick suspending [1] the Articles in the Constitution of the Movement relating to the General Committee. The proposed experiment included a scheme for a conference of all the controlling committees, and also an arrangement for training student members of sub-committees. This was accepted by the General Committee and adopted by the business meeting, Swanwick, July 1927.

The air reverberated by this date with discussions about the future, and personal issues began to bulk rather more largely than was satisfactory, especially the question whether a group of the rather more senior secretaries on the staff would be the people to take over the leadership of the Movement in my place, and whether the leadership would come to them before they were too old for it. As a new generation of students was now represented on the General Committee it seemed wise that they should not be plunged into a discussion about changes in personnel until they had some clear ideas about the administration of the Movement, so I again provided a memorandum on the reorganization of the Movement and the questions that needed consideration. This was discussed in September 1927, accepted and some points added to it, and J. H. Grummitt, Owen Griffith, Amy Buller and I were appointed as a sub-committee to prepare an outline for the Christmas meeting, dealing with the questions which needed attention at once.

Just before this meeting the Auxiliary Movement Committee, with Miss Fairfield's approval, wrote to the General Committee and asked it to release her after the quadrennial conference, 1929, to enable her to become one of the secretaries of the Auxiliary Movement. This request produced a long discussion on the General Committee, and it was ultimately decided that the question of Miss Fairfield's retirement must depend

---

[1] The scheme has been modified since, but the Articles relating to the composition of the General Committee continue to be suspended while experiments are tried.

upon someone being found who could be trained to be her successor, but on condition that such a worker was secured it was agreed she should be released from the post of Assistant General Secretary at midsummer 1929.

The General Committee having decided this matter, went on to appoint yet another reorganization committee, and asked it to consider first of all the relation of the secretaries to the General Committee, the training of secretaries, the need for better organized financial work on behalf of the Movement, and the nature and work of the general secretariat. The committee asked Miss Fairfield to become convener of this new reorganization committee and to regard it as an important piece of work to be done for the Movement before she retired from it. The other members appointed were J. H. Grummitt, Eleanora Iredale, Edwin Barker, Hugh Martin, Hugh Warner and T. Tatlow, with two former secretaries—Leslie Hunter and Mrs John Lewis.

This was the most effective of all the reorganization committees and had a strange history, for it not only did its own work but secured fresh secretaries, did business in connection with the National Appeal Fund, and attended to many other things outside its province! It issued a series of memoranda to the General Committee from early in 1928 to the end of 1929, dealing with staff, finance, the S.V.M.U., the Theological College Department, publications, choice and training of secretaries, the Student Movement House, the Movement's Councils.

All this time discussion went on about staff. Early in the discussion I suggested to the Reorganization Committee that I should retire from the general secretaryship in the summer of 1929 and should become chairman of the Movement, in which position I could help the new team to get into their stride, do more adequately the consultative work which was constantly asked of me, edit *The Student Movement* and write the history of the Movement. This suggestion met with general approval.

The question of the general secretariat was now urgent. Miss Fairfield was anxious that there should be no delay after the quadrennial conference, 1929, in allowing her to take up work for the Auxiliary Movement, and I wanted to pass to the chairmanship at the same time. Who should succeed? Miss Mackinnon was reported to be returning from China and she was invited to succeed Miss Fairfield. As to the chief position of leadership, the General Committee decided that it would not appoint another general secretary but a team, nevertheless it began to discuss " the new secretary." Some held that he should be an experienced man who had won his spurs in another field of work, others that he should be " a much younger man, relying for help and training on the experienced secretaries available." Many people were suggested and no decision made. The matter was discussed at Easter and the General Committee met again at Swanwick to discuss it.

Opinion was moving in favour of a much younger group of secretaries on the headquarters staff of the Movement, and " with the whole conception of a group of younger secretaries at headquarters there went the idea of much more intimate team work amongst those engaged in administration." [1] No decision was taken, but at the business meeting at Swanwick, July 1928, the whole question of reorganization was put before the Movement for the first time. Robert Mackie, as chairman of the General Committee, told the conference that a reorganization committee was at work, that I had asked to be .allowed to retire from the general secretaryship in the summer of 1929, and that I had been invited to take the chairmanship.

The General Committee was in a position of freedom as regards future staff. Miss Fairfield and I, who were the only secretaries on a permanent basis, were vacating our secretaryships, various agreements with nearly all the rest of the staff for stated terms of service would be completed within a year or two.

The movement of opinion during the spring and

[1] S.C.M. General Committee Minute.

summer of 1928 in favour of a young general secretariat
conditioned the decisions of the General Committee as
regards secretaries whose terms of office were expiring,
and as a result it was decided not to offer fresh appointments to some whom at one time all thought I should
leave behind me in the leadership of the Movement.

During the summer I became anxious about one
matter. It seemed to me vital that the services of Hugh
Martin should not be lost to the Movement, and matters
were moving in a direction which looked as if the
position he would be expected to occupy under a new
administration might not be acceptable to him. Further,
I knew he was constantly being offered appointments
outside the Movement. If he left and Cockin, Dobson,
Grummitt and I were gone, there would be no one to
whom the General Committee could turn for help in
safeguarding its important publishing business. When
the General Committee met in September I proposed that
an incorporated body with a board of directors should
be created, with Hugh Martin as managing director, to
take over the publishing work from the General Committee, a body always quite unsuited to guide the highly
technical work of publishing. This proposal met with
immediate acceptance and Hugh Martin, assisted by
A. Walker, worked out plans for the Student Christian
Movement Press, Limited.

At the September meeting of the General Committee the Reorganization Committee was reconstituted,
and it was asked to deal with the work of the councils,
financial policy, the future of the S.V.M.U., the Schools
Department and Publication Department, the policy of
the Movement as regards conferences of all kinds, and
the reorganization of the Theological Department. As
to the general secretariat, one or two people recently in
college were approached, and other names of people
already on the staff discussed, but no appointment made
until January 1929, when Robert C. Mackie, who had
been on the General Committee since 1922 and Scottish
secretary since 1925, was appointed secretary of the

General Committee and leader of the new general secretariat, which was for an interim period to consist of R. C. Mackie, Eric Fenn, Catherine Mackinnon and Amy Buller. I was delighted at Mackie's appointment. I had longed at some stages of the discussion to throw my weight into the scales and try to secure his appointment. I was sure he was the right man. But I took no share in the discussions, as I was convinced that the decision should be made by the younger element in the Movement. It was a great joy that they chose a man whom I personally liked, and one I was sure was the right man for the post. The new arrangement was put into operation on September 1st 1929.

It had again fallen to my lot to write a revised set of proposals for the reorganization of the committee work of the Movement. A preamble stated the general principles on which the actual proposals were based, as follows :

1. While maintaining the unity of the British Movement, it has seemed wise to provide for a greater measure of devolution than has been in operation in the past. The unity of the Movement can only be real and valuable in so far as the national and regional elements within the British Isles are encouraged to do their own work and make their individual contributions to the life of the whole Movement. This means the giving of greater scope and added responsibility to the National and Regional Councils hitherto established, and, by putting England on the same basis as the other countries in giving her a Council of the same status as the others, making it possible for the General Committee truly to represent the life and thought of the Movement throughout Great Britain and Ireland, without undue preoccupation with the affairs of any one portion of the field.

2. There has always been an element of democracy in the administration of the Student Movement, and this has worked better perhaps in practice than it appeared in the theory of government underlying the Constitution. But the proposals we now make will distribute the responsibilities of democracy more widely than has been the case in our recent practice. Instead of the General Committee

being elected by the business meeting—a body that rarely knows more than a portion of the nominees—it is proposed that the majority of the members of the committee be appointed direct by the various Councils.

3. A Movement which employs some thirty-five secretaries must give attention to the best way in which those secretaries can be related to the governing body. Obviously all the secretarial staff cannot be on a committee without making a student majority impossible, or the committee itself far too large for working purposes. Hence the only way in which secretaries can take their part effectively in the counsels of the Movement will be through the functioning of the various Councils, and their relation to the General Committee.

The proposals included the creation of an English Council to take the place of the modern universities conference, and a General Committee to consist of members appointed by the Councils, Theological College Department, the S.V.M.U., the S.C.M. secretaries, the School Department and five co-opted members, with the general secretaries *ex-officio*. A Standing Committee like, but smaller than, the old Reference Committee was to be retained.

These proposals were adopted by the business meeting, Swanwick, 1929, and are still in force.

In the autumn of 1931 a further step was taken towards the complete transference of the leadership of the Student Movement to a younger group of men and women, as first planned in 1929. Robert Mackie and I decided to suggest that I should retire from the chairmanship of the General Committee in favour of a younger man, while remaining chairman of the Movement and editor of *The Student Movement*, and in this capacity continuing my services as consultant on the Movement's greater concerns. At the same time we reminded the General Committee that they must begin to think of a question of the new editor for *The Student Movement*.

The General Committee agreed to these proposals, and John Maud became chairman, but, alas, not for as long as we desired. He seems to collect travelling fellowships and the like ! In his place Dorothy Emmet was appointed—the third woman who has occupied the chair of the General Committee.

In May 1933 Eric Fenn became Editor of *The Student Movement*, and the last act in the reorganization of the Movement was thus accomplished.

The transference of the general secretaryship has been accomplished without fuss or confusion. I am well content, for I see work to which I gave some of the best years of my life to building up safely transferred to the younger generation.

CHAPTER XLIV

THOUGHT AND LIFE FROM 1925-33

IN the autumn of 1925 I wrote a paragraph in the editorial column of *The Student Movement* which was quoted by the General Committee in its Annual Report nearly a year later, as describing the situation in the student world. The paragraph might have been written five or six years earlier or five or six years later, in neither case would it have needed alteration. It ran thus :

> The world into which a freshman steps to-day when he enters college is very different to that into which the men and women who founded the Student Christian Movement came. Everything moves more rapidly, so everyone tries to fit more into his day—more work, more social activities, and more general interests. The result is that there is more strain, and, in consequence, beliefs and character tend to mature more slowly. There are far more people openly ready to inquire and learn about the spiritual aspects of life, and the nature and claims of Christianity. Those who speak for the Church carry far less weight, even with those who claim to be Christians, than used to be the case. People used to be divided into those who accepted Christianity and those who did not, and those who accepted Christianity accepted it without much questioning of what the Christian Church had to say about it. To-day the atmosphere is different ; it is not an atmosphere of either belief or disbelief, it is one of uncertainty.

The last decade has been one of uncertainty about the Christian faith. More and more students come to college with little or no Church allegiance, and without the foundation of a religious home life. The result of this is ignorance of the fundamentals of Christianity. Even those who call themselves Christians are uncertain

as to what they should believe.   They do not know the
Bible, and they know very little about the doctrines of
Christianity.

The Movement has made valiant efforts to help people,
and a certain number each year do learn a great deal
about the Faith, but the difficulties are very great.
Student life is an exhausting business.   There is nothing
quiet or studious about the universities.   Life is one
unceasing whirl and bustle from morning until night.
It is a marvel how students manage to secure sufficient
quiet to learn their own " shop."   When it comes to
asking for serious study of the Bible and Christian
doctrine, response is hard to secure.

> The crowded lecture or lessons table and the voracity of
> the mechanism created by science for the diminishing
> reserve of leisure leave no time for general reading or
> thought, and in the assignment of priorities religion at best
> gets the odd sweeping.[1]

A woman student came to see me a little time ago
about some difficulties that were troubling her, and
after trying to help her I suggested she should read a
book I named, whereat the girl melted into tears.   On
inquiry I found the cause was that she felt so overwhelmed already by all the demands upon her that she
could not bear the thought of trying to meet one more.
I think she was typical.   People sometimes complain
that students won't read and study seriously that they
may know what Christianity teaches.   It is not slackness
so much as overpressure.

The Student Movement has been rather less than
more successful in getting thorough study done in
recent years.   The General Committee in 1926 deplored
" the decline of study "[2] in the Movement, but on the
whole it still declines.   A careful reading of the reports
of the Movement for the last four or five years reveals

[1] *The Life of a Modern University*, chapter by Sir Charles Grant
Robertson, p. 73.
[2] *Annual Report, S.C.M.*, 1925-26, p.16.

that less and less is said about study.   It is hard now to
get facts.   The Bible study secretary in 1921 gave up
asking for statistical records of the number of students
in study circles, on the ground that there was such a
variety of study that statistics were little guide to the
situation.   The social and missionary study secretaries
of the day followed his example, and my protests were
of no avail.   I thought then, and am more sure now,
that they were wrong.   Statistics are of limited value,
but they do serve as a thermometer and show whether
things are going up or down.   To-day no one in the
Movement knows what is the real situation about study.
The best guess one can make is that there is very little
serious study, and that most so-called study circles are
discussion circles.   The Student Movement needs more
study secretaries.   It needs to consider how best to get
at the facts as to what study is being done, and it needs
new methods.   Probably tutorial classes · would be a
success if carefully adjusted to student conditions.

The student field is certainly not less promising soil
than it was.   The years after the war were difficult.
The revolt against authority of all kinds, the suspicion
of Christian doctrine, and a good deal of crankiness of
temperament made the work of the Movement difficult.
There has been a recovery of steadiness and good temper
in the last few years.   Students have been responsive to
anything well done designed to help them to understand
the Christian faith and to live the Christian life.   They
have come more and more to quiet days, crowded
to university missions, and besieged the quadrennial
conference at Edinburgh, in January 1933, for places.
Never did the Movement have to do so little to fill a
quadrennial conference with men and women, never
did it have so long a waiting list of men and women
ready to fill any last minute vacancy.

Students have become steadily more pacifist as regards
war each year.   They are more and more perplexed in
face of Western civilization, feel its evils and defects
keenly, and are ready for great social and economic

changes. Communism is a source of interest to many, but there is no anti-religious movement in the colleges of this country. On the contrary, the situation seems ripe for a far-reaching religious movement. I believe such a movement must have its roots in better teaching of religion, and religion in all its aspects. There have been times when some of the leaders of the Movement in recent years have suggested solving the problem of complexity, in view of the limitation of time and strength of students, by trying to reduce the area of thought covered by the Movement. The Movement has ever-growing interests, it makes ever-growing demands upon its members. Our history is a continuous record of the widening comprehension of the relevance of Christ to all aspects of human life. This expansion has had its dangers. It has led to diffusion of interest and a super-ficial acquaintance with a variety of subjects. Anything that was novel has tended to absorb the attention of some college S.C.M.s and cause neglect of effort to gain a fundamental knowledge of the meaning and claims of Christianity. The cure does not seem to be the return to a gospel of individual salvation, but an attempt to get students to take things one after another, and not to go in for everything at once, as is too often the case in discussion groups.

Life is complex, and there is no use pretending it is simple. But students can be helped to take one thing at a time, and college S.C.M.s can be taught to provide for students at different stages. If this is to happen, however, the Churches and the Movement will have to work much more closely together. Such co-operation ought to result in an adequate staff of workers in the colleges and in really good tutorial class work. The Student Movement has trained senior men before now to speak effectively at its conferences. It ought also to be able to provide the training in student psychology and in tendencies in current student thought for selected clergy and ministers who would make available in the colleges the truth the Christian Church has to give.

George Cockin saw the need for good study, and did all that one man could be expected to do to promote it. Tutorial work of different kinds and in different places has shown what could be done, *e.g.* the Rev. J. K. Mozley's [1] work for the students of Reading University, or the Rev. H. A. A. Kennedy's careful training of Bible circle leaders in Edinburgh University.

Related to this question is the training of Student Movement secretaries. George Cockin started a ten days' reading party each autumn for Student Movement secretaries in 1925, which has been carried on ever since. It was a move in the right direction, but the different degrees of religious knowledge among those on the S.C.M. staff tends to make discussion too diffuse, and more differentiated teaching is needed for those who have had no theological training.

Another attempt at training has been made by introducing at the summer conference a " special course " of a definitely Biblical and theological character for selected college S.C.M. leaders. The first of these was held in 1926 at Swanwick, when fifty students attended; Canon Streeter and Dr Underwood were the lecturers, and George Cockin was in general charge.

As to the happenings of the last few years apart from those recorded in the special chapters devoted to them, a few must be noted; readers, however, must remember that this record of the Movement's life takes little notice of its day to day work. Thousands of letters, tens of thousands of circulars, callers innumerable pass in and out of Annandale. Conferences, retreats, committees are without end. The activities of the S.C.M. branches—meetings, study groups, discussions—all concerned with the purpose of the Movement to win men and women to personal faith in God as revealed in Jesus Christ, to build up their lives in that faith and to help them to understand the world in which they are to serve God are carried steadily forward.

[1] Afterwards Canon of St Paul's Cathedral.

The International House in Glasgow was opened on October 14th 1925 by Sir Donald Macalister, and I was sent to speak on behalf of the General Committee, and carried their message of congratulations to those in Glasgow who had worked successfully for the opening of this house, especially to Mr Aiman, the first warden, without whose valiant efforts it would never have been opened. Jim Aiman went to Glasgow after experience of foreign student work in Edinburgh to see what could be done for foreign students, especially Indians, being himself an Indian. Quickly making up his mind that an international house, where Oriental and Scottish students could meet, was a necessity of the situation, he pressed for action by the Y.M.C.A. and Student Movement. The result was that this house was opened under the joint auspices of the Y.M.C.A. and the Movement. The Scotsman, without whose help and practical sympathy in interesting other business men in Glasgow the house would never have been opened, was Mr G. W. Service. All interested in the house are in his debt.

The Student Movement in Ireland opened the year 1926 by sharing in a conference in Dublin with the Irish Christian Fellowship and the Christian Citizenship Councils of Belfast and Dublin, when the needs and problems of Irish life were studied in the light of Christian principles. Things were ripe in Ireland for such a conference—" Towards a Better Ireland," it was called. People were conscious of two things, said Bolton Waller, " first, that self-government is a much more difficult enterprise than we had earlier imagined ; second, that our citizens, taken as a whole, are but poorly equipped for the enterprise." In both Northern Ireland and in the Free State there was a great deal of pessimism. The first excitement of the new political condition was over, political leaders were all distrusted, and there was a general apathy about matters of public concern and lack of effort to deal with actual problems.

The conference was an attempt to apply Christianity. Urban and industrial problems, including industrial civilization, the labour movement, unemployment, re-creation, rural economics and life, education, both child and adult, were all on the programme. Ireland as a world-partner, and the inter-relation of North and South, together with the responsibilities of citizenship, were all dealt with. "Ireland in the Purposes of God" was Professor Davey's subject on the first night. Well-known Irish leaders like Mr Smith Gordon, Miss Cunningham, Senator Douglas, Bolton Waller and Professor R. M. Henry were assisted in the speaking by Mr Kenneth Lindsay, Canon C. E. Raven and Dr R. W. Livingstone. The conference was marked by fair-mindedness—not always a mark of gatherings in Ireland—thoroughness and optimism. Its evening meetings were open to the public and drew large crowds. It certainly helped many students in their preparation for life.

In England the General Strike during May, arising out of conflict in the coal industry, was a warning to us of the desperate tension between capital and labour. Students reacted in very different ways. Some just felt the excitement of the time and delighted to leave their studies and drive tube trains or milk lorries. Others were too near the workers, and watched the struggle anxiously without taking any part. Eight Student Movement secretaries sent a letter from Annandale to the Christian Unions, urging that all members of the Movement should " help to promote the spirit of peace by abstaining from ill-considered speech, and from imputing motives to any parties to the dispute which they themselves would repudiate, by discharging any duties we feel incumbent upon us in a spirit that none can regard as provocative, by trying to understand the position of different parties in the dispute, and by trying each in our own circle to create an atmosphere in which it will become easier rather than more difficult for a settlement to be made." It was a time of great individual and national testing.

When the year 1927 opened, it was Wales this time, not Ireland, that held a conference on national needs and problems. The reason why the conference was held at this time was much the same as the reason for holding an Irish conference a year before. After a period of optimism and fair prosperity the country had been plunged in gloom.

The problems of Welsh life were grave. The distribution of mineral wealth in the country led to an unbalanced distribution of population. Two counties in South Wales had over one-half of the population crowded together in their narrow valleys and industrial towns. Much of this crowded life was sordid. There had also been a revolution in thought which affected the old love of the people for the Churches and their leadership, and which produced new ferment in the sphere of national aspirations. What was the true vocation of Wales?

The title of the conference was " The Nation in the Purpose of God." It was held from January 3rd to 8th at Alexandra Hall, Aberystwyth, and was arranged by the Welsh Council of the Student Movement and Urdd-y-Deyrnas, Owen Griffith being its leader as well as secretary. Two hundred students and senior people attended, and the conference was one of the most representative of different points of view ever assembled in Wales. The changes in Welsh life were not covered up. Miners, professors, educationists and literary men each spoke their mind. Mr Mainwaring, hot from the Rhondda, sore from industrial defeat, poverty and victimization, poured out the doctrines of Karl Marx and denounced the vanity of culture. It was the first public treatment of communism on a Student Movement platform, and the speaker asked for communism. Other programmes were put forward for national life, and the Christian call for a dedicated nation sounded. Different points of view brought out the difficulties and the disunity in Wales. The deep religious note was never for long absent, and the conference knew that whatever aspect of Welsh life it dealt with, it was dealing with God.

One of the fruits of the work of the International

House in Glasgow was the first East and West Conference, held from March 30th to April 4th, at Ardenconnel, Rhu, under the chairmanship of Dr E. B. Ludlam. The organizer of the conference was J. S. Aiman, and the subject racial relationships. The conference sessions—and still more the conference life— helped to an increase of real understanding between students of different nationalities.

The Movement lost Edith Thornton in the autumn, she resigned on account of ill-health after thirteen years as private secretary to the general secretary. The resolution of the General Committee, expressing appreciation and gratitude for her work, said that " her interest and devotion had extended to every side of the life of the Movement, and she has been the intimate friend of many members of the staff. In addition to her own work, she has always had a particular concern for the missionary work of the Movement, she has devoted herself to the routine of producing the magazine, and she has played a large part in the setting up and organization of the quadrennial and summer conferences."

The reference to her concern for missionary work was specially appropriate; at one point she was invited to become missionary secretary, which was a tribute to her missionary knowledge and interest, in view of the fact that she had never been to college and the Movement only offered its secretaryships to students. We tried hard to get her to accept the missionary secretaryship, but behind a striking appearance and a manner that indicated a competent personality, she was always nervous about anything in the nature of public work. Although an excellent speaker, and immensely popular on the rare occasions when she was persuaded to talk in a college, such appearances took so much out of her that she would not do this kind of work. The fact, however, that she did not want a more prominent position, and yet was a woman of first-class ability, made her an extremely valuable private secretary, and when she was forced by very serious illness, which ended fatally in

1929, to retire, the burden of work thrown back upon me was almost crushing.

An idea which had been discussed under the guidance of Dr Rutgers before the war was put into operation in January 1928, and a meeting of the general secretaries of all the European Student Movements affiliated to the Federation was assembled at Hàrdenbroek, Holland, as guests of the Dutch Student Movement. It was decided to constitute the body as the European Council of the Federation. I was appointed chairman and Dr Kullmann secretary.

We exchanged information as to religious conditions in our respective fields, discussed different aspects of our work and made plans for certain European Federation activities. This European Council is now a regular part of the work of the Federation and has met annually: Swanwick 1929, Paris 1930, Nauheim 1931, Bad Boll 1932, Melrose 1933. Its meetings have increased in value and the European Movements have been drawn together. The last meeting I attended at Nauheim, near Coblence, in 1931, marked a great advance. We were closer together and the range of interests covered was more extensive. On my resignation, R. C. Mackie was elected chairman at the Bad Boll meeting, 1932.

The lack of international student leadership had given some of us concern for some time. At the Peking Conference it looked as if the Federation was going to give a strong lead in the sphere of international relationships, and use the tremendous latent potency in its membership scattered all over the world to mould student opinion. But the High Leigh committee meeting was ineffective about international affairs and the Nyborg committee meeting was no better, so I determined to say what I thought in *The Student Movement*. I wrote an editorial under the title " Does the Federation want World Peace ? " recalling what the Student Movement had done for foreign missions, and continued :

But we are profoundly dissatisfied. Youth ought to be impulsive, passionate and active ; always making experiment, always doing new things, always pushing on. The leadership of the World's Student Christian Federation has grown younger and younger each year, but in spite of that its lead has not increased in vigour, imagination or courage, In what single great cause has it rallied its constituent movements since the war? At the time of the Peking Committee Meeting and Conference it looked as if it would give the students of the world a lead in relation to the question of war. A fine enthusiasm was shown at the conference and excellent resolutions were passed; students of all lands were found to be eager to follow a lead in working against the causes that make for war among the nations. . . .

A changing and widely scattered body like the Federation needs articulate and urgent and eager leadership A resolute and determined group of leaders with passionate convictions and a gift for bold and daring statemanship, and a belief that God had given some definite things to the Federation to do, would draw a response from the students of the world which would be far greater in volume and effect to-day than the response which has sent fourteen thousand volunteers in a generation into the service of the missionary societies.

Ought we not as a world movement to tackle with real vigour and urgency the whole question of war? . . .

Should not every Student Movement in the Federation be training its members to think of war as the greatest social evil in the world, and training them to believe that it can be brought to an end, and that they ought to strive together to bring this about. . . .

We have every reason in the World's Student Christian Federation for a whole-hearted campaign against war, our belief in God as the Father of all men, with the brotherhood of all men as an inevitable consequence of that belief, our respect and goodwill for one another as members of the World's Student Christian Federation, and our interest in everything that will reduce human suffering and promote human well-being. All these are mighty reasons for a whole-hearted and sustained endeavour to rally the students of the world on the side of disarmament and world peace.[1]

The Student Movement in the United States responded to this challenge, asked us to arrange a joint conference

[1] *The Student Movement*, Editorial, vol. xxx. pp. 121-22.

and offered to send a delegation across the Atlantic.
Twenty-five men and women subsequently met, half
from each side of the Atlantic.   Francis P. Miller came
as representative of the Federation.   A number of
practical suggestions to the British and American Student
Movement were prefaced by the following statement :

As representatives of the Student Christian Movements
of Great Britain and Ireland and the United States of
America, and as members of the World's Student Christian
Federation, we believe that the most progressive and
enlightened elements in the East and the West have become
convinced that war should no longer be used as an instrument of public policy, but should be eliminated from the
life of the nations as a social evil.

We unanimously favour the adoption of the treaty to
abolish war as an instrument of national policy, and agree
to carry to our Movements the urgent request that they
assist in creating a public opinion favourable to its adoption
and application.   We regard this treaty as representing the
beginning of a new day in the relations between nations,
and as affording an ideal opportunity for working towards
the development of effective agencies for international co-
operation and the active association of our respective nations
with such agencies.

We realize that the outlawry of war means the outlawry
of the causes of war, and we call upon our Student Movements to study these causes and to provide their members
with the incentive to devote their lives to their removal.
We are aware that the present status of our two nations
with regard to each other and to the rest of the world lays
an especially heavy burden upon the Christian groups in
both countries.   While considering the relations between
our two countries, we are not unmindful of our relations
with other nations, and particularly of our association with
mandated and subject peoples and of our obligation to
ensure justice.[1]

From that time on increasing attention has been given
to the question of disarmament in the Student Movements in Great Britain, France, Holland, Czechoslovakia
and the United States of America, and the secretariat of
the Federation has taken a full share in the efforts the

[1] *The Student Movement*, vol. xxxi. p. 33.

Christian organizations have made both to move public opinion in favour of world disarmament and to represent existing Christian opinion to the World Disarmament Conference at Geneva.

The year 1929 was an eventful one. First came the quadrennial at Liverpool. Its title was " The Purpose of God in the Life of the World." It was unusually well prepared for in the colleges, the result of the study department suggesting concentration on the *Epistle to the Ephesians*, with the guidance of studies by George Cockin and *A Philosophy from Prison* by F. R. Barry. The study department often suggests too many books and subjects ; a single subject appealed to students with excellent results.

It was the fourth time we had been to Liverpool, and the welcome of the University, City and Churches was as cordial as ever. Morning prayers in the Cathedral was a new feature, otherwise we met as before in the Philharmonic Hall, using the Y.M.C.A. gymnasium as a conference club and the University classrooms for groups after tea, which were held at a " quadrennial " for the first time.

Solicitude for the King, who was seriously ill, was universal, and the first act of the conference on assembling was to pray for him. A telegram of sympathy to the Queen was acknowledged within a few hours, conveying Her Majesty's thanks for " the kind message of sympathy and good wishes."

R. O. Hall made an excellent chairman and his conduct of the evening services earned the gratitude of all. T. Z. Koo of China was again with us, and the chief addresses were given by the Archbishop-elect of York (Dr Temple), Canons C. E. Raven and Spanton, Revs. F. R. Barry, C. F. Andrews, W. R. Maltby, J. S. Whale, Messrs John Macmurray and J. H. Oldham. The Archbishop-elect gave the conference, three days immediately before his enthronement at York, one of the best addresses and its heartiest laugh. Mr Barry, speaking before him, remarked that his business was to roll the pitch for the Archbishop, whereupon Dr Temple, as he came forward to follow Barry, remarked, " By nature and by art I am far more qualified than Mr Barry to be a roller—it is required of rollers that they be cylindrical." Everyone roared as they looked from the lean figure of Barry to the portly form of the Archbishop !

The programme had been planned in the main on the lines of " Glasgow 1921 " and " Manchester 1925." Freedom and friendship for all the world were ideas that ran through all that was said and found fullest expression in the address of John Macmurray, which deeply moved the conference. As the human race has developed in self-consciousness, man's instinct for fellowship and freedom has asserted itself, yet the world finds itself drawn by a desire for domination and in the grip of a selfish un-lovingness. The strange contradiction and conflict was never more apparent than to-day. Humanity longs for freedom, and yet men strive for domination over their fellows. God calls us to freedom and fellowship, and has set men in families and in nations that they may love and serve one another and help one another to true freedom.

But God does not " buy men nor coerce men, nor overawe men." God's method with men is friendship. It is as the reality of the friendship of God enters the heart and mind of a man that he begins to realize how great God's method is and how much is involved in his use of freedom. Jesus Christ still stands in the midst of history with a message and a power which assures those who have ears to hear that God's purpose for the world is undefeated. Will men accept the friendship and freedom God offers, and then with His purpose for human life accepted as central, will they go where and do what that purpose requires them ?

There was a total conference membership of 2008 persons (1438 British students, 139 from abroad, and 431 professors, tutors, speakers, missionaries, etc.), and these represented 198 British universities and colleges and 38 countries.

The conference was a call " to tread the way of friendship into the heart of the world in this hour of destiny." [1] It made a deep impression on the delegates present and was accounted as great an occasion as previous conferences had been.

The next event of the year was the reopening of Annandale on April 11th by Mr E. R. Peacock, representing the three trustees of the National Appeal Fund—the Rt. Hon. Stanley Baldwin, M.P., Prime Minister ; Sir Robert Kindersley, Director of the Bank of England ; and Dr Montague James, the Provost of Eton College. A service of dedication followed, led by J. O. Dobson, Hugh Martin and T. Tatlow. The dedicatory prayer was taken by Archbishop Lord Davidson of Lambeth. This was his last visit to us.

A number of gifts were received for the new house, which cost £17,428. Viscount Astor's gifts were the fireplace and moulding which beautify the refectory, and also its furniture ; the secretaries' lounge was furnished by Lord Maclay ; former chairmen of the Movement presented two oak tables for the committee room ; an ikon was made and presented by the Russian Student Christian Movement in Emigration ; a group of secretaries, past and present, presented a cross, and the kitchen staff a Bible, in memory of Edith Thornton ; while a consecrated altar was loaned to the chapel by the House of the Sacred Mission, Kelham. The letter in which Father Kelly, on behalf of the House of the Sacred Mission, offered the altar through Miss Fairfield to the Movement is of such interest that it should be produced.

House of the Sacred Mission,
Kelham, Newark-on-Trent,
March 25th, 1929.

Dear Miss Fairfield,

I have shown your letter to the Fr. Prior. The altar in question is not at present in use. We should like you to feel how much we sympathize with S.C.M. and its work, how grateful we feel for its kindness, and the help we have

[1] *The Purpose of God in the Life of the World*, p. 12.

had from it.   If your people would like to have the altar
in their chapel—all the more since it has passed through
our hands—it would be no less a pleasure to us in some
way to contribute.

You do and will realize our feeling that this is a dedicated
altar.   And we realize your difficulties as a meeting-place of
many minds who do not think alike.

If you would like to have it there, I have been trying to
think out a way in which it might be done.   If we make
what might seem to be an offer with reservations, I want
to point out at the start that they are meant to meet your
difficulties as much as to meet our own.

How would it be if we agree to *lend* it to you quite openly
—*until* you have, make, find, or decide on, something of
your own ?

On our side, if the S.S.M. should want it, it can ask for
its return.   But—I am thinking mainly of S.C.M.—there
may be friends and visitors who would dislike it ; you can
reply to them, equally uncommitted, " Yes, it is a Church
altar.   We do not use it as such, and have no Church licence
for celebrations.   We did not think it right to ask for one.
But it is lent to us by friends, who were glad to do something."

If you find it creates trouble, you also are free to send it
back.   You can tell your critics so (if anyone is critical).

If at any time these difficulties pass away, and common
celebrations become possible, you can ask the S.S.M. to
make it a gift.   Perhaps the day is less far off than some
people think.   The S.C.M. has done so much to bring it
nearer—and I will add emphatically for my own part—that
S.C.M. has done so much more to bring it nearer by refusing
to snatch at it.   I am not an authority of S.S.M., least of
all an authority of the future, but when the time does come,
I have no doubt the authorities of S.S.M. will say the gift
is well earned.   In the meanwhile, I hope the loan is
prophesying of unity.

We should *prefer* that the cross and candlesticks went
with the altar to which they belong.   Possibly if you
explained that they were part of the whole setting, people
might not object, but—if your friends think otherwise—
we might keep them for you.

I should like a copy of this letter kept convenient to the
chapel, to prevent possible misunderstandings.

Yours sincerely in Christ,

HERBERT KELLY.

3 I

At the meeting of the General Committee in June 1929 Hugh Martin laid before it a scheme for the future development of the publishing work of the Movement. This was the formation of the Student Christian Movement Press, Limited, to be governed by a board of twelve directors. It was decided that the friends of the Movement should be asked to provide capital for the new company in the form of preference shares paying a dividend limited to 5 per cent., and that all the ordinary shares should be held by the Student Christian Movement. After valuation of the existing stock it was agreed that this should be handed to the new company in return for 3000 ordinary £1 shares. By this arrangement the Student Movement retains the ultimate control of the company and receives the profits of the Press in the form of dividends on the ordinary shares.

The directors chosen for the new company were all either former members of the Movement, or senior friends. They were :

> Canon Tatlow, Chairman of S.C.M. and Rector of All Hallows, Lombard Street.
> F. W. Bain, Esq., Executive Director of Brunner, Mond & Co., Ltd.
> Canon F. A. Cockin, Canon of Southwark and Diocesan Missioner.
> The Rev. J. O. Dobson, Missionary Secretary of the S.C.M.
> The Rev. F. A. Iremonger, formerly Editor of *The Guardian*.
> Dr A. D. Lindsay, Master of Balliol College, Oxford.
> The Rev. Hugh Martin, Managing Director and Editor.
> A. G. Pite, Esq., Headmaster of Weymouth College.
> Miss Ruth Rouse, Secretary of the Missionary Council of the Church Assembly.
> The Rev. Canon E. Gordon Selwyn, Editor of *Theology*.
> The Rev. Edward Shillito, Literary Superintendent of the London Missionary Society.
> The Rev. W. S. Tindal, Study Secretary of S.C.M.
> Alexander Walker, Esq., Business Director.
> The Rev. W. M. Wightman, Director of Education, Church of Scotland.

Canon Tatlow was appointed chairman and Mr F. R. Reader secretary of the Press.

In order to ensure contact between the managing director and the Student Christian Movement a clause was inserted in the articles of association to the effect that the offices of the managing director should be at the headquarters of the Student Christian Movement.

As the Press needed capital, it asked friends of the Movement to subscribe £7500 in 5 per cent. preference shares of £5 each. This amount was quickly over-subscribed.

The Press and the Student Movement House Club both wanted more space, so it was decided that the Student Movement Press should have new offices, and the directors purchased the lease of 58 Bloomsbury Street, W.C.

At the same time changes were made in the Student Movement House, a sum of money being provided by the National Appeal Fund which enabled the Managing Committee to redecorate the house, improve the club rooms and carry out some alterations making it more suitable for the use of the club.

While the summer brought changes in administration, it also gave the Movement a new Aim and Basis, which is dealt with elsewhere. When the autumn of 1929 came we were without Zoë Fairfield and George Cockin. Miss Fairfield had been a secretary for twenty years, and when she became such had already much experience in the work of the Movement. During her years of service there was no side of the Movement's work which she did not help. Before she joined the staff her work among London women students and fine art students had put them in her debt. At different times she led the Movement in its thought about training colleges and education, Bible study, social questions, inter-national relationships, and in its work for foreign students and fine art and music students. She was the chief maker of the programmes for four quadrennial and a score of summer conferences. She led the

Auxiliary for ten years before she became its secretary. The evangelistic and missionary policy of the Movement owed much to her initiative. No one was more often the convener of S.C.M. sub-committees and few were as effective, for she could weld a group of people into a fellowship with a capacity to create as could no one else who has served the Movement. The Theological College Department made her its secretary at one period, and the Student Movement House its chairman. She was for years the chief link between the S.C.M. in both Ireland and Wales and the centre of the Movement.

This catalogue, by no means complete, will give some idea of her place in the Movement. I often wondered whether she or Douglas Thornton had the greater creative gift. I don't know, but of this I am sure : no other secretaries ever equalled their genius for producing new ideas and harnessing them to effective work.

Miss Fairfield's active and versatile intelligence, while always at the service of the Movement, was still more at the service of individuals. Her capacity for friendship seemed without bounds. She disliked sentiment, and people in a mood of self-pity—wanting a little comfort—would find her probing into the cause of their state and sometimes offering a more drastic remedy than that for which they looked. Her friendship has an astringent quality in it. I have never known anyone who could be counted upon for help with greater certainty than Zoë Fairfield. Two qualities that marked all she did were those of courage and disinterestedness. It was no use going to her for encouragement in a timid or cautious course of action. She has immense courage and always advocated the courageous course. So it was, too, in the matter of disinterestedness—I use a word to which she has given a great content for many people. I never knew her think of relationships and situations in terms of herself.

I asked her once to write on "The Importance of being Impersonal" for *The Student Movement*. It was a short paper but pregnant. "The first element," she wrote, " in the power to be impersonal about oneself is to look oneself clearly in the face and cut oneself dead." I often marvelled at the capacity of one with so much personality to efface herself. Most people with much personality push themselves a good deal. Deeply-rooted faith in God, courage, versatility, brains and a capacity for rendering disinterested service to causes and number-less individuals made it a great privilege to work with her. The Student Movement has not replaced her, that it cannot do, but it can always be thankful that her twenty years' work for it has enriched it with what Bill Paton has characterized as " a magnificent piece of service." [1]

It was a heavy loss to the Movement that George Cockin's term of service ended at this time. He had been on the staff for fifteen years. Educated at Marl-borough School, University College, Oxford, and Cud-desdon College, he joined the staff of the Movement after having spent three years on " short service " at Delhi. His first post was that of foreign student secretary, to which he was appointed in 1914. He gave the work of the Movement for students from overseas a new place in its life and thought. His reports and memo-randa are still the basis of the Movement's work for students from other lands. He was leader of this side of the Movement's work for seven years, but to say this would give no real idea of his place in the life of the Student Movement.

Every secretary has always fallen into one of two categories : the man who does his own work, or the man who always thinks of the Movement as a whole and who, while doing his own work, never lets the picture of what the whole Movement is aiming at slip from his vision. George was emphatically of the latter category. His mind ranged over the whole policy of the Movement and he was always eager to know what any of us was doing or thinking. This breadth of

[1] *The Student Movement*, vol. xxxi., p. 205, " Zoë Fairfield," by William Paton.

outlook and interest, together with a deep capacity for understanding and sympathy, made him the friend and confidant of innumerable secretaries and students.

When, in 1921, he became the first apologetics study secretary of the Movement, he passed to work he had wanted to do for some time and for which he proved himself well fitted. He became far more than an apologetics' specialist. He guided the whole study policy of the Movement from 1921 to 1929, and when during this period the study staff was reduced for financial reasons, he became responsible for all the Bible and doctrinal study of the Movement.

He devoted himself with untiring patience to men who had intellectual difficulties about Christianity, and won the confidence of the questioning students who filled the colleges after the war more than any other secretary. " When in difficulties send for George Cockin " became the practical motto of the leaders of the S.C.M. in the universities. He was extraordinarily good with groups of students on the outside fringe of Christianity. He knew how to find common ground on which to meet them with success. There is a very large body of men and women all over the world who remember him with special gratitude.

His capacity for interpreting people of very different points of view to one another was an asset to the Federation, which has found him irreplaceable so far. He was invited by students to many lands and undertook periods of service in Canada, Czechoslovakia, Poland and India, while he was with the Movement. He did not disappoint the Movements that secured his help.

It is not possible to record all he did, which ranged from looking after the men's colleges in London towards the close of the war, to lecturing at the Student Movement House, but a word must be said about his conduct of the last Aim and Basis discussion which lasted for several years. It was the most difficult, in some ways, of all that had gone before, and more than once the situation might have broken had it not been for the

patience and thoroughness of George Cockin.   He could
be nervous and over-anxious on occasions, but when
need arose his patience was apparently unfathomable,
and he had his reward in the confidence and gratitude
of a goodly company.

The academic year 1930-31 started without the
services of J. O. Dobson, who had been a member of
the staff for eight years.   His first three years were spent
as secretary of the East and West Friendship Committee.
He was its first secretary.   As he had his office at
Annandale and was accorded all the privileges of a
Student Movement secretary, no one thought of him
except as such, though he received his appointment
from, and was paid by, the East and West Friendship
Committee.   J. O. Dobson laid down lines of close co-
operation between this committee and the Student
Movement which have been of great value to both
organizations.   After three years' work for foreign
students he became missionary secretary of the Movement, a position he held for five years, and one in
which he did more than any one else in the years since
the war to cement the Movement's friendly relationships with the headquarters of the great missionary
societies.

Dobson always took a great interest in all that was
happening in the Movement.   The majority of secretaries
find that their particular work is as much as they can
manage, and, although it is unusual if any of them are
not intelligently interested in all that the Movement is
doing, only an occasional man and woman here and
there has had the capacity to understand and make their
own departments of the Movement's life and thought
for which they were not directly responsible.   Such
people have always been invaluable to their colleagues
for consultative purposes, and are the people who have
preserved and enriched the continuous life and growth
of the Movement.   J. O. Dobson was one of these people.
He had considerable knowledge of international affairs
and kept himself specially closely informed in relation

to India. A Congregationalist by denomination, he was a strong churchman and the work of the Theological College Department, as well as the position of the Movement in relation to questions of unity, had his interest and sympathetic understanding. He is a good reviewer of books and has real distinction as a writer, as a reference to his books and also his articles in *The Student Movement* bears witness.

In 1932 Mr and Mrs Christmas, who had taken care of Annandale—house and garden—for twenty years, retired, leaving a memory of kindly and faithful service for us all behind them.

The political situation in India has been a topic of frequent discussion in Student Movement circles for the last three years. When the late K. T. Paul was in London for the Round-Table Conference convened by the Government, the leaders of the Student Movement saw a great deal of him. We had published a book of his some years before on *The British Connection with India*, and knew how deeply he longed that the two countries might find the way to a readjustment of their relationships, so that they could be contented and self-respecting friends within the British Commonwealth. In the autumn of 1930 the International Council of the Movement had a long discussion on the relationship of Great Britain and India when he was present, together with Paul Runganadhan, who was working jointly for International Student Service and the World's Student Christian Federation, and Mr J. S. Aiman, the warden of the Indian Students' Union and Hostel, both of them old friends of our Movement. The outcome of this meeting was a decision to send the following letter to the Student Movement in India :

To the Members of the
    Student Christian Association
        of India, Burma and Ceylon.

Dear Friends,
    We, the members of the General Committee of the Student Christian Movement of Great Britain and Ireland, meeting

in session at a time when the relations between the Indian and British people have reached a most critical stage, desire to offer you our sincere greetings, and the assurance of our sympathy and prayers at this time of peculiar difficulty in India.

We believe that we express the conviction of the great majority of our members when we declare our full sympathy with the desire of the people of India to control Indian affairs. We feel India's desire for real freedom to be in the spirit of our faith.

We know that you in India are passing through a period of intense unrest and strain which is bringing pain and suffering upon large numbers of your people, that thousands of men and women have gone to prison, and that violence has been used by some on both sides. We hate violence on the part of any.

We are convinced that, especially at a time such as this, all Christians are called to exercise a ministry of reconciliation and to be alive to the moral issues involved. We recognize that you and some of our own nation are facing this task as members of the Christian community in India under very difficult circumstances. On our part we propose to call our members to the same task and to a sympathetic understanding of the present situation, and that by prayer and study we may be prepared to exercise an intelligent and quickened Christian witness.

We greatly value the friendship that has existed between your Association and our Movement, both in Britain and in India. Whatever may be the political settlement of the future, we hope that our friendship and co-operation may be broadened and deepened.

As we send you this message we pray that through this time of strain and suffering we of the Student Christian Movements of India and Britain may realize more truly the meaning of our vocation in the world, and of our fellowship together in the service of Christ and His Kingdom.

On behalf of the General Committee,

I am,

Yours sincerely,

ROBERT C. MACKIE.

The decision to hold a quadrennial conference in January 1933 was reached at the Easter meeting, 1931, and a couple of months later a special meeting was convened to discuss its programme. Robert Mackie wanted to take the conference to Edinburgh, and as it would be the first quadrennial that anybody had organized except myself since 1896, we thought that as a Scotsman he was wise in making the suggestion, provided it evoked a sympathetic response in Edinburgh. By the autumn of 1931 we had abundant evidence that the Church and University in Edinburgh would give us a warm welcome. The conference was limited to two thousand, which was the capacity of the Assembly Hall of the Church of Scotland, and this number of delegates was found without any difficulty.

The conference was remarkable for the intensity of the attention of its members to all that was put before them. As ever, the programme was closely relevant to the world situation. The challenge of communism to all weakness and ineffectiveness in the Christian Church was clear and compelling. None of the features of previous quadrennials were omitted. The division of the conference into groups for a period each day that they might discuss the speeches was continued. This was first done at "Liverpool 1929." On this occasion much care was taken to train the group leaders, the major responsibility being borne by Eric Fenn.

The evening meetings dealt with the fundamental verities of the Christian faith, and the speakers handled their themes with greater assurance and won a deeper response from the students than in any of the quadrennial conferences held since the war.

The new general secretariat, consisting of Robert Mackie, Francis House and Catherine Mackinnon, organized the conference with a skill which assured the Movement's friends that the change of staff at the centre which gave the Movement a young team had been achieved without loss of efficiency.

When speaking of efficiency one's mind turns to the staff of clerks at Annandale.

The Movement has always been served with great loyalty by the group of men and women who compose its clerical staff. This staff has grown from one stenographer, when I joined the Movement, to a body of over twenty accountants, private secretaries, stenographers and juniors at the present time. Some have served a number of years : F. R. Reader, secretary of the S.C.M. Press, S. R. Hepper, senior accountant—both came to the Movement as junior clerks after leaving school; the former has served over twenty-five and the latter over twenty years, while Miss Lucking has been the one constant element on the London college staff for twenty years.

I must also make mention of two men who have served the Movement for many years. Walter Saunders, F.C.A., became auditor in 1894, and what any of us know of accountancy we learned from him. His patience and wisdom have been unfailing. R. L. Barclay succeeded Charles Harford Battersby, the first treasurer, in 1897. He has seen many changes and discussed with us many bold proposals regarding finance and has always been one of those ready for advance. We have had in Robin Barclay a friend who has always shared in our aspirations for the Movement, and one who has always been with us in spirit as God has called us to go forward.

The place of *The Student Movement* in the life of the S.C.M. is an important one. We centre our corporate life as a Movement in our summer conferences and once in a student generation in an international and missionary conference ; but all the year round the thought of the Movement is expressed and interpreted in *The Student Movement*. Anything that is moving the hearts and minds of the leaders is reflected in the magazine.

A study of the thirty-four volumes of it which have appeared show that it has reflected the thoughts of many of the leaders of the Christian Churches in the British Isles as well as that of the Movement's leaders. Names of men now famous appear at the foot of paragraphs of S.C.M. College news, some of whom later contribute articles, and some of them now belong to the whole Church of Christ.

CHAPTER XLV

THE AIM OF THE STUDENT MOVEMENT
AND HOW IT IS CARRIED OUT

THE theme of this book is how the Student Movement has thought about its work and tried to do it during the last forty years. But an attempt must be made to say something about the work of the Movement from day to day at the present time in the universities and colleges, and the conditions under which it is carried on.

If a college S.C.M. is sometimes found which is content to be one of a number of college societies it is not a characteristic branch of the Movement. The Movement " stands for something that is indispensable to every man. Religion is not something to be taken up as an extra, as one may decide between the rival claims of football or hockey." [1] The Movement does not want to see in a college a S.C.M. set as there may be a hockey set. " Christ is for all sorts and conditions of men, and wherever the Student Movement has not learnt to present Him to the entire body of students, it has to that extent failed." [1]

There can be no question about the need for the Movement. Student days are days of intense mental activity and of readjustment to whole new realms of thought and life, before unrealized. It is for most men the time for taking the great decisions of life, for the determination of ideals and standards of value.

The Movement has to do its work over and over again. On an average the student population of the college world is completely changed every three years. This rapid change in the constituency of the Movement

[1] *Annual Report, S.C.M.,* 1922-23, pp. 7-8.

explains the fluctuating fortunes of the different college branches. Almost everything depends upon the leaders for the time being, and branches which are weak and ineffective one year may be strong and vigorous the next. The reverse, unhappily, is also true. It is difficult to conserve policy and make it continuous from year to year. Here the travelling and intercollegiate secretaries render invaluable help. These secretaries are also often able to advise and guide in the choice of local leaders. Students know a first-class man when they have such in their midst, but when it comes to choosing the best possible leaders from an average lot, mistakes are often made. A Student Movement secretary with a gift for " spotting " good leaders from among first and second year men is invaluable, he is also somewhat rare. In spite of all the difficulties of continuity, the policy of the Movement does develop as it is passed on from generation to generation, a fact to which this book bears witness.

If lack of continuity is one difficulty, another is the non-residential character of most of our British universities. Oxford, Cambridge, Dublin and Durham are residential, but the other English, Scottish, Welsh and Irish universities where the majority of students are studying are non-residential in the main, though Reading University has all its students in hostels, and most of the modern universities have an increasing number of hostels. Being non-residential means that a large body of students live at home with the interests of two communities pulling at them—home and college. Living at home often also means two long and tiring journeys daily in crowded trains. Others live in lodgings; on the whole these are the poorest students, and lodgings scattered over a great city, lodgings in which students are not encouraged by landladies to entertain their friends, do not add to the value of university life.

Non-residence is the rule with the great medical schools attached to the London hospitals, though there are exceptions in the case of a few students. Technical, music and fine art colleges are also non-residential, but training, agricultural and theological colleges are usually residential.

The modern universities all have crowded curricula, and one who has been educated at an ancient university finds, with dismay, that students who began lectures at 9 a.m. are sometimes still being lectured at 5 p.m. Life is lived at high pressure, and the physical strain of travelling in crowded trains and tubes, with long hours of lectures and work in laboratories, the anxieties of examinations on which much depends from a family and financial point of view, tends to make students put up a shield of indifference against any attempt to add religion to the already excessive demands of life. Hostels usually improve conditions and greatly facilitate the work of the Movement.

The S.C.M. is as well supported, as a rule, as the more important societies and far better than most. A university may have more than 50 different student societies with as high as 70 per cent. of its entire body of students supporting no society at all. The latest available figures, those for 1932, show that in a university and college field of some 70,000 to 75,000 students of all kinds—44,000 of them being university students—the Student Movement has 210 branches at work, 78 among men and 132 among women. In these there are 3186 men members and 6514 women members. There are 72 theological colleges " associated " with the Movement, containing 3056 students. The total membership of the Movement is thus 12,756. In addition it has some groups in touch with it in fine art and music schools.

The Student Volunteer Missionary Union has been joined by 7102 [1] students since it was started, and of this number 2246 men and 1243 women have become missionaries; 1500 members are in college for further preparation or temporarily hindered from service abroad,

[1] These figures are correct to July 1933.

and the remainder will not be available for missionary work. The reason which has prevented the great majority from going abroad has been rejection by the missionary societies on grounds of health.

What is it that a college S.C.M. actually does ? It has first of all to introduce itself and what it stands for to the new students each year, and all freshmen are invited to a gathering where this is done. This gathering varies from college to college, producing its best results, as far as bringing freshmen into the Movement is concerned, if the leaders have the courage of their convictions and make it an occasion the primary purpose of which is to explain the Movement to the freshman and give him some idea of its central purpose. The most successful type of meeting has never varied much during the forty years' experience of the Movement. The first part of the evening is social, refreshments and conversation interspersed with music, then come one or two of the leaders of the Student Movement in college, who explain its objects and programme, and a favourite speaker to students concludes with a direct Christian message encouraging the freshman to take his stand as a Christian in college. That has always been the most effective kind of meeting, although time and again student leaders become timid about the drawing power of the Christian message and feel that they must attract students by a dance, or some other form of entertainment, which becomes the chief event of the evening. Sometimes a freshmen's social of this kind will draw very large numbers, but nothing much comes of it except the feeling that everybody has had a pleasant time.

The most important work of the college S.C.M. begins once the freshmen's meeting is over. That is the collecting of people for study circles and the starting of these circles. The study work of the Movement is its backbone. The study circle has been a method in continuous use from the inception of the Movement. It is a group of eight to a dozen students, who meet regularly for an hour once a week during term to compare the results of their study. The success of a study circle depends upon the care with which members prepare for it. It sometimes happens that no one does much preparation, in which case the circle may succeed in holding together until the end of the term, but its value to members is small. A few people in it studying regularly will always save a circle, while if everyone prepares regularly the circle will be a success ; the meetings of some circles are more highly prized by members than anything else they attend in college.

The study secretaries of the Movement spend much time and thought in planning text-books and either writing them or getting them written, preparing outline studies to guide leaders, and arranging at the beginning of each summer term for the training of leaders. Good leaders are not easy to find, but the average student who has to be used for leadership, if given a certain amount of training, can be considerably assisted in his task.

The subjects of study vary a great deal. The Movement tries to get all its branches to do a certain amount of study of Christian doctrine or the Bible (or both), missionary, international and social study each year. A small branch may only have one or two study circles, a large one may have twenty meeting each week. The handling of its study work by a college S.C.M. tends to vary a good deal from time to time, according to the ability of the leaders. If the leadership is good there will be a variety of circles studying the Bible, doctrinal, missionary, international and social subjects : leaders will have been trained, circles will start work early in the term, and students who are likely to work well together will be arranged in groups. If leadership is poor, the circles will probably be late in starting, the leaders untrained, people put into circles without much selection and, as likely as not, unsuitable subjects chosen. It is by no means uncommon to find students extremely ignorant about the Bible beginning with the Book of Daniel !

The Movement has had a very varied experience with regard to general meetings, but on the whole the general meeting addressed by a speaker from outside the college, a member of staff or Student Movement secretary, and open to any student who likes to attend, is a regular feature of the programme of each branch of the Movement. At one time every branch had a general meeting of this kind once a week. Nowadays, however, they are much less frequent and the standard of speaking is greatly improved. The selection of subjects for general meetings, even now, is much less effective than it might be in many places. Committees are apt to choose a subject because some member has heard it treated at a sectional meeting at a summer conference of the Movement, or simply because someone suggests a topic and it is accepted without much reflection. Subjects chosen without adequate reasons bulk rather too largely in programmes, and there is not always that careful study of the spiritual needs of the students in college which is necessary before good programmes can be made. There is still much to be done in relating general meetings to the rest of the work of many college S.C.M.'s. Sometimes, for example, one wonders, in visiting a college, whether it has occurred to anybody that there ought to be a relationship between the study circle work and the general meetings.

The general meeting is often addressed by a speaker the General Committee of the Movement has secured for a tour of the colleges. Missionaries and social workers are sent round to talk about the need for workers at home and abroad. Perhaps hardly enough has been said about the platform which the college branches of the Movement provide for the Christian Church. Clergy, ministers, missionaries and social workers address over four thousand meetings annually, at the lowest computation, under the auspices of the Movement. Missionaries of the great societies of the Anglican, Presbyterian and Free Churches are secured, not merely for single meetings, but to tour the colleges

3 K

and by speech and personal intercourse stir students to missionary interest. Most of the missionaries selected for this work nowadays have been leaders of college S.C.M.'s themselves in their own student days, and are well qualified to interest students.

In order to help students to think about society at home, economists, social workers and others are in constant demand as speakers. The study-conference method is used a good deal, groups of students are billeted in or near a social settlement for two or three days, when it is possible to combine lectures and visits to cinemas, housing areas, factories and the like, so that students may study on the spot how the masses earn their livelihood, are housed, and what recreation is available for them.

A good deal has been said elsewhere about evangelistic work, which students refer to either as " mission " or " campaign," or " religion and life week," according to the fashion of the day. The Student Movement has never achieved the ideal which at one time its committee named, of having a mission in each university centre once in a student generation, but if this ideal has not been universally attained, the Movement has come very near fulfilling it, for a study of the last twenty-five years shows that there has been a consistent attempt to present the Christian gospel to the students of the British Isles by the Movement. It must not be forgotten that the evangelistic effect of the summer conferences has always been considerable. There are many students feeling their way towards the Christian faith who join study circles and are brought by fellow students to a summer conference, who there make the decision to commit themselves to Christ.

Almost every college S.C.M. arranges regularly some gathering of its members for prayer. A considerable proportion of them have daily prayer-meetings. This is one of the most enduring of the Movement's activities. These meetings are often very small, yet they swell to large dimensions if there is some special effort in college, such as a mission. I have again and again seen a prayer-meeting attended regularly by a handful of people become a daily prayer-meeting of anything up to nearly a hundred students for weeks before a mission. Colleges vary very much in the way they conduct this particular activity. It is usually held for a quarter of an hour about middle-day. It may be in a classroom or in church near the college. Some universities have given the S.C.M. a room of its own in which it is held. Again, it may be in the form of morning prayers, students coming to college half an hour before lectures begin, usually at 9 o'clock, to meet for prayer. Sometimes the meeting is a guided intercession, where the leader alone is vocal, and sometimes it is an extempore prayer-meeting. It may be a fellowship of silence.

Quiet days and half-days have been successfully introduced in a number of places in recent years, some senior friend being invited to act as leader. At these quiet days there will be several addresses interspersed with periods for prayer, private reading and meditation. These quiet days are much appreciated and are on the increase.

Another common activity of the college S.C.M.'s is what is often called a retreat. It is a misnomer, but the word came into use to distinguish a week-end gathering, which was designed to provide opportunity for quiet and personal spiritual help for those attending, from one convened for speeches and discussion apart from any special devotional purpose. A more suitable term for these gatherings would be " retreat-conferences." Usually some senior friend comes to give one or more addresses of a devotional character. Care is taken to make the devotional element an important part of the gathering, but far from being a retreat in silence, there is a great deal of talking. The students value the opportunity of exchanging experiences and views with one another and with their leader as they sit under a tree in summer, or round a fire in winter. These gatherings may centre in the cultivation of the spiritual life, or may aim at helping a group to do a piece of more thorough Bible or doctrinal study than is possible in the rush of college life, or may have a more varied programme, interspersing devotional and apologetic with international, missionary or social topics. They are usually held away from college in some place where the students can live together for a day or two. For the last twenty years they have been a very important factor in the development of Christian thought, character and activity among students.

Another kind of conference which is common is the pre-terminal conference, where in some cases the committee of the college S.C.M., and in others the committee joined by study circle leaders, or even by any members able to attend, meet to prepare themselves for the S.C.M. work of the coming term. The Aim and Basis of the Movement, the different kinds of study work and other S.C.M. activities will usually come in for consideration at a gathering of this kind. A pre-terminal conference may last for a day, or three days, and is usually held in the university, although sometimes, like the retreat-conference, it may be held away from the university in some country place.

One occasion that is universally observed is the Day of Prayer for Students, appointed by the World's Student Christian Federation. For many years this day has been the third Sunday in February. Sometimes it is observed simply by a gathering for prayer, sometimes by more than one meeting, and occasionally an attempt is made to reach the whole university in the name of the World's Student Christian Federation with the Christian message. In the latter case there will be a gathering of members of the Movement for united prayer and praise, and one or two more meetings, or services, open to all students.

The majority of college branches of the Movement make good use of its literature and the literature itself has grown steadily, both in quantity and quality, as the years have gone by. Nowadays college leaders expect to get literature descriptive of the Movement and guides

to all kinds of meetings and study circles supplied automatically from Annandale, and know that the catalogue
of the Student Christian Movement Press contains the
names of books available for dealing with the different
kinds of subjects that students are expected to study in relation to the Christian faith.   The Movement's magazine,
The Student Movement, although it has a larger circulation
outside the colleges than within them, is read by most
of the keener members of the Movement.   The circulation is, on the whole, rather poor in the colleges in
relation to the membership, probably not more than one
member in eight is a subscriber.   On the other hand,
a large proportion of the copies subscribed for are read
by many students, and a request for a show of hands
of readers of the magazine at a Student Movement
gathering invariably produces a far larger show of hands
than a study of the subscription list suggests would be
likely.

If the members of the Movement look to its headquarters for literature, they also look to it for conferences, and they are not disappointed.   Not less than two
thousand students attend Student Movement conferences
in a normal year, the chief being two general conferences
for students at Swanwick, an officers' conference at
Swanwick to help to prepare students to lead the college
branches, and a general conference in Wales.   Sometimes
Scotland has its own conference, and sometimes the
Scots come to Swanwick.   In addition to these there
are always a number of local conferences.   In the
year of a quadrennial conference about three thousand
five hundred students attend conferences during the
year.

I have often heard students and others attempt to
describe a Student Movement conference, and when
listening have realized afresh what a difficult thing it
is to do.   What makes a conference is its atmosphere,
and no words can really describe the atmosphere of a
conference.   Perhaps the best description ever given
was that by Dr Cairns.   " It is a spirit of laughter and

of prayer." Even to look at a student conference does one good. Youth, vitality and good fellowship are in themselves extraordinarily attractive. The uninitiated are sometimes afraid of Student Movement conferences because they think that there will be an atmosphere of forced piety, emotionalism and "heartiness," but acquaintance with them soon dispels such fears. People are much too interested in the great questions of God and man and the world that are being spoken to by some of the ablest Christian leaders in the country to want to simulate piety. Anyone who knows students knows that they are afraid of emotionalism and disapprove of and suspect the minority among their fellow students who favour it, and as for heartiness natural spirits are too high for anyone to be tempted to ape them.

The fear of giving play to the emotions is specially true of women students, who douche the men with criticism if they show any signs of what they call emotionalism. There is a tendency in the Student Movement to give the emotions rather less than their proper place in its gatherings, but this does not interfere with the spirit of good fellowship, and a Student Movement conference is always simply bursting with high spirits, and yet high spirits that are never allowed to get out of hand, as sometimes happens when students rag. More than once Father Kelly has said that the most Christian thing about the summer conference at Swanwick was its ragging. The Student Movement knows how to rag to the glory of God. Sports' day, or camp meals provide occasions for the expression of student humour in all kinds of ways, but in forty years there have not been more than two or three occasions on which something has been said or done which afterwards seemed, to those concerned, unworthy of the Movement. It is in this kind of setting that students listen to addresses and lectures for hours, meet for corporate devotion and discuss in large and small groups, with some of the great Christian leaders of the day, the great matters of religion and life with that deadly earnestness which students, more than any other class in the community, concentrate on such discussions.

Leadership for the Student Christian Movement has always been of vital importance.   The idea that it arose spontaneously in the universities and grew in an easy way by its own momentum is far from the truth.   It began because a very small group of resolute men believed God had given them work to do among their fellow students.   It developed because one here and another there saw new tasks for it.   The communication of their visions and the stimulation and education of the student rank and file has always called for incessant labour on the part of those to whom the call to lead the Movement has come.   Students are accessible to truth, and they will follow leaders they trust, but leaders are essential.

Leadership has come from two groups working together in the Movement—the General Committee and the secretaries of the Movement.

The General Committee has always met for a three- or four-day meeting in the end of September, round about Christmas and at Easter, each year.

There is nothing I know of in the least like a meeting of the General Committee.   It was once a very small group and is now a large and representative one, but it has not changed in essential characteristics during the thirty-six years I have known it.   The outstanding quality is vitality—everyone, or almost everyone, is of student age.   People are very different : variety in speech if nothing else tells one that.   Eton and New College produce a different accent from Coleraine and Queen's University, Belfast, or from King Edward VI Grammar School and Birmingham University.   There are differences of race and politics and church.   Here is a Presbyterian who thinks there is but one real Kirk, there a Free Churchman who is looking forward to preaching the Word, and here is an Anglo-Catholic rejoicing in the Catholic movement.   It is difficult for a newcomer to discover who everybody is, for one hears only an occasional surname, and one must get to know who are Edwin, Robert, Moira, John, Dorothy, Eric and so on. " Mr " and " Miss " was the regular usage between the sexes until the middle of the world war, when the common stress and anxiety and the need of all for sympathy swept away titles, and we came to use each other's Christian names simply and naturally, and have done so ever since.

Secretaries who, by election or *ex officio* rights, are on the committee are full members of it. It is soon apparent to the newcomer that no time is wasted on formalities. Methods are businesslike and the level of debate is high. Students come straight from the colleges, and know what their fellow students think, and, as a rule, say what that is with directness. The General Committee is also surprisingly well informed. There is always someone who knows all about the Lindsay Commission Report, the content of the Encyclical of the last Lambeth Conference, the significance of the Ordinances in India, the theology of Karl Barth, the doings of the World Economic Conference, etc. There is a flood of talk, most of it relevant, but the Committee means to act, and the chairman can get decisions when the topic is well explored, and the line to be taken has become clear. When the Committee is at its best it always laughs a good deal. I always felt anxious when laughter was absent. The spirit of laughter and of prayer are a good combination, and are, as a rule, found together in the Movement.

The secretary of the General Committee is an outstanding figure, speaking often as he puts issue after issue before the committee, but when the subjects which have special secretaries attached to them are taken the secretary concerned leads the debate—social, missionary, Bible, or the like. But the people whose words get most attention when a big subject is up for discussion, like the programme of a quadrennial conference or the subjects to be dealt with in evangelistic campaigns, are the students. They have the insight into the mind of the colleges, and the more experienced the S.C.M. secretary the more carefully he listens to what they have to say, for he knows that the mind of the colleges is in a constant state of change, and that he can hope to be of use only if he can keep in touch with it and understand it. Newcomers still in their teens sometimes think that the attentive silence in which their first nervous utterance is received is politeness, to encourage a new hand. It may be, but it is far more likely to be due to a sense of the vital importance of understanding the student mind of the hour.

The items on the agenda, perhaps forty during the three-day meeting, may be romped through with shouts of " agreed," or one item may take a day, to the growing anxiety of the chairman. But you can't hurry the General Committee on what it thinks an important issue. It never reaches its decisions by taking a vote. That is untrue if taken literally, for it votes constantly on small questions, whether a grant shall be for £10 or £15, to decide the date of a conference, etc., but if the spirit of the statement is taken it is absolutely true. On all major questions the Committee proceeds by the method of universal consent. It threshes the subject out until it is agreed. It may defer the question for thought and prayer. The one thing it will not have is an outvoted minority. So no one is anxious: if one is in a minority on an important issue one will get time to state one's case, and restate it and convince the whole body, if one can, or else be convinced oneself. We owe an incalculable debt to the men who first made the Movement, and who believed that if men in fellowship with one another and with God were seeking the inspiration of the Holy Spirit, and trying to offer to God such gifts as they had, they would be led to unity of purpose and action. The method is slow at times, and sometimes questions have to wait for settlement, but new light often comes when the way seems dark, and a higher synthesis is found again and again of views that seemed in final opposition.

It is from a body of this kind that the leadership of the Movement comes.

Last, but by no means least, comes the Movement's method of holding together as a Movement and transmitting its message. It is through the work of the Student Movement secretary. Sometimes an uninitiated senior looks at the income and expenditure account of the Movement and shakes his head, saying, with disapproval, " You spend too much on secretaries' salaries." The right reply to such a critic is to point out to him that we really do not spend our money on anything else, and then to explain to him why the Movement spends most of what its members can give or collect on secretaries' salaries—salaries are usually just large enough to make ends meet—on a building in which they can plan their work, on their travelling bills, on expenses of student committees which meet to guide the secretaries in their work, on typists and the like to enable them to clear off their administrative work as quickly as possible in order that they may get on with their real task. It is only the uninitiated who think of Student Movement secretaries as people who sit in offices and dictate business letters. Students like to choose words that say too little rather than too much about anything which they think important, and so they have chosen to call their leaders " secretaries." If these secretaries were to be given really descriptive titles, perhaps pastors would be the best word. There is no secretary, no matter what his position in the Movement, whose main preoccupation is not helping students to understand the Christian faith and live the Christian life.

The Movement has developed a definite theory about its staff as a result of its experience, and holds that the ideal staff contains three elements. There are a small number who continue in office for some time and maintain the traditions of the Movement, and its effective continuity as an organization. The second element is composed of people who have expert knowledge ; we generally refer to it as the study staff, people who by training and personal preference have competence in a particular subject—the Bible, Christian doctrine, apologetics, foreign missions, social or international questions. These not only guide the study work that is done in the colleges, but they watch for the best books and preserve contacts of all kinds, with societies and individuals who are leading thought in relation to the subjects for which they are responsible. As a result of these contacts and of their own work the study secretaries affect in a great variety of ways the life of the Movement. Their contribution is given not only during their visits to college S.C.M's. to speak to members, or to meet with leaders of study circles, but also at conferences, on the committees and sub-committees of the Movement and at the luncheon-table at Annandale. When the study staff of the Movement is at full strength, its influence upon the whole life of the Movement is immense.

The third and largest element on the staff of the Movement is that which consists of men and women straight from college, who give the Movement two or three years' service before they enter upon their life-work. They have almost all proved themselves effective leaders of college S.C.M's. They know the mind of the present student generation. It is their task to take hold of the policy of the Movement, through committee meetings and conference with the study secretaries, and to interpret it to the present generation of students. Some of the larger university centres have one or more of these younger men and women as their own residential secretary. This is the case in Liverpool, Manchester, London, Edinburgh and Glasgow. Places which have no resident secretary are served by travelling secretaries. The districts of these secretaries vary from time to time. The aim of the General Committee is that each area should have one or more secretaries of its own—Ireland, Scotland, Wales, London, the North of England and the South of England.

The work of the secretary differs somewhat according to whether he is resident or a traveller who visits several college centres.   If he (or she) is a travelling secretary, he is constantly making speeches, meeting different committees, talking to the secretaries of the different departments of a college S.C.M. about their work, occasionally visiting study circles and dealing all the time with personal problems of students.   He has on his mind the securing of well-selected delegations to conferences, some care for Student Movement finances, the circulation of the magazine and Student Movement literature, as well as an effort to improve the activities of each S.C.M. branch he visits.

If, on the other hand, he is a resident or intercollegiate secretary he will make fewer public speeches, but, on the other hand, he will organize many of the activities of the university S.C.M., will have much to do with the training and leadership of study circles, and will devote much time to helping individuals.   He may initiate new circles and lead such for a time.   He will help other colleges, e.g. training, technical, fine art, etc., in the university city in which he is located.   He will also get to know the staff, and his contact with sympathetic members of staff will be closer than is possible in the case of a travelling secretary.

Too little has been said in this book about the immense help a large number of members of staff in almost all our universities and colleges have been to the Movement. From lecturers and demonstrators, through the ranks of professors up to vice-chancellors and principals the Movement has been helped increasingly all through its course by the teachers.   The number of friends of the Movement on the teaching staff of our institutions of higher learning in the British Isles at the present time runs well into four figures.   As for the heads of colleges, an unsympathetic head is very rare.   There is no Student Movement in the world which has the co-operation and sympathy of the teaching staff of its universities and colleges to anything like the same extent as is the case in Great Britain and Ireland.   The nervous intercollegiate secretary starting his work soon finds, if he is wise enough to visit members of staff whose names are given him, that he has amongst them many staunch friends. How different it all is from the days when we were pioneering the Movement ! It was a new phenomenon in most colleges. Academic heads were nervous as to what students interested in religion might do, and also anxious about what might happen if they were friendly when the institution for which they were responsible was on a non-religious foundation. Those days are gone, and there is only one criticism to be made, and that is that the Student Movement makes nothing like the use it might make in many parts of the field of the help and sympathy of teachers.

The travelling and intercollegiate secretaries are constantly helped in person in their work in the colleges and at conferences by all the other secretaries of the Movement. Even the members of the general secretariat, whose work centres at Annandale, have always been away from the centre for a considerable time each year— the office man takes his full share in the Movement's work among students in college. It may be his business to be at Annandale as much as possible from the point of view of those who want to find him there to discuss their work with him, but the Movement's office men find that they are in constant demand in the colleges.

Whatever the office a secretary holds, whether head-quarters, study, travel or intercollegiate, he will spend a great deal of his time helping students with their own lives. The help asked will depend to some extent on the secretary concerned, obviously the missionary secretary is specially sought out by students thinking of missionary service and wanting advice about it. The apologetic study secretary, if the Movement has one, will have more people go to him about intellectual difficulties than go to other secretaries, and so on. But in the main it is true that every secretary has to deal with a flood of questions about the spiritual life, the intellectual understanding of Christianity, college work, work for the Student Movement, home difficulties, sex, engagement, marriage and ethical questions of all kinds.   He has to advise relating to college problems and evils, and in all this he receives confidences of innumerable men and women every year.   If constantly helping individuals to live their lives in relation to the Christian gospel is to exercise a cure of souls, then there is no Student Movement secretary, man or woman, who does not exercise the cure of souls on a large scale.

The Student Movement suffers from one very grave defect at the present time ; it has too small a staff.   In the years immediately after the war it came very near having an adequate staff, and the day seemed to be in sight when the staff would be adequate.   But with the increase of depression and money harder to come by, the staff has shrunk in size and, what is quite as important, has had to be cheapened—that is to say, the committee felt itself forced to avoid appointing men who are married and unable to retain more than a very few married men on its staff.   The Movement still suffers from having had to dispense with the services, nearly ten years ago now, of J. R. Coates, its Bible study secretary, and H. A. Mess, its social study secretary. Both these men were experts with considerable experience and were invaluable.   But they had growing families, and the Movement was forced to replace one of them by a younger man at a smaller salary, the other it has never been able to replace.   With over forty years' experience behind it the Movement has a fair knowledge of what ought to be aimed at and what its methods ought to be in carrying out that aim, and we all know that at the present time it is suffering badly for want of an adequate study staff.   All that Leslie Hunter [1] said to the General Committee not far short of twenty years ago, and all that George Cockin [2] said five years ago about the importance of an adequate study staff, is

[1] Now the Venerable the Archdeacon of Northumberland.
[2] Now the Rev. F. A. Cockin, Vicar of St Mary-the-Virgin, Oxford.

being constantly emphasized as true by the Movement's experience. At one time or another it has had on its staff study and specialist secretaries who have been responsible for missionary study among men, missionary study among women, social study, Bible study, doctrinal and apologetic study, special work among training college students, medical students (men) and medical students (women), technical college students, fine art and music students. It needs all these specialist and study secretaries, and what has it got at the present time? One study secretary, one specialist among medical students and half the time of a man on social and industrial questions. Again, an adequate staff demands at least one man and one woman in each of the large modern universities, and one man in the smaller, giving all their time as intercollegiate secretaries.

Some time before the war the Movement thought it was on the road to an adequate staff in London. University College had its own secretary. S. H. Wood, who is now in the Board of Education, first held this office. There were two secretaries working among men generally and a man among foreign students. There was also one woman. It was hoped that this was the beginning of a staff that could be built up until it was adequate. At the present time there are about twice as many students in London as there were before the war, and there is one woman and three men in London, one of them being the medical specialist referred to above. There are at least thirty thousand students in over forty colleges in London. Is it any wonder that the London secretaries often feel dazed by the immensity of the task they have to tackle ?

It is not a hopeless prospect to look for adequate staffing of the Student Christian Movement of Great Britain and Ireland. A staff of round about fifty men and women, instead of about thirty which we have at the present time, is required. If the staff were adequate it would do far more than double the effectiveness of the work. It would be nearer the truth to say it would multiply it by four.   At present the Movement needs a round sum of £20,000 per annum.   If it was adequately staffed it would need from, say, £30,000 to £35,000 per annum.   I always hope the day will come when the Churches will make it their business to see that as long as the Movement is effective it is given an adequate supply of men and money.   I relate the supply of men as well as of money definitely to the Churches and their help, because while the Movement will continue to find a large proportion of its staff among its members as they leave college, it needs for its staff a certain proportion of young men who have had two or three years' experience in the ministry.   At present it is almost impossible to get these men.   None except the best that can be found are any use for student work, and not unnaturally they are just the people the Churches hold on to.   It is only on very rare occasions that it has proved possible to detach a man and bring him back for student work, but every man who comes back, when he returns —I do not say to church work, because if ever there was church work this student work is it—to work for a congregation or a parish, he will bring some with him into the ministry, and he will have trained many laymen for the service of the Church.

This statement of how the Movement works is a plain account of what it does to help British students to understand the Christian faith and live the Christian life. Special departments of its work, such as work for theological students, Oriental and Overseas students generally, the Student Movement House in London and the International House in Glasgow, are all dealt with elsewhere in this book.

There is one omission I would remedy before I conclude.   I have written incidentally about the World's Student Christian Federation, but have nowhere described the nature and extent of its organization, or attempted to estimate its importance as an auxiliary to the forces of the Christian Church in the world.   The subject needs a volume, but some things should be said.

GENERAL COMMITTEE OF THE WORLD'S STUDENT CHRISTIAN FEDERATION
AT WOUDSCHOTEN, HOLLAND, 1932

The World's Student Christian Federation grew from the simple idea that if it was good for individual Christians in a college to band themselves in an organization to understand the Christian faith and live the Christian life, and also good that such organizations in many colleges should federate to form a national Student Christian Movement, it would also be good to federate such national Student Christian Movements. A World's Student Christian Federation composed of national Student Christian Movements could interchange experience and help one another in a variety of ways, and together they could extend the Movement into countries where there was no Christian organization among students. With this simple idea the Federation started in 1895. It had wonderful leadership at first from John R. Mott, and then from him in combination with Ruth Rouse, until shortly after the World War. Commencing with five national Movements, it now comprises twenty-two, with four Corresponding Movements, that is to say, Movements which want to enter the Federation and which are being helped by it to qualify for membership by becoming sufficiently representative and strong to be fairly regarded as national.

The membership of the national Student Christian Movements in the Federation is a difficult figure to arrive at owing to uncertainty about statistics in one or two countries in recent years, but speaking generally there are from two and a half to three million students in the thirty countries in the East and West where there are universities and other institutions of higher learning. This generalization omits only Russia of all the lands that have students. Between 250,000 and 300,000 of the world's students in universities and institutions of higher learning are members of the World's Student Christian Federation, and thousands more come under its influence. In Great Britain, for example, we return our membership as 12,000, but on the lowest estimate 20,000 of our students come under the direct influence of the Movement through taking part in its activities. It is the same elsewhere in the world.

Each national Movement in the Federation preserves its autonomy. Once a Movement is admitted the only requirement made of it is that its basis be maintained in harmony with that of the Federation, which is " To lead students to the Christian faith in God—Father, Son and Holy Spirit according to the Scriptures, and to live as true disciples of Jesus Christ."

Each Movement has one or more places on the General Committee of the Movement, according to the size and nature of its student field; for example, as the British Isles comprises four countries it has the right to appoint five members to the General Committee. This committee meets once every two years and has an Executive which meets annually. Its staff has varied from two to four secretaries in recent years. Its present secretaries, Dr W. A. Visser 't Hooft and M. Pierre Maury, are well known in our Movement, and come in and out amongst us as freely as our own secretaries. Hugh Martin is the Federation's treasurer, and it is no light task to manage accounts in the currencies of all the world. The chairman, as I have already stated, is Francis P. Miller. It also has a number of special workers, student leaders in different parts of the world, who give stretches of time when they work under its direction. The special workers at present are nine in number and represent eight different nationalities. It needs a far larger staff but its income is provided by affiliated Movements, and as most of these have had a hard struggle to maintain their own work in recent years, the amount they have been able to allot to the Federation produces a total far less than is really needed to do its work adequately. Its organ is *The Student World*.

The most important work of the Federation is pioneering in lands where there is no Student Christian Movement, or helping in countries where it is small and weak. This it does through visitation by its secretaries and special workers, arranging conferences and providing special literature.

The countries to which special attention has been given in recent years are Austria, the Balkan States, Esthonia, Latvia, Italy, Spain and the Dutch East Indies.

The Federation, in addition to its pioneering work, has led the thought of the national Movements along three lines in particular since the world war in addition to helping them in their regular work in university and college branches.

First, it has enabled them to come into contact with Churches not represented in their own country, and thus caused them to become more deeply concerned with the question of Christian unity. In Great Britain we owe our present contact with members of the Russian and Bulgarian Orthodox Churches and several Lutheran Churches to the Federation. Thus the Federation has helped to enrich our life as a Movement as well as to teach us to look for the unity of all the Churches of Christ.

The Œcumenical Commission of the Federation has for some years brought together from time to time Anglicans, Calvinists, Lutherans, Orthodox and Roman Catholics for frank discussion and interchange of spiritual experience. This is proving valuable pioneer work in the cause of reunion.

Second, the Federation has stimulated national movements to " lead students to realize that the principles of Christ should rule in international relationships " by affording opportunities for Christian fellowship in cases where nations and races are in danger of being estranged from each other. Those whom the Federation has brought together have not been denationalized people, but students who will become leaders in their own countries, and who have been eager to discuss with the nationals of countries with which their people were in a state of tension those questions, however difficult, which were producing the tension. Over and above this, the

Federation has done much to arouse students to definite action for disarmament and international reconciliation. When the World Conference on Disarmament assembled in February 1932 in Geneva, James Frederick Green, an undergraduate from Yale University, spoke not only the mind of American and British students, whom he was specially commissioned to represent, but the mind of the whole Federation, when, after presenting a number of formal petitions from student bodies—including the S.C.M.—asking for a substantial reduction of armaments, he said :

In transmitting these petitions, I should hardly be speaking with the candour of the New World if I did not discuss some of the questions which are constantly being debated in every dormitory, club, and fraternity house in America and England. We never cease to ask—Were those ten million young men, who loved life as whole-heartedly as ourselves, the victims of an illusion when they fell to earth only a few years ago ? Must the insanity known as war be repeated within our generation at the cost of our lives ? Most important, what is to be our answer to the Government in case of mobilization for war ? No doubt, it may be considered unwise, even impertinent, to raise these issues ; yet I would be playing traitor to my constituency were I to remain silent. Perhaps students may rush in where diplomats fear to tread.

After contemplating the events preceding the catastrophe of 1914, we remain unconvinced as to the wisdom of our predecessors. Fourteen years after the Armistice the glamour and heroism of that period fail to impress us, even when inscribed in gilt on stone memorials. The swords have lost their brilliance ; the helmets and shiny buttons are tarnished. In fact, the whole glorious temple of Mars has crumbled into ashes. We respect the noble war dead ; but we question the judgment of those responsible for their death.

Organized slaughter, we realize, does not settle a dispute ; it merely silences an argument. We insist that for violence be substituted juridical control through the World Court and executive action through the League of Nations. If we are to evolve an international order out of anarchy, we must renounce nationalism and drastically curtail the absolute sovereignty of states.

The other speakers have much at stake ; we have even more, for we are literally fighting for our lives. I stand before you as attorney for the defence, pleading for a reprieve. It is my generation which will be called upon to surrender all we consider worth while in life, in order to become targets for machine-gun bullets and victims for the latest poisonous gas. It is the young men and women of my age who will be commanded to commit suicide. It is my generation which will be requested to destroy the best of human culture, perhaps civilization itself, for causes which future historians will discover to be erroneous, if not utterly stupid or actually vicious. We have thus lost interest in being prepared for cannon fodder.

In a sense, I am presenting an ultimatum rather than a petition. The students whom I represent are watching critically every action of this conference. For behind your deliberations stands staring down at us the spectre of death. We desire to live and to live at peace. We desire to construct a world society providing freedom, equal opportunity, and a sense of security. We desire to make possible for every human being full development of personality in terms of the highest human and spiritual values we know. Those of us who have retained a concept of a loving and purposeful God, desire to live in peace lives which will reflect that concept. We are therefore petitioning you for a substantial reduction of armaments, in order that we may have a civilization in which to forward this creative purpose.

In the third place, the Federation has given time and energy to the international discussion of the Christian Gospel and its presentation to students to-day. At a time when great divergencies in tendencies of thought threaten to make the Christian witness ineffective, and when only a common Christian message can hope to deal with the forces of the modern world, this work first carried on by the " Message Commission," and now by the Federation's " Commission on Christian Faith and Life," is of special importance for the future, not only of the Federation but also of the Christian Church.

The Federation provides a medium of exchange between Christian students the world over. The knowledge of ideas and methods that arise in one Movement pass with extraordinary rapidity all over the world. Also students migrate in large numbers from one country to another, and this has been a means of extending the influence of the Movement.

It is remarkable the degree in which students of one Movement feel at home with members of another. We were told again and again during the war by student-soldiers from Australia and New Zealand how the circles in which they felt most at home when on furlough in England were those of the Student Movement.

Leaders of the Dutch, German, French, Czecho-slovak and other Continental Student Movements have for years passed in and out of Annandale as freely and happily as our own British secretaries. Not least important are the ties that bind us Occidentals to Oriental friends. The Easterner and the Westerner in the main have not learned how to make friends. These unaffected and deep personal friendships between East and West have really been a new thing in the world. When I think of S. K. Datta, Ariam Williams, John Matthai, A. A. Paul, Rallia Ram, Ralla Ram, V. S. Azariah, F. E. Mendis, T. Kagawa, Michi Kawai, Yana Shidachi, Sochi Saito, T. Z. Koo, David Yui, 'Aunt' Kwok, C. T. Wang, T. C. Chao, K. L. Chau, Sandy Hsia, Max Yergan, Audrey Jeffers, they are not to me a strange group of black and yellow men and women, but friends who, if any of them were to enter this study of mine where I write, would be welcomed with delight, and the prospect of sitting down to the kind of talk which is only possible between friends who know they have all the most fundamental things in life in common.

I have looked helplessly again and again at the vast piles of letters, memoranda, reports that are on my files, and wished I could distil their interest, friendship and wonder for these pages. There is hardly a country in the world with which I have not corresponded about student life and the Kingdom of God. Every European country from Russia to Spain and from France to the Black Sea ; India, Ceylon, the Dutch East Indies ; China,

Korea and Japan; the Philippines, Jamaica, Trinidad; North and South America; Australia, Tasmania, New Zealand; Egypt, West Africa, South Africa—they are all represented, most of them by hundreds and some by thousands of letters in those files.   Many of my correspondents I have seen and many more I have never seen, but they all write as friends.   No words can express the strength of the tie that binds men and women in all lands who have entered at all deeply into the life of a national Student Christian Movement, and through such into the fellowship of the World's Student Christian Federation.

APPENDICES

APPENDICES

THESE Appendices are, in the main, the work of Miss Violet Latford, to whom I am also indebted for the Index and much help in the preparation of the whole volume.—T. T.

I

MEN AND WOMEN WHO HAVE SERVED THE S.C.M. AS SECRETARIES

This list of those who have served the S.C.M. as secretaries, does not attempt to provide life histories. It records name, university or college, office held in S.C.M. and present occupation, adding, in the case of those whose S.C.M. service is some time past, some indication of their chief activity in life.

B.A. and M.A. degrees are not included, nor theological colleges except in the case of theological secretaries.

Present titles are given for convenience in identification.

AARON, APPADURAI. Madras University. Warden, International Student House, Glasgow, from 1929.

ADAMS, DAVID T. Hertford College, Oxford. London Sec., 1924-5. Member of staff, Prince of Wales College, Achimota. Sec., Temperance Legislation League.

AIMAN, JAMES S. St Paul's College, Calcutta. Sec., Shakespeare Hut, London, 1922-3. Indian Student Sec., Scottish Y.M.C.A., 1923-5. Founder and first Warden, International Student House, Glasgow, 1925-9. Warden, Indian Students' Union and Hostel, Gower Street, London, W.C.

AIRD, LIONEL. Armstrong College, Newcastle. Sec., East and West Friendship Council, London, from 1928.

ALLEN, REV. GEOFFREY FRANCIS. University College, Oxford. Inter-coll. Sec., Liverpool, 1926-8. Fellow and Tutor, Lincoln College, Oxford.

ANDERSON, REV. A. M. Edinburgh Univ. Educ. Sec., S.V.M.U., 1897-8. Church of Scotland missionary, Blantyre, from 1900.

ANDERSON, ELAINE (Mrs D. M. Thornton). Non-coll. Sub-editor, *Student Volunteer*, 1895-8. C.M.S. missionary, Cairo. Foreign Secretary, women, C.M.S., London.

ANDERSON, D.D., REV. FRANK. Exeter College, Oxford. I.U.C.U. Trav. Sec., 1893-4. S.V.M.U., Trav. Sec., 1894-5. B.C.C.U. Trav. Sec., 1895-6. Y.M.C.A., Bombay. Incumbent, St Luke's, Crumlin, Ontario.

ANDERSON, KATHLEEN. Queen Margaret College, Glasgow. Sec., Edinburgh, Dunfermline, and St Andrews, from 1932.

ANGUS, REV. G. H. C. Christ's College, Cambridge. London Sec., 1911-14. Principal, Serampore College, India.

ATKINSON, MAUD (Mrs David T. Adams). Royal College of Music, London. Sub-Warden, Student Movement House, 1919-24.

ASHTON, REV. PHILIP. Manchester University. Inter-coll. Sec., Manchester, 1919-20. Minister, Charlotte Street Congregational Church, Carlisle.

BACHMANN, REV. H. Zurich Univ. Foreign Student Sec., 1920-21. Minister in Switzerland.

BAINES, REV. HARRY W. Balliol College, Oxford. Trav. Sec., England, 1927-9. Inter-coll. Sec., Oxford, and curate of St Mary the Virgin, Oxford, from 1930.

BAKER, GILBERT. Christ Church, Oxford. London Sec. from 1932.

BAND, REV. STEPHEN. University Coll., Liverpool. Trav. Sec., 1902-3. Minister, Presbyterian Church, Singapore.

BANNERMAN, MARGARET (Mrs D. B. Donald). Aberdeen University. Inter-coll. Sec., Aberdeen, women, 1920-2.

BARCLAY, C.B.E., ROBERT LEATHAM. Trinity College, Cambridge. Hon. Treasurer from 1897. Director, Barclay's Bank, Ltd.

BARKER, EDWIN. Sheffield University. Inter-coll. Sec., Leeds, 1927-30. Social Study Sec. and Inter-coll. Sec., Birmingham, 1930-1. Social and International Study Sec., 1931-2. Social Study Sec. and part-time with Auxiliary Movement from 1932.

BARKER, REV. T. M. Trinity College, Dublin, and Queen's College, Belfast. Irish Sec., 1911-13 and 1931-2. Irish Presbyterian Mission, Moukden, Manchuria.

BARNES, DR J. A. P. St Bartholomew's Hospital. London Sec., 1900-1. Private practice, Tottenham.

BARRIE, FREDA. Queen Margaret College, Glasgow. Inter-coll. Sec., Glasgow, 1914-5. Trav. Sec., Scotland, 1919-21. Lady Superintendent, High School, Dundee.

BATTERSBY, M.D., C. F. HARFORD. Trinity College, Cambridge. St Bartholomew's Hospital. Nigeria C.M.S., 1890-2. Hon. Treas., B.C.C.U., 1894-7. First Principal of Livingstone College, London. Medical Officer, C.M.S. Died July 1925.

BENNITT, REV. A. J. Clare College, Cambridge. Inter-coll. Sec., Newcastle, 1930-3. St Paul's College, Hong Kong.

BEWSHER, REV. ROBERT. Wadham College, Oxford. International Relations Sec., 1921-3. S.P.G. missionary, Jamshedpur, India.

BIGNOLD, GLADYS (Mrs Reid). Edinburgh Univ. Inter-coll. Sec., Edinburgh, 1915-8.

BLAXALL, REV. A. W. Keble College, Oxford. Sec. for Serbian Students, 1916-8. Sec., Diocesan Board of Missions, Capetown.

BOND, REV. F. W. Christ's College, Cambridge. Inter-coll. Sec., Liverpool, from 1931.

BOULLEN, M.Sc., RACHEL. Manchester University. Inter-coll. Sec., Manchester, 1915-7. Headmistress, Leyton County High School.

BOWLER, ENID (Mrs Donald Wilson). Bedford College, London. Trav. Sec., England and Wales, 1922-4.

BRADNACK, B. O. Brasenose College, Oxford. Inter-coll. Sec., Newcastle, 1921-3. Master, Dean Close School, Cheltenham.

BRANTS, MRS JEAN. Edinburgh University. Sub-Warden, Student Movement House, London, 1924-32.

BRETHERTON, MARGARET A. (Mrs Pittendrigh). Bedford College, London. Trav. Sec., British Isles, Gen. Coll. Dept. and S.V.M.U., 1904-6. Asst. Sec., S.C.M., 1906-8. Y.W.C.A., Madras. Died 1917.

BROWN, ALICE. Trinity College, Dublin. Irish Council Sec., 1930-2.

BROWN, DOROTHY E. Girton College, Cambridge. Trav. Sec., British Isles, 1907-9. Sec., Overseas Committee, Y.W.C.A. of Great Britain.

BRUCE, MICHAEL. Edinburgh University. International Sec., Edinburgh, from 1932.

BULLER, AMY. Birkbeck College, London. Inter-coll. Sec., women, Manchester, 1921-2. London Sec., 1922-8. Asst. Sec., S.C.M., 1928-9. General Secretariat, 1929-31. Warden, University Hall, Liverpool.

BURGE, MARGARET (Mrs Papazoꞏ loff). Girton College, Cambridge, Auxiliary Sec., 1921-2.

BURTT, LUCY. Bedford College, London. Member of staff, Municipal Training College, Brighton. Training Coll. Sec., 1928-30. Member of staff, Yenching University, Peiping, China.

BUTCHER, REV. CANON L. B. Sidney Sussex Coll., Cambridge. Gen. Sec., S.V.M.U. and B.C.C.U., 1895-6. C.M.S. missionary in India from 1896 to 1914 and from 1923. Asst. Sec., C.M.S., 1914-9. Candidates Sec., C.M.S., 1919-23.

CARGIN, REV. WILLIAM M. Trinity College, Dublin. Trav. Sec., S.V.M.U., 1909-12. Minister, Presbyterian Church, Ardglass, Co. Down.

CARSWELL, RENA (Mrs S. K. Datta). Queen Margaret College, Glasgow. Inter-coll. Sec., Glasgow, 1908-9. Trav. Sec., S.V.M.U., 1909-10. Sec., International Student Service.

CHESHIRE, F. M. St John's College, Cambridge. Asst. Sec., L.I.C.C.U., 1910-11. Indian Educational Service, 1911-32. Master at St George's School, Harpenden.

CLARKE, REV. OLIVER F. Hertford College, Oxford. Inter-coll. Sec., Oxford, 1924-7. Christa Seva Sangha, India. Member of staff, Liddon House, London.

CLIMIE, ALLINA J. Queen Margaret College, Glasgow. Inter-coll. Sec., women, Aberdeen and Glasgow, 1921-3.

COATES, REV. JOHN R. Peterhouse, Cambridge. Bible Study Sec., 1919-23. Member of staff, Selly Oak Colleges.

COCKIN, REV. F. A. University College, Oxford. Foreign Student Sec., 1916-21. Apologetic and Doctrinal Study Sec., 1921-9. Canon missioner of Southwark Cathedral and Warden of College of St Saviour's, Carshalton, 1929-33. Vicar of St Mary the Virgin, Oxford.

COEY, MABEL SALLY. Queen's University, Belfast. Inter-coll. Sec., Birmingham, 1924-6. Staff, Indian Student Y.W.C.A., 1926-32. Missionary Sec. from 1932.

COX, CLARENCE R. Manchester University. Asst. Sec., 1912-3. Died of wounds in Egypt, April 1917.

COYSH, B.Sc., F.G.S., A. W. Bristol University. Inter-coll. Sec., Sheffield, 1927-9. Master at Ramsey Grammar School, Isle of Man, 1929-31. Yardley Sec. Sch., Birmingham.

CRAIG, C. STUART. University College, Nottingham. Inter-coll. Sec., Manchester, from 1932.

CRASKE, REV. F. W. T. King's College, London. Inter-coll. Sec., Manchester, 1927-9. International Relations Sec. and Curate of All Hallows, Lombard Street, 1929-30. London Sec. and Curate of All Hallows, Lombard Street, 1930-32. Vicar of Read-in-Whalley, Lancs.

CURRIE, JOSEPHINE. London School of Economics. Warden, Student Movement House, London, 1922-6 and 1932-3.

DALLIMORE, VENERABLE H. E. Liverpool University. Inter-coll. Sec., Liverpool, 1907-10. C.M.S. missionary, Nigeria, 1910-20. Inter-coll. Sec., Liverpool, 1920-22. Archdeacon of Ade-Ekiti, Lagos, West Africa.

DATTA, M.B., Ch.B., S. K. Punjab University, India, and Edinburgh University. Trav. Sec., 1906-7. Asst. Sec., 1907-8. Y.M.C.A., India. Principal, Forman Christian College, Lahore, India.

DAVIDSON, REV. MICHAEL N. Christ's College, Cambridge. Inter-coll. Sec., Manchester, 1925-7. C.M.S. missionary, Onitsha, Nigeria, West Africa.

DAVIES, D.Litt., REV. CANON A. W. University College, Oxford.

Trav. Sec., 1903-4. Sometime Principal, St John's College, Agra. Vice-Chancellor, Agra University. General Sec. of the Missionary Council of the National Assembly, Church of England, from 1929.

DAVIES, REV. E. TEGLA. University College, Bangor. Editor of *Yr Efrydydd* from 1931.

DAVIES, OLWEN (Mrs Wilkins). University College, Aberystwyth. Welsh Sec., 1925-9.

DICKEY, REV. ROBERT S. Trinity College, Dublin. Irish Sec., 1916-7. Missionary, Irish Presbyterian Mission, Gujerat, India.

DIXON, MARY I. (Mrs F. G. Healey). Girton College, Cambridge. Trav. Sec., N. England and Ireland, 1929-31. English Presbyterian Mission, Formosa.

DOBSON, REV. JAMES O. University College, London. Sec., East and West Friendship Committee, 1921-5. Missionary Sec., 1925-30. Minister of Friary Congregational Church, West Bridgford, Notts.

DONALD, D. B. Aberdeen University. Inter-coll. Sec., Aberdeen, 1922-3. Died Jan. 1933 as result of wounds received in World War.

DOREY, ELFREDA (Mrs W. S. Tindal). Slade School of Art. Sec. for fine art students, 1924-7.

DOUGALL, REV. J. W. C. Glasgow University. Inter-coll. Sec., Glasgow, 1920-1. Sometime Principal of Jeanes School, Livingstonia. Educ. adviser to the Missions of Kenya and Uganda.

DRYBURGH, REV. GEORGE M. Glasgow University. Theol. Coll. Trav. Sec., 1921-2. Minister, Church of Scotland, Dunfermline.

DUGARD, REV. DONALD. Didsbury College, Manchester. Theol. Coll. Trav. Sec., 1930-3. Minister, Methodist Church, Armadale, West Lothian.

DUNCAN, REV. HARRY C. Edinburgh University. Gen. Sec., 1897-8. Church of Scotland Mission, Darjeeling.

DUNCAN, REV. JOHN M. B. Edinburgh University. Gen. Sec., 1901-2. Minister of Tynecastle, Edinburgh.

DYER, REV. RICHARD P. Liverpool University. Inter-coll. Sec., Liverpool, 1913-5. Staff, Queen's Coll., Nassau, British W. Indies.

DYSON, WILLIAM H. King's College, Cambridge. Theol. Coll. Trav. Sec., 1914-5. Killed in France, July 1916.

EDMINSON, JANET (Mrs R. D. Rees). Newnham College, Cambridge. London Sec., 1918-20. Shanghai, China.

EDWARDS, D.D., REV. PROF. D. MIALL. Memorial College, Brecon. Editor, *Yr Efrydydd*, 1920-8.

EDMONDS, E. WYKEHAM. Keble College, Oxford. Sub-Warden, Student Movement House, London, 1931-2. Fellow of St Augustine's College, Canterbury.

EDMUNDS, CRAYDEN. St John's College, Cambridge. Gen. Sec., S.V.M.U. and B.C.C.U., 1894-5. British and Foreign Bible Society, Calcutta, 1895-1900. British and Foreign Bible Society, London, 1900-1911. Died, April 1911.

EDWARDS, JOHN T. University College, Bangor. Inter-coll. Sec., Liverpool, 1922-4. Insurance official, Liverpool, London and Globe Insurance Co.

EDWARDS, L. JOHN. Leeds University. Inter-coll. Sec., Birmingham, 1928-9. W.E.A. lecturer, Leeds.

ELLERSHAW, HELEN. St Christopher's College, Blackheath. Sub-Warden, Student Movement House, London, 1930-2. Working with Rev. J. W. Parkes in Geneva.

ELLIS, TOM I. University College, Aberystwyth, and Jesus College, Oxford. Sec., Welsh Council, 1923-4. Headmaster, Rhyl County School.

ENGESTROM, MAY VON (Mrs Sjoding). Uppsala University, Sweden. Asst. Warden, Student Movement House, London, 1925-6.

ENNIS, ALFRED. Trinity College, Dublin. Irish Sec. from 1932.

EVANS, REV. EMRYS O. University College, Bangor. Welsh Sec., 1926-8. Minister, Cong. Church, Newtown, Montgomeryshire.

EVANS, REV. R. EMRYS. University College, Aberystwyth. Welsh Sec., 1924-5. Minister, C.M. Church, West Kirby.

EVANS, KATHLEEN B. Bristol University. Trav. Sec., England (part), 1912-4. L.M.S. Missionary, Shanghai, China.

EWAN, REV. GEORGE. Edinburgh University and New College, Edinburgh. Theol. Coll. Trav. Sec., 1912-3. Church of Scotland Mission, Calcutta. Died 1923.

FAIRFIELD, ZOË B. Slade School of Art. Sec., Guild of Helpers, Y.W.C.A., 1907-9. Asst. Gen. Sec., 1909-29. Gen. Sec., Auxiliary Movement, from 1929.

FENN, B.Sc., REV. JOHN ERIC. Imperial College of Science and Technology. Asst. Sec., 1926-9. General Secretariat, 1929-32. Study Sec. from 1932. Editor, *The Student Movement*, from 1933.

FINNEGAN, TOM. Queen's University, Belfast, and St John's College, Cambridge. Irish Sec., 1926-30. Professor of Classics, Magee M'Crae College, Londonderry.

FORBES, HILDA G. Queen Margaret College, Glasgow. Warden, South Park House, Glasgow, 1919-30.

FOX, CHRISTOPHER STORRS. Jesus College, Cambridge. Inter-coll. Sec., Manchester, 1929-31. Staff, H.M. Borstal Institution, Rochester.

FRASER, REV. A. G. Trinity College, Oxford. Trav. Sec., S.V.M.U., 1898-9. Sometime Principal, Trinity College, Kandy, now Principal, Achimota College, Accra.

FRASER, D.D., VERY REV. DONALD. Glasgow University. S.V.M.U. Trav. Sec., 1893-4. B.C.C.U. Trav. Sec., 1894-5. Missionary, Livingstonia, 1899-25. Moderator, U.F.C.S., 1922-3. Chaplain to the King in Scotland. Joint Foreign Mission Sec., Church of Scotland. Died August 20th, 1933.

FRASER, JEAN. Newnham College, Cambridge. London Sec. from 1932.

GAGE, ARTHUR S. University College, Cardiff. Welsh Sec., 1915-7. Warden, Swarthmore Hall, Plymouth.

GAIRDNER, REV. CANON W. H. TEMPLE. Trinity College, Oxford. Trav. Sec., B.C.C.U., British Isles, 1897-9. C.M.S. missionary, Cairo. Died, May 1928.

GARSIDE, CONSTANCE. Bedford College, London. London Sec., 1913-6. War work for Y.W.C.A. Sec., Foreign Dept., Y.W.C.A., 1927-8. Died, February 1931.

GAUDIN, ALEC. DE G. Christ's College, Cambridge. Trav. Sec., England, 1923-4, also Ireland, 1924-5. Irish Sec., 1925-6. Assistant Master, Trent College.

GLASS, A. BEATRICE (Mrs A. G. Fraser). Newnham College, Cambridge. Trav. Sec., British Isles B.C.C.U. and S.V.M.U., 1897-9. Achimota College, Accra.

GRANT, REV. A. C. Glasgow University. Trav. Sec., British Isles, B.C.C.U., 1906-7. Missionary, U.F.C.S., India. Torpedoed and drowned in s.s. Persia, Dec. 1915.

GRANT, CONSTANCE. Newnham College, Cambridge. Foreign Student Sec., London, 1919-20. Napier, New Zealand.

GRANT, REV. DONALD. Edinburgh University. Scottish Sec., 1915-8. European Student Relief, 1920-5. Gen. Sec., S.C.M., New Zealand, 1925-9. International F.O.R., Vienna, 1929-33. Trav. Sec., the Auxiliary Movement, from 1933.

GRAY, D.D., REV. A. HERBERT. Edinburgh University. Presbyterian minister, Glasgow and Manchester. Evangelistic Sec., 1921-4. Minister, Presbyterian Church, Crouch Hill, 1924-32.

GRDANITCHSKY, FATHER DAMASKIN. Serbia. Trav. Sec. among members of Serbian Orthodox Church in British Universities, 1917-9.

GREGG, REV. J. B. Trinity College, Dublin. Trav. Sec., England, 1925-7. Curate of St George's, Cullercoats. Died May 1930.

GREENE, E. A. King's College, London. Asst. Sec., L.I.C.C.U., 1911-2.

GRIEVE, REV. GEORGE E. Liverpool University. Inter-coll. Sec., Newcastle, 1926-8. Minister, Rhodes Street Methodist Church, Halifax.

GRIFFITH, REV. OWEN.   University College, Cardiff.   Welsh Sec., 1919-32.

GRIFFITHS, HILDA (Mrs C. Williams).   University College, Aberystwyth.   Welsh Sec., 1917-20.

GRIMWOOD, FRANK S.   Reading University.   Foreign Student Sec. and Sub-Warden, Student Movement House, 1930. L.C.C. Lecturer.

GRUMMITT, J. H.   Gonville and Caius College, Cambridge.   Sec., Schools Dept., 1923-33, also Asst. Sec., 1928-9.   Headmaster, Victoria College, Jersey.

HAIGH, GWENNETH.   University College, London.   Trav. Sec., N. England and Wales, 1924-5.   Member of staff, Battersea Polytechnic.

HALL, RIGHT REV. RONALD O.   Brasenose College, Oxford. Inter-coll. Sec., Newcastle, Durham, and Sunderland, 1920-1. Missionary Sec., 1921-5.   Bishop of Victoria, Hong Kong.

HAMILTON, BERTA.   St Andrews Univ.   Inter-coll. Sec., Manchester, 1914-5.   Social Service, Canada.

HARDIE, ARCHIBALD G.   Trinity College, Cambridge.   Trav. Sec., England, from 1932.

HARDIE, RIGHT REV. W. G.   Emmanuel College, Cambridge. Trav. Sec., S.V.M.U., 1901-2.   Bishop of Jamaica.

HARNETT, KATHLEEN (Mrs J. W. Woodhouse).   Lady Margaret Hall, Oxford.   Missionary Sec., 1919-21.

HARRIS, CHARLOTTE.   University College, Dundee.   Inter-coll. Sec., St Andrews and Dundee, 1923-4.   Inter-coll. Sec., Aberdeen, 1924-5.   Mistress, Eastern School, Broughty Ferry.

HARRISON, KATHLEEN (Mrs J. E. Fenn).   Newnham College, Cambridge.   Trav. Sec., S. England and Ireland, 1923-5. London Sec., 1925-7.

HAWKES, REV. S. F.   Wadham College, Oxford.   Trav. Sec., B.C.C.U., 1898-9.   Sometime vicar, St Mary's, Johannesburg. Died, Sidmouth, November 1930.

HEAWOOD, GEOFFREY L.   Wadham College, Oxford.   London Sec., 1922-4.   Headmaster, County School for Boys, Bromley, Kent.

HEMINGWAY, M.R.C.S., L.R.C.P., MARY I. (Mrs Hemingway-Rees).   Birmingham University.   Sec. for women medical students, 1918-9.

HENDERSON, A. ISABEL (Mrs Craig).   Glasgow University.   Inter-coll. Sec., Glasgow, 1909-11.

HENDERSON, HELEN S.   Edinburgh University.   Trav. Sec., Scotland, 1930-3.

HENRIOD, B.D., REV. HENRI LOUIS.   Neuchâtel, Marburg and Bâle Universities.   Foreign Student Sec., 1917-20.   Sec., W.S.C.F., 1920-32.   From 1932, Gen. Sec., World Alliance for International Friendship through the Churches and Sec., Universal Christian Council for Life and Work.

HESLAM, MARGARET (Mrs M'Ewan Lawson). Manchester University. Inter-coll. Sec., women, Manchester, 1912-3.

HITCHCOCK, LOUISE. Glasgow University. Inter-coll. Sec., Glasgow, and first Warden, South Park House, Glasgow, 1917-9.

HODGES, MAY E.. Non-coll. Trav. Sec., British Isles, 1894-6.

HODKIN, REV. HEDLEY. Sheffield University. Inter-coll. Sec., Sheffield, 1925-7. Minister, Methodist Church, Horley.

HOLLAND, F.R.C.S., C.I.E., HENRY T. Edinburgh University. Trav. Sec., B.C.C.U., 1899-1900. C.M.S. Hospital, Quetta.

HOLLAND, REV. CANON W. E. S. Magdalen College, Oxford. Trav. Sec., B.C.C.U., British Isles, 1896-7. Missionary, India, 1899-1933. Founded Oxford and Cambridge Hostel (now Holland Hall), Allahabad. Principal, St Paul's College, Calcutta, and Kottayam College, Travancore, and staff Alwaye College, Travancore. Principal, St John's College, Agra. Rector, St Mary Woolnoth, London, E.C.

HOLMES, JASPER. Jesus College, Cambridge. Inter-coll. Sec., Cambridge, 1912-3. Master, Charterhouse School.

HOLTBY, REV. EDWARD B. Manchester University. Foreign Student Sec., Manchester, 1916-9. Vicar of Christ Church, Southchurch.

HOPKIRK, REV. F. S. Emmanuel College, Cambridge. Foreign Student Sec., 1926-9. Vicar of Layer-de-le-Haye, Colchester.

HORSTEAD, REV. CANON JAMES LAWRENCE CECIL. Durham University. Inter-coll. Sec., Durham, 1923-6. Principal, Fourah Bay College, Sierra Leone.

HOULDER, HOWARD F. St John's College, Oxford. Trav. Sec., British Isles, 1909-11. Director, Howard Houlder & Partners, Ltd.

HOUSE, FRANCIS. Wadham College, Oxford. Inter-coll. Sec., Manchester, 1931-2. General Secretariat from 1932.

HOWARD, REV. ARTHUR E. Queen's College, Oxford. Trav. Sec., N. England, 1919-20. Trav. Sec., England, 1920-1. Presbyterian minister, Wavertree, Liverpool.

HOYTE, M.R.C.S., L.R.C.P., STANLEY. Westminster Hospital. Asst. Sec., L.I.C.C.U., 1910-1. Med. Sup., Wilson Mem. Hosp., Ping Yang Fu.

HUNTER, VENERABLE L. S. New College, Oxford. Theol. Coll. Trav. Sec., 1913-4. Bible Study Sec., 1914-9. Literary Sec., 1919-21. Archdeacon of Northumberland and Canon Residentiary of Newcastle-on-Tyne.

INSKIP, NORA (Mrs Geoffrey Heawood). St Hilda's College, Oxford. Trav. Sec., S. England, 1921-3. London Sec., 1923-5.

IREDALE, ELEANORA.   Sorbonne, Paris.   Associate Finance Sec., 1924-32.   Sec., Christian Social Council, from 1932.

IRVINE, F. R.   Armstrong College, Newcastle.   Foreign Student Sec., 1920-1.   Member of staff, Prince of Wales College, Achimota.

JACKSON, LAURA.   Newnham College, Cambridge.   Missionary Sec., 1925-6.   Member of staff, Women's Christian College, Madras, 1921-5 and 1926-32.   S.P.G., Educ. Missy., Trichinopoly, S. India, from 1933.

JACKSON, REV. G. BASIL.   Manchester University.   Foreign Student Sec., 1923-5.   Member of staff, Training College, Peradeniya, Ceylon.

JANES, B.D., REV. MAX.   London University.   London Sec., 1924-5.   Minister, Stoke Newington Congregational Church.

JARDINE, KENNETH W. S.   Corpus Christi College, Oxford.   Sec., East and West Friendship Committee, 1925-8.   Staff member, Holland Hall, Allahabad, 1921-4 and 1928-33.   From 1933, Missionary Sec., S.C.M.

JAYS, M.R.C.S., L.R.C.P., TOM.   St Thomas's Hospital.   Trav. Sec., S.V.M.U., 1900-1.   London Sec., 1901-2.   Previously C.M.S. missionary, West Africa, now Principal, Livingstone College, Leyton.

JONES, REV. PRINCIPAL J. MORGAN.   Mansfield College, Oxford. Editor, *Yr Efrydydd*, 1928-31.   Principal, Bala Bangor College, Bangor.

KEMP, BRIAN C. L.   Corpus Christi College, Oxford.   Inter-coll. Sec., Oxford, and then Sec., Ireland, 1923-4.   Tutor and Head of Science Dept., Wellington College, Berks.

KEMPTHORNE, RIGHT REV. L. S.   University College, London. Sec., L.I.C.C.U., 1909-10.   Bishop of Polynesia.

KILBORN, REV. TREVOR H. H.   University College, Leicester. Trav. Sec., England, 1930-2.   Curate of All Hallows, Lombard Street, and Sec., The Auxiliary Movement, from 1932, also Sec., Friends of Reunion from 1933.

KIRK, D.D., REV. CANON KENNETH E.   St John's College, Oxford. Foreign Student Sec., London, 1909-10.   Sec., L.I.C.C.U., 1910-2.   Regius Professor of Moral and Pastoral Theology, and Canon of Christ Church, Oxford.

KIRKWOOD, KENNETH.   Toronto University.   International Relations Sec., 1923.

KNOTT, REV. ALAN G.   Manchester University.   Inter-coll. Sec., Manchester, 1912-4.   Minister of Bishop's Stortford Congregational Church.

LATHAM, ELEANOR. St Hugh's College, Oxford. Sec., Student Movement House, London, 1930-2. Sec., Agricultural Camps Committee.

LENWOOD, MAIDA (Mrs Duncan Leith). Somerville College, Oxford. Trav. Sec., British Isles, 1906-7. Sec. for women's work, Methodist Missionary Society.

LENWOOD, REV. FRANK. Corpus Christi College, Oxford. Theol. Coll. Trav. Sec., 1900-1901. Missionary of L.M.S. in Benares, India, 1909-12. Foreign Sec., L.M.S., 1912-25. Minister of Greengate Congregational Church, Plaistow, from 1926.

LEWARS, REV. J. M. Edinburgh University. Inter-coll. Sec., Edinburgh, 1921-2. Church of Scotland missionary, Port Harcourt, Nigeria.

LEWIS, JOHN H. Trinity College, Cambridge. Trav. Sec., N. England and Ireland, 1921-3. Underwriter at Lloyds, London.

LEWIS, REV. T. J. University College, Cardiff. Welsh Sec., 1913-5. Minister, Presbyterian Church of Wales, Beechwood Park, Newport, Mon.

LINDSAY, ELLA B. (Mrs Floyer). Edinburgh University. Inter-coll. Sec., Glasgow, 1924-7. Calabar, West Africa.

LISTER, REV. HUGH. Trinity College, Cambridge. London Sec., 1931-2.

LOMAS, REV. R. H. Manchester University. Inter-coll. Sec., Manchester, 1914-5. Minister of St Francis-on-the-Hill, Barry, S. Wales.

M'AULAY, GRACE (Mrs L. S. Hunter). Girton College, Cambridge. Trav. Sec., England (part), 1916-9.

M'COLM, REV. W. S. Glasgow University. Inter-coll. Sec., Aberdeen, St Andrews, and Dundee, 1926-31, also Edinburgh, 1930-1. Minister of St Andrew's Church, Newburgh, Fife.

MACDONALD, O.B.E., REV. R. G. Aberdeen University. Scottish Sec., 1912-5. English Trav. Sec., 1915. War service, Y.M.C.A., France, 1915-8. Scottish Sec., 1919-21. Minister of St Columba's Church, Brechin.

MACDONALD-SMITH, MARY. Edinburgh University. Trav. Sec., N. England and Ireland, 1931-3. Student, Women's Missionary College, Edinburgh.

MACINTOSH, JESS (Mrs Dundas). Edinburgh University. Inter-coll. Sec., Edinburgh, 1912.

MACKENZIE, FLORENCE. Girton College, Cambridge. Inter-coll. Sec., Edinburgh, 1910-2. Principal, Women's Missionary College, Edinburgh.

M'KERROW, MARGARET E. (Mrs A. S. Crichton). Queen Margaret College, Glasgow. Trav. Sec., British Isles, 1905-6.

MACKIE, REV. ROBERT C. Glasgow University. Scottish Sec., 1925-9. General Secretariat, from 1929.

MACKINNON, CATHERINE. Queen Margaret College, Glasgow. Inter-coll. Sec., Glasgow, 1911-4. Trav. Sec., 1915-8. Scottish Sec., 1918-9. Missionary Sec., 1929-30. General Secretariat, 1929-32. Sometime Y.W.C.A. Sec., China. Now Principal of Carey Hall, Selly Oak.

MACKWORTH, JOAN. Bedford College, London. London Sec., 1928-32. Medical student at Bristol University.

MACLEAN, HELEN B. K. Glasgow University. Inter-coll. Sec., Glasgow, 1919-21. Church of Scotland missionary, Moukden, Manchuria.

MACLEAN, D.D., REV. J. H. Glasgow University. Editor, *The Student Volunteer*, 1893-5. Church of Scotland missionary at Conjeveram, India.

MACLEAN, M.B., G. T. Glasgow University. General Sec., 1900-1901. Private practice, Muswell Hill.

McLEISH, J. MARJORIE. Queen Margaret College, Glasgow. Sometime teaching, welfare work, etc. Warden, South Park House, Glasgow, from 1930.

MACNICOL, HELEN. Edinburgh University. Scottish Sec., 1929-32. General Secretariat and bursar at Annandale from 1933.

MADGE, GERTRUDE. Lady Margaret Hall, Oxford. Missionary Sec., 1923-5. Sister at the House of the Epiphany, Barisal, E. Bengal.

MARTIN, REV. HUGH. Glasgow University. Educational Sec., 1914-7. Asst. Sec., 1917-23. Asst. and Literary Sec., 1923-9. Managing Director and Editor, S.C.M. Press, Ltd., from 1929. Treasurer, World's Student Christian Federation, from 1928.

MERRYLEES, MEG. St Andrews University. Inter-coll. Sec., Glasgow, 1927-9. Trav. Sec., Scotland, 1929-30. Sec., Westminster Housing Association.

MESS, Ph.D., HENRY A. London University. Social Study Sec., 1919-23. Director, Tyneside Council of Social Service.

MILFORD, REV. T. R. Magdalen College, Oxford. Inter-coll. Sec., Liverpool, 1924-6. Lecturer, St John's College, Agra, India.

MILLER, FRANCIS P. Washington University, U.S.A., and Trinity College, Oxford. International Relations Sec., 1921-2. Chairman of the World's Student Christian Federation from 1929. Lecturer in Yale Divinity School.

MILLER, JEAN. John Hassal School of Art, London. Sec., Auxiliary Movement, 1927-9. Warden, Presbyterian Settlement, London, E.

MILLER, M.R.C.S., L.R.C.P., WALTER R. St Bartholomew's Hospital. Trav. Sec., S.V.M.U., 1896-7. C.M.S. missionary, Nigeria.

MITCHELL, REV. ROBIN I. Edinburgh University. Inter-coll. Sec., Edinburgh, 1931-3. Minister of Rathen Church, Aberdeenshire.

MOBERLY, OLIVE (Mrs F. A. Cockin). Lady Margaret Hall, Oxford. London Sec., 1917-21.

MORISON, MARGARET (Mrs Arthur Campbell). Edinburgh University. Inter-coll. Sec., Edinburgh, St Andrews and Dundee, 1920-3.

MORLEY, REV. F. DOUGLAS. Handsworth College. Foreign Student Sec., 1913-4. Chaplain, Royal Air Force.

MOULE, Rev. G. H. Clare College, Cambridge. Educational Sec., S.V.M.U., 1898-1900. Incumbent, Immanuel Church, Tokyo, Japan.

MOWLL, GLADYS. Newnham College, Cambridge. Trav. Sec., 1910-2. St Stephen's Hospital, Delhi.

MURRAY, A. VICTOR. Magdalen College, Oxford. Inter-coll. Sec., Oxford, 1913-6. Trav. Sec., British Isles, 1916-20. Inter-coll. Sec., Manchester, 1920-2. Lecturer in Education in the Selly Oak Colleges, Birmingham, 1922-33. Professor of Education, University College, Hull.

NASH, ARNOLD S. Liverpool University. Inter-coll. Sec., Sheffield, 1930-2. London Sec. from 1932.

NEILL, MOIRA. Trinity College, Dublin. Trav. Sec., S. England from 1932.

NEWBIGIN, LESSLIE. Queens' College, Cambridge. Inter-coll. Sec., Glasgow, 1931-3, also Scottish Council Sec., 1932-3. Student at Westminster College, Cambridge.

NUTTALL, M.D., HAROLD. Edinburgh University. Inter-coll. Sec., Edinburgh, 1897-8. General practice, Colwyn Bay.

OLDHAM, D.D., J. H. Trinity College, Oxford. Gen. Sec., 1896-7. Y.M.C.A., Lahore, 1897-1900. Educational Sec., 1908-9. Secretary, International Missionary Council.

OLDHAM, REV. HARRY W. Central Technical College. London Sec., 1898-1900. Sometime Missionary, English Presbyterian Church, Swatow, China. Church of Scotland minister at Tain.

O'NEILL, REV. F. W. S. Queen's and Assembly's Colleges, Belfast. Trav. Sec., B.C.C.U. (for theological colleges), 1896-7. Irish Presbyterian Mission, Moukden, Manchuria.

OTTER, REV. ANTHONY. Trinity College, Cambridge. London Sec., 1925-31. Vicar of Lowdham, Notts.

OVERTON, EDITH E. Somerville College, Oxford. Trav. Sec., British Isles, 1900-1. Sometime with Z.B.M.M. and Y.W.C.A. First Warden, Student Movement House, London, 1917-22.

OWEN, EIRIAN MORGAN. Girton College, Cambridge. Trav. Sec., S. England, 1927-9. Trav. Sec., Wales, 1930-1 General Secretariat, 1932-3.

OWENS, GWEN (Mrs J. H. Lewis). Newnham College, Cambridge. Trav. Sec., S. England, 1919-20. Trav. Sec., S. England and Wales, 1920-1. Trav. Sec., Ireland and Wales, 1921-3. International Relations Sec., 1924-5.

PAGE, REV. E. MURRAY. University College, London, and Regent's Park College. Theol. Coll. Trav. Sec., 1910-2. Campaign Sec. (part-time), 1913-4. Minister of North Finchley Baptist Church.

PAINTER, P. I. Jesus College, Oxford. International Relations Sec., 1925-6. World's Y.M.C.A., Geneva, 1926-32.

PARKER, RUTH. University College, Aberystwyth. Trav. Sec., Wales, from 1931.

PARKES, REV. J. W. Hertford College, Oxford. International Relations Sec., 1923-5. International Relations Sec. and Asst. Warden, Student Movement House, 1925-6. Warden, Student Movement House, 1926-8. Staff, International Student Service.

PARTINGTON, REV. HOWARD. Lancashire Independent College, Manchester. Inter-coll. Sec., Manchester, 1911-2. Congregational Minister at Nottingham.

PASSMORE, IRENE (Mrs Donald Grant). Edinburgh University. Inter-coll. Sec., Manchester and Belfast, 1919-21.

PELLY, REV. RICHARD L. Clare College, Cambridge. Bible Study Sec., 1911-4. Trav. Sec., 1914-5. Rector, St Paul's School, Darjeeling.

PATON, REV. WILLIAM. Pembroke College, Oxford. Central Volunteer Sec. and Mission Study Sec., S.V.M.U., 1911-3. Asst. Sec. and Miss. Sec., 1913-9. Miss. Sec., 1919-21. Sometime Gen. Sec., Nat. Christian Council of India, Burma, and Ceylon. Now Sec., International Missionary Council and Editor, *International Review of Missions*.

PHILIP, JANET (Mrs Basil Thornley). Royal Holloway College. Trav. Sec., N. England and Ireland, 1927-9.

PHILLIPS, F.R.C.S., WALTER. Queen's University, Belfast. Trav. Sec., S.V.M.U., 1902-3. In charge I.P. Mission Hospital, Newchwang, N. China.

PITE, M.C., A. G. Trinity College, Cambridge. London Sec., 1921-2. Asst. Sec., 1922-3. Asst. and Finance Sec., 1923-5. Headmaster, Weymouth College.

POLHILL-TURNER, REV. A. T. (now Polhill). Trinity College, Cambridge. Trav. Sec., S.V.M.U., 1892-3. With China Inland Mission to 1928. Vicar of Furneaux Pelham, 1928-32. Public Preacher, Dio. St Albans, from 1932.

POPE, BEATRICE. Royal Holloway College. London Sec., 1920-1. Member of staff, St Stephen's College, Hong Kong.

POWELL, JOYCE. Newnham College, Cambridge. Auxiliary Sec., 1922-3. Librarian, Sussex County Libraries.

PRICE, MOLLY. Oxford Home Student. Sub-Warden, Student Movement House, London, 1929-30. International Relations Sec., 1930-2. Secretarial work.

PRYS, ELINED (Mrs Walter Kotschnig). University College, Aberystwyth and Newnham College, Cambridge. Welsh Sec., 1923-4.

RAMSBOTHAM, DOROTHY (Mrs Anthony Otter). St Hilda's College, Oxford. Trav. Sec., S. England and Ireland, 1925-7. London Sec., 1927-9.

RAMSBOTHAM, REV. JOHN. Corpus Christi College, Cambridge. Trav. Sec., England, 1929-30. Missionary Sec., 1930-2. Chaplain, Wells Theological College.

RAVEN, REV. CANON E. E. St John's College, Cambridge. Inter-coll. Sec., Cambridge, 1913-4. Dean of St John's College, Cambridge, and Canon Theol., Liverpool Cathedral.

READ, MARGARET. Newnham College, Cambridge. India Y.W.C.A., 1919-24. International Relations Sec., 1925-9. Anthropological Research.

REES, REV. RONALD D. Trinity College, Oxford. London Sec., 1915-7. Royal Artillery, 1917-9. London Sec., 1919-22. Sec., Nat. Christian Council of China.

REEVES, REV. R. AMBROSE. Sidney Sussex College, Cambridge, and House of the Resurrection, Mirfield. Trav. Sec., Theol. Coll. Dept., 1927-31. Rector, St Margaret's, Leven, Fife.

RETTIE, JAMES. Yale University, U.S.A. Sub-Warden, Student Movement House, London, from 1932.

RICHARDSON, REV. ALAN. Liverpool University. Inter-coll. Sec., Liverpool, 1928-31. Chaplain, Ripon Hall, Oxford.

RITCHIE, JOHN. Manchester University. Inter-coll. Sec., Manchester, 1924-5.

ROBERTSON, M.D., BERKELEY H. Glasgow University. Trav. Sec., British Isles, 1904-5. Sometime U.F.C.S., Livingstonia. Private practice, Glasgow.

ROBERTSON, REV. W. S. A. Queens' College and Westcott House, Cambridge. Trav. Sec., Theol. Coll. Dept., 1923-7. Christa Seva Sangha, India. Vicar of St Ives, Hunts.

ROBSON, M.B., Ch.B., AGNES R. (Mrs Donald Fraser). Queen Margaret College, Glasgow. Trav. Sec., B.C.C.U. and S.V.M.U., 1899-1900. Sometime medical missionary, Livingstonia.

ROUSE, C. RUTH. Girton College, Cambridge. Editor, *The Student Volunteer*, 1895-6. Trav. Sec., B.C.C.U. and S.V.M.U., 1896-7. Trav. Sec., S.V.M.F.M. and College Y.W.C.A. of U.S.A. and Canada, 1897-9. Missionary Settlement for University Women, India, 1899-1902. Sec., W.S.C.F., 1904-24. Asst. Sec., Missionary Council of National Assembly of Church of England, from 1925.

ROY, ANDREW T. Washington and Lee Univ., U.S.A. International Relations Sec., 1929-30. Missionary in China.
ROYAARDS, LOUISE (Mrs Alexander Walker). Somerville College, Oxford. Asst. Sec., 1919-20. Foreign Student Sec., 1920-4.
RUSSELL, M.B., B.Ch., G. L. Edinburgh University. Sec., Medical Students, London, from 1932.
RUTHERFORD, REV. JOYCE. Liverpool University. Trav. Sec., N. England, 1925-7. Candidates Sec., L.M.S.

SAUNDERS, UNA M. Somerville College, Oxford. Trav. Sec., British Isles, 1906-10. Sometime Gen. Sec., Y.W.C.A., Canada. World's Y.W.C.A., Geneva.
SCARLETT, ERIC YORK. College of Technology, Manchester. Trav. Sec. for Technical Colleges, 1922-4. L.M.S. Missionary, China, 1924. Killed by bandits in China, April 1930.
SCOTT, B.D., REV. WARREN H. Pennsylvania University, U.S.A. International Relations Sec., 1930-3.
SEDGWICK, WINIFRED M. Somerville College, Oxford. Trav. Sec., British Isles, 1903-5. Sec., S.C.M., Geneva and Moscow, 1905-9. Trav. Sec., S.C.M., 1909-14. Warden, Y.W.C.A. Training Centre, 1915-20. Died, August 1922.
SÉLINCOURT, AGNES DE. Girton College, Cambridge. Missionary Settlement for University Women, Bombay. Principal, Lady Muir Memorial College, Allahabad. S.V.M.U. Sec., 1910-3. Principal of Westfield College from 1913-7. Died, August 1917.
SHANN, LETTICE M. Westfield College, London. S.V.M.U. Sec., 1914-9. C.M.S. missionary, India. Died, July 1930.
SHAW, REV. VERNON G. H. Clare College, Cambridge. Trav. Sec., S.V.M.U., 1913-4. Warden, Oxford and Cambridge Hostel, Allahabad, 1915-8 and 1921-2. St John's Coll., Agra, 1919-21. English Presbyterian Mission, Bengal, 1923-7. Vicar of St Barnabas, Mossley Hill, Liverpool.
SILCOCK, HARRY T. Oriel College, Oxford. Trav. Sec., S.V.M.U., 1905-6. F.F.M.A. missionary, China, 1908-20. Gen. Sec., F.F.M.A., 1920-32. Adviser to Chinese Students under Universities' China Committee.
SMITH, ALICE A. Edinburgh University. Inter-coll. Sec., Edinburgh, 1912-5.
SMITH, ERNEST. Liverpool University. Inter-coll. Sec., Liverpool, 1911-3.
SMITH, JAMES W. D. Glasgow University. Inter-coll. Sec., Glasgow, 1921-2. Scottish Sec., 1922-4. Sec., United Council for Missionary Education.
SOUTHWELL, LORNA V. St Hugh's College, Oxford. Trav. Sec., 1914-6. London Sec., 1916-8. Headmistress, St George's School, Clarens, Switzerland.
SPENCER, REV. MALCOLM. Corpus Christi and Mansfield Colleges,

Oxford. Trav. Sec., Theological Dept., 1906-9. Asst. Gen. Sec., 1909-10. Social Service Sec., 1910-4. Joint Sec., Christian Social Council.

SPICER, R. H. Hertford College, Oxford. Sub-Warden, Student Movement House, London, 1932-3.

SQUIRE, HELEN (Mrs Stansfeld). Royal Holloway College. London Sec., 1912-3.

STEPHENS, AMELIA (Mrs Taffs). Royal Holloway College. Trav. Sec., 1912-5. Y.W.C.A., New Delhi, India.

STEVEN, DOROTHY (Mrs R. C. Mackie). Edinburgh University and Newnham College, Cambridge. Missionary Sec., 1921-3. Inter-coll. Sec., Edinburgh and Glasgow, 1923-4. Scottish Sec., 1924-6.

STEVENS, REV. ALAN W. Mansfield College, Oxford. Student Missionary Campaign Sec., 1907-10. Minister of St Paul's St. Congregational Church, Aberdeen.

STEVENSON, LILIAN S. Slade School of Art. Editor, *The Student Volunteer*, 1896-8. Editor, *The Student Movement*, 1898-1900 and 1902-3. Editorial Sec., 1899-1900. Chairman of Exec., International Fellowship of Reconciliation.

STEWART, MARJORIE. Queen's University, Belfast. Sec., Irish Council, 1923-5. Sec., University Women's "Camps" for Schoolgirls, 1928-31.

STUART, M.B., C.M., EMMELINE M. Queen Margaret College, Glasgow. Trav. Sec., S.V.M.U., 1895-6. C.M.S. missionary in Persia.

SUTTON, FLORENCE. St Hugh's College, Oxford. Sometime Y.W.C.A., China. International Relations Sec. and East and West Friendship Council Sec. from 1932.

SYMONS, W. G. Exeter College, Oxford. Inter-coll. Sec., Birmingham, from 1932.

TAIT, JAMES. Glasgow University. Inter-coll. Sec., Glasgow, 1929-31. Staff, H.M. Borstal Institute, Feltham.

TATLOW, D.D., REV. CANON TISSINGTON. Trinity College, Dublin. Trav. Sec., S.V.M.U., 1897-8. Gen. Sec., 1898-1900 and 1903-29. Editor, *The Student Movement*, 1900-2 and 1904-33. Educational Sec., S.V.M.U., 1900-8. Chairman, 1929-33. Hon. Chaplain, S.C.M., from 1933. Vice-chairman, W.S.C.F., 1922-8. Chairman, I.S.S., from 1926. Rector of All Hallows, Lombard Street, with St Dionis, Backchurch, St Leonard's, Eastcheap, and St Benet, Gracechurch, and Honorary Canon of Canterbury Cathedral.

TAUNTON, PHYLLIS (Mrs S. H. Wood). Westfield College, London. Trav. Sec., 1918-21. London Sec., 1921-2.

TAYLOR, REV. C. W. G. Edinburgh University. Trav. Sec., British Isles, 1900-2. London Sec., 1904-6. Minister of St George's, Edinburgh.

TAYLOR, REV. H. V.   Assembly's College, Belfast, and Wadham College, Oxford.   Trav. Sec., Theological Dept., 1899-1900. U.F.C.S. missionary, Lovedale, 1900-3.   Moderator, Presbyterian Church of South Africa, 1922.

TEASDELL, KITTY.   School of Art, Cardiff.   Sec. for Fine Art Students, London, 1927-8.

THOMAS, CICELY (Mrs W. E. S. Holland).   Westfield College, London.   Asst. Finance Sec., 1923-4.

THOMAS, REV. OLIVER.   University College, Aberystwyth.   Welsh Sec., 1909-13.   Sec., Foreign Missions Committee, Presbyterian Church in Wales.

THOMAS, REV. W. C.   Leeds University.   Trav. Sec., England, 1912-4.   Vicar of Eastwood, Rotherham.

THOMPSON, W. E. S.   Queens' College, Cambridge.   Inter-coll. Sec., Cambridge, 1914-5.   Died 1915.

THORNTON, REV. DOUGLAS M.   Trinity College, Cambridge. Educ. Sec., S.V.M.U., 1896-7.   C.M.S., Cairo.   Died, Sept. 1907.

TINDAL, REV. W. S.   Glasgow University.   Study Sec., 1927-32. Minister of Kilcreggan, Dumbartonshire.

TOWERS, M.R.C.S., L.R.C.P., AGNES ELSIE.   Girton College, Cambridge and Birmingham University.   Sec. for women medical students, 1919-20.   L.M.S. missionary, Lester Chinese Hospital, Shanghai.

TRAFFORD, REV. MARTYN.   Glasgow University and Mansfield College, Oxford.   Trav. Sec., Theol. College Dept., 1908-10. Died, August 1910.

TREVELYAN, A.R.C.M., A.R.C.O., MARY.   Royal College of Music, London.   Extension Sec., Student Movement House, 1932-3. Acting Warden, 1933.

TURNER, REV. ASHLEY D.   King's College, London.   Trav. Sec., S. England, 1921-3.   Vicar of St Martin, Dagenham.

TURNER, M.B., Ch.B., W. Y.   Glasgow University.   Trav. Sec., S.V.M.U., 1904-5.   Church of Scotland missionary, Nyasaland.

TYNDALE-BISCOE, REV. W. FRANCIS.   Trinity College, Oxford. Inter-coll. Sec., Leeds, 1925-7.   Curate, St Andrew's, Catford.

UNDERHILL, MURIEL M.   Oxford Home Student.   Trav. Sec., 1901-3.   Z.B.M.M. missionary, India, 1904-23.   *International Review of Missions* from 1923.

VENN, B.Sc., HUBERT J. P.   University College, London.   London Sec., 1912-3.

WADE, MARGARET (Mrs W. E. Wilkinson).   Girton College, Cambridge.   Missionary Sec., 1930-2.

WALKER, ALEXANDER. Non-coll. Business Sec., 1919-29. Business Director, S.C.M. Press, Ltd., from 1929.

WALLACE, REV. JOHN A. V. Trinity College, Cambridge. London Sec., 1918-9. Vicar, St George's, Camberwell, and Warden of Trinity College Mission.

WALLER, REV. BOLTON C. Trinity College, Dublin. Irish Sec., 1912-4 and 1920-1. Curate of Holy Trinity Church, Rathmines, Dublin.

WARD, WALTER. University College, Aberystwyth, and Merton College, Oxford. Asst. Sec., 1909-12. Solicitor, practising in Ipswich.

WARNER, REV. CHARLES W. Keble College, Oxford. London Sec., 1925-8. Warden, Student Movement House, London, 1928-31. Curate, St John the Evangelist, Lambeth.

WARNER, DOROTHEA L. Froebel Institute, London. Trav. Sec., Training Colleges, 1908-10.

WARNER, REV. HUGH. Oriel College, Oxford. Inter-coll. Sec., Birmingham, 1926-8. Vicar of Bishopthorpe, York.

WEIR, M.B., M.R.C.S., L.R.C.P., HUGH H. Trinity College, Cambridge. Trav. Sec., S.V.M.U., 1899-1900. S.P.G. missionary, Korea. Sec., Medical Missions Dept., S.P.G., London.

WHITEHORN, REV. ROY D. Trinity and Westminster Colleges, Cambridge. Asst. Sec., 1921-2. Sec., Theol. Coll. Dept., 1921-3. London Sec., 1922-3. English Presbyterian minister, Oxford.

WHYTE, CAPTAIN J. DUDLEY. University College, London. Sec., L.I.C.C.U. ,1913-4. Killed in France, July 1916.

WHYTE, M.D., REV. G. DUNCAN. Edinburgh University. Inter-coll. Sec., Edinburgh, 1900-1. English Presbyterian missionary, China, 1903-23. Died, Nov. 1923.

WIGRAM, M.B., B.Ch., LOFTUS E. Trinity College, Cambridge. Asst. Sec., 1899-1900. Sometime C.M.S. missionary, Peshawar. Now in private practice at Chingford.

WILDER, D.D., REV. ROBERT P. Princeton University, U.S.A. Missionary, India, 1892-7. Student work, U.S.A., 1897-9. Student work, India, 1899-1902. Student Vol. Miss. Sec., Scandinavia, 1903-4. Trav. Sec., S.V.M.U., 1905-6. London Sec., 1906-7. Trav. Sec., British Isles, 1907-8. Evangelistic Sec., 1908-15. Foreign Student Sec., 1915-6. Gen. Sec., S.V.M.F.M., for U.S.A. and Canada, 1916-27. Sec., Near East Christian Council, 1927-33.

WILKINSON, REV. A. H. Manchester University. Inter-coll. Sec., Manchester, 1910-1. C.M.S. missionary at Miencheo, 1914-9. Chentu University, 1919-24. Sec., British and Foreign Bible Society.

WILLIAMS, REV. A. TUDNO. University College, Bangor. Trav. Sec., Wales, 1931-3.

WILLIAMS, B.D., E. ARIAM. Serampore College, India, and Edinburgh University. Trav. Sec., 1919-20. International Relations Sec., 1923-4. With Rabindranath Tagore, Shanteniketan Ashram.

WILLIAMS, M.B., B.Sc., M.R.C.S., L.R.C.P., O.B.E., VERY REV. F. GARFIELD H. St Bartholomew's Hospital. London Sec., 1907-8. Treas., W.S.C.F., 1906-8. Student Sec., Y.M.C.A., Calcutta, 1908-10. C.M.S. missionary, India. Sec., Missionary Council of the National Assembly of Church of England, 1924-9. Dean of Manchester from 1931.

WILLIAMS, REV. W. P. W. Trinity College, Dublin. Gen. Sec., 1902-3. C.M.S. missionary, Fuhkien.

WILLIAMSON, M.D., J. RUTTER. Edinburgh University. Trav. Sec., S.V.M.U., 1895-6. Missionary, Church of Scotland, India. Government Service, London.

WILLIS, REV. EDGAR A. Hackney and New College, London. Sec., Schoolboys' Christian Association from 1931.

WILSON, C. DONALD. Christ's College, Cambridge. Inter-coll. Sec., Leeds, 1923-4; also Sheffield, 1924-5. Partner, Wilson & Co., Sheffield.

WILSON, GERTRUDE M. (Mrs Frank Lenwood). Girton College, Cambridge. Trav. Sec., B.C.C.U. and S.V.M.U., 1899-1900.

WISEWOULD, REV. P. A. Melbourne University, Australia. London Sec., 1920-1. Asst. Chaplain, Trinity Grammar School, Kew, Melbourne, Australia.

WITTEN, A. MARY. Southlands Training College. London Sec., 1921-2. Training College Sec., 1922-3. Sometime Prince of Wales College, Achimota. From 1933 St Christopher's Training College, Madras, India.

WITZ, KATHLEEN T. Alexandra College, Dublin. Sec., Irish Council, 1917-20. Gen. Sec., Federation of University Women's " Camps " for Schoolgirls.

WOOD, SYDNEY H. University College, London. Sec., S.C.M. University College, 1907-8. Sec., L.I.C.C.U., 1908-9. Board of Education, Whitehall.

WOODHOUSE, REV. JACK W. University College, Oxford. Trav. Sec., British Isles, 1907-9. Vicar of Christ Church, Luton.

WRONG, MARGARET. Toronto University and Somerville College, Oxford. Sec., W.S.C.F., 1921-5. Missionary Sec., 1926-9. Sec., International Committee on Christian Literature for Africa.

WYNNE, NORA. University College, Bangor. Welsh Trav. Sec., 1914-5. From 1915 Chief Welfare Supervisor and Employment Manager, Carr & Co., Ltd., Carlisle.

Young, M.C., Rev. W. P. Edinburgh University. United Free Church of Scotland missionary, Livingstonia, 1912-5. Trav. Sec., Theol. Coll. Dept., 1919-20. Scottish Sec., 1920-2. Principal, Livingstonia Institute, Nyasaland.

Zernov, Ph.D., Nicolas. Belgrade University, Serbia, and Keble College, Oxford. Sec., Russian S.C.M. in Emigration, 1926-9. Travelling as Russian Orthodox Church visitor, British theological colleges, from 1932.

II

UNIVERSITIES AND COLLEGES IN WHICH THE S.C.M. HAS BEEN ORGANISED

Name in brackets=former title of institution.
M=Men.   W=Women.
The date is that of affiliation of Society in College to the S.C.M.
* Indicates that S.C.M. work in College has ceased.

ENGLAND

BATH
Domestic Science Training Coll. 1931
BEDFORD
Froebel Training Coll. 1921
*Physical Training Coll. 1925
BINGLEY
Training Coll. 1921
BIRMINGHAM
University (Mason Coll.), M. 1896; W. 1896
*School of Art 1899
Selly Oak Group of Colls. 1911
Anstey Physical Training Coll. 1922
BISHOP'S STORTFORD
*Hockerill Training Coll. 1916
BOLTON
*Training Coll. 1910
BRADFORD
Technical Coll., M. 1903; W. 1922
Coll. of Art and Crafts 1923
BRIGHTON
Diocesan Training Coll. 1929
Municipal Training Coll. 1915
BRISTOL
University, M. 1894; W. 1895
*School of Art 1900

BRISTOL
*Training Coll., M. 1907; W. 1901
CAMBRIDGE
University 1893
Girton Coll. 1895
Newnham Coll. 1895
Homerton Coll. 1895
Training Coll. ('Teachers' Coll.) 1895
CHELTENHAM
*Ladies' Coll. 1908
Training Coll., M. 1896; W. 1896
CHESTER
Training Coll. 1911
CHICHESTER
*Bishop Otter Memorial Coll. 1924
CREWE
Cheshire County Training Coll., M. 1925; W. 1913
DARLINGTON
Training Coll. 1900
DERBY
Training Coll. 1912
DUDLEY
Training Coll. 1912
DURHAM
University, M. 1895;

DURHAM
*St Hild's Coll., W. 1908
Bede Coll. 1923
Neville's Cross Coll. 1921

EXETER
University Coll. (Royal Albert Memorial Coll.) 1903
St Luke's Coll. 1921

GLOUCESTER
Training Coll. of Domestic Science 1920

HEREFORD
Training Coll. 1904

HUDDERSFIELD
Technical Coll. 1922

HULL
*University Coll. 1931
Municipal Training Coll., W. 1913 ; M. 1915
*Technical Coll. 1923

LANCASTER
*School of Arts and Crafts

LEEDS
University (Yorkshire Coll.), M. 1897 ; W. 1896
College of Art, W. 1906 ; M. 1913
Training Coll. 1911
Yorkshire Training Coll. of Housecraft 1931

LEICESTER
University Coll. 1922
Domestic Science Training Coll. 1930

LINCOLN
Diocesan Training Coll. 1922

LIVERPOOL
University, M. 1896 ; W. 1896
*School of Art 1909
Edgehill Training Coll. 1907
F. L. Calder Coll. of Domestic Science 1921
Josephine Butler Memorial House 1929
Warrington Training Coll. 1926

LONDON
Avery Hill Training Coll. 1908
Bedford Coll. 1896
Bergman Osterberg Physical Training Coll., Dartford, 1924
Berridge House 1924
Birkbeck Coll. 1919
[1] Bloomsbury School of Art, 1898
Borough Road Training Coll. 1899
[1] Central Technical Coll. 1896
*Central School of Arts and Crafts 1925
Charing Cross Hospital 1900
Chelsea Coll. of Physical Education 1927
Clapham High School Training Coll. 1904
London Instit. of Education (London Day Training Coll.) 1908
[1] Datchelor Training Coll. 1905
East London Coll. 1909
*Faraday House 1907
[2] Finsbury Technical Coll. 1900
Froebel Coll. 1898
Furzedown Training Coll. 1917
Gipsy Hill Training Coll. 1919
Goldsmith's Coll., M. 1908 ; W. 1907
*Goldsmith's Coll. School of Art 1911
Graystoke Place Training Coll. 1920
*Guildhall School of Music, 1908
*Guy's Hospital 1895
*Hillcroft Coll. 1920
[1] Home and Colonial Training Coll. 1900
Imperial Coll. of Science and Technology 1912
King's Coll. and Hospital, M. 1896

3 N

LONDON
   King's College for Women
      1905
   King's Coll. of Household
      and Social Science 1918
   *Livingstone Coll. 1897
   London Hospital 1894
   Maria Grey Training Coll.
      1899
   *Middlesex Hospital 1895
   National Training Coll. of
      Domestic Subjects 1923
   Rachel Macmillan Training
      Coll. 1920
   Royal Academy of Art 1897
   Royal Academy of Music 1912
   *Royal Coll. of Music 1911
   *Royal Coll. of Art, M. 1897;
      W. 1900
   2 Royal Coll. of Science 1897
   Royal Free Hospital 1920
   Royal Holloway Coll. 1900
   *Royal Normal Coll. for the
      Blind, M. 1898; W. 1901
   St Bartholomew's Hospital
      1894
   St Gabriel's Coll. 1927
   St Katharine's Coll., Totten-
      ham 1914
   St Mark and St John, Chelsea
      1924
   St Mary's Hospital 1894
   *St Mary's Training Coll.,
      Lancaster Gate 1908
   St Thomas's Hospital 1894
   London School of Economics
      1911
   *Slade School of Art 1897
   Southlands Training Coll.
      1910
   Stockwell Training Coll. 1912
   London School of Medicine
      for Women 1895
   *Trinity Coll. of Music 1906
   University Coll., M. 1895;
      W. 1898
   University Coll. Hospital
      1908

LONDON
   Westminster Training Coll.
      1916
   *Westminster Hospital 1894
   Westfield Coll. 1896
   Whitelands Training Coll.
      1920
LOUGHBOROUGH
   Technical College 1921

MANCHESTER
   University (Owens Coll.), M.
      1896; W. 1896
   College of Domestic Science
      1921
   *Municipal School of Art, M.
      1906; W. 1906
   *Municipal Day Training Coll.
      1911
   College of Technology 1905

NEWCASTLE
   Armstrong Coll., M. 1906;
      W. 1901
   Durham University College
      of Medicine, M. 1900; *W.
      1906
   Kenton Lodge Training Coll.
      1922
   School of Cookery 1931
NORTHAMPTON
   *Technical Coll. 1924
NORWICH
   Training Coll. 1932
NOTTINGHAM
   University Coll., M. 1897;
      W. 1896
   *School of Art, M. 1901; W.
      1899

OXFORD
   University 1893
   1 Cherwell Hall 1906
   Home Students 1896
   Lady Margaret Hall 1906
   Oxford Education Dept. 1929
   St Hugh's Coll. 1910
   St Hilda's Coll. 1910
   Somerville Coll. 1896

APPENDICES

PETERBOROUGH
St Peter's Training Coll. 1922
PLYMOUTH
Technical Coll. 1923
PORTSMOUTH
Municipal Training Coll. 1910
Municipal Coll. 1913

READING
University, M. 1906; W.
1904

SAFFRON WALDEN
Training Coll. 1904
SALOP
*Harper Adams Agric. Coll.
1920
SALTLEY
Training Coll. 1922
SANDHURST
*Royal Military Coll. 1897
SHEFFIELD
University (Firth Coll.), M.
1897; W. 1897.
City Training Coll., M. 1907;
W. 1907
*School of Art, M. 1900; W.
1899
SOUTHAMPTON
University Coll., M. 1903;
W. 1904
SUNDERLAND
*Training Coll., M. 1910; W.
1910
*Technical Coll. 1918
SUTTON BONINGTON
Midland Agricultural College
1929
SWANLEY
*Horticultural College 1899

TRURO
Diocesan Training Coll. 1917

WAKEFIELD
College of Art 1930

WYE
*South Eastern Agricultural
Coll. 1930

YORK
St John's Coll. 1911

SCOTLAND

ABERDEEN
University, M. 1893; W. 1898
[1] Church of Scotland Training
Coll. 1898
[1] Free Church Normal Coll.
1899
School of Art 1921
School of Domestic Science
Training College 1925
DUNDEE
University Coll., M. 1900;
W. 1903
Training Coll., M. 1909; W.
1915
DUNFERMLINE
College of Hygiene and
Physical Education 1929
EDINBURGH
University, Medical Faculty,
M. 1893; Arts, M. 1895;
W. 1896
*College of Art, M. 1903; W.
1900
[3] School of Medicine for
Women 1896
*Royal College of Surgeons
1896
[1] Free Church Training Coll.
1896
[1] Church of Scotland Training
Coll. 1896
St George's Training Coll.
1916
Provincial Training College
(Moray House) 1895
College of Domestic Science
1930

GLASGOW
  University 1893
  Queen Margaret Coll. 1896
  *School of Art, M. 1910 ; W. 1909
  [1] Anderson's Coll. 1895
  [1] United Presbyterian Church Training Coll. 1895
  [1] Free Church Training Coll., M. 1896 ; W. 1895
  [1] Froebel Students 1913
  [3] St Mungo's Coll. 1895
  Royal Technical Coll. 1913
  West of Scotland Agric. Coll. 1920
  [1] Church of Scotland Training Coll. 1900
  Provincial Training Coll. 1907
ST ANDREWS
  University, M. 1895 ; W. 1897

WALES

ABERYSTWYTH
  University Coll., M. 1893 ; W. 1895
BANGOR
  University Coll., M. 1893 ; W. 1895
  Normal Coll., M. 1912 ; W. 1913
CARDIFF
  University Coll., M. 1895 ; W. 1895
  *Technical Coll. 1923
  School of Art 1924
CARMARTHEN
  Training Coll. 1909
  Presbyterian Coll. 1915
  Myrdden Coll. 1931

GLAMORGAN
  Barry Training Coll. 1931
LAMPETER
  St David's Coll. 1909
NEWPORT
  Caerleon Training Coll. 1914
SWANSEA
  University Coll. 1921
  Training Coll. 1897
TREFOREST
  *School of Mines 1923

IRELAND

BELFAST
  Queen's University (Queen's Coll.), M. 1894; W. 1895
  [1] University Classes 1896
  Stranmillis Training Coll., M. 1924 ; W. 1923
CORK
  *Queen's Coll. 1903
DUBLIN
  Trinity Coll. 1893
  *Royal Coll. of Science 1905
  *Royal Coll. of Surgeons, M. 1904 ; W. 1898
  Church of Ireland Training Coll. 1904
  Alexandra Coll. 1903
  [4] Marlborough St. Training Coll. 1894
  *Metropolitan School of Art, W. 1899
GALWAY
  *Queen's Coll., M. 1896 ; W. 1905
LONDONDERRY
  McCrea Magee Coll., M. 1896; W. 1906

[1] College closed.
[2] Now amalgamated with Imperial College of Science and Technology.
[3] Merged in University.
[4] Transferred to Belfast as Stranmillis Training College.

ASSOCIATED THEOLOGICAL COLLEGES

ENGLAND

Anglican

BIRKENHEAD
St Aidan's College
BURGH
St Paul's College
CAMBRIDGE
Ridley Hall
Westcott House
CANTERBURY
St Augustine's College
CHESHUNT
Bishop's College
CHICHESTER
Theological College
ELY
Theological College
KELHAM
House of the Sacred Mission
LICHFIELD
Theological College
LINCOLN
Bishop's Hostel
LONDON
King's College
St John's Hall, Highbury
MANCHESTER
Egerton Hall
MIRFIELD
College of the Resurrection
ISLE OF MAN
Bishop Wilson Theol. Coll.
OXFORD
Cuddesdon College
Ripon Hall
Wycliffe Hall
St Stephen's House
SALISBURY
Theological College
WARMINSTER
St Boniface College
WELLS
Theological College

Baptist

BRISTOL
Baptist College
LEEDS
Rawdon College
LONDON
Regents Park College
Spurgeon's College
MANCHESTER
Baptist College

Congregational

BRADFORD
United College
BRISTOL
Western College
CAMBRIDGE
Cheshunt College
LONDON
Hackney and New College
MANCHESTER
Lancs. Indep. College
NOTTINGHAM
Paton Congreg. College
OXFORD
Mansfield College

Church of Christ

BIRMINGHAM
Overdale College

Moravian

MANCHESTER
The College, Fairfield

Methodist

BIRMINGHAM
Handsworth College

MANCHESTER
Didsbury College
Hartley College
Methodist College, Victoria Park

CAMBRIDGE
Wesley House

LONDON
Richmond College

LEEDS
Headingley Coll.

Presbyterian

CAMBRIDGE
Westminster College

IRELAND

Anglican

DUBLIN
Trinity Coll. (Divinity School)

Presbyterian

BELFAST
Assembly's College

Wesleyan Methodist

BELFAST
Edgehill College

SCOTLAND

Anglican

EDINBURGH
Coates Hall

Baptist

GLASGOW
Scottish Baptist Theol. Coll.

Congregational

EDINBURGH
Scottish Congregational Coll.

Presbyterian

ABERDEEN
University (Divinity Faculty)
Alford Place College

EDINBURGH
University (Divinity Faculty)
New College

GLASGOW
University (Divinity Faculty)
Trinity College

ST ANDREWS
St Mary's College

WALES

Anglican

LLANDAFF
St Michael's College

Baptist

BANGOR
North Wales Baptist College

CARDIFF
South Wales Baptist College

Calvinistic Methodist

ABERYSTWYTH
Calvinistic Methodist College

BALA
Calvinistic Methodist College

TREVECCA
College, Talgarth

Congregational

BRECON
Memorial College

BANGOR
Bala Bangor College

Ministerial Preparatory School

CLYNNOG
Clywd College

ASSOCIATED WOMEN'S THEOLOGICAL COLLEGES

Anglican

BIRMINGHAM
College of the Ascension

LONDON
Deaconess House, Clapham
St Christopher's College
St Catherine's Deaconess
House

PORTSMOUTH
St Andrew's House

WANTAGE
St Michael's

Methodist

ILKLEY, YORKS.
Deaconess House

Presbyterian

EDINBURGH
Women's Missionary College

INDEX

INDEX

Any title used below is that held at the time the reference to its holder is made, and therefore not necessarily his present title.

A

Academic work and S.C.M., 599
Adriani, Dr J. H., 341-3
Africa Group, 674
Africa Waiting, 85
Aim and Basis (*see* under Basis)
Aim of Movement, 20, 31, 38, 49, 65, 146, 209, 256, 330-5, 353, 360, 483-4, 626, 628, 633, 817, 860 *et seq.*
Aim revised, 1905, 256
Aiman, J. S., 299, 839, 856
Aird, Lionel, 699
All Hallows, Lombard Street, E.C., 653, 826
Allen, Clifford, 727
America—
Missionary study in, 82, 83
Summer Conferences, 17-20, 34, 42, 221
Student Volunteer Conferences, 70
United States of, 1, 16-20, 34, 80, 220, 686, 844
Watchword of S.V.M.U., 75, 104
Anderson, Frank, 50, 62-4, 68, 71, 103, 115
Andover Seminary, 3
Andrews, Rev. C. F., 139-40, 142, 298, 303-4, 846
Anglican Fellowship, 463-4, 729-30, 737
Anglo-American relations, 701, 844
Anglo-Russian relations—
Conferences, 781-5
Fellowship of St Alban and St Sergius founded, 783-5

Anglo-Russian relations—
Appointment of Dr Nicolas Zernov, 785
Angus, C. F., 525, 668
Angus, G. H. C., 283, 295
Annandale, 465, 826, 848
Apologetics—
Introduction to Summer Conference programme of, 215, 260
First lectures on, 259, 321
Literature on, 401-2
Need for, 424-7
First Sub-committee, 434-5
Archdall, H. K., 414, 429, 464
Army and Religion Enquiry, 588-90, 771
Arnold, T. W., 568
Art Students' C.U. (*see* Fine Art)
Artist and Religion, The, 600
Ashwell, Lena, 601
Aubrey, Rev. M. E., 808
Australian S.C.M., 79, 392, 414, 571, 678
Auxiliary Movement, The—
Genesis of, 727-9
Founded, April 1912, 728
Conference on "Students and the Church," April 1918, 731-7
New constitution adopted, May 1919, 738
Membership, 728, 731, 738, 748
widened to include non-students, 739-41
Conferences, 738, 742, 747
Full-time secretary appointed, 740
Secretaries, 729, 740, 741, 744, 748

Printed by Turnbull & Spears, Edinburgh